ROYAL HISTORICAL SOCIETY

ANNUAL
BIBLIOGRAPHY
OF
BRITISH AND IRISH
HISTORY

ROYAL HISTORICAL SOCIETY

in association with the Institute of Historical Research

ANNUAL
BIBLIOGRAPHY
OF
BRITISH AND IRISH
HISTORY

PUBLICATIONS OF 2000

GENERAL EDITOR:

AUSTIN GEE

Ian W. Archer   H.V. Bowen   Antoine Capet   David Crouch
Bernadette Cunningham   Virginia Davis   C.C. Eldridge
Austin Gee   Stanley Ireland   James Kirk   David Pratt
Huw Pryce   Rosemary Sweet   Miles Taylor

OXFORD
UNIVERSITY PRESS

OXFORD
UNIVERSITY PRESS

Great Clarendon Street, Oxford OX2 6DP

Oxford University Press is a department of the University of Oxford.
It furthers the University's objective of excellence in research, scholarship,
and education by publishing worldwide in

Oxford New York

Athens Auckland Bangkok Bogotá Buenos Aires Cape Town
Chennai Dar es Salaam Delhi Florence Hong Kong Istanbul Karachi
Kolkata Kuala Lumpur Madrid Melbourne Mexico City Mumbai Nairobi
Paris São Paulo Shanghai Singapore Taipei Tokyo Toronto Warsaw

and associated companies in Berlin Ibadan

Oxford is a registered trade mark of Oxford University Press
in the UK and in certain other countries

Published in the United States
by Oxford University Press Inc., New York

British Library Cataloguing in Publication Data

Data available

Library of Congress Cataloging in Publication Data
data available
ISBN 0–19–924917–2

1 3 5 7 9 10 8 6 4 2

Typeset by Hope Services (Abingdon) Ltd.
Printed in Great Britain
on acid-free paper by
Biddles Ltd.,
Guildford & King's Lynn

CONTENTS

Contents

Contents

Contents

Contents

PREFACE

The Annual Bibliography of the Royal Historical Society is designed primarily to serve the urgent needs of scholars. Total coverage and refinements of arrangement have been subordinated to speed of production. Nevertheless, the bibliography aims to be as comprehensive as possible: this year's volume includes 1926 books and 4775 articles by 6022 authors. More than 700 journals are searched annually for relevant articles, and those which regularly yield titles for 2000 are listed below, before the index of authors. This volume further supplements the *Royal Historical Society Bibliography on CD-ROM: The History of Britain, Ireland, and the British Overseas* (Oxford University Press, 1998), which includes publications down to 1992. A description of the Society's bibliography project, including information about the classification scheme, is available on the Internet at www.ihrinfo.ac.uk/rhs/bibwel.html

The subdivisions of sections are standardised; searchers are advised to use those subsections in conjunction with the four indices. The indices form an important part of the book and cover, as far as is practicable, all major subjects of the books and articles listed, whether or not they figure in the titles. The counties listed in identifying places are in general those predating the reorganisations of 1974 and 1975. A list of abbreviations of county names precedes the Index of Places.

Articles and essays in collective works are as far as possible listed individually in the appropriate subsections, with a cross-reference to the full details of the volume in section A. Reprinted articles and brief reports (in, for example, archaeological reports or exhibition catalogues) are not normally itemised separately, and where this is the case the fact is noted. Apart from the short list of standard abbreviations which follows this preface, these 'A' numbers are the only abbreviated form of publication details.

Items covering more than two sections are listed in section B; any items which extend over two sections normally appear in the first appropriate section and are cross-referenced at the head of the second. Within each subsection the items are arranged in alphabetical order of authors. To keep the bibliography within bounds, items in sections N 'Empire to 1783' and P 'Empire and Commonwealth post 1783' are included only if they contribute substantially to British or Irish history. These sections do not seek to provide a bibliography of the internal history of places subject to imperial control.

The library staff of the Institute of Historical Research have, as in every year, undertaken the searches without which the compilation of the Bibliography would be completely impracticable. Keith Manley's work in gathering references has been especially important, as has the work of Mrs Shirley Warner. The section editors too carry a heavy burden of searching and checking a wide range of publications. The British Library has given permission to reproduce in edited form records from its 'Inside' database. Thanks are also due to the historians and many publishers who supplied details of their publications. Any corrections, additions or suggestions would be gratefully received by the editor, at the Institute of Historical Research, Senate House, University of London, Malet Street, London WC1E 7HU, or by electronic mail at rhsbib@ihrinfo.ac.uk.

ABBREVIATIONS

Arch.	Archaeological
B.	Bulletin
BAR	British Archaeological Reports
c.	*circa*
CBA	Council for British Archaeology
comp.	compiler(s)
d.	died
ed.	editor(s)
edn.	edition
fl.	*floruit*
Inst.	Institute
J.	Journal
no.	number
ns	new series
P.	Proceedings or Press
Q.	Quarterly
R.	Review
rev.	revised
ser.	series
Soc.	Society
T.	Transactions
Univ.	University
UP	University Press

A. COLLECTIVE VOLUMES

1. Addison, Paul; Crang, Jeremy A. (eds.) *The burning blue: a new history of the Battle of Britain* (London: Pimlico, 2000), 292p.
2. Airs, Malcolm (ed.) *The later eighteenth century country house: the proceedings of a conference under the joint directorship of Edward Chaney and Malcolm Airs held at the Department for Continuing Education, the University of Oxford, 10–12 January 1997* ([Oxford]: University of Oxford, Department for Continuing Education, 1997), 240p.
3. Airs, Malcolm (ed.) *The Victorian great house* (Oxford: Department of Continuing Education, Oxford University, 2000), vi, 164p.
4. Alan, Leslie (ed.) *Theoretical Roman archaeology & architecture: the third conference proceedings* (Glasgow: Cruithne, 1999), 212p.
5. Aldous, Richard; Lee, Sabine (eds.) *Harold Macmillan: aspects of a political life* (Basingstoke: Macmillan, 1999), xv, 258p.
6. Ansprenger, Franz; Hiery, Hermann; Kampmann, Christoph (eds.) *Imperium / Empire / Reich: Ein Konzept politischer Herrschaft im deutsch-britischen Vergleich. An Anglo-German comparison of a concept of rule* (Prince Albert Studies, 16) (Munich: K.G. Saur, 1999), 211p.
7. Arnold, Dana (ed.) *The metropolis and its image: constructing identities for London, c.1750–1950* (Oxford: Blackwell, 1999), 176p.
8. Atkinson, John Andrew; Banks, Iain; MacGregor, Gavin (eds.) *Townships to farmsteads: rural settlement studies in Scotland, England and Wales* (BAR British series, 293) (Oxford: British Archaeological Reports, 2000), vii, 243p.
9. Aurell, Martin (ed.) *La cour Plantagenêt (1154–1204). Actes du Colloque tenu à Thouars du 30 avril au 2 mai 1999* (Poitiers: Centre d'Études Supérieures de Civilisation Médiévale, 2000), 364p.
10. Baranzini, Mauro; Besomi, Daniele (eds.) *Macroeconomia* (Lugano: Università della Svizzera italiana, 1999).
11. Barbe, Jean-Paul; Bernecker, Roland (eds.) *Les intellectuels européens face à la campagne d'Italie, 1796–1798. Actes du colloque international de l'université de Nantes, 7–8 mars 1997* (Münster: Nodus Publikationen, 1999).
12. Barnard, Toby; Fenlon, Jane (eds.) *The Dukes of Ormonde, 1610–1745* (Woodbridge: Boydell, 2000), x, 279p.
13. Behlmer, George K.; Leventhal, Fred M. (eds.) *Singular continuities: tradition, nostalgia, and society in modern Britain* (Stanford (CA): Stanford University Press, 2000), xi, 277p.
14. Bernard, George W. *Power and politics in Tudor England* (Aldershot and Burlington (VT): Ashgate, 2000), 240p. [Some of the items are reprinted and are not itemised here.]

A: Collective Volumes

15. Bielenberg, Andy (ed.) *The Irish diaspora* (Harlow: Longman, 2000), vi, 368p.
16. Birke, Adolf M. (eds.) *Deutschland und Großbritannien = Britain and Germany: historische Beziehungen und Vergleiche = historical relations and comparisons*, eds. Franz Bosbach & Hermann Hiery (Prince Albert Research Publications, 1) (München: Saur, 1999), xiii, 298p.
17. Bjorn, Claus (ed.) *Social and political identities in western history* (Copenhagen: Academic Press, 1994), 266p.
18. Black, Ronald; Gillies, William; Ó Maolalaigh, Roibeard (eds.) *Celtic connections: proceedings of the Tenth International Congress of Celtic Studies*, vol. 1: *Language, literature, history, culture* (East Linton: Tuckwell, 1999). [Publication of volume 2 has been abandoned.]
19. Boemeke, Manfred M.; Feldman, Gerald D.; Glaser-Schmidt, Elisabeth (eds.) *The Treaty of Versailles: a reassessment after seventy-five years* (Cambridge: Cambridge University Press, 1998), 645p.
20. Bonifas, Gilbert (ed.) *Lecture(s) de la ville—The City as Text. Proceedings of the Newcastle-upon-Tyne Conference, September 1999* (Nice: Publications de la Faculté des Lettres de Nice, 2000).
21. Brewer, Richard J. (ed.) *Roman fortresses and their legions: papers in honour of George C. Boon, FSA, FRHistS* (London and Cardiff: Society of Antiquaries of London and the National Museum & Galleries of Wales, 2000), xvii, 187p.
22. Brinkley, Douglas; Facey-Crowther, David R. (eds.) *The Atlantic Charter* (New York: St. Martins Press, 1994), 225p.
23. Britnell, Richard H. (ed.) *Daily life in the middle ages* (Stroud: Sutton, 1998), vi, 234p.
24. Brivati, Brian; Heffernan, Brian (eds.) *The Labour Party: a centenary history* (Basingstoke: Macmillan, 2000), xxii, 512p.
25. Brock, Peter; Socknat, Thomas Paul (eds.) *Challenge to Mars: essays on pacifism from 1918 to 1945* (Toronto (Ont) and London: University of Toronto Press, 1999), xviii, 474p.
26. Brower, Charles (ed.) *World War Two in Europe: the final year. A collection of papers presented at a Symposium held at Middelburg, Netherlands, June 1–3, 1994* (New York: St Martins Press, 1998)
27. Brown, Stewart J.; Miller, David W. (eds.) *Piety and power in Ireland 1760–1960: essays in honour of Emmet Larkin* (Belfast and Notre Dame (IN): Institute of Irish Studies, Queen's University of Belfast and the University of Notre Dame Press, 2000), x, 304p.
28. Burke, Kathleen; Stokes, Melvyn (eds.) *The United States and the European alliance since 1945* (Oxford: Berg, 1999), vii, 324p.
29. Burke, Peter; Harrison, Brian; Slack, Paul (eds.) *Civil histories: essays presented to Sir Keith Thomas* (Oxford: Oxford University Press, 2000), xiv, 399p.
30. Burkhauser, Jude (ed.) *Glasgow girls: women in art and design, 1880–1920*, revised edn. (Edinburgh and Cape May (NJ): Canongate and Red Ochre, 1993), 263p. [1st published 1990.]
31. Campbell, Alan; Fishman, Nina; McIlroy, John (eds.) *British trade unions and industrial politics*, vol.1: *The post-war compromise, 1945–64* (London: Ashgate, 1999), 352p.

2

32. Campbell, Alan; Fishman, Nina; McIlroy, John (eds.) *British trade unions and industrial politics*, vol.2: *The high tide of trade unionism, 1964–79* (London: Ashgate, 1999), 400p.

33. Canny, Nicholas P.; Illick, Joseph E.; Nash, Gary B. (eds.) *Empire, society, and labor: essays in honor of Richard S. Dunn* ([s.l.]: Pennsylvania Historical Association, 1997), 372p. [Special supplemental issue of *Pennsylvania History* 64 (1997).]

34. Capet, Antoine; Romanski, Philippe; Sy-Wonyu, Aïssatou (eds.) *États de New York* (Publications de l'université de Rouen, 273) (Rouen: Presses de l'université, 2000).

35. Capet, Antoine; Pichardie, Jean-Paul (eds.) *Les années Wilson (1964–1970)* [the Wilson Years] (Publications de l'université de Rouen, 257) (Rouen: Presses de l'Université, 1999), 253p.

36. Carey, John; Koch, John T.; Lambert, Pierre-Yves (eds.) *Ildánach Ildírech: a festschrift for Proinsias Mac Cana* (Celtic Studies Publications, 4) (Andover and Aberystwyth: Celtic Studies Publications, 1999).

37. Carré, Jacques (ed.) *Les visiteurs du pauvre: Anthologie d'enquêtes britanniques sur la pauvreté urbaine (XXIe-XXe siècles)* [The poor man's visitors: an anthology of British enquiries into urban poverty (19th-20th centuries)] (Paris: Karthala, 2000), 262p.

38. Catterall, Peter; Seymour-Ure, Colin; Smith, Adrian (eds.) *Northcliffe's legacy: aspects of the British popular press, 1896–1996* (Basingstoke: Macmillan in association with the Institute of Contemporary British History, 2000), xii, 237p.

39. Catterall, Peter; Kaiser, Wolfram; Walton-Jordan, Ulrike (eds.) *Reforming the constitution: debates in twentieth-century Britain* (London and Portland (OR): Frank Cass, 2000), xiii, 304p.

40. Cavanagh, Dermot; Kirk, Tim (eds.) *Subversion and scurrility: popular discourse in Europe from 1500 to the present* (Aldershot: Ashgate, 2000), ix, 210p.

41. Charles-Edwards, T.M.; Owen, Morfydd E.; Russell, Paul (eds.) *The Welsh king and his court* (Cardiff: University of Wales Press on behalf of the History and Law Committee of the Board of Celtic Studies, 2000), ix, 603p.

42. Charlot, Monica (ed.) *Pauvreté et inégalités en Grande-Bretagne de 1942 à 1990* (Paris: Ophrys, 2000), 157p.

43. Clark, Peter (ed.) *The Cambridge urban history of Britain*, vol.2: *1540–1840* (Cambridge: Cambridge University Press, 2000), xxvii, 906p.

44. Clark, Stuart (ed.) *The Annales school: critical assessments*, vol. II: *The Annales school and historical studies* (London and New York: Routledge, 1999), xv, 557p.

45. Clark, Stuart (ed.) *The Annales school: critical assessments*, vol. IV: *Febvre, Bloch and other Annales historians* (London and New York: Routledge, 1999), xiii, 341p.

46. Collette, Christine; Bird, Stephen (eds.) *Jews, Labour and the Left, 1918–48* (Aldershot: Ashgate, 2000), viii, 186p.

47. Collini, Stefan; Whatmore, Richard; Young, Brian W. (eds.) *History, religion, and culture: British intellectual history 1750–1950* (Cambridge: Cambridge University Press, 2000), viii, 289p.

48. Collins, Timothy (ed.) *Decoding the landscape: papers read at the inaugural conference of the Centre for Landscape Studies*, 2nd revised edn. (Galway: Centre for Landscape Studies, Social Sciences Research Centre, University College Galway, 1997), x, 168p.

49. Collinson, Patrick; Craig, John (eds.) *The Reformation in English towns, 1500–1640* (Basingstoke: Macmillan, 1998), ix, 335p.

50. Comerford, R.V.; Delaney, Enda (eds.) *National questions: reflections on Daniel O'Connell and contemporary Ireland* (Dublin: Wolfhound, 2000).

51. Connolly, S.J. (ed.) *Political ideas in eighteenth-century Ireland* (Dublin: Four Courts, 2000), 236p.

52. Cooter, Roger; Harrison, Mark; Sturdy, Steve (eds.) *Medicine and modern warfare* (Clio Medica, 55) (Amsterdam and Atlanta (GA): Editions Rodolpi, 1999), 285p.

53. Corsini, Carlo A.; Viazzo, Paolo (eds.) *The decline of infant and child mortality: the European experience 1750–1990* (The Hague: Martinus Nijhoff, 1997), xxxi, 258p.

54. Coss, Peter R. (ed.) *The moral world of the law* (Cambridge and New York: Cambridge University Press, 2000), xi, 262p.

55. Cottam, Sally (ed.) *TRAC 94: proceedings of the fourth annual Theoretical Roman Archaeology Conference, held at the Department of Archaeology, University of Durham, 19th & 20th March, 1994* (Oxford: Oxbow, 1994), 150p.

56. Crawford, Barbara E. (ed.) *Scotland in dark age Europe: the proceedings of a day conference held on 20 February 1993* (St Andrews: Committee for Dark Age Studies, University of St Andrews, 1994), [113]p.

57. Cronin, Mike; Regan, John M. (eds.) *Ireland: the politics of independence, 1922–49* (Basingstoke: Macmillan, 2000), x, 237p.

58. Cruickshanks, Eveline (ed.) *The Stuart courts* (Stroud: Sutton, 2000), xv, 288p.

59. Cullen, Mary; Luddy, Maria (eds.) *Women, power and consciousness in 19th-century Ireland: eight biographical studies* (Dublin: Attic Press, 1995), 304p.

60. Davis, Michael T. (ed.) *Radicalism and revolution in Britain, 1775–1848: essays in honour of Malcolm I. Thomis* (Basingstoke and New York: Macmillan and St. Martin's Press, 2000), xv, 242p.

61. Day, John Terhune; Lund, Eric; O'Donnell, Anne M. (eds.) *Word, church, and state: Tyndale quincentenary essays* (Washington (DC): Catholic University of America Press, 1998), xxiv, 343p.

62. de Gruchy, John W. (ed.) *The London Missionary Society in Southern Africa: historical essays in celebration of the bicentenary of the LMS in Southern Africa, 1799–1999* (Cape Town: David Philip, 1999).

63. Deighton, Anne (ed.) *Building postwar Europe: national decision-makers and European institutions, 1948–63* (Basingstoke and New York: Macmillan and St. Martin's Press in association with St. Antony's College, Oxford, 1995), xxviii, 187p.

64. Delumeau, Jean (ed.) *L'Acceptation de l-autre, de Édit de Nantes à nos jours* (Paris: Fayard, 2000).

65. Diederiks, Herman A.; Reeder, David (eds.) *Cities of Finance* (Amsterdam: North-Holland, 1996).

66. Ditchburn, David; Brotherstone, Terry (eds.) *Freedom and authority: Scotland c.1050–c.1650: historical and historiographical essays presented to Grant G. Simpson* (East Linton: Tuckwell, 2000), 256p.

67. Dobranski, Stephen B.; Rumrich, John Peter (eds.) *Milton and heresy* (Cambridge: Cambridge University Press, 1998), x, 272p.

68. Dor, Juliette; Johnson, Lesley; Wogan-Browne, Jocelyn (eds.) *New trends in feminine spirituality: the holy women of Liege and their impact* (Turnhout: Brepols, 1999), xii, 350p.

69. Dormois, Jean-Pierre; Dintenfass, Michael (eds.) *British industrial decline* (Routledge Explorations in Economic History, 10) (London and New York: Routledge, 1999), xii, 234p.

70. Dresser, Madge; Ollerenshaw, Philip (eds.) *The making of modern Bristol* (Tiverton: Redcliffe, 1996), x, 246p.

71. Driver, Felix; Gilbert, David (eds.) *Imperial cities: landscape, display and identity* (Manchester: Manchester University Press, 1999), viii, 283p.

72. Duffy, Seán (ed.) *Medieval Dublin I: proceedings of the Friends of Medieval Dublin Symposium 1999* (Dublin: Four Courts, 2000), 237p.

73. Duppler, Jörg; Groß, Gerhard P. (eds.) *Kriegsende 1918: Ereignis, Wirkung, Nachwirkung* (München: Oldenbourg, 1999), ix, 398p. [Im Auftrag des Militärgeschichtlichen Forschungsamtes. Beiträge zur Militärgeschichte, 53.]

74. Edwards, John; Révauger, Jean-Paul (eds.) *Employment and citizenship in Britain and France* (Aldershot: Ashgate, 2000), xiii, 267p.

75. English, Richard; Kenny, Michael (eds.) *Rethinking British decline* (Basingstoke: Macmillan, 2000), xiv, 315p.

76. Eustance, Claire; Ryan, Joan; Ugolini, Laura (eds.) *A suffrage reader: charting directions in British suffrage history* (London and New York: Leicester University Press, 2000), ix, 214p.

77. Ewan, Elizabeth; Meikle, Maureen (eds.) *Women in Scotland, c.1100–c.1750* (East Linton: Tuckwell, 1999), xxx, 272p.

78. Fabech, Charlotte; Ringtved, Jytte (eds.) *Settlement and landscape: proceedings of a conference in Århus, Denmark, May 4–7 1998* (Moesgård: Jutland Archaeological Society, 1999), 500p.

79. Fentress, Elizabeth (ed.) *Romanization and the city: creation, transformation, and failures. Proceedings of a conference held at the American Academy in Rome to celebrate the 50th anniversary of the excavations at Cosa, 14–16 May 1998* (Journal of Roman Archaeology, Supplementary Series, 38) (Portsmouth (RI): Journal of Roman Archaeology, 2000).

80. Fincham, Garrick; Harrison, Geoff; Holland, René; Revell, Louise (eds.) *TRAC: Proceedings of the Ninth Annual Theoretical Roman Archaeology Conference, Durham 1999* (Oxford: Oxbow, 2000), x, 141p.

81. Fletcher, Anthony J.; Hussey, Stephen (eds.) *Childhood in question: children, parents and the state* (Manchester: Manchester University Press, 1999), 177p.

82. Fox, Robert (ed.) *Thomas Harriot: an Elizabethan man of science* (Aldershot and Burlington (VT): Ashgate, 2000), xii, 317p.

83. Fraser, T.G. (ed.) *The Irish parading tradition: following the drum* (Basingstoke: Macmillan, 2000), xi, 209p.

A: Collective Volumes

84. Frison, Danièle (ed.) *Pauvreté et inégalités en Grande-Bretagne de 1942 à 1990* (Paris: Ellipses, 2000), 285p.
85. Frost, Alan; Samson, Jane (eds.) *Pacific empires: essays in honour of Glyndwr Williams* (Carlton South (Vic): Melbourne University Press, 1999), xii, 334p.
86. Funari, Pedro Paulo A.; Hall, Martin; Jones, Siân (eds.) *Historical archaeology: back from the brink* (London and New York: Routledge, 1999), xx, 350p.
87. Galloway, James A. (ed.) *Trade, urban hinterlands and market integration, c.1300–1600: a collection of working papers* (London: Centre for Metropolitan History, Institute of Historical Research, 2000), x, 109p.
88. Gameson, Richard (ed.) *St Augustine and the conversion of England* (Stroud: Sutton, 1999), viii, 436p.
89. Geake, Helen; Kenny, Jonathan (eds.) *Early Deira: archaeological studies of the East Riding in the fourth to ninth centuries AD* (Oxford and Oakville (CT): Oxbow Books, 2000), xi, 140p.
90. Gladstone, David (ed.) *Before Beveridge: welfare before the welfare state* (Choice in Welfare, 47) (London: Institute of Economic Affairs Health and Welfare Unit, 1999), vii, 139p.
91. Gooch, John (ed.) *The Boer War: Direction, Experience and Image* (London and Portland (OR): Frank Cass, 2000), xxi, 310p.
92. Gosman, M.; Vanderjagt, A.; Veenstra, J. (eds.) *Propagation of power in the medieval west* (Mediaevalia Groningana, 23) (Groningen: Egbert Forsten, 1997).
93. Gramich, Katie; Hiscock, Andrew (eds.) *Dangerous diversity: the changing faces of Wales: essays in honour of Tudor Bevan* (Cardiff: University of Wales Press, 1998), xx, 220p.
94. Griffiths, Paul; Jenner, Mark S.R. (eds.) *Londinopolis: essays in the cultural and social history of early modern London* (Manchester and New York: Manchester University Press, 2000).
95. Guex, Sébastien (ed.) *La Suisse et les Grandes Puissances 1914–1945: relations économiques avec les Etats-Unis, la Grande-Bretagne, l'Allemagne et la France* [Switzerland and the great powers 1914–1945: economic relations with the United States, Great Britain, Germany and France] (Publications du Centre d'histoire économique et sociale de l'Université de Genève, 14) (Geneva: Droz, 1999), 494p.
96. Guy, John A. *Politics, law and counsel in Tudor and early Stuart England* (Aldershot: Ashgate Variorum, 2000). [Not continuously paginated. Reprints; only those not previously noted are itemised here.]
97. Hadfield, Andrew; Hope, Andrew (eds.) *Reformation*, vol.4 (Aldershot: Ashgate, 1999).
98. Hansen, Mogens Herman (ed.) *A comparative study of thirty city-state cultures: an investigation conducted by the Copenhagen Polis Centre* (Historisk-filosofiske Skrifter, 21) (Copenhagen: Reitzels and Det Kongelige Danske Videnskabernes Selskab / Royal Danish Academy of Sciences and Letters, 2000), 636p.
99. Haseldine, Julian. *Friendship in medieval Europe* (Stroud: Sutton, 1999), xxiii, 287p.

100. Hawkes, Jane; Mills, Susan (eds.) *Northumbria's golden age* (Stroud: Sutton, 1999), xii, 452p.
101. Heinemann, Winfried; Wiggershaus, Norbert (eds.) *Das internationale Krisenjahr 1956. Polen, Ungarn, Suez* [The international year of crises 1956: Poland, Hungary, Suez] (München: Oldenbourg, 1999), xxix, 722p. [Im Auftrag des Militärgeschichtlichen Forschungsamtes. Beiträge zur Militärgeschichte, 48.]
102. Hen, Y.; Innes, M. (eds.) *The uses of the past in the early middle ages* (Cambridge: Cambridge University Press, 2000).
103. Henriet, Patrick; Legras, Anne-Marie (eds.) *Au cloître et dans le monde: Femmes, hommes et sociétés (IXe-XVe siècle). Mélanges en l'honneur de Paulette L'Hermitte-Leclercq (Cultures et civilisations médiévales, XXIII)* (Paris: Presses de l'université de Paris-Sorbonne, 2000).
104. Hewitt, Virginia (ed.) *The banker's art: studies in paper money* (London: British Museum, 1995), 168p.
105. Hitchcock, Tim; Cohen, Michèle (eds.) *English masculinities, 1660–1800* (London: Addison Wesley, 1999), x, 268p.
106. Holm, Poul; Starkey, David John; Thór, Jón Th. (eds.) *The North Atlantic fisheries, 1100–1976: national perspectives on a common resource* (Fiskeri- og sofartsmuseets studieserie, 7) (Esbjerg: North Atlantic Fisheries History Association, 1996), 208p.
107. Holtfrerich, Carl-Ludwig. *Emergence of modern central banking from 1918 to the present* (Aldershot: Ashgate, 1999), [xi], 385p.
108. Hongzhen, W. (ed.) *Comparative planetology: geological education: history of geology* (Beijing: VSP, 1997).
109. Hooke, Della; Burnell, Simon Paul (eds.) *Landscape and settlement in Britain, AD 400–1066* (Exeter: University of Exeter Press, 1994), xi, 156p.
110. Houwen, L.A.J.R.; MacDonald, Alasdair A. (eds.) *Beda Venerabilis: historian, monk & Northumbrian* (Mediaevalia Groningana, 19) (Groningen: E. Forsten, 1996), ix, 179p.
111. Howell, David W.; Morgan, Kenneth O. (eds.) *Crime, protest and police in modern British society: essays in memory of David J.V. Jones* (Cardiff: University of Wales Press, 1999), x, 248p.
112. Hurst, Henry. *The Coloniae of Roman Britain: new studies and a review. Papers of a conference held at Gloucester on 5–6 July, 1997* (Journal of Roman Archaeology, supplementary series, 36) (Portsmouth (RI): Journal of Roman Archaeology, 1999), 196p.
113. Jackson, Gordon; Williams, David Malcolm (eds.) *Shipping, technology, and imperialism: papers presented to the third British-Dutch maritime history conference* (Aldershot: Scolar, 1996), xiv, 285p.
114. Jefferies, Henry A.; Devlin, Ciarán (eds.) *History of the diocese of Derry from earliest times* (Dublin: Four Courts, 2000), 304p.
115. Jefferys, Kevin (ed.) *Leading Labour: from Keir Hardie to Tony Blair* (London: I.B. Tauris, 1999), 235p.
116. Jones, Vivien (ed.) *Women and literature in Britain, 1700–1800* (Cambridge: Cambridge University Press, 2000), 344p.
117. Joyner, David (ed.) *Coding theory and cryptography: from Enigma and Geheimschreiber to quantum theory* (New York: Springer, 2000), vi, 256p.

118. Jupp, Peter; Magennis, Eoin (eds.) *Crowds in Ireland, c.1720–1920* (Basingstoke: Macmillan, 2000), xii, 277p.
119. Kaeuper, Richard W. (ed.) *Violence in medieval society* (Woodbridge: Boydell, 2000), xiii, 226p.
120. Keller, Katherine Z.; Schiffhorst, Gerald J. (ed.) *The witness of times: manifestations of ideology in seventeenth century England* (Pittsburgh (PA): Duquesne University Press, 1993), x, 308p.
121. Kelly, James; Keogh, Dáire (eds.) *History of the Catholic diocese of Dublin* (Dublin: Four Courts, 2000), x, 390p.
122. Kidd, Alan J.; Nicholls, David (eds.) *Gender, civic culture, and consumerism: middle-class identity in Britain, 1800–1940* (Manchester: Manchester University Press, 1999), xi, 223p.
123. Kidd, Alan J.; Nicholls, David (eds.) *The making of the British middle class? Studies of regional and cultural diversity since the eighteenth century* (Stroud: Sutton, 1998), xl, 312p.
124. Killingray, David; Omissi, David Enrico (eds.) *Guardians of empire: the armed forces of the colonial powers c.1700–1964* (Manchester: Manchester University Press, 1999), 259p.
125. Kinane, Vincent; Walsh, Anne (eds.) *Essays on the history of Trinity College Library Dublin* (Dublin: Four Courts, 2000), 206p.
126. King, Carla (ed.) *Famine, land and culture in Ireland* (Dublin: University College Dublin Press, 2000), 227p.
127. Knighton, C.S.; Loades, David Michael (eds.) *The Anthony Roll of Henry VIII's navy: Pepys MS 2991 and British Library Add MS 22047 with related material* (Navy Records Society occasional publications, 2) (Aldershot: Ashgate, 2000), xix, 198p. [Edition of illustrations of Henry VIII's ships in 1546, with details of ordnance.]
128. Körner, Martin (ed.) *Stadtzerstörung und Wiederaufbau. Zerstörung durch die Stadtherrschaft, innere Unruhen und Kriege / Destruction and reconstruction of towns: destruction by the lord's power, internal troubles and war / Destruction et reconstruction des villes: destruction par le pouvoir seigneurial, les troubles internes et les guerres*, vol. 2 (Bern, Stuttgart and Wien: Paul Haupt, 2000).
129. Kranz, J.; Reiter, J. (eds.) *Drogi do Europy* [Visions of Europe] (Warsaw: Center for International Relations, 1998).
130. Laidlaw, James (ed.) *The Auld Alliance: France and Scotland over 700 years* (Edinburgh: University of Edinburgh Press, 1999), 160p.
131. Lake, Peter; Questier, Michael (eds.) *Conformity and orthodoxy in the English church, c.1560–1660* (Woodbridge: Boydell, 2000), xx, 296p.
132. Lane, Ann; Temperley, Howard (eds.) *The rise and fall of the grand alliance, 1941–45* (Basingstoke: Macmillan, 1995), xvi, 264p.
133. Larratt Keefer, Sarah; O'Keeffe, Katherine O'Brien (eds.) *New approaches to editing Old English verse* (Cambridge: D.S. Brewer, 1998), viii, 126p.
134. Lawrence, C.H. (ed.) *The English church and the Papacy in the middle ages* (Stroud: Sutton, 1999), xii, 259p. [Reprint of 1965 collection of essays, with a new chapter by Veronica Ortenberg.]
135. Leventhal, Fred M.; Quinault, Roland E. (eds.) *Anglo-American attitudes: from revolution to partnership* (Aldershot: Ashgate, 2000), xi, 313p.

136. Liedtke, Rainer; Wendehorst, Stephan (eds.) *The emancipation of Catholics, Jews and Protestants: Minorities and the nation state in nineteenth-century Europe* (Manchester: Manchester University Press, 1999), x, 223p.

137. Litvack, Leon; Hooper, Glenn (eds.) *Ireland in the nineteenth century: regional identity* (Dublin: Four Courts, 2000), 247p.

138. Louis, Wm. Roger (ed.) *More adventures with Britannia: personalities, politics and culture in Britain* (Austin (TX) and London: University of Texas Press and I.B. Tauris, 1998), x, 388p.

139. Lowry, Donal (ed.) *The South African war reappraised* (Manchester: Manchester University Press, 2000).

140. Lualdi, Katharine Jackson; Thayer, Anne T. (eds.) *Penitence in the age of reformations* (Aldershot: Ashgate, 2000), xvi, 276p.

141. Maddicott, J.R.; Palliser, D.M. (eds.) *The medieval state: essays presented to James Campbell* (London and Rio Grande (OH): Hambledon, 2000), xlii, 262p.

142. Mäkelä, Tomi (ed.) *Music and nationalism in 20th-century Great Britain and Finland* (Hamburg: von Bockel, 1997), 243p.

143. Marolda, E.J. (ed.) *FDR and the US Navy* (Basingstoke and New York: Macmillan and St Martin's Press, 1998), vi, 202p.

144. Marotti, Arthur F. (ed.) *Catholicism and anti-Catholicism in early modern English texts* (Macmillan: Basingstoke, 1999).

145. Matthew, Colin (ed.) *The nineteenth century: the British Isles: 1815–1901* (The Short Oxford History of the British Isles) (Oxford: Oxford University Press, 2000), xiv, 342p.

146. Mayer, Thomas F. *Cardinal Pole in European context* (Variorum Collected Studies series, CS686) (Aldershot: Ashgate, 2000), 350p. [All but one item reprinted; those not previously noted are itemised.]

147. McClendon, Muriel C.; Ward, Joseph P.; MacDonald, Michael (eds.) *Protestant identities: religion, society, and self-fashioning in post-Reformation England* (Stanford (CA): Stanford University Press, 1999), xiii, 372p.

148. McCray, P. (ed.) *The prehistory and history of glassmaking technology* (Westerville (OH): American Ceramic Society, 1998).

149. Miller, Naomi J.; Yavneh, Naomi (eds.) *Maternal measures: figuring caregiving in the early modern period* (Aldershot: Ashgate, 2000), xvi, 374p.

150. Mills, Coralie M.; Coles, Geraint (eds.) *Life on the edge: human settlement and marginality* (Oxbow monograph, 100) (Oxford: Oxbow, 1998), xii, 187p.

151. Milne, Kenneth (ed.) *Christ Church Cathedral, Dublin: a history* (Dublin: Four Courts, 2000), xxi, 420p.

152. Milward, A.; Deighton, A. (eds.) *Acceleration, deepening and enlarging: the EEC, 1957–1963* (Baden Baden: Nomos, 1999).

153. Minnis, Alastair J.; Morse, Charlotte C.; Turville-Petre, Thorlac (eds.) *Essays on Ricardian literature: in honour of J.A. Burrow* (Oxford: Clarendon, 1997), xv, 358p.

154. Mitchell, Fraser (ed.) *Human interactions with the Irish quaternary: abstracts of the Annual Symposium of the Irish Association for Quaternary*

Studies held at Geological Survey of Ireland, Beggar's Bush, Dublin, 22nd November 1996 ([Dublin]: IQUA, 1996), [33]p.

155. Moir, Martin; Peers, Douglas M.; Zastoupil, Lynn (eds.) *J.S. Mill's encounter with India* (Toronto (Ont): Toronto University Press, 1999), xii, 264p.

156. Morello, Nicoletta (ed.) *Volcanoes and history: proceedings of the 20th INHIGEO Symposium, Napoli-Eolie-Catania (Italy), 19–25 September 1995* (Genova: Brigati, 1998).

157. Morgan, Hiram (ed.) *Political ideology in Ireland, 1541–1641* (Dublin: Four Courts, 1999), 264p.

158. Morris, Christopher W. (ed.) *The social contract theorists: critical essays on Hobbes, Locke, and Rousseu* (Lanham (MD): Rowman & Littlefield, 1999), xiv, 244p.

159. Morris, Robert John; Trainor, Richard Hughes (eds.) *Urban governance: Britain and beyond since 1750* (Aldershot: Ashgate, 2000), xiv, 254p.

160. Mowbray, Donald; Purdie, Rhiannon; Wei, Ian P. *Authority and community in the middle ages* (Stroud: Sutton, 1999), xviii, 187p.

161. Müller, Rolf-Dieter; Volkmann, Hans-Erich (eds.) *Die Wehrmacht: Mythos und Realität* [myth and reality] (München: Oldenbourg, 1999), xiii, 1318p. [Im Auftrag des Militärgeschichtlichen Forschungsamtes.]

162. Mullally, Evelyn; Thompson, John (eds.) *The court and cultural diversity: selected papers from the eighth triennial congress of the International Courtly Literature Society, the Queen's University of Belfast, 26 July–1 August 1995* (Woodbridge: D.S. Brewer, 1997), x, 426p.

163. Muller, James W. (ed.) *Churchill's "Iron Curtain" speech fifty years later* (Columbia (MO) and London: University of Missouri Press, 1999), xviii, 180p.

164. Myrone, Martin; Peltz, Lucy (eds.) *Producing the past: aspects of antiquarian culture and practice 1700–1850* (Aldershot and Brookfield (VT): Ashgate, 1999), xxiii, 214p.

165. Nash, David S.; Taylor, Antony (eds.) *Republicanism in Victorian society* (Stroud: Sutton, 2000), 192p.

166. Neufeld, Michael J.; Berenbaum, Michael (eds.) *The bombing of Auschwitz: should the Allies have attempted it?* (New York: St Martin's Press in association with the United States Holocaust Memorial Museum, 2000), xvii, 350p. [Includes documents.]

167. Norquay, Glenda; Smyth, Gerry (eds.) *Space & place: the geographies of literature* (Liverpool: Liverpool John Moores University Press, 1997), 414p.

168. Numbers, Ronald L.; Stenhouse, John (ed.) *Disseminating Darwinism: the role of place, race, religion, and gender* (Cambridge: Cambridge University Press, 1999), xi, 300p.

169. Offner, Arnold A.; Wilson, Theodore A. (eds.) *Victory in Europe 1945: from world war to Cold War* (Lawrence (KS): University Press of Kansas, 2000), x, 308p.

170. Ohlmeyer, Jane H. (ed.) *Political thought in seventeenth-century Ireland: kingdom or colony* (Cambridge: Cambridge University Press in association with the Folger Institute, Washington, DC, 2000), xvii, 290p.

171. Orlin, Lena Cowen (ed.) *Material London, ca.1600* (Pittsburgh (PA): University of Pennsylvania Press, 2000), 400p.

172. Osmaston, H. (ed.) *Recent research on Ladakh 4 & 5: proceedings of the 4th and 5th International Colloquia on Ladakh* (London: School of Oriental and African Studies, 1995), viii, 429p.

173. Overmans, Rüdiger (ed.) *In der Hand des Feindes: Kriegsgefangenschaft von der Antike bis zum Zweiten Weltkrieg* (Köln: Böhlau, 1999), xii, 551p. [In Verbindung mit dem Arbeitskreis Militärgeschichte e.V.]

174. Palliser, David M. (ed.) *The Cambridge urban history of Britain*, vol. 1: *600–1540* (Cambridge: Cambridge University Press, 2000).

175. Paviot, Jacques; Verger, Jacques (eds.) *Guerre, pouvoir et noblesse au Moyen Âge. Mélanges en l'honneur de Philippe Contamine (Cultures et civilisations médiévales, XXII)* (Paris: Presses de l'université de Paris-Sorbonne, 2000).

176. Platt, Peter G. (ed.) *Wonders, marvels, and monsters in early modern culture* (Newark (DE) and London: University of Delaware Press and Associated University Presses, 1999), 341p.

177. Prevenier, W.; de Hemptinne, T. (eds.) *La diplomatique urbaine en Europe au moyen âge. Actes du congrès de la Commission internationale de Diplomatique, Gand, 25–29 août 1998* (Leuven and Apeldoorn, 2000).

178. Purvis, June; Holton, Sandra Stanley (eds.) *Votes for women* (London and New York: Routledge, 2000), xiii, 297p.

179. Randall, Adrian; Charlesworth, Andrew (eds.) *Moral economy and popular protest: crowds, conflict and authority* (Basingstoke: Macmillan, 2000), xiii, 280p.

180. Reinink, Adriaan Wessel (ed.) *Memory and oblivion: proceedings of the XXIXth International Congress of the History of Art held in Amsterdam, 1–7 September 1996* (Dordrecht and Norwell (MA): Kluwer Academic, 1999), xiv, 1114p.

181. Révauger, Jean-Paul. *Pauvreté et inégalités en Grande-Bretagne de 1942 à 1990* (Paris: Éditions du Temps, 2000), 159p.

182. Richardson, Roger Charles (ed.) *The changing face of English local history* (Aldershot: Ashgate, 2000), vi, 218p.

183. Richardson, Roger Charles (ed.) *The English civil wars: local aspects* (Stroud: Sutton, 1997), ix, 342p.

184. Ridgway, Christopher; Williams, Robert (eds.) *Sir John Vanbrugh and landscape architecture in baroque England 1690–1730* (Stroud: Sutton in association with the National Trust, 2000), 242p.

185. Ritter, Gerhard A.; Wende, Peter (eds.) *Rivalität und Partnerschaft: Studien zu den deutsch-britischen Beziehungen im 19. und 20. Jahrhundert. Festschrift für Anthony J. Nicholls* (Veröffentlichungen des Deutschen Historischen Instituts London, 46) (Paderborn: Schöningh, 1999), 375p.

186. Roberts, Michael; Clarke, Simone (eds.) *Women and gender in early modern Wales* (Cardiff: University of Wales Press, 2000), xiv, 320p.

187. Rundkvist, Martin (ed.) *Grave matters: eight studies of first millennium AD burials in Crimea, England and southern Scandinavia: papers from a session held at the European Association of Archaeologists fourth annual meeting in Göteborg 1998* (BAR, International Series, 181) (Oxford: Archaeopress, 1999), v, 110p.

11

188. Ryan, Ray (ed.) *Writing in the Irish Republic: literature, culture, politics, 1949–99* (Basingstoke and New York: Macmillan and St. Martin's Press, 2000), x, 289p.

189. Salmon, J.H.M. *Ideas and contexts in France and England from the Renaissance to the Romantics* (Aldershot: Ashgate, 2000), 320p. [Reprints; only those not previously noted are itemised.]

190. Schleissner, Margaret Rose (ed.) *Manuscript sources of medieval medicine: a book of essays* (Garland Reference Library of the Humanities, 1576) (New York and London: Garland, 1995), xii, 212p.

191. Sharp, Alan; Stone, Glyn (eds.) *Anglo-French relations in the twentieth century: rivalry and cooperation* (London and New York: Routledge, 1999), 368p.

192. Sharpe, Kevin (ed.) *Remapping early modern England: the culture of seventeenth-century politics* (Cambridge: Cambridge University Press, 2000), xvi, 475p. [All but one essay reprints.]

193. Shepard, Alexandra; Withington, Phil (eds.) *Communities in early modern England: networks, place, rhetoric* (Manchester and New York: Manchester University Press, 2000).

194. Slater, T.R. (ed.) *Towns in decline, AD 100–1600* (Aldershot: Ashgate, 2000), xii, 325p.

195. Smith, John (ed.) *Administering empire: the British colonial service in retrospect. Proceedings of a conference jointly sponsored by the University of London and the Corona Club held at the Senate House on 27th and 28th May 1999 under the auspices and direction of the Institute of Historical Research and the Institute of Commonwealth Studies* (London: University of London Press, 1999), xiv, 350p.

196. Smyth, Alfred P. (ed.) *Seanchas: studies in early and medieval Irish archaeology, history and literature in honour of Francis J. Byrne* (Dublin: Four Courts, 2000), xxiii, 478p.

197. Spensky, Martine (ed.) *Universalisme, particularisme et citoyenneté dans les Iles Britanniques* [Universalism, particularism and citizenship in the British Isles] (Paris: L'Harmattan, 2000), 179p.

198. Spufford, Margaret. *Figures in the landscape: rural society in England, 1500–1700* (Variorum Collected Studies series, CS666) (Aldershot: Ashgate, 2000), xii, 364p.

199. Stobart, Jon Vernon; Owens, Alastair (eds.) *Urban fortunes: property and inheritance in the town, 1700–1900* (Aldershot: Ashgate, 2000), xiii, 241p.

200. Strachan, Hew (ed.) *The British army, manpower and society into the twenty-first century* (London: Cass, 2000), 288p.

201. Stuchtey, Benedikt; Wende, Peter (eds.) *British and German historiography, 1750–1950: traditions, perceptions and transfers* (Oxford: Oxford University Press, 2000), viii, 438p.

202. Tanner, Duncan; Thane, Pat; Tiratsoo, Nick (eds.) *Labour's first century* (Cambridge: Cambridge University Press, 2000), x, 418p.

203. Taylor, Simon (ed.) *Kings, clerics and chronicles in Scotland, 500–1297: essays in honour of Marjorie Ogilvie Anderson on the occasion of her ninetieth birthday* (Dublin: Four Courts, 2000), 208p.

204. Thacker, Alan (ed.) *Medieval archaeology, art and architecture at Chester* (Conference Transactions, British Archaeological Association, 22) (Leeds: Maney, 2000), xv, 189p.

205. Thompson, Benjamin (ed.) *Monasteries and society in medieval Britain: proceedings of the 1994 Harlaxton Symposium* (Harlaxton Medieval Studies, 6) (Stamford: Paul Watkins, 1999), xii, 368p.

206. Walker, Harlan (ed.) *Cooks & other people: proceedings of the Oxford Symposium on Food and Cookery, 1995* (Totnes: Prospect Books, 1995), 311p.

207. Walker, Harlan (ed.) *Fish: food from the waters. Proceedings of the Oxford Symposium on Food and Cookery 1997* (Totnes: Prospect Books, 1998), 335p.

208. Walker, Harlan (ed.) *Food on the move: proceedings of the Oxford Symposium on Food and Cookery, 1996* (Totnes: Prospect Books, 1997), 336p.

209. Wallace, David John (ed.) *The Cambridge history of medieval English literature* (Cambridge: Cambridge University Press, 1999), xxv, 1043p.

210. Waller, Philip J. (ed.) *The English urban landscape* (Oxford and New York: Oxford University Press, 2000), 352p.

211. Walsh, Margaret (ed.) *Working out gender: perspectives from labour history* (Aldershot: Ashgate, 1999), xii, 235p.

212. Whitton, Timothy (ed.) *Le New Labour: Rupture ou continuité?* (Rennes: Presses universitaires de Rennes, 2000), 282p.

213. Wilson, Pete; Wilmott, Tony (eds.) *The late Roman transition in the north: papers from the Roman Archaeology Conference, Durham 1999* (BAR British Series, 299) (Oxford: Archaeopress, 2000), iv, 94p.

214. Winks, Robin William (ed.) *The Oxford history of the British Empire*, vol. 5: *Historiography* (Oxford: Oxford University Press, 1999), xxiv, 731p.

215. Wischermann, Clemens; Shore, Elliott (eds.) *Advertising and the European city: historical perspectives* (Aldershot: Ashgate, 2000), xviii, 225p.

216. Woolner, David B. (ed.) *The second Quebec Conference revisited: waging war, formulating peace: Canada, Great Britain, and the United States in 1944–1945* (Basingstoke and New York: Macmillan and St Martin's Press, 1998), xiii, 210p.

217. Wordie, J. Ross (ed.) *Agriculture and politics in England, 1815–1939* (Basingstoke: Macmillan, 2000), vii, 260p.

218. Wrigley, Chris (ed.) *The First World War and the international economy* (Cheltenham and Northampton (MA): Edward Elgar, 2000), x, 221p.

219. Wyse Jackson, Patrick N. (ed.) *Science and engineering in Ireland in 1798: a time of revolution: proceedings of a symposium organised by the National Committee for the History and Philosophy of Science, 4th November 1998* (Dublin: Royal Irish Academy, 2000), viii, 83p.

220. Young, Suzanne M.M.; Pollard, A. Mark; Budd, P.; Ixer, Robert A. (eds.) *Metals in antiquity* (BAR International Series, 792) (Oxford: Archaeopress, 1999), xii, 348p.

221. Zell, Michael (ed.) *Early modern Kent 1540–1640* (Kent history project, 5) (Woodbridge: Boydell and Kent County Council, 2000), x, 340p.

B. LONG PERIODS

A. *General*

222. Abalain, Hervé. *Le Pays de Galles: Identité, modernité* [Wales: Identity, Modernity] (Crozon: Éditions Armeline, 2000), 300p.

223. Anderson, David. 'John Muir birthplace, Dunbar' [history of the site at 126–28 High Street], *Transactions of the East Lothian Antiquarian and Field Naturalists' Society* 24 (2000), 1–7.

224. Andrews, D.D. (ed.) 'Historic buildings notes and surveys 1998', *Essex Archaeology and History* 3rd ser. 30 (1999), 232–49.

225. Aughton, Peter. *Bristol: a people's history* (Lancaster: Carnegie, 2000), vi, 266p.

226. Ballie, Bruce. *History of Dollar* (Dollar: Dollar Museum Trust, 1998), vi, 153p.

227. Benvie, James R. *A Benvie chronicle: a Scottish, local and family history from Pictish past to the 20th century* (Forfar: Baneuer, 1998), x, 180p.

228. Black, Jeremy. *A new history of England* (Stroud: Sutton, 2000), xii, 308p.

229. Black, Jeremy. *A new history of Wales* (Stroud: Sutton, 2000), x, 246p.

230. Bodey, Hugh. 'The office at 7 Cathedral Close, Exeter' [the office of the Devonshire Association], *Devonshire Association Report and Transactions* 131 (1999), 267–74.

231. Colley, Linda. 'The significance of the frontier in British history', A138.

232. Currie, Christopher K. 'Polesden Lacey and Ranmore Common estates, near Dorking: an archaeological and historical survey', *Surrey Archaeological Collections* 87 (2000), 49–84.

233. Gardiner, Julie (ed.) *Resurgam!: archaeology at Stonehouse, Mount Batten, and Mount Wise regeneration areas, Plymouth* (Salisbury: Wessex Archaeology, 2000), xvi, 312p.

234. Gilkes, Oliver J. 'Excavations at Rocky Clump, Stanmer Park, Brighton, 1951–1981', *Sussex Archaeological Collections* 135 (1997), 113–25.

235. Glen, Duncan. *A new history of Cambuslang* (Kirkcaldy: Akros, 1998), 152p.

236. Griffiths, W.B. 'Excavations at the New Quay, Berwick upon Tweed, 1996', *Archaeologia Aeliana* 5th ser. 27 (1999), 75–108.

237. Lowe, Raymond. *Reflections of a bygone age: a brief history of Allington and Burton in the parish of Rossett* (Wrexham: RLP, 1998), 112p.

238. Luffingham, John (ed.) *Boxgrove: history of a Sussex village* (Chichester: Boxgrove History Group, 2000), 144p.

239. Mackinder, Anthony; Blatherwick, Simon. *Bankside: excavations at Benbow House, Southwark, London, SE1* (MoLAS archaeology studies, 3) (London: Museum of London Archaeology Service, 2000), viii, 68p.

240. McKinley, Jacqueline I. 'Excavations at Tinney's Lane, Sherborne, Dorset', *Proceedings of the Dorset Natural History and Archaeological Society* 121 (1999), 53–67.

241. Moore, Peter. 'Excavations at the site of West Court Manor House, Chalk', *Archaeologia Cantiana* 119 (1999), 353–67.

242. Moran, Madge. 'Shootrough Farm, Cardington, Shropshire (SO 490964)',
      Shropshire History and Archaeology 74 (1999), 43–50.
243. Newlyn, Doreen. *This goodly house: its people and its times, 1733 to 1953*
      [Chapel Allerton] (Leeds: WAC, 1998), 234p.
244. Nolan, Brian. *Eminent Roffensians*, 4th edn. ([Rochester]: Old Roffensian
      Society, 1998), 52p.
245. Oakey, Niall; Spoerry, Paul. *Excavations at Orchard Lane, Huntingdon,
      1994 Proceedings of the Cambridge Antiquarian Society* 85 (1996), 123–58p.
246. Palmer, Stuart C. 'Archeological excavations in the Arrow Valley,
      Warwickshire', *Birmingham and Warwickshire Archaeological Society
      Transactions* 103 (1999), 1–230.
247. Palmer, Susann. 'Excavations of previously unknown buildings in the
      grounds of St Stephen's Vicarage', *Proceedings of the Dorset Natural
      History and Archaeological Society* 121 (1999), 69–75.
248. Patchett, John H. 'Queenshead c.1385–1845: a history from the Wakefield
      Court Rolls', *Transactions of the Halifax Antiquarian Society* ns 8 (2000),
      47–64.
249. Rawlings, Mick. 'Excavations at Ivy Street and Brown Street, Salisbury,
      1994', *Wiltshire Archaeological and Natural History Magazine* 93 (2000),
      20–62.
250. Richardson, Roger Charles. 'Introduction: the changing face of English
      local history', A182.
251. Roberts, O. 'Joe Boumphrey of Tranmere and Abersoch', *Maritime Wales*
      21 (2000), 109–111.
252. Roberts, O. 'The Pile of Foudrey and Lewis Morris', *Maritime Wales* 21
      (2000), 52–54.
253. Rogers, Kenneth. 'Yet more about Cumberwell' [House near Bradford-on-
      Avon], *Wiltshire Archaeological and Natural History Magazine* 93 (2000),
      249–54. [See also G.J. Kidson, 'More about Cumberwell', *Wiltshire
      Archaeological and Natural History Magazine* 54 (1952), 279–88.]
254. Schama, Simon. *A history of Britain*, vol.1: *At the edge of the world? 300
      BC—AD 1603* (London: BBC, 2000), 416p.
255. Scott, Frank T. 'Commercial Road area, Hawick: a historical study 1998'
      [Register of addresses, owners, etc.], *Hawick Archaeological Society
      Transactions* (1999), 35–52.
256. Sinclair, J.N. *A brief history of the Orkneys* (London: Minerva, 2000), xiii,
      157p.
257. Stamper, Paul; Croft, R.A. *The South Manor area* (Wharram: a study of
      settlement on the Yorkshire Wolds, 8; York University Archaeological
      Publications, 10) (York: University of York, 2000), xiv, 223p.
258. Stead, Miriam. *Wrotham Place: a history* (London: Haggerston, 1998),
      70p.
259. Teasdale, J.A. 'An archaeological investigation of the town wall between
      St. Andrew's Street and St. Andrew's Churchyard, Newcastle upon Tyne',
      Archaeologia Aeliana 5th ser. 27 (1999), 29–43.
260. Turbutt, Gladwyn. *History of Derbyshire* (Merton Priory, 1999), 4 pts.
261. Walker, Frank Arneil. *Argyll and Bute* (Buildings of Scotland) (London:
      Penguin, 2000), xviii, 683p.

262. Woodward, Stuart. *Further reflections on Ticknall and Calke* ([Ticknall]: Ticknall Preservation and Historical Society, 1998), 33p.
263. Wyatt, Peter; Stanes, Robin (eds.) *Uffculme: a Devon town from Tudor times* (Uffculme: Short Run Press for the Uffculme Archive Group, 1997), xv, 323p.

B. *Historiography and Historical Methods*

See also 355 (B)

264. Anonymous. 'Guide to the special collections of the John Rylands University Library of Manchester', *Bulletin of the John Rylands University Library of Manchester* 80:2 (1999), 1–381.
265. Anonymous. 'Bibliography: Literary [and] historical', *Recusant History* 25:2 (2000), 365–71.
266. Betteridge, Alan. 'Preservation and interpretation: archives and the Halifax Antiquarian Society', *Transactions of the Halifax Antiquarian Society* ns 8 (2000), 190–207.
267. Bierton, Graham; Hayes, Graham. 'An excavation at Shoelands, Puttenham', *Surrey Archaeological Collections* 87 (2000), 169–74.
268. Bristow, Joy (comp.) *The local historian's glossary and vade mecum*, 2nd edn. (Centre for Local History Record Series, 8) (Nottingham: Department of Adult Education, University of Nottingham, 1994), x, 277p. [1st published 1990.]
269. Burke, Peter. 'Reflections on the historical revolution in France: the *Annales* school and British social history', A44, 284–94. [1st published in *Review* 1 (1978), 147–56.]
270. Cockin, Tim. *The Staffordshire encyclopaedia: a secondary source index on the history of the old county of Stafford, celebrating its curiosities, peculiarities and legends* (Barlaston, Stoke-on-Trent: Malthouse, 2000), xxvi, 771p.
271. Crabb, S. 'Dronfield's local history zone', *The Local Historian* 30:3 (2000), 183–86.
272. Everitt, Alan. 'New avenues in English local history', A182.
273. Finberg, H.P.R. 'The local historian and his theme', A182.
274. Fisher, Deborah C. *Who's who in Welsh history* (Swansea: Christopher Davies, 1997), 187p.
275. Fraser, Antonia. 'The value of biography in history', *The Historian* [London] 66 (2000), 4–9.
276. Gee, Austin (ed.) *Royal Historical Society annual bibliography of British and Irish history: publications of 1999* (Oxford: Oxford University Press, 2000), xiii, 535p.
277. Gibson, William. 'Recent work in history and archives 1998–99', *Archives* 24:101 (1999), 71–78.
278. Gibson, William. 'Recent work in local history and archives 1999', *Archives* 25:103 (2000), 161–71.
279. Graham, T.W. 'A list of articles on Scottish history published during the year 1998', *Scottish Historical Review* 79:1 (2000), 87–96.

280. Grant, Alexander. 'A list of essays on Scottish history published during the years 1997–1998', *Scottish Historical Review* 79:1 (2000), 97–104.

281. Haigh, Donald. 'Wakefield Gate (the Alta Via): a re-appraisal', *Transactions of the Halifax Antiquarian Society* ns 8 (2000), 14–46.

282. Hodgson, John R. (ed.) *A guide to special collections of the John Rylands University Library of Manchester* (Manchester: John Rylands University Library of Manchester, 1999), 272p.

283. Hoskins, W.G. 'English local history: the past and the future', A182.

284. Hudson, Pat. 'A new history from below: computers and the maturing of local and regional history', A182.

285. Kain, Roger J.P.; Ravenhill, William L.D. (eds.) *Historical atlas of southwest England* (Exeter: University of Exeter Press, 1999), xxii, 564p.

286. Kenyon, John R. 'Post-medieval Britain and Ireland in periodic literature in 1998', *Post-Medieval Archaeology* 33 (1999), 288–95.

287. Kenyon, John R. 'Post-medieval periodic literature in Britain and Ireland in 1999', *Post-Medieval Archaeology* 34 (2000), 392–8.

288. Kitching, Christopher. 'The National Register of Archives: adapting to meet researchers' needs in the twenty-first century', *Recusant History* 25:2 (2000), 356–60.

289. List and Index Society. *Master Harvey's exhibits: Duchess of Norfolk's deeds (C115)* (List and Index Society, 274) ([Kew?]: List and Index Society, 1999), [242]p.

290. Marchant, D. 'The East Yorkshire Heritage Library: history at your fingertips', *The Local Historian* 30:3 (2000), 178–82.

291. Martin, G.H.; Clare, T.; Shotter, D.C.A. 'A retrospective', *Transactions of the Cumberland & Westmorland Antiquarian & Archaeological Society* 100 (2000), 261–72.

292. Miller, S. 'A bibliography of the Revd. Walter Gregor's publications', *Northern Scotland* 20 (2000), 149–66.

293. Murray, Hugh (comp.) 'A York bibliography, part 5', *York Historian* 16 (1999), 59–68.

294. Murray, Hugh (comp.). 'A York bibliography, part 6', *York Historian* 17 (2000), 72–84.

295. Neighbour, O.W. 'The Tyson collection', *British Library Journal* 24:2 (1998), 269–77.

296. Richardson, John. *The local historian's encyclopedia*, 3rd edn. (2000).

297. Roper, Michael. 'The Public Record Office and sources for the history of the Halifax area', *Transactions of the Halifax Antiquarian Society* ns 8 (2000), 214–22.

298. Sewell, Pat. 'West Yorkshire Archive Service, Calderdale: archive accessions, 1999', *Transactions of the Halifax Antiquarian Society* ns 8 (2000), 231–4.

299. Smith, John; Backouche, Isabelle. 'Current bibliography of urban history', *Urban History* 26 (1999), 441–87.

300. Spufford, Peter (ed.) *Index to the probate accounts of England and Wales*, 2 vols. (Index Library, 112–13) (London: British Record Society, 1999).

301. Thackray, John C. *A guide to the official archives of the Natural History Museum, London* (London: Society for the History of Natural History on behalf of the Natural History Museum, 1998), xix, 174p.

302. Turvey, R.K.; Freeman, Peter (comps.) 'Articles relating to the history of Wales published mainly in 1997', *Welsh History Review* 19:4 (1999), 781–91.
303. Willetts, Pamela Joan. *Catalogue of manuscripts in the Society of Antiquaries of London* (Woodbridge: D.S. Brewer, 2000), xxv, 619p.
304. Williams, David H. *Catalogue of seals in the National Museum of Wales*, II: *Ecclesiastical, monastic and collegiate seals with a supplement concerning Wales* (Cardiff: National Museums & Galleries of Wales, 1998), ix, 67p.

C. Population and Environment

See also 501, 508 (B)

305. Aston, Mick; Bond, James. *The landscape of towns*, revised edn. (Stroud: Sutton, 2000), 259p. [1st published London: Dent, 1976.]
306. Breeze, Andrew. 'The names of Bellshill, Carmichael, Lauder and Soutra', *Innes Review* 51:1 (2000), 72–79.
307. Cameron, Kenneth. *English place names* (London: Batsford, 1996), 256p.
308. Clark, John F.M. 'The Irishmen of birds' [house sparrows], *History Today* 50:10 (2000), 16–17.
309. Coates, Richard. 'Thoughts on L'Ancresse, Guernsey', *Nomina* 23 (2000), 75–78.
310. De Lisle, David de Garis. 'The regional impact of population change in Guernsey', *La Société Guernesiaise Report and Transactions* 24 (1999), 703–13.
311. Doyle, Barry. 'Research in urban history', *Urban History* 27:2 (2000), 283–91.
312. Fleming, Andrew. 'A lost Swaledale vaccary and a palimpsest of place names', *Northern History* 36 (2000), 159–62.
313. Garwood, Adam. 'A medieval pit group in Epping: an evaluation at the Co-op site, rear of 237–55 High Street, Epping', *Essex Archaeology and History* 3rd ser. 30 (1999), 262–6.
314. Gelling, Margaret. *Signposts to the past: place-names and the history of England*, 3rd edn. (Chichester: Phillimore, 1997), 281p.
315. Gray, Ronald; Stubbings, Derek. *Cambridge street-names: their origins and associations* (Cambridge: Cambridge University Press, 2000), xix, 159p.
316. Kearns, G. 'Maps, models and registers: the historical geography of the population of England', *Journal of Historical Geography* 26:2 (2000), 298–304.
317. Megaw, Ruth; Megaw, Vincent. 'Celtic connections past and present: Celtic ethnicity ancient and modern', A18, 19–81.
318. Muir, Richard. 'Pollards in Nidderdale: a landscape history', *Rural History* 11 (2000), 95–111.
319. Osborne, Graham; Hobbs, Graham. *The place-names of Eastern Gwent* (Abertillery: Old Bakehouse Publications, 1998), 112p.
320. Parsons, David N.; Styles, Tania; Hough, Carole (eds.) *The vocabulary of English place-names: A-Box* (Nottingham: Centre for English Name-Studies, 1997), xix, 155p.

321. Parsons, David N.; Styles, Tania (eds.) *The vocabulary of English place-names: Brace-Cæster* (Nottingham: Centre for English Name-Studies, 2000), xviii, 177p.
322. Phillpotts, C. 'Landscape into townscape: an historical and archaeological investigation of the Limehouse area, east London', *Landscape History* 21 (1999), 59–76.
323. Pryce, W.T.R. 'A migration typology and some topics for the research agenda', *Family & Community History* 3 (2000), 65–80.
324. Ryan, P.M. 'Woodham Walter hall; its site and setting', *Essex Archaeology and History* 3rd ser. 30 (1999), 178–95.
325. Shoard, Marion. 'Access to the countryside', *History Today* 50:9 (2000), 16–18.
326. Sydeserff, David. 'East Lothian field names: some researches into past and present names', *Transactions of the East Lothian Antiquarian and Field Naturalists' Society* 23 (1996), 87–104.
327. Taylor, Christopher. *Fields in the English landscape*, revised & updated edn. (Stroud: Sutton, 2000), 174p. [1st published London: Dent, 1975.]
328. Taylor, Christopher. *Parks and gardens of Britain: a landscape history from the air* (Edinburgh: Edinburgh University Press, 1998), vii, 224p.
329. Thirsk, Joan (ed.) *The English rural landscape* (Oxford: Oxford University Press, 2000), 352p.
330. Thomas, James. 'The great bustard in Wiltshire: flight into extinction?', *Wiltshire Archaeological and Natural History Magazine* 93 (2000), 63–70.
331. Waller, Philip J. 'The English urban landscape: yesterday, today, and tomorrow', A210, 11–31.

Da. *Social Life and Conditions*

See also 381, 413, 417 (B)

332. Abrams, Lynn. ' "The best men in Shetland": women, gender and place in peripheral communities', *Cornish Studies* 8 (2000), 97–114.
333. Ashelford, Jane. *The art of dress: clothes and society, 1500–1914* (London: National Trust, 1996), 320p.
334. Baker-Jones, Leslie. *Princelings, privilege and power: the Tivyside gentry in their community* (Llandysul: Gwasg Gomer, 1999), 376p.
335. Behlmer, George K. 'Character building and the English family: continuities in social casework, ca.1870–1930', A13, 58–74.
336. Birley, Derek. *A social history of English cricket* (London: Aurum, 1999), x, 388p.
337. Blaikie, A. 'Migration and cultural identity: within and beyond the nation. A review article', *Northern Scotland* 20 (2000), 179–188.
338. Curtis-Bennett, Susan. *The Curtis-Bennett chronicle* (Chichester: Phillimore, 1998).
339. Domville, Edward Alan. *The Mawdsleys of the Moss* (Southport: Limited Edition, 1998), vi, 148p.
340. Elder, Eilen. 'The Peacock family archive: an interpretive survey', *Lincolnshire History and Archaeology* 34 (1999), 41–45.

341. Fortescue, Lady Margaret. 'Recollections of the Fortescue family', *Devonshire Association Report and Transactions* 131 (1999), 1–10.

342. Halliday, S. 'The Loraines of Kirkharle: the decline and resurgence of a Northumbrian upper gentry family', *Northern History* 36 (2000), 73–82.

343. Jupp, Peter C.; Gittings, Clare. *Death in England: an illustrated history* (Manchester: Manchester University Press, 1999), xiv, 282p.

344. Richardson, Joan. 'The origin of the Carews: an update', *Genealogists' Magazine* 26 (1999), 245–9.

345. Sayer, Karen. *Country cottages: a cultural history* (Manchester: Manchester University Press, 2000), 229p.

346. Sellar, W. David H.; Mclean, Alasdair. *The Highland clan MacNeacail (MacNicol): a history of the Nicolsons of Scorrybreac*, ed. C.B. Harman Nicholson (Waternish (Skye): Maclean, 1999), xvi, 80p.

347. Swinburne, L. 'Dancing with the mermaids: ship's biscuit and portable soup', A208, 309–20.

348. Sydeserff, David. 'The Hepburns of Kingston', *Transactions of the East Lothian Antiquarian and Field Naturalists' Society* 24 (2000), 9–22.

349. Thane, Pat. '"An untiring zest for life": images and self-images of old women in England', *Journal of Family History* 25 (2000), 235–47.

350. Thane, Pat. *Old age in English history: past experiences, present issues* (Oxford: Oxford University Press, 2000), x, 536p.

351. Webley, John. *The Scotts of Thirlestane: the story of John Scott of Thirlestane, his Buccleuch ancestry and his descendents, the Scott Elliots of Larriston and the Napiers* (Horsmonden: The author, 2000), 217p.

Db. *Social Structure*

See also 310 (B)

352. Aldous, Vivienne E. *My ancestors were freemen of the City of London* (London: Society of Genealogists, 1999), vii, 133p.

353. Alvarez Borge, Ignacio. *Comunidades locales y transformaciones sociales en la Alta Edad Media. Hampshire (Wessex) y el sur la Castille, un estudio comparativo* [Local communities and social transformations in the high middle ages: a comparative study of Hampshire and Castille] (Logroño: Universidad de La Rioja, 1999), 198p.

354. Floate, Sharon Sillers. *My ancestors were gypsies* (London: Society of Genealogists, 1999), 89p.

355. Razzell, Peter. 'Evaluating the same name technique as a way of measuring burial register reliability in England', *Local Population Studies* 64 (2000), 8–22.

356. Runciman, W.G. 'Is there always an underclass?', *Proceedings of the British Academy* 101 (1999), 273–88.

357. Wenzerul, Rosemary (ed.) *A beginner's guide to Jewish genealogy in Great Britain* (London: The Jewish Genealogical Society of Great Britain, 2000), 80p.

Dc. *Social Policy and Welfare*

See also 350 (B)

358. Bornat, Joanna (ed.) *Oral history, health and welfare* (London: Routledge, 2000), x, 314p.
359. Hanley, Hugh. *Thomas Hickman's Charity, Aylesbury: a tercentenary history, 1698–1998* (Oxford: Leopard's Head, 2000), viii, 117p.
360. Micale, Mark S. '*The history of Bethlem*' [review article], *Social History of Medicine* 13:1 (2000), 153–62.

Ea. *Economic Activity and Organisation*

See also 458 (B)

361. Anonymous. 'Transport records deposited in 1998', *Journal of Transport History* 3rd ser. 21:2 (2000), 209–13.
362. Adeeb, Yasmin; Bennett, John. 'British labour history publications in 1998', *Labour History Review* 64 (1999), 314–34.
363. Adeeb, Yasmin; Bennett, John (comps.) 'Theses and dissertations on British and Irish Labour History, 1998', *Labour History Review* 64 (1999), 290–4.
364. Aldcroft, Derek Howard; Sutcliffe, Anthony (eds.) *Europe in the international economy 1500 to 2000* (London: Edward Elgar, 1999), xi, 289p.
365. Attard, Bernard. 'Making a market: the jobbers of the London Stock Exchange, 1800–1986', *Financial History Review* 7:1 (2000), 5–24.
366. Bannerman, N. 'Fish trap types', *Maritime Wales* 21 (2000), 7–22.
367. Bhanji, Sadru. 'Limeburning in Exeter and Exe estuary parishes: a documentary study', *Devonshire Association Report and Transactions* 131 (1999), 165–98.
368. Bhanji, Sadru. 'The involvement of Exeter and the Exe estuary in piracy', *Devonshire Association Report and Transactions* 130 (1998), 23–49.
369. Bonson, Tony (ed.) *Millstones to megawatts: a bibliography for industrial historians: the publications of Dr D.G. Tucker* (Congleton: Midland Wind & Water Mills Group, 1999), 68p.
370. Britnell, Richard H.; et al. (comps.) 'Review of periodical literature published in 1998', *Economic History Review* 2nd ser. 53 (2000), 127–75.
371. Bullen, Mark. 'The Newport customs house', *Maritime Wales* 19 (1997–98), 56–69.
372. Collett, Janet. 'Annual list of articles on agrarian history, 1998', *Agricultural History Review* 48:1 (2000), 104–13.
373. Cottingham, Ann. *The hostelries of Henley: or an account of the alehouses, beerhouses, breweries, hostelries, hotels, inns, malthouses, public houses, taverns and typpling houses in the town of Henley on Thames* (Shiplake: The author, 2000), 335p.
374. Cubbon, M. 'A remarkable decade of Manx coin hoards, 1972–1982', *Isle of Man Natural History and Antiquarian Society Proceedings* 11:1 (1997–99), 29–50.

375. Davey, P.J. 'Medieval and later pottery from the Isle of Man', *Isle of Man Natural History and Antiquarian Society Proceedings* 11:1 (1997–99), 91–114.

376. Dawson, David; Kent, Oliver. 'Reduction fired low-temperature ceramics' [reconstruction of kilns], *Post-Medieval Archaeology* 33 (1999), 164–78.

377. Dean, Ann. *Foudland: slate quarriers and crofters in Aberdeenshire* (Insch: The author, 1998), 72p.

378. Douglas, Roy. *Taxation in Britain since 1660* (Basingstoke: Macmillan, 1999), xii, 174p.

379. Dyer, Christopher. 'Alternative approaches to the history of agriculture' [review article], *Past & Present* 168 (2000), 254–62.

380. Gill, M.; Harvey, W. 'Weights and measures used in the lead industry', *British Mining* 61 (1998), 129–40.

381. Hale, Matthew; Hawkins, Richard; Partridge, Michael (comps.) 'List of publications on the economic and social history of Great Britain and Ireland published in 1999', *Economic History Review* 2nd ser. 53:4 (2000), 783–820.

382. Hall, Phillip. 'Royal revenues' [1760–1999], *History Today* 50:2 (2000), 26–28.

383. Hesse, Mary. 'Field systems in southwest Cambridgeshire: Abington Pigotts, Litlington and the Mile Ditches', *Proceedings of the Cambridge Antiquarian Society* 89 (2000), 49–58.

384. Hill, N.A. 'Nevill Holt: the development of an English country house', *Archaeological Journal* 156 (1999), 246–93.

385. Howkins, Richard A. 'Bibliography in business history', *Business Archives* 80 (2000), 57–63.

386. Humphrey, Thomas M. *Money, exchange, and production: further essays in the history of economic thought* (Cheltenham: Edward Elgar, 1998), ix, 178p.

387. Ide, Isabel. '"A very pretty seat": Erlestoke Park, 1780–1999', *Wiltshire Archaeological and Natural History Magazine* 93 (2000), 9–19.

388. Keene, Derek. 'The financial district of the City of London: continuity and change, 1300–1871', A65, 279–302.

389. Lampard, Nigel S. *A history of South Newton water mill* ([Lyndhurst?]: The author, 1998), 52p.

390. Larn, Richard; Larn, Bridget. *Shipwreck index of the British Isles*, vol. 4: *Scotland; Index to volumes 1–4* (London: Lloyd's Register of Shipping, 1998), 227p.

391. Lefeber, L. 'Classical vs. neoclassical economic thought in historical perspective: the interpretation of processes of economic growth and development', *History of Political Thought* 21:3 (2000), 525–42.

392. Lenfestey, Hugh. 'Saints Farm and Fief Fortescu: a revised historical perspective', *La Société Guernesiaise Report and Transactions* 24 (1999), 620–34. [With reply, no.397.]

393. Llewellyn, Charles. *The mill's life: from the Domesday book to the millennium* (London: Robson, 1997), viii, 197p.

394. Lowe, M.C. 'Devon local carriers', *Devonshire Association Report and Transactions* 130 (1998), 111–36.

395. Mayhew, Nicholas J. *Sterling: the rise and fall of a currency* (London: Allen Lane, 1999), xiv, 305p.

396. McCann, John. *The dovecotes of Suffolk* (Ipswich: Suffolk Institute of Archaeology and History, 1998), 128p.

397. McCormack, John A. 'Saints Farm and Fief Fortescu: a reply' [to no.392], *La Société Guernesiaise Report and Transactions* 24 (1999), 635–40.

398. McIntosh, Tania. *The decline of Stourbridge Fair, 1770–1934* (Friends' Papers, 2) (Leicester: Friends of the Department of English Local History, University of Leicester, 1998), 43p.

399. Melton, Nigel; Scott, Keith. 'Polesworth: a north Warwickshire country pottery', *Post-Medieval Archaeology* 33 (1999), 94–126.

400. Michie, Ranald C. *The London Stock Exchange: a history* (Oxford: Oxford University Press, 1999), xiii, 672p.

401. Moriceau, Jean-Marc. 'La terre et les paysans en France et en Grande-Bretagne aux XVIIe et XVIIIe siecles: un parcours bibliographique critique. Pte. 2', *Histoire et Sociétés Rurales* 10 (1998), 105–238.

402. Orbell, John. 'The historical archives of ING Barings', *Financial History Review* 7:1 (2000), 89–104.

403. Poitras, Geoffrey. *The early history of financial economics, 1478–1776: from commercial arithmetic to life annuities and joint stocks* (London: Edward Elgar, 2000), 544p.

404. Polkinghorn, Bette; Thomson, Dorothy Lampen. *Adam Smith's daughters: eight prominent women economists from the eighteenth century to the present*, revised edn. (Cheltenham: Edward Elgar, 1998), xi, 130p. [1st published 1973.]

405. Poussou, Jean-Pierre. 'L'"agriculture alternative": à propos d'un livre de Joan Thirsk', *Histoire et Sociétés Rurales* 12 (1999), 131–47.

406. Ransom, Bill. 'The descent and dispersion of the manor of Ilsington', *Devonshire Association Report and Transactions* 131 (1999), 105–22.

407. Richmond, Lesley. 'Balancing rights and interests: the ethics of business archives', *Business Archives* 79 (2000), 29–41.

408. Robertson, Iain A. *The Tay salmon fisheries since the eighteenth century* (Glasgow: Cruithne, 1998), xiv, 463p.

409. Robinson, Robb; Starkey, David J. 'The sea fisheries of the British isles, 1376–1976: a preliminary survey', A106, 121–43.

410. Roe, M. 'Swan Bank colliery', *British Mining* 61 (1998), 22–32.

411. Ross, Duncan M. 'British business history: a review of the periodical literature for 1998', *Business History* 42:2 (2000), 1–16.

412. Sambrook, Pamela A. *The country house kitchen 1650–1900: skills and equipment for food provisioning* (Food and Society, 8) (Stroud: Alan Sutton in association with the National Trust, 1996), xi, 266p.

413. Sharpe, Pamela (ed.) *Women's work: the English experience, 1650–1914* (London: Arnold, 1998), xii, 368p.

414. Sinclair, David. *The pound: a biography* (London: Century, 2000), 298p.

415. Smith, R. 'Smelt mills of the Yorkshire dales: Keld Heads and Preston mills', *British Mining* 61 (1998), 42–62.

416. Stammers, M.K. 'The Welsh sloop', *Maritime Wales* 21 (2000), 55–58.

417. Stapleton, Barry; Thomas, James Harry. *Gales: a study in brewing, business and family history* [George Gale & Co.] (Aldershot: Ashgate, 2000), xii, 192p.

418. Thorold, Peter. *The London rich: the creation of a great city from 1666 to the present* (London: Viking, 1999), ix, 403p.

419. Todd, Daniel. 'Retreat from specialisation: a coal port's search for sustainability', *Journal of Transport History* 3rd ser. 21:2 (2000), 168–90.

420. Tyler, Kieron. 'The production of tin-glazed ware on the north bank of the Thames: excavations at the site of the Hermitage Pothouse, Wapping', *Post-Medieval Archaeology* 33 (1999), 127–63.

421. Williams, Katherine. 'Major accessions to repositories in 1998 relating to labour history', *Labour History Review* 64 (1999), 307–13.

422. Yamey, B.S. 'The "particular gain or loss upon each article we deal in": an aspect of mercantile accounting, 1300–1800', *Accounting, Business & Financial History* 10:1 (2000), 1–12.

Eb. *Technology*

See also 448 (B)

423. Brown, J.K. 'Design plans, working drawings, national styles: engineering practice in Great Britain and the United States, 1775–1945', *Technology and Culture* 41:2 (2000), 195–238.

424. Dekker, Elly; Ackermann, Silke; Lippincott, Kristen; van der Merwe, Pieter; Blyzinsky, Maria (comp.) *Globes at Greenwich: a catalogue of the globes and armillary spheres in the National Maritime Museum, Greenwich* (Oxford: Oxford University Press and the National Maritime Museum, 1999), xi, 592p.

425. Proctor, J.; Sabel, K.; Meddens, F.M. 'Post-medieval brick clamps at New Cross in London', *Post-Medieval Archaeology* 34 (2000), 187–202.

426. Ravenhill, Mary R.; Rowe, Margery M. (eds.) *Early Devon maps: maps of lands and estates in Devon before 1700* (Exeter: Friends of Devon's Archives, 2000), vi, 58p.

427. Russell, Colin Archibald (ed.) *Chemistry, society and environment: a new history of the British chemical industry* (Cambridge: Royal Society of Chemistry, 2000), xvi, 372p.

Fa. *Media and Communication*

428. Hellyer, Roger. *Ordnance Survey small-scale maps: indexes, 1801–1998* (Kerry (Montgomeryshire): David Archer, 1999), xxiv, 264p.

Fb. *Science and Medicine*

See also 427 (B)

429. Fauvel, John; Flood, Raymond; Wilson, Robin (eds.) *Oxford figures: 800 years of the mathematical sciences* (Oxford: Oxford University Press, 2000), 296p.

430. Hunter, Andrew (ed.) *Thornton and Tully's scientific books, libraries, and collectors: a study of bibliography and the book trade in relation to the history of science*, 4th edn. (Aldershot: Ashgate, 2000), xii, 405p. [3rd edn. published 1971.]
431. Oldroyd, David Roger. *Sciences of the earth: studies in the history of mineralogy and geology* (Collected Studies, CS628) (Aldershot: Ashgate, 1998).
432. Rice, A.L. *Voyages of discovery: three centuries of natural history exploration* (London: Scriptum Editions in association with the Natural History Museum, 2000), 335p.
433. Rose, Frank Clifford (ed.) *A short history of neurology: the British contribution, 1660–1910* (Oxford: Butterworth-Heinemann, 1999), ix, 282p.

Fc. *Ideas and Learning*

See also 460, 479 (B)

434. Aldrich, Richard. 'Educational standards in historical perspective', *Proceedings of the British Academy* 102 (2000), 39–68.
435. Bendall, A. Sarah; Brooke, Christopher Nugent Lawrence; Collinson, Patrick. *A history of Emmanuel College, Cambridge* (Woodbridge: Boydell, 2000), xvii, 741p.
436. Hobbs, Jean M.F. *The log books of Ware St. Mary's Schools* (Ware: Ware Society, 1997), 117p.
437. Korte, Barbara. *English travel writing from pilgrimages to the postcolonial explorations* (Basingstoke: Macmillan, 2000), vii, 218p. [Translation of *Der englische Reisebericht. Von der Pilgerfahrt bis zur Postmoderne* (Darmstadt: Wissenschaftliches Buchgesellschaft, 1996).]
438. Roach, J. 'The Sheffield boys' and girls' charity schools, 1706–1962', *Journal of Educational Administration and History* 31 (1999), 114–29.

Fd. *Culture and the Arts*

See also 487 (B)

439. Ashbee, Andrew; Harley, John (eds.) *The cheque books of the Chapel Royal, with additional material from the manuscripts of William Lovegrove and Marmaduke Alford* (Aldershot: Ashgate, 2000), 2 vols. [Edition by Edward F. Rimbault published 1872.]
440. Barker, Nicolas; Jervis, Simon. *Treasures from the libraries of National Trust country houses* (New York: Royal Oak Foundation and the Grolier Club, 1999), 179p.
441. Beeson, Mark. 'A history of Dartmoor theatre. Part two: 1661–1999', *Devonshire Association Report and Transactions* 131 (1999), 139–64.
442. Bengtson, Jonathan B. 'Benefaction registers in Oxford libraries', *Library History* 16 (2000), 143–52.
443. *The British Library catalogue of additions to the manuscripts: 1956–65, 3 vols.* (London: British Library, 2000), xvi, 1692p. [Additional manuscripts 48989–53708; Egerton manuscripts 3725–3776; Additional charters and

rolls 75435–75577; Detached seals and casts CCI. 1–124; Part 1: Descriptions; part 2: Index A-K; Part 3: Index L-Z.]

444. Burnett, T.A.J. *The British Library catalogue of the Ashley manuscripts*, 2 vols.: 1. *Inscriptions*; 2. *Index* (London: British Library, 1999).

445. Clarke, R. 'Medieval timber buildings in Chipping Ongar: excavation at the south side of the Pleasance car park, 1995', *Essex Archaeology and History* 3rd ser. 30 (1999), 154–77.

446. Cox, Philip. *Reading adaptations: novels and verse narratives on the stage, 1790–1840* (Manchester: Manchester University Press, 2000), vii, 184p.

447. Donaldson, William. *The highland pipe and Scottish society, 1750–1950: transmission, change and the concept of tradition* (East Linton: Tuckwell, 2000), x, 518p.

448. Dunn, Michael. 'The art and history of lead rainwater heads in the City of York', *York Historian* 17 (2000), 2–16.

449. Easthope, Antony. *Englishness and national culture* (London: Routledge, 1999), x, 243p.

450. Farrar, Maurice. *The Gilbert & Sullivan alphabet of artistes: a performance record of D'Oyly Carte personnel, 1875–1982* (Ayr: Rhosearn, 1999), xxvii, 267p.

451. Freeman, Michael. 'The history of museums in Ceredigion', *Ceredigion* 13:3 (1999–99), 64–90.

452. Fyfe, Gordon. *Art, power and modernity: English art insitutions, 1750–1950* (London: Leicester University Press, 2000), ix, 212p.

453. Hellinga, Lotte; Trapp, Joseph Burney (eds.) *The Cambridge history of the book in Britain*, vol.3: *1400–1557* (Cambridge: Cambridge University Press, 1999), xxiv, 743p.

454. Herrmann, Frank. *The English as collectors: a documentary sourcebook*, 2nd edn. (New Castle (DE) and London: Oak Knoll and John Murray, 1999), xlviii, 461p. [1st published New York: W.W. Norton, 1972.]

455. Hüllen, Werner. *English dictionaries, 800–1700: the topical tradition* (Oxford: Clarendon, 1999), xiv, 525p.

456. Keynes, Simon. 'The cult of King Alfred the Great', *Anglo-Saxon England* 28 (1999), 225–356.

457. Parkinson-Bailey, John J. *Manchester: an architectural history* (Manchester: Manchester University Press, 2000), xviii, 366p.

458. Pearson, Lynn F. *British breweries: an architectural history* (London: Hambledon, 1999), xii, 256p.

459. Penoyre, Jane; Penoyre, John. 'Some Bruton town houses', *Somerset Archaeology and Natural History* 140 (1997), 121–32.

460. Petford, A.J. 'Architecture and education: the buildings of Hipperholme Grammar School 1661–1907', *Transactions of the Halifax Antiquarian Society* ns 8 (2000), 65–92.

461. Shattock, Joanne (ed.) *The Cambridge bibliography of English literature*, 3rd edn., 4 vols. (Cambridge: Cambridge University Press, 2000), 1536p.

462. Strong, Roy. *The spirit of Britain: a narrative history of the arts* (London: Hutchinson, 1999), xi, 708p.

G. Religious Belief, Practice and Organisation

See also 357 (B)

463. Anonymous. 'Cumulative index to volumes XXVI–XXXV', *Jewish Historical Studies* 35 (1998), 347–453.

464. Anonymous. 'Major accessions to repositories in 1999 relating to Roman Catholicism', *Recusant History* 25:2 (2000), 360–5.

465. Anonymous. *Ministers of the Church of Scotland from 1560 to 1929: an index to Fasti ecclesiæ Scoticanæ*, vol.2: *E-K: first draft* (Edinburgh: Peter Bell, 1999)

466. Adams, Bernard. 'The Latin epitaphs in Brecon Cathedral', *Brycheiniog* 31 (1998–99), 31–42.

467. Andrews, D.D. (ed.) 'Church miscellany 1998', *Essex Archaeology and History* 3rd ser. 30 (1999), 250–7.

468. Aylmer, Gerald E.; Tiller, John Eric (eds.) *Hereford Cathedral: a history* (London: Hambledon, 2000), xxxii, 672p.

469. Bateman, Nick; Miles, Adrian. 'St Lawrence Jewry from the 11th to 19th centuries', *Transactions of the London and Middlesex Archaeological Society* 50 (1999), 109–43.

470. Bronstein, Jamie. 'Rethinking the "readmission": Anglo-Jewish history and the immigration crisis', A13, 28–42.

471. Brown, Roger Lee. *Llandaff figures and places: aspects of the ecclesiastical history of Llandaff* (Welshpool: Gwasg Eglwys y Trallwng, 1998), 76p.

472. Brown, Roger Lee. *Pews, benches and seats: being a history of the church pew in Wales* (Welshpool: Gwasg Eglwys y Trallwng, 1998), 77p.

473. Chadwick, Henry; Ward, Allison (eds.) *Not angels but Anglicans: a history of Christianity in the British Isles* (Norwich: Canterbury, 2000), ix, 303p.

474. Champ, Judith F. *The English pilgrimage to Rome: a dwelling for the soul* (Leominster: Gracewing, 2000), xii, 230p.

475. Clarke, J.N. 'Horncastle baptists', *Lincolnshire Past & Present* 40 (2000), 6–9.

476. Doe, Norman; Hill, Mark; Ombres, Robert (eds.) *English canon law: essays in honour of Bishop Eric Kemp* (Cardiff: University of Wales Press, 1998), xvii, 153p.

477. Dugdale, D.S. *Manx church origins* (Felinfach: Llanerch, 1998), 214p.

478. Dymond, David. 'God's disputed acre' [the use of churchyards], *Journal of Ecclesiastical History* 50 (1999), 464–97.

479. Eaton, Deborah Hayward. 'Information in the stones, a library building as history: St. Peter-in-the-East, St. Edmund Hall, Oxford', *Library History* 15 (1999), 137–47.

480. Gilmore, Alec. *A dictionary of the English Bible and its origins* (Sheffield: Sheffield Academic, 2000), 192p.

481. Hale, A. '"In the eye of the sun": the relationship between the Cornish Gorseth and esoteric Druidry', *Cornish Studies* 8 (2000), 182–196.

482. Harvey, A.D. 'Baluster-cornered box tombs', *Journal of the Warburg and Courtauld Institutes* 62 (1999), 287–95.

483. Humphery-Smith, Cecil R. (ed.) *The Phillimore atlas and index of parish registers*, 2nd edn. (Chichester: Phillimore, 1995), 306p.
484. Jones, Kathleen. *The saints of the Anglican calendar* (Norwich: Canterbury, 2000), xiv, 368p.
485. Kerry, David A.; Cornell, Evelyn (eds.) *A guide to theological and religious studies: collections of Great Britain and Ireland* (Cambridge: Association of British Theological and Philosophical Libraries, 1999), iv, 272p.
486. Kirk, James (ed.) *The church in the Highlands* (Edinburgh: Scottish Church History Society, 1998), vii, 176p.
487. Knapp, Alexander. 'The influence of German music on United Kingdom synagogue practice', *Jewish Historical Studies* 35 (1998), 167–98.
488. Mackley, Roderick (ed.) *The church of Pitsea St Michael: research project 1994–1995* (Transactions of the Rochford Hundred Field Archaeology Group, 2) (Leigh on Sea: Rochford Hundred Field Archaeology Group, [1998?]), ii, 55p.
489. McCann, John. *Essays on the Lodge of Stirling, ancient and modern: a quadricentennial review of Lodge 'Antient' Stirling* ([Stirling]: [The author], 1998), vii, 50p.
490. Orme, Nicholas. *The saints of Cornwall* (Oxford: Oxford University Press, 2000), xvii, 302p.
491. Palmer, Martin; Palmer, Nigel. *Sacred Britain: a guide to the sacred sites and pilgrim routes of England, Scotland & Wales* (London: Piatkus, 1997), 319p.
492. Parry, J.P.; Taylor, Stephen. 'Introduction: Parliament and the Church of England from the Reformation to the twentieth century', *Parliamentary History* 19 (2000), 1–13.
493. Pounds, Norman John Greville. *A history of the English parish: the culture of religion from Augustine to Victoria* (Cambridge: Cambridge University Press, 2000), [xxvi], 593p.
494. Richardson, Ruth; Shoesmith, Ron (eds.) *A definitive history of Dore Abbey* (Woonton Almeley (Herefordshire): Logaston, 1997), ix, 240p.
495. Sansbury, Ruth. *Beyond the blew stone: 300 years of Quakers in Newcastle* (Newcastle upon Tyne: Newcastle upon Tyne Preparative Meeting, 1998), 278p.
496. Simpson, John H. 'The history of Yester church', *Transactions of the East Lothian Antiquarian and Field Naturalists' Society* 23 (1996), 13–34.
497. Waszak, Peter. 'King's Cliffe: the Catholic connection', *Northamptonshire Past and Present* 53 (2000), 49–58.
498. Williams, Brian. 'The evaluation of clergy livings', *Lincolnshire Past & Present* 40 (2000), 13–15.

Ha. *Law and Order*

499. Bush, Jonathan A.; Wijffels, Alain A. (eds.) *Learning the law: teaching and the transmission of law in England, 1150–1900* (London: Hambledon, 1999), xxv, 417p.
500. Cowley, Richard. *Guilty m'lud!: the criminal history of Northamptonshire* (Kettering: Peg and Whistle, 1998), xii, 200p.

501. Kershaw, Roger; Pearsall, Mark. *Immigrants and aliens: a guide to sources on UK immigration and citizenship* (Public Record Office readers' guide, 22) (Kew: PRO, 2000), xiii, 130p.

502. Kynell, Kurt von S. *Saxon and medieval antecedents of the English common law* (Lewiston (NY): Mellen, 2000), xi, 250p.

503. Sherman, Brad; Bently, Lionel. *The making of modern intellectual property law: the British experience, 1760–1911* (Cambridge: Cambridge University Press, 1999), xx, 242p.

Hb. Public Administration

504. Mason, John F. 'Bridgnorth Town Clerks from 1525/6–1974', *Shropshire History and Archaeology* 74 (1999), 29–31.

Hc. Political and Constitutional

See also 456, 492 (B)

505. Birke, Adolf M.; Brechten, Magnus (eds.) *Politikverdrossenheit: der Parteienstaat in der historischen und gegenwärtigen Diskussion: ein deutsch-britischer Vergleich = Disillusioned with politics: party government in the past and present discussion: an Anglo-German comparison* (Prinz-Albert-Studien, 12) (München and New Providence: K.G. Saur, 1995), 136p.

506. Daunton, Martin. 'Virtual representation: *The History of Parliament* on CD-ROM', *Past & Present* 167 (2000), 238–61.

507. Davidson, Neil. *The origins of Scottish nationhood* (London: Pluto, 2000), vii, 264p.

508. Feldman, David. 'L'immigration, les immigrés et l'État en Grande-Bretagne aux XIXe et XXe siècles' [Immigration, immigrants and the State in Britain in the 19th and 20th centuries], *Le Mouvement Social* 188 (1998), 43–60.

509. Foster, Sally; Macinnes, Allan I.; MacInnes, Ranald (eds.) *Scottish power centres from the early middle ages to the twentieth century* (Glasgow: Cruithne, 1998), vi, 250p.

510. Goldsmith, M.M. 'Republican liberty considered', *History of Political Thought* 21:3 (2000), 543–60.

511. Kent, Susan Kingsley. *Gender and power in Britain, 1640–1990* (London: Routledge, 1999), xii, 364p.

512. MacCormick, N. 'The English Constitution, the British State, and the Scottish anomaly', *Proceedings of the British Academy* 101 (1999), 289–308.

513. Morgan, Kenneth O. 'Consensus and conflict in modern Welsh history', A111, 16–41.

514. Nolan, Michael Patrick; Sedley, Stephen. *The making and remaking of the British Constitution: the Radcliffe lectures at the University of Warwick for 1996–97* (London: Blackstone, 1997), [xiii], 142p.

515. Prochaska, Frank K. *The republic of Britain, 1760–2000* (London: Allen Lane, 2000), xix, 292p.

J. Military

516. Anonymous. 'Major accessions to repositories in 1998 relating to the British Army', *Journal of the Society for Army Historical Research* 78 (2000), 56–60.

517. Guy, Alan James; Thomas, R.N.W.; De Groot, Gerard J. (eds.) *Military miscellany 1: manuscripts from the Seven Years War, the First and Second Sikh Wars and the First World War* (Publications of the Army Records Society, 12) (Stroud: Sutton for the Army Records Society, 1997), 449p.

518. Heathcote, Thomas Anthony. *The British field marshals 1763–1997: a biographical dictionary* (London: Leo Cooper, 1999), xvi, 368p.

519. Lewis, Jon E. (ed.) *The mammoth book of war diaries and letters: life on the battlefield in the words of the ordinary soldier, 1775–1991* (London: Robinson, 1998), x, 498p.

520. Public Record Office. *Using army records* (Richmond: Public Record Office, 2000), 64p.

521. Sheldon, Matthew. *Guide to the manuscript collection of the Royal Naval Museum* (Portsmouth: Royal Naval Museum, 1997), iv, 77p.

522. Sutton, John D. (ed.) *Wait for the waggon: the story of the Royal Corps of Transport and its predecessors, 1794–1993* (Barnsley: Leo Cooper, 1998), xxxii, 448p.

523. Thompson, Julian. *The Royal Marines: from sea soldiers to a special force* (London: Sidgwick & Jackson, 2000), xv, 699p.

524. Williams, Geoffrey. *Stronghold Britain: four thousand years of British fortifications* (Stroud: Sutton, 1999), viii, 264p.

K. Foreign Affairs

525. Hoare, James E. (ed.) *Britain & Japan: biographical portraits*, vol. 3 (Richmond: Japan Library, 1999), xviii, 397p. [Vols. 1 and 2 edited by Ian Nish.]

526. Nish, Ian; Kibata, Yoichi (eds.) *The history of Anglo-Japanese relations, 1600–2000: the political-diplomatic dimension*, 2 vols.: 1. *1600–1930*; 2. *1931–2000* (Basingstoke: Macmillan, 2000).

527. Stibbe, Matthew. 'A dialogue of the deaf?: historiographical connections between Britain and Germany, c.1750–2000' [conference report], *German History* 18 (2000), 86–93.

C. ROMAN BRITAIN

A. General and Archaeology

See also 254 (B); 554, 565 (C); 4995 (J)

528. Anonymous. 'Shudy Camps Roman villa', *Journal of the Haverhill and District Archaeological Group* 7:1 (1999), 28–39.

529. Booth, Paul. 'Ralegh Radford and the Roman villa at Ditchley: a review', *Oxoniensia* 64 (2000 for 1999), 39–49.
530. Bosanko, John. 'The Romans in east Devon', *Devonshire Association Report and Transactions* 130 (1998), 1–13.
531. Braund, David. 'Britain AD 1' [Portrait of Britain at the time of the Roman invasions], *History Today* 50:1 (2000), 7–13.
532. Connor, Aileen; Buckley, Richard. *Roman and medieval occupation at Causeway Lane, Leicester* (Leicester Archaeological Monographs, 5) (Leicester: University of Leicester, 1999), xiv, 385p.
533. Dark, Kenneth. 'The late Roman transition in the north: a discussion', A213, 81–88.
534. Davenport, Peter. *Archaeology in Bath: excavations 1984–1989* (British Archaeological Reports, British series, 284) (Oxford: Bath Archaeological Trust / Archaeopress, 1999), vi, 168p.
535. Ford, Steve; et al. 'The excavation of a Roman trackway and field system at Three Locks Golf Course, Stoke Hammond, Buckinghamshire, 1994', *Records of Buckinghamshire* 40 (1998–2000), 35–54.
536. Fulford, Michael; Timby, Jane. *Late iron-age and Roman Silchester: excavations on the site of the Roman Forum-Basilica, 1977, 1980–86* (Britannia monograph, 15) (London: Society for the Promotion of Roman Studies, 2000), xxvi, 613p.
537. Glass, Helen J. 'Archaeology of the Channel Tunnel rail line', *Archaeologia Cantiana* 119 (1999), 189–220.
538. Heard, Kieron. 'Romano-British occupation site near Downe, Kent', *London Archaeologist* 9:4 (2000), 110–15.
539. Henig, Martin; Booth, Paul. *Roman Oxfordshire* (Stroud: Sutton, 2000), xii, 244p.
540. Houliston, Mark. 'Excavations at the Mount Roman villa, Maidstone, 1994', *Archaeologia Cantiana* 119 (1999), 71–172.
541. Huntley, J.P. 'Late Roman transition in the north: the palynological evidence', A213, 67–72.
542. Salway, Peter. 'Roman Oxfordshire', *Oxoniensia* 64 (2000 for 1999), 1–22.
543. Scott, Eleanor. *A gazetteer of Roman villas in Britain* (Leicester Archaeology Monographs, 1) (Leicester: University of Leicester, School of Archaeological Studies, 1993), ix, 209p.
544. Sidwell, Jane. 'Environmental archaeology in London 1995–8, part 2', *London Archaeologist* 9:4 (2000), 95–101.
545. Wacher, John. *A portrait of Roman Britain* (London: Routledge, 2000), viii, 139p.
546. Wacher, John. *Roman Britain* (Stroud: Sutton, 1998), xv, 320p.

B. *Historiography and Historical Methods*

See also 540, 544, 546, 596–8, 605, 612, 632, 633, 649, 686 (C); 1629 (F)

547. Biggins, J.A.; Taylor, D.J.A. 'The Roman Fort at Stanwix, Carlisle: a geophysical survey', *Transactions of the Cumberland & Westmorland Antiquarian & Archaeological Society* 100 (2000), 279–81.

548. Booth, Paul; Lawrence, Steve. 'Ashford, Westhawk Farm', *Current Archaeology* 168:14.12 (2000), 478–81.

549. Caruana, Ian. 'Observations in the vicus of Stanwix Roman Fort on the site of the Miles MacInnes Hall, 1986', *Transactions of the Cumberland & Westmorland Antiquarian & Archaeological Society* 100 (2000), 55–78.

550. Clarke, Simon. 'A quantitative analysis of the finds from the Roman fort of Newstead: some preliminary findings', A55, 72–82.

551. Cool, H.E.M. 'The parts left over: material culture and the fifth century', A213, 47–65.

552. Dobney, Keith; Hall, Allan; Kenward, Harry. 'It's all garbage . . . a review of bioarchaeology in the four English *colonia* towns', A112, 15–35.

553. Faulkner, Neil. 'Change and decline in Romano-British towns', A194, 25–50.

554. Faulkner, Neil. *The decline and fall of Roman Britain* (Stroud: Tempus, 2000), 192p.

555. Fulford, Michael. 'Human remains from the north gate, Silchester: an "early" and a "late" radiocarbon date from the city', *Britannia* 31 (2000), 356–58.

556. Fulford, Michael; Clarke, Amanda. 'Silchester and the end of Roman towns', *Current Archaeology* 161:14.5 (1999), 176–80.

557. Going, C.J.; Hunn, J.R. *Excavations at Boxfield Farm, Chells, Stevenage, Hertfordshire* (Hertfordshire Archaeological Trust, report, 2) (Hertford: Hertfordshire Archaeological Trust, 1999), viii, 165p.

558. Hingley, Richard. 'The imperial context of Romano-British studies and proposals for a new understanding of social change', A86, 137–50.

559. Isserlin, Raphael M.J. 'An archaeology of brief time: monuments and seasonality in Roman Britain', A55, 45–56.

560. Johns, Catherine. 'Romano-British precious-metal hoards: some comments on Martin Millett's paper' [no.563], A55, 107–17.

561. Jones, Michael J. 'Roman Lincoln: changing perspectives', A112, 101–12.

562. Lakin, Dave. 'A Romano-British site at Summerton Way, Thamesmead, London Borough of Bexley', *Archaeologia Cantiana* 119 (1999), 311–41.

563. Millett, Martin. 'Treasure: interpreting Roman hoards', A55, 99–106. [With comments, no.560.]

564. Reece, Richard. '*Colonia* in context: *Glevum* and the *civitas Dobunnorum*', A112, 73–85.

565. Shotter, David C.A. 'The Roman conquest of the north-west', *Transactions of the Cumberland & Westmorland Antiquarian & Archaeological Society* 100 (2000), 33–53.

566. Spaul, J. 'Two problems from Roman Scotland: Genunia and Cohors II Tungrorum', *Transactions of the Dumfriesshire and Galloway Natural History and Antiquarian Society* 74 (2000), 47–54.

567. Stallibrass, Sue. 'How little we know, and how much there is to learn: what can animal and human bones tell us about the late Roman transition in northern England?', A213, 73–79.

568. Stallibrass, Sue. 'On the outside looking in: a view of animal bones in Roman Britain from the north west frontier', A150, 53–60.

569. Swan, Vivien G. 'The Twentieth Legion and the history of the Antonine Wall reconsidered', *Proceedings of the Society of Antiquaries of Scotland* 129 (1999), 399–480.
570. Timby, Jane. 'Pottery supply to Gloucester *colonia*', A112, 37–44.
571. Tully, Devon. 'The application of GIS to the study of settlement patterns: Silchester, a case study', A80, 104–17.
572. Waldron, Tony; Taylor, G. Michael; Rudling, David. 'Sexing of Romano-British baby burials from the Beddingham and Bignor villas', *Sussex Archaeological Collections* 137 (1999), 71–79.

C. Population and Environment

See also 539, 543, 546, 548, 553, 556, 561, 650, 687 (C)

573. Alexander, John; Pullinger, Joyce. 'Roman Cambridge: excavations on Castle Hill 1956–1988', *Proceedings of the Cambridge Antiquarian Society* 88 (1999), 3–268.
574. Clarke, Simon; Wise, Alicia. 'Evidence for extramural settlement north of the Roman fort at Newstead (Trimontium), Roxburghshire', *Proceedings of the Society of Antiquaries of Scotland* 129 (1999), 373–91.
575. Conquest, Robert. 'A note on the *"Civitas"* and *"Polis"* names of Scotland: an alternative approach', *Britannia* 31 (2000), 347–50.
576. Crummy, Philip. 'Colchester: making towns out of fortresses and the first urban fortifications in Britain', A112, 89–100.
577. Fulford, Michael. 'Civic space at Silchester (*Calleva Atrebatum*)', A112, 161–66.
578. Fulford, Michael. 'Veteran settlement in 1st-century Britain and the foundations of Gloucester and Lincoln', A112, 177–80.
579. Hanley, Robin. *Villages in Roman Britain*, revised edn. (Princes Risborough: Shire Archaeology, 2000), 64p.
580. Hassall, Mark; Hurst, Henry. 'Soldier and civilian: a debate on the bank of the Severn', A112, 181–89.
581. Hurst, Henry. 'The fortress coloniae of Roman Britain: Colchester, Lincoln and Gloucester', A79, 105–14.
582. Hurst, Henry. 'Topography and identity in *Glevum colonia*', A112, 113–35.
583. Jones, Michael J. 'Lincoln and the British fora in context', A112, 167–74.
584. Le Duc, Gwenaël. 'The colonisation of Britanny from Britain: new approaches and questions', A18, 133–51.
585. Maier, Bernhard. 'Zu den celtischen Namen von Carlisle und Colchester' [On the Celtic names of Carlisle and Colchester], *Beiträge zur Namenforschung* 32 (1997), 281–5.
586. McDermot, J. 'Evidence of Roman Southampton's hinterland at the new magistrate's court, London Road', *Proceedings of the Hampshire Field Club and Archaeological Society* 54 (1999), 183–88.
587. Oosthuizen, Susan. 'Prehistoric fields into medieval furlongs?: evidence from Caxton, Cambridgeshire', *Proceedings of the Cambridge Antiquarian Society* 86 (1997), 145–52.
588. Ottaway, Patrick. 'York: the study of a late Roman *colonia*', A112, 136–50.

589. Palliser, David M. 'The origins of British towns', A174, 17–26.
590. Price, Eddie G. *Frocester, a Romano-British settlement, its antecedents and successors*, vol.1: *The sites* (Stonehouse: Gloucester & District Archaeological Research Group, 2000), xxiii, 262p.
591. Rippon, Stephen. 'Landscapes in context: the exploitation and management of coastal resources in southern and eastern Britain during the 1st millennium AD', A78, 225–36.
592. Rowley, A.R. 'The origins of the name of *Craven*', *Beiträge zur Namenforschung* 34 (1999), 25–45.
593. Shotter, David C.A. 'The Roman contribution' [to the English urban landscape], A210, 32–54.
594. Stallibrass, Sue. 'Cattle, culture, status and soldiers in northern England', A80, 64–73.
595. Strickland, T.J. 'What kind of community existed at Chester during the hiatus of the 2nd century?', *Journal of Roman Archaeology*, supplementary series 34 (1999), 105–9.
596. White, Roger. 'Wroxeter and the transformation of late-Roman urbanism', A194, 96–119.
597. Wilson, Pete. 'Cataractonium (Catterick): the end of a Roman town?', A213, 25–32.
598. Wilson, Pete. 'Catterick', *Current Archaeology* 166:14.10 (1999), 378–86.
599. Woolf, A. 'Adventus, patrocinium and the urban landscape in Roman Britain', A4, 33–47.

Da. *Social Life and Conditions*

See also 530, 537, 544, 552, 639 (C)

600. Allason-Jones, Lindsay. 'Women and the Roman army in Britain', *Journal of Roman Archaeology*, supplementary series 34 (1999), 41–51.
601. Déry, Carol A. 'Food and the Roman army: travel, transport, and transmission (with particular reference to the province of Britannia)', A208, 84–96.
602. Eckardt, Hella. 'Illuminating Roman Britain', A80, 8–21.
603. Ferris, Iain; Jones, R. 'Transforming an elite: reinterpreting late Roman Binchester', A213, 1–12.
604. Holman, D. 'Roman cremation burials at Sandwich 1846', *Kent Archaeological Review* 138 (1999), 170–74.
605. Kenward, Harry. 'Pubic lice (Pthirus pubis L.) were present in Roman and medieval Britain', *Antiquity* 73 (1999), 911–14.
606. King, M. 'Roman cemetery at Lockham', *Kent Archaeological Review* 135 (1999), 112–15.
607. Meadows, Karen I. 'You are what you eat: diet, identity and Romanisation', A55, 133–40.
608. Oxford Archaeological Trust. 'Springhead Roman cemetery', *Current Archaeology* 168:14.12 (2000), 458–59.
609. Parry, Charles. 'Iron-age, Romano-British and medieval occupation at Bishop's Cleeve, Gloucestershire: excavations at Gilder's Paddock 1989 and

1990–1', *Transactions of the Bristol and Gloucestershire Archaeological Society* 117 (1999), 89–118.
610. Rahtz, Philip; Hirst, Sue; Wright, Susan M. *Cannington cemetery: excavations 1962–3 of the prehistoric, Roman, post-Roman and later features of Cannington Park Quarry, nr. Bridgewater, Somerset* (Britannia Monographs, 17) (London: Society for the Promotion of Roman Studies, 2000), xxiii, 516p.
611. Sherlock, David. 'The backs of Roman spoons in Britain', *Britannia* 31 (2000), 365–70.

Db. *Social Structure*

See also 594, 640 (C)

612. Fincham, Garrick. 'Romanisation, status and landscape: extracting a discrepant perspective from survey data', A80, 30–36.
613. Matthews, K.J. 'Britannus/Britto: Roman ethnographies, native identities, labels, and folk devils', A4, 14–32.

Ea. *Economic Activity and Organisation*

See also 532, 535–6, 539, 546, 549, 552, 557, 570, 573, 590, 630, 650–2, 660, 667, 671, 674 (C)

614. Brickstock, R.J. 'Coin supply in the north in the late Roman period', A213, 33–37.
615. Brown, A.G.; Meadows, Iain. 'Roman vineyards in Britain: finds from the Nene Valley and new research', *Antiquity* 74:285 (2000), 491–92.
616. Davies, Jeffrey L.; Driver, T.G. 'The discovery of a Roman coin hoard at Salem, Trefeurig, Aberystwyth', *Ceredigion* 13:3 (1999), 1–4.
617. Evans, Jeremy. 'The end of Roman pottery in the north', A213, 39–46.
618. MacMahon, Ardle. '*Taberna* economics', A80, 44–52.
619. Price, Jennifer. *The social context of glass production in Roman Britain*, A148, 331–48.
620. Rippon, Stephen. 'The Romano-British exploitation of coastal wetlands: survey and excavation on the north Somerset Levels, 1993–7', *Britannia* 31 (2000), 69–200.
621. Roskams, Steve. 'The hinterlands of Roman York: present patterns and future strategies', A112, 45–72.
622. Schrüfer-Kolb, Irene. 'Environmental use and landscape: Roman iron production in the east Midlands in its context', A78, 268–69.
623. Schrüfer-Kolb, Irene. 'Roman iron production in the east Midlands, England', A220, 227–33.
624. Shields, Glen. 'The course of the London to Brighton Roman road south of Burgess Hill', *Sussex Archaeological Collections* 137 (1999), 81–90.
625. Shotter, David C.A. 'Recent finds of Roman coins in Cumbria', *Transactions of the Cumberland & Westmorland Antiquarian & Archaeological Society* 100 (2000), 276–9.

626. Swan, Vivien G.; Philpott, Robert A. 'Legio XXVV and tile production at Tarbock, Merseyside', *Britannia* 31 (2000), 55–67.
627. Waddelove, Edmund. *The Roman roads of north Wales: recent discoveries* (Ruthin: Waddelove, 1999), xi, 332p.
628. Walsh, Michael. 'Roman maritime activities around Britain: what is the evidence and how might it be enhanced?', A80, 53–63.
629. Willis, Steven. 'Roman imports into late iron age British societies: towards a critique of existing models', A55, 141–48.

Eb. *Technology*

See also 538, 573, 590 (C)

630. Evans, C.J.; Jenks, W.E.; White, R.H. 'Romano-British kilns at Meole Brace (Pulley), Shropshire', *Shropshire History and Archaeology* 74 (1999), 1–27.
631. Frere, Sheppard. 'A *limitatio* of Icenian territory?', *Brittania* 31 (2000), 350–55.

Fc. *Ideas and Learning*

See also 560, 563, 607, 629, 668 (C), 1629 (F)

632. Collis, John. 'George Buchanan and the Celts in Britain', A18, 91–107.
633. Hassall, Mark. 'Pre-Hadrianic dispositions in Britain', A21, 51–65.
634. Hingley, Richard. 'Britannia, origin myths and the British empire', A55, 11–23.

Fd. *Culture and the Arts*

See also 528–30, 532, 535–8, 540, 544, 549–51, 557, 560, 569, 573, 609, 611, 620, 666–7, 674, 681 (C)

635. Bates, Sarah. 'Excavations at Quidney Farm, Saham Toney, Norfolk 1995', *Britannia* 31 (2000), 201–37.
636. Cool, H.E.M. 'The significance of snake jewellery hoards', *Britannia* 31 (2000), 29–40.
637. de la Bédoyère, Guy. *Pottery in Roman Britain* (Shire Archaeology, 79) (Princes Risborough: Shire Archaeology, 2000), 72p.
638. Elliot, J. Walter; Henig, Martin. 'Further engraved gemstones from Newstead (Trimontium) Roxburghshire', *Proceedings of the Society of Antiquaries of Scotland* 129 (1999), 393–8.
639. Ellis, Simon. 'Lighting in late Roman houses', A55, 65–71.
640. Ferris, Iain. 'Insignificant others: images of barbarians on military art from Roman Britain', A55, 24–31.
641. Gilkes, Oliver J. 'The bathhouse of Angmering Roman villa: a reconsideration of its sequence and context', *Sussex Archaeological Collections* 137 (1999), 59–69.

642. Gurney, D. 'Four Roman multiple bow brooches from Norfolk', *Norfolk Archaeology* 43:1 (1998), 177–79.

643. Henig, Martin; Cleary, Robert; Purser, Philip. 'A Roman relief of Mercury and Minerva from Aldsworth, Gloucestershire', *Britannia* 31 (2000), 362–63.

644. Henig, Martin; Cannon, Martin. 'A sceptre-head for the Matres cult and other objects from west Berkshire', *Britannia* 31 (2000), 358–62.

645. Henig, Martin. 'Artistic patronage and the Roman military community in Britain', *Journal of Roman Archaeology*, supplementary series 34 (1999), 150–64.

646. Henig, Martin. 'Bignor Roman villa', *British Archaeology* 51 (2000), 20–23.

647. Henig, Martin. 'Chester and the art of the Twentieth Legion', A204, 1–15.

648. Hurst, Henry. 'Civic space at Glevum', A112, 152–60.

649. Knight, Jeremy K. 'Late Roman and post-Roman Caerwent: some evidence from metalwork', *Archaeologia Cambrensis* 145 (1998 for 1996), 34–66.

650. Laing, Jennifer. *Art and society in Roman Britain* (Wren's Park Publishing, 2000), ix, 188p. [1st published Stroud: Sutton, 1997.]

651. Langley, Richard; Drage, Christopher. 'Roman occupation at Little Chester, Derby: salvage excavation and recording by the Trent and Peak Archaeological Trust, 1986–90', *Derbyshire Archaeological Journal* 120 (2000), 123–287.

652. Luckett, Larry. 'Investigation of a Roman villa site at Euridge Manor Farm, Colerne', *Wiltshire Archaeological and Natural History Magazine* 93 (2000), 218–32.

653. Makepeace, G.A. 'Prehistoric and Roman material from the Brassington area of Derbyshire: "the Radford collection"', *Derbyshire Archaeological Journal* 120 (2000), 87–100.

654. Oxford Archaeological Trust. 'Thurnham Roman villa', *Current Archaeology* 168:14.12 (2000), 454–47.

655. Reynolds, Julie. 'A bronze figurine of Hercules from St. Paul's Churchyard, London', *Britannia* 31 (2000), 363–65.

656. Rush, Peter; Dickinson, Brenda; Hartley, Brian; Hartley K.F. *Roman Castleford, excavations 1974–85*, vol.3: *The pottery* (Leeds: West Yorkshire Archaeology Service, 2000), xiii, 278p.

657. Sawyer, Jennifer. 'The excavation of a Romano-British site at Burgess Hill, West Sussex', *Sussex Archaeological Collections* 137 (1999), 49–58.

658. Scott, Sarah. *Art and society in fourth-century Britain: villa mosaics in context* (Oxford: Oxford University School of Archaeology, 2000), 192p.

659. Smith, Derek. 'The wall paintings of the town-house in the *vicus* outside the Roman fort at Malton, north Yorkshire', *Yorkshire Archaeology* 72 (2000), 7–15.

660. Tomber, Roberta; Williams, David. 'Egyptian amphorae in Britain and the western provinces', *Britannia* 31 (2000), 41–54.

661. Trott, Kevin. 'A rescue excavation on the Brading Roman villa coach park, Isle of Wight', *Proceedings of the Hampshire Field Club and Archaeological Society* 54 (1999), 189–215.

662. Witts, Patricia. 'Mosaics and room-function: the evidence from some fourth-century Romano-British villas', *Britannia* 31 (2000), 291–324.

G. Religious Belief, Practice and Organisation

See also 546, 636, 643–4, 650, 655 (C); 5076 (J)

663. Aldhouse-Green, Miranda J. 'Pagan Celtic religion and early Celtic myth: connections or coincidence?', A18, 82–90.
664. Clarke, Simon. 'In search of a different Roman period: the finds assemblage at the Newstead military complex', A80, 22–29.
665. Ferris, I.M. 'Alchemy of suffering: hope and faith beyond the healing art in Roman Britain', A4, 1–13.
666. Painter, Kenneth. 'The Water Newton silver: votive or liturgical', *Journal of the British Archaeological Association* 152 (1999), 1–23.
667. Williams, David. 'Wanborough Roman temple', *Current Archaeology* 167:14.11 (2000), 434–47.
668. Zoll, Amy L. 'Patterns of worship in Roman Britain: double-named deities in context', A55, 32–44.

Hc. Political and Constitutional

669. Kulikowski, Michael. 'Barbarians in Gaul, usurpers in Britain', *Britannia* 31 (2000), 325–45.

J. Military

See also 530, 547, 566, 569, 573–4, 576, 581, 600, 645, 651 (C)

670. Bird, D.G. 'The Claudian invasion campaign reconsidered', *Oxford Journal of Archaeology* 19 (2000), 91–104.
671. Birley, Robin. *The early wooden forts: the excavations of 1973–76 and 1985–89, with some additional details from the excavations of 1991–93* (Vindolanda Research Reports, 1) ([Hexham]: Roman Army Museum Publications for the Vindolanda Trust, 1994), xii, 158p.
672. Black, E.W. 'Sentius Saturninus and the Roman invasion of Britain', *Britannia* 31 (2000), 1–10.
673. Crow, Jim. 'High Rochester—life beyond the wall', *Current Archaeology* 164:14.8 (1999), 290–4.
674. Dore, J.N.; Wilkes, J.J. 'Excavations directed by J.D. Leach and J.J. Wilkes on the site of a Roman fortress at Carpow, Perthshire, 1964–79', *Proceedings of the Society of Antiquaries of Scotland* 129 (1999), 481–575.
675. Frere, S.S. 'M. Maenius Agrippa, the *Expeditio Britannica* and Maryport', *Britannia* 31 (2000), 23–28.
676. Fulford, Michael. 'The organization of legionary supply: the Claudian invasion of Britain', A21, 41–50.
677. Glendinning, B.D.; Dunwell, A.J. 'Excavations of the Gask frontier tower and temporary camp at Blackhill Wood, Ardoch, Perth and Kinross', *Britannia* 31 (2000), 255–90.
678. Hodgson, Nick. 'The Stanegate: a frontier rehabilitated', *Britannia* 31 (2000), 11–22.

679. Hodgson, Nick; Griffiths, Bill. 'Wallsend: where did they keep the horses in Roman forts?', *Current Archaeology* 164:14.8 (1999), 284–89.
680. Hoffmann, Birgitta. 'Use of space and variability of ground plans: a study of legionary centurions' quarters', A55, 83–89.
681. Howard-Davis, Christine; Buxton, K. *Roman forts in the Fylde: excavations at Dowbridge, Kirkham* (Lancaster: Centre for North West Regional Studies, Lancaster University, 2000), xii, 106p.
682. Keppie, Lawrence. 'Legio VIIII in Britain: the beginning and the end', A21, 83–100.
683. Lowe, C.E.; Moloney, R. 'Excavation of the Roman temporary camps at Dullatur, north Lanarkshire', *Britannia* 31 (2000), 239–53.
684. Manning, W.H. 'The fortresses of *Legio XX*', A21, 69–81.
685. Wilmott, Tony. 'Birdoswald and its landscape', *Current Archaeology* 164:14.8 (1999), 298–302.
686. Wilmott, Tony. 'The late Roman transition at Birdoswald and on Hadrian's Wall', A213, 13–23.
687. Woodside, Robert; Crow, James. *Hadrian's Wall: an historic landscape* (National Trust, 1999), 164p.

D. ENGLAND 450–1066

A. *General*

See also 254 (B)

688. Wood, Michael. *In search of England: journeys into the English past* (London: Viking, 1999), xvi, 336p.

B. *Historiography and Historical Methods*

See also 304 (B); 605, 649 (C); 773, 841, 904 (D)

689. Conner, Patrick W. 'Beyond the ASPR: electronic editions of Old English poetry', A133, 109.
690. Dobney, Keith; Hall, Allan; Kenward, Harry. 'The bioarchaeology of Anglo-Saxon Yorkshire: present and future perspectives', A89, 133–40.
691. Fulford, Michael; Handley, Mark; Clark, Amanda. 'An early date for Ogham: the Silchester Ogham Stone rehabilitated', *Medieval Archaeology* 44 (2000), 1–23.
692. Irving, Edward B. (Jr.) 'Editing Old English verse: the ideal', A133, 11–20.
693. O'Keeffe, Katherine O'Brien. 'Introduction' [New approaches to editing Old English verse], A133, 1–10.
694. Scragg, D.G. 'Towards a new Anglo-Saxon poetic records', A133, 67–78.
695. Spence, Craig. '"Citie . . . of stickes": toward a material history of medieval London', *Transactions of the London and Middlesex Archaeological Society* 50 (1999), 98–107.

C. Population and Environment

See also 587, 589, 591–2 (C); 690, 783, 786, 798, 845, 866, 918, 920 (D)

696. Andrews, Phil; Mepham, Lorraine; Smith, Rachael Seager. 'Excavations in Wilton, 1995–6: St. John's Hospital and South Street', *Wiltshire Archaeological and Natural History Magazine* 93 (2000), 181–204.
697. Astill, Grenville. 'General survey 600–1300', A174, 27–50.
698. Bailey, K.A. 'Buckinghamshire parish names', *Records of Buckinghamshire* 40 (2000), 55–72.
699. Bassett, Steven. 'Anglo-Saxon Birmingham', *Midland History* 25 (2000), 1–27.
700. Batey, C.E. 'Aspects of rural settlement in northern Britain', A109, 69–94.
701. Blair, John. 'Small towns 600–1270', A174, 245–72.
702. Blake, Martin. 'Assessing the evidence for the earliest Anglo-Saxon place-names in Bedfordshire', *English Place-Name Society Journal* 32 (2000), 5–20.
703. Bond, C.J. 'Settlement, land use and estate patterns on the Failand Ridge, north Somerset: a preliminary discussion', A109, 115–52.
704. Breeze, Andrew. 'Gaelic elements in early Northumberland: the place-name *Tarset* and *cumeman* ("serf")', *Archaeologia Aeliana* 5th ser. 27 (1999), 25–27.
705. Brodt, Bärbel. 'East Anglia' [urban history], A174, 639–56.
706. Butler, Chris. *Saxon settlement and earlier remains at Friars Oak, Hassocks, West Sussex* (BAR, British Series, 295) (Oxford: Archaeopress, 2000), iii, 81p.
707. Cessford, Craig. 'Relations between the Britons of southern Scotland and Anglo-Saxon Northumbria', A100, 150–60.
708. Cleary, S.E. 'Changing constraints on the landscape AD 400–600', A109, 11–26.
709. Coates, Richard. 'Plardiwick', *English Place-Name Society Journal* 32 (2000), 21–22.
710. Coates, Richard. '*Box* in English place-names', *English Studies* 80 (1999), 2–45.
711. Cole, Ann. '*Ersc*: distribution and use of this Old English place-name element', *English Place-Name Society Journal* 32 (2000), 27–39.
712. Cole, Ann; Cumber, Janey; Gelling, Margaret. 'Old English *merece* "wild celery, smallage" in place-names', *Nomina* 23 (2000), 141–8.
713. Courtney, Paul. 'Saxon and medieval Leicester: the making of an urban landscape', *Transactions of the Leicestershire Archaeological and Historical Society* 72 (1998), 110–45.
714. Dark, Petra. *The environment of Britain in the first millennium AD* (London: Duckworth, 2000), x, 211p.
715. Dietz, K. 'Die ortsnamen *Freshwater, Friskney* und die Etymologie von neuenglisch *fresh* "frisch"' [The place names *Freshwater, Friskney* and the etymology of modern English *fresh*], *Beiträge zur Namenforschung* 34 (1999), 159–71.
716. Dyer, Christopher; Slater, T.R. 'The Midlands' [urban history], A174, 609–38.

717. Egan, Geoff. 'Material from a millenium: detritus from a developing city', *Transactions of the London and Middlesex Archaeological Society* 50 (1999), 29–37.

718. Forsberg, R. *The place name* Lewes: *a study of its early spellings and etymology* (Uppsala: Ubsaliensis S. Academia [Uppsala University Press], 1997), 66p.

719. Fox, Harold. 'The Wolds: before about 1500', MM123.

720. Gardiner, Mark; Greatorex, Christopher. 'Archaeological excavations in Steyning, 1992–95: further evidence for the evolution of a late Saxon town', *Sussex Archaeological Collections* 135 (1997), 143–71.

721. Hinton, David A. 'Decay and revival: early medieval urban landscapes', A210, 55–73.

722. Hinton, David A. 'The large towns 600–1300', A174, 217–44.

723. Holt, Richard. 'Society and population 600–1300', A174, 79–104.

724. Hooke, Della. 'Reconstructing Anglo-Saxon landscapes in Warwickshire', *Birmingham and Warwickshire Archaeological Society Transactions* 100 (1996), 99–116.

725. Hooke, Della. 'The mid-late Anglo-Saxon period: settlement and land use', A109, 95–114.

726. Hough, Carole. 'Carolside in Berwickshire and *Carelholpit* in Lincolnshire', *Nomina* 23 (2000), 79–86.

727. Hough, Carole. 'Cheveley and Chaff Hall: a reconsideration of OE *ceaf* in place-names', *Nottingham Medieval Studies* 43 (1999), 21–32.

728. Hough, Carole. 'Place-name evidence for two Middle English words', *Notes and Queries* 47:1 (2000), 6–7.

729. Hough, Carole. 'The place-name Pitchcombe', *English Place-Name Society Journal* 32 (2000), 50–52.

730. Insley, John. 'Harby: a place-name complex in the Danelaw', *Studia Neophilologica* 70 (1998), 9–23.

731. Keene, Derek. 'London from the post-Roman period to 1300', A174, 187–216.

732. Keene, Derek. 'The medieval urban landscape, AD 900–1540', A210, 74–98.

733. Keene, Derek. 'The south-east of England' [urban history, 600–1540], A174, 545–82.

734. Kermode, Jennifer. 'Northern towns', A174, 657–80.

735. Kristensson, Gillis. 'The place-name Owermoigne (Dorset)', *Notes and Queries* 47:1 (2000), 5–6.

736. Kristensson, Gillis. 'The place-name Yarnfield (Wiltshire)', *Notes and Queries* 47:1 (2000), 4–5.

737. Leahy, Kevin. 'The middle Saxon site at Flixborough, North Lincolnshire', A100, 87–94.

738. Malim, Tim; et al. 'New evidence on the Cambridgeshire Dykes and Worsted Street Roman road', *Proceedings of the Cambridge Antiquarian Society* 85 (1996), 27–122.

739. Morris, Christopher D.; et al. 'Recent work at Tintagel', *Medieval Archaeology* 43 (1999), 206–15.

740. Mortimer, Richard. 'Village development and ceramic sequence: the middle to late Saxon village at Lordship Lane, Cottenham, Cambridgeshire', *Proceedings of the Cambridge Antiquarian Society* 89 (2000), 5–33.

741. Palliser, David M.; Slater, T.R.; Dennison, E. Patricia. 'The topography of towns 600–1300', A174, 153–86.

742. Powlesland, Dominic. 'The Anglo-Saxon settlement at West Heslerton, North Yorkshire', A100, 55–65.

743. Powlesland, Dominic. 'West Heslerton settlement mobility: a case of static development', A89, 19–26.

744. Rahtz, Philip. 'Anglo-Saxon Yorkshire: current research problems', A89, 1–9.

745. Reynolds, Andrew. *Later Anglo-Saxon England: life and landscape* (Stroud: Tempus, 1999), 192p.

746. Richards, Julian D. 'Anglo-Saxon settlement and archaeological visibility in the Yorkshire wolds', A89, 27–39.

747. Richards, Julian D. 'Anglo-Saxon settlements of the Golden Age', A100, 44–54.

748. Richards, Julian D.; et al. 'Cottam: an Anglian and Anglo-Scandinavian settlement on the Yorkshire wolds', *Archaeological Journal* 156 (1999), 1–111.

749. Richards, Julian D. 'What's so special about "productive sites"? Middle Saxon settlements in Northumbria', *Anglo-Saxon Studies in Archaeology and History* 10 (1999), 71–80.

750. Rose, P.; Preston-Jones, A. 'Changes in the Cornish countryside AD 400–1100', A109, 51–68.

751. Sandred, K.I. 'Det engelska *stead* och het nordiska *stad* "kant, rand"' [English *stead* and Scandinavian *stad* 'edge, verge'], *Namn och Bygd* 87 (1999), 47–55.

752. Slater, T.R. 'The south-west of England' [urban history, 600–1540], A174, 583–608.

753. Spoerry, Paul. 'The topography of Anglo-Saxon Huntingdon: a survey of the archaeological and historical evidence', *Proceedings of the Cambridge Antiquarian Society* 89 (2000), 35–47.

754. Stopford, Jennie. 'The case for archaeological research at Whitby', A89, 99–107.

755. Suzuki, Seiichi. *The quoit brooch style and Anglo-Saxon settlement: a casting and recasting of cultural identity symbols* (Woodbridge: Boydell, 2000), xiv, 218p.

756. Taylor, Alison; Duhig, Corinne; Hines, John. 'An Anglo-Saxon cemetery at Oakington, Cambridgeshire', *Proceedings of the Cambridge Antiquarian Society* 86 (1997), 57–90.

757. Treveil, Philip; Burch, Mark. 'Number 1 Poultry and the development of medieval Cheapside', *Transactions of the London and Middlesex Archaeological Society* 50 (1999), 55–60.

758. Ulmschneider, Katharina. 'Archaeology, history, and the Isle of Wight in the middle Saxon period', *Medieval Archaeology* 43 (1999), 19–44.

759. Van de Noort, Robert. 'Where are Yorkshire's "Terps"? Wetland exploitation in the early medieval period', A89, 121–31.

760. Watts, Victor. 'Some place-name distributions', *English Place-Name Society Journal* 32 (2000), 53–72.

761. Webb, Alf (ed.) *Early medieval Dean: the Forest of Dean and west Gloucestershire, 409 to 1272 A.D.* (Lydney: Dean Archaeological Group, 2000), 62p.

D. Social

See also 605, 609 (C); 749, 807, 829, 872, 883, 909, 915, 929 (D); 5023, 5025 (J)

762. Abramson, Philip. 'A re-examination of a Viking Age burial at Beacon Hill, Aspatria', *Transactions of the Cumberland & Westmorland Antiquarian & Archaeological Society* 100 (2000), 79–88.
763. Campbell, James. 'Britain: AD 500', *History Today* 50:2 (2000), 29–35.
764. Campbell, James. 'Power and authority 600–1300', A174, 51–78.
765. Crawford, Sally. *Childhood in Anglo-Saxon England* (Stroud: Sutton, 1999), xviii, 198p.
766. Cubitt, Catherine. 'Virginity and misogyny in tenth- and eleventh-century England', *Gender & History* 12 (2000), 1–32.
767. Ford, W.J. 'Anglo-Saxon cemeteries along the Avon valley', *Birmingham and Warwickshire Archaeological Society Transactions* 100 (1996), 59–98.
768. Geake, Helen. 'When were hanging bowls deposited in Anglo-Saxon graves?', *Medieval Archaeology* 43 (1999), 1–18.
769. Lebecq, Stéphane. 'England and the continent in the sixth and seventh centuries: the question of logistics', A88, 59–67.
770. Lucy, Samantha J. 'Changing burial rites in Northumbria AD 500–750', A100, 12–43.
771. Lucy, Samantha J. 'Early medieval burials in east Yorkshire: reconsidering the evidence', A89, 11–18.
772. Lucy, Samantha J. *The Anglo-Saxon way of death* (Stroud: Sutton, 2000), v, 210p.
773. Lucy, Samantha J. 'The early Anglo-Saxon burial rite: moving towards a contextual understanding', A187, 33–40.
774. Stoodley, N. 'From the cradle to the grave: age organization and the early Anglo-Saxon burial rite', *World Archaeology* 31:3 (2000), 456–72.
775. Stoodley, Nick. *The spindle and the spear: a critical enquiry into the construction and meaning of gender in the early Anglo-Saxon burial rite* (BAR, British series, 288) (Oxford: British Archaeological Reports, 1999), ix, 251p.
776. Ward-Perkins, Bryan. 'Why did the Anglo-Saxons not become more British?', *English Historical Review* 115 (2000), 513–33.
777. Williams, H.M.R. 'Placing the dead: investigating the location of wealthy barrow burials in seventh century England', A187, 57–86.

Ea. *Economic Activity and Organisation*

See also 700, 703, 714, 935 (D); 1023, 1057 (E)

778. Bailey, K.A. '*Vendere potuit*: "He could sell", to coin a Domesday phrase', *Records of Buckinghamshire* 40 (2000), 73–88. [Refers mostly to pre-Conquest conditions.]
779. Blackmore, Lyn. 'Aspects of trade and exchange evidenced by recent work on Saxon and medieval pottery from London', *Transactions of the London and Middlesex Archaeological Society* 50 (1999), 38–54.

780. Booth, James. 'Northumbrian coinage and the productive site at South Newbald ("Sancton")', A89, 83–97.

781. Bowsher, David; Malcolm, Gordon. 'Excavations at the Royal Opera House: middle Saxon London', *Transactions of the London and Middlesex Archaeological Society* 50 (1999), 4–11.

782. Britnell, Richard H. 'The economy of British towns 600–1300', A174, 105–26.

783. Cox, Margaret; et al. 'Early-medieval hemp retting at Glasson Moss, Cumbria in the context of the use of *Cannabis sativa* during the historic period', *Transactions of the Cumberland & Westmorland Antiquarian & Archaeological Society* 100 (2000), 131–50.

784. Gardiner, M. 'Shipping and trade between England and the continent during the eleventh century', *Anglo-Norman Studies* 22 (2000), 71–94.

785. Gifford, Edwin; Gifford, Joyce. 'The art of Anglo-Saxon shipbuilding', A100, 78–86.

786. Hall, R.A. 'The decline of the *Wic?*', A194, 120–36.

787. Hines, J. 'Coins and runes in England and Frisia in the seventh century', *Amsterdamer Beitrage zur Alteren Germanistik* 45 (1996), 47–62.

788. Hough, Carole. 'Cattle-tracking in the Fonthill letter', *English Historical Review* 115 (2000), 864–92.

789. Kent, Oliver. 'Ceramic finds from archaeological excavations at Glastonbury Abbey', *Somerset Archaeology and Natural History* 140 (1997), 73–104.

790. Leahy, Kevin. 'Middle Anglo-Saxon metalwork from South Newbald and the "productive site" phenomenon in Yorkshire', A89, 51–82.

791. Mackreth, D.F. 'Peterborough, from St Aethelwold to Martin de Bec, c.970–1155', A205, 137–56.

792. Mainman, A.J.; Rogers, Nicola S.H. *Craft, industry and everyday life: finds from Anglo-Scandinavian York* (Archaeology of York, 17/14) (York: Council for British Archaeology, 2000), 1869–2072p.

793. Mills, Susan. '(Re)constructing Northumbrian timber buildings: the Bede's World experience', A100, 66–72.

794. Morris, Carole A. *Wood and woodworking in Anglo-Scandinavian and medieval York* (The archaeology of York, 17:13) (York: Council for British Archaeology, 2000), 2073–2452, xiii p.

795. Palliser, David M. 'Introduction' [urban history, 600–1540], A174, 3–16.

796. Palliser, David M. 'Conclusion' [urban history, 600–1540], A174, 741–46.

797. Thier, Katrin. 'The cobles: Celtic boats in Anglo-Saxon Northumbria?', *Mariner's Mirror* 86 (2000), 131–9.

798. Ulmschneider, Katharina. 'Settlement, economy and the "productive" site: middle Anglo-Saxon Lincolnshire A.D. 650–780', *Medieval Archaeology* 44 (2000), 53–72.

799. Watson, Bruce. 'Medieval London Bridge and its role in the defence of the realm', *Transactions of the London and Middlesex Archaeological Society* 50 (1999), 17–22.

800. Wroe-Brown, Robin. 'The Saxon origins of Queenhithe', *Transactions of the London and Middlesex Archaeological Society* 50 (1999), 12–16.

Eb. *Technology*

801. Inker, Peter. 'Technology as active material culture: the quoit-brooch style', *Medieval Archaeology* 44 (2000), 25–52.

F. *Intellectual, Cultural and the Arts*

See also 445, 456 (B); 649 (C), 689, 692–4, 755, 793, 844, 846–7, 852–3, 855–7, 860, 863, 868, 870, 873, 876, 878–9, 885–6, 889, 893, 901, 896, 903–4, 905, 907 (D); 1068 (E); 5032, 5034, 5037 (J)

802. Barrow, Julia. 'Churches, education and literacy in towns 600–1300', A174, 127–52.
803. Brantley, Jessica. 'The iconography of the Utrecht Psalter and the Old English *Descent into Hell*', *Anglo-Saxon England* 28 (1999), 43–63.
804. Bryant, Richard; Viner, David. 'A late Saxon sculptural fragment from All Saints' Church, Somerford Keynes', *Transactions of the Bristol and Gloucestershire Archaeological Society* 117 (1999), 155–8.
805. Budny, Mildred. 'The *Biblia Gregoriana*', A88, 237–84.
806. Cambridge, Eric. 'The architecture of the Augustinian mission', A88, 202–36.
807. Cramp, Rosemary. 'The Northumbrian identity', A100, 1–11.
808. D'Aronco, M.A.; Cameron, Malcolm Lawrence (eds.) *The Old English illustrated pharmacopoeia* (Copenhagen: Rosenkilde & Bagger, 1998), 64p. [British Library Cotton Vitellius C III (facsimile; plates I–XXV, fols.11r–85v.]
809. Doane, A.N. 'Spacing, placing and effacing: scribal textuality and Exeter riddle 30 a/b', A133, 45–66.
810. Dodwell, Charles Reginald. *Anglo-Saxon gestures and the Roman stage* [prepared for publication by Timothy Graham] (Cambridge Studies in Anglo-Saxon England, 28) (Cambridge: Cambridge University Press, 2000), xvii, 171p.
811. Emms, Richard. 'The scribe of the Paris Psalter', *Anglo-Saxon England* 28 (1999), 179–85.
812. Everson, Paul; Stocker, David. 'A newly identified figure of the Virgin from a late Anglo-Saxon rood at Great Hale, Lincolnshire', *Antiquaries Journal* 80 (2000), 285–94.
813. Farr, Carol A. 'The shape of learning at Wearmouth-Jarrow: the diagram pages in the "Codex Amiatinus"', A100, 336–44.
814. Fjalldal, Magnús. *The long arm of coincidence: the frustrated connection between 'Beowulf' and 'Grettis' saga* (Toronto (Ont) and London: University of Toronto Press, 1998), ix, 176p.
815. Gameson, Richard. 'The earliest books of Christian Kent', A88, 313–73.
816. Gerritsen, Johan. 'What use are the Thorkelin transcripts of *Beowulf*?', *Anglo-Saxon England* 28 (1999), 23–42.
817. Grocock, Christopher. 'Bede and the golden age of Latin prose in Northumbria', A100, 371–82.

818. Gwara, Scott. 'Canterbury affiliations of London, British Library MS Royal 7D. XXIV and Brussels, Bibliotheque Royale MS 1650 (Aldhelm's *Prosa de virginitate*)', *Romanobarbarica* 14 (1997), 359–74.

819. Hall, R.A.; et al. 'The Ripon jewel', A100, 268–80.

820. Hawkes, Jane. 'Anglo-Saxon sculpture: questions of context', A100, 204–25.

821. Henderson, Isabel. 'The Dupplin cross: a preliminary consideration of its art-historical context', A100, 161–77.

822. Holder, Arthur. '(Un)dating Bede's "De Arte Metrica"', A100, 390–95.

823. Horden, Peregrine. 'The millennium bug: health and medicine around the year 1000', *Social History of Medicine* 13:2 (2000), 201–20.

824. MacGregor, Arthur. 'A seventh-century pectoral cross from Holderness, East Yorkshire', *Medieval Archaeology* 44 (2000), 217–22.

825. Keefer, Sarah Larratt. 'Respect for the book: a reconsideration of "form", "content" and "context" in two vernacular poems', A133, 21–44.

826. Lang, James. 'The apostles in Anglo-Saxon sculpture in the age of Alcuin', *Early Medieval Europe* 8 (1999), 271–82.

827. Lang, James. 'The imagery of the Franks Casket: another approach', A100, 247–55.

828. MacLean, Douglas. 'Northumbrian vine-scroll ornament and the "Book of Kells"', A100, 178–90.

829. Magennis, Hugh. *Anglo-Saxon appetites: food and drink and their consumption in Old English and related literature* (Dublin: Four Courts, 1999), 195p.

830. Marsden, Richard. 'The gospels of St Augustine', A88, 285–312.

831. Martin, Geoffrey. 'A forgotten early Christian symbol illustrated by three objects associated with St. Cuthbert', *Archaeologia Aeliana* 5th ser. 27 (1999), 21–23.

832. Meaney, Audrey L. 'The practice of medicine in England about the year 1000', *Social History of Medicine* 13:2 (2000), 221–37.

833. Netzer, Nancy. 'The "Book of Durrow": the Northumbrian connection', A100, 315–26.

834. Neuman de Vegvar, Carol. 'The travelling twins: Romulus and Remus in Anglo-Saxon England', A100, 256–67.

835. O'Donnell, Dan. 'A Northumbrian version of "Cædmon's Hymn" (*eordu*-recension) in Brussels, Bibliothèque Royale MS 8245–57 ff. 62r2–v1: identification, edition and filiation', A110, 139–65.

836. O'Donoghue, Heather (ed. & reviser). *Beowulf: the fight at Finnsburh*, translated by Kevin Crossley-Holland (Oxford: Oxford University Press, 1999), xxxviii, 128p.

837. Okasha, Elisabeth. 'The inscribed stones from Hartlepool', A100, 113–25.

838. Philpott, Robert A. 'Recent Anglo-Saxon finds from Merseyside and Cheshire and their archaeological significance', *Medieval Archaeology* 43 (1999), 194–202.

839. Porter, David W. 'The earliest texts with English and French', *Anglo-Saxon England* 28 (1999), 87–110.

840. Scheil, Andrew P. 'Anti-Judaism in Ælfric's *Lives of Saints*', *Anglo-Saxon England* 28 (1999), 65–86.

841. Szarmach, Paul E. 'Abbot Ælfric's rhythmical prose and the computer age', A133, 95–108.
842. Webster, Leslie. 'The iconographic programme of the Franks Casket', A100, 227–46.
843. Youngs, Susan. 'A Northumbrian plaque from Asby Winderwath, Cumbria', A100, 281–95.

G. *Religious Belief, Practice and Organisation*

See also 737, 803, 805–6, 809–10, 812–13, 815, 817, 820–1, 824–5, 828, 830, 833, 835, 840–1, 897, 911–14, 916, 925, 932 (D); 1072, 1178, 1186, 1192, 1213, 1226, 1231 (E); 5076 (J); 5448 (L)

844. Allen, Michael Idomir. 'Bede and Frechulf at medieval St Gallen', A110, 61–80.
845. Blair, John. 'Saint Cuthman, Steyning and Bosham', *Sussex Archaeological Collections* 135 (1997), 173–92.
846. Blokhuis, B.A. 'Bede and Ælfric: the sources of the homily on St Cuthbert', A110, 107–38.
847. Bonner, Gerald. 'Bede: scholar and spiritual teacher', A100, 365–70.
848. Brown, George Hardin. 'The church as non-symbol in the age of Bede', A100, 359–64.
849. Burnell, Simon; James, Edward. 'The archaeology of conversion on the continent in the sixth and seventh centuries: some observations and comparisons with Anglo-Saxon England', A88, 83–106.
850. Clayton, Mary. *The Apocryphal Gospels of Mary in Anglo-Saxon England* (Cambridge: Cambridge University Press, 1998), xi, 355p.
851. Clemoes, Peter (ed.) *Ælfric's Catholic homilies: the first series: text* (Early English Text Society, supplementary ser., 17) (Oxford: Oxford University Press, 1997), xxii, 562p.
852. Cross, J.E. 'Bede's influence at home and abroad: an introduction', A110, 17–29.
853. Cubitt, Catherine. 'Memory and narrative in the cult of early Anglo-Saxon saints', A102, 29–66.
854. Daniels, Robin. 'The Anglo-Saxon monastery at Hartlepool, England', A100, 105–12.
855. Davidse, Jan. 'On Bede as Christian historian', A110, 1–15.
856. DeGregorio, Scott. 'The Venerable Bede on prayer and contemplation', *Traditio* 54 (1999), 1–39.
857. Emms, Richard. 'The early history of Saint Augustine's Abbey, Canterbury', A88, 410–28.
858. Foot, Sarah. 'The role of the minster in earlier Anglo-Saxon society', A205, 35–58.
859. Foot, Sarah. *Veiled women*, 2 vols. 1: *The disappearance of nuns from Anglo-Saxon England*; 2: *Female religious communities in England, 871–1066* (Aldershot: Ashgate, 2000).
860. Gameson, Fiona. 'Goscelin's *Life* of Augustine of Canterbury', A88, 391–409.

861. Gameson, Richard. 'Augustine of Canterbury: context and achievement', A88, 1–40.

862. Gatch, Milton McC. *Eschatology and Christian nurture: themes in Anglo-Saxon and medieval religious life* (Aldershot: Ashgate, 2000), xiii, 330p. [Collected papers, all previously published: not individually itemised.]

863. Glaeske, Keith. 'Eve in Anglo-Saxon retellings of the harrowing of hell', *Traditio* 54 (1999), 81–101.

864. Grant, N. 'Saint Petroc in Devon', *Devon Historian* 61 (2000), 10–16.

865. Hill, Joyce. 'The *Litaniae maiores* and *minores* in Rome, Francia and Anglo-Saxon England: terminology, texts and traditions', *Early Medieval Europe* 9:2 (2000), 211–46.

866. Holdsworth, C. 'Bishoprics, monasteries and the landscape c.AD 600–1066', A109, 27–49.

867. Hood, Allan B.E. 'Lighten our darkness: Biblical style in early medieval Britain and Ireland' [review article], *Early Medieval Europe* 8 (1999), 283–96.

868. Howlett, David. 'A response to "Lighten our darkness"' [no.867], *Early Medieval Europe* 9:1 (2000), 85–92.

869. Jansen, A.M. 'Bede and the legends of St Oswald', A110, 167–78.

870. Jones, Christopher. 'The book of the liturgy in Anglo-Saxon England', *Speculum* 73 (1998), 659–702.

871. Jones, Christopher A. 'A liturgical miscellany in Cambridge, Corpus Christi College', *Traditio* 54 (1999), 103–40.

872. Karkov, Catherine E. 'Whitby, Jarrow and the commemoration of death in Northumbria', A100, 126–35.

873. Lang, Jim. 'Monuments from Yorkshire in the age of Alcuin', A89, 109–19.

874. Laynesmith, Mark D. 'Stephen of Ripon and the Bible: allegorical and typological interpretations of the *Life of St Wilfrid*', *Early Medieval Europe* 9:2 (2000), 163–82.

875. Lenker, Ursula. *Die Westsächsiche Evangelienversion und die Perikopenordnungen im Angelsächsischen England* [The West Saxon Gospels and the gospel-lectionary in Anglo-Saxon England] (Texte und Untersuchungen zur englischen Philologie, 20) (München: W. Fink, 1997), xxiii, 548p.

876. Lenker, Ursula. 'The West Saxon Gospels and the gospel-lectionary in Anglo-Saxon England: manuscript evidence and liturgical practice', *Anglo-Saxon England* 28 (1999), 141–78.

877. Loyn, Henry Royston. *The English church, 940–1154* (Harlow: Longman, 2000), x, 174p.

878. Lutterkort, Karl. 'Beda hagiographicus: meaning and function of mairacle stories in the *Vita Cuthberti* and the *Historia ecclesiastica*', A110, 81–106.

879. Mackay, Thomas W. 'Augustine and Gregory the Great in Bede's commentary on the Apocalypse', A100, 396–405.

880. Markus, R.A. 'Augustine and Gregory the Great', A88, 41–49.

881. Marner, Dominic. *St Cuthbert: his life and cult in medieval Durham* (London: British Library, 2000), 112p.

882. McAleer, J. Philip. *Rochester Cathedral 604–1540: an architectural history* (Toronto (Ont) and London: University of Toronto Press, 1999), xxiv, 314p.

883. Meens, Rob. 'Questioning ritual purity: the influence of Gregory the Great's answers to Augustine's queries about childbirth, menstruation and sexuality', A88, 174–86.

884. Michelli, Perette. 'What's in the cupboard? Ezra and Matthew reconsidered', A100, 345–58.

885. Norton, Christopher. 'The Anglo-Saxon Cathedral at York and the topography of the Anglian city', *Journal of the British Archaeological Association* 151 (1998), 1–42.

886. O'Carragain, Eamonn. 'The necessary distance: "Imitatio Romae" and the Ruthwell cross', A100, 191–203.

887. Orme, Nicholas. 'Two unusual Devon saints', *Devon Historian* 51 (1995), 10–13.

888. Ortenberg, Veronica. 'The Anglo-Saxon church and the Papacy', A134, 31–62.

889. Orton, Fred. 'Northumbrian sculpture (the Ruthwell and Bewcastle monuments): questions of difference', A100, 216–26.

890. Parsons, David. 'Odda's Chapel, Deerhurst: place of worship or royal hall?', *Medieval Archaeology* 44 (2000), 225–8.

891. Parsons, David. 'Willibrord's "Frisian" mission and the early churches in Utrecht', A100, 136–49.

892. Pfaff, Richard W. 'The Anglo-Saxon bishop and his book', *Bulletin of the John Rylands University Library of Manchester* 81:1 (1999), 3–24.

893. Raw, Barbara C. 'The Office of the Trinity in the Crowland Psalter (Oxford, Bodleian Library, Douce 296)', *Anglo-Saxon England* 28 (1999), 185–200.

894. Rollason, David. 'Monasteries and society in early medieval Northumbria', A205, 59–74.

895. Rollason, David (ed.) *Symeon of Durham: Libellus de Exordio atque Procursu istius, hoc est Dunhelmensis, Ecclesie: Tract on the origins and progress of this the Church of Durham* (Oxford: Clarendon, 2000), xcv, 353p.

896. Rushforth, Rebecca. 'A Cambridge fragment of Aldhelm: CUL MS Add. 4219', *Transactions of the Cambridge Bibliographical Society* 11:4 (1999), 449–62.

897. Rushforth, Rebecca. 'The medieval hagiography of St Cuthburg', *Analecta Bollandiana* 118 (2000), 291–324.

898. Scharer, Anton. 'The Gregorian tradition in early England', A88, 187–201.

899. Smith, William. 'Iwi of Wilton: a forgotten saint', *Analecta Bollandiana* 117 (1999), 297–318.

900. Stancliffe, Clare. 'The British church and the mission of Augustine', A88, 107–51.

901. Stansbury, Mark. 'Source-marks in Bede's Biblical commentaries', A100, 383–89.

902. Thacker, Alan. 'In Gregory's shadow? the pre-conquest cult of St Augustine', A88, 374–90.

903. Thacker, A.T. 'Bede and the Irish', A110, 31–59.

904. Toswell, M.J. 'How pedantry meets intertextuality: editing the Old English metrical psalter', A133, 79–94.

905. Toswell, M.J. 'St. Martial and the dating of late Anglo-Saxon manuscripts', *Scriptorium* 51 (1997), 3–14.
906. Verey, Christopher D. 'Lindisfarne or Rath Maelsigi? the evidence of the texts', A100, 327–35.
907. Withers, Benjamin C. 'Unfulfilled promise: the rubrics of the Old English prose Genesis', *Anglo-Saxon England* 28 (1999), 111–39.
908. Wood, Ian. 'Augustine and Gaul', A88, 68–82.

H. Politics, Administration and Law

See also 502 (B); 758, 777, 842, 861, 869, 877, 880, 898, 900, 936 (D); 5095, 5105 (J)

909. Barrow, J. 'Friends and friendship in Anglo-Saxon charters', A99, 106–23.
910. Behr, Charlotte. 'The origins of kingship in early medieval Kent', *Early Medieval Europe* 9:1 (2000), 25–52.
911. Brooks, Nicholas. *Anglo-Saxon myths: state and church, 400–1066* (London and Rio Grande (OH): Hambledon, 2000), xvi, 308p. [Collected papers, not individually itemized; includes one new chapter: 'The English origin myth', pp. 79–89; plus a new postscript on the period 1973–98 (pp. 202–15), added to 'Anglo-Saxon charters: a review of work 1953–73', pp. 181–202.]
912. Conn, M.A. 'Rites of king-making in tenth-century England', A92, 111–28.
913. Corning, Caitlin. 'The baptism of Edwin, King of Northumbria: a new analysis of the British tradition', *Northern History* 36 (2000), 5–16.
914. Cubitt, Catherine. 'Sites and sanctity: revisiting the cult of murdered and martyred Anglo-Saxon royal saints', *Early Medieval Europe* 9:1 (2000), 53–83.
915. Haywood, John. *The vikings* (Stroud: Sutton, 1999), vii, 166p.
916. Higham, Nicholas J. 'Dynasty and cult: the utility of Christian mission to Northumbrian kings between 642 and 654', A100, 95–104.
917. Higham, Nicholas J. 'King Edwin of the Deiri: rhetoric and the reality of power in early England', A89, 41–49.
918. Higham, Nicholas J. '*Imperium* in early Britain: rhetoric and reality in the writings of Gildas and Bede', *Anglo-Saxon Studies in Archaeology and History* 10 (1999), 31–36.
919. Insley, Charles. 'Politics, conflict and kinship in early eleventh-century Mercia', *Midland History* 25 (2000), 28–42.
920. Maddicott, J.R. 'Two frontier states: Northumbria and Wessex, *c*.650–750', A141, 25–45.
921. Oakeshott, Michael. 'Saxon South Cerney', *Transactions of the Bristol and Gloucestershire Archaeological Society* 117 (1999), 119–26.
922. O'Brien, Bruce R. *God's peace and king's peace: the laws of Edward the Confessor* (Philadelphia (PA): University of Pennsylvania Press, 1999), xv, 305p.
923. Peddie, John. *Alfred: warrior king* (Stroud: Sutton, 1999), xv, 224p.
924. Scharer, Anton. *Herrschaft und Repräsentation. Studien zur Hofkultur König Alfreds des Grossen* [Rule and representation. Studies on the court culture of King Alfred the Great] (Vienna: R. Oldenbourg, 2000), 151p.

925.   Thacker, Alan. '*Peculiaris Patronus Noster*: the saint as patron of the state in the early middle ages', A141, 1–24.
926.   Tyler, Elizabeth M. '"The eyes of the beholders were dazzled"?: treasure and artifice in *Encomium Emmae Reginae*', *Early Medieval Europe* 8 (1999), 247–70.
927.   Walker, Ian W. *Mercia and the making of England* (Stroud: Sutton, 2000), xix, 236p.
928.   Williams, Ann. 'Britain: AD 1000', *History Today* 50:3 (2000), 35–41.
929.   Williams, Ann. *Kingship and government in pre-Conquest England c.500–c.1066* (Basingstoke and New York: Macmillan and St Martin's Press, 1999), xxvii, 243p.
930.   Wormald, Patrick. *The making of English law: King Alfred to the twelfth century*, vol. 1: *Legislation and its limits* (Oxford: Blackwell, 1999), xviii, 574p.
931.   Yorke, Barbara. *The Anglo-Saxons* (Stroud: Sutton, 1999), x, 118p.
932.   Yorke, Barbara. 'The reception of Christianity at the Anglo-Saxon royal courts', A88, 152–73.

J. *Military*

933.   Cathers, K. 'Hierarchy or anarchy: an examination of the leadership structures within the Anglo-Saxon military', A92, 97–110.
934.   Lawson, M.K. 'Observations upon a scene in the Bayeux Tapestry, the Battle of Hastings and the military system of the late Anglo-Saxon state', A141, 73–91.
935.   Swanton, M.J. 'King Alfred's ships: text and context', *Anglo-Saxon England* 28 (1999), 1–22.

K. *Foreign Affairs*

See also 784 (D)

936.   Charles-Edwards, T.M. ' "The continuation of Bede", *s.a.* 750: high-kings, kings of Tara and "Bretwaldas" ', A196, 137–45.
937.   Harris, Jonathan. 'Wars and rumours of wars: England and the Byzantine world in the eighth and ninth centuries', *Mediterranean Historical Review* 14:2 (1999), 29–46.
938.   Van Houts, Elisabeth. 'Hereward and Flanders', *Anglo-Saxon England* 28 (1999), 201–23.

E. ENGLAND 1066–1500

A. General

See also 254 (B); 688 (D); 1269 (E)

939. Ambrisco, A.S. 'Cannibalism and cultural encounters in Richard Coeur de Lion', *Journal of Medieval and Early Modern Studies* 29:3 (1999), 499–528.
940. Britnell, Richard H. 'Introduction' [Daily life in the middle ages], A23, 1–4.
941. Hallam, Elizabeth (ed.) *Chronicles of the age of chivalry* (London: Salamander, 2000), 320p. [Brief extracts from chronicles with brief essays on varied subjects.]
942. Higgins, Iain Macleod. *Writing east: the 'travels' of Sir John Mandeville* (Philadelphia (PA): University of Pennsylvania Press, 1997), ix, 335p.
943. Morley, Beric M.; Miles, Daniel W.H. 'Nave roof, chest and door of the church of St Mary, Kempley, Gloucestershire: dendrochronological dating', *Antiquaries Journal* 80 (2000), 294–6.

B. Historiography and Historical Methods

See also 304 (B); 605 (C); 695 (D); 1004, 1282 (E); 5297 (L)

944. Cholakian, Rouben C. 'The Bayeux Tapestry: is there more to say?', *Annales de Normandie* 47 (1997), 43–50.
945. Collier, H. 'Richard Hill: a London compiler', A162, 319–29.
946. Freeman, Elizabeth. 'Aelred of Rievaulx's "De bello standardii": Cistercian historiography and the creation of community memories', *Cîteaux* 49 (1998), 5–28.
947. Harvey, D.C. 'Continuity, authority and the place of heritage in the medieval world', *Journal of Historical Geography* 26:1 (2000), 47–59.
948. Kay, Richard. 'Walter of Coventry and the Barnwell Chronicle', *Traditio* 54 (1999), 141–67.
949. Philpott, Mark. 'Eadmer, his archbishops and the English state', A141, 93–107.
950. Raftis, J. Ambrose. 'Marc Bloch's comparative method and the rural history of mediaeval England', A45, 63–79.
951. Roling, Bernd. 'Der Historiker als Apologet der Weltverachtung: die "Historia Anglorum" des Heinrich von Huntingdon', *Frühmittelalterliche Studien* 33 (1999), 125–68.

C. Population and Environment

See also 313 (B), 697, 701, 705, 713, 716–17, 719, 722–3, 726, 731–4, 741, 752, 757, 783 (D); 996, 1000, 1037 (E)

952. Altenberg, Karin. 'Space and community on medieval Dartmoor and Bodmin Moor: interim report', *Medieval Settlement Research Group Annual Report* 14 (1999), 26–28.

953. Barron, Caroline M. 'London 1300–1540', A174, 395–440.

954. Breeze, Andrew. 'The name of Hergest, near Kington', *Radnorshire Society Transactions* 69 (1999), 176–77.

955. Conheeney, Jan. 'Reconstructing the demography of medieval London from studies on human skeletal material: problems and potential', *Transactions of the London and Middlesex Archaeological Society* 50 (1999), 78–86.

956. Creighton, Oliver H. 'Early castles and rural settlement patterns: insights from Yorkshire and the east midlands', *Medieval Settlement Research Group Annual Report* 14 (1999), 29–33.

957. Cunnington, W.E. 'The field-names of Kingsbury (Middlesex)', *English Place-Name Society Journal* 32 (2000), 41–46.

958. Dyer, Christopher. 'Rural settlements in medieval Warwickshire', *Birmingham and Warwickshire Archaeological Society Transactions* 100 (1996), 117–32.

959. Gardiner, Mark. 'The characterization of medieval Wealden settlements: excavations at Ivenden, Combe Farm, Mayfield, East Sussex', *Sussex Archaeological Collections* 136 (1998), 95–110.

960. Graham, David; Graham, Audrey. 'The moated site at South Park Farm, Grayswood', *Surrey Archaeological Collections* 87 (2000), 127–45.

961. Grainger, Ian. 'Excavations at Battle Bridge Lane in 1995: medieval and early post-medieval development along Tooley Street, Southwark', *Surrey Archaeological Collections* 87 (2000), 1–47.

962. Harvey, D.C. 'Landscape organization, identity and change: territoriality and hagiography in medieval west Cornwall', *Landscape Research* 25:2 (2000), 201–12.

963. Hough, Carole. 'The field-name *Felterrode*', *English Place-Name Society Journal* 32 (2000), 47–49.

964. Jones, Evan T.; Laughton, J.; Clark, P. *Northampton in the late middle ages: the archaeology and history of a Midland town* (Centre for Urban History, Working Paper, 10) (Leicester: Centre for Urban History, University of Leicester, 2000), 139p.

965. Kermode, Jennifer. 'The greater towns 1300–1540', A174, 441–66.

966. Lavender, N.J. 'Bronze Age and medieval sites at Springfield, Chelmsford: excavations near the A12 Boreham Interchange, 1993', *Essex Archaeology and History* 3rd ser. 30 (1999), 1–43.

967. Lilley, Keith. 'Mapping the medieval city: plan analysis and urban history' [Coventry], *Urban History* 27:1 (2000), 5–30.

968. Newman, R.M.; Hair, Nick J.; Howard-Davis, Christine L.E.; Brooks, C.; White, A. 'Excavations at Penrith Market, 1990', *Transactions of the Cumberland & Westmorland Antiquarian & Archaeological Society* 100 (2000), 105–30.

969. Oosthuizen, Susan; James, N. 'The South-West Cambridgeshire Project: interim report 1998–9', *Medieval Settlement Research Group Annual Report* 14 (1999), 17–25.

970. Postles, David. 'Migration and mobility in a less mature economy: English internal migration, c. 1200–1350', *Social History* 25:3 (2000), 285–99.

971. Rigby, S.H. 'Gendering the Black Death: women in later medieval England' [review article], *Gender & History* 12:3 (2000), 745–54.

972.   Sabin, Richard; Bendrey, Robin; Riddler, Ian. 'Twelfth-century porpoise remains from Dover and Canterbury', *Archaeological Journal* 156 (1999), 363–70.

973.   Schofield, John; Stell, Geoffrey. 'The built environment 1300–1540', A174, 371–94.

974.   Sharp, B. 'The food riots of 1347 and the medieval moral economy', A179, 33–54.

975.   Stevens, Simon. 'Excavations at the Old Post Office site, 15–17 High Street, Crawley, West Sussex', *Sussex Archaeological Collections* 135 (1997), 193–208.

976.   Thomson, J.A.F. 'Scots in England in the fifteenth century', *Scottish Historical Review* 79:1 (2000), 1–16.

977.   White, William. 'Publishing the peopling of medieval London', *Transactions of the London and Middlesex Archaeological Society* 50 (1999), 87–90.

978.   Williams, Alan; Wood, Philip. 'Excavation in Durham's Old Borough, 1995', *Archaeologia Aeliana* 5th ser. 27 (1999), 45–74.

Da. *Social Life and Conditions*

See also 347 (B); 605, 609 (C); 766 (D); 950, 1015, 1117, 1280 (E); 1378, 1413 (F)

979.   Bennett, Judith M. *A medieval life: Cecilia Penifader of Brigstock, c.1295–1344* (Boston (MA) and London: McGraw-Hill College, 1999), x, 147p.

980.   Bleakley, H.H. 'Some additional thoughts on Ockham's right reason: an addendum to Coleman', *History of Political Thought* 21:4 (2000), 565–605.

981.   Bullón-Fernández, Maria. *Fathers and daughters in Gower's Confessio Amantis: authority, family, state, and writing* (John Gower Society publications, 5) (Cambridge: Brewer, 2000), viii, 241p.

982.   Buxton, M. 'Fish-eating in medieval England', A207, 51–59. [Includes recipes.]

983.   Collard, Judith. 'Gender and genealogy in English illuminated Royal genealogical rolls from the thirteenth century', *Parergon* ns 17:2 (2000), 11–34.

984.   Finke, Laurie A. *Women's writing in English: medieval England* (London: Longman, 1999), x, 251p.

985.   Hawkes, Emma. 'Younger sons, illegitimate sons and the law: a study of three Yorkshire gentry families, 1480–1540', *Parergon* ns 17:2 (2000), 125–46.

986.   Heslop, David; Harbottle, Barbara. 'Chillingham Church, Northumberland: the South Chapel and the Grey tomb', *Archaeologia Aeliana* 5th ser. 27 (1999), 123–34.

987.   Hieatt, C.B. 'A cook of 14th-century London: Chaucer's Hogge of Ware', A206, 138–43.

988.   Kelly, H.A. 'Bishop, prioress, and bawd in the stews of Southwark', *Speculum* 75:2 (2000), 342–88.

989. Kitsikopoulos, Harry. 'Standards of living and capital formation in pre-plague England: a peasant budget model', *Economic History Review* 2nd ser. 53:2 (2000), 237–61.

990. Mercer, Malcolm. 'Lancastrian loyalism in Kent during the Wars of the Roses', *Archaeologia Cantiana* 119 (1999), 221–43.

991. Riddy, Felicity. 'Nunneries, communities and the revaluation of domesticity' [review article], *Gender & History* 12:3 (2000), 755–62.

992. Rycraft, A. '"Messing about in boats": the York Chamberlain's accounts, 1444–5', A208, 258–64.

993. Voaden, Rosalynn; Volf, Stephanie. 'Visions of my youth: representations of the childhood of medieval visionaries', *Gender & History* 12:3 (2000), 665–84. [Mainly considers French and Italian visionaries, but includes Richard Rolle.]

994. Woolgar, Christopher Michael. *The great household in late medieval England* (New Haven (CT): Yale University Press, 1999), x, 248p.

Db. *Social Structure*

See also 1163, 1282 (E)

995. Barron, W.R.J. (ed.) *The Arthur of the English: the Arthurian legend in medieval English life and literature* (Cardiff: University of Wales Press, 1998), xvii, 395p.

996. Bolton, J.L. 'Irish migration to England in the late middle ages: the evidence of 1394 and 1440', *Irish Historical Studies* 125 (2000), 1–21.

997. Bothwell, James S. '"Escheat with heir": guardianship, upward mobility, and political reconciliation in the reign of Edward III', *Canadian Journal of History* 35:2 (2000), 241–74.

998. Carpenter, D.A. 'The second century of English feudalism', *Past & Present* 168 (2000), 30–71.

999. Einbinder, Susan L. 'Meir b. Elijah of Norwich: persecution and poetry among medieval English Jews', *Journal of Medieval History* 26:2 (2000), 145–162.

1000. Jones, E.D. 'Some Spalding priory vagabonds of the twelve-sixties', *Historical Research* 73 (2000), 93–104.

1001. McCarthy, Conor. 'The position of widows in the later fourteenth-century English community and the Wife of Bath's prologue', A160, 101–15.

1002. McGee Morganstern, Anne. *Gothic tombs of kinship in France, the Low Countries, and England* (University Park (PA): Penn State University Press, 2000), xix, 252p.

1003. Powell, W.R. 'What use are "manorial descents"?: The case of Stebbing, 1066–1545', *Essex Archaeology and History* 3rd ser. 30 (1999), 144–53.

1004. Purser, T.S. 'The origins of English feudalism?: an episcopal land-grant revisited' [1085 grant from Bishop Losinga of Hereford to Roger de Lacy], *Historical Research* 72 (2000), 80–92.

1005. Stell, P.M. 'Forenames in thirteenth- and fourteenth-century Yorkshire: a study based on a biographical database generated by computer', *Medieval Prosopography* 20 (1999), 95–128.

1006. Strickland, Debra Higgs. 'Monsters and Christian enemies', *History Today* 50:2 (2000), 45–51.

1007. Swabey, ffiona. *Medieval gentlewoman: life in a widow's household in the later middle ages* (Stroud: Sutton, 1999), xiii, 210p.

1008. Watkins, Andrew. 'Peasants in Arden', A23, 83–102.

1009. Whittle, Jane; Yates, Margaret. '"*Pays rél or pays légal*"?: contrasting patterns of land tenure and social structure in eastern Norfolk and western Berkshire, 1450–1600', *Agricultural History Review* 48:1 (2000), 1–26.

1010. Wilkinson, Louise. 'Pawn and political player: observations on the life of a thirteenth-century countess', *Historical Research* 73:181 (2000), 105–23.

1011. Williams, A. 'Lost worlds: Kentish society in the eleventh century', *Medieval Prosopography* 20 (1999), 51–74.

Dc. *Social Policy and Welfare*

See also 764 (D)

1012. Britnell, Richard H. 'York under the Yorkists', A23, 175–94.

Ea. *Economic Activity and Organisation*

See also 388, 422 (B); 778–9, 782–4, 791, 794–6, 799 (D); 1157, 1259 (E); 1527 (F)

1013. Andrews, Phil; Mepham, Lorraine. 'Excavations at Vale's Lane, Devizes, 1996–7', *Wiltshire Archaeological and Natural History Magazine* 93 (2000), 241–8.

1014. Arnold, Hilary. 'The kitchens of medieval York: the evidence of the inventories', *York Historian* 16 (1999), 2–9.

1015. Bardsley, Sandy. 'Women's work reconsidered: gender and wage differentiation in late medieval England', *Past & Present* 165:1 (1999), 3–29.

1016. Brand, Paul. 'Jews and the law in England, 1275–90', *English Historical Review* 115 (2000), 1138–58.

1017. Britnell, Richard H. 'The economy of British towns 1300–1540', A174, 313–34.

1018. Britnell, Richard H. 'Urban demand in the English economy, 1300–1600', A87, 1–21.

1019. Campbell, Bruce M.S. *English seigniorial agriculture, 1250–1450* (Cambridge Studies in Historical Geography, 31) (Cambridge: Cambridge University Press, 2000), xxvi, 517p.

1020. Childs, Wendy R. 'Irish merchants and seamen in late medieval England', *Irish Historical Studies* 32:125 (2000), 22–43.

1021. Childs, Wendy R. 'The commercial shipping of south-western England in the later fifteenth-century', *Mariner's Mirror* 83:2 (1997), 272–92.

1022. Chrystall, F. 'The classification of field systems by shape and function', A8, 117–29.

1023. Comninel, G.C. 'English feudalism and the origins of capitalism', *Journal of Peasant Studies* 27:4 (2000), 1–53.

1024. Dobson, Barrie. 'General survey 1300–1540' [urban history of Britain], A174, 273–90.

1025. Dyer, Christopher. 'Small towns 1270–1540', A174, 505–40.

1026. Dyer, Christopher. 'Trade, urban hinterlands and market integration, 1300–1600', A87, 103–9.

1027. Edwards, David; Hall, David. 'Medieval pottery from Cambridge: sites in the Bene't Street—Market area', *Proceedings of the Cambridge Antiquarian Society* 86 (1997), 153–68.

1028. Ellaby, Roger. 'The Horley demesne of Reigate Priory', *Surrey Archaeological Collections* 87 (2000), 147–55.

1029. Emery, Anthony. *Greater medieval houses of England Wales 1300–1500*, vol. 2: *East Anglia, Central England and Wales* (Cambridge: Cambridge University Press, 1999), xv, 724p.

1030. Fenton, A. 'The adaptation of tools and techniques to ridge and furrow fields', A8, 167–72.

1031. Fox, H.S.A.; Padel, O.J. (eds.) *The Cornish lands of the Arundells of Lanherne, fourteenth to sixteenth centuries* (Devon and Cornwall Record Society, ns, 41) (Exeter: Devon and Cornwall Record Society, 2000), clv, 279p.

1032. Fryde, E. 'Economic depression in England in the second and third quarters of the fifteenth century: effective resistances of tenant to landlords as one of its consequences: defiances and rent strikes', A119, 215–26.

1033. Galloway, James A. 'Metropolitan market networks: London's economic hinterland in the later middle ages', *Transactions of the London and Middlesex Archaeological Society* 50 (1999), 91–97.

1034. Galloway, James A. 'One market or many? London and the grain trade of England', A87, 23–42.

1035. Gardiner, Mark. 'Vernacular buildings and the development of the later medieval domestic plan in England', *Medieval Archaeology* 44 (2000), 159–79.

1036. Gem, R. 'Romanesque architecture in Chester, c.1075–1117', A204, 31–44.

1037. Greeves, Tom; Rowe, Alan. 'Four deserted medieval settlements on Buckland Down, West Devon', *Devonshire Association Report and Transactions* 131 (1999), 71–80.

1038. Harris, R.B. 'The origins of the Chester rows', A204, 132–51.

1039. Higham, J. 'The relationship between the abbey and town of Peterborough from 1200 to the reformation', A205, 157–76.

1040. Hislop, Malcolm. 'John Lewyn of Durham: a north country master mason of the 14th century', *Journal of the British Archaeological Association* 151 (1998), 170–89.

1041. Hopcroft, R.L.; Emigh, R.J. 'Divergent paths of agrarian change: eastern England and Tuscany compared', *Journal of European Economic History* 29 (2000), 9–51.

1042. Hyland, Ann. *The horse in the middle ages* (Stroud: Sutton, 1999), xii, 180p.

1043. James, Tom Beaumont; Roberts, Edward. 'Winchester and late medieval urban development: from palace to pentice', *Medieval Archaeology* 44 (2000), 181–200.

1044. Jones, Evan T. 'River navigation in Medieval England', *Journal of Historical Geography* 26:1 (2000), 60–74p. [With response, no.1050.]

1045. Jones, Malcolm. 'The names given to ships in fourteenth- and fifteenth-century England', *Nomina* 23 (2000), 23–36.

1046. Keen, Laurence. 'Monastic urban speculation: the Cistercians and medieval Charmouth', *Proceedings of the Dorset Natural History and Archaeological Society* 121 (1999), 17–21.

1047. Keene, Derek. 'Changes in London's economic hinterland as indicated by debt cases in the Court of Common Pleas', A87, 59–81.

1048. Kowaleski, Maryanne. 'Port towns: England and Wales 1300–1540', A174, 467–94.

1049. Kowaleski, Maryanne. 'The expansion of the south-western fisheries in late medieval England', *Economic History Review* 2nd ser. 53:3 (2000), 429–54.

1050. Langdon, J. 'Inland water transport in medieval England—the view from the mills: a response to Jones' [no.1044], *Journal of Historical Geography* 26:1 (2000), 75–82p.

1051. Lewis, C. 'Medieval settlement in Hampshire and the Isle of Wight', A8, 78–89.

1052. Lomas, Richard. 'A priory and its tenants', A23, 103–24.

1053. Mackie, F.P. 'The clerical poll tax of 1379 in the diocese of Carlisle: a reassessment', *Transactions of the Cumberland & Westmorland Antiquarian & Archaeological Society* 100 (2000), 151–60.

1054. Moesgaard, Jens-Christian. 'La monnaie comme moyen de propagande: le cas de la France lancastrienne 1417–1450' [Currency as a propaganda medium: the case of Lancastrian France], *Bulletin Trimestriel de la Société Géologique de Normandie et des Amis du Muséum du Havre* 84:3–4 (1997), 83–90.

1055. Munro, John. 'A maze of medieval monetary metrology: determining mint weights in Flanders, France and England from the economics of counterfeiting, 1388–1469', *Journal of European Economic History* 29 (2000), 173–99.

1056. Nightingale, Pamela. 'Norwich, London, and the regional integration of Norfolk's economy in the first half of the fourteenth century', A87, 83–101.

1057. Ormrod, Mark. 'The English state and the Plantagenet empire, 1259–1360: a fiscal perspective', A141, 197–214.

1058. Palliser, D.M. 'Towns and the English state, 1066–1500', A141, 127–45.

1059. Ramsay, N. 'Medieval graffiti at Vale Royal Abbey, Cheshire', A204, 167–69.

1060. Stern, Derek V. *A Hertfordshire demesne of Westminster Abbey: profits, productivity and weather*, ed. Christopher Thornton. (Studies in Regional and Local History, 1) (Hatfield: University of Hertfordshire Press, 2000), lviii, 256p.

1061. Stocker, David. '"A very goodly house longging to Sutton . . .": a reconstruction of "John of Gaunt's Palace", Lincoln', *Lincolnshire History and Archaeology* 34 (1999), 5–15.

1062. Swanson, Heather. *Medieval British towns* (Basingstoke and New York: Macmillan and St Martin's Press, 1999), 161p.

1063. Thacker, Alan. 'The early medieval city and its buildings' [Chester], A204, 16–30.
1064. Threlfall-Holmes, Miranda. 'Late medieval iron production and trade in the north-east', *Archaeologia Aeliana* 5th ser. 27 (1999), 109–22.
1065. Tipping, Richard. 'Palaeoecological approaches to historical problems: a comparison of sheep-grazing intensities in the Cheviot Hills in the medieval and later periods', A8, 130–44.
1066. Ward, Jennifer. 'Townswomen and their households', A23, 27–42.

Eb. *Technology*

See also 5029 (J)

1067. Loewen, Brad. 'Bayonne, 1419: lapstraking and moulded frames in the same hull?', *Mariner's Mirror* 83:2 (1997), 328–30.

Fa. *Media and Communication*

See also 1110 (E)

1068. Briggs, Charles F. 'Literacy, reading, and writing in the medieval West', *Journal of Medieval History* 26:4 (2000), 397–420.
1069. Connolly, Margaret. 'Books connected with Battle Abbey before the dissolution: some new discoveries', *The Library* 7th ser. 1:2 (2000), 119–32.
1070. Lerer, Seth. 'William Caxton', A209, 720–38.
1071. McCarren, Vincent P.; Moffatt, Douglas (eds.) *A guide to editing Middle English* (Ann Arbor (MI): University of Michigan Press, 1998), x, 338p.
1072. Thompson, Benjamin. 'Introduction: monasteries and medieval society', A205, 1–34.

Fb. *Science and Medicine*

1073. Burnett, Charles; Ronca, Italo; Mantas España, Pedro; Abeele, Baudouin van den (ed. and trans.) *Adelard of Bath, Conversations with his Nephew: 'On the Same and the Different', 'Questions on Natural Science', and 'On Birds'*, ed. and transl. by Charles Burnett. (Cambridge: Cambridge University Press, 1998), lii, 287p.
1074. Farley, M.H. 'Her own creature: religion, feminist criticism, and the functional eccentricity of Margery Kempe', *Exemplaria* [Binghampton] 11:1 (1999), 1–22.
1075. Getz, Faye Marie. *Medicine in the English middle ages* (Princeton (NJ): Princeton University Press, 1998), xiv, 174p.
1076. Goldie, M.B. 'Psychosomatic illness and identity in London, 1416–1421: Hoccleve's Complaint and Dialogue with a Friend', *Exemplaria* [Binghampton] 11:1 (1999), 23–52.
1077. Hiatt, Alfred. 'The cartographic imagination of Thomas Elmham', *Speculum* 75 (2000), 859–86.
1078. Rawcliffe, Carole. 'Hospital nurses and their work', A23, 43–64.

1079.   Taavitsainen, I. 'Metadiscursive practices and the evolution of early English medical writing 1375–1550', *Language and Computers* 30 (2000), 191–208.
1080.   Taviner, Mark; Thwaites, Guy; Gant, Vanya. 'The English sweating sickness, 1485–1551', *New England Journal of Medicine* 336:8 (1997), 580–82.
1081.   Voigts, L.E. 'Multitudes of Middle English medical manuscripts, or the Englishing of science and medicine', A190, 183–95.

Fc. Ideas and Learning

See also 980 (E)

1082.   Boureau, Alain. 'Richard Southern: a landscape for a portrait', *Past & Present* 165:1 (1999), 218–29.
1083.   Bowers, R. 'The almonry schools of the English monasteries, c.1265–1540', A205, 177–222.
1084.   Danbury, E. 'The intellectual life of the Abbey of St Werburgh, Chester, in the middle ages', A204, 107–20.
1085.   Edden, Valerie. *Manuscripts in Midland libraries* (The index of Middle English prose, handlist, 15) (Woodbridge: D.S. Brewer, 2000), xxvi,110p.
1086.   Embree, Dan (ed.) *The chronicles of Rome: an edition of the Middle English chronicle of popes and emperors and the Lollard chronicle* (Woodbridge: Boydell, 1998), x, 310p.
1087.   Galloway, Andrew. 'Writing history in England', A209, 255–83.
1088.   Genet, Jean-Philippe. 'Le vocabulaire politique du *Policratus* de Jean de Salisbury: le prince et le roi', A9, 187–215.
1089.   Gillingham, John. 'Royal newsletters, forgeries and English historians: some links between court and history in the reign of Richard I', A9, 171–86.
1090.   Greatrex, Joan. 'Rabbits and eels at high table: monks of Ely at the University of Cambridge, c.1337–1539', A205, 312–28.
1091.   Orme, Nicholas. 'Children and literature in medieval England', *Medium Aevum* 68 (1999), 218–46.
1092.   Otter, Monika. '1066: the moment of transition in two narratives of the Norman Conquest', *Speculum* 74 (1999), 565–86.
1093.   Spencer, H.L. 'The study of medieval English preaching: what next?', *Medium Aevum* 69:1 (2000), 104–9.
1094.   Swan, Mary; Treharne, Elaine M. (eds.) *Rewriting Old English in the twelfth century* (Cambridge Studies in Anglo-Saxon England, 30) (Cambridge: Cambridge University Press, 2000), x, 213p.
1095.   Woods, Marjorie Curry; Copeland, Rita. 'Classroom and confession', A209, 376–406.

Fd. *Culture and the Arts*

See also 445, 456 (B); 609 (C); 995, 1202 (E); 1697, 1731, 1734, 1752 (F)

1096.   Aers, David. '*Vox populi* and the literature of 1381', A209, 432–53.

1097. Allen, Ruth. 'The pageant of history: a re-interpretation of the 13th-century building at King John's House, Romsey, Hampshire', *Medieval Archaeology* 43 (1999), 74–114.

1098. Ashbee, Andrew. 'Groomed for service: musicians in the Privy Chamber at the English court, c.1495–1558', *Early Music* 25 (1997), 185–97.

1099. Badham, Sally. 'Monumental brasses and the Black Death: a reappraisal', *Antiquaries Journal* 80 (2000), 207–47.

1100. Barber, Luke. 'The excavation of land adjacent to the Old Farmhouse, Pevensey, East Sussex, 1994', *Sussex Archaeological Collections* 137 (1999), 91–120 + microfiche.

1101. Beeson, Mark. 'A history of Dartmoor Theatre. Part one: 1325–1660', *Devonshire Association Report and Transactions* 130 (1998), 137–77.

1102. Benson, C. David; Blanchfield, Lynne S. *The manuscripts of Piers Plowman: the B-version* (Cambridge: D.S. Brewer, 1997), 339p.

1103. Binski, Paul. 'A note on the Hutton Conyers charter and related Fenland manuscript illumination', *Antiquaries Journal* 80 (2000), 296–302.

1104. Bitterling, Klaus. *Of Shrifte and Penance: the ME prose translation of Le manuel des péchés* (Middle English Texts, 29) (Heidelberg: Universitätsverlag C. Winter, 1998), 232p.

1105. Blacker, J. '"Dame Custance la gentil": Gaimar's portrait of a lady and her books', A162, 109–19.

1106. Burrow, Colin. 'The experience of exclusion: literature and politics in the reigns of Henry VII and Henry VIII', A209, 793–820.

1107. Clarke, C.P.; Lavender, N.J. (ed.) 'Moat Cottage, The Street, Pleshey: excavations 1988', *Essex Archaeology and History* 3rd ser. 30 (1999), 266–72.

1108. Clopper, Lawrence M. 'English drama: from ungodly *ludi* to sacred play', A209, 739–66.

1109. Cooper, Helen (ed. & abridged). *Le Morte Darthur: the Winchester manuscript* (Oxford: Oxford University Press, 1998), xxxiii, 576p.

1110. Crane, Susan. 'Anglo-Norman cultures in England, 1066–1460', A209, 35–60.

1111. Creighton, Oliver H. 'Early castles in the medieval landscape of Wiltshire', *Wiltshire Archaeological and Natural History Magazine* 93 (2000), 105–19.

1112. Dennison, L. 'Monastic or secular? The artist of the Ramsay Psalter, now at Holkham Hall, Norfolk', A205, 223–61.

1113. Downing, Mark. 'A "Westminster workshop" effigy at Leckhampstead Church, Buckinghamshire', *Records of Buckinghamshire* 40 (2000), 89–96.

1114. Edwards, A.S.G. 'John Shirley and the emulation of courtly culture', A162, 309–18.

1115. Gilchrist, Roberta. 'Norwich Cathedral: a biography of the north Transept', *Journal of the British Archaeological Association* 151 (1998), 107–36.

1116. Green, Richard Firth. *A crisis of truth: literature and law in Ricardian England* (Philadelphia (PA): Pennsylvania University Press, 1998), xvi, 496p.

1117. Grenville, Jane. *Medieval housing* (London: Leicester University Press, 1997), viii, 230p.

1118. Heighway, Carolyn; Mychalysin, Pascal. 'Masons' marks on Gloucester cathedral tower', *Transactions of the Bristol and Gloucestershire Archaeological Society* 117 (1999), 159–63.

1119. Holton-Krayenbuhl, Anne. 'The Prior's Lodging at Ely', *Archaeological Journal* 156 (1999), 294–341.

1120. Impey, Edward. 'The seigneurial residence in Normandy, 1125–1225: an Anglo-Norman tradition?', *Medieval Archaeology* 43 (1999), 45–73.

1121. Isserlin, Raphael M.J. 'The Carmelite Friary at Maldon: excavations 1990–91', *Essex Archaeology and History* 3rd ser. 30 (1999), 44–143.

1122. Johnson, Lesley; Wogan-Browne, Jocelyn. 'National, world and women's history: writers and readers in post-conquest England', A209, 92–121.

1123. King, Edmund (ed.) *William of Malmesbury: Historia Novella. The contemporary history* (Oxford: Clarendon, 1998), cxiv, 143p.

1124. Klein, Peter. 'The Poppyhead at Ludlow: boy bishop and Lord of Misrule?', *Shropshire History and Archaeology* 74 (1999), 77–82.

1125. Knight, Stephen Thomas. *Robin Hood: a complete study of the English outlaw* (Oxford: Blackwell, 1994), xi, 308p.

1126. Lachaud, Frédérique. 'Un "miroir au prince" méconnu: le De nobilitatibus, sapienciis et prudenciis regum de Walter Milemete (vers 1326–1327)', A175, 401–10.

1127. Lewis, Anthony. 'Stained glass from Glastonbury', *Somerset Archaeology and Natural History* 140 (1997), 61–67.

1128. Malyschko, Olga E. 'Three newly-discovered fragments at Worcester Cathedral: another "magnus liber organi" flyleaf', *Scriptorium* 5298 (1998), 66–82.

1129. Martin, David; Martin, Barbara. 'Adapting houses to changing needs: multi-phased medieval and transitional houses in eastern Sussex', *Sussex Archaeological Collections* 137 (1999), 121–32.

1130. Olson, Glending. 'Geoffrey Chaucer', A209, 566–88.

1131. Oosterwijk, Sophie. 'Lost, found and lost again?: the continuing enigma of the Gisborough Priory effigies', *Journal of the British Archaeological Association* 151 (1998), 190–202.

1132. Panayotova, Stella. 'Cuttings from an unknown copy of the *Magna Glossatura* in a Wycliffite Bible (British Library, Arundel MS. 104)', *British Library Journal* 25:1 (1999), 85–100.

1133. Renevey, D. 'The name poured out: margins, illuminations and miniatures as evidence for the practice of devotions to the name of Jesus in late medieval England', *Analecta Cartusiana* 130:9 (1997 for 1995), 127–48.

1134. Rigg, A.G. 'Propaganda of the Hundred Years War: poems on the battles of Crecy and Durham (1346): a critical edition', *Traditio* 54 (1999), 169–211.

1135. Rogers, Nicholas. 'Monuments to monks and monastic servants', A205, 262–76.

1136. Staley, L. 'Gower, Richard II, Henry of Derby, and the business of making culture', *Speculum* 75:1 (2000), 68–96.

1137. Strohm, Paul. 'Hoccleve, Lydgate and the Lancastrian court', A209, 640–61.

1138. Sutton, Anne. 'Dress and fashions c.1470', A23, 5–26.

1139. Thurley, Simon. 'Royal lodgings at the Tower of London 1216–1327', *Architectural History* 38 (1995), 36–57.

1140. Walker, John L. 'Fyfield Hall: a late twelfth-century aisled hall rebuilt c.1400 in the archaic style', *Archaeological Journal* 156 (1999), 112–42.

1141. Warren, Michelle R. *History on the edge: Excalibur and the borders of Britain, 1100–1300* (Medieval Cultures, 22) (Minneapolis (MN): University of Minnesota Press, 2000), xiii, 302p.

1142. Watkins, John. 'The allegorical theatre: moralities, interludes and Protestant drama', A209, 767–92.

1143. Weldon, James. 'Jousting for identity: tournaments in Thomas Chestre's *Sir Launfal*', *Parergon* ns 17:2 (2000), 107–24.

1144. Wetherbee, Winthrop. 'John Gower', A209, 589–609.

1145. Williamson, Magnus. 'The early Tudor court, the provinces and the Eton choirbook', *Early Music* 25 (1997), 229–43.

1146. Williman, Daniel. 'Some additional provenances of Cambridge Latin manuscripts', *Transactions of the Cambridge Bibliographical Society* 11:4 (1999), 427–48.

1147. Woods, M.C. 'Shared books: primers, psalters, and the adult acquisition of literacy among devout laywomen and women in orders in late medieval England', A68, 177–94.

G. *Religious Belief, Practice and Organisation*

See also 469 (B); 769, 802, 881–2, 894 (D); 1093, 1095, 1101, 1133, 1237, 1244, 1279, 1296 (E); 1854 (F); 5065, 5067, 5076–7 (J)

1148. Bateman, Nick. 'The dedication of Guildhall chapel', *Transactions of the London and Middlesex Archaeological Society* 50 (1999), 23–28.

1149. Bennett, Nicholas H. (ed.) *The registers of Bishop Henry Burghersh, 1320–1342*, vol.1: *Institutions to benefices in the archdeaconries of Lincoln, Stow and Leicester* (Publications of the Lincoln Record Society, 87) (Woodbridge: Boydell, 1999).

1150. Bozoky, Edina. 'Le culte des saints et des reliques dans la politique des premiers rois Plantagenêt', A9, 277–91.

1151. Bryant, Geoffrey F.; Hunter, Vivien M. *'How thow schalt thy paresche preche': John Myrc's instructions for parish priests*, part 1: *Introduction and text* (Barton-on-Humber: Workers' Educational Association, 1999), i, 107p.

1152. Burgess, Clive. 'London parishes: development in context', A23, 151–74.

1153. Burgess, Clive. 'The churchwardens' accounts of St Andrew Hubbard, Eastcheap, and their implications', *Transactions of the London and Middlesex Archaeological Society* 50 (1999), 61–66.

1154. Burman, Thomas E. '*Tafsī* and translation: traditional Arabic Qur'ān exegesis and the Latin Qur'āns of Robert of Ketton and Mark of Toledo', *Speculum* 73 (1998), 703–32.

1155. Burton, Janet. 'Priory and parish: Kirkham and its parishioners, 1496–7', A205, 329–47.

1156. Burton, Janet. 'The estates and economy of Rievaulx Abbey in Yorkshire', *Cîteaux* 49 (1998), 29–94.

1157. Burton, Janet. *The monastic order in Yorkshire, 1069–1215* (Cambridge Studies in Medieval Life and Thought, 4th ser., 40) (Cambridge: Cambridge University Press, 1999), xxii, 354p.

1158. Cannon, Christopher. 'Monastic productions', A209, 316–48.

1159. Cather, S.; Park, D.; Pender, R. 'Henry III's wall paintings at Chester Castle', A204, 170–89.

1160. Catto, J.I. 'A radical preacher's handbook, c.1383', *English Historical Review* 115 (2000), 893–904.

1161. Colvin, Howard. 'The origin of chantries', *Journal of Medieval History* 26:2 (2000), 163–73.

1162. Copsey, Richard. 'Simon Stock and the scapular vision', *Journal of Ecclesiastical History* 50:4 (1999), 652–83. [English saint in France; dates obscure.]

1163. Crouch, David J.F. *Piety, fraternity, and power: religious gilds in late medieval Yorkshire, 1389–1547* (Woodbridge: York Medieval, 2000), xi, 331p.

1164. Davey, P.J. (ed.) *Rushen Abbey, Ballasalla, Isle of Man: first archaeological report* (Douglas: Centre for Manx Studies, 1999), iii, 105p.

1165. Davidson, Carol F. 'Change and change back: the development of English parish church chancels', *Studies in Church History* 35 (1999), 65–77.

1166. Davis, Virginia. *Clergy in London in the late middle ages: a register of clergy ordained in the diocese of London based on episcopal ordination lists 1361–1539* (London: Centre for Metropolitan History, Institute of Historical Research, 2000), x, 76p.

1167. Dobson, Barrie. 'English and Welsh monastic bishops: the final century, 1433–1533', A205, 348–67.

1168. Dowling, Maria. *Fisher of men: a life of John Fisher, 1469–1535* (Basingstoke: Macmillan, 1999), 232p.

1169. not used.

1170. Dutton, M.L. 'Chaucer's two nuns', A205, 296–311.

1171. Evans, Christopher; Dickens, Alison; Richmond, D.A.H. 'Cloistered communities: archaeological and architectural investigations in Jesus College, Cambridge, 1988–97', *Proceedings of the Cambridge Antiquarian Society* 86 (1997), 91–144.

1172. Everard, J.A. 'The foundation of an alien priory at Linton, Cambridgeshire', *Proceedings of the Cambridge Antiquarian Society* 86 (1997), 169–74.

1173. Fleming, John V. 'The friars and medieval English literature', A209, 349–75.

1174. Fletcher, S. 'Cardinal Marco Barbo as protector of English interests at the Roman Curia in the late fifteenth century', *Downside Review* 118 (2000), 27–44.

1175. Flight, Colin. 'Parish churches in the diocese of Rochester, c.1320–c.1520', *Archaeologia Cantiana* 119 (1999), 285–310.

1176. Freeman, Elizabeth. 'Wonders, prodigies and marvels: unusual bodies and the fear of heresy in Ralph of Coggeshall's *Chronicon Anglicanum*', *Journal of Medieval History* 26:2 (2000), 127–43.

1177. Glasscoe, Marion (ed.) *The medieval mystical tradition: England, Ireland and Wales. Exeter Symposium, July 1999* (Cambridge: D.S. Brewer, 1999), 268p.
1178. Gouttebroze, Jean-Guy. 'Deux modèles de sainteté royale: Edouard le Confesseur et saint Louis', *Cahiers de Civilisation Médiévale* 42 (1999), 243–58.
1179. Greatrex, J. 'Prosopographical perspectives, or What can be done with five thousand monastic biographies?', *Medieval Prosopography* 20 (1999), 129–46.
1180. Hanham, Alison. 'Text and subtext: Bishop John Russell's parliamentary sermons', *Tradito* 54 (1999), 301–22.
1181. Harper-Bill, Christopher. *The register of John Morton, Archbishop of Canterbury 1486–1500*, vol.3: *Norwich sede vacante, 1499* (Canterbury and York Society, 89) (Woodbridge: Canterbury and York Society, 2000), xii, 324p.
1182. Harvey, Margaret M. *The English in Rome, 1362–1420: portrait of an expatriate community* (Cambridge: Cambridge University Press, 1999), x, 278p.
1183. Hayden, J.M. 'Religious reform and religious orders in England, 1490–1540: the case of the Crutched Friars', *Catholic Historical Review* 86:3 (2000), 420–38.
1184. Hoare, P.G.; Sweet, C.S. 'The orientation of early medieval churches in England', *Journal of Historical Geography* 26:2 (2000), 162–73.
1185. James, Josephine M. 'The Norman Benedictine alien Priory of St George, Modbury, AD c.1135–1480', *Devonshire Association Report and Transactions* 131 (1999), 81–103.
1186. Jones, Graham. 'Authority, challenge and identity in three Gloucestershire saints' cults', A160, 117–37.
1187. Justice, Steven. 'Lollardy', A209, 662–89.
1188. Kemp, Brian R. (ed.) *English episcopal acta, 18: Salisbury, 1078–1217* (Oxford: Oxford University Press, 1999), cxxiii, 213p.
1189. Kemp, Brian R. (ed.) *English episcopal acta, 19: Salisbury, 1217–1228* (Oxford: Oxford University Press, 2000), xxvi, 490p.
1190. Lachaud, Frédérique. 'Les soieries importées en Angleterre (fin XIIe et XIIIe siècles)', *Techniques et Cultures* 34 (1999), 179–92.
1191. Laurent, Françoise. *Plaire et édifier: les récits hagiographiques composés en Angleterre aux XIIe et XIIIe siècles* (Paris: Champion, 1998), 630p.
1192. Lawton, David. 'Englishing the Bible, 1066–1549', A209, 454–84.
1193. Lee, Paul. 'Orthodox parish religion and chapels of ease in late medieval England: the case of St George's chapel in Gravesend', *Archaeologia Cantiana* 119 (1999), 55–70.
1194. Lewis, Katherine J. *The cult of St Katherine of Alexandria in late medieval England* (Woodbridge: Boydell, 2000), xviii, 286p.
1195. Little, Katherine C. 'Catechesis and castigation: sin in the Wycliffite sermon cycle', *Traditio* 54 (1999), 213–44.
1196. Long, R. James; O'Carroll, Maura. *The life and works of Richard Fishacre OP: prolegomena to the edition of his commentary on the* Sentences. (Veröffentlichungen der Komission für die Herausgabe

Ungedruckter Texte aus der Mittelalterlichen Geisteswelt, 21) (Munich: Bayerische Akademie der Wissenschaften, 1999), 235p.

1197. Lorrey, Haidee. 'Religious authority, community boundaries and the conversion of the Jews in medieval England', A160, 85–99.

1198. Lundgren, Karen; Thurlby, Malcolm. 'The Romanesque Church of St Nicholas, Studland (Dorset)', *Proceedings of the Dorset Natural History and Archaeological Society* 121 (1999), 1–16.

1199. Maneuvrier, Christophe. 'Un acte oublié de Henry II Plantagenêt pour l'évêché de Lisieux, confirmé par Richard Coeur de Lion', *Bulletin de la Société Historique de Lisieux* 40 (1997), 12–16.

1200. Meale, Carol M. 'Women's piety and women's power: Chaucer's prioress reconsidered', A153, 39–60.

1201. Medcalf, Stephen. 'The world and heat of Thomas Usk', A153, 222–51.

1202. Morgan, N. 'Texts and images of Marian devotion in English twelfth-century monasticism, and their influence on the secular church', A205, 117–36.

1203. Nicholson, H. 'Following the path of the Lionheart: the De ortu Walwanii and the Itinerarium peregrinorum et gesta regis Ricardi', *Medium Aevum* 69:1 (2000), 21–33.

1204. Nicholson, H.J. 'Margaret de Lacy and the Hospital of St John at Aconbury, Herefordshire' [in the early 13th century], *Journal of Ecclesiastical History* 50:4 (1999), 629–51.

1205. Oliva, Marilyn. 'All in the family?: monastic and clerical careers among family members in the late middle ages', *Medieval Prosopography* 20 (1999), 161–80.

1206. Pedersen, Sarah. 'Piety and charity in the painted glass of late medieval York', *Northern History* 36 (2000), 33–42.

1207. Pobst, Phyllis E. (ed.) *The register of William Bateman, Bishop of Norwich, 1344–1355*, vol.2 (Canterbury and York Society, 90) (Woodbridge: Boydell, 2000), 248p.

1208. Postles, David. 'Defensores Astabimus: Garendon Abbey and its early benefactors', A205, 97–116.

1209. Pritchard, Gillian. 'Religion and the Paston family', A23, 65–82.

1210. Rasche, Ulrich. 'The early phase of appropriation of parish churches in medieval England', *Journal of Medieval History* 26:3 (2000), 213–37.

1211. Renshaw, Alison. 'The authoritative conscience: the functions and significance of the conscience in three religious manuals for the layman', A160, 139–52.

1212. Riches, Samantha. '"Seynt George, on whom alle Englond hath byleve"', *History Today* 50:10 (2000), 46–51.

1213. Rollason, L. 'The Liber Vitae of Durham and lay association with Durham Cathedral Priory in the later middle ages', A205, 277–95.

1214 Rosenthal, J.T. 'Margery Kempe and medieval anti-Judaic ideology', *Medieval Encounters* 5:3 (1999), 409–20.

1215 Rosenthal, J.T. 'The northern clergy: clerical wills and family ties', *Medieval Prosopography* 20 (1999), 147–60.

1216. Rosser, Gervase. 'Urban culture and the church 1300–1540', with Scottish material by E. Patricia Dennison, A174, 335–70.

1217. Rowlands, Kenneth. *The friars: a history of the British medieval friars* (Lewes: Book Guild, 1999), xiv, 377p.

1218. Rushton, Neil S. 'Parochialization and patterns of patronage in 11th-century Sussex', *Sussex Archaeological Collections* 137 (1999), 133–52.

1219. Sayers, Jane Eleanor. 'Peter's throne and Augustine's chair: Rome and Canterbury from Baldwin (1184–90) to Robert Winchelsey (1297–1313)', *Journal of Ecclesiastical History* 51:2 (2000), 249–66.

1220. Sloane, Barney. 'Reversing the dissolution: reconstructing London's medieval monasteries', *Transactions of the London and Middlesex Archaeological Society* 50 (1999), 67–77.

1221. Smith, David M. (ed.) *The Church in medieval York: records edited in honour of Professor Barrie Dobson* (Borthwick texts and calendars, 24) (York: University of York, Borthwick Institute of Historical Research, 1999), viii, 168p.

1222. Smith, David M. (ed.) *The acta of Hugh of Wells: Bishop of Lincoln 1209–1235* (Lincoln Record Society, 88) (Woodbridge: Boydell, 2000), liii, 256p.

1223. Somerset, Fiona E. 'Vernacular argumentation in *The Testimony of William Thorpe*', *Mediaeval Studies* 58 (1996), 207–41.

1224. Spurrell, Mark. 'The promotion and demotion of whole relics', *Antiquaries Journal* 80 (2000), 67–85.

1225. Stacey, Robert C. 'Anti-semitism and the medieval English state', A141, 163–77.

1226. Stanton, R. 'National martyrs and willing heroes: piety and patriotism in two English saints' lives', *Mediaevalia Groningana* 23 (1997), 191–204.

1227. Stork, Nancy P. 'Did Margery Kempe suffer from Tourette's syndrome?', *Mediaeval Studies* 59 (1997), 261–300.

1228. Swanson, R.N. 'Letters of confraternity and indulgence in late medieval England', *Archives* 25 (2000), 40–57.

1229. Urry, William. *Thomas Becket: his last days* (Stroud: Sutton, 1999), xv, 192p.

1230. Ward, S. 'The friaries in Chester, their impact and legacy', A204, 121–31.

1231. Webb, Diana. *Pilgrimage in medieval England* (London: Hambledon, 2000), 256p.

1232. Webb, Diana. 'The saint of Newington: who was Robert le Bouser?', *Archaeologia Cantiana* 119 (1999), 173–88.

1233. Whiteford, P. '"Chosen to be þi derlyng": the anticipation of heaven in a fifteenth-century Middle English meditation', *Medium Aevum* 69:1 (2000), 80–91.

1234. Wild, Chris; Howard-Davis, Christine. 'Excavations at Priory Gardens, Cartmel', *Transactions of the Cumberland & Westmorland Antiquarian & Archaeological Society* 100 (2000), 161–80.

1235. Winstead, Karen A. (ed.) *Chaste passions: medieval English virgin martyr legends* (Ithaca (NY): Cornell University Press, 2000), 201p.

Ha. *Law and Order*

See also 502 (B); 930 (D); 1263, 1325 (E)

1236. Bohna, M.L. 'Political and criminal violence in fifteenth-century England', A119, 91–104.
1237. Boureau, Alain. 'How law came to the monks: the use of law in English society at the beginning of the thirteenth century', *Past & Present* 167 (2000), 29–74.
1238. Brand, Paul. 'Inside the courtroom: lawyers, litigants and justices in England in the later middle ages', A54, 91–112.
1239. Cooper, Alan. 'The king's four highways: legal fiction meets fictional law', *Journal of Medieval History* 26:4 (2000), 351–70.
1240. Fraser, Constance M. 'The Northumberland Eyre of 1293', *Northern History* 36 (2000), 17–32.
1241. Green, Richard Firth. 'Medieval literature and law', A209, 407–31.
1242. Groot, Roger. 'When suicide became felony', *Journal of Legal History* 21:1 (2000), 1–20.
1243. Hanawalt, Barbara A. 'Violence in the domestic milieu of late medieval England', A119, 197–214.
1244. Haren, Michael J. 'The will of Master John de Belvoir, official of Lincoln', *Mediaeval Studies* 58 (1996), 119–47.
1245. Haskett, Timothy S. '"I have ordeyned and make my testament and last wylle in tis forme": English as a testamentary language, 1387–1450', *Mediaeval Studies* 58 (1996), 149–206.
1246. Hopkinson, Aileen M. (ed.) *The rolls of the 1281 Derbyshire eyre* (Derbyshire Record Society, 27) (Chesterfield: Derbyshire Record Society, 2000), lxx, 310p.
1247. Hudson, John. 'Court cases and legal arguments in England, c.1066–1166', *Transactions of the Royal Historical Society* 6th ser. 10 (2000), 91–116.
1248. Hyams, P. 'Does it matter when the English began to distinguish between crime and tort?', A119, 107–28.
1249. Neville, Cynthia J. 'The courts of the Prior and the Bishop of Durham in the later middle ages', *History* 85 (2000), 216–31.
1250. Ohlgren, Thomas H. (ed.) *A book of medieval outlaws: ten tales in modern English* (Stroud: Sutton, 2000), xxix, 346p.
1251. Phelan, A. 'Trailbaston and attempts to control violence in the reign of Edward I', A119, 129–40.
1252. Phillips, S. 'Simon de Montfort (1265), the Earl of Manchester (1644), and other stories: violence and politics in thirteenth- and early fourteenth-century England', A119, 79–90.
1253. Seabourne, Gwen; Seabourne, Alice. 'The law on suicide in medieval England', *Journal of Legal History* 21:1 (2000), 21–48.
1254. Summerson, Henry. 'Suicide and the fear of the gallows', *Journal of Legal History* 21:1 (2000), 49–56.
1255. Sutton, A.F. 'Malory in Newgate: a new document', *The Library* 7th ser. 1:3 (2000), 243–62.

1256.   Tucker, P. 'The early history of the Court of Chancery: a comparative study', *English Historical Review* 115 (2000), 791–811.

Hb. *Public Administration*

See also 1292 (E); 5452 (L)

1257.   Biggs, D. 'A Plantagenet revolution in government?: the officers of central government and the Lancastrian usurpation of 1399', *Medieval Prosopography* 20 (1999), 191–211.
1258.   Brooker, Janice; Flood, Susan (eds.) *Hertfordshire lay subsidy rolls, 1307 and 1334* (Hertfordshire Record Society, 14) ([Hertfordshire]: Hertford-shire Record Society, 1998), 204p.
1259.   Davies, Matthew. 'Artisans, guilds and government in London', A23, 125–50.
1260.   Gordon-Kelter, Janice; Rice Young, Charles. 'The poor scholar v. the able debtor: ploughing the rough ground of due process', *Journal of Medieval History* 26:2 (2000), 175–87.
1261.   Heiser, Richard R. 'Castles, constables, and politics in late twelfth-century English governance', *Albion* 32:1 (2000), 19–36.
1262.   Hinton, David A. '"Closing" and the later middle ages', *Medieval Archaeology* 43 (1999), 172–82.
1263.   Huscroft, Richard. 'The correspondence of Robert Burnell, Bishop of Bath and Wells and Chancellor of Edward I', *Archives* 25 (2000), 16–39.
1264.   Jenks, S. 'The lay subsidies and the state of the English economy (1275–1334)', *Vierteljahrschrift für Sozial- und Wirtschaftsgeschichte* 85 (1998), 1–39.
1265.   Knight, Gershom A. *The great roll of the pipe for the sixth year of the reign of King Henry III, Michaelmas 1222* (Pipe Roll Society, 89) (London: Pipe Roll Society, 1999), xvi, 344p.
1266.   Richardson, Malcolm. *The medieval Chancery under Henry V* (Special Series, 30) (Kew: List and Index Society, 1999), 139p.
1267.   Rigby, S.H.; Ewan, Elizabeth. 'Government, power and authority 1300–1540', A174, 291–312.
1268.   White, Graeme J. *Restoration and reform, 1153–1165: recovery from civil war in England* (Cambridge Studies in Medieval Life and Thought, 46) (Cambridge: Cambridge University Press, 2000), xvii, 248p.

Hc. *Political and Constitutional*

See also 926 (D); 1016, 1088–9, 1268 (E); 2005, 2074 (F); 5092, 5094, 5096, 5105 (J)

1269.   Anonymous. 'Politics and the English people in the early fourteenth cen-tury', *Costerus* 113 (1998), 99–128.
1270.   Astell, Ann W. *Political allegory in late medieval England* (Ithaca (NY) and London: Cornell University Press, 1999), xii, 218p.
1271.   Aurell, Martin. 'La cour Plantagenêt: entourage, savoir et civilité', A9, 9–46.

1272. Baume, Andrew. 'Gisors et la Normandie anglaise 1419–1449', *Cahiers de la Société Historique et Géographique du Bassin de l'Epte* 40 (1997), 47–54.

1273. Bevan, Bryan. *Henry VII: the first Tudor king* (London: Rubicon, 2000), xi, 148p.

1274. Billoré, Maïté. 'La noblesse normande dans l'entourage de Richard Ier', A9, 151–66.

1275. Burchall, Michael. 'The Conqueror's choice' [William de Braose's estates in Sussex], *Genealogists' Magazine* 26:10 (2000), 377–80.

1276. Campbell, Bruce. 'Portrait of Britain: AD 1300', *History Today* 50:6 (2000), 10–17.

1277. Carlson, David R. 'The civic poetry of Abbot John Whethamstede of St. Albans (†1465)', *Mediaeval Studies* 61 (1999), 205–42.

1278. Chauvenet, Frédérique. 'L'entourage de Richard Coeur de Lion en Poitou et en Aquitaine', A9, 137–49.

1279. Chibnall, Marjorie. *Piety, power and history in medieval England and Normandy* (Variorum Collected Studies series, CS683) (Aldershot: Ashgate, 2000), xiv, 346p. [Individual essays not itemised.]

1280. Cloulas, Ivan. 'Le douaire de Bérengère de Navarre, veuve de Richard Coeur de Lion, et sa retraite au Mans', A9, 89–94.

1281. Coote, Lesley; Thornton, Tim. 'Richard, son of Richard: Richard III and political prophecy', *Historical Research* 73:182 (2000), 321–30.

1282. Crouch, David J.F. *The reign of King Stephen, 1135–1154* (Harlow: Longman, 2000), xiv, 384p.

1283. Dace, R. 'Bertram de Verdun: royal service, land and family in the late twelfth century', *Medieval Prosopography* 20 (1999).

1284. Driver, J.T. 'A "perillous, covetous man": the career of Thomas Tropenell Esq. (c. 1405–88), a Wiltshire lawyer, parliamentary burgess and builder of Great Chalfield', *Wiltshire Archaeological and Natural History Magazine* 93 (2000), 82–89.

1285. Duggan, Anne J. '*Ne in dubium*: the official record of Henry II's reconciliation at Avranches, 21 May 1172', *English Historical Review* 115 (2000), 643–58.

1286. Everard, Judith. *Brittany and the Angevins: province and empire, 1158–1203* (Cambridge: Cambridge University Press, 2000), xiv, 242p.

1287. Gill, Louise. *Richard III and Buckingham's rebellion* (Stroud: Sutton, 1999), viii, 184p.

1288. Golding, Brian. 'Portrait of Britain: AD 1100', *History Today* 50:4 (2000), 10–17.

1289. Greenway, Diana (ed. & trans.) *Henry, Archdeacon of Huntingdon, 'Historia Anglorum': the history of the English people* (Oxford: Clarendon, 1996), clxxii, 899p.

1290. Hicks, Michael A. 'Bastard feudalism, overmighty subjects and idols of the multitude during the Wars of the Roses', *History* 85:279 (2000), 386–403.

1291. Hicks, Michael A. 'From megaphone to microscope: the correspondence of Richard Duke of York with Henry VI in 1450 revisited', *Journal of Medieval History* 25 (1999), 243–56.

1292. Hivergneaux, Marie. 'Aliénor d'Aquitaine: le pouvoir d'une femme à la lumière de ses chartes (1152–1204)', A9, 63–87.

1293. Hudson, John. 'Henry I and counsel', A141, 109–26.

1294. Huscroft, Richard. *Royal charter witness lists of Edward I, (1272–1307)* (Kew: List and Index Society, 2000), 197p.

1295. Keats-Rohan, Katharine S.B. 'Domesday Book and the Malets: patrimony and the private histories of public lives', *Nottingham Medieval Studies* 41 (1997), 13–56.

1296. Kerby-Fulton, Kathryn. 'Prophecy and suspicion: closet radicalism, reformist politics, and the vogue for Hildegardiana in Ricardian England', *Speculum* 75:2 (2000), 318–41.

1297. King, Edmund. 'Stephen of Blois, Count of Mortain and Boulogne', *English Historical Review* 115 (2000), 271–96.

1298. Laborderie, Olivier; Maddicott, J.R.; Carpenter David A. 'The last hours of Simon de Montfort: a new account', *English Historical Review* 115 (2000), 378–412.

1299. Magee, J. 'Sir William Elmham and the recruitment for Henry Despenser's Crusade of 1383', *Medieval Prosopography* 20 (1999), 181–90.

1300. Mason, Emma. 'Portrait of Britain: AD 1200', *History Today* 50:5 (2000), 39–45.

1301. Mayer, Hans Eberhard. 'A ghost ship called *Frankenef*: King Richard I's German itinerary', *English Historical Review* 115 (2000), 134–44.

1302. Mercer, Malcolm. 'Driven to rebellion?: Sir John Lewknor, dynastic loyalty and debt', *Sussex Archaeological Collections* 137 (1999), 153–9.

1303. Offler, Hilary Seton. *Church and crown in the fourteenth century: studies in European history and political thought*, ed. A.I. Doyle (Variorum Collected Studies series, CS692) (Aldershot: Ashgate, 2000), xxxvii, 336p. [Reprints, not itemised.]

1304. Page, Mark. 'Cornwall, Earl Richard, and the Barons' War', *English Historical Review* 115 (2000), 21–38.

1305. Saul, Nigel. 'Britain 1400', *History Today* 50:7 (2000), 38–43.

1306. Saul, Nigel. 'The Sussex gentry and the oath to uphold the acts of the Merciless Parliament', *Sussex Archaeological Collections* 135 (1997), 221–39.

1307. Sharman, Ian C. *Thomas Langley: the first spin doctor (c.1353–1437): a political biography of the fifteenth century's greatest statesman* ([s.l.]: Dovecote-Renaissance, 1999), xvi, 253p.

1308. Stafford, Pauline. '*Cherchez la femme*: queens, queens' lands and nunneries: missing links in the foundation of Reading Abbey', *History* 85 (2000), 4–27.

1309. Studd, Robin. *An itinerary of Lord Edward* (List & Index Society, 284) (Kew: List and Index Society, 2000), 134p.

1310. Sumption, Jonathan. *The Hundred Years War]*, 2 vols. I: *Trial by battle;* II: *Trial by fire (London: Faber & Faber, 1990–92)*.

1311. Tanner, H.J. 'Reassessing King Stephen's continental strategies', *Medievalia et Humanistica* 26 (1999), 101–18.

1312. Thompson, Kathleen. 'Lords, castellans, constables and dowagers: the rape of Pevensey from 11th to the 13th century', *Sussex Archaeological Collections* 135 (1997), 209–20.

1313.   Thompson, Kathleen. 'Richer of Laigle and the Rape of Pevensey', *Sussex Archaeological Collections* 136 (1998), 201.
1314.   Tolmie, S. 'Quia Hic Homo Multa Signa Facit. Henry V's royal entry into London, November 23, 1415', *Mediaevalia Groningana* 23 (1997), 363–403.
1315.   Turner, Ralph V. 'The households of the sons of Henry II', A9, 49–62.
1316.   Vincent, Nicholas. 'King Henry II and the Poitevins', A9, 103–35.
1317.   Vincent, Nicholas. 'William Marshal, King Henry II and the honour of Châteauroux', *Archives* 25 (2000), 1–15.
1318.   Walker, S. 'Between Church and Crown: Master Richard Andrew, King's Clerk', *Speculum* 74:4 (1999), 956–91.
1319.   Walker, Simon. 'Rumour, sedition and popular protest in the reign of Henry IV', *Past & Present* 166 (2000), 31–65.

J. Military

See also 1310 (E); 5100 (J)

1320.   Curry, Anne. *The battle of Agincourt: sources and interpretations* (Woodbridge: Boydell, 2000), xiv, 474p.
1321.   Grummitt, David. 'The defence of Calais and the development of gunpowder weaponry in England in the late fifteenth century', *War in History* 7:3 (2000), 253–72.
1322.   Haydon, E. 'Castle Hill at Widworthy', *Devon Historian* 50 (1995), 18–23.
1323.   Impey, Edward. 'The buildings on the Motte at Kilpeck Castle, Herefordshire', *Archaeologia Cambrensis* 146 (2000 for 1997), 101–84.
1324.   Jones, Christopher; Eyre-Morgan, Graham; Palmer, Stuart; Palmer, Nicholas. 'Excavations in the outer enclosure of Boteler's Castle, Oversley, Alcester, 1992–93', *Birmingham and Warwickshire Archaeological Society Transactions* 101 (1997), 1–98.
1325.   Strickland, M. 'A law of arms or a law of treason? Conduct in a war in Edward I's campaigns in Scotland, 1296–1307', A119, 39–78.

K. Foreign Affairs

See also 784 (D)

1326.   Jörn, Nils. *'With money and bloode': der Londoner Stalhof im Spannungsfeld der englisch-hansischen Beziehungen im 15. und 16. Jahrhundert* [The London steelyard in 15th- and 16th-century Anglo-Hanseatic relations] (Quellen und Darstellungen zur hansischen Geschichte, neue Folge, 50) (Cologne: Böhlau, 2000), x, 628p.
1327.   Summerfield, T. 'The political songs in the Chronicles of Pierre de Langtoft and Robert Mannying', A162, 139–48.
1328.   Weiler, Björn. 'Matthew Paris, Richard of Cornwall's candidacy for the German throne, and the Sicilian business', *Journal of Medieval History* 26 (2000), 71–92.

F. ENGLAND AND WALES 1500–1714

A. *General*

See also 254 (B)

1329. Bartlett, Kenneth R. 'Travel and translations: the English and Italy in the sixteenth century', *Annali d'Italianistica* 14 (1996), 493–506.
1330. Chandler, John Howard (ed.) *Travels through Stuart Britain: the adventures of John Taylor, the water poet* (Stroud: Sutton, 1999), xii, 308p.
1331. Chard, Chloe. *Pleasure and guilt on the Grand Tour: travel writing and imaginative geography, 1600–1830* (Manchester: Manchester University Press, 1999), ix, 278p.
1332. Gunn, Steven. 'Britain 1500', *History Today* 50:8 (2000), 38–44.
1333. Miller, John. 'Britain 1600', *History Today* 50:9 (2000), 35–43.
1334. Macinnes, Allan. 'Britain 1700', *History Today* 50:10 (2000), 39–45.
1335. Renaud, Emma. *L'Angleterre au XVIIe siècle* [England in the 17th century] (Rennes: Presses universitaires de Rennes, 1997), 171p.
1336. Wagner, John A. *Historical dictionary of the Elizabethan world: Britain, Ireland, Europe, and America* (Chicago: Fitzroy Dearborn, 1999), xxxix, 392p.

B. *Historiography and Historical Methods*

See also 304 (B); 1629 (F); 5001 (J)

1337. Bernard, George W. 'History and postmodernism', A14, 217–30.
1338. Richardson, Roger Charles. *The debate on the English revolution*, 3rd edn. (Manchester: Manchester University Press, 1998), x, 262p. [1st published 1977.]

C. *Population and Environment*

See also 313 (B); 757 (D); 953, 961, 965, 973 (E); 2157–8, 2162, 2164 (G); 5003, 5012, 5014–15 (J)

1339. Adams, Bernard. 'The parish register of Talachddu 1601–1640', *Brycheiniog* 32 (2000), 61–70.
1340. Alvey, Norman. 'Growth in the population of St. Albans from the seventeenth to the nineteenth centuries', *The Local Historian* 30:3 (2000), 150–159.
1341. Barry, Jonathan. 'South-west' [the urban history of Britain, 1540–1840], A43, 67–92.
1342. Bearman, Robert. 'Stratford's fires of 1594 and 1595 revisited', *Midland History* 25 (2000), 180–90.
1343. Borsay, Peter. 'Early modern urban landscapes, 1540–1800', A210, 99–124.

1344. Bower, Jacqueline. 'Kent towns, 1540–1640', A221, 141–76.
1345. Chalklin, C.W. 'South-east' [urban history of Britain, 1540–1840], A43, 49–66.
1346. Clark, Peter. 'Introduction' [urban history of Britain, 1540–1840], A43, 1–30.
1347. Clark, Peter. 'Conclusion' [Urban history of Britain 1540–1840], A43, 831–36.
1348. Coates, Richard. 'The Sinodun Hills, Little Wittenham, Berkshire', *English Place-Name Society Journal* 32 (2000), 23–25.
1349. Corfield, Penelope J. 'East Anglia' [urban history of Britain, 1540–1840], A43, 31–48.
1350. Dyer, Alan. 'Midlands' [urban history of Britain, 1540–1840], A43, 93–110.
1351. Fleming, Peter. 'The emergence of modern Bristol', A70, 1–24.
1352. French, H.R. 'Urban agriculture, commons and commoners in the seventeenth and eighteenth centuries: the case of Sudbury, Suffolk', *Agricultural History Review* 48:2 (2000), 171–99.
1353. Griffiths, Paul. 'Politics made visible: order, residence and uniformity in Cheapside, 1600–45', A94, 176–96.
1354. Griffiths, Paul; Landers, John; Pelling, Margaret; Tyson, R. 'Population and disease, estrangement and belonging 1540–1700', A43, 195–33.
1355. Hudson, Pat; King, Steve. 'Two textile townships, c.1660–1820: a comparative demographic analysis', *Economic History Review* 2nd ser. 53:4 (2000), 706–41.
1356. Jack, Sybil M. 'Ecological destruction in the 16th century: the case of St Leonards Forest', *Sussex Archaeological Collections* 135 (1997), 241–7.
1357. Jenkins, Philip. 'Wales' [urban history of Britain, 1540–1840], A43, 133–50.
1358. Jenner, Mark S.R. 'From conduit community to commercial network? Water in London, 1500–1725', A94, 250–72.
1359. Langton, John. 'Urban growth and economic change: from the late seventeenth century to 1841', A43, 453–90.
1360. Reed, Michael. 'The urban landscape 1540–1700', A43, 289–314.
1361. Sharpe, Pamela. 'Population and society 1700–1840', A43, 491–528.
1362. Slack, Paul. 'Great and good towns 1540–1700', A43, 347–76.
1363. Slack, Paul. 'Perceptions of the metropolis in seventeenth-century England', A29, 161–80.
1364. Taylor, C.C. 'An archaeological field survey of Wothorpe, Cambridgeshire', *Proceedings of the Cambridge Antiquarian Society* 85 (1996), 161–70.
1365. Walton, John K. 'North' [urban history of Britain, 1540–1840], A43, 111–32.
1366. Watts, Sylvia. 'The significance of colonisation in two north Shropshire parishes: Wem and Whitchurch, c.1560–1660', *Midland History* 25 (2000), 61–77.
1367. Whyte, Ian D. *Migration and society in Britain, 1550–1830* (Basingstoke: Palgrave, 2000), 208p.

Da. *Social Life and Conditions*

See also 198 (A); 347 (B); 2099 (F); 2171, 2178 (G); 2753 (H); 5021 (J)

1368.   Bain, P.; Black, M. 'A glance at the life of Sir Kenelm Digby, knight, at his cookbook called "the Closet Opened", and a peep into a contemporary manuscript', A206, 27–34.

1369.   Barry, Jonathan. 'Bristol pride: civic identity in Bristol, c.1640–1775', A70, 25–47.

1370.   Ben-Amos, Ilana Krausman. '"Good works" and social ties: helping the migrant poor in early modern England', A147, 125–40.

1371.   Ben-Amos, Ilana Krausman. 'Reciprocal bonding: parents and their off-spring in early modern England', *Journal of Family History* 25:3 (2000), 291–312.

1372.   Boulton, Jeremy. 'Theatrical cultures in early modern London', *Urban History* 27:1 (2000), 89–104.

1373.   Bray, Alan; Rey, Michel. 'The body of the friend: continuity and change in masculine friendship in the seventeenth century', A105, 65–84.

1374.   Broad, John. 'Housing the rural poor in southern England, 1650–1850', *Agricultural History Review* 48:2 (2000), 151–70.

1375.   Clark, Peter. *British clubs and societies c.1580–1800: the origins of an associational world* (Oxford: Clarendon, 2000), xvii, 516p.

1376.   Clarke, Simone; Roberts, Michael. 'Guide to sources and further reading', A186, 291–99.

1377.   Cliffe, John Trevor. *The world of the country house in seventeenth-century England* (New Haven (CT) and London: Yale University Press, 1999), viii, 232p.

1378.   Clifford, H. 'Oxford college cooks, 1400–1800', A206, 59–67.

1379.   Courtney, Paul. 'Lord's Place, Leicester: an urban aristocratic house of the 16th century', *Transactions of the Leicestershire Archaeological and Historical Society* 74 (2000), 37–58.

1380.   Crane, Mary Thomas. '"Players in your huswifery, and huswives in your beds": conflicting identities of early modern English women', A149, 212–23.

1381.   Crawford, Patricia. 'Women's dreams in early modern England', *History Workshop Journal* 49 (2000), 129–42.

1382.   Crawford, Patricia; Gowing, Laura (eds.) *Women's worlds in seventeenth-century England: a sourcebook* [edition of documents] (London: Routledge, 2000), xviii, 314p.

1383.   Cressy, David. 'Conflict, consensus, and the willingness to wink: the erosion of community in Charles I's England', *Huntington Library Quarterly* 61 (2000 for 1998), 131–49.

1384.   Dabhoiwala, Faramerz. 'The pattern of sexual immorality in seventeenth- and eighteenth-century London', A94, 86–106.

1385.   Davin, A. 'What is a child?', A81, 15–36.

1386.   Dawson, Mark S. 'Histories and texts: refiguring the diary of Samuel Pepys', *Historical Journal* 43:2 (2000), 407–32.

1387.   Dench, Susan (ed.) *Index to the wills proved in the Consistory Court of*

Carlisle, 1661–1750 (Index Library, 110) (London: British Record Society, 1998), xiii, 374p.

1388.   Dillon, Janette. *Theatre, court and city, 1595–1610: drama and social space in London* (Cambridge: Cambridge University Press, 2000), x, 187p.

1389.   Dolan, Frances E. 'Marian devotion and maternal authority in seventeenth-century England', A149, 282–92.

1390.   Foyster, Elizabeth A. 'Boys will be boys? Manhood and aggression, 1660–1800', A105, 151–66.

1391.   Foyster, Elizabeth A. *Manhood in early modern England: honour, sex and marriage* (London: Longman, 1999), xi, 247p.

1392.   Foyster, Elizabeth A. 'Silent witnesses? Children and the breakdown of domestic and social order in early modern England', A81, 57–73.

1393.   Gowing, Laura. '"The freedom of the streets": women and social space, 1560–1640', A94, 130–53.

1394.   Green, Adrian; Schadla-Hall, R. Tim. 'The building of Quenby Hall, Leicestershire: a reassessment', *Transactions of the Leicestershire Archaeological and Historical Society* 74 (2000), 21–36.

1395.   Griffiths, Paul. 'Meanings of nightwalking in early modern England', *Seventeenth Century* 13:2 (1998), 212–38.

1396.   Heal, Felicity; Holmes, Clive. '"Prudentia ultra Sexum": Lady Jane Bacon and the management of her families', A147, 100–24.

1397.   Hitchcock, Tim; Cohen, Michèle. 'Introduction' [English masculinities, 1660–1800], A105, 1–22.

1398.   Hitchcock, Tim. 'Sociability and misogyny in the life of John Cannon, 1684–1743', A105, 25–43.

1399.   Hole, Robert. 'Incest, consanguinity and a monstrous birth in rural England, January 1600', *Social History* 25:2 (2000), 183–99.

1400.   Houlbrooke, Ralph. 'Civility and civil observances in the early modern English funeral', A29, 67–85.

1401.   Houlbrooke, Ralph. 'Death in childhood: the practice of the "good death" in James Janeway's A Token for Children', A81, 37–56.

1402.   Howard, Maurice. 'Inventories, surveys and the history of great houses 1480–1640', *Architectural History* 41 (1998), 14–29. List of inventories of great houses.]

1403.   Hubert, Maria. *Christmas in Shakespeare's England* (Stroud: Sutton, 1998), 152p. [An anthology of miscellaneous sources.]

1404.   Huggett, Jane E. 'Rural costume in Elizabethan Essex: a study based on the evidence from wills', *Costume* 33 (1999), 74–88.

1405.   Ingram, Martin. 'Sexual manners: the other face of civility in early modern England', A29, 87–109.

1406.   Jenner, Mark S.R.; Griffiths, Paul. 'Introduction' [Londinopolis: essays in the cultural and social history of early modern London], A94, 1–23.

1407.   Lane, Belden C. 'Two schools of desire: nature and marriage in seventeenth-century Puritanism', *Church History* 69:2 (2000), 372–402.

1408.   Langford, Paul. *Englishness identified: manners and character, 1650–1850* (Oxford: Oxford University Press, 2000), x, 389p.

1409.   Levey, Santina M. 'References to dress in the earliest account book of Bess of Hardwick', *Costume* 34 (2000), 13–24.

1410. Marschner, Joanna. 'Mary II: her clothes and textiles', *Costume* 34 (2000), 44–50.

1411. Mendelson, Sara. 'The civility of women in seventeenth-century England', A29, 111–25.

1412. Munro, Ian. 'The city and its double: plague time in early modern London', *English Literary Renaissance* 30:2 (2000), 241–61.

1413. O'Hara, Diana. *Courtship and constraint: rethinking the making of marriage in Tudor England* (Manchester and New York: Manchester University Press, 2000), xii, 276p.

1414. Orlin, Lena Cowen. 'Boundary disputes in early modern London', A171, 344–76.

1415. Orlin, Lena Cowen. 'Introduction' [Material London, ca.1600], A171, 1–13.

1416. Phillippy, Patricia. 'London's mourning garment: maternity, mourning and royal succession', A149, 319.

1417. Pritchard, R.E. *Shakespeare's England* (Stroud: Sutton, 1999), iv, 252p. [Anthology of source material.]

1418. Purdue, A. William. *Merchants and gentry in north-east England, 1650–1830: the Carrs and the Ellisons* (Sunderland: University of Sunderland Press, 1999), xxi, 273p.

1419. Roberts, Michael. '"More prone to be idle and riotous than the English"? Attitudes to male behaviour in early modern Wales', A186, 259–90.

1420. Roberts, Michael. 'Introduction' [Women and gender in early modern Wales], A186, 1–13.

1421. Schofield, John. 'The topography and buildings of London, ca. 1600', A171, 296–321.

1422. Schwarz, Kathryn. 'Mother love: clichés and amazons in early modern England', A149, 293–305.

1423. Shepard, Alexandra. 'Contesting communities? "Town" and "gown" in Cambridge, *c.*1560–1640', A193, 216–34.

1424. Shepard, Alexandra. 'Manhood, credit and patriarchy in early modern England c.1580–1640', *Past & Present* 167 (2000), 75–106.

1425. Shoemaker, Robert B. 'Reforming male manners: public insult and the decline of violence in London, 1660–1740', A105, 133–50.

1426. Shoemaker, Robert B. 'Separate spheres? Ideology and practice in London gender relations, 1660–1740', A147, 266.

1427. Sim, Alison. *Pleasures and pastimes in Tudor England* (Stroud: Sutton, 1999), 188p.

1428. Spufford, Margaret. 'Isaac Archer's Chippenham: a postscript', A198, 151–54.

1429. Stoyle, Mark J. '"Whole streets converted to ashes": property destruction in Exeter during the English Civil War', A183, 129–44. [1st published in *Southern History* 16 (1994), 69–84.]

1430. Sul, H. 'The King's Book of Sports: the nature of leisure in early modern England', *International Journal of the History of Sport* 17:4 (2000), 167–179.

1431. Terry, Reta A. '"Vows to the blackest devil": Hamlet and the evolving code of honor in early modern England', *Renaissance Quarterly* 52:4 (1999), 1070–86.

1432. Thomas, Richard. 'Feasting at Worcester Cathedral in the seventeenth century: a zooarchaeological and historical approach', *Archaeological Journal* 156 (1999), 342–58.

1433. Turner, David. '"Nothing is so secret but shall be revealed": the scandalous life of Robert Foulkes', A105, 169–92.

1434. Tyson, Blake. 'Twenty cruck buildings at Skelsmergh, Kendal, c. 1600', *Transactions of the Cumberland & Westmorland Antiquarian & Archaeological Society* 100 (2000), 181–206.

1435. Walker, Garthine. '"Strange kind of stealing": abduction in early modern Wales', A186, 50–74.

1436. Waller, Maureen. *1700: scenes from London life* (London: Hodder & Stoughton, 2000), vii, 388p.

Db. *Social Structure*

See also 1003, 1009 (E); 1361, 1637 (F); 2302 (G); 5938 (N)

1437. Archer, Ian W. 'Social networks in Restoration London: the evidence of Samuel Pepys's diary', A193, 76–94.

1438. Barton, P.G. 'Sir Rowland Hayward and the Heyward Family of Trawscoed Hall, Guilsfield', *Montgomeryshire Collections* 88 (2000), 37–52.

1439. Berkhout, Carl T. 'Adrian Stokes, 1519–1585', *Notes and Queries* 47:1 (2000), 27–28.

1440. Bianchi, Serge; Biard, Michel; et al. *La terre et les paysans en France et en Grande-Bretagne du début du XVIIe à la fin du XVIIIe siècle* [The land, the farmers and the peasantry in France and Britain from the early 17th to the late 18th century] (Paris: Armand Colin, 1999), 346p.

1441. Chevet, Jean-Michel. *La terre et les paysans en France et en Grande-Bretagne du début du XVIIe à la fin du XVIIIe siècle*, 2 vols.: 1. *Les hommes et les structures foncières*; 2. *Les hommes et la production* [The land, the farmers and the peasantry in France and Britain from the early 17th to the late 18th century. 1: The men and ownership structures. 2: The men and production] (Paris: Messene, 1998).

1442. Dickinson, Patric L. 'The heralds' visitation of Gloucestershire 1682–3', *Transactions of the Bristol and Gloucestershire Archaeological Society* 117 (1999), 11–33.

1443. Evans, M.J. Crossley. 'The maternal ancestry of Sir Hans Sloane (1660–1753), and the household of Ann Hamilton (c 1612–1689), Countess of Clanbrassil', *Antiquaries Journal* 80 (2000), 302–8.

1444. Forster, Joy. 'The lost children of Bedfordshire's Pilgrim Fathers: the Tilley family of the "Mayflower"', *Genealogists' Magazine* 26 (2000), 332–5.

1445. French, H.R. '"Ingenious & learned gentlemen": social perceptions and self-fashioning among parish elites in Essex, 1680–1740', *Social History* 25 (2000), 44–66.

1446. French, H.R. 'Social status, localism and the "middle sort of people" in England 1620–1750', *Past & Present* 166 (2000), 66–99.

1447. French, H.R. 'The search for the "middle sort of people" in England, 1600–1800' [historiographical review], *Historical Journal* 43 (2000), 277–93.

1448. Hadfield, Andrew. 'Literature, politics and national identity in sixteenth century England', *Mitteilungen—Johann Wolfgang Goethe Universität Zentrum zur Erforschung der Frühen Neuzeit, Beiheft* 2 (1995), 260–71.

1449. Hanley, Hugh. 'Probate and the church courts in Buckinghamshire in the Civil War era', *Records of Buckinghamshire* 40 (2000), 97–106.

1450. Hindle, Steve. 'A sense of place? Becoming and belonging in the rural parish, 1550–1650', A193, 96–114.

1451. Hipkin, Stephen. 'Tenant farming and short-term leasing on Romney Marsh, 1587–1705', *Economic History Review* 2nd ser. 53:4 (2000), 646–76.

1452. Holiday, P.G. 'Land sales and repurchases in Yorkshire after the Civil Wars, 1650–70', A183, 287–308. 1st published in *Northern History* 5 (1970), 67–92.]

1453. Howard, Jean E. 'Women, foreigners, and the regulation of urban space in *Westward Ho*', A171, 150–67.

1454. Jones, Judith (ed.) *Monmouthshire wills: proved in the Prerogative Court of Canterbury 1560–1601* (South Wales Record Society, 12) (Cardiff: South Wales Record Society, 1997), vii, 256p.

1455. Larguier, Gilbert; et al. *La terre et les paysans en France et en Grande-Bretagne de 1600 à 1800* [The land, the farmers and the peasantry in France and Britain, 1600–1800] (Paris: Ellipses, 1999), 223p.

1456. Marshall, Tristan. *Theatre and empire: Great Britain on the London stages under James VI and I* (Manchester and New York: Manchester University Press, 2000), viii, 211p.

1457. Mikalachki, Jodi. *The legacy of Boadicea: gender and nation in early modern England* (London: Routledge, 1998), xi, 202p.

1458. Morgan, Gerald. 'A note on Brecon probate accounts', *Brycheiniog* 31 (1998–99), 43–47.

1459. Poussou, Jean-Pierre. *La terre et les paysans en France et en Grande-Bretagne aux XVIIe et XVIIIe siècles* [The land, the farmers and the peasantry in France and Britain in the 17th and 18th centuries] (Paris: SEDES/CNED, 1999), 607p.

1460. Sale, A.J.H. *Cheltenham probate records, 1660–1740* (Gloucestershire record ser., 12) (Gloucester: Bristol and Gloucestershire Archaeological Society, 1999), xxxi, 231p.

1461. Shrank, Cathy. 'Rhetorical constructions of a national community: the role of the King's English in mid-Tudor writing', A193, 180–98.

1462. Spufford, Margaret. *Contrasting communities: English villages in the sixteenth and twentieth centuries* (Stroud: Sutton, 2000), xxxv, 374p.

1463. Tumbleson, Raymond D. *Catholicism in the English Protestant imagination: nationalism, religion, and literature, 1660–1745* (Cambridge: Cambridge University Press, 1998), ix, 254p.

1464. Williams, Alison M.A. 'Patterns of inheritance and attitudes to women revealed in wills: the Tonbridge area 1500–1560', *Archaeologia Cantiana* 119 (1999), 245–68.

1465.   Withington, Phil; Shepard, Alexandra. 'Introduction: communities in early modern England', A193, 1–15.
1466.   Zell, Michael. 'Landholding and the land market in early modern Kent', A221, 39–74.

Dc. Social Policy and Welfare

1467.   Ben-Amos, Ilana Krausman. 'Gifts and favors: informal support in early modern England', *Journal of Modern History* 72:2 (2000), 295–338.
1468.   Birtles, Sara. 'Common land, poor relief and enclosure: the use of manorial resources in fulfilling parish obligations 1601–1834', *Past & Present* 165:1 (1999), 74–106.
1469.   Boulton, Jeremy. '"It is extreme necessity that makes me do this": some "survival strategies" of pauper households in London's West End during the early eighteenth century', *International Review of Social History* supplement 8 (2000), 47–70.
1470.   Boulton, Jeremy. 'The poor among the rich: paupers and the parish, in the West End, 1600–1724', A94, 197–25.
1471.   Broad, John. 'Parish economies of welfare, 1650–1834', *Historical Journal* 42:4 (1999), 985–1006.
1472.   MacGregor, Arthur. 'The household out of doors: the Stuart court and the animal kingdom', A58, 86–117.

Ea. Economic Activity and Organisation

See also 378, 388, 412, 418, 422 (B); 795–6, 799 (D); 1017–18, 1023–6, 1033–4, 1045, 1047–8 (E); 1358, 1366, 1418, 1451, 1715, 1723, 1763, 1978 (F); 2234, 2247, 2252–3, 2286, 2556 (G)

1473.   Allen, J.R.L. 'An early post-medieval timber setting and subrectangular diggings in Late Flandrian estuarine sediments, Romney Great Wharf, Cardiff (formerly Monmouthshire)', *Archaeologia Cambrensis* 145 (1998 for 1996), 152–68.
1474.   Andrewes, Jane. 'Industries in Kent, c.1500–1640', A221, 105–39.
1475.   Archer, Ian W. 'Material Londoners?', A171, 174–92.
1476.   Arel, Maria Salomon. 'Masters in their own house: the Russian merchant élite and complaints against the English in the first half of the seventeenth century', *Slavonic and East European Review* 77 (1999), 401–47.
1477.   Ash, Eric H. '"A perfect and an absolute work": expertise, authority, and the rebuilding of Dover harbor, 1579–1583', *Technology and Culture* 41:2 (2000), 239–68.
1478.   Barnard, John. 'The Stationers' stock 1663/4 to 1705/6: psalms, psalters, primers and ABCs', *The Library* 7th ser. 21:4 (1999), 369–75.
1479.   Beckett, John; Smith, Catherine. 'Urban renaissance and consumer revolution in Nottingham, 1688–1750', *Urban History* 27:1 (2000), 31–50.
1480.   Besly, Edward. 'A Civil War hoard from Tregwynt, Pembrokeshire', *British Numismatic Journal* 68 (1998), 119–36.

1481. Boulton, Jeremy. 'Food prices and the standard of living in London in the "century of revolution", 1580–1700', *Economic History Review* 2nd ser. 53:3 (2000), 455–92.

1482. Boulton, Jeremy. 'London 1540–1700', A43, 315–46.

1483. Bourne, W.R.P. 'Information in the Lisle letters from Calais in the early sixteenth century relating to the development of the English bird trade', *Archives of Natural History* 26:3 (1999), 349–68.

1484. Cooke, W.D.; Tavman-Yilmaz, M.B. 'Hand knitting, frame knitting and rotary frame knitting in the 17th, 18th and 19th centuries', *Textile History* 30:2 (1999), 199–206.

1485. Cox, Gregory Stevens. *St Peter Port, 1680–1830: the history of an international entrepôt* (Woodbridge: Boydell, 1998), xix, 247p.

1486. Dyer, Alan. 'Small market towns 1540–1700', A43, 425–50.

1487. Fairclough, K.R. 'The Cordwell family: gunpowder producers at Chilworth 1636–1650', *Surrey Archaeological Collections* 87 (2000), 113–26.

1488. Fairclough, K.R. 'The East India Company and gunpower production in England, 1625–1636', *Surrey Archaeological Collections* 87 (2000), 95–111.

1489. Friedman, Alice T. 'Inside/out: women, domesticity, and the pleasures of the city', A171, 232–50.

1490. Glennie, Paul; Whyte, Ian. 'Towns in an agrarian economy 1540–1700', A43, 167–94.

1491. Goodacre, John. *The transformation of a peasant economy: townspeople and villagers in the Lutterworth area, 1500–1700* (Aldershot: Scolar Press, 1994), xix, 322p.

1492. Harris, Dan G. 'Francis Sheldon in Denmark 1686–1690', *Mariner's Mirror* 83:3 (1997), 293–302.

1493. Harvey, John H. 'The English nursery flora, 1677–1723', *Garden History* 26:1 (1998), 60–101.

1494. Keene, Derek. 'Material London in time and space', A171, 55–74.

1495. Langton, John. 'Proletarianization in the industrial revolution: regionalism and kinship in the labour markets of the British coal industry from the seventeenth to the nineteenth centuries', *Transactions of the Institute of British Geographers* 25:1 (2000), 31–49.

1496. Lemire, Beverly. '"In the hands of work women": English markets, cheap clothing and female labour, 1650–1800', *Costume* 33 (1999), 23–35.

1497. Lessen, Marvin. 'Cromwellian coin tools in the Royal Mint Museum', *British Numismatic Journal* 68 (1998), 157–60.

1498. Lloyd, T.H. 'Early Elizabethan investigations into exchange and the value of sterling, 1558–1568', *Economic History Review* 2nd ser. 53 (2000), 60–83.

1499. Mayer, Thomas F. 'Cardinal Pole's finances: the property of a reformer', A146, XV: 1–16.

1500. Newman, Christine M. 'Employment on the estates of the Priory of Durham, 1494–1519: the Priory as an employer', *Northern History* 36 (2000), 43–58.

1501. Pearce, Jacqueline; Tomber, Roberta. 'Evidence for the early 16th-century Surrey-Hampshire border ware industry from the City of London', *Medieval Ceramics* 21 (1997), 43–59.

1502.   Pennell, Sara. '"Great quantities of gooseberry pye and baked clod of beef": victualling and eating out in early modern London', A94, 228–49.

1503.   Redwood, Pamela. 'Early seventeenth-century mercers in Brecon', *Brycheiniog* 32 (2000), 71–84. [Includes shop inventory, c.1633.]

1504.   Rieuwerts, H. 'Early gunpowder work in Longe or Cromford Sough, Derbyshire, 1662–1663 and 1676–1680', *Mining History* 13:6 (1998), 1–5.

1505.   Roscow, J.R. 'The development of Castletown 1601 to 1703', *Isle of Man Natural History and Antiquarian Society Proceedings* 11:1 (1997/99), 5–28.

1506.   Sacks, David Harris. 'London's dominion: the metropolis, the market economy, and the state', A171, 20–54.

1507.   Sacks, David Harris; Lynch, Michael. 'Ports 1540–1700', A43, 377–424.

1508.   Samuel, Edgar. 'Gems from the Orient: the activities of Sir John Chardin (1643–1713) as a diamond importer and East India merchant', *Proceedings of the Huguenot Society of Great Britain & Ireland* 27:3 (2000), 351–68.

1509.   Scammell, G. 'British merchant shipbuilding, c.1500–1750', *International Journal of Maritime History* 11:1 (1999), 27–52.

1510.   Scammell, Lorna. 'Town versus country: the property of everyday consumption in the late seventeenth and early eighteenth centuries', A199, 26–49.

1511.   Schneider, Jane. 'Fantastical colors in foggy London: the new fashion potential of the late sixteenth century', A171, 109–27.

1512.   Sickinger, Raymond L. 'Regulation or ruination: Parliament's consistent pattern of mercantilist regulation of the English textile trade, 1660–1800', *Parliamentary History* 19:2 (2000), 211–32.

1513.   Spufford, Margaret. 'General view of the rural economy of the county of Cambridge', *Proceedings of the Cambridge Antiquarian Society* 89 (2000), 69–85.

1514.   Spufford, Margaret. 'The cost of apparel in seventeenth-century England and the accuracy of Gregory King', *Economic History Review* 2nd ser. 53:4 (2000), 677–705.

1515.   Spurgeon, C.J.; Thomas, Howard J. 'Marsh House, Aberthaw: a seventeenth-century fortified tobacco store in Glamorgan', *Archaeologia Cambrensis* 146 (2000 for 1997), 127–37.

1516.   Spurgeon, C.J.; Roberts, D.J.; Thomas, Howard J. 'Salt House, Port Eynon: a sixteenth-century saltworks in Gower', *Archaeologia Cambrensis* 146 (2000 for 1997), 117–26.

1517.   Styles, John. 'Product innovation in early modern London', *Past & Present* 168 (2000), 124–69.

1518.   Ternstrom, Myrtle. 'The ownership of Lundy by Sir Richard Grenville and his descendants, 1577–1775', *Devonshire Association Report and Transactions* 130 (1998), 65–80.

1519.   Thirsk, Joan. 'Agriculture in Kent, 1540–1640', A221, 75–103.

1520.   Thirsk, Joan. 'England's provinces: did they serve or drive material London?', A171, 97–108.

1521.   Turner, Gerard L'Estrange. 'The government and the English optical glass industry, 1650–1850', *Annals of Science* 57:4 (2000), 399–414.

1522.   Umfreville, J. 'Emergence of the malting industry in Henley-on-Thames', *Oxfordshire Local Historian* 5 (1997–98), 12–17.

1523. Wardle, Patricia. '"Divers necessaries for his Majesty's use and service": seamstresses to the Stuart kings', *Costume* 31 (1997), 16–27.

1524. Webb, Cliff. *Carmen's Company, 1668, 1678–1800* (London livery company apprenticeship registers, 29) (London: Society of Genealogists, 2000), vi, 77p.

1525. Wells, John; Wills, Douglas. 'Revolution, restoration, and debt repudiation: the Jacobite threat to England's institutions and economic growth', *Journal of Economic History* 60:2 (2000), 418–41.

1526. White, Andrew. 'Pottery making at Silverdale and Arnside', *Transactions of the Cumberland & Westmorland Antiquarian & Archaeological Society* 100 (2000), 285–91.

1527. Woodward, Donald. 'Early modern servants in husbandry revisited', *Agricultural History Review* 48:2 (2000), 141–50.

1528. Wrigley, E.A. 'The divergence of England: the growth of the English economy in the seventeenth and eighteenth centuries', *Transactions of the Royal Historical Society* 6th ser. 10 (2000), 117–41.

1529. Youngs, Deborah. 'Estate management, investment and the gentleman landlord in later medieval England', *Historical Research* 73:181 (2000), 124–41.

Eb. *Technology*

1530. Bendall, A. Sarah. 'Estate management, maps and map-making in Oxford and Cambridge 1580–1640', *History of Universities* 15 (1999), 123–54.

1531. King, P.W. 'The cupola near Bristol: smelting lead with pitcoal', *Somerset Archaeology and Natural History* 140 (1997), 37–51.

Fa. *Media and Communication*

See also 1069 (E); 2133 (F); 2302 (G); 5030–1 (J)

1532. Baudry, Samuel. 'Acte de lecture et idéologie de la culture selon Joseph Addison', *Bulletin de la société d'études anglo-américaines des XVIIe et XVIIIe siècles* 48 (1999), 177–96.

1533. Berry, Helen. 'An early coffee house periodical and its readers: the *Athenian Mercury*, 1691–1697', *London Journal* 25:1 (2000), 14–33.

1534. Borot, Luc. 'L'escapade espagnole de Charles et Buckingham: Un feuilleton d'actualité dans les nouvelles à la main de Joseph Mead en 1623' [Charles and Buckingham's Spanish escapade: a current affairs serial in Joseph Mead's newsletters, 1623], *Bulletin de la société d'études anglo-américaines des XVIIe et XVIIIe siècles* 50 (2000), 193–208.

1535. Boulard, Claire. *Presse et socialisation féminine en Angleterre de 1690 à 1750: Conversations à l'heure du thé* [Press and female socialisation in England, 1690–1750: tea-time conversations] (Paris: L'Harmattan, 2000), 536p.

1536. Boulard, Claire. 'The Lover ou la passion transitoire' [The Lover or transient passion], *Bulletin de la société d'études anglo-américaines des XVIIe et XVIIIe siècles* 50 (2000), 219–32.

1537. Breeze, Andrew. 'Dr Siôn Dafydd Rhys and Chinese printing', *Transactions of the Honourable Society of Cymmrodorion* ns 6 (1999), 9–13.

1538. Brooks, Douglas A. *From playhouse to printing house: drama and authorship in early modern England* (Cambridge: Cambridge University Press, 2000), xviii, 293p.

1539. Bryant-Quinn, Paul. '"To preserve our language": Gruffydd Roberts and Morys Clynnog', *Journal of Welsh Religious History* 8 (2000), 16–34.

1540. Carron, Helen. 'William Sancroft (1617–93): a seventeenth-century collector and his library', *The Library* 7th ser. 1:3 (2000), 290–307.

1541. Cusack, Bridget (ed.) *Everyday English, 1500–1700: a reader* (Edinburgh: Edinburgh University Press, 1998), xvi, 351p.

1542. Descargues, Madeleine. 'Le Spectator à la recherche d'équilibres précaires' [The Spectator in search of a precarious equilibrium], *Bulletin de la société d'études anglo-américaines des XVIIe et XVIIIe siècles* 50 (2000), 247–59.

1543. Devereux, Edward James. *A bibliography of John Rastell* (Montreal: McGill-Queen's University Press, 1999), xvi, 183p.

1544. Duval, Gilles. 'John Dunton (libraire et auteur, 1659–1733) ou la versatilité' [John Dunton, bookseller and author], *Bulletin de la société d'études anglo-américaines des XVIIe et XVIIIe siècles* 50 (2000), 209–18.

1545. Janssen, Frans A. 'The first English and the first Dutch printer's manual: a comparison', *Quaerendo* 30 (2000), 154–63.

1546. Johns, Adrian. 'Miscellaneous methods: authors, societies and journals in early modern England', *British Journal for the History of Science* 33:2:116 (2000), 159–86.

1547. Johnson, V.S. '"The valiant champion Lieut-General Cromwell"; "So perfect a hater of images": Oliver Cromwell and the civil war press', *Renaissance Papers* (1999), 125–36.

1548. Kiessling, Nicolas K. 'The library of Anthony Wood from 1681 to 1999', *Bodleian Library Record* 16 (1999), 470–98. [Includes Wood's guide to arrangement of his printed books in his attic study rooms, 1681.]

1549. Leedham-Green, Elisabeth Somerville; Fehrenbach, Robert J. *Private libraries in renaissance England: a collection and catalogue of Tudor and early Stuart book-lists*, vol.4 (Medieval & Renaissance Texts & Studies, 148) (Binghamton (NY): Medieval & Renaissance Texts & Studies, 1995), xxx, 348p.

1550. Llwyd, Rheinallt. 'Meirionnydd a'r fasnach lyfrau Gymrdeg: y cysylltiadan rynnor' [The Merioneth book trade, 1546–1695], *Journal of the Merioneth Historical and Record Society* 13 (2000), 227–42.

1551. Luborsky, Ruth Samson; Ingram, Elizabeth Morley. *A guide to English illustrated books, 1536–1603*, 2 vols. (Medieval and Renaissance Texts and Studies, 166) (Tempe (AZ): Medieval and Renaissance Texts and Studies, 1998).

1552. Lucas, Peter J. 'Sixteenth-century English spelling reform and the printers in continental perspective: Sir Thomas Smith and John Hart', *The Library* 7th ser. 1:1 (2000), 3–21.

1553. Lynch, Beth. 'Mr. Smirke and "Mr. Filth": a bibliographic case study in nonconformist printing', *The Library* 7th ser. 1:1 (2000), 46–71.

1554. Malcolm, Neol. 'Charles Cotton, translator of Hobbes's *De Cive*', *Huntington Library Quarterly* 61 (2000 for 1998), 259–87.
1555. Peck, Linda Levy. 'Building, buying, and collecting in London, 1600–1625', A171, 268–89.
1556. Rogers, Shef. 'The use of royal licences for printing in England, 1695–1760: a bibliography', *The Library* 7th ser. 1:2 (2000), 133–92.
1557. Scott-Warren, Jason. 'Reconstructing manuscript networks: the textual transactions of Sir Stephen Powle', A193, 18–37.
1558. Sharpe, Kevin. *Reading revolutions: the politics of reading in early modern England* (New Haven (CT): Yale University Press, 2000), xiv, 358p.
1559. Spiller, Elizabeth A. 'Reading through Galileo's telescope: Margaret Cavendish and the experience of reading', *Renaissance Quarterly* 53:1 (2000), 192–221.
1560. Tournu, Christophe. 'Le Bon Livre, le Livre, les livres. L'Areopagitica de John Milton: De la liberté de la presse à la presse de la liberté' [The Good Book, the Book, books. John Milton's Areopagitica: from freedom of the press to press of freedom], *Bulletin de la société d'études anglo-américaines des XVIIe et XVIIIe siècles* 48 (1999), 41–54.
1561. Tudeau-Clayton, Margaret. 'Richard Carew, William Shakespeare, and the politics of translating Virgil in early modern England and Scotland', *International Journal of the Classical Tradition* 5:4 (1999), 507–27.

Fb. *Science and Medicine*

See also 433 (B); 1079–80 (E); 2317, 2324 (G)

1562. Anderson, T. 'Documentary and artistic evidence for congenital conditions from sixteenth century England', *International Journal of Osteoarchaeology* 7:6 (1997), 625–27.
1563. Aspin, Richard. 'Who was Elizabeth Okeover?', *Medical History* 44:4 (2000), 531–40.
1564. Bacon, Francis. *Instauratio magna: last writings*, ed. Graham Rees (Oxford: Clarendon, 2000), xcvi, 363p.
1565. Batho, Gordon R. 'Thomas Harriot and the Northumberland household', A82, 28–47.
1566. Ben-Chaim, Michael. 'The value of facts in Boyle's experimental philosophy', *History of Science* 38:1:119 (2000), 57–77.
1567. Bennett, J.A. 'Instruments, mathematics, and natural knowledge: Thomas Harriot's place on the map of learning', A82, 137–52.
1568. Bicks, Caroline. 'Midwiving virility in early modern England', A149, 49–64.
1569. Brooke, John Hedley. '"Wise men nowadays think otherwise": John Ray, natural theology and the meanings of anthropocentrism', *Notes & Records of the Royal Society* (of London) 54:2 (2000), 199–213.
1570. Burton, Robert. *The anatomy of melancholy*, vol. 4: *Commentary*, eds. J.B. Bamborough & Martin Dodsworth (Oxford: Clarendon, 1998), xvi, 362p.
1571. Burton, Robert. *The anatomy of melancholy*, vol. 5: *Commentary from part 1, sect. 2, memb. 4, subs. 1 to the end of the second partition*, eds. J.B. Bamborough & Martin Dodsworth (Oxford: Clarendon, 2000), xiv, 312p.

1572. Clay, John. 'Robert Boyle: a Jungian perspective', *British Journal for the History of Science* 32:3 (1999), 285–98.

1573. Clucas, Stephen. 'Thomas Harriot and the field of knowledge in the English Renaissance', A82, 93–136.

1574. Cook, Harold John. *Trials of an ordinary doctor: Joannes Groenevelt in seventeenth-century London* (Baltimore: Johns Hopkins University Press, 1994), xviii, 301p.

1575. Dils, Joan A. 'Epidemics, mortality and the Civil War in Berkshire, 1642–6', A183, 144–55. [1st published in *Southern History* 11 (1989), 40–52.]

1576. Evenden, Doreen A. *The midwives of seventeenth-century London* (Cambridge: Cambridge University Press, 2000), xi, 260p.

1577. Figlio, Karl. 'Psychoanalysis and the scientific mind: Robert Boyle', *British Journal for the History of Science* 32:3 (1999), 299–314.

1578. Fox, Robert. 'Introduction: Thomas Harriot. An Elizabethan man of science', A82, 1–8.

1579. Gatti, Hilary. 'The natural philosophy of Thomas Harriot', A82, 64–92.

1580. Glisson, Francis. *From Anatomia hepatis (the anatomy of the liver), 1654*, ed. Andrew R. Cunningham (Cambridge Wellcome Texts and Documents, 3) (Cambridge: Wellcome Unit for the History of Medicine, 1993), vii, 221p.

1581. Harkness, Deborah E. *John Dee's conversations with angels: cabala, alchemy and the end of nature* (Cambridge: Cambridge University Press, 1999), xiii, 252p.

1582. Harris, Frances. 'The manuscripts of John Evelyn's "Elysium Britannicum"', *Garden History* 25:2 (1997), 131–37.

1583. Hunter, Michael. 'Robert Boyle (1627–91): a suitable case for treatment?', *British Journal for the History of Science* 32:3 (1999), 261–76.

1584. Janacek, Bruce. 'Thomas Tymme and natural philosophy: prophecy, alchemical theology, and the Book of Nature', *Sixteenth Century Journal* 30 (1999), 987–1007.

1585. Kahr, Brett. 'Robert Boyle: a Freudian perspective on an eminent scientist', *British Journal for the History of Science* 32:3 (1999), 277–84.

1586. Keller, E. 'Making up for losses: the workings of gender in William Harvey's De Generatione Animalium', *Women's Studies* 27:2 (1998), 131–162.

1587. Lloyd, Howell A. '"Famous in the field of number and measure": Robert Recorde, renaissance mathematician', *Welsh History Review* 20:2 (2000), 254–82.

1588. Mandelbrote, Scott. 'The religion of Thomas Harriot', A82, 246–79.

1589. Nichols, Richard. *Robert Hooke and the Royal Society* (Lewes: Book Guild, 1999), x, 138p.

1590. North, John D. 'Stars and atoms', A82, 186–228.

1591. Paster, Gail Kern. 'Purgation as the allure of mastery: early modern medicine and the technology of the self', A171, 193–205.

1592. Pelling, Margaret. 'Defensive tactics: networking by female medical pratitioners in early modern London', A193, 38–53.

1593. Pelling, Margaret. 'Skirting the city? Disease, social change and divided households in the seventeenth century', A94, 154–75.

1594. Pesic, Peter. 'Wrestling with Proteus: Francis Bacon and the "torture" of nature', *Isis* 90:1 (1999), 81–94.

1595. Porter, Stephen. *The great plague* (Stroud: Sutton, 1999), viii, 213p.

1596. Roche, John J. 'Harriot, Oxford, and twentieth-century historiography', A82, 229–45.

1597. Roos, Anna Marie. 'Luminaries in medicine: Richard Mead, James Gibbs, and solar and lunar effects on the human body in early modern England', *Bulletin of the History of Medicine* 74:3 (2000), 433–57.

1598. Rowlands, Peter. *Newton and the concept of mass energy* (Liverpool: Liverpool University Press, 1990), 34p.

1599. Seltman, Muriel. 'Harriot's algebra: reputation and reality', A82, 153–85.

1600. Snobelen, Stephen D. 'Isaac Newton, heretic: the strategies of a Nicodemite', *British Journal for the History of Science* 32:4 (1999), 381–420.

1601. Stedall, Jacqueline Anne. 'Ariadne's thread: the life and times of Oughtred's Clavis', *Annals of Science* 57:1 (2000), 27–60.

1602. Stirland, Ann. *Raising the dead: the skeleton crew of Henry VIII's great ship, the* Mary Rose. (Chichester: John Wiley, 2000), xviii, 183p.

1603. Trevor-Roper, Hugh. 'Harriot's physician: Theodore de Mayerne', A82, 48–63.

1604. Trubowitz, Rachel. '"But blood whitened": nursing mothers and others in early modern Britain', A149, 82.

1605. Wilding, Michael. *Raising spirits, making gold and swapping wives: the true adventures of Dr John Dee and Sir Edward Kelly* (Nottingham: Shoestring, 1999), 495p. [1st published Sydney: Abbot Bentley, 1999.]

Fc. *Ideas and Learning*

See also 1083, 1090 (E); 1462, 1787, 1915 (F); 4074 (I)

1606. Appelbaum, Robert. '"O Power. . .": Gerrard Winstanley and the limits of Communist poetics', *Prose Studies* 22:1 (1999), 39–58.

1607. Armitage, David. 'The political economy of Britain and Ireland after the Glorious Revolution', A170, 221–43.

1608. Baldwin, Geoff. 'The "public" as a rhetorical community in early modern England', A193, 199–215.

1609. Barley, M.W.; Train, K.S. 'Robert Thoroton', A182, 52–68. [Originally formed the introduction to reprint of Thoroton's *Antiquities of Nottinghamshire* (Wakefield, 1972).]

1610. Beddard, Robert A. 'A projected Cromwellian foundation at Oxford and the "true reformed Protestant interest", c.1657–8', *History of Universities* 15 (1999), 155–92.

1611. Blayney, Peter W.M. 'John Day and the bookshop that never was', A171, 322–43.

1612. Burns, William E. 'The king's two monstrous bodies: John Bulwer and the English revolution', A176, 187–202.

1613. Christen, Richard S. 'Boundaries between liberal and technical learning: images of seventeenth-century English writing masters', *History of Education Quarterly* 39 (1999), 31–50.

1614. Cohen, Joshua. 'Structure, choice, and legitimacy: Locke's theory of the state', A158, 143–66.

1615. Coleman, W.O. 'The significance of John Locke's medical studies for his economic thought', *History of Political Economy* 32:4 (2000), 711–32.

1616. Cromartie, Alan. 'Theology and politics in Richard Hooker's thought', *History of Political Thought* 21 (2000), 41–66.

1617. Dhuicq, Bernard. 'Aphra Behn, écrivain professionnel: Du plagiat aux droits d'auteur' [Aphra Behn, professional writer: from plagiary to copyright], *Bulletin de la société d'études anglo-américaines des XVIIe et XVIIIe siècles* 50 (2000), 51–65.

1618. Ducros, David. '"Books for Travailers": L'initiation au voyage dans l'Angleterre élisabéthaine et jacobéenne', *Bulletin de la société d'études anglo-américaines des XVIIe et XVIIIe siècles* 48 (1999), 161–76.

1619. Dunan, Anne. 'Le châtiment de Dorothy Mately: Mise en livre des histoires de jugement' [Dorothy Mateley's punishment: making stories of judgements from God into books], *Bulletin de la société d'études anglo-américaines des XVIIe et XVIIIe siècles* 50 (2000), 31–49.

1620. Fellows-Jensen, Gillian. 'John Aubrey, pioneer onomast?', *Nomina* 23 (2000), 89–106.

1621. Fudge, Erica. *Perceiving animals: humans and beasts in early modern English culture* (Basingstoke and New York: Macmilland and St Martin's Press, 2000), x, 232p.

1622. Gauthier, David. 'Hobbes's social contract', A158, 59–71.

1623. Gauthier, David. 'Why ought one obey God? Reflections on Hobbes and Locke', A158, 73–95.

1624. Glaisyer, Natasha. 'Readers, correspondence and communities: John Houghton's *A Collection for Improvement of Husbandry and Trade* (1692–1703)', A193, 235–51.

1625. Goldie, Mark (ed.) *The reception of Locke's Politics: from the 1690's to the 1830's* (London: Pickering & Chatto, 1999), 6 vols. [1. *The Glorious Revolution defended, 1690–1704; 2. Patriarchalism and the social contract, 1703–1710; 3. Civic virtue and political reform, 1720–1775; 4. Age of the American and French Revolutions, 1776–1838; 5. The church, dissent, and religious toleration, 1689–1831; 6. Wealth, property, and commerce, 1696–1832.*]

1626. Goldsmith, M.M. 'Hobbes's "mortall God": Is there a fallacy in Hobbes's theory of sovereignty?', A158, 23–39.

1627. Hamilton, Donna B. 'Richard Verstegan's A Restitution of Decayed Intelligence (1605): a Catholic antiquarian replies to John Foxe, Thomas Cooper, and Jean Bodin', *Prose Studies* 22:1 (1999), 1–38.

1628. Hampton, Jean. 'The failure of Hobbes's social contract argument', A158, 41–57.

1629. Hepple, Leslie W. 'Sir Robert Cotton, Camden's *Britannia* and the early history of Roman Wall studies', *Archaeologia Aeliana* 5th ser. 27 (1999), 1–19.

1630. Hobbes, Thomas. *Leviathan*, ed. Richard Tuck, revised student edn. (Cambridge and New York: Cambridge University Press, 1996), xciii, 519p. [1st edn. 1991.]

1631. Hume, Robert. 'Voluntary education 1660–1833: the Shropshire evidence', *Shropshire History and Archaeology* 74 (1999), 51–64.

1632. Jenner, Mark S.R. 'Civilization and deodorization? Smell in early modern English culture', A29, 127–44.

1633. Kavka, Gregory S. 'Hobbes's war of all against all', A158, 1–22.

1634. Knight, Caroline. 'The travels of the Rev. Sir George Wheler', *The Georgian Group Journal* 10 (2000), 21–35.

1635. Kusukawa, Sachiko. 'The Historia Piscium (1686)', *Notes & Records of the Royal Society* (of London) 54:2 (2000), 179–97.

1636. Lösch, Doris. *Property, order und civil war. zum Diskurs über Eigentum in England 1580–1649* [The discourse on property in England] (Berlin: Bodenheim, 1999), 319p.

1637. Ludington, Charles C. 'From ancient constitution to British empire: William Atwood and the imperial crown of England', A170, 244–70.

1638. Magnusson, L. 'The language of mercantilism: the English economic discussion during the seventeenth century', *Sociology of the Sciences* 20 (1996), 163–88.

1639. Manry, Marie-Agnès. 'Bacon ou les trois livres: Livre de Dieu, livre de la nature, livre de la science' [Bacon or the three books: Book of God, book of nature, book of science], *Bulletin de la société d'études anglo-américaines des XVIIe et XVIIIe siècles* 48 (1999), 7–26.

1640. Martin, Ian. 'The manuscript and editorial traditions of William Thomas's *The Pilgrim*', *Bibliothèque d'Humanisme et Renaissance* 59 (1997), 621–41.

1641. Mayhew, Robert. 'Edmund Gibson's editions of *Britannia*: dynastic chorography and the particularist politics of precedent, 1695–1722', *Historical Research* 73:182 (2000), 239–61.

1642. McCrea, Adriana Alice Norma. *Constant minds: political virtue and the Lipsian paradigm in England, 1584–1650* (Toronto (Ont) and London: University of Toronto Press, 1997), xxxi, 342p.

1643. McGee, J. Sears. 'The mental world of Sir Richard Berkeley', A147, 85–89.

1644. McLaren, Anne N. *Political culture in the reign of Elizabeth I: queen and commonwealth 1558–1585* (Cambridge and New York: Cambridge University Press, 1999), ix, 272p.

1645. More, Sir Thomas. *Utopia: Latin text and English translation*, eds. George M. Logan, Robert M. Adams & Clarence H. Miller (Cambridge and New York: Cambridge University Press, 1994), xlvi, 290p.

1646. Muldrew, Craig. 'From a "light cloak" to an "iron cage": historical changes in the relation between community and individualism', A193, 156–77.

1647. Myers, Peter C. *Our only star and compass: Locke and the struggle for political rationality* (Lanham (MD): Rowman & Littlefield, 1999), xiv, 269p.

1648. Peacey, Jason T. 'Nibbling at *Leviathan*: politics and theory in England in the 1650s', *Huntington Library Quarterly* 61 (2000 for 1998), 241–57.

1649. Piggott, Stuart. 'William Camden and the Britannia', A182, 12–29. [1st published in the *Proceedings of the British Academy*.]

1650. Pittion, Jean-Paul. 'Ni livres ni gazettes: traduction et représentation de l'événement français dans les occasionnels anglais (1588–1590 et 1617)' [Not books or gazettes: translation and representation of French events in English pamphlets], *Bulletin de la société d'études anglo-américaines des XVIIe et XVIIIe siècles* 50 (2000), 9–29.

1651. Power, M.J. 'John Stow and his London', A182, 30–31. [1st published in the *Journal of Historical Geography* 11.]

1652. Pyle, Andrew (ed.) *The dictionary of seventeenth-century British philosophers*, 2 vols. (Bristol: Thoemmes, 2000), xxi, 932p.

1653. Rae, Thomas H.H. *John Dury and the royal road to piety* (Studia irenica, 37) (Frankfurt am Main: P. Lang, 1998), 365p.

1654. Reeves, Eileen. 'As good as gold: the mobile earth and early modern economics', *Journal of the Warburg and Courtauld Institutes* 62 (1999), 126–66.

1655. Rockett, William. '*Britannia*, Ralph Brooke, and the representation of privilege in Elizabethan England', *Renaissance Quarterly* 53:2 (2000), 474–99.

1656. Roux, Louis. 'Histoire et théâtre: Richard II, Thomas More, Shakespeare', *Bulletin de la société d'études anglo-américaines des XVIIe et XVIIIe siècles* 49 (1999), 7–24.

1657. Rudolph, Julia. 'Rape and resistance: women and consent in seventeenth-century English legal and political thought', *Journal of British Studies* 39:2 (2000), 157–84.

1658. Salmon, J.H.M. 'Oliver Cromwell and the French Romantics', A189, XIX: 1–9.

1659. Sarasohn, Lisa T. 'Was *Leviathan* a patronage artifact?', *History of Political Thought* 21:4 (2000), 606–31.

1660. Schochet, Gordon. '"Guards and fences": property and obligation in Locke's political thought', *History of Political Thought* 21:3 (2000), 365–89.

1661. Simmons, John. 'Locke's state of nature', A158, 97–120.

1662. Simmons, John. 'Political consent', A158, 121–41.

1663. Vidmar, John. 'John Lingard's history of the English Reformation: history or apologetics?', *Catholic Historical Review* 85 (1999), 383–419.

1664. Ward, Joseph P. 'Godliness, commemoration, and community: the management of provincial schools by London trade guilds', A147, 141–57.

1665. Wilson, Jenny. *Ralegh's History of the world: its purpose and political significance* (Occasional paper, 28) (Durham: Thomas Harriot Seminar, [1999]), 40p.

1666. Woolfson, Jonathan. *Padua and the Tudors: English students in Italy, 1485–1603* (Cambridge: James Clarke & Co., 1998), xii, 322p.

1667. Young, John T. *Faith, medical alchemy, and natural philosophy: Johann Moriaen, reformed intelligencer and the Hartlib circle* (Aldershot: Ashgate, 1998), xv, 278p.

1668. Youngs, Deborah. 'The medieval commonplace book: the example of the commonplace book of Humphrey Newton of Newton and Pownall, Cheshire (1466–1536)', *Archives* 25 (2000), 58–73.

1669. Zagorin, Perez. 'Hobbes without Grotius', *History of Political Thought* 21 (2000), 16–40.

Fd. *Culture and the Arts*

See also 439, 445 (B); 609 (C); 1098, 1101, 1106, 1108, 1121, 1125, 1135, 1145 (E); 1973 (F); 2397, 2401, 2466 (G); 5043, 5057–8, 5060 (J)

1670.   Alcock, N.W. 'Innovation and conservatism: the development of Warwickshire houses in the late 17th and 18th centuries', *Birmingham and Warwickshire Archaeological Society Transactions* 100 (1996), 133–54.

1671.   Alsop, J.D. 'New light on Richard Steele', *British Library Journal* 25:1 (1999), 23–34.

1672.   Arnold, Janet. 'Serpents and flowers: embroidery designs from Thomas Trevelyon's miscellanies of 1608 and 1616', *Costume* 34 (2000), 7–12.

1673.   Austern, Linda Phyllis. '"My mother musicke": music and early modern fantasies of embodiment', A149, 239–81.

1674.   Biddle, Martin. 'The gardens of Nonsuch: sources and dating', *Garden History* 27:1 (1999), 145–83.

1675.   Blair, W.J. 'Some 17th and 18th century houses in Leatherhead', *Leatherhead & District Local History Society Proceedings* 6:1 (1997), 16–28.

1676.   Blezzard, Judith; Palmer, Frances. 'King Henry VIII: connoisseur, performer and composer of music', *Antiquaries Journal* 80 (2000), 249–72.

1677.   Briggs, C. Stephen. 'Aberglasney: the theory, history and archaeology of a post-medieval landscape', *Post-Medieval Archaeology* 33 (1999), 242–84.

1678.   Bristol, Michael. 'Sacred literature and profane religion: the modernity of Herbert of Cherbury', A120, 14–33.

1679.   Browne, Sylvia (ed.) *Women's writing in Stuart England* (Stroud: Sutton, 1999), xii, 260p. [Contains Dorothy Leigh, *The Mothers Blessing* (1616); Elizabeth Joscelin, manuscript mother's legacy; Elizabeth Richardson, *A Ladies Legacie to her Daughters* (1645).]

1680.   Buck, Anne. 'Clothing and textiles in Bedfordshire inventories, 1617–1620', *Costume* 34 (2000), 25–38.

1681.   Campbell, Heather. 'Bringing forth wonders: temporal and divine power in *The Tempest*', A120, 69–89.

1682.   Chaundy-Smart, D.H. 'The moral Shecinah: chancel decorations in Caroline London', *Anglican and Episcopal History* 69:2 (2000), 193–210.

1683.   Cockerham, P. '"On my grave a marble stone": early modern Cornish memorialization', *Cornish Studies* 8 (2000), 9–39.

1684.   Cressy, David. *Travesties and transgressions in Tudor and Stuart England: tales of discord and dissension* (Oxford: Oxford University Press, 2000), xi, 351p.

1685.   Downes, Kerry. 'Vanbrugh over fifty years', A184, 1–11.

1686.   Elsky, Martin. 'Microhistory and cultural geography: Ben Jonson's "To Sir Robert Wroth" and the absorption of local community in the Commonwealth', *Renaissance Quarterly* 53:2 (2000), 500–28.

1687.   Esterly, David. *Grinling Gibbons and the art of carving* (London: V & A, 1998), 224p.

1688.   Findlay, Alison; Williams, Gwen; Hodgson-Wright, Stephanie J. '"The play is ready to be acted": women and dramatic production, 1570–1670', *Women's Writing* 6:1 (1999), 129–48.

1689.   Geraghty, Anthony. 'Nicholas Hawksmoor and the Wren City church steeples', *The Georgian Group Journal* 10 (2000), 1–14.

1690.   Geuter, Ruth. '"The silver hand": needlework in early modern Wales', A186, 159–85.

1691.   Gouk, Penelope. *Music, science and natural magic in seventeenth-century England* (New Haven (CT) and London: Yale University Press, 1999), xii, 308p.

1692.   Grantley, Darryll. *Wit's pilgrimage: drama and the social impact of education in early modern England* (Aldershot: Ashgate, 2000), 270p.

1693.   Gurr, Andrew. 'The authority of the Globe and the Fortune', A171, 251–67.

1694.   Harding, Vanessa. 'Reformation and culture 1540–1700', A43, 263–88.

1695.   Hayward, Maria. 'Luxury or magnificence? Dress at the court of Henry VIII', *Costume* 30 (1996), 37–46.

1696.   Hearn, Karen. 'A fatal fertility? Elizabethan and Jacobean pregnancy portraits', *Costume* 34 (2000), 39–43.

1697.   Henderson, Paula. 'The architecture of the Tudor garden', *Garden History* 27:1 (1999), 54–72.

1698.   Hiscock, Andrew. '"To the honour of that nation": Ben Jonson and the masquing of Wales', A93, 37–63.

1699.   Howard, Skiles. *The politics of courtly dancing in early modern England* (Amherst (MA): University of Massachusetts Press, 1998), xii, 222p.

1700.   Hughes, A. Lloyd. 'Y cerddi i'r "Barwn Owain" o Dolgellau' [Poems in honour of Lewis Owen], *Journal of the Merioneth Historical and Record Society* 13 (2000), 286–95.

1701.   Ingram, Randall. 'First words and second thoughts: Margaret Cavendish, Humphrey Moseley, and "the Book"', *Journal of Medieval and Early Modern Studies* 30:1 (2000), 101–24.

1702.   Jacques, David. 'The compartment system in Tudor England', *Garden History* 27:1 (1999), 32–53.

1703.   Jacques, David. 'The formal garden', A184, 31–48.

1704.   James, Susan; van der Stighelen, Katlijne. 'New discoveries concerning the portrait of the family of William Brooke, 10th Lord Cobham, at Longleat House', *Dutch Crossing* 23:1 (1999), 66–101.

1705.   Jones, Ann Rosalind; Stallybrass, Peter. '"Rugges of London and the Diuell's band": Irish mantles and yellow starch as hybrid London fashion', A171, 128–49.

1706.   Keates, Jonathan. *Purcell: a biography* (London: Chatto & Windus, 1995), xi, 304p.

1707.   Keller, Katherine Z. 'Introduction' [manifestations of ideology in seventeenth century England], A120, 1–13.

1708.   Kelliher, Hilton. 'Dryden attributions and texts from Harley MS. 6054', *British Library Journal* 25:1 (1999), 1–22.

1709.   Kinney, Arthur F. 'Imagination and ideology in *Macbeth*', A120, 148–73.

1710.   Kisby, Fiona. 'A courtier in the community: new light on the biography of William Cornish, Master of the Choristers in the English Chapel Royal, 1509–1523', *Bulletin of the Society for Renaissance Studies* 16 (1999),

8–17. [Includes copy of the will of Margaret Stevins (d. 1508), from whom Cornish purchased property.]

1711.   Kisby, Fiona. 'Royal minstrels in the city and suburbs of early-Tudor London: professional activities and private interests', *Early Music* 25 (1997), 199–221.

1712.   Klein, Peter. 'The Churchman monument: further evidence of religious hermeticism at Munslow', *Shropshire History and Archaeology* 74 (1999), 83–88.

1713.   Knight, Stephen Thomas (ed.) *Robin Hood: the Forresters manuscript, British Library Additional MS 71158* [with a manuscript description by William Hilton Kelliher] (Woodbridge: Brewer, 1998), xxix, 173p.

1714.   Laird, Mark. 'Exotics and botanical illustration', A184, 93–113.

1715.   Leapman, Michael. *The ingenious Mr Fairchild: the forgotten father of the flower garden* (London: Headline, 2000), 280p.

1716.   Lehmann, Gilly. 'Le livre de cuisine en Angleterre aux XVIIe et XVIIIe siècles: Par qui, pour qui?' [The cookery book in 17th and 18th century England: By whom? For whom?], *Bulletin de la société d'études anglo-américaines des XVIIe et XVIIIe siècles* 48 (1999), 89–102.

1717.   Leith-Ross, Prudence. 'The garden of John Evelyn at Deptford', *Garden History* 25:2 (1997), 138–52.

1718.   Lewalski, Barbara Kiefer. *The life of John Milton: a critical biography* (Oxford: Blackwell, 2000), xvii, 777p.

1719.   Lindley, David. 'Courtly play: the politics of Chapman's *The Memorable Masque*', A58, 43–58.

1720.   Linstrum, Derek. 'Remembering Vanbrugh', A184, 192–214. [Vanbrugh's influence on later architects.]

1721.   Lynch, Jack. 'Betwixt two ages cast: Milton, Johnson, and the English Renaissance', *Journal of the History of Ideas* 61:3 (2000), 397–413. [On the reception of Milton.]

1722.   MacIntyre, Jean. 'Buckingham the masquer', *Renaissance and Reformation* 22:3 (1998), 59–82.

1723.   Martin, Catherine Gimelli. 'Angels, alchemists and exchange: commercial ideology in court and city comedy, 1596–1610', A120, 121–47.

1724.   McVeagh, John. *Thomas Durfey and Restoration drama: the work of a forgotten writer* (Aldershot: Ashgate, 2000), 240p.

1725.   Mendle, Michael. 'An enduring discourse community? Some studies in early modern English history and culture' [review article], *Renaissance Quarterly* 53:1 (2000), 222–38.

1726.   Merryweather, James. 'The minstrels' pillar in St. Mary's Church, Beverley: a Tudor portrait of the York Waites?', *York Historian* 16 (1999), 10–15.

1727.   Mowl, Timothy. 'Antiquaries, theatre and early medievalism', A184, 71–92.

1728.   Mowl, Timothy. *Gentlemen and players: gardeners of the English landscape* (Stroud: Sutton, 2000), xv, 218p.

1729.   Musson, Ann; Thorp, John. *Topsham houses, warehouses and trades: 1700s and earlier* (Topsham: F.A. Musson, 1998), iv, 20p. [Photographs of buildings.]

1730. Nuttall, A.D. 'Two political poems: Marvell's "Horatian Ode" and Yeats's "No Second Troy"', *Proceedings of the British Academy* 105 (2000), 115–30.

1731. Oosthuizen, Susan M.; Taylor, C.C. 'Rediscovery of a vanished garden in Bassingbourn, Cambridgeshire, and the impact of the Lynne family on the medieval landscape', *Proceedings of the Cambridge Antiquarian Society* 89 (2000), 59–67.

1732. Pattacini, L. 'Andre Mollet, royal gardener in St James's Park, London', *Garden History* 26:1 (1998), 3–18.

1733. Patterson, Annabel. 'Imagining new worlds: Milton, Galileo and the "good old cause"', A120, 238–60.

1734. Powell, Nia. 'Women and strict-metre poetry in Wales', A186, 129–58.

1735. Ridgway, Christopher. 'Rethinking the picturesque', A184, 172–91.

1736. Ridgway, Maurice H. 'The church plate of the diocese of St Asaph', *Archaeologia Cambrensis* 145 (1998 for 1996), 1–14.

1737. Roberts, Judith. 'Stephen Switzer and water gardens', A184, 154–71.

1738. Roberts, Judith. 'The gardens of the gentry in the late Tudor period', *Garden History* 27:1 (1999), 89–108.

1739. Rudick, Michael (ed.) *The poems of Sir Walter Ralegh: a historical edition* (Renaissance English Text Society, 7th ser., 23) (Tempe (AZ): Arizona Center for Medieval and Renaissance Studies, 1999), lxxviii, 239p.

1740. Ruffatti, Alessio. 'Italian musicians at the Tudor Court: were they really Jews?', *Jewish Historical Studies* 35 (1998), 1–14.

1741. Rutledge, Douglas. 'The politics of disguise: drama and political theory in the early seventeenth century', A120, 90–120.

1742. Schleiner, Louise. 'Lady Falkland's reentry into writing: Anglo-Catholic consensual discourse and her *Edward II* as historical fiction', A120, 201–17.

1743. Schofield, John. 'City of London gardens, 1500–c.1620', *Garden History* 27:1 (1999), 73–88.

1744. Siddons, Michael Powell. 'The heraldic carving at Gregynog', *Montgomeryshire Collections* 88 (2000), 53–62.

1745. Sinfield, Alan. '*Poetaster*, the author, and the perils of cultural production', A171, 75–89.

1746. Skretkowicz, Victor. 'Mary Sidney Herbert's Antonius, English philhellenism and the Protestant cause', *Women's Writing* 6:1 (1999), 7–26.

1747. Sloan, Kim. *A noble art: amateur artists and drawing masters c.1600–1800* (London: British Museum, 2000), 256p. [Exhibition catalogue.]

1748. Solkin, David H. 'Isaac Fuller's *Escape of Charles II*: a Restoration tragicomedy', *Journal of the Warburg and Courtauld Institutes* 62 (1999), 199–240.

1749. Sondergard, Sid. '"This giant has wounded me as well as thee": reading Bunyan's violence and/as authority', A120, 218–37.

1750. Soo, Lydia M. *Wren's 'tracts' on architecture and other writings* (Cambridge: Cambridge University Press, 1998), xv, 320p.

1751. Spink, Ian. *Henry Lawes: Cavalier songwriter* (Oxford: Oxford University Press, 2000), xix, 172p.

1752. String, Tatiana C. 'Some observations on trends in the recent historiography of Tudor Art' [review article], A97, 251–55.

1753.   Strong, Roy. 'The Renaissance garden in England reconsidered: a survey of two decades of research on the period 1485–1642', *Garden History* 27:1 (1999), 1–9.

1754.   Sutton, James M. 'The decorative program at Elizabethan Theobalds: educating an heir and promoting a dynasty', *Studies in the Decorative Arts* 7:1 (2000), 33–64.

1755.   Thomas, Gwyn. 'John Griffith, Llanddyfnan, bardd o'r ail ganrif ar bymtheg', *Transactions of the Honourable Society of Cymmrodorion* ns 6 (1999), 14–37.

1756.   Thurley, Simon. 'A country seat fit for a king: Charles II, Greenwich and Winchester', A58, 214–39.

1757.   Trapp, J.B. 'The likeness of William Tyndale', A97, 21–50.

1758.   Travitsky, Betty S. 'Relations of power, relations to power, and power(ful) relations: Mary Fage, Robert Fage, and "Fames Roule"', *Medieval and Renaissance Texts and Studies* 213 (1999), 95–114.

1759.   White, Adam. 'A biographical dictionary of London tomb sculptors c.1560–c.1660', *Walpole Society* 61 (1999), 1–162.

1760.   Whittle, Elisabeth. 'The Tudor gardens of St. Donat's Castle, Glamorgan, south Wales', *Garden History* 27:1 (1999), 109–26.

1761.   Williams, Robert. 'Fortified gardens', A184, 49–70.

1762.   Williams, Robert. 'Vanbrugh's India and his mausolea for England', A184, 114–30.

1763.   Williamson, Tom. 'Estate management and landscape design', A184, 12–30.

1764.   Wilson, Jean. 'Elite commemoration in early modern England: reading funerary monuments', *Antiquity* 74:284 (2000), 413–23.

1765.   Wood, Jeremy. 'Taste and connoisseurship at the court of Charles I: Inigo Jones and the work of Giulio Romano', A58, 118–40.

1766.   Woodhouse, Elisabeth. 'Kenilworth, the Earl of Leicester's pleasure grounds following Robert Laneham's letter', *Garden History* 27:1 (1999), 127–44.

1767.   Woodhouse, Elisabeth. 'Spirit of the Elizabethan garden', *Garden History* 27:1 (1999), 10–31.

1768.   Worsley, Giles. '"After ye antique": Vanbrugh, Hawksmoor and Kent', A184, 131–53.

G. Religious Belief, Practice and Organisation

See also 469, 492, 495 (B); 658 (C); 882 (D); 1072, 1101, 1153, 1164, 1167, 1192–3, 1213, 1216, 1220 (E); 1407, 1446, 1462, 1510, 1742, 1746, 1966, 2025, 2065, 2095 (F); 2178, 2500, 2512 (G); 5075, 5077 (J); 5227 (K); 5393, 5397 (L)

1769.   Aberth, John; Randolph, Gregory. 'England's counter-reformation: the changing historiography of English religious history', *Downside Review* 117 (1999), 273–92.

1770.   Adolph, Anthony R.J.S. 'Papists' horses and the Privy Council 1689–1720', *Recusant History* 24 (1998), 55–75.

1771.   Allen, Richard. '"Taking up her daily cross": women and the early Quaker movement in Wales, 1653–1689', A186, 104–28.

1772.   Almasy, Rudolph P. 'Tyndale Menedemus', A61, 128–40.
1773.   Atkinson, Colin B.; Atkinson, Jo B. 'The identity and life of Thomas Bentley, compiler of *The monument of matrones* (1582)', *Sixteenth Century Journal* 31:2 (2000), 323–48.
1774.   Auksi, Peter. '"Borrowing from the shepherds": Tyndale's use of folk wisdom', A61, 115–27.
1775.   Auksi, Peter. 'Reason and feeling as evidence: the question of "proof" in Tyndale's thought', A97, 1–20.
1776.   Barnett, Mary Jane. 'From the allegorical to the literal (and back again): Tyndale and the allure of allegory', A61, 63–73.
1777.   Baskerville, S.K. 'Puritans, revisionists, and the English Revolution', *Huntington Library Quarterly* 61 (2000 for 1998), 151–71.
1778.   Berlin, Michael. 'Reordering rituals: ceremony and the parish, 1520–1640', A94, 47–66.
1779.   Botelho, Lynn A. (ed.) *Churchwardens' accounts of Cratfield, 1640–1660* (Suffolk Records Society, 42) (Woodbridge: Boydell & Brewer, 1999), xi, 177p.
1780.   Bowen, Geraint. *Welsh recusant writings* (Cardiff: University of Wales Press, 1999), 87p.
1781.   Bowers, Roger. 'The Chapel Royal, the first Edwardian Prayer Book, and Elizabeth's settlement of religion, 1559', *Historical Journal* 43:2 (2000), 317–44.
1782.   Burgess, Glenn. 'Was the Civil War a war of religion? The evidence of political propaganda', *Huntington Library Quarterly* 61 (2000 for 1998), 173–201.
1783.   Byford, Mark. 'The birth of a protestant town: the process of reformation in Tudor Colchester, 1530–1580', A49, 23–47.
1784.   Capp, Bernard. 'Transplanting the Holy Land: Diggers, Fifth Monarchists, and the New Israel', *Studies in Church History* 36 (2000), 288–98.
1785.   Carter, Patrick. 'Economic problems of provincial urban clergy during the reformation', A49, 147–58.
1786.   Carter, Patrick. 'Parliament, convocation and the granting of clerical supply in early modern England', *Parliamentary History* 19 (2000), 14–26.
1787.   Chibi, Andrew A. 'The schooling of Henry VIII's bishops: a comparative examination', *Archiv für Reformationsgeschichte* 91 (2000), 354–72.
1788.   Clancy, Thomas H. 'A content analysis of English Catholic books, 1615–1714', *Catholic Historical Review* 86:2 (2000), 258–72.
1789.   Clark, James Andrew. 'Corrupt prelates in Tyndale and Shakespeare', A61, 287–306.
1790.   Clark, James G. 'Reformation and reaction at St Albans Abbey, 1530–58', *English Historical Review* 115 (2000), 297–328.
1791.   Coffey, John. *Persecution and toleration in Protestant England, 1558–1689* (Harlow: Longman, 2000), xii, 244p.
1792.   Collins, Jeffrey R. 'Christian ecclesiology and the composition of Leviathan: a newly discovered letter to Thomas Hobbes', *Historical Journal* 43 (2000), 217–31. [Includes text of letter from Anglican cleric Robert Payne to Thomas Hobbes.]

1793.   Collins, Jeffrey R. 'The Restoration bishops and the royal supremacy', *Church History* 68 (1999), 549–80.

1794.   Collinson, Patrick. 'The shearman's tree and the preacher: the strange death of merry England in Shrewsbury and beyond', A49, 205–20.

1795.   Como, David R.; Lake, Peter. 'Puritans, Antinomians and Laudians in Caroline London: the strange case of Peter Shaw and its contexts', *Journal of Ecclesiastical History* 50:4 (1999), 684–715.

1796.   Como, David R. 'Puritans, predestination and the construction of orthodoxy in early seventeenth-century England', A131, 64–87.

1797.   Como, David R. 'The kingdom of Christ, the kingdom of England, and the kingdom of Traske: John Traske and the persistence of radical Puritanism in early Stuart England', A147, 63–82.

1798.   Como, David R. 'Women, prophecy, and authority in early Stuart Puritanism', *Huntington Library Quarterly* 61 (2000 for 1998), 203–22.

1799.   Coogan, Robert. '"From the chin upward, above St. Francis": More, Tyndale, and the Franciscans', A61, 217–27.

1800.   Cooper, Tim. 'The Antinomians redeemed: removing some of the "radical" from mid-seventeenth-century English religion', *Journal of Religious History* 24:3 (2000), 247–62.

1801.   Cooper, Tim. *The last generation of English Catholic clergy: parish priests in the Diocese of Coventry and Lichfield in the early sixteenth century* (Woodbridge: Boydell, 1999), xii, 236p.

1802.   Corns, Thomas N. 'Milton's antiprelatical tracts and the marginality of doctrine', A67, 39–48.

1803.   Corthell, Ronald. 'Robert Persons and the writer's mission', A144, 35–62.

1804.   Cosmos, Georgia. 'Huguenot storytellers in London in the 18th century', *Proceedings of the Huguenot Society of Great Britain & Ireland* 27:3 (2000), 403–17.

1805.   Coulton, Barbara. 'Implementing the Reformation in the urban community: Coventry and Shrewsbury 1559–1603', *Midland History* 25 (2000), 43–60.

1806.   Cressy, David. 'Different kinds of speaking: symbolic violence and secular iconoclasm in early modern England', A147, 19–42.

1807.   Cross, Claire. 'Religion in Doncaster from the Reformation to the Civil War', A49, 48–62.

1808.   Cummings, Brian. 'The theology of translation: Tyndale's grammar', A61, 36–59.

1809.   Cunich, Peter. 'Dissolution and de-conversion: institutional change and individual response in the 1530s', *International Medieval Research* 5 (1998), 25–42.

1810.   Cunich, Peter. 'The dissolution of the chantries', A49, 159–74.

1811.   Daniell, David. '"Gold, silver, ivory, apes and peacocks"' [Word, church, and state: Tyndale quincentenary essays], A61, 5–25.

1812.   Davies, Adrian. *The Quakers in English society 1655–1725* (Oxford: Oxford University Press, 2000), 262p.

1813.   Day, John Terhune. 'Tyndale and Frith on Tracy's Will and Justification', A61, 162–82.

1814. DeCoursey, Matthew. 'The semiotics of narrative in *The Obedience of a Christian Man*', A61, 74–86.
1815. Dick, John A.R. 'Posthumous revisions in Tyndale's *The Parable of the Wicked Mammon* and *The Practice of Prelates*', A61, 307–21.
1816. Dobranski, Stephen B.; Rumrich, John Peter. 'Introduction: heretical Milton', A67, 1–20.
1817. Dobranski, Stephen B. 'Licensing Milton's heresy', A67, 139–58.
1818. Dolan, Frances E. '"The wretched subject the whole town talks of": representing Elizabeth Cellier (London, 1680)', A144, 218–58.
1819. English, John C. 'John Hutchinson's critique of Newtonian heterodoxy', *Church History* 68 (1999), 581–97.
1820. Fallon, Stephen M. '"Elect above the rest": theology as self-representation in Milton', A67, 93–116.
1821. Fincham, Kenneth. 'Clerical conformity from Whitgift to Laud', A131, 125–58.
1822. Fincham, Kenneth. 'William Laud and the exercise of Caroline ecclesiastical patronage', *Journal of Ecclesiastical History* 51:1 (2000), 69–93.
1823. Flick, Andreas. 'Huguenots in the Electorate of Hanover and their British links', *Proceedings of the Huguenot Society of Great Britain & Ireland* 27:3 (2000), 335–50.
1824. Foster, Andrew. 'Archbishop Richard Neile revisited', A131, 159–78.
1825. Fox, Adam. 'Religious satire in English towns, 1570–1640', A49, 221–40.
1826. Freeman, Thomas. 'Demons, deviance and defiance: John Darrell and the politics of exorcism in late Elizabethan England', A131, 34–63.
1827. Freeman, Thomas S. 'Fate, faction, and fiction in Foxe's *Book of Martyrs*', *Historical Journal* 43:3 (2000), 601–24.
1828. Gibbens, Lilian. 'Roman Catholic tradesmen in London, 1681', *Catholic Ancestor* 8 (2000), 58–62.
1829. Greene, J.P. 'The impact of the dissolution on monasteries in Cheshire: the case of Norton', A204, 152–66.
1830. Griffin, Eric R. 'Daniel Brevint: French preacher to the king in exile', *Anglican and Episcopal History* 69:3 (2000), 295–314.
1831. Griggs, Burke W. 'Remembering the Puritan past: John Walker and Anglican memories of the English civil war', A147, 158–91.
1832. Gucer, Kathryn. '"Not heretofore extant in print": where the mad ranters are', *Journal of the History of Ideas* 61:1 (2000), 75–95.
1833. Gunn, Steven. 'Edmund Dudley and the Church', *Journal of Ecclesiastical History* 51:3 (2000), 509–26.
1834. Haigh, Christopher. 'The taming of reformation: preachers, pastors and parishioners in Elizabethan and early Stuart England', *History* 85:280 (2000), 572–88.
1835. Hale, John K. 'Milton and the rationale of insulting', A67, 159–75.
1836. Hammond, Gerald. 'Tyndale's knowledge of Hebrew: from the Old Testament to the New', A61, 26–35.
1837. Harrison, Brian A. *A Tudor journal: the diary of a priest in the Tower, 1580–1585* (London: St. Pauls, 2000), 240p.
1838. Higgs, Laquita M. *Godliness and governance in Tudor Colchester* (Ann Arbor (MI): University of Michigan Press, 1998), xiii, 434p.

1839. Hodgetts, Michael. 'A topographical index of hiding places, part 2', *Recusant History* 24 (1998), 1–54.

1840. Holien, Thomas R. 'Conversion and its consequences in the life and letters of Nicholas Sheterden', A147, 43–62.

1841. Holt, Geoffrey. 'Some chaplains at the Stuart court, Saint-Germain-en-Laye', *Recusant History* 25:1 (2000), 43–51.

1842. Houlbrooke, Ralph. 'Funeral sermons and assurance of salvation: conviction and persuasion in the case of William Lord Russell of Thornhaugh', A97, 119–38.

1843. Howson, Barry. 'Eschatology in sixteenth and seventeenth century England', *Evangelical Quarterly* 70:4 (1998), 325–50.

1844. Jowitt, Claire. '"Inward" and "outward" Jews: Margaret Fell, circumcision and women's preaching', A97.

1845. Kay, Dennis. 'Who says "miracles are past"? Some Jacobean marvels and the margins of the known', A176, 164–86.

1846. Kemp, Theresa D. 'Translating (Anne) Askew: the textual remains of a sixteenth-century heretic and saint', *Renaissance Quarterly* 52:4 (1999), 1021–45.

1847. Kerrigan, William. 'Milton's kisses', A67, 117–38.

1848. King, John N. 'Milton's Paradise of Fools: ecclesiastical satire in Paradise Lost', A144, 198–217.

1849. Kingsley, Margery. 'Interpreting providence: the politics of jeremiad in Restoration polemic', A176, 251–70.

1850. Kinney, Arthur F. 'Skelton and Tyndale: men of the cloth and of the word', A61, 275–86.

1851. Kirkus, M. Gregory. 'Great aunt and great niece: two 17th/18th century members of the Bedingfield family' [York Catholic community], *Recusant History* 25:1 (2000), 29–42.

1852. Knighton, C.S. (ed.) *Acts of the Dean and Chapter of Westminster, 1543–1609, part 2: 1560–1609* (Westminster Abbey record series, 2) (Woodbridge: Boydell, 1999), xvi, 327p.

1853. Knowles, Nigel. *Richard Baxter of Kidderminster* (Bewdley: Star and Garter, 2000), viii, 96p. [Reprints essays by Thomas Cave: 'Richard Baxter and Kidderminster', pp.11–27, and 'Richard Baxter (1615–1662)', pp.29–70.]

1854. Kümin, Beat A. 'Voluntary religion and reformation change in eight urban parishes', A49, 175–89.

1855. Lake, Peter. 'Moving the goal posts? Modified subscription and the construction of conformity in the early Stuart church', A131, 179–205.

1856. Lake, Peter; Questier, Michael. 'Puritans, Papists, and the "public sphere" in early modern England: the Edmund Campion affair in context', *Journal of Modern History* 72:3 (2000), 587–627.

1857. Lamburn, David J. 'Politics and religion in early modern Beverley', A49, 64–78.

1858. Lamburn, David J. *The laity and the church: religious developments in Beverley in the first half of the sixteenth century* (Borthwick Papers, 97) (York: Borthwick Institute of Historical Research, University of York, 2000), 29p.

1859. Lewalski, Barbara Kiefer. 'How radical was the young Milton?', A67, 49–74.
1860. Litzenberger, Caroline. 'The coming of protestantism to Elizabethan Tewkesbury', A49, 79–93.
1861. Liu, Tai. 'The founding of the London Provincial Assembly, 1645–47', A183, 37–62. [1st published in *Guildhall Studies in London History* 3:2 (1978).]
1862. Lloyd, Richard. 'Music at the parish church of St Mary at Hill, London', *Early Music* 25 (1997), 221–26.
1863. Loewenstein, David. 'Treason against God and state: blasphemy in Milton's culture and *Paradise Lost*', A67, 176–98.
1864. Longhorn, Victor. 'The ancestry of Blessed Richard Langhorne 1624–1679', *Catholic Ancestor* 8 (2000), 51–57.
1865. Lund, Eric. 'Tyndale and Frith on the eucharist as sign and memorial', A61, 183–96.
1866. Luttmer, Frank. 'Persecutors, tempters and vassals of the Devil: the unregenerate in Puritan practical divinity', *Journal of Ecclesiastical History* 51:1 (2000), 37–68.
1867. MacCulloch, Diarmaid. *Tudor church militant: Edward VI and the Protestant Reformation* (London: Allen Lane, 1999), xviii, 283p.
1868. MacCulloch, Diarmaid. 'Worcester: a cathedral city in the reformation', A49, 94–112.
1869. Macfarlane, Alan. 'Civility and the decline of magic', A29, 145–59.
1870. Maltby, Judith. 'From *Temple* to *Synagogue*: "old" conformity in the 1640s-1650s and the case of Christopher Harvey', A131, 88–120.
1871. Marc'hadour, Germain. 'Tyndale and Fisher's 1521 sermon against Luther', A61, 145–61.
1872. Marotti, Arthur F. 'Alienating Catholics in early modern England: recusant women, Jesuits and ideological fantasies', A144, 1–34.
1873. Martin, Jeanette. 'Leadership and priorities in Reading during the reformation', A49, 113–29.
1874. Matar, Nabil I. *Islam in Britain, 1558–1685* (Cambridge: Cambridge University Press, 1998), xi, 163p.
1875. Matar, Nabil I. *Turks, Moors, and Englishmen in the age of discovery* (New York: Columbia University Press, 1999), xi, 268p.
1876. Mayer, Thomas F. '"Heretics be not in all things heretics": Cardinal Pole, his circle, and the potential for toleration', A146, I: 107–24. [1st published in *Beyond the Persecuting Society: Religious Toleration before the Enlightenment*, eds. J.C. Laursen & C.J. Nederman (Philadelphia, 1992).]
1877. Mayer, Thomas F. 'A stiking-plaster saint? Autobiography and hagiography in the making of Reginald Pole', A146, XII: 205–22. [1st published in *The Rhetoric of Life-Writing*, ed. T.F. Mayer & D.R. Woolf (Ann Arbor, 1995).]
1878. Mayer, Thomas F. 'An unknown diary of Julius III's conclave by Bartolomeo Stella, a servant of Cardinal Pole', A146, V: 345–75.
1879. Mayer, Thomas F. 'The war of the two saints: the conclave of Julius III and Cardinal Pole', A146, IV: 1–21. [Revised English version of 'Il fallimento di una candidatura: il partito della riforma, Reginald Pole e il conclave di Giulio III'.]

1880.   McClendon, Muriel C.; Ward, Joseph P. 'Introduction: Religion, society and self-fashioning in post-Reformation England', A147, 1–15.

1881.   McClendon, Muriel C. 'Reconsidering the Marian persecution: the urban context', A147, 195–210.

1882.   McClendon, Muriel C. *The quiet reformation: magistrates and the emergence of Protestantism in Tudor Norwich* (Stanford (CA): Stanford University Press, 1999), xv, 340p.

1883.   McCoog, Thomas M. 'Robert Parsons and Claudio Acquaviva: correspondence', *Archivum Historicum Societatis Iesu* 68 (1999), 79–182.

1884.   McCutcheon, Elizabeth. 'The prison letters of More and Tyndale', A61, 243–55.

1885.   McMahon, Susan. 'John Ray (1627–1705) and the Act of Uniformity 1662', *Notes & Records of the Royal Society* (of London) 54:2 (2000), 153–78.

1886.   Milton, Anthony. 'A qualified intolerance: the limits and ambiguities of early Stuart anti-Catholicism', A144, 85–115.

1887.   Morgan, D. Densil. 'John Myles (1621–83) and the future of Ilston's past: Welsh Baptists after three and a half centuries', *Baptist Quarterly* 38 (1999), 176–84.

1888.   Morrill, John Stephen. 'The English church in the seventeenth century', *History Review* 30 (1998), 18–23.

1889.   Mueller, Janel. 'Milton on heresy', A67, 21–38.

1890.   Muldoon, Andrew R. 'Recusants, Church-Papists, and "comfortable" missionaries: assessing the post-Reformation English Catholic community', *Catholic Historical Review* 86:2 (2000), 242–57.

1891.   Murphy, Clare M. 'The Turks in More and Tyndale', A61, 228–42.

1892.   Ogier, Daryl M. 'Night revels and werewolfery in Calvinist Guernsey', *Folklore* 109 (1998), 53–62.

1893.   Oldridge, Darren. 'Protestant conceptions of the devil in early Stuart England', *History* 85 (2000), 232–46.

1894.   Oldridge, Darren. *The devil in early modern England* (Stroud: Sutton, 2000), 224p.

1895.   Oliva, Marilyn. 'Unsafe passage: the state of the nuns at the dissolution and their conversion to secular life', *International Medieval Research* 5 (1998), 87–104.

1896.   Overell, M.A. 'Vergerio's anti-Nicodemite propaganda and England, 1547–1558', *Journal of Ecclesiastical History* 51:2 (2000), 296–318.

1897.   Overhoff, Jürgen. 'The theology of Thomas Hobbes's *Leviathan*', *Journal of Ecclesiastical History* 51:3 (2000), 527–55.

1898.   Parish, Helen L. '"Then May the Deuyls of Hell be Sayntes Also": the medieval Church in sixteenth century England', A97, 71–91.

1899.   Parish, Helen L. *Clerical marriage and the English reformation* (Aldershot: Ashgate, 2000), xii, 276p.

1900.   Parker, Douglas H. 'Tyndale's Biblical hermeneutics', A61, 87–101.

1901.   Parker, Kenneth L. 'Richard Greenham's "spiritual physicke": the comfort of afflicted consciences in Elizabethan pastoral care', A140, 71–83.

1902.   Pasquarello, Michael. 'John Jewel: preaching prelate', *Anglican and Episcopal History* 69:3 (2000), 276–94.

1903. Patterson, W.B. 'New approaches to the English Reformation' [review essay], *Renaissance Quarterly* 52:4 (1999), 1132–8.

1904. Percy, Martyn. *Introducing Richard Hooker and the laws of ecclesiastical polity* (London: Darton, Longman & Todd, 1999), 56p.

1905. Pinilla, Ignacio Garcia; Nelson, Jonathan Lort. 'Una carta de Francisco de Enzinas (Dryander) en el martirologio de John Foxe', *Bibliothèque d'Humanisme et Renaissance* 61 (1999), 515–28.

1906. Plowden, Alison. *Danger to Elizabeth: the Catholics under Elizabeth I* (Stroud: Sutton, 1999), 254p. [1st published 1973.]

1907. Plunket, Francis. 'The life of Francis Tregian (1548–1608)', *British Historical Society of Portugal Annual Report* 26 (1999), 140–65. [An edition of Francis Plunket's life of Tregian, published in Lisbon in 1655.]

1908. Poole, Kristen. *Radical religion from Shakespeare to Milton: figures of nonconformity in early modern England* (Cambridge: Cambridge University Press, 2000), xiii, 272p.

1909. Puterbaugh, Joseph. '"Your selfe be judge and answer your selfe": formation of Protestant identity in *A conference betwixt a mother a devout Recusant and her sonne a zealous Protestant*', *Sixteenth Century Journal* 31:2 (2000), 419–32.

1910. Questier, Michael C.; Healy, Simon. '"What's in a name?": A Papist's perception of Puritanism and conformity in the early seventeenth century', A144, 137–53.

1911. Questier, Michael C. 'Conformity, Catholicism and the law', A131, 237–61.

1912. Questier, Michael C. 'What happed to English Catholicism after the English Reformation?', *History* 85 (2000), 28–47.

1913. Razovsky, Helaine. 'Remaking the Bible: English Reformation spiritual conduct books', *Renaissance and Reformation* 22:4 (1998), 5–25.

1914. Rigney, James. 'Anti-clerical slander in the English Civil War: John White's First Century of Scandalous and Malignant Priests', A40, 93–105.

1915. Rivers, Isabel. *Reason, grace and sentiment: a study of the language of religion and ethics in England, 1660–1780*, vol.2 (Cambridge and New York: Cambridge University Press, 2000) [Vol. 1 published 1991.]

1916. Rowlands, Marie B. '"Rome's snaky brood": Catholic yeomen, craftsmen and townsmen in the west Midlands, 1600–1641', *Recusant History* 24 (1998), 147–65.

1917. Rowlands, Marie B. 'The allegiances and loyalties of three Catholic priests in the late seventeenth century', *Midland History* 25 (2000), 78–97.

1918. Roye, William. *A brefe dialoge bitwene a Christen father and his stobborne sonne: the first Protestant catechism published in English*, eds. Douglas Harold Parker and Bruce Krajewski (Toronto and London: University of Toronto Press, 1999), 305p.

1919. Rumrich, John Peter. 'Milton's Arianism: why it matters', A67, 75–92.

1920. Russell, Conrad. 'Parliament, the Royal Supremacy and the Church', *Parliamentary History* 19 (2000), 27–37.

1921. Sands, Kathleen R. 'The doctrine of transubstantiation and the English Protestant dispossession of demons', *History* 85:279 (2000), 446–62.

1922. Sauer, Elizabeth. 'The politics of performance in the inner theater: *Samson Agonistes* as closet drama', A67, 199–216.

1923.   Sena, Margaret. 'William Blundell and the networks of Catholic dissent in post-Reformation England', A193, 54–75.

1924.   Sharpe, James A. *The bewitching of Anne Gunter: a horrible and true story of football, witchcraft, murder and the king of England* (London: Profile, 1999), xvi, 238p.

1925.   Sheils, William; Sheils, Sarah. 'Textiles and reform: Halifax and its hinterland', A49, 130–43.

1926.   Sheils, W.J. 'The altars in York Minster in the early sixteenth century', *Studies in Church History* 35 (1999), 104–15.

1927.   Shell, Alison. 'Multiple conversion and the Menippean self: the case of Richard Carpenter', A144, 154–97.

1928.   Skinner, David. 'Discovering the provenance and history of the Caius and Lambeth choirbooks', *Early Music* 25 (1997), 245–62.

1929.   Smith, David L. 'Oliver Cromwell, the first Protectorate Parliament and religious reform', *Parliamentary History* 19 (2000), 38–48.

1930.   Snape, Michael Francis. 'Poverty and the northern clergy in the eighteenth century: the parish of Whalley, 1689–1789', *Northern History* 36 (2000), 83–98.

1931.   Snocle, Edith. '"His open side our book": meditations and education in Elizabeth Grymeston's Miscelanea Meditations Memoratives', A149, 163–75.

1932.   Sommerville, C. John. 'Interpreting seventeenth-century English religion as movements', *Church History* 69:4 (2000), 749–69.

1933.   Spicer, Andrew. *The French-speaking reformed community and their church in Southampton, 1567–c.1620* (Southampton Records Series, 39) (Southampton: University of Southampton, 1997), xii, 198p.

1934.   Spinks, Bryan D. 'Evaluating liturgical continuity and change at the Reformation: a case study of Thomas Muntzer, Martin Luther, and Thomas Cranmer', *Studies in Church History* 35 (1999), 151–71.

1935.   Stafford, William S. 'Tyndale's voice to the laity', A61, 105–14.

1936.   Stavreva, Kirilka. 'Fighting words: witch-speak in late Elizabethan docu-fiction', *Journal of Medieval and Early Modern Studies* 30:2 (2000), 309–38.

1937.   Suggett, Richard. 'Witchcraft dynamics in early modern Wales', A186, 75–103.

1938.   Tennant, Philip. 'Parish and people: south Warwickshire in the Civil War', A183, 157–86. [1st published in *Warwickshire History*.]

1939.   Tittler, Robert. 'Reformation, resources and authority in English towns: an overview', A49, 190–201.

1940.   Tyacke, Nicholas. 'Lancelot Andrewes and the myth of Anglicanism', A131, 5–33.

1941.   Usher, Brett. 'Expedient and experiment: the Elizabethan lay reader', *Studies in Church History* 35 (1999), 185–98.

1942.   Vercruysse, Jos E. 'Latomus and Tyndale's trial', A61, 197–214.

1943.   Walker, Claire. 'Prayer, patronage, and political conspiracy: English nuns and the Restoration', *Historical Journal* 43 (2000), 1–23.

1944.   Walsham, Alexandra. '"Domme preachers"?: post-reformation English Catholicism and the culture of print', *Past & Present* 168 (2000), 72–123.

1945. Walsham, Alexandra. '"Yielding to the extremity of the time": conformity, orthodoxy and the post-Reformation Catholic community', A131, 211–36.

1946. Walsham, Alexandra. *Providence in early modern England* (Oxford: Oxford University Press, 1999), xvi, 387p.

1947. Watkins, John. '"Out of her ashes may a second phoenix rise": James I and the legacy of Elizabethan anti-Catholicism', A144, 116–36.

1948. Westbrook, Vivienne. 'Speaking as men commonly use: William Whittingham's 1557 New Testament', A97, 51–70.

1949. Williams, Michael E. 'The English Catholic educational diaspora in Europe from the 1560s to the French Revolution', *Aspects of Education* 47 (1992), 3.

1950. Wiseman, S. 'Margaret Cavendish among the prophets: performance ideologies and gender in and after the English civil war', *Women's Writing* 6:1 (1999), 95–112.

1951. Worth, Roland H. (Jr.) *Church, monarch and Bible in sixteenth century England: the political context of biblical translation* (Jefferson (NC): McFarland, 2000), v, 202p.

1952. Wykes, David L. 'From David's psalms to Watts's hymns: the development of hymnody among Dissenters following the Toleration Act', *Studies in Church History* 35 (1999), 227–39.

1953. Wyly, Thomas J. 'Tyndale as interpreter of Henrician politics', A61, 259–74.

1954. Yates, Julian. 'Parasitic geographies: manifesting Catholic identity in early modern England', A144, 63–84.

1955. Zell, Michael. 'The coming of religious reform', A221, 177–206.

1956. Zell, Michael. 'The establishment of a Protestant church', A221, 207–44.

Ha. *Law and Order*

See also 502 (B); 1252 (E); 1911 (F); 2541, 2548, 2553, 2556 (G); 5080 (J)

1957. Baker, John Hamilton. *The common law tradition: lawyers, books and the law* (London: Hambledon, 2000), xxxiv, 404p.

1958. Campagna, Norbert. 'Das Gesetz, die Richter und die Gesetzesauslegung im *Leviathan*: über ein vernächlässigtes Thema in der Hobbesschen Rechtsphilosophie', *Der Staat* 38 (1999), 519–46.

1959. Capp, Bernard. 'Arson, threats of arson, and incivility in early modern England', A29, 197–213.

1960. Carlile, Dianne. '"A comon and sottish drunkard you have been": prosecutions for drunkenness in the York courts c.1660–1725', *York Historian* 16 (1999), 32–44.

1961. Child, Sarah. 'Rackenford goes to Chancery: an outbreak of litigation in an Elizabethan rural parish' [property disputes, c.1570], *Devonshire Association Report and Transactions* 131 (1999), 123–38.

1962. Fudge, Erica. 'Monstrous acts: bestiality in early modern England', *History Today* 50:8 (2000), 20–25.

1963. Fumerton, Patricia. 'London's vagrant economy: making space for "low" subjectivity', A171, 206–25.

1964. Garratt, Harold J.H. *Eckington: the court rolls*, vol. 4: *1633–1694* (Huddersfield: The author, 2000), x, 244p.

1965. Gaskill, Malcolm. *Crime and mentalities in early modern England* (Cambridge: Cambridge University Press, 2000), xiii, 377p.

1966. Gaskill, Malcolm. 'Witches and witchcraft prosecutions, 1560–1660', A221, 245–78.

1967. Griffiths, Paul. 'Overlapping circles: imagining criminal communities in London, 1545–1645', A193, 115–33.

1968. Hipkin, Stephen. '"Sitting on his penny rent": conflict and right of common in Faversham Blean, 1595–1610', *Rural History* 11 (2000), 1–35.

1969. Ingram, Martin. 'Law, litigants and the construction of "honour": slander suits in early modern England', A54, 134–60.

1970. Kesselring, Krista. 'Abjuration and its demise: the changing face of royal justice in the Tudor period', *Canadian Journal of History* 24 (1999), 345–58.

1971. Palmer, William. 'Scenes from provincial life: history, honor, and meaning in the Tudor north', *Renaissance Quarterly* 53:2 (2000), 425–48.

1972. Powell, Damian X. *Sir James Whitelocke's Liber Famelicus 1570–1632: law and politics in early Stuart England* (Frankfurt am Main: Peter Lang, 2000), 264p.

1973. Staub, Susan C. 'Early modern Medea: representations of child murder in the street literature of seventeenth-century England', A149, 333–47.

1974. Thomas, Phillip V. 'Rogues and vagabonds in Elizabethan York', *York Historian* 16 (1999), 16–31.

1975. Towner, E.; Towner, J. 'Developing the history of unintentional injury: the use of coroners' records in early modern England', *Injury Prevention* 6:2 (2000), 102–5.

1976. Wales, Tim. 'Thief-takers and their clients in later Stuart London', A94, 67–84.

Hb. *Public Administration*

See also 1267 (E); 2171, 2557 (G); 3389 (H)

1977. Barry, Jonathan. 'Civility and civic culture in early modern England: the meanings of urban freedom', A29, 181–96.

1978. Cramsie, John. 'Commercial projects and the fiscal policy of James VI and I', *Historical Journal* 43:2 (2000), 345–64.

1979. Hyde, Patricia; Harrington, Duncan. *Hearth tax returns for Faversham Hundred, 1661–1671: with supporting documents* (Faversham Hundred records, 2) (Folkestone: Arden Enterprises, 1998), 173p.

1980. Marshall, Alan. *The strange death of Edmund Godfrey: plots and politics in Retoration London* (Stroud: Sutton, 1999), xiv, 241p.

1981. Patterson, Catherine F. *Urban patronage in early modern England: corporate boroughs, the landed elite, and the crown, 1580–1640* (Stanford (CA): Stanford University Press, 1999), viii, 337p.

1982. Robinson, W.R.B. 'Sir Richard Herbert (d. 1539) of Montgomery, part 2', *Montgomeryshire Collections* 88 (2000), 1–23.

1983. Rodgers, Mary; Wallace, May (eds.) *Norwich landgable assessment 1568–70* (Norfolk Record Society, 63) (Norfolk: Norfolk Record Society, 1999), ix, 180p.

1984. Zell, Michael L. 'Kent's Elizabethan JPs at work', *Archaeologia Cantiana* 119 (1999), 1–43.

Hc. *Political and Constitutional*

See also 492 (B); 926 (D); 1273 (E); 1512, 1525, 1686, 1741, 2138 (F); 2587 (G); 3531 (H); 5099 (J); 5246, 5261 (K)

1985. Archer, Ian W. 'Politics and government 1540–1700', A43, 235–62.

1986. Archer, Ian W. 'Popular politics in the sixteenth and early seventeenth centuries', A94, 26–46.

1987. Ashdown, Dulcie M. *Tudor cousins: rivals for the throne* (Stroud: Sutton, 2000), xiv, 252p.

1988. Aylmer, Gerald E. 'Patronage at the court of Charles II', A58, 191–202.

1989. Barber, Sarah. *A revolutionary rogue: Henry Marten and the English republic* (Stroud: Sutton, 2000), xi, 228p.

1990. Barclay, Andrew. 'Charles II's failed restoration: administrative reform below stairs, 1660–4', A58, 158–70.

1991. Bennett, Martyn. *A historical dictionary of the British and Irish civil wars 1637–1660* (Historical Dictionaries of War, Revolution, and Civil Unrest, 14) (Chicago (IL) and London: Fitzroy Dearborn, 2000), xxi, 253p.

1992. Bergeron, David Moore. *King James & letters of homoerotic desire* (Iowa City: University of Iowa Press, 1999), viii, 251p.

1993. Bernard, George W. 'Amy Robsart', A14, 161–74.

1994. Bernard, George W. 'Architecture and politics in Tudor England', A14, 175–90.

1995. Bernard, George W. 'Court and government', A14, 129–33.

1996. Bernard, George W. 'Introduction' [Power and politics in Tudor England], A14, 1–19.

1997. Bernard, George W. 'New perspectives or old complexities?', *English Historical Review* 115 (2000), 113–20.

1998. Bernard, George W. 'The continuing power of the Tudor nobility', A14, 20–50. [Revised version of *The Tudor Nobility*.]

1999. Blackwood, B.G. 'Parties and issues in the Civil War in Lancashire and East Anglia', A183, 261–85. [1st published in *Northern History* 29 (1993), 99–122.]

2000. Brimacomb, Peter. *All the queen's men: the world of Elizabeth I* (Stroud: Sutton, 2000), 214p.

2001. Bush, Michael; Bownes, David. *The defeat of the pilgrimage of grace: a study of the postpardon revolts of December 1536 to March 1537 and their effect* (Hull: University of Hull Press, 1999), xv, 476p.

2002. Bush, Michael L. 'Protector Somerset and the 1549 rebellions: a post-revision questioned', *English Historical Review* 115 (2000), 103–12.

2003. Button, Andrea E. 'Royalist women petitioners in south-west England, 1655–62', *Seventeenth Century* 15:1 (2000), 53–66.

2004. Callow, John. *The making of James II: the formative years of a fallen king* (Stroud: Sutton, 2000), ix, 373p.

2005. Cameron, Andrea. 'Tudor and Stuart Royal visits in and around Hounslow Heath', *Transactions of the London and Middlesex Archaeological Society* 50 (1999), 145–51.

2006. Clark, Jonathan Charles Douglas. *English society 1660–1832: religion, ideology and politics during the ancien regime*, 2nd edn. (Cambridge: Cambridge University Press, 2000), xii, 580p. [1st published as *English Society 1688–1832* (1985).]

2007. Condren, Conal. 'The date of Cavendish's advice to Charles II', *Parergon* ns 17:2 (2000), 147–50.

2008. Coote, Stephen. *Royal survivor: a life of Charles II* (London: Hodder & Stoughton, 1999), xiii, 396p.

2009. Corp, Edward. 'The Jacobite court at Saint-Germain-en-Laye: etiquette and the use of the royal apartments', A58, 240–55.

2010. Coulton, Barbara. 'Thomas Hunt of Shrewsbury and Boreatton 1599–1669', *Shropshire History and Archaeology* 74 (1999), 33–42.

2011. Cox, Nick. 'Rumors and risings: plebeian insurrection and the circulation of subversive discourse in the 1590s', A40, 43–57.

2012. Croft, Pauline. 'The Catholic gentry, the Earl of Salisbury and the baronets of 1611', A131, 262–81.

2013. Cruickshanks, Eveline. 'Introduction' [the Stuart courts], A58, 1–12.

2014. Cruickshanks, Eveline. *The Glorious Revolution* (Basingstoke: Palgrave, 2000), 126p.

2015. Cuddy, Neil. 'Reinventing monarchy: the changing structure and political function of the Stuart court, 1603–88', A58, 59–85.

2016. de Groot, Jerome. 'Commerce, religion, loyalty: Royalist Newcastle upon Tyne, 1642–1644', *Archaeologia Aeliana* 5th ser. 27 (1999), 135–44.

2017. Donagan, Barbara. 'Family and misfortune in the English Civil War: the sad case of Edward Pitt', *Huntington Library Quarterly* 61 (2000 for 1998), 223–40.

2018. Doran, Susan. 'Revenge her foul and most unnatural murder?: the impact of Mary Stewart's execution on Anglo-Scottish relations', *History* 85:280 (2000), 589–612.

2019. Durkin, Neil. 'His praeludiary weapons: mocking Colonel Hewson before and after the Restoration', A40, 106–24.

2020. Durston, Christopher. '"Settling the hearts and quieting the minds of all good people": the major-generals and the Puritan minorities of interregnum England', *History* 85 (2000), 247–67.

2021. Eales, Jacqueline. 'The rise of ideological politics in Kent, 1558–1640', A221, 279–313.

2022. Everitt, Alan. 'The local community and the Great Rebellion', A183, 14–36. [1st published 1969.]

2023. Furdell, Elizabeth Lane. 'Dilucidating *The Dilucidator*: published epistolary commentary and the "Glorius Revolution"' [Orange propaganda], *Quaerendo* 30 (2000), 51–63.

2024. Geiter, Mary K. 'William Penn and Jacobitism: a smoking gun?' [depositions, 1691], *Historical Research* 73:181 (2000), 213–18.

2025. Guy, John A. 'Henry VIII and the *Praemunire* manoeuvres of 1530–1531', A96, VII: 481–503. [1st published in the *English Historical Review* 97 (1982).]

2026. Guy, John A. 'The King's Council and political participation', A96, 121–47. [1st published in *Reassessing the Henrician Age: Humanism, Politics and Reform, 1500–1550*, eds. A. Fox & J.A. Guy (Oxford, 1986).]

2027. Guy, John A. 'Thomas More and Christopher St German: the battle of the books', A96, VIII: 95–120. [1st published in *Reassessing the Henrician Age: Humanism, Politics and Reform, 1500–1550*, eds. A. Fox & J.A. Guy (Oxford, 1986).]

2028. Guy, John A. 'Wolsey's Star Chamber: a study in archival reconstruction', A96, III: 169–80. [1st published in the *Journal of the Society of Archivists* 5:3 (1975).]

2029. Hammer, Paul E.J. 'Sex and the Virgin Queen: aristocratic concupiscence and the court of Elizabeth I', *Sixteenth Century Journal* 31:1 (2000), 77–98.

2030. Hammer, Paul E.J. *The polarisation of Elizabethan politics: the political career of Robert Devereux, second earl of Essex, 1585–1597* (Cambridge: Cambridge University Press, 1999), xviii, 449p.

2031. Harris, Jonathan. 'The Grecian Coffee House and political debate in London 1688–1714', *London Journal* 25:1 (2000), 1–13.

2032. Harris, Tim. 'The legacy of the English Civil War: rethinking the revolution', *European Legacy* 5:4 (2000), 501–14.

2033. Herman, Peter C. 'Rastell's Pastyme of People: monarchy and the law in early modern historiography', *Journal of Medieval and Early Modern Studies* 30:2 (2000), 275–308.

2034. Hopper, Andrew J. '"The popish army of the north": Anti-Catholicism and Parliamentarian allegiance in civil war Yorkshire, 1642–46', *Recusant History* 25:1 (2000), 12–28.

2035. Hopper, Andrew J. 'The Clubmen of the West Riding of Yorkshire during the First Civil War: "Bradford club-law"', *Northern History* 36 (2000), 59–72.

2036. Hoppit, Julian. *A land of liberty?: England, 1689–1727* (Oxford: Clarendon, 2000), xix, 580p.

2037. Howell, Roger. 'Newcastle and the nation: the 17th-century experience', A183, 309–29. [1st published in *Archaeologia Aeliana*, 5th ser. 8 (1980), 17–34.]

2038. Hughes, Ann. *The causes of the English civil war*, 2nd edn. (Basingstoke and New York: Macmillan and St Martin's Press, 1998), viii, 206p. [1st published 1991.]

2039. Hunt, Margaret R. 'Wives and marital "rights" in the Court of Exchequer in the early eighteenth century', A94, 107–29.

2040. Hutton, Ronald. *The British republic 1649–1660*, 2nd edn. (Basingstoke: Palgrave, 2000), xxvi, 176p. [1st published 1990.]

2041. Hyde, Patricia; Zell, Michael. 'Governing the county', A221, 7–38.

2042. Ives, Eric. 'Marrying for love: the experience of Edward IV and Henry VIII', *History Today* 50:12 (2000), 48–53.

2043. Jones, Michael A. 'Cultural boundaries within the Tudor state: Bishop Rowland Lee and the Welsh settlement of 1536', *Welsh History Review* 20:2 (2000), 227–53.

2044. Kennedy, D.E. *The English revolution, 1642–49* (Basingstoke: Palgrave, 2000), 192p.

2045. Key, Newton E.; Ward, Joseph P. '"Divided into parties": exclusion crisis origins in Monmouth', *English Historical Review* 115 (2000), 1159–83.

2046. Knoppers, Laura Lunger. *Constructing Cromwell: ceremony, portrait and print, 1645–1661* (Cambridge: Cambridge University Press, 2000), xiii, 249p.

2047. Knowles, James. '"To scourge the arse / Jove's marrow so had wasted": scurrility and the subversion of sodomy', A40, 74–92.

2048. Kuin, Roger. 'Sir Philip Sidney's model of the statesman', A97, 93–117.

2049. Kyle, Chris R. '"It beeing not fitt to bee without a lawe": expiring laws continuance acts, 1604–1641', *Parliamentary History* 19:2 (2000), 195–210.

2050. Latham, Agnes Mary Christabel; Youings, Joyce A. (eds.) *The letters of Sir Walter Ralegh* (Exeter: University of Exeter Press, 1999), lxiii, 403p.

2051. Lindley, Keith; Scott, David. *The journal of Thomas Juxon, 1644–1647* (Camden, 5th ser., 13) (Cambridge: Cambridge University Press, 1999), x, 214p.

2052. Loades, David. 'The reign of Edward VI: an historiographical survey', *The Historian* [London] 67 (2000), 22–25.

2053. Macleod, John. *Dynasty: the Stuarts 1560–1807* (London: Sceptre, 1999), xiii, 386p.

2054. Madway, Lorraine. '"The most conspicuous solemnity": the coronation of Charles II', A58, 141–57.

2055. Malden, John. 'A secret diary', *York Historian* 17 (2000), 17–29.

2056. Marcus, Leah. 'Elizabeth the writer', *History Today* 50:10 (2000), 36–38.

2057. McGrath, Patrick. 'Bristol and the Civil War', A183, 91–128. [1st published by the Bristol Branch of the Historical Association, 1981.]

2058. McGurk, John. *The Tudor monarchies, 1485–1603* (Cambridge: Cambridge University Press, 1999), iv, 124p.

2059. McJimsey, Robert. 'Crisis management: parliament and political stability, 1692–1719', *Albion* 31:4 (1999), 559–88.

2060. McRae, Andrew. 'The verse libel: popular satire in early modern England', A40, 50–73.

2061. Miller, John. *After the Civil Wars: English politics and government in the reign of Charles II* (Harlow: Longman, 2000), ix, 318p.

2062. Milton, Philip. 'John Locke and the Rye House Plot', *Historical Journal* 43:3 (2000), 647–68.

2063. Morgan, Prys. 'Wild Wales: civilizing the Welsh from the sixteenth to the nineteenth centuries', A29, 265–83.

2064. Myers, Nick. 'Hercule Gaulois, Great Britain's Solomon—myths of persuasion, styles of authority', A58, 29–42.

2065. Nowack, Thomas S. 'Propaganda and the pulpit: Robert Cecil, William Barlow and the Essex and gunpowder plots', A120, 34–52.

2066. Parker, Derek. *Nell Gwyn* (Stroud: Sutton, 2000), xii, 212p.

2067. *Calendar of patent rolls 34 Elizabeth: part I to part XV (C66/1379–1394)* (List and Index Society, 272) (Kew: List and Index Society, 1999), 222p.

2068. *Calendar of patent rolls 35 Elizabeth: part I to part IX (C66/1395–1404)* (Kew: List and Index Society, 2000), 178p.

2069. Patterson, Catherine F. 'Corporations, cathedrals and the Crown: local dispute and royal interest in early Stuart England', *History* 85:280 (2000), 546–71.

2070. Peacey, Jason T. 'John Lilburne and the Long Parliament', *Historical Journal* 43:3 (2000), 625–46.

2071. Peacey, Jason T. 'Marchamont Nedham and the Lawrans letters' [on the fate of Charles I], *Bodleian Library Record* 17:1 (2000), 24–35.

2072. Peacey, Jason T. 'The exploitation of captured royal correspondence and Anglo-Scottish relations in the British civil wars, 1645–46', *Scottish Historical Review* 79:2 (2000), 213–32.

2073. Phillips, C.B. 'The royalist north: the Cumberland and Westmorland gentry, 1642–60', A183, 239–59. [1st published in *Northern History* 14 (1978), 169–92.]

2074. Plowden, Alison. *The house of Tudor* (Stroud: Sutton, 1998), xii, 276p.

2075. Plowden, Alison. *The young Elizabeth*, revised edn. (Stroud: Sutton, 1999), 238p.

2076. Plowden, Alison. *Tudor women*, revised edn. (Stroud: Sutton, 1998), 187p.

2077. Pursell, Brendan C. 'James I, Gondomar and the dissolution of the Parliament of 1621', *History* 85:279 (2000), 428–45.

2078. Richardson, Roger Charles. 'Introduction: local historians and the English Civil Wars', A183, 1–13.

2079. Robinson, Paul. 'Some copper alloy objects from the west country depicting the arms of the Commonwealth', *Post-Medieval Archaeology* 33 (1999), 285–7.

2080. Roots, Ivan. 'The 1650s' [historiographical review], *Historian* 65 (2000), 23–26.

2081. Scott, David. 'The Barwis affair: political allegiance and the Scots during the British Civil Wars', *English Historical Review* 115 (2000), 843–63.

2082. Scott, Jonathan. *England's troubles: seventeenth-century English political instability in European context* (Cambridge: Cambridge University Press, 2000), xii, 546p.

2083. Seel, Graham E. *Regicide and republic: England 1603–1660* (Cambridge: Cambridge University Press, 2000), 218p.

2084. Shagan, Ethan H. '"Popularity" and the 1549 rebellions revisited', *English Historical Review* 115 (2000), 121–33.

2085. Sharpe, Kevin. '"So hard a text"?: images of Charles I, 1612–1700', *Historical Journal* 43:2 (2000), 383–406.

2086. Sharpe, Kevin. 'Remapping early modern England: from revisionism to the culture of politics', A192, 3–37.

2087. Smail, John. 'Local politics in restoration England: religion, culture and politics in Oliver Heywood's Halifax', A147, 234–48.

2088. Smuts, R. Malcolm. *Culture and power in England, 1585–1685* (Basingstoke and New York: Macmillan and St Martin's Press, 1999), xi, 201p.

2089. Starkey, David. *Elizabeth: apprenticeship* (London: Chatto & Windus, 2000), xii, 339p.

2090.   *State papers domestic: Charles I to James II (SP16–SP31)* [unpaginated] (List and Index Society, 273) (Kew: List and Index Society, 1999)

2091.   Stoyle, Mark J. '"The Gear rout": the Cornish rising of 1648 and the second Civil War', *Albion* 32:1 (2000), 37–58.

2092.   Styles, Philip. 'The city of Worcester during the Civil Wars, 1640–60', A183, 187–238. [1st published in *Studies in seventeenth-century west Midlands history*, ed. Philip Styles (Kineton, 1978), 213–57, 295–305.]

2093.   Swett, Katherine W. '"Born of my land": identity, community and faith among the Welsh in early modern London', A147, 249–65.

2094.   Thornton, Tim. 'Dynasty and territory in the early modern period: the princes of Wales and their western British inheritance', *Welsh History Review* 20:1 (2000), 1–33.

2095.   Thornton, Tim. 'Opposition drama and the resolution of disputes in early Tudor England: Cardinal Wolsey and the Abbot of Chester', *Bulletin of the John Rylands University Library of Manchester* 81:1 (1999), 25–47.

2096.   Tumbleson, Raymond D. 'The triumph of London: Lord Mayor's Day pageants and the rise of the City', A120, 53–68.

2097.   Turner, Dorothy. 'Royalism, romance, and history in Boscobel: or, The History of His Sacred Majesties Most Miraculous Preservation', *Prose Studies* 22:1 (1999), 59–70.

2098.   Warnicke, Retha M. *The marrying of Anne of Cleves* (Cambridge: Cambridge University Press, 2000), xv, 343p.

2099.   Weil, Rachel Judith. *Political passions: gender, the family and political argument in England, 1680–1714* (Manchester: Manchester University Press, 1999), ix, 262p.

2100.   Weiser, Brian. 'Access and petitioning during the reign of Charles II', A58, 203–13.

2101.   Williams, Glanmor. 'Sir John Pryse of Brecon', *Brycheiniog* 31 (1998–99), 49–63.

2102.   Withington, Phil. 'Citizens, community and political culture in Restoration England', A193, 134–55.

2103.   Wynne, Sonya. 'The mistresses of Charles II and Restoration court politics', A58, 171–90.

2104.   Young, Michael B. *King James VI and I and the history of homosexuality* (Basingstoke: Macmillan, 1999), ix, 221p.

J. *Military*

See also 1602 (F); 2616 (G); 5108 (J)

2105.   Adair, John. *By the sword divided: eyewitness accounts of the English Civil War*, 2nd edn. (Stroud: Sutton, 1998), 240p. [1st edn. 1983.]

2106.   Ashley, Maurice. *The English Civil War*, revised edn. (Stroud: Alan Sutton, 1996), xiv, 202p. [1st published 1974.]

2107.   Barratt, John. *Cavaliers: the royalist army at war, 1642–1646* (Stroud: Sutton, 2000), xii, 244p.

2108.   Bennell, John. 'The oared vessels' [The Anthony Roll of Henry VIII's navy: Pepys MS 2991 and British Library Add MS 22047 with related material], A127, 34–58.

2109.   Bennett, Martyn. *The civil wars experienced: Britain and Ireland, 1638–61* (London and New York: Routledge, 2000), xxvi, 277p.

2110.   Bhanji, Sadru. 'Topsham Fort' [in the Civil War period], *Devon Historian* 52 (1996), 12–17.

2111.   Coster, Will. 'Massacre and codes of conduct in the English Civil War', *War and Genocide* 1 (1999), 89–106.

2112.   Davies, J.D. 'The Revenge of Llanelli: a Welsh privateer in the 17th century', *Maritime Wales* 21 (2000), 45–51.

2113.   Gaunt, Peter. *The Cromwellian gazetteer*, new edn. (Stroud: Sutton, 2000), xiv, 241p. [1st published 1987.]

2114.   Hainsworth, D. Roger; Churches, Christine. *The Anglo-Dutch naval wars, 1652–1674* (Stroud: Sutton, 1998), viii, 212p.

2115.   Harding, Richard. *Seapower and naval warfare, 1650–1830* (London: UCL Press, 1999), xx, 356p.

2116.   Howes, Audrey; Foreman, Martin. *Town and gun: the 17th-century defences of Hull* (Kingston upon Hull: Kingston, 1999), iii, 207p.

2117.   Hudson, Roger (ed.) *The grand quarrel: women's memoirs of the English Civil War* (Stroud: Sutton, 2000), xxxviii, 256p. [1st published London: Folio Society, 1993.]

2118.   Hyde, Patricia; Harrington, Duncan. *Faversham Tudor & Stuart muster rolls* (Faversham Hundred records, 3) (Folkestone: Arden Enterprises, 2000), xxxvi, 216p.

2119.   Knighton, C.S. 'Introduction: the manuscript and its compiler' [The Anthony Roll of Henry VIII's navy: Pepys MS 2991 and British Library Add MS 22047 with related material], A127, 3–14.

2120.   Knighton, C.S. 'Some Pepysian addenda at Magdalene College, Cambridge', *Mariner's Mirror* 86 (2000), 148–56.

2121.   Loades, David Michael. 'The ordnance' [The Anthony Roll of Henry VIII's navy: Pepys MS 2991 and British Library Add MS 22047 with related material], A127, 12–14.

2122.   Moore, Peter. 'Tilbury Fort: a post-medieval fort and its inhabitants', *Post-Medieval Archaeology* 34 (2000), 3–104.

2123.   Morris, M. 'Naval cordage procurement in early modern England', *International Journal of Maritime History* 11:1 (1999), 81–100.

2124.   Nusbacher, Aryeh J.S. 'Civil supply in the civil war: supply of victuals to the new model army on the Naseby campaign, 1–14 June 1645', *English Historical Review* 115 (2000), 145–60.

2125.   Ostwald, J. 'The "decisive" Battle of Ramillies, 1706: prerequisites for decisiveness in early modern warfare', *Journal of Military History* 64:3 (2000), 649–78.

2126.   Payne, Ann. 'An artistic survey' [The Anthony Roll of Henry VIII's navy: Pepys MS 2991 and British Library Add MS 22047 with related material], A127, 20–27.

2127.   Phillips, Gervase. 'Irish *ceatharnaigh* in English service, 1544–1550 and the development of "Gaelic warfare"', *Journal of the Society for Army Historical Research* 78:315 (2000), 163–72.

2128.   Plas, T. van der. 'Een Italiaans bankierszoon in de Nederlanden: Federico Spinola en de zeeoorlog tegen Engeland en de Republiek (1593–1603)' [An Italian banker's son in the Netherlands: Federico Spinola and the naval war between England and the Dutch republic], *Belgisch Tijdschrift voor Militaire* 31 (1996), 5–6, 81–108.

2129.   Richardson, W.A.R. 'An Elizabethan pilot's charts (1594): Spanish intelligence regarding the coasts of England and Wales and the end of the XVIth century', *Journal of Navigation* 53:2 (2000), 313–27.

2130.   Versfelt, H.J. 'De Munsterse inval van 1665', *Nieuwe Drentse Volksalmanak* 116 (1999), 1–20.

2131.   Vine, Stuart; Hildred, Alexzandra. 'The evidence of the Mary Rose excavation' [The Anthony Roll of Henry VIII's navy: Pepys MS 2991 and British Library Add MS 22047 with related material], A127, 15–19.

2132.   Webb, John. 'The siege of Portsmouth in the Civil War', A183, 63–90. [1st published in Portsmouth Papers, 7 (1969).]

2133.   Wilson, Timothy; Hayward, Maria. 'The flags' [The Anthony Roll of Henry VIII's navy: Pepys MS 2991 and British Library Add MS 22047 with related material], A127.

2134.   Wroughton, John. *An unhappy civil war: the experiences of ordinary people in Gloucestershire, Somerset and Wiltshire, 1642–1649* (Bath: Lansdown Press, 1999), viii, 312p.

K. *Foreign Affairs*

See also 1326 (E); 2059, 2077 (F)

2135.   Banderier, Gilles. 'L'*Advis au roy de la Grande Bretagne*: un texte inedit d'Agrippa d'Aubigné' [Edition of MS in Yelverton collection in the British Library], *Bibliothèque d'Humanisme et Renaissance* 61 (1999), 509–14.

2136.   Burton, Jonathan. 'Anglo-Ottoman relations and the image of the Turk in Tamburlaine', *Journal of Medieval and Early Modern Studies* 30:1 (2000), 125–56.

2137.   Doran, Susan. *England and Europe in the sixteenth century* (Basingstoke and New York: Macmillan and St Martin's Press, 1999), xvii, 145p.

2138.   Gojosso, Éric. 'La constitution anglaise à l'aune de la Fronde (1649–1653)' [The British constitution as seen by the Fronde leaders], *Revue française d'histoire des idées politiques* 12 (2000), 229–50.

2139.   Hartley, Janet. '"Losing my best days": Charles Whitworth, first British ambassador to Russia' [1705–10], *History Today* 50:6 (2000), 40–46.

2140.   Osborne, Toby. 'Abbot Scaglia, the Duke of Buckingham and Anglo-Savoyard relations during the 1620s', *European History Quarterly* 30:1 (2000), 5–32.

2141.   Walker, Roger M.; Liddell, W.H. (comps.) *The papers of Sir Richard Fanshawe, Bart.* (Leeds: W.S. Maney and London Borough of Barking and Dagenham, 1999), 134p. [Calendar of correspondence.]

G. BRITAIN 1714–1815

A. General

See also 243 (B); 1331 (F); 2636, 2639 (H); 5117 (K)

2142. Black, Jeremy. 'Britain 1800', *History Today* 50:11 (2000), 29–37.
2143. Cervantes, Xavier. *L'Angleterre au XVIIIe siècle* (Rennes: Presses universitaires de Rennes, 1998), 171p.
2144. Douglas, Hugh. *The private passions of Bonnie Prince Charlie*, revised edn. (Stroud: Sutton, 1998), xv, 316p. [1st published 1995.]
2145. Dziembowski, Edmond. 'La France et la Grande-Bretagne pendant les années 1750: aux portes d'une nouvelle modernité' [France and Britain in the 1750s: on the eve of a new modernity], *Franco-British Studies* 28 (1999), 67–86.
2146. Mason, H. 'Voltaire and Sir Everard Fawkener', *British Journal for Eighteenth-Century Studies* 23:1 (2000), 1–12.
2147. Rak, J. 'The improving eye: eighteenth-century picturesque travel and agricultural change in the Scottish highlands', *Studies in Eighteenth-Century Culture* 27 (1998), 343–64.
2148. Selwood, Ann. 'Reynold Davies of Bodwigiad, Penderyn and Streatham, London 1752–1820', *Brycheiniog* 32 (2000), 102–11.
2149. Thomas, Emlyn. *Georgian Chichester*, vol.1 (Middleton-on-Sea (Ssx): The author, 2000), 116p.
2150. Wright, Esmond. 'Benjamin Franklin: an American in London', *History Today* 50:3 (2000), 18–25.

B. Historiography and Historical Methods

See also 304 (B); 1338 (F); 2197, 2209 (G)

2151. Borsay, Peter. *The image of Georgian Bath, 1700–2000: towns, heritage, and history* (Oxford: Oxford University Press, 2000), xi, 434p.
2152. Phillips, Mark Salber. 'Historical distance and the historiography of eighteenth-century Britain', A47, 31–47.
2153. Thirsk, Joan. 'Edward Hasted as historian', A182. [1st published in *Archaeologia Cantiana* 111 (1993), 1–15.]
2154. Young, Brian William. 'Religious history and the eighteenth-century historian' [review article], *Historical Journal* 43:3 (2000), 849–68.

C. Population and Environment

See also 313 (B); 1340–1, 1343, 1345–52, 1355, 1357–9, 1361, 1365, 1367 (F); 2649, 2657 (H); 3630 (I); 5012, 5014 (J); 5141 (K)

2155. Anderson, James. 'Urban development as a component of government policy in the aftermath of the Napoleonic War', *Construction History* 15 (1999), 23–38.

2156. Arnold, Dana. 'London Bridge and its symbolic identity in the Regency metropolis: the dialectic of civic and national pride', A7, 79–100.
2157. Clark, Peter. 'Small towns 1700–1840', A43, 733–74.
2158. Ellis, Joyce. 'Regional and county centres 1700–1840', A43, 673–704.
2159. Haines, Robin; Shlomowitz, Ralph. 'Explaining the mortality decline in the eighteenth-century British slave trade', *Economic History Review* 2nd ser. 53:2 (2000), 262–83.
2160. Hayman, Richard; Horton, Wendy; White, Shelley. *Archaeology and conservation in Ironbridge* (CBA research report, 123) (York: Council for British Archaeology, 1999), xvii, 221p.
2161. McKellar, Elizabeth. 'Peripheral visions: alternative aspects and rural presences in mid-eighteenth century London', A7, 29–47.
2162. Reed, Michael. 'The transformation of urban space 1700–1840', A43, 615–40.
2163. Russell, R.C. 'Parliamentary enclosure, common rights and social change: evidence from the parts of Lindsey in Lincolnshire', *Journal of Peasant Studies* 27:4 (2000), 54–111.
2164. Schwarz, Leonard. 'London 1700–1840', A43, 641–72.
2165. Schwarz, Leonard. 'Residential leisure towns in England towards the end of the eighteenth century', *Urban History* 27:1 (2000), 51–61.
2166. Smith, Catherine. 'Urban improvement in the Nottinghamshire market town 1770–1840', *Midland History* 25 (2000), 98–114.

Da. *Social Life and Conditions*

See also 347 (B); 1369, 1374–5, 1378, 1384, 1387, 1390, 1397–8, 1406, 1408, 1418–20, 1425–6 (F); 2213–14, 2221, 2370, 2446, 2497 (G); 2684, 2705, 2709, 2721, 2753 (H); 5021 (J); 5159–60 (K); 5926 (N)

2167. Beale, Norman; Beale, Elaine. 'Looking for Dr Ingen Housz: the evidence for the site and nature of the burial, in Calne, of the famous Dutch physician and scientist of the eighteenth century', *Wiltshire Archaeological and Natural History Magazine* 93 (2000), 120–30.
2168. Brailsford, Dennis. *A taste for diversions: sport in Georgian England* (Cambridge: Lutterworth, 1999), 252p.
2169. Cameron, A.D. 'Living in Teviotdale. 1. An estate and its people 1750 to c.1770', *Hawick Archaeological Society Transactions* (1999), 9–29.
2170. Carter, Philip. 'James Boswell's manliness', A105, 111–30.
2171. Clark, Jonathan Charles Douglas. 'Protestantism, nationalism, and national identity, 1660–1832' [historiographical review], *Historical Journal* 43 (2000), 249–76.
2172. Clarke, Simone. 'Visions of community: Elizabeth Baker and late eighteenth-century Merioneth', A186, 234–58.
2173. Cohen, Michèle. 'Manliness, effeminacy and the French: gender and the construction of national character in eighteenth-century England', A105, 44–62.
2174. Davison, Lesley. 'Spinsters were doing it for themselves: independence and the single woman in early eighteenth-century rural Wales', A186, 186–209.

2175. Duff, V.M. 'Early English women novelists testify to the law's manifest cruelties against women before the Marriage Act of 1753', *Women's Studies* 29:5 (2000), 583–618.

2176. Finn, Margot. 'Men's things: masculine possession in the consumer revolution', *Social History* 25:2 (2000), 133–55.

2177. Gammon, J. '"A denial of innocence": female juvenile victims of rape and the English legal system in the eighteenth century', A81, 74–95.

2178. Gregory, Jeremy. '*Homo religiosus*: masculinity and religion in the long eighteenth century', A105, 85–110.

2179. Harvey, Karen. '"The majesty of the masculine-form": multiplicity and male bodies in eighteenth-century erotica', A105, 193–214.

2180. Ingram, Allan. 'Sanity, madness and the people next door: neighbours and normalcy in eighteenth-century England', *Le spectateur européen* 1 (2000), 75–90.

2181. Knight, Ronald D. *Hambledon's cricket glory*, vol. 19: *1795–1796* (Weymouth: The author, 1998), 127p.

2182. Langford, Paul. 'Politics and manners from Sir Robert Walpole to Sir Robert Peel', *Proceedings of the British Academy* 94 (1997), 103–26.

2183. Langford, Paul. 'The English as reformers: foreign visitors' impressions, 1750–1850', *Proceedings of the British Academy* 100 (1999), 101–20.

2184. Leneman, Leah. 'Marriage north of the border', *History Today* 50:4 (2000), 20–25.

2185. Money, John. 'Country matters: the fall and rise of Sylvanus Urban in 18th century England', *Canadian Journal of History* 35:1 (2000), 93–98. [Review of Carl Estabrook, *Urbane and rustic England: cultural ties and social spheres in the provinces 1660–1780* (Manchester University Press, 1998).]

2186. Moore, Lucy. *Con men and cutpurses: scenes from the Hogarthian underworld* (London: Allen Lane, 2000), xvii, 299p.

2187. Mueller, J.C. 'Fallen men: representations of male impotence in Britain', *Studies in Eighteenth Century Culture* 28 (1998), 85–102.

2188. Passmore, Susan C. 'A fresh look at the diary (1776–86) of Elizabeth Baker, Dolgellau. Part 2', *Journal of the Merioneth Historical and Record Society* 13 (2000), 243–64.

2189. Perry, Ruth. 'Women in families: the great disinheritance', A116, 111–34.

2190. Pocock, Tom. *Nelson's women* (London: Deutsch, 1999), x, 278p.

2191. Poole, Steve. 'To be a Bristolian: civic identity and the social order, 1750–1850', A70, 76–95.

2192. Russell, G. '"Faro's daughters": female gamesters, politics, and the discourse of finance in 1790s Britain', *Eighteenth-Century Studies* 33:4 (2000), 481–504.

2193. Seleski, Patty. 'Identity, immigration, and the state: Irish immigrants and English settlement in London, 1790–1840', A13, 11–27.

2194. Sherbo, Arthur. 'Isaac Reed's diaries, 1762–1804: a source book', *Notes and Queries* 47:2 (2000), 213–16.

2195. Stolberg, M. 'An unmanly vice: self-pollution, anxiety, and the body in the eighteenth century', *Social History of Medicine* 13:1 (2000), 1–22.

2196.   Stolberg, M. 'Self-pollution, moral reform, and the venereal trade: notes on the sources and historical context of *Onania* (1716)', *Journal of the History of Sexuality* 9:1–2 (2000), 37–61.

2197.   Tosh, John. 'The old Adam and the new man: emerging themes in the history of English masculinities, 1750–1850', A105, 217–38.

2198.   Trumbach, Randolph. *Sex and the gender revolution*, vol. 1: *Heterosexuality and the third gender in Enlightenment London* (Chicago (IL) and London: University of Chicago Press, 1998), 509p.

2199.   Warner, J.; Ivis, F. 'Gin and gender in early eighteenth-century London', *Eighteenth Century Life* 24:2 (2000), 85–105.

2200.   Wells, R. 'The moral economy of the English countryside', A179, 209–72.

2201.   Willes, M. 'The cooks (and others) at Erddig', A206, 296–306.

Db. *Social Structure*

See also 1361, 1438, 1440–1, 1447, 1455, 1459–60, 1463 (F); 2200, 2271, 2302, 2404, 2489, 2537, 2544, 2550, 2612 (G); 2768, 2793, 2798 (H); 5940 (N)

2202.   Anonymous. 'Of roses white and red: the Robinsons and Dales and a network of 18th century secular priests in Lancashire and Yorkshire', *Catholic Ancestor* 8:1 (2000), 13–24.

2203.   Caunce, Stephen. 'Not sprung from princes: middling society in eighteenth-century west Yorkshire', A123, 19–41.

2204.   Chater, Kathy. 'Hidden from history: black people in parish records', *Genealogists' Magazine* 26:10 (2000), 381–4.

2205.   Chater, Kathy. 'Where there's a will' [Perceptions of black Britons in the 18th century], *History Today* 50:4 (2000), 26–27.

2206.   Eagles, Robin. *Francophilia in English society, 1748–1815* (Basingstoke: Macmillan, 2000), 229p.

2207.   Gould, Eliga H. *The persistence of empire: British political culture in the age of the American Revolution* (Chapel Hill (NC): University of North Carolina Press, 2000), xxiv, 262p.

2208.   Harris, Bob. 'Praising the middling sort? Social identity in eighteenth-century British newspapers', A123, 1–18.

2209.   Kidd, Alan J.; Nicholls, David. 'Introduction: the making of the British middle class?', A123, xv.

2210.   Lane, Penelope. 'Women, property and inheritance: wealth creation and income generation in small English towns, 1750–1853', A199, 172–94.

2211.   Leneman, Leah. '"No unsuitable match": defining rank in eighteenth and early nineteenth-century Scotland', *Journal of Social History* 44 (1999), 665–82.

2212.   Lewis, Brian. '"A republic of Quakers": the radical bourgeoisie, the state and stability in Lancashire, 1789–1851', A123, 72–91.

2213.   Maurer, Shawn Lisa. *Proposing men: dialectics of gender and class in the eighteenth century English periodical* (Stanford (CA): Stanford University Press, 1998), viii, 306p.

2214.   Stobart, Jon. 'Social and geographical contexts of property transmission in the eighteenth century', A199, 108–30.

2215.   Warner, Jessica; Ivis, Frank; Demess, Andree. 'A predatory social struc-
        ture: informers in Westminster, 1737–1741', *Journal of Interdisciplinary
        History* 30 (2000), 617–34.
2216.   Woodley, Roger. 'Professionals: early episodes amongst architects and
        engineers', *Construction History* 15 (1999), 15–22.
2217.   Worsley, Giles. 'The financial problems of Sir Thomas Robinson', *The
        Georgian Group Journal* 10 (2000), 15–20.

Dc. *Social Policy and Welfare*

See also 1468, 1470–1 (F); 2331, 2340, 2457, 2576 (G); 2802, 2807, 2819 (H)

2218.   Alcock, J.P. '"God sends meat, but the Devil sends cooks", or "a solitary
        pleasure": the travels of the Honourable John Byng through England and
        Wales in the late 18th century', A208, 14–31.
2219.   Carré, Jacques. 'Frederick Morton Eden et l'asile des indigents d'Oxford
        en 1795' [Frederick Morton Eden and the Oxford workhouse in 1795
        (from *The State of the Poor*, 1797)], A37, 11–19.
2220.   Cole, R.C. 'Alexander Bicknell and the Royal Literary Fund', *Notes and
        Queries* 47:2 (2000), 211–13.
2221.   Hallas, C.S. 'Poverty and pragmatism in the northern uplands of England:
        the North Yorkshire Pennines, c.1770–1900', *Social History* 25 (2000),
        67–84.
2222.   Ingram, Allan. 'Insanity in the city: London and lunacy in the eighteenth
        century', A20, 23–36.
2223.   Jones, Peris. *Making ends meet: (poor relief in 18th century Mangotsfield)*
        (Bristol: Downend Local History Society, 1998), 52p.
2224.   Pitofsky, A. 'The warden's court martial: James Oglethorpe and the poli-
        tics of eighteenth-century prison reform', *Eighteenth Century Life* 24:1
        (2000), 88–102.
2225.   Wittering, S. 'How reliable are the government poor law returns?', *The
        Local Historian* 30:3 (2000), 160–164.

Ea. *Economic Activity and Organisation*

See also 378, 388, 408, 412, 418, 422 (B); 1023 (E); 1358, 1418, 1478–9, 1484–5,
        1493, 1495–6, 1502, 1509, 1512, 1517–18, 1521, 1524, 1527–8, 1763 (F);
        2159, 2176, 2242, 2345, 2503, 2551, 2556, 2624 (G); 2832, 2872, 2887, 2918,
        2948 (H); 5176 (K); 5950 (N)

2226.   Barker, David; Horton, Wendy. 'The development of the Coalport china-
        works: analysis of ceramic finds', *Post-Medieval Archaeology* 33 (1999),
        3–93.
2227.   Barrow, Tony. 'Corn, carriers and coastal shipping: the shipping and
        trade of Berwick and the borders, 1730–1830', *Journal of Transport
        History* 3rd ser. 21:1 (2000), 6–27.
2228.   Beauroy, Jacques. 'Les Coke de Holkham Hall et l'essor du "Norfolk sys-
        tem of husbandry"', *Histoire et Sociétés Rurales* 10 (1998), 9–45.

2229. Bennison, B.R. 'The size and arrangement of brewing in north-eastern England, 1800–1830', *Northern History* 36 (2000), 99–112.

2230. Billington, Vivien. 'Woad-growing in Northampton', *Northamptonshire Past and Present* 53 (2000), 59–70.

2231. Brown, D. '"Persons of infamous character": the textile pedlars and the role of peddling in industrialization', *Textile History* 31:1 (2000), 1–26.

2232. Cessford, A. 'An eighteenth century clay pipe production site at Caerleon', *Monmouthshire Antiquary* 14 (1998), 41–55.

2233. Cliff, Kenneth. 'Mr Lock, hatter to Admiral Lord Nelson', *Costume* 33 (1999), 98–104.

2234. Colvin, Howard Montagu. 'The Townesends of Oxford: a firm of Georgian master masons and its accounts', *The Georgian Group Journal* 10 (2000), 43–60.

2235. De Bruyn, F. 'Het groote tafereel der dwaasheid and the Speculative Bubble of 1720: a bibliographical enigma and an economic force', *Eighteenth Century Life* 24:1 (2000), 62–87.

2236. De Marchi, N.; Van Miegroet, H.J. 'Ingenuity, preference, and the pricing of pictures: the Smith-Reynolds connection', *History of Political Economy* 31 (suppl.) (2000), 379–412.

2237. Dilley, Robert S. 'The enclosure awards of Cumberland: a statistical list', *Transactions of the Cumberland & Westmorland Antiquarian & Archaeological Society* 100 (2000), 225–40.

2238. Douglas, Alistair. 'Excavations at Rainbow Quay, an 18th-century whale rendering plant, Rotherhithe, London', *Post-Medieval Archaeology* 33 (1999), 179–93.

2239. Dresser, Madge. 'Squares of distinction, webs of interest: gentility, urban development and the slave trade in Bristol, c.1673–1820', *Slavery & Abolition* 21:3 (2000), 21–47.

2240. Fremdling, Rainer. 'Transfer patterns of British technology to the Continent: The case of the iron industry', *European Review of Economic History* 4:2 (2000), 195–222.

2241. Gambles, Anna. 'Free Trade and State formation: the political economy of fisheries policy in Britain and the United Kingdom circa 1780–1850', *Journal of British Studies* 39:3 (2000), 288–316.

2242. Guillery, Peter. 'The further adventures of Mary Lacy', *The Georgian Group Journal* 10 (2000), 61–9.

2243. Guillery, Peter. 'The further adventures of Mary Lacy: "seaman", ship-wright, builder', *History Workshop Journal* 49 (2000), 212–20.

2244. Hair, Paul Edward Hedley (ed.) *Coals on rails, Or the reason of my wrighting: the autobiography of Anthony Errington, a Tyneside colliery waggon and waggonway wright, from his birth in 1778 to around 1825* (Liverpool: Liverpool University Press, 2000), 288p.

2245. Hair, Paul Edward Hedley. 'Slavery and liberty: the case of the Scottish colliers', *Slavery & Abolition* 21:3 (2000), 136–151.

2246. Hampson, Rodney. *Pottery references in* The Staffordshire Advertiser, *1795–1865* (Hanley: Northern Ceramic Society, 2000), xiii, 121p.

2247. Hannah, Leslie. 'The moral economy of business: a historical perspective on ethics and efficiency', A29, 285–99.

2248. Harley, C. Knick; Crafts, N.F.R. 'Simulating the two views of the British Industrial Revolution', *Journal of Economic History* 60:3 (2000), 819–41. [Response: no.2281]

2249. Hawkings, David T. 'Little used sources and new discoveries: 2. Silver Plate Tax and Carriage Tax', *Genealogists' Magazine* 26 (1999), 212.

2250. Hayman, Richard; Horton, Wendy. *Ironbridge: history & guide* (Stroud: Tempus, 1999), 176p.

2251. Herbert, Nicholas. 'Stroud tradesmen in an age of enterprise, 1770–1832', *Transactions of the Bristol and Gloucestershire Archaeological Society* 117 (1999), 127–39.

2252. Hewlings, Richard. 'Women in the building trades, 1600–1850: a preliminary list', *The Georgian Group Journal* 10 (2000), 70–83.

2253. Jackson, Gordon. 'Ports 1700–1840', A43, 705–32.

2254. Lawson, J. 'Thomas Dodds—18th century mining visionary or profiteer?', *British Mining* 61 (1998), 119–28.

2255. Lewis, W.J. 'James Baker and the Pool Quay Smelthouse', *Montgomeryshire Collections* 88 (2000), 25–35.

2256. Little, J.I. 'Agricultural improvement and Highland clearance: the Isle of Arran 1766–1829', *Scottish Economic & Social History* 19:2 (1999), 132–47.

2257. Mitchison, Rosalind. 'The Athelstaneford Case' [embezzlement of the parish poor fund, 1726–30], *Transactions of the East Lothian Antiquarian and Field Naturalists' Society* 23 (1996), 45–47.

2258. Morgan, Kenneth. 'The economic development of Bristol, 1700–1850', A70, 48–75.

2259. Moss, Michael S. 'Lagan and Clyde shipbuilding', A113, 177–88.

2260. Murray, Athol L. 'The Scottish Mint after the recoinage, 1709–1836', *Proceedings of the Society of Antiquaries of Scotland* 129 (1999), 861–86.

2261. Murray, Hugh. 'Sedan chairs in York', *York Historian* 17 (2000), 30–46.

2262. Offen, Karl H. 'British logwood extraction from the Mosquitia: the origin of a myth', *Hispanic American Historical Review* 80 (2000), 113–35.

2263. Oxley, G.W. 'Robert Whitworth (1737–99): canal engineer of Calderdale', *Transactions of the Halifax Antiquarian Society* ns 8 (2000), 93–104.

2264. Pearce, Jacqueline. 'A late 18th-century inn clearance assemblage from Uxbridge, Middlesex', *Post-Medieval Archaeology* 34 (2000), 144–86.

2265. Pearson, Robin. 'Ein Wachstumsrätsel: Feuerversicherung und die wirtschaftliche Entwicklung Grossbritanniens 1700–1850' [A growth puzzle: fire insurance and British economic development 1700–1850], *Zeitschrift für Unternehmensgeschichte* 44 (1999), 218–34.

2266. Perkins, R. 'Shipbuilding at Torquay', *Devon Historian* 61 (2000), 17–24.

2267. Pointon, M. 'Dealer in magic: James Cox's Jewelry Museum and the economics of luxurious spectacle in late-eighteenth-century London', *History of Political Economy* 31 (suppl.) (2000), 423–451.

2268. Pollard, Sidney. *Essays on the industrial revolution in Britain* (Variorum Collected Studies series, CS665) (Aldershot: Ashgate, 2000), 350p.

2269. Porter, D. 'A peculiar but uninteresting country: China and the discourse of commerce in eighteenth-century England', *Eighteenth Century Studies* 33:2 (2000), 181–200.

2270. Powell, Christopher. '"Cobing and Helling": a Georgian building firm at work', *Construction History* 15 (1999), 3–14.

2271. Rule, J. 'Industrial disputes, wage bargaining and the moral economy', A179, 166–86.

2272. Sanger, C.W. 'The impact of the American Revolutionary War on Scottish northern whaling: the Dunbar factor', *Northern Scotland* 20 (2000), 71–86.

2273. Sharp, S. 'The Alderson lead merchants and pewterers of London', *British Mining* 59 (1997), 75–78.

2274. Sharpe, Pamela. *Adapting to capitalism: working women in the English economy, 1700–1850* (Basingstoke: Palgrave, 2000), 240p. [Reprint of 1996 edition, with new preface and corrections.]

2275. Shirlaw, Jean H. 'Potters at Morrison's Haven c.1750–1833 and the Gordons at Bankfoot 1795–1840', *Transactions of the East Lothian Antiquarian and Field Naturalists' Society* 24 (2000), 29–37.

2276. Simonton, Deborah. 'Gendering work in eighteenth-century towns', A211, 29–47.

2277. Smail, John. *Merchants, markets and manufacture: the English wool textile industry in the eighteenth century* (Basingstoke: Macmillan, 1999), x, 198p.

2278. Smout, T. Christopher. 'The history of the Rothiemurchus Woods in the eighteenth century', *Northern Scotland* 15 (1995), 19–31.

2279. Stammers, Michael. 'The hand maiden and victim of agriculture: the port of Wells-next-the-Sea, Norfolk, in the eighteenth and nineteenth centuries', *Mariner's Mirror* 86 (2000), 60–65.

2280. Stirk, Nigel. 'Manufacturing reputations in late eighteenth-century Birmingham', *Historical Research* 73:181 (2000), 142–55.

2281. Temin, Peter. 'A response to Harley and Crafts' [no.2248], *Journal of Economic History* 60:3 (2000), 842–46.

2282. Teuteberg, Hans J. 'Britische Frühindustrialisierung und kurhannoversches Reformbewusstsein im späten 18. Jahrhundert' [Early British industrialisation and late eighteenth-century Hanoverian reform awareness], *Vierteljahrschrift für Sozial- und Wirtschaftsgeschichte* 86 (1999), 153–80.

2283. Thick, Malcolm. 'The contrasting histories of Florence fennel, Spanish cardoons, broccoli and celeriac in England from the early eighteenth century until the 1970s', A206, 204–14.

2284. Thomas, James Harry. 'Portsmouth: gateway to eighteenth century India', *Journal of Regional and Local Studies* 19:2 (1999), 5–29.

2285. Thomas, James Harry. 'The Isle of Wight and the East India Company 1700–1840: some connections considered', *The Local Historian* 30:1 (2000), 4–22.

2286. Trinder, Barrie. 'Industrialising towns 1700–1840', A43, 805–30.

2287. Tucker, Keith. *A scratch in Glamorganshire: George the founder (1765–1832): a study of the life of George Tennant, projector of the Neath and Swansea, Red Jacket and Junction Canals (better known as the Tennant Canal)* (Cilfrew: Historical Projects, 1998), xx, 338p.

2288. Wallace, E.K. 'The needs of strangers: friendly societies and insurance societies in late eighteenth-century England', *Eighteenth Century Life* 24:3 (2000), 53–72.

2289.   Zablotney, S. 'Production and reproduction: commerce in images in late-eighteenth-century London', *History of Political Economy* 31 (suppl.) (2000), 413–422.

Eb. *Technology*

See also 423 (B); 2216, 2611 (G); 2973 (H)

2290.   Ashworth, William J. 'England and the machinery of reason 1780 to 1830', *Canadian Journal of History* 35:1 (2000), 1–36.
2291.   Money, John. 'Industrial espionage and technology transfer' [review article], *International History Review* 22:3 (2000), 611–18.
2292.   Moore, J. 'Many years servant to the town: James Barrie and the eighteenth century mapping of Glasgow', *Scottish Geographical Magazine* 113:2 (1997), 105–22.
2293.   Roberts, O. 'Lewis Morris' Universal Tide Table 1723', *Maritime Wales* 20 (1999), 7–11.
2294.   van Laun, John; Bick, David. 'South Wales plateways 1788–1860', *Antiquaries Journal* 80 (2000), 321–31.

Fa. *Media and Communication*

See also 1535, 1548, 1556 (F); 2208, 2346, 2530, 2627 (G); 5769 (M)

2295.   Bandry, Anna. 'The Visitor, the Inspectress, Selima, Obadiah et Tristram, ou comment s'anime le *Public Ledger* en 1760–1761' [How the Public Ledger came to life], *Bulletin de la société d'études anglo-américaines des XVIIe et XVIIIe siècles* 50 (2000), 283–98.
2296.   Barker, Hannah. *Newspapers, politics and English society, 1700–1850* (Harlow: Longman, 2000), 246p.
2297.   Baudino, Isabelle. 'La presse et le développement du marché de l'art à Londres dans la première moitié du XVIIIe siècle' [The press and the development of the art market in London in the first half of the 18th century], *Bulletin de la société d'études anglo-américaines des XVIIe et XVIIIe siècles* 50 (2000), 233–45.
2298.   Bending, Stephen. 'The true rust of the Barons' Wars: gardens, ruins, and the national landscape', A164, 83–93.
2299.   Colclough, S. '"A catalogue of my books": the library of John Dawson (1692–1765), "exciseman and staymaker", c. 1739', *Publishing History* 47 (2000), 45–66.
2300.   Dingwall, Helen M. '"To be insert in the *Mercury*": medical practitioners and the press in eighteenth-century Edinburgh', *Social History of Medicine* 13 (2000), 23–44.
2301.   Marks, P.J.M. 'The Edwards of Halifax bindery', *British Library Journal* 24:2 (1998), 184–218.
2302.   Massil, Stephen. 'The Huguenot Royal librarians: Henri Justel, Francois Vallotton, and Claudius Amyand', *Proceedings of the Huguenot Society of Great Britain & Ireland* 27:3 (2000), 369–81.

2303. Parsloe, John. 'The first issue of Samuel Rudder's *The history and antiquities of Gloucester*', *Transactions of the Bristol and Gloucestershire Archaeological Society* 117 (1999), 163–6.

2304. Pedley, Mary Sponberg (ed.) *The map trade in the late eighteenth century: letters to the London map sellers Jefferys and Faden* (Oxford: Voltaire Foundation, 2000), xiv, 197p.

2305. Pitcher, Edward W.R. *Discoveries in periodicals, 1720–1820: facts and fictions* (Lewiston (NY): E. Mellen, 2000), 702p.

2306. Prescott, S.; Spencer, J. 'Prattling, tattling and knowing everything: public authority and the female editorial persona in the early essay-periodical', *British Journal for Eighteenth-Century Studies* 23:1 (2000), 43–58.

2307. Russell, Terence M. *The encyclopaedic dictionary in the eighteenth century: architecture, arts and crafts*, 5 vols.: 1. John Harris, *Lexicon Technicum, incorporating works of Sir Francis Bacon and Sir Henry Wotton*; 2. Ephraim Chambers *Cyclopaedia*; 3. *The Builder's Dictionary*; 4. Samuel Johnson, *A Dictionary of the English Language*; 5. A Society of Gentlemen, *Encyclopaedia Britannica* (Aldershot: Ashgate, 1997).

2308. Saunderson, B. 'English and the French enlightenment', *Aspects of Education* 47 (1992), 19–37.

2309. Spier, J.; Kagan, J. 'Sir Charles Frederick and the forgery of ancient coins in eighteenth-century Rome', *Journal of the History of Collections* 12:1 (2000), 35–90.

2310. Starkey, Patricia Margaret (ed.) *Riches into art: Liverpool collectors 1770–1880: essays in honour of Margaret T. Gibson* (Liverpool: Liverpool University Press, 2000), 70p.

2311. Strien, Kees van. 'Thomas Hollis and his donation to Leiden University Library, 1759–70', *Quaerendo* 30 (2000), 3–34.

2312. Suarez, M.F. 'English book sale catalogues as bibliographical evidence: methodological considerations illustrated by a case study in the provenance and distribution of Dodsley's collection of poems, 1750–1795', *The Library* 7th ser. 21:4 (1999), 321–60.

Fb. *Science and Medicine*

See also 433 (B); 1597 (F); 2300, 2482, 2534 (G); 3017, 3032 (H)

2313. Allan, D.G.C. 'William Shipley in Northampton c.1747–1754', *Northamptonshire Past and Present* 53 (2000), 31–37.

2314. Bates, David L. '*Naturae accedere partes*: the Northampton Philosophical Society revisited', *Northamptonshire Past and Present* 53 (2000), 19–30.

2315. Bivins, R. 'Expectations and expertise: early British responses to Chinese medicine', *History of Science* 37 (1999), 459–89.

2316. Borsay, Anne. 'An example of political arithmetic: the evaluation of spa therapy at the Georgian Bath Infirmary, 1742–1830', *Medical History* 44 (2000), 149–72.

2317. Borsay, Peter. 'Health and leisure resorts 1700–1840', A43, 775–804.

2318. Cleevely, R.J. 'A note on John Hawkins (1761–1841) and the Hawkins archive', *Archives of Natural History* 27:2 (2000), 261–68.

2319. Coote, J.; Gathercole, P.; Meister, N.; Rogers, T.; Midgley, F. '"Curiosities sent to Oxford": the original documentation of the Forster collection at the Pitt Rivers Museum', *Journal of the History of Collections* 12:2 (2000), 177–92.

2320. Crawford, Catherine. 'Patients' rights and the law of contract in eighteenth-century England', *Social History of Medicine* 13:3 (2000), 381–410.

2321. Dean, D.R. 'Italian volcanoes and English observers', A156, 99–122.

2322. Dolan, Brian. *Exploring European frontiers: British travellers in the age of Enlightenment* (Basingstoke: Macmillan, 2000), xi, 232p.

2323. Edmondson, J.; Hill, C. 'The Linnean Society's Smith Herbarium: a resource for eighteenth-century garden history research', *Garden History* 27:2 (1999), 244–52.

2324. Elliott, Paul. 'The birth of public science in the English provinces: natural philosophy in Derby, c.1690–1760', *Annals of Science* 57:1 (2000), 61–100.

2325. Evans, E.D. 'Lewis Morris's aristocratic connections', *National Library of Wales Journal* 31:2 (1999), 121–4.

2326. Forrester, John M. 'The origins and fate of James Currie's cold water treatment for fever', *Medical History* 44 (2000), 57–74.

2327. Fritscher, B. 'Volcanoes and the "wealth of nations": relations between the emerging sciences of political economy and geology in 18th century Scotland', A156, 209–28.

2328. Frost, Alan; Williams, Glyndwr. 'The beginnings of Britain's exploration of the Pacific Ocean in the eighteenth century', *Mariner's Mirror* 83:2 (1997), 410–18.

2329. Harrison, M. 'From medical astrology to medical astronomy: sol-lunar and planetary theories of disease in British medicine, c.1700–1850', *British Journal for the History of Science* 33:1 (2000), 25–48.

2330. Henderson, D.M. 'James Robertson, an eighteenth century discoverer of Scotland', *Botanical Journal of Scotland* 46:4 (1994), 693–93.

2331. King, Steven; Weaver, Alan. 'Lives in many hands: the medical landscape in Lancashire, 1700–1820', *Medical History* 44 (2000), 173–200.

2332. Mason, P. 'Ethnographic portraiture in the eighteenth century: George Psalmanaazaar's drawings of Formosans', *Eighteenth Century Life* 23:3 (1999), 58–76.

2333. McAllister, M.E. 'Stories of the origin of syphilis in eighteenth-century England: science, myth, and prejudice', *Eighteenth Century Life* 24:1 (2000), 22–44.

2334. Millburn, John R. *Adams of Fleet Street, instrument makers to King George III* (Aldershot: Ashgate, 2000), xix, 420p.

2335. Poolman, Kenneth. *The Speedwell voyage: a tale of piracy and mutiny in the eighteenth century* (Annapolis (MD): Naval Institute Press, 1999), 190p.

2336. Porter, Roy. 'Medicine & progress: the late eighteenth century view', *Transactions of the Medical Society of London* 114 (1999), 31–41.

2337. Rousseau, G.S.; Haycock, D. 'The jew of Crane Court: Emanuel Mendes da Costa (1717–91), natural history and natural excess', *History of Science* 38:2 (2000), 127–70.

2338.   Russell, Colin Archibald. 'Aristocracy and alkali: the 18th century peer, Archibald Cochrane, laid important foundations for the modern chemical industry', *Chemistry in Britain* 35:12 (1999), 31–32.
2339.   Wallis, R. 'Cross-currents in astronomy and navigation: Thomas Hornsby, FRS (1733–1810)', *Annals of Science* 57:3 (2000), 219–240.

Fc. *Ideas and Learning*

See also 1631, 1915 (F); 2327, 2336–7, 2445, 2461, 2467, 2510 (G); 3118, 3131, 3138 (H)

2340.   Alves, H.O. 'Wondering about wonders: Paine, Constâncio and *The Age of Reason, 1794–97'*, A60, 84–95.
2341.   Baillie, James. *Routledge philosophy guidebook to Hume on morality* (London: Routledge, 2000), ix, 226p.
2342.   Blouet, O.M. 'Bryan Edwards, F.R.S., 1743–1800', *Notes & Records of the Royal Society* (of London) 54:2 (2000), 215–22.
2343.   Burr, S.J. 'Inspiring lunatics: biographical portraits of the Lunar Society's Erasmus Darwin, Thomas Day, and Joseph Priestley' [review essay], *Eighteenth Century Life* 24:2 (2000), 111–27p. [Review essay of Desmond G. King-Hele *Erasmus Darwin: a life of unequalled achievement* (London: Giles de la Mare, 1999), P. Rowlandson on Thomas Day and Robert E. Schofield, *The Enlightenment of Joseph Priestley* (University Park: Pennsylvania State University Press, 1998).]
2344.   Chézaud, Patrick. 'Mary Wollstonecraft, féministe néo-classique', *Bulletin de la société d'études anglo-américaines des XVIIe et XVIIIe siècles* 49 (1999), 255–68.
2345.   Churchman, N. 'Public debt policy and public extravagance: the Ricardo-Malthus debate', *History of Political Economy* 31:4 (1999), 653–74.
2346.   Cohen, Michèle. 'Gender and the learning of French in eighteenth century England', *Aspects of Education* 47 (1992), 38–41.
2347.   Deane, S. 'Factions and fictions: Burke, colonialism and revolution', *Bullán: an Irish Studies Review* 4:2 (2000), 5–26.
2348.   Descargues, Madeleine. 'Forme et vie de la prédication chez Sterne: Les Sermons et l'idée de bonheur', *Bulletin de la société d'études anglo-américaines des XVIIe et XVIIIe siècles* [Numéro spécial: Hommage à Paul Denizot] (1999), 61–70.
2349.   Dunthorne, Hugh. 'Beccaria and Britain', A111, 73–96.
2350.   Dwyer, John; Sher, Richard B. (eds.) *Sociability and society in eighteenth-century Scotland* (Edinburgh: Mercat, 1993), xi, 252p. [1st published as *Eighteenth-Century Life* 15:1–2 (1991); not itemised.]
2351.   Fyfe, Aileen. 'Reading children's books in late eighteenth-century dissenting families', *Historical Journal* 43:2 (2000), 453–74.
2352.   Gallagher, Susan E. *The rule of the rich? Adam Smith's argument against political power* (University Park (PA): Pennsylvania State University Press, 1998), vii, 141p.
2353.   Gee, A.J.M. 'Thomas Robert Malthus and Samuel Hollander: a review', *Scottish Journal of Political Economy* 47:2 (2000), 198–212. [Reviews

Samuel Hollander, *The Economics of Thomas Robert Malthus* (Toronto, 1997).]

2354. Griswold, Charles L. (Jr.) *Adam Smith and the virtues of enlightenment* (Cambridge: Cambridge University Press, 1998), xiv, 412p.

2355. Haycock, David. '"A small journey into the country": William Stukeley and the formal landscapes of Stonehenge and Avebury', A164, 67–79.

2356. Heffernan, T. 'Feminism against the east/west divide: Lady Mary's Turkish embassy letters', *Eighteenth Century Studies* 33:2 (2000), 201–16.

2357. Hivet, Christine. 'Mary Wollstonecraft, la Révolution française et A Vindication of the Rights of Woman', *Bulletin de la société d'études anglo-américaines des XVIIe et XVIIIe siècles* 49 (1999), 269–81.

2358. Kerhervé, Alain. "La bibliothèque virtuelle d'une grande dame du XVIIIe siècle: Les livres dans la correspondance de Mary Delany (1700–1788)' [An 18th century Lady's virtual library: books in Mary Delaney's correspondence], *Bulletin de la société d'études anglo-américaines des XVIIe et XVIIIe siècles* 50 (2000), 137–66.

2359. Lafon, Sylvie. 'Si loin, si proche: Les Highlands, les Lowlands et le «complexe d'éloignement» de l'Écosse des Lumières' [So far, so near: the 'distance complex' of Enlightenment Scotland], *Le spectateur européen* 1 (2000), 59–74.

2360. Lai, Cheng-chung (ed.) *Adam Smith across nations: translations and receptions of* The Wealth of Nations (Oxford: Oxford University Press, 1999), xxxiii, 446p. [Includes reprinted articles on the reception of *The Wealth of Nations* in China, Denmark, France, Germany, Italy, Japan, Portugal, Russia, Spain and Sweden.]

2361. Leduc, Guyonne. *L'éducation des Anglaises au XVIIIe siècle: la conception de Henry Fielding* [The education of English women in the 18th century: Fielding's conception] (Paris: L'Harmattan, 1999), 415p.

2362. Loussouarn, Sophie. 'La littérature enfantine en Angleterre au XVIIIe siècle' [English 18th-century juvenile literature], *Bulletin de la société d'études anglo-américaines des XVIIe et XVIIIe siècles* 50 (2000), 99–114.

2363. Martin, Raymond; Barresi, John. *Naturalization of the soul: self and personal identity in the eighteenth century* (London: Routledge, 1999), xi, 203p.

2364. McNally, D. 'Political economy to the fore: Burke, Malthus and the Whig response to popular radicalism in the age of the French Revolution', *History of Political Thought* 21:3 (2000), 427–48.

2365. Miller, D.P. '"Puffing Jamie": the commercial and ideological importance of being a "philosopher" in the case of the reputation of James Watt (1736–1819)', *History of Science* 38:1 (2000), 1–24.

2366. Motooka, Wendy. *The age of reasons: quixotism, sentimentalism, and political economy in eighteenth-century Britain* (London: Routledge, 1998), xiii, 282p.

2367. Nippel, W. 'Gibbon and German historiography', A201, 67–82.

2368. Oz-Salzburger, Fania. 'Adam Ferguson's histories in Germany: English liberty, Scottish vigour, and German rigour', A201, 49–66.

2369. Peltz, Lucy; Myrone, Martin. 'Introduction: "mine are the subjects rejected by the historian": antiquarianism, history and the making of modern culture', A164, 1–13.

2370.   Porter, Roy. *Enlightenment: Britain and the making of the modern world* (London: Allen Lane, 2000), xxiv, 727p.
2371.   Potkay, Adam. *The passion for happiness: Samuel Johnson and David Hume* (Ithaca (NY): Cornell University Press, 2000), xv, 241p.
2372.   Richardson, Roger Charles. 'Writing urban history in the eighteenth century: Milner's Winchester', A182, 83–93.
2373.   Smith, Sarah J. 'Retaking the register: women's higher education in Glasgow and beyond, c.1796–1845', *Gender & History* 12:2 (2000), 310–35.
2374.   Smyth, Orla. 'Books within books: What did Clarissa Harlowe read? A note on the history of reading practices', *Bulletin de la société d'études anglo-américaines des XVIIe et XVIIIe siècles* 48 (1999), 103–22.
2375.   Springborg, Patricia. *Astell: political writings* (Cambridge and New York: Cambridge University Press, 1996), xlviii, 289p. [Contains *Some Reflections upon Marriage, A Fair Way with the Dissenters* and *An Impartial Enquiry into the Causes of Rebellion and Civil War.*]
2376.   Stuchtey, Benedikt. 'Introduction: towards a comparative history of Anglo-German historiographical traditions and transfers', A201, 1–24.
2377.   van den Dungen, P. 'The Abbe de Saint-Pierre and the English "Irenists" of the 18th century (Penn, Belliers, and Bentham)', *International Journal on World Peace* 17:2 (2000), 395–414.
2378.   Wilson, Geoffrey. 'A plethora of parks: mainly Merton examples', *English Place-Name Society Journal* 32 (2000), 73–75.

Fd. *Culture and the Arts*

See also 439, 445, 447, 456 (B); 816 (D); 1670, 1675, 1677, 1685, 1690, 1703, 1714, 1716, 1720–1, 1727–9, 1734–5, 1737, 1747, 1761–3, 1768 (F); 2161, 2213, 2220, 2301, 2307, 2355, 2361, 2369, 2394, 2486, 2521, 2523, 2554, 2585, 2596, 2610, 2627 (G); 3148, 3221 (H); 5043, 5058, 5060 (J); 5984 (N)

2379.   Adshead, David. 'A "modern Italian loggia" at Wimpole Hall', *The Georgian Group Journal* 10 (2000), 150–63.
2380.   Asleson, Robyn (ed.) *A passion for performance: Sarah Siddons and her portraitists* (Los Angeles (CA): J. Paul Getty Museum, 1999), xvii, 142p.
2381.   Baker, M. 'Public fame or private remembrance? The portrait bust and modes of commemoration in eighteenth-century England', A180, 527–36.
2382.   Balderston, Gordon. 'The genesis of "Edward Salter ætatis 6"', *The Georgian Group Journal* 10 (2000), 175–205.
2383.   Ballaster, Ros. 'Women and the rise of the novel: sexual prescripts', A116, 197–216.
2384.   Baridon, Michel. 'L'architecture, le paysage et la naissance du pittoresque: le rôle de Vanburgh' [Architecture, landscaping and the birth of the picturesque: Vanburgh's role], *Bulletin de la société d'études anglo-américaines des XVIIe et XVIIIe siècles* 51 (2000), 141–50.
2385.   Barker, Jeremy. 'Sir James Thornhill's obelisk at Thornhill', *Proceedings of the Dorset Natural History and Archaeological Society* 121 (1999), 140–2.

2386. Baudino, Isabelle. 'Vie des femmes artistes à Londres au XVIIIe siècle: de l'ombre à la lumière?' [The life of female artists in 18th century London: from shade to light?], *Bulletin de la société d'études anglo-américaines des XVIIe et XVIIIe siècles* [Numéro Spécial: Hommage à Paul Denizot] (1999), 245–60.

2387. Brant, Clare. 'Varieties of women's writing', A116, 285–305.

2388. Bristol, Kerry. 'The painted rooms of "Athenian" Stuart', *The Georgian Group Journal* 10 (2000), 164–74.

2389. Brushe, John. 'The building of Clare College Chapel', *The Georgian Group Journal* 10 (2000), 84–91.

2390. Burke, Edmund. *On empire, liberty, and reform: speeches and letters*, ed. David Bromwich (New Haven (CT): Yale University Press, 2000), viii, 525p.

2391. Carré, Jacques. 'Colen Campbell et la négociation des formes: un tournant de l'opinion architecturale en 1715', *Bulletin de la société d'études anglo-américaines des XVIIe et XVIIIe siècles* [Numéro Spécial: Hommage à Paul Denizot] (1999), 261–76.

2392. Carré, Jacques. 'Le jardin urbain au XVIIIe siècle' [The 18th century urban garden], *Bulletin de la société d'études anglo-américaines des XVIIe et XVIIIe siècles* 51 (2000), 185–200.

2393. Cervantes, Xavier. '«The famous painter of views Canaletti of Venice»: Canaletto entre l'Italie et l'Angleterre' [Canaletto between Italy and England], *Le spectateur européen* 2 (2000), 111–34.

2394. Chalklin, Christopher William. 'Quarter Sessions building in Lancashire, 1770–1830', *The Georgian Group Journal* 10 (2000), 92–121.

2395. Chézaud, Patrick. 'Culture et nature au XVIIIe siècle, ou le sens du jardin' [Culture and nature in the 18th century, or the sense of gardening], *Bulletin de la société d'études anglo-américaines des XVIIe et XVIIIe siècles* 51 (2000), 129–40.

2396. Christie, Christopher. *The British country house in the eighteenth century* (Manchester: Manchester University Press, 2000), xv, 333p.

2397. Clark, Peter; Houston, R.A. 'Culture and leisure 1700–1840', A43, 575–614.

2398. Collier, Patrick. '"The lawless by force . . . the peaceable by kindness": strategies of social control in Charlotte Brontë's *Shirley* and the *Leeds Mercury*', *Victorian Periodicals Review* 32 (1999), 279–98.

2399. Colvin, Howard Montagu. 'Lease or demolish? The problem of the redundant country house in Georgian England', A2, 100–13.

2400. Coombs, D. 'The garden at Carlton House of Frederick Prince of Wales and Augusta Princess and Dowager of Wales', *Garden History* 25:2 (1997), 153–77.

2401. Cowell, F. 'Adam Holt (1691?-1750): his work at Coopersdale House, Essex', *Garden History* 26:2 (1998), 214–17.

2402. Cumberland, George. *An attempt to descibe Hafod*, ed. & intr. Jennifer Macve and Andrew Sclater ([Aberystwyth?]: Ymddiriedolaeth Yr Hafod / Hafod Trust, 1996), 17, vii, 50p. [Facsimile of 1796 edition, with new introduction and notes.]

2403. Curl, James Stevens. 'Young's Night Thoughts and the origins of the garden cemetery', *Journal of Garden History* 14:2 (1994), 92.

2404. Davis, Leith. *Acts of union: Scotland and the literary negotiation of the British nation, 1707–1830* (Stanford (CA): Stanford University Press, 1998), viii, 219p.

2405. Degott, Pierre. 'Le livret d'oratorio au XVIIIe siècle: Quelle sorte de livre?' [The 18th century oratorio libretto: what sort of a book?], *Bulletin de la société d'études anglo-américaines des XVIIe et XVIIIe siècles* 50 (2000), 81–98.

2406. Degott, Pierre. 'Paysages musicaux et musiques paysagères: la musique dans les jardins d'agrément de Londres au XVIIIe siècle' [Musical landscapes and landscaping musics: music in 18th-century London pleasure gardens], *Bulletin de la société d'études anglo-américaines des XVIIe et XVIIIe siècles* 51 (2000), 201–214.

2407. Doody, Margaret Anne. 'Women poets of the eighteenth century', A116, 217–37.

2408. Dubois, Pierre. 'Un livre sur la musique: Le Mausolée obscur de Sir John Hawkins', *Bulletin de la société d'études anglo-américaines des XVIIe et XVIIIe siècles* 48 (1999), 123–38.

2409. Dugaw, Dianne. 'Women and popular culture: gender, cultural dynamics, and popular prints', A116, 263–84.

2410. Dupuy, Pascal. 'La campagne d'Italie dans les gravures anglaises sous le Directoire: diffusion et interprétations (1796–1798)' [The French campaign of Italy in British prints at the time of the Directory], A11, 209–31.

2411. Dupuy, Pascal. 'La caricature anglaise face à la France en révolution (1789–1802)' [British caricature and Revolutionary France], *Dix-huitième Siècle* 32 (2000), 307–20.

2412. Dupuy, Pascal. 'Promis'd Horrors: la mort dans la caricature contre-révolutionnaire anglaise (1789–1799)' [Death in British anti-French-Revolution caricature], *Sociétés et Représentations* 10 (2000), 119–33.

2413. Ellis, Joyce. 'Georgian town gardens', *History Today* 50:1 (2000), 38–45.

2414. Ellis, Osian. 'John Parri (c.1710–82): "y tehor dall"', *Transactions of the Honourable Society of Cymmrodorion* ns 6 (1999), 38–65.

2415. Erskine-Hill, Howard (ed.) *Alexander Pope: selected letters* (Oxford: Oxford University Press, 2000), xxv, 405p.

2416. Fairer, D. 'Historical criticism and the English canon: A Spenserian dispute in the 1750s', *Eighteenth Century Life* 24:2 (2000), 43–64.

2417. Farrant, John H. 'James Lambert, Senior and Junior, landscape painters of Lewes', *Sussex Archaeological Collections* 135 (1997), 249–63.

2418. Feibel, J. 'Vortigern, Rowena, and the ancient Britons: historical art and the Anglicization of national origin', *Eighteenth Century Life* 24:1 (2000), 1–21.

2419. Fergus, Jan. 'Women readers: a case study', A116, 155–78.

2420. Fernandez Poza, M. 'A propósito de Mary Wollstonecraft', *Cuadernos de Historia Contemporanea* 20 (1998), 273–84.

2421. FitzPatrick, P.J. 'Richard Dawes (1708–1766), classical scholar and Tynesider. Pt. 1', *Archaeologia Aeliana* 5th ser. 27 (1999), 145–54.

2422. Forbes, D. '"Dodging and watching the natural incidents of the peasantry": genre painting in Scotland 1780–1830', *Oxford Art Journal* 23:2 (2000), 79–94.

2423. France, Peter; Renwick, John. 'France and Scotland in the eighteenth century', A130, 89–104.

2424. Friedman, Terry. 'The transformation of York Minster, 1726–42', *Architectural History* 38 (1995), 69–90.

2425. Furbank, Philip N. 'Defoe, the De la Faye letters and Mercurius Politicus', *British Journal for Eighteenth-Century Studies* 23:1 (2000), 13–19.

2426. Goldgar, Anne. 'The British Museum and the virtual representation of culture in the eighteenth century', *Albion* 32:2 (2000), 195–231.

2427. Gow, Ian. 'Archerfield: the reconstruction of Robert Adam's last interior', *Scottish Archives* 5 (1999), 49–56. [Registers of Entailed Estates as a source for architectural history.]

2428. Grundy, Isobel. '(Re)discovering women's texts', A116, 179–96.

2429. Guest, Harriet. 'Eighteenth-century femininity: "a supposed sexual character"', A116, 46–68.

2430. Gurstein, Rochelle. 'Taste and "the conversible world" in the eighteenth century', *Journal of the History of Ideas* 61:2 (2000), 203–22.

2431. Halimi, Suzy. 'Lecture d'un jardin anglais: Stowe (Buckinghamshire)' [Interpreting an English garden], *Bulletin de la société d'études anglo-américaines des XVIIe et XVIIIe siècles* 51 (2000), 151–66.

2432. Hall, E. '"Mr Brown's directions": Capability Brown's landscaping at Burton Constable (1767–82)', *Garden History* 23:2 (1995), 145–76.

2433. Hargraves, N.K. 'National history and "philosophical" history: character and narrative in William Robertson's History of Scotland', *History of European Ideas* 26:1 (2000), 19–33.

2434. Harman, Claire. *Fanny Burney: a biography* (London: HarperCollins, 2000), xxviii, 430p.

2435. Harris, John. 'The Duchess of Beaufort's "Observations on places"', *The Georgian Group Journal* 10 (2000), 36–42.

2436. Hart, Kevin. 'Economic acts: Johnson in Scotland', *Eighteenth Century Life* 16:1 (1992), 94.

2437. Haycock, David. '"The cabal of a few designing members": the presidency of Martin Folkes, PRS, and the society's first charter', *Antiquaries Journal* 80 (2000), 273–84.

2438. Jenkins, John. *Mozart and the English connection* (London: Cygnus Arts, 1998), xii, 171p.

2439. Kahan, Jeffrey. *Reforging Shakespeare: the story of a theatrical scandal* (Bethleham and London: Lehigh University Press and Associated University Presses, 1998), 271p.

2440. Koehler, M. 'Friedrich Karl von Hardenberg's (1696–1763) journeys to England and his contribution to the introduction of the English landscape garden to Germany', *Garden History* 25:2 (1997), 212–18.

2441. Korshin, Paul (ed.) *The Age of Johnson: a scholarly annual*, vol. 9 (New York: AMS Press, 1998), xvii, 439p.

2442. Krysmanski, Bernd W. *A Hogarth bibliography, 1697–1997* (Hildesheim: Olms, 1999), 2 vols.

2443. Laird, Mark; Harvey, John H. 'The garden plans for 13 Upper Gower Street, London: a conjectural review of the planting, upkeep and long-term maintenance of a late eighteenth-century town garden' [Richard

Twiss' garden proposal for Francis Douce], *Garden History* 25:2 (1997), 189–211.

2444. Llewellyn, Sacha. '"Inventory of her grace's things, 1747"—the dress inventory of Mary Churchill, 2nd Duchess of Montague', *Costume* 31 (1997), 49–67.

2445. Macmillan, Duncan. 'Art and philosophy: Scotland and France in the age of the Enlightenment', A130, 105–24.

2446. Marschner, Joanna. 'Queen Caroline of Ansbach: attitudes to clothes and cleanliness, 1727–1737', *Costume* 31 (1997), 28–37.

2447. Martinet, Marie-Madeleine. '"Darke against light will make a landscape caminare": lumière et animation en peinture' [Light and animation in English 18th century painting], *Bulletin de la société d'études anglo-américaines des XVIIe et XVIIIe siècles* [Numéro spécial: Hommage à Paul Denizot] (1999), 233–44.

2448. Martinet, Marie-Madeleine. 'Ceci n'est pas un discours sur le jardin anglais' [This is not a discourse on the English garden], *Bulletin de la société d'études anglo-américaines des XVIIe et XVIIIe siècles* 51 (2000), 113–28.

2449. McDowell, Paula. 'Women and the business of print', A116, 135–54.

2450. McIlvanney, L. 'Robert Burns and the Ulster-Scots literary revival of the 1790s', *Bullán: an Irish Studies Review* 4:2 (2000), 125–144.

2451. McPherson, H. 'Picturing tragedy: Mrs. Siddons as the tragic muse revisited', *Eighteenth-Century Studies* 33:3 (2000), 401–30.

2452. Meir, J. 'Sanderson Miller and the landscaping of Wroxton Abbey, Farnborough Hall and Honington Hall', *Garden History* 25:1 (1997), 81–106.

2453. Messenger, Ann. *Woman and poet in the eighteenth century: the life of Mary Whateley Darwall (1738–1825)* (New York: AMS Press, 1999), xii, 273p.

2454. Mieder, W. '"A man of fashion never has recourse to proverbs": Lord Chesterfield's tilting at proverbial windmills', *Folklore* 111:1 (2000), 23–42.

2455. Moore, D. 'Ossian, chivalry and the politics of genre: the case of Fingal King of Morven, a knight-errant', *British Journal for Eighteenth-Century Studies* 23:1 (2000), 21–35.

2456. Moore, Donald. 'Thomas Pennant's view of the landscape', *Archaeologia Cambrensis* 146 (2000 for 1997), 138–77.

2457. Morrissey, Lee. 'Sexuality and consumer culture in eighteenth century England: "mutual love from pole to pole" in the London Merchant', *Restoration and 18th Century Theatre Research* 13:1 (1998), 25–40.

2458. Mowl, Timothy; Earnshaw, Brian. *An insular rococo: architecture, politics and society in Ireland and England, 1710–1770* (London: Reaktion, 1999), ix, 358p.

2459. Mueller, U. 'Rousham: a transcription of the steward's letters 1738–42', *Garden History* 25:2 (1997), 178–88.

2460. Murphy, Norman D.H. 'Bolton parish library and others: the record of a lost resource', *Transactions of the East Lothian Antiquarian and Field Naturalists' Society* 23 (1996), 87–104.

2461. Myrone, Martin. 'Graphic antiquarianism in eighteenth-century Britain: the career and reputation of George Vertue (1684–1756)', A164, 35–49.

2462. Nurse, Bernard. 'George Cruikshank's *The Antiquarian Society*, 1812, and Sir Henry Charles Englefield', *Antiquaries Journal* 80 (2000), 316–21.

2463. Nussbaum, Felicity A. 'Women and race: "a difference of complexion"', A116, 69–90.

2464. Ogée, Frédéric. '«A work to wonder at»: essence et existence du «jardin-paysage» anglais' [Essence and existence of the English landscape garden], *Études anglaises* 53:4 (2000), 428–41.

2465. Paulson, Ronald. *The life of Henry Fielding* (Oxford: Blackwell, 2000), 400p.

2466. Peltz, Lucy. 'Aestheticizing the accidental city: antiquarianism, modernity and the representation of London in the long eighteenth century', A7, 6–28.

2467. Peltz, Lucy. 'The extra-illustration of London: the gendered spaces and practices of antiquarianism in the late eighteenth century', A164, 115–28.

2468. Pitman, Liz. 'Gilded angels: the eighteenth century funeral monuments of the Brute family of Llanbedr', *Brycheiniog* 32 (2000), 85–101.

2469. Raven, James; Forster, Antonia; Schöwerling, Rainer (eds.) *The English novel 1770–1829: a bibliographical survey of prose fiction published in the British Isles* (Oxford: Oxford University Press, 2000), 2 vols.

2470. Redford, Bruce; Goldring, Elizabeth (eds.) *James Boswell's Life of Johnson: an edition of the original manuscript*, vol.2: *1766–1776* (Edinburgh: Edinburgh University Press, 1998), xviii, 303p.

2471. Révauger, Cécile. 'William Hogarth et la franc-maçonnerie: jeux de lumière' [Hogarth and freemasonry], *Bulletin de la société d'études anglo-américaines des XVIIe et XVIIIe siècles* [Numéro Spécial: Hommage à Paul Denizot] (1999), 277–92.

2472. Richardson, J. 'John Gay, The Beggar's Opera, and forms of resistance', *Eighteenth Century Life* 24:3 (2000), 19–30.

2473. Roberts, J. 'Cusworth Park: the making of an eighteenth-century designed landscape', *Landscape History* 21 (1999), 77–93.

2474. Roscoe, Ingrid. 'Peter Scheemakers', *Walpole Society* 61 (1999), 163–304.

2475. Shaw, T. 'John Swinton, F.R.S., identified as the author of a 1734 travel journal', *Notes & Records of the Royal Society* (of London) 53 (1999), 295–304.

2476. Sherbo, Arthur. 'Isaac Reed's diaries and the theatrical scene in eighteenth-century England', *Restoration and 18th Century Theatre Research* 14:1 (1999), 61–73.

2477. Silvester, B.; Pitman, Liz. 'Eighteenth-century stonemasons in the Black Mountains', *Church Archaeology* 2 (1998), 29–34.

2478. Smallwood, Angela J. 'Elizabeth Inchbald and the «jostling race»: adaptations of French comedy for the London stage in the 1780s and 1790s', *Le spectateur européen* 2 (2000), 207–22.

2479. Smallwood, Angela J. 'Women and the theatre', A116, 238–62.

2480. Smart, Alastair. *Allan Ramsay: a complete catalogue of his paintings*, ed. John Ingamells (New Haven (CT): Yale University Press, 1999), 432p.

2481. Smiles, Sam. 'British antiquity and antiquarian illustration', A164, 55–64.

2482. Stevenson, Christine. 'Hogarth's mad king and his audiences', *History Workshop Journal* 49 (2000), 24–44.

2483. Sutherland, Kathryn. 'Writings on education and conduct: arguments for female improvement', A116, 25–45.

2484. Sweet, Rosemary. 'John Nichols and his circle', *Transactions of the Leicestershire Archaeological and Historical Society* 74 (2000), 1–20.

2485. Toft, Robert. *Heart to heart: expressive singing in England 1780–1830* (Oxford: Oxford University Press, 2000), xv, 198p.

2486. Tyack, Geoffrey. 'The making of the Radcliffe Observatory', *The Georgian Group Journal* 10 (2000), 122–40.

2487. Wagner, Eve-Marie. 'Un jardin en Avignon (1743–1746): Lady Mary Wortley Montagu et la création d'un domaine à soi' [A garden in Avignon: the creation of a domain of one's own], *Bulletin de la société d'études anglo-américaines des XVIIe et XVIIIe siècles* 49 (1999), 341–61.

2488. Walker, Richard. 'Henry Bone's pencil drawings in the National Portrait Gallery', *Walpole Society* 61 (1999), 305–67.

2489. Walker, W. 'Ideology and Addison's Essays on the Pleasures of the Imagination', *Eighteenth Century Life* 24:2 (2000), 65–84.

2490. Willson, A.B. 'Alexander Pope's grotto in Twickenham', *Garden History* 26:1 (1998), 31–59.

2491. Wright, Paul. 'Vile Saxons and ancient Britons: Wordsworth, the ambivalent Welsh tourist', A93, 64–82.

G. *Religious Belief, Practice and Organisation*

See also 492, 495 (B); 1770, 1812, 1819, 1823, 1869, 1875, 1915, 1930, 1937, 1949 (F); 2154, 2178, 2257, 2573, 2582 (G); 3283, 3290, 3359 (H); 5075 (J); 5237 (K); 5992 (N); 6395 (P)

2492. Ball, Andrew. 'A chaplain in Wellington's Army: Fr. Edmund Winstanley', *British Historical Society of Portugal Annual Report* 26 (1999), 107–12.

2493. Bostridge, Ian. 'Music, reason, and politeness: magic and witchcraft in the career of George Frideric Handel', A29, 251–63.

2494. Chamberlain, Jeffrey Scott. *Accommodating high churchmen: the clergy of Sussex, 1700–1745* (Urbana (IL): University of Illinois Press, 1997), xv, 192p.

2495. Cornwall, Robert. 'The rite of confirmation in Anglican thought during the eighteenth century', *Church History* 68 (1999), 359–72.

2496. Ditchfield, G.M. '"Incompatible with the very name of Christian": English Catholics and Unitarians in the age of Milner', *Recusant History* 25:1 (2000), 52–73.

2497. Dresser, Madge. 'Protestants, Catholics and Jews: religious difference and political status in Bristol, 1750–1850', A70, 96–123.

2498. Eddy, G.T. 'Formica contra Leonem: an eighteenth century conflict reassessed', *Methodist History* 38:2 (2000), 71–81.

2499. Finestein, Israel. 'The Jews in Hull, between 1766 and 1880', *Jewish Historical Studies* 35 (1998), 33–93.

2500. Freiberg, Malcolm. 'Going Gregorian, 1582–1752: a summary view' [calendar reform], *Catholic Historical Review* 86 (2000), 1–19.

2501.   Gibson, William T. 'Patronage and connection: the career of the Rev. William Talbot (1720–1811), Chancellor of Salisbury', *British Library Journal* 25:1 (1999), 77–84.

2502.   Guérin, Pierre. 'Compléments sur les jésuites anglais de Liège: note sur la famille Gal', *Cahier Historique de Fléron* 37:4 (1997), 43–54.

2503.   Guérin, Pierre. 'Difficultés financières des jésuites anglais de Liège de 1741 à 1749' [Financial difficulties of the English Jesuits in Liège, 1741–1749], *Cahier Historique de Fléron* 37:1 (1997), 14–21.

2504.   Hall, Richard Andrew; Richardson, Sarah. *The Anglican clergy and Yorkshire politics in the eighteenth century* (Borthwick paper, 94) (York: Borthwick Institute of Historical Research University of York, 1998), 34p.

2505.   Hall, Stuart G. 'Patristics and reform: Thomas Rattray and *The ancient liturgy of the Church of Jerusalem*', *Studies in Church History* 35 (1999), 240–60.

2506.   Haydon, Colin. '"The mouth of Hell": religious discord at Brailes, Warwickshire, c.1660–c.1800', *The Historian* [London] 68 (2000), 23–27.

2507.   Hindmarsh, D. Bruce. '"My chains fell off, my heart was free": early Methodist conversion narrative in England', *Church History* 68 (1999), 910–29.

2508.   Holt, Geoffrey. '"Haeres . . . Thomae More cancellarii": Fr Thomas More 1722–1795', *Recusant History* 24 (1998), 76–88.

2509.   Homan, Roger. 'Mission and fission: the organization of Huntingtonian and Calvinistic Baptist causes in Sussex in the 18th and 19th centuries', *Sussex Archaeological Collections* 135 (1997), 265–82.

2510.   Johnson, David. *Hume, holism, and miracles* (Ithaca (NY): Cornell University Press, 1999), 106, ix p.

2511.   Jones, P. 'The Qualified Episcopal chapels of the north-east of Scotland 1689–1898', *Northern Scotland* 20 (2000), 47–70.

2512.   Juster, Susan. 'Mystical pregnancy and holy bleeding: visionary experience in early modern Britain and America', *William and Mary Quarterly* 3rd ser. 57:2 (2000), 249–88.

2513.   Kirkus, M. Gregory. '"Yes, my Lord": some eighteenth and nineteenth century bishops and the Institute of the Blessed Virgin Mary', *Recusant History* 24 (1998), 171–92.

2514.   Leighton, C.D.A. 'Antichrist's revolution: some Anglican apocalypticists in the age of the French wars', *Journal of Religious History* 24:2 (2000), 125–42.

2515.   Litton, Pauline. 'Return of papists, 1767: some Yorkshire returns', *Catholic Ancestor* 8 (2000), 65–72.

2516.   Lovegrove, Deryck. '"A set of men whose proceedings threaten no small disorder": The Society for Propagating the Gospel at Home, 1798–1808', *Scottish Historical Review* 79:1 (2000), 61–81.

2517.   Lovegrove, Deryck. 'The mirage of authenticity: Scottish Independents and the reconstruction of a New Testament Order of Worship, 1799–1808', *Studies in Church History* 35 (1999), 261–74.

2518.   MacDonald, Ian R. *Aberdeen and the Highland church (1785–1900)* (Edinburgh: St Andrew's Press, 2000), xix, 294p.

2519.   Mack, Phyllis. 'Religious dissenters in Enlightenment England', *History Workshop Journal* 49 (2000), 1–23.

2520.   Mason, Margaret J. 'The Blue Nuns in Norwich: 1800–1805', *Recusant History* 24 (1998), 89–122.

2521.   Mayhew, R. 'William Gilpin and the Latitudinarian picturesque', *Eighteenth Century Studies* 33:3 (2000), 349–66.

2522.   Nockles, Peter B. '"The difficulties of Protestantism": Bishop Milner, John Fletcher and Catholic apologetic against the Church of England in the era from the first Relief Act to Emancipation, 1778–1830', *Recusant History* 24 (1998), 193–236.

2523.   Penelhum, Terence. *Themes in Hume: the self, the will, religion* (Oxford: Clarendon, 2000), xix, 294p.

2524.   Petch, Joyce. 'The Methodists in Huntington 1797–1900', *York Historian* 16 (1999), 45–58.

2525.   Philip, W.J.U. 'The marrow and the dry bones: ossified orthodoxy and the battle for the gospel in eighteenth-century Scottish Calvinism', *Scottish Bulletin of Evangelical Theology* 15:1 (1997), 27–37.

2526.   Phillips, Dewi Z.; Tessin, Timothy (eds.) *Religion and Hume's legacy* (Basingstoke: Macmillan, 1999), xx, 282p. [Papers from the 1997 Claremont Conference on the Philosophy of Religion.]

2527.   Pocock, J.G.A. 'Gibbon and the primitive church', A47, 48–67.

2528.   Prunier, Clotilde. 'L'éducation et le Livre: Controverses religieuses en écosse au XVIIIe' [Education and the Good Book: religious controversies in 18th-century Scotland], *Bulletin de la société d'études anglo-américaines des XVIIe et XVIIIe siècles* 50 (2000), 67–79.

2529.   Rogal, Samuel J. *A biographical dictionary of 18th century Methodism*, vol.10: *X-Z, appendices* (Lewiston (NY): E. Mellen, 1999), lxi, 313p.

2530.   Stott, Anne. 'Hannah More and the Blagdon controversy, 1799–1802' [Thomas Bere, curate of Blagdon, Somerset], *Journal of Ecclesiastical History* 51:2 (2000), 319–46.

2531.   Taylor, Stephen. 'Whigs, Tories and anticlericalism: ecclesiastical courts legislation in 1733', *Parliamentary History* 19:3 (2000), 329–56.

2532.   Watts, John. *Scalan: the forbidden college 1716–1799* (East Linton: Tuckwell, 1999), viii, 276p.

2533.   Welch, Edwin. 'Lady Glenorchy's church at Exmouth', *Devonshire Association Report and Transactions* 130 (1998), 15–21.

2534.   White, Eryn M. 'Women, religion and education in eighteenth-century Wales', A186, 210–33.

2535.   Womersley, David. 'Gibbon's religious characters', A47, 69–90.

Ha. *Law and Order*

See also 502 (B); 1965 (F); 2177, 2186, 2191, 2215, 2320, 2335, 2629 (G); 3368, 3377, 3383 (H); 6399 (P)

2536.   Barrell, John. *Imagining the king's death: figurative treason, fantasies of regicide 1793–1796* (Oxford: Oxford University Press, 2000), xvii, 737p.

2537. Bohstedt, John. 'The pragmatic economy, the politics of provisions and the "invention" of the food riot tradition in 1740', A179, 55–92.

2538. Braun, Guido. 'Scheid, Neckar et Dupal: la connaissance du droit public allemand en France et en Grande-Bretagne (1741–1754)', *Francia* 27:2 (2000), 213–47.

2539. Coldham, Peter Wilson. 'Oxfordshire prisoners. Part I: 1753–69', *Genealogists' Magazine* 26 (2000), 335–9. [Convicts transported to America.]

2540. Coldham, Peter Wilson. 'Oxfordshire prisoners. Part II: 1770–75', *Genealogists' Magazine* 26:10 (2000), 388–9. [Extracts from *Jackson's Oxford Journal*.]

2541. Cooke, Jessica; Horwitz, Henry. *Samples of Exchequer and equity pleadings and suits: 1685–86, 1734–35, 1784–85 and 1819* (Kew: List and Index Society, 2000), 244p.

2542. Edelstein, Laurie. 'An accusation easily to be made?: rape and malicious prosecution in eighteenth-century England', *American Journal of Legal History* 42:4 (1998), 351–90.

2543. Gould, Jack. 'The Culworth Gang', *Northamptonshire Past and Present* 53 (2000), 38–48.

2544. Hay, D. 'Moral economy, political economy and law', A179, 93–122.

2545. Howell, David W. 'Riots and public disorder in eighteenth-century Wales', A111, 42–72.

2546. Lemmings, David. *Professors of the law: barristers and English legal culture in the eighteenth century* (Oxford: Oxford University Press, 2000), xiv, 399p.

2547. Leneman, Leah. 'Defamation in Scotland, 1750–1800', *Continuity and Change* 15:2 (2000), 209–34.

2548. McGowen, Randall. 'From pillory to gallows: the punishment of forgery in the age of the financial revolution', *Past & Present* 165:1 (1999), 107–40.

2549. Oakes, Jonathan. 'York and the rebel prisoners, 1745–1752', *York Historian* 17 (2000), 47–61.

2550. Randall, Adrian; Charlesworth, Andrew. 'The moral economy: riots, markets and social conflict', A179, 1–32.

2551. Sanderson, Elizabeth C. 'Nearly new: the second-hand clothing trade in eighteenth-century Edinburgh', *Costume* 31 (1997), 38–48.

2552. Selley, Gill. 'A murder mystery in eighteenth-century Woodbury', *Devonshire Association Report and Transactions* 130 (1998), 51–64.

2553. Sharpe, J.A. 'Civility, civilizing processes, and the end of public punishment in England', A29, 215–30.

2554. Shevlin, E.F. '"Imaginary productions" and "minute contrivances": law, fiction, and property in eighteenth-century England', *Studies in Eighteenth Century Culture* 28 (1998), 131–54.

2555. Skinner, Gillian. 'Women's status as legal and civic subjects: "a worse condition than slavery itself"?', A116, 91–110.

2556. Stirk, Nigel. 'Arresting ambiguity: the shifting geographies of a London debtors' sanctuary in the eighteenth century', *Social History* [London] 25:3 (2000), 316–29.

Hb. *Public Administration*

See also 2166, 2171, 2241 (G); 3389, 3391, 3393 (H)

2557.   Douglas, Hugh. *Jacobite spy wars: moles, rogues and treachery* (Stroud: Sutton, 1999), xvii, 269p.

2558.   Lloyd, Campbell F. 'The search for legitimacy: universities, medical licensing bodies and governance in Glasgow and Edinburgh from the late eighteenth to the late nineteenth centuries', A159, 198–210.

2559.   Panton, F.H. 'Canterbury Court of Guardians: eighteenth century—a postscript', *Archaeologia Cantiana* 119 (1999), 343–51.

2560.   Simms, B. 'Reform in Britain and Prussia, 1797–1815: (confessional) fiscal-military state and military-agrarian complex', *Proceedings of the British Academy* 100 (1999), 79–100.

2561.   *Treasury Board: papers 1775–1779, T 1/512–555* (List and Index Society, 277) (Kew: List and Index Society, 2000). [The final volume in the series, completing the *Calendar of Treasury Papers* and *Calendar of Treasury Books* (vols. 240, 244, 250, 256 and 275–276).]

2562.   *Treasury Board: papers, 1775–1776 (T 1/512–527)* (List and Index Society, 275) (Kew: List and Index Society, 1999), 133p.

2563.   *Treasury Board: papers, 1777–1779 (T 1/528–555)* (List and Index Society, 276) (Kew: List and Index Society, 1999), 211p.

2564.   *Treasury Board: papers, 1780–1788 (T 1/556–664)* (Kew: List and Index Society, 2000), 173p.

Hc. *Political and Constitutional*

See also 492, 513, 515 (B); 1512, 2006, 2036, 2039, 2053, 2059, 2063 (F); 2212, 2504, 2531, 2545, 2623, 2625, 2631 (G); 3359, 3490 (H); 5940, 6008 (N); 6501 (P)

2565.   Black, Jeremy. 'Eighteenth-century English politics: recent work', *Albion* 32:2 (2000), 248–72.

2566.   Bourke, R. 'Edmund Burke and Enlightenment sociability: justice, honour and the principles of government', *History of Political Thought* 21:4 (2000), 632–56.

2567.   Chalus, Elaine. 'Elite women, social politics, and the political world of late eighteenth-century England', *Historical Journal* 43:3 (2000), 669–98.

2568.   Clark, Anna; Richardson, Sarah (eds.) *History of suffrage, 1760–1867* (London: Pickering & Chatto, 2000), 6 vols.

2569.   Conway, Stephen. *The British isles and the American War of Independence* (Oxford: Oxford University Press, 2000), vii, 407p.

2570.   Cruickshanks, Eveline. 'The second duke of Ormonde and the Atterbury Plot', A12, 243–53.

2571.   Davis, Michael T. '"Good for the public example": Daniel Isaac Eaton, prosecution, punishment and recognition, 1793–1812', A60, 110–32.

2572.   Davis, Michael T. '"That odious class of men called democrats": Daniel Isaac Eaton and the Romantics 1794–1795', *History* 84 (1999), 74–92.

2573. Ditchfield, G.M. 'Ecclesiastical legislation during the ministry of the Younger Pitt, 1783–1801', *Parliamentary History* 19 (2000), 64–80.

2574. Emsley, Clive. 'The pop-gun plot, 1794', A60, 56–68.

2575. Farmer, Lindsay. *Criminal law, tradition and legal order: crime and the genius of Scots law, 1747 to the present* (Cambridge: Cambridge University Press, 1997), xi, 207p.

2576. Fruchtman, J. (Jr.) 'Two doubting Thomases: the British progressive enlightenment and the French revolution', A60, 30–40.

2577. Gibson, John S. *The gentle Lochiel: the Cameron chief and Bonnie Prince Charles* (Edinburgh: National Museums of Scotland, 1998), 96p.

2578. Graham, Jenny. *The nation, the law and the king, reform politics in England, 1789–1799* (Lanham (MD), New York and Oxford: University Press of America, 2000), 2 vols.

2579. Guyatt, M. 'The Wedgwood slave medallion: values in eighteenth-century design', *Journal of Design History* 13:2 (2000), 93–105.

2580. Hall, Richard Andrew. 'Voting communities in the West Riding of Yorkshire in the early eighteenth century', *Parliaments, Estates & Representation* 20 (2000), 91–110.

2581. Hanham, Andrew. '"So few facts": Jacobites, Tories and the Pretender', *Parliamentary History* 19:2 (2000), 233–58.

2582. Haydon, Colin. 'Parliment and popery in England, 1700–1780', *Parliamentary History* 19 (2000), 49–63.

2583. Hayton, D.W. 'Dependence, clientage and affinity: the political following of the second duke of Ormonde', A12, 211–41.

2584. Hellmuth, Eckhart. 'Why does corruption matter? Reforms and reform movements in Britain and Germany in the second half of the eighteenth century', *Proceedings of the British Academy* 100 (1999), 5–24.

2585. Hole, Robert. 'Hannah More on literature and propaganda, 1788–1799', *History* 85:280 (2000), 613–33.

2586. Hoppit, Julian. 'An embarrassment of riches', *Parliamentary History* 18 (1999), 189–205. [Review article on the *History of Parliament on CD-ROM* (Cambridge University Press with the History of Parliament Trust, 1998).]

2587. Innes, Joanna; Rogers, Nicholas. 'Politics and government 1700–1840', A43, 529–74.

2588. Jenks, Timothy. 'Contesting the hero: the funeral of Admiral Lord Nelson', *Journal of British Studies* 39:4 (2000), 422–53.

2589. Jones, Clyve. 'Jacobites under the beds: Bishop Francis Atterbury, the Earl of Sunderland and the Westminster School dormitory case of 1721', *British Library Journal* 25:1 (1999), 35–54.

2590. Jupp, Peter. 'Britain and the Union, 1797–1801', *Transactions of the Royal Historical Society* 6th ser. 10 (2000), 197–220.

2591. Kulisheck, P.J. 'The "lost" Pelham papers', *Archives* 24:101 (1999), 37–43.

2592. Laws, W. 'An eighteenth-century carpetbagger: Banstaple's MP, Thomas Whetham', *Devon Historian* 60 (2000), 3–7.

2593. Macleod, Emma Vincent. 'The influence of the French Revolution in Scotland', A130, 125–42.

2594. Mee, J. 'The political showman at home: reflections on popular radicalism and print culture in the 1790s', A60, 41–55.

2595. Mitchell, L.G. 'The Whigs, the people, and reform', *Proceedings of the British Academy* 100 (1999), 25–42.

2596. Phillips, Michael. 'William Blake in Lambeth', *History Today* 50:11 (2000), 18–28.

2597. Pocock, J.G.A. 'The Union in British history', *Transactions of the Royal Historical Society* 6th ser. 10 (2000), 181–96.

2598. Rogers, Nicholas. 'Burning Tom Paine: loyalism and counter-revolution in Britain, 1792–1793', *Histoire Sociale / Social History* 32 (1999), 139–71.

2599. Scrivener, M. 'John Thelwall's political ambivalence: reform and revolution', A60, 69–83.

2600. Semmel, Stuart. 'British radicals and "legitimacy": Napoleon in the mirror of history', *Past & Present* 167 (2000), 140–75.

2601. Shaw, John Stuart. *The political history of eighteenth-century Scotland* (Basingstoke: Macmillan, 1999), vii, 151p.

2602. Stewart, James A. (Jr.) 'Lost Highland manuscripts and the Jacobite rebellion of 1745–46', A18, 287–308.

2603. Turner, B. 'A loyal Englishman? John Lloyd and aspects of oath-taking in 1812', A60, 133–42.

2604. Turner, Michael J. *The age of unease: government and reform in Britain, 1782–1832* (Stroud: Sutton, 2000), x, 310p.

J. *Military*

See also 517 (B); 2115–16, 2120, 2122 (F); 2410, 2492 (G); 3539, 3557 (H); 5108 (J); 5940 (N)

2605. Blake, Nicholas; Lawrence, Richard. *The illustrated companion to Nelson's navy* (London: Chatham, 1999), 207p.

2606. Carman, William Y. 'A Grenadier cap of 1745', *Journal of the Society for Army Historical Research* 78:315 (2000), 161–2.

2607. Colfer, W. 'Lieutenant Colonel Charles Bevan, Kings Own Royal Lancaster Regiment. 4th Foot 1786–1811', *British Historical Society of Portugal Annual Report* 26 (1999), 77–102.

2608. Cormack, Andrew. 'Captain Henry Mark Mason, 19th Light Dragoons, c.1760', *Journal of the Society for Army Historical Research* 78 (2000), 1–2.

2609. Day, Alan. 'A Russian army on Guernsey and Jersey (1799)', *Review of the Guernsey Society* 53:2 (1997), 40–45. [Originally appeared in *Army Quarterly & Defence Journal* 126 (1996).]

2610. Ennis, Daniel J. 'Naval impressment in Tobias Smollett's *Roderick Random*', *Albion* 32:2 (2000), 232–47.

2611. Goodwin, Peter. 'The development of the orlop deck of HMS *Victory*', *Mariner's Mirror* 83:2 (1997), 460–6.

2612. Hill, John (comp.) *Hertfordshire militia lists: Cheshunt, combining Street, Woodside and Waltham Cross Ward* (Militia ser., 97–100) ([St. Albans]: Hertfordshire Family Population History Society, 1999), 4 vols.

2613. Krajeski, Paul C. *In the shadow of Nelson: the naval leadership of Admiral Sir Charles Cotton, 1753–1812* (Westport (CT) and London: Greenwood, 2000), xx, 219p.

2614. Light, Kenneth H. 'The Portuguese and British navies 1750–1815', *British Historical Society of Portugal Annual Report* 26 (1999), 37–48.

2615. Lincoln, Margarette. 'Naval ship launches as public spectacle 1773–1854', *Mariner's Mirror* 83:2 (1997), 466–72.

2616. Linney-Drouet, C.A. 'British military dress from contemporary newspapers, 1682–1799: extracts from the notebook of the Revd Percy Sumner', *Journal of the Society for Army Historical Research* 78:314 (2000), 81–101.

2617. Macinnes, Allan I. 'Slaughter under trust: clan massacres and British state formation', *War and Genocide* 1 (1999), 127–48.

2618. Malcomson, Robert. 'HMS *St Lawrence*: the freshwater first-rate', *Mariner's Mirror* 83:2 (1997), 419–33.

2619. Pringle, Denys; Ewart, Gordon; Ruckley, Nigel. '". . . an old pentagonal fort built of stone": excavation of the battery wall at Fort Charlotte', *Post-Medieval Archaeology* 34 (2000), 105–43.

2620. Quinault, Roland. 'The French invasion of Pembrokeshire in 1797: a bicentennial assessment', *Welsh History Review* 19:4 (1999), 618–42.

2621. Robertson, James. *The first Highlander: Major-General David Stewart of Garth CB* (East Linton: Tuckwell, 1997), 199p.

2622. Sloss, Janet. *A small affair: the French occupation of Menorca during the Seven Years War* (Tetbury: Bonaventura, 2000), xiv, 96p.

K. Foreign Affairs

See also 2059 (F); 2284, 2410–12, 2423, 2445, 2593 (G); 3576 (H); 6687 (P)

2623. Bacot, Guillaume. 'Rousseau et la nation anglaise: "en dire le mal ainsi que le bien"' [Rousseau and the British nation: 'say what is bad as well as what is good'], *Revue française d'histoire des idées politiques* 12 (2000), 251–64.

2624. Bower, Peter. 'Economic warfare: banknote forgery as a deliberate weapon', A104, 46–63. [British forgery of French assignats as a means of destabilising the revolutionary regime.]

2625. Boyer, Pierre-Xavier. 'Raison et tradition: le cas anglais chez les idéologues' [Reason and tradition: the English case among the ideologues], *Revue française d'histoire des idées politiques* 12 (2000), 287–306.

2626. Cetre, F.O. 'Beresford, Marshall of Portugal', *British Historical Society of Portugal Annual Report* 26 (1999), 123–33.

2627. Dupuy, Pascal. 'Le 18 Brumaire en Grande-Bretagne: le témoignage de la presse et des caricatures' [The 18 Brumaire coup as represented in the British press and caricatures], *Annales historiques de la Révolution Française* 4 (1999), 773–87.

2628. Fidler, David P.; Welsh, Jennifer M. (eds.) *Empire and community: Edmund Burke's writings and speeches on international relations* (Boulder (CO): Westview, 1999), xv, 353p.

2629. Harding, Nicholas B. 'North African piracy, the Hanoverian carrying trade, and the British state, 1728–1828', *Historical Journal* 43 (2000), 25–47.

2630. Kremeier, Jarl. 'Drei Audienzen des englischen Gesandten Onslow Burrish bei Fürstbishof Friedrich Karl von Schönborn in den Jahren 1745 und 1746' [Three audiences of the British ambassador Onslow Burrish with the Prince-Bishop [of Franconia] Friedrich Karl von Schönborn in 1745 and 1746], *Mainfränkisches Jahrbuch für Geschichte und Kunst* 50 (1998), 76–86.

2631. Tillet, Édouard. 'Modèle anglais et modèle américain de l'Ancien régime à la Révolution: l'exemple de Jean-Nicolas Démeunier' [British model and American model from the Ancien Regime to the Revolution: the example of Démeunier], *Revue française d'histoire des idées politiques* 12 (2000), 265–86.

H. BRITAIN 1815–1914

A. *General*

See also 243 (B); 1331 (F); 3597 (I); 5117 (K)

2632. Briggs, Asa. 'Britain 1900', *History Today* 50:12 (2000), 31–37.
2633. Davis, John. 'Modern London', A210, 125–50.
2634. Ifans, Dafydd. 'Francis Kilvert and Wales', *Transactions of the Honourable Society of Cymmrodorion* ns 6 (1999), 66–89.
2635. Clinton, Catherine (ed.) *Fanny Kemble's journals* (Cambridge (MA): Harvard University Press, 2000), 201p.
2636. Knox, William W. *The industrial nation: work, culture and society in Scotland, 1800–present* (Edinburgh: Edinburgh University Press, 1999), xv, 368p.
2637. Matthew, Colin. 'Introduction: the United Kingdom and the Victorian century, 1815–1901' [The nineteenth century: the British Isles 1815–1901], A145, 1–40.
2638. Matthew, Colin. 'Conclusion: *fin-de-siècle*', A145, 293–99.
2639. Pugh, Martin. *Britain since 1789: a concise history* (Basingstoke and New York: Macmillan and St Martin's Press, 1999), x, 254p. [1st published as *Storia della Gran Bretagna, 1789–1990* (Roma: La Nuova Italia Scientifica, 1997).]
2640. Ziegler, Philip. *Britain then & now* [the Francis Frith Collection] (London: Weidenfeld & Nicolson, 1999), 429p.

B. *Historiography and Historical Methods*

See also 304 (B); 1338 (F); 2151, 2197 (G); 3523, 3532 (H); 3605, 3611 (I)

2641. Boase, Frederic. *Modern English biography: containing many thousand concise memoirs of persons who have died since the year 1850. With an index of the most interesting matter* (Bristol: Thoemmes, 2000), 6 vols. [1st published London, 1892–1921.]

2642. Dintenfass, Michael. 'Converging accounts, misleading metaphors and persistent doubts: reflections on the historiography of Britain's "decline"', A69, 7–26.

2643. Kidd, Alan J. 'Between antiquary and academic: local history in the nineteenth century', A182.

2644. Mitchell, Rosemary. *Picturing the past: English history in text and image, 1830–1870* (Oxford: Clarendon, 2000), xi, 314p.

2645. Parker, Christopher. *The English idea of history from Coleridge to Collingwood* (Aldershot: Ashgate, 2000), [vii], 244p.

2646. Soffer, Reba N. 'Was it possible to be a good Catholic, a good Englishman, and a good historian?', A138.

2647. Wawn, Andrew. *The Vikings and the Victorians: inventing the old north in nineteenth-century Britain* (Cambridge: Brewer, 2000), xiii, 434p.

2648. Weiner, G. 'Harriet Martineau and her contemporaries: past studies and methodological questions on historical surveys of women', *History of Education* 29:5 (2000), 389–404.

C. Population and Environment

See also 1340–1, 1345–7, 1349–50, 1355, 1357, 1359, 1361, 1365, 1367 (F); 2155–8, 2162–4, 2166 (G); 3209 (H); 3630 (I); 5012, 5014 (J); 5141 (K)

2649. Archer, Ian; Jordan, Spencer; Ramsey, Keith (comps.) *Abstract of Bristol historical statistics*, 4 parts.: 1. *Poor law 1835–1948*; 2. *Unemployment 1910–1997*; 3. *Political representation and Bristol's elections 1700–1997*; 4. *Health 1838–1995* (Bristol: Bristol Historical Databases Project, University of West of England, 1997).

2650. Basu, P. 'Sites of memory—sources of identity: landscape-narratives of the Sutherland clearances', A8, 225–36.

2651. Beckett, J. 'Chronicling the British industrial city' [review article], *Journal of Urban History* 26:1 (1999), 83–91.

2652. Cullen, L.M. 'Ireland and Scotland: famines and migrants' [review article], *Scottish Economic & Social History* 19:2 (1999), 155–62.

2653. Deacon, B. 'A forgotten migration stream: the Cornish movement to England and Wales in the nineteenth century', *Cornish Studies* 6 (1998), 96–117.

2654. Driver, Felix; Gilbert, David. 'Imperial cities: overlapping territories, intertwined histories', A71, 1–17.

2655. Duncan, C.J.; Duncan, S.R.; Scott, S. 'The dynamics of scarlet fever epidemics in England and Wales in the 19th century', *Epidemiology and Infection* 117:3 (1996), 493–99.

2656. Eckstein, Briony; Hinde, Andrew. 'Measuring fertility within marriage between 1841 and 1891 using parish registers and the census enumerators' books', *Local Population Studies* 64 (2000), 38–53.

2657. Hassan, John. 'Dealing with coastal pollution in health resorts in England and Wales, 1800–1960: policies and politics of local authorities', *Jahrbuch für Europäische Verwaltungsgeschichte* 11 (1999), 163–82.

2658. Hennock, E. Peter. 'The urban sanitary movement in England and Germany, 1838–1914: a comparison', *Continuity and Change* 15:2 (2000), 269–96.

2659. Hogg, Jimmy. 'Cockenzie and Port Seton: from village to burgh 1860–1914', *Transactions of the East Lothian Antiquarian and Field Naturalists' Society* 23 (1996), 35–44.

2660. Howells, Gary. 'Emigration and the new Poor Law: the Norfolk emigration fever of 1836', *Rural History* 11:2 (2000), 145–64.

2661. Kinchin, Juliet; Bird, Liz; Howarth, Thomas. 'Second city of the empire: Glasgow 1880–1920', A30, 27–42.

2662. le Pard, Gordon. 'The Great Storm of 1824', *Proceedings of the Dorset Natural History and Archaeological Society* 121 (1999), 23–36.

2663. Martin, Moira. ' "A future not of riches but of comfort": the emigration of pauper children from Bristol to Canada, 1870–1915', *Immigrants & Minorities* 19:1 (2000), 25–52.

2664. Michie, Ranald C. 'The City of London: functional and spatial unity in the nineteenth century', A65, 189–206.

2665. Morris, Robert John. 'The industrial town', A210, 175–208.

2666. Nicholls, Alice. 'Fenland ague in the nineteenth century', *Medical History* 44:4 (2000), 513–30.

2667. Reid, A. 'Locality or class? Spatial and social differentials in infant and child mortality in England and Wales, 1895–1911', A53, 129–54.

2668. Schwarz, Bill. 'Afterword: postcolonial times: the visible and the invisible', A71, 268.

2669. Skillen, Brian S. 'Land use and urban history in the Glasgow context', *Scottish Archives* 5 (1999), 57–62.

2670. Swift, R. 'Historians and the Irish: recent writings on the Irish in nineteenth-century Britain', *Immigrants & Minorities* 18:2–3 (1999), 14–39.

2671. Tyack, Geoffrey. 'The public face' [of the English urban landscape], A210, 290–315.

2672. Verrinder, D. 'Why did England and Wales suffer accelerated population decline in the late nineteenth century?', *Nutrition and Health* 8:4 (1992), 223.

2673. Withers, C.W.J. 'Authorizing landscape: "authority", naming and the Ordnance Survey's mapping of the Scottish Highlands in the nineteenth century', *Journal of Historical Geography* 26:4 (2000), 532–54.

2674. Woods, R.; Williams, N.; Galley, Chris. 'Differential mortality patterns among infants and other young children: the experience of England and Wales in the nineteenth century', A53, 57–72.

2675. Woods, R.; Shelton, N. 'Disease environments in Victorian England and Wales', *Historical Methods* 33:2 (2000), 73–82.

Da. *Social Life and Conditions*

2676. Bartley, Paula. 'Moral regeneration: women and the civic gospel in Birmingham, 1870–1914', *Midland History* 25 (2000), 143–61.

2677. Battarel, Myriam. 'James Phillips Kay et la condition des ouvriers d'usine à Manchester en 1832' [James Phillips Kay and the condition of factory workers in Manchester in 1832 (from *The Moral and Physical Condition of the Working Classes employed in the Cotton Manufacture in Manchester*, 1832)], A37, 33–40.

2678. Blaen, Angela. '"A form of love": the traditional healing of Donald Hannaford, Devon farmer', *Devonshire Association Report and Transactions* 131 (1999), 253–8.

2679. Blondeau, Aurélie. 'Andrew Mearns et William Carnall Preston: L'âpre plainte des exclus de Londres (1883)' [*The Bitter Cry of Outcast London*, 1883], A37, 78–97.

2680. Booth, Alison. 'The lessons of the medusa: Anna Jameson and collective biographies of women', *Victorian Studies* 42 (1999), 257–88.

2681. Boussahba-Bravard, Myriam. 'E. Mahler et E.F. Rathbone analysent le paiement des marins de Liverpool et le sort de leur famille en 1911' [E. Mahler and E.F. Rathbone's analysis of Liverpool seamen's pay and their families' plight, 1911 (from *Payment of Seamen: The present System—How the Wives Suffer*, 1911)], A37, 133–43.

2682. Breward, Christopher. 'Sartorial spectacle: clothing and masculine identities in the imperial city, 1860–1914', A71, 238–53.

2683. Bunyan, Stephen. 'A shy lady and her estates: a study of the Hon. M.G. Constance Nisbet Hamilton Ogilvy 1843–1920', *Transactions of the East Lothian Antiquarian and Field Naturalists' Society* 23 (1996), 113–29.

2684. Burnett, John. *Liquid pleasures: a social history of drinks in modern Britain* (London: Routledge, 1999), 224p.

2685. Burton, Valerie. 'Whoring, drinking sailors: reflections on masculinity from the labour history of nineteenth-century British shipping', A211, 84–101.

2686. Busteed, Mervyn A. '"Persons who are in a species of exile": varieties of Irishness amongst Irish migrants in mid-nineteenth century Manchester', A167, 57–75.

2687. Butterill, Carol. 'The temperance movement in York: 1830–1845', *York Historian* 17 (2000), 62–71.

2688. Campbell, J.D. '"Training for sport is training for war": sport and the transformation of the British army, 1860–1914', *International Journal of the History of Sport* 17:4 (2000), 21–58.

2689. Carré, Jacques. 'Les pauvres et le mariage à Lambeth (Londres) en 1913 selon Maud Pember Reeves' [The poor and marriage in Lambeth 1913 according to Maud Pember Reeves (from *Round about a Pound a Week*, 1913)], A37, 145–55.

2690. Chinn, Carl. *From little acorns grow: 150 years of the West Bromwich Building Society* (Studley: Brewin, 1999), 206p.

2691. Chinn, Carl. *Homes for people: council housing and urban renewal in Birmingham, 1849–1999* (Studley: Brewin, 1999), 192p.

2692. Clegg, Edward K. 'At the dawn of the new century: extracts from the diary of William Henry Stott (1852–1935) of West Vale for 1900', *Transactions of the Halifax Antiquarian Society* ns 8 (2000), 150–68.

2693. Craig, Simon. 'Riding high' [Arthur Linton and drug abuse in sport, c.1896], *History Today* 50:7 (2000), 18–19.

2694. Crowther, Janice E.; Crowther, Peter A. (eds.) *The diary of Robert Sharp of South Cave: life in a Yorkshire village 1812–1837* (Oxford: Oxford University Press for the British Academy, 1997), lvi, 667p.

2695. D'Cruze, Shani (ed.) *Everyday violence in Britain, 1850–1950: gender and class* (Harlow: Longman, 1999), xii, 233p.

2696. Durack, John; Gilbert, George; Marks, John. *The bumps: an account of the Cambridge University bumping races 1827–1999* (Cambridge: G. Gilbert, 2000), vi, 133p.

2697. Ellenberger, Nancy W. 'Constructing George Wyndham: narratives of aristocratic masculinity in fin-de-siècle England', *Journal of British Studies* 39:4 (2000), 487–517.

2698. Evans, R.H. 'Fathers, sons and brothers: two Victorian families', *Transactions of the Leicestershire Archaeological and Historical Society* 72 (1998), 146–53.

2699. Fern, Khinlyn. 'Visitors' book for the Loyalty Theatre, Dorchester', *Proceedings of the Dorset Natural History and Archaeological Society* 121 (1999), 145–50.

2700. Gates, Barbara T. *Kindred nature: Victorian and Edwardian women embrace the living world* (Chicago (IL) and London: University of Chicago Press, 1998), xv, 293p.

2701. Gillies, Midge. *Marie Lloyd: the one and only* (London: Gollancz, 1999), xii, 338p.

2702. Gorlach, M. 'Attitudes towards British English dialects in the 19th century', *Leeds Studies in English* 30 (1999), 137–64.

2703. Guillaume, André. 'Henry Mayhew parmi les Irlandais des rues à Londres au milieu du XIXe siècle' [Henry Mayhew among Irish costermongers in mid 19th-century London (from *London Labour and the London Poor*, 1851)], A37, 41–75.

2704. Hagen, Grace. 'Women and poverty in south west Wales, 1834–1914', *Llafur* 7:3–4 (1999), 21–34.

2705. Hallas, Christine. *Rural responses to industrialization: the North Yorkshire Pennines 1790–1914* (New York: Peter Lang, 1999), x, 348p.

2706. Hammerton, A.J. 'The English weakness? Gender, satire and "moral manliness" in the lower middle class, 1870–1920', A122, 164–82.

2707. Harvey, A.D. 'Prostitution in Cardiff in 1908', *Archives* 25:103 (2000), 117–22.

2708. Hibbert, Christopher. *Queen Victoria: a personal history* (London: HarperCollins, 2000), xviii, 557p.

2709. Hilton, Matthew. *Smoking in British popular culture, 1800–2000: perfect pleasures* (Manchester: Manchester University Press, 2000), xii, 284p.

2710. Holt, Ysanne. 'London types', *London Journal* 25:1 (2000), 34–51.

2711. Hopkins, Eric. *Industrialisation and society: a social history, 1830–1951* (London: Routledge, 2000), x, 308p.

2712. Howarth, Janet. 'Gender, domesticity, and sexual politics', A145, 163–94.

2713. Howell, P. 'A private Contagious Diseases Act: prostitution and public space in Victorian Cambridge', *Journal of Historical Geography* 26:3 (2000), 376–402.

2714. Huggins, Mike J. 'Culture, class and respectability: racing and the English middle classes in the nineteenth century', *International Journal of the History of Sport* 11:1 (1994), 19.

2715. Huggins, Mike J. *Flat racing and British society, 1790–1914: a social and economic history* (London: Cass, 2000), xv, 270p.

2716. Huggins, Mike J. 'More sinful pleasures?: leisure, respectability and the male middle classes in Victorian England', *Journal of Social History* 33 (1999), 585–600.

2717. Huggins, Mike J. 'The first generation of street bookmakers in Victorian England', *Northern History* 36 (2000), 129–45.

2718. Hunt, Karen. 'Negotiating the boundaries of the domestic: British socialist women and the politics of consumption', *Women's History Review* 9:2 (2000), 389–410.

2719. Jarvie, G. 'Sport, Gaelic nationalism and Scottish politics 1879–1920', *Liikuntatieteellisen Seuran Julkaisu* 134 (1999), 156–63.

2720. Johnes, Martin. '"Poor Man's Cricket": baseball, class and community in south Wales c.1880–1950', *International Journal of the History of Sport* 17:4 (2000), 153–66.

2721. Jones, Dot. *Statistical evidence relating to the Welsh language 1801–1911* (Cardiff: University of Wales Press, 1998), xiv, 519p.

2722. Judge, R. 'The "country dancers" in the Cambridge Comus of 1908', *Folklore* 110 (1999), 25–38.

2723. Kanya-Forstner, M. 'Defining womanhood: Irish women and the Catholic church in Victorian Liverpool', *Immigrants & Minorities* 18:2–3 (1999), 168–88.

2724. Lamplugh, Lois. *Parson Jack Russell of Swimbridge* (Swimbridge: Wellspring, 1994), 27p.

2725. Larsen, Timothy. 'Thomas Cook, Holy Land pilgrims, and the dawn of the modern tourist industry', *Studies in Church History* 36 (2000), 329–42.

2726. Laybourn, Keith (ed.) *Social conditions, status and community, 1860–c.1920* (Stroud: Sutton, 1997), viii, 241p.

2727. Lelong, O. 'The prospect of the sea: responses to forced coastal resettlement in nineteenth century Sutherland', A8, 217–24.

2728. Levine-Clark, Marjorie. 'Dysfunctional domesticity: female insanity and family relationships among the West Riding poor in the mid-nineteenth century', *Journal of Family History* 25:3 (2000), 341–61.

2729. Lindsay, Jean. '"Feed my lambs": an account of child poverty in north Wales in the late Victorian era', *Caernarvonshire Historical Society Transactions* 61 (2000), 89–97.

2730. Lipkes, Jeff. 'Virtue and necessity: the bonds of marriage and the political economy of J.S. Mill and F.W. Newman', *Albion* 31:4 (1999), 589–609.

2731. Logan, Deborah. 'An "outstretched hand to the fallen": *The Magdalen's Friend* and the Victorian reclamation movement. Pt. 1', *Victorian Periodicals Review* 30 (1997), 368–87.

2732. Logan, Deborah. 'An "outstretched hand to the fallen": *The Magdalen's Friend* and the Victorian reclamation movement. Pt. 2', *Victorian Periodicals Review* 31 (1998), 125–41.

2733. Maas, H. 'Pacifying the workman: Ruskin and Jevons on labor and popular culture', *History of Political Economy* 31 (suppl.) (2000), 85–120.

2734. Mandler, Peter. 'Mansions of England: the public status of the private house 1830–1880', A3.

2735. McCready, Richard B. 'Revising the Irish in Scotland: the Irish in nineteenth- and early twentieth-century Scotland', A15, 37–50.

2736. O'Leary, Paul. *Immigration and integration: the Irish in Wales, 1798–1922* (Cardiff: University of Wales Press, 2000), xv, 340p.

2737. Parratt, C.M. 'Making leisure work: women's rational recreation in late Victorian and Edwardian England', *Journal of Sport History* 26:3 (1999), 471–88.

2738. Pécastaing-Boissière, M. 'Les actrices travesties à l'époque victorienne' [Actresses in breeches roles in the Victorian era], *Cahiers victoriens et édouardiens* 51 (2000).

2739. Perkin, Joan. 'From strolling player to banker-duchess', *History Today* 50:10 (2000), 19–28.

2740. Perry, R. '"The breadwinners": gender, locality and diversity in late Victorian and Edwardian Cornwall', *Cornish Studies* 8 (2000), 115–126.

2741. Picker, John M. 'The soundproof study: Victorian professionals, work space, and urban noise', *Victorian Studies* 42:3 (2000), 427–53.

2742. Pooley, C.G.; Turnbull, J. 'Moving through the city: the changing impact of the journey to work on intra-urban mobility in XIXth century Britain', *Annales de Démographie Historique* (1999), 127–50.

2743. Prunet, Monique. 'Charles Booth et la condition des dockers de Londres en 1889' [Charles Booth and the London dockers' condition in 1889 (from *Life and Labour of the People in London*, 1889–1902)], A37, 99–120.

2744. Ranfurley, Hermione countess of. *The ugly one: the childhood memoirs of Hermione, Countess of Ranfurly, 1913–1939* (London: Michael Joseph, 1998), 201p.

2745. Ravilious, C.P. 'Brighton's public chess room, 1873–1914', *Sussex Archaeological Collections* 135 (1997), 283–96.

2746. Rendel, Margherita. 'Households in Torquay headed by women in 1851', *Devonshire Association Report and Transactions* 131 (1999), 199–220.

2747. Ring, Jim. *How the English made the Alps* (London: John Murray, 2000), xii, 288p.

2748. Ritchie, A. 'The origins of bicycle racing in England: technology, entertainment, sponsorship, and advertising in the early history of the sport', *Journal of Sport History* 26:3 (1999), 489–520.

2749. Roderick, Gordon W. 'Self-improvement and the Welsh mineworker', *Llafur* 7:3–4 (1999), 35–49.

2750. Sigel, L.Z. 'Filth in the wrong people's hands: postcards and the expansion of pornography in Britain and the Atlantic world, 1880–1914', *Journal of Social History* 33:4 (2000), 859–86.

2751. Smith, Pete. 'Welbeck Abbey and the 5th Duke of Portland: eccentricity or philanthropy?', A3.

2752. Sokoll, Thomas. 'Negotiating a living: Essex pauper letters from London, 1800–1834', *International Review of Social History* supplement 8 (2000), 19–46.

2753. Stevens, Catrin. '"The funeral made the attraction": the social and economic functions of funerals in nineteenth-century Wales', A93, 83–104.

2754. Teo, Hsu-Ming. 'Women's travel, dance, and British metropolitan anxieties, 1890–1939', *Gender & History* 12:2 (2000), 366–400.

2755. Thomas, J. 'The adulteress's "egg": infidelity and maternity in past and present', *Nineteenth Century Contexts* 21:3 (1999), 371–94.

2756. Thompson, Brian John William. *A monkey among crocodiles: the life, loves and lawsuits of Mrs Georgina Weldon* (London: HarperCollins, 2000), xvi, 304p.

2757. Trezise, S. 'The Celt, the Saxon and the Cornishman: stereotypes and counter-stereotypes of the Victorian period', *Cornish Studies* 8 (2000), 54–68.

2758. Tromp, Marlene. *The private rod: marital violence, sensation, and the law in Victorian Britain* (Charlottesville (VA) and London: University Press of Virginia, 2000), x, 289p.

2759. Tusan, Michelle Elizabeth. 'Inventing the new woman: print culture and identity politics during the fin-de-siècle', *Victorian Periodicals Review* 31 (1998), 169–82.

2760. Twells, A. '"A Christian and civilised land": the British middle class and the civilising mission, 1820–42', A122, 47–64.

2761. Tyrrell, Alex. 'Samuel Smiles and the woman question in early Victorian Britain', *Journal of British Studies* 39:2 (2000), 185–216.

2762. Walton, John K. 'The pleasures of urbanity', A210, 269–89.

2763. Whitton, Timothy. 'Seebohm Rowntree distingue pauvreté primaire et pauvreté secondaire à York en 1899' [Seebohm Rowntree distinguishes between primary and secondary poverty in York, 1899 (from *Poverty: A Study of Town Life*, 1901)], A37, 11–19.

2764. Wilton, Iain. *C.B. Fry: an English hero* (London: Richard Cohen, 1999), xiv, 498p.

2765. Windholz, Anne M. 'An emigrant and a gentleman: imperial masculinity, British magazines, and the colony that got away' [the United States of America], *Victorian Studies* 42:4 (2000), 631–58.

Db. *Social Structure*

See also 1361, 1438, 1443 (F); 2200, 2209–10, 2212, 2404 (G); 2933 (H); 6192 (P)

2766. Bagenal, T.B. 'Mortality rate estimates of Gunnerside lead miners from the censuses', *British Mining* 59 (1997), 79–88.

2767. Belchem, John; Hardy, Nick. 'Second metropolis: the middle class in early Victorian Liverpool', A123, 58–71.

2768. Belchem, John. 'The Liverpool-Irish enclave', *Immigrants & Minorities* 18:2–3 (1999), 128–46.

2769. Black, Alistair. 'Skeleton in the cupboard: social class and the public library in Britain through 150 years', *Library History* 16 (2000), 3–12.

2770. Busteed, Mervyn A. 'Little islands of Erin: Irish settlement and identity in mid-nineteenth-century Manchester', *Immigrants & Minorities* 18:2–3 (1999), 94–127.

2771. Claeys, Gregory. 'The "survival of the fittest" and the origins of social Darwinism', *Journal of the History of Ideas* 61:2 (2000), 223–40.

2772. Crossick, Geoffrey. 'La bourgeoisie britannique an 19e siècle: recherches, approches, problématiques', *Annales* 53 (1998), 1089–130.

2773. Davis, Graham. 'The Irish in Britain, 1815–1939', A15, 19–36.

2774. di Felice, P. 'Italians in Manchester 1891–1939: settlement and occupations', *The Local Historian* 30:2 (2000), 88–104.

2775. Dintenfass, Michael. 'Service, loyalty and leadership: the life tales of British coal masters and the culture of the middle class, c.1890–1950', A123, 214–27.

2776. Dintenfass, Michael. 'The voice of industry and the ethos of decline: business citizenship, public service and the making of a British industrial élite', A69, 175–88.

2777. Finestein, Israel. *Anglo-Jewry in changing times: studies in diversity, 1840–1914* (London: Vallentine Mitchell, 1999), xvi, 265p.

2778. Garrard, John; Parrott, Vivienne. 'Craft, professional and middle-class identity: solicitors and gas engineers, c.1850–1914', A123, 148–68.

2779. Gray, Robert. 'The platform and the pulpit: cultural networks and civic identities in industrial towns, c.1850–70', A123, 130–47.

2780. Grayson, Ruth. 'Who was master? Class relationships in nineteenth-century Sheffield', A123, 42–57.

2781. Gritt, A.J. 'The census and the servant: a reassessment of the decline and distribution of farm service in early nineteenth-century England', *Economic History Review* 2nd ser. 53 (2000), 84–106.

2782. Gunn, S. 'The middle class, modernity and the provincial city: Manchester, c.1840–80', A122, 112–28.

2783. Gunn, S. 'The public sphere, modernity and consumption: new perspectives on the history of the English middle class', A122, 12–33.

2784. Hall, Lesley A. *Sex, gender and social change in Britain since 1880* (Basingstoke: Macmillan, 2000), [viii], 254p.

2785. Holmes, Heather. '"An abject and deplorable existence": problems faced by Irish women migratory potato workers in Scotland in the early twentieth century', *Folk Life* 38 (2000), 42–55.

2786. Jennings, Paul. 'Occupations in the nineteenth century censuses: the drink retailers of Bradford, West Yorkshire', *Local Population Studies* 64 (2000), 23–37.

2787. Lahiri, Shompa. *Indians in Britain: Anglo-Indian encounters, race, and identity: 1880–1930* (London: Cass, 2000), xviii, 249p.

2788. MacRaild, Donald M. 'Crossing migrant frontiers: comparative reflections on Irish migrants in Britain and the United States during the nineteenth century', *Immigrants & Minorities* 18:2–3 (1999), 40–70.

2789. MacRaild, Donald M. 'Introduction: The Great Famine and beyond: Irish migrants in Britain in the nineteenth and twentieth centuries', *Immigrants & Minorities* 18:2–3 (1999), 1–13.

2790. Mandler, Peter. '"Race" and "nation" in mid-Victorian thought', A47, 224–44.

2791. Miles, Andrew. *Social mobility in nineteenth- and early twentieth-century England* (Basingstoke and New York: Macmillan and St Martin's Press, 1999), xiv, 262p.

2792. Morris, Robert John. 'Reading the will: cash economy capitalists and urban peasants in the 1830s', A123, 113–29.

2793. Neal, F. 'The foundations of the Irish settlement in Newcastle upon Tyne: the evidence in the 1851 census', *Immigrants & Minorities* 18:2–3 (1999), 71–93.

2794. Nicholas, Tom. 'Wealth making in the nineteenth and early twentieth century: the Rubinstein hypothesis revisited', *Business History* 42:2 (2000), 155–68. [With response, no.2796.]

2795. Quail, John M. 'From personal patronage to public school privilege: social closure in the recruitment of managers in the United Kingdom from the late nineteenth century to 1930', A123, 169–85.

2796. Rubinstein, William D. 'Wealth making in the late nineteenth and early twentieth centuries: a response', *Business History* 42:2 (2000), 141–54. [Responds to no.2794.]

2797. Smith, John. 'Urban elites c. 1830–1930 and urban history', *Urban History* 27:2 (2000), 255–75.

2798. Spencer, D. 'Reformulating the "closed" parish thesis: associations, interests, and interaction', *Journal of Historical Geography* 26:1 (2000), 83–98.

2799. Winstanley, Michael. 'Owners and occupiers: property, politics and middle-class formation in early industrial Lancashire', A123, 92–112.

2800. Woollard, Matthew. 'The classification of occupations in the 1881 census of England and Wales', *History and Computing* 10:1–3 (1998), 17–36.

2801. Worship, Vanessa. 'Cotton factory or workhouse: Poor Law assisted migration from Buckinghamshire to northern England, 1835–1837', *Family & Community History* 3 (2000), 33–48.

Dc. *Social Policy and Welfare*

See also 1468, 1471 (F); 2221, 2225 (G); 3751, 3758 (I)

2802. Beale, Norman. *Is that the doctor?: a history of the Calne GPs* (Calne: The author, 1998), 95p.

2803. Bradshaw, Jonathan; Sainsbury, Roy (eds.) *Getting the measure of poverty: the early legacy of Seebohm Rowntree* (Aldershot: Ashgate, 2000), xiv, 274p.

2804. Cherry, Stephen. 'Hospital Saturday, workplace collections and issues in late nineteenth-century hospital funding', *Medical History* 44:4 (2000), 461–88.

2805. Cody, Lisa Forman. 'The politics of illegitimacy in an age of reform: women, reproduction, and political economy in England's new Poor Law of 1834', *Journal of Women's History* 11 (2000), 131–56.

2806. Doody, G.A.; Beveridge, A.; Johnstone, E.C. 'Poor and mad: a study of patients admitted to the Fife and Kinross District Asylum between 1874 and 1899', *Psychological Medicine* 26:5 (1996), 887–97.

2807. Duckworth, Jeannie Shorey. 'The Cheltenham Female Orphan Asylum',
       Transactions of the Bristol and Gloucestershire Archaeological Society
       117 (1999), 141–9.
2808. Durbach, Nadja. '"They might as well brand us": working-class resistance
       to compulsory vaccination in Victorian England', *Social History of
       Medicine* 13 (2000), 45–62.
2809. Fisk, Audrey. 'Diversity within the friendly society movement 1834–1911:
       the value to community studies', *Family & Community History* 3 (2000),
       19–31.
2810. Gazeley, Ian; Newell, Andrew. 'Rowntree revisited: poverty in Britain,
       1900', *Explorations in Economic History* 37:2 (2000), 174–88.
2811. Gorsky, Martin. *Patterns of philanthropy: charity and society in nineteenth-
       century Bristol* (Royal Historical Society studies in history, ns)
       (Woodbridge: Royal Historical Society, 1999), xiv, 274p.
2812. Guilcher, Goulven. 'Le Parlement enquête sur la gestion d'un asile lon-
       donien en 1815' [Parliament enquires into the management of a London
       workhouse in 1815 (from *On the State of Mendicity in the Metropolis*
       (1815)], A37, 21–31.
2813. Harris, Jose. 'Political thought and the welfare state 1870–1940: an intel-
       lectual framework for British social policy', A90, 43–63. [1st published in
       Past & Present 135 (1992).]
2814. Jackson, Louise A. '"Singing birds as well as soap suds": the Salvation
       Army's work with sexually abused girls in Edwardian England', *Gender &
       History* 12 (2000), 107–26.
2815. Jackson, Louise A. 'Family, community and the regulation of child sexual
       abuse: London, 1870–1914', A81, 133–51.
2816. Levine-Clark, Margorie. 'Engendering relief: women, ablebodiedness, and
       the new Poor Law in early Victorian England', *Journal of Women's
       History* 11 (2000), 107–30.
2817. Lindsay, P. 'Overcoming false dichotomies: Mill, Marx and the Welfare
       State', *History of Political Thought* 21:4 (2000), 657–81.
2818. Marriott, John. 'Sweep them off the streets' [the London poor], *History
       Today* 50:8 (2000), 26–28.
2819. Pinches, Sylvia M. 'Lay charities in the diocese of Birmingham,
       1800–1918', *Catholic Ancestor* 8 (2000), 73–83.
2820. Roberts, Owen. 'The politics of health and the origins of Liverpool's Lake
       Vyrnwy water scheme, 1871–92', *Welsh History Review* 20:2 (2000),
       308–35.
2821. Sheard, Sally. 'Profit is a dirty word: the development of public baths and
       wash-houses in Britain 1847–1915', *Social History of Medicine* 13 (2000),
       63–85.
2822. Thane, Pat. 'The working class and state "welfare" in Britain, 1880–1914',
       A90, 86–112. [1st published in the *Historical Journal* 27:4 (1984).]

Ea. *Economic Activity and Organisation*

See also 378, 388, 408, 412, 418 (B); 1418, 1484–5, 1495, 1521, 1527–8 (F); 2226–7, 2229, 2238–9, 2241, 2244, 2246–8, 2250, 2252–3, 2258–9, 2265–6, 2268, 2273–5, 2279, 2281, 2283, 2286, 2345 (G); 2683, 2748, 2776, 2972, 3129–30, 3388, 3583, 3592 (H); 3791, 3814, 3824, 3870, 3873, 3887, 4004 (I); 6259 (P)

2823. Aldcroft, Derek Howard; Oliver, Michael J. *Trade unions and the economy: 1870–2000* (Aldershot: Ashgate, 2000), xi, 222p.

2824. Alford, B.W.E. 'Flagging or failing? British economic performance, 1880–1914', A69, 85–100.

2825. Andrews, Frank W.G. 'Employment on the railways in east Kent, 1841–1914', *Journal of Transport History* 3rd ser. 21:1 (2000), 54–72.

2826. Andrews, Ken. *Mr Bowler of Bath: Victorian entrepreneur and engineer* (Bristol: The author, 1998), 96p.

2827. Armstrong, John; Stevenson, Julie. 'Liverpool to Hull—by sea?', *Mariner's Mirror* 83:2 (1997), 150–68.

2828. Armstrong, John. 'Transport', A210, 209–32.

2829. Arnold, A.J. '"Of not much significance?" The inclusion of naval and foreign business in the UK shipbuilding output series, 1825–1914', *International Journal of Maritime History* [St John's, Newfoundland] 11:2 (1999), 61–86.

2830. Bagenal, T.B. *Miners and farmers: the agricultural holdings of the lead miners at Heights, Gunnerside, in north Yorkshire* (British Mining, 62) (Keighley: Northern Mine Research Society, 1999), 53p.

2831. Baldwin, T.J. *Cash flow and corporate finance in Victorian Britain: cases from the British coal industry, 1860–1914* (Exeter: University of Exeter Press, 2000), v, 152p.

2832. Bellamy, Joyce M.; Saville, John; Martin, David E. *Dictionary of labour biography*, vol.10 (Basingstoke: Macmillan, 2000), 288p.

2833. Blaszak, Barbara J. 'The gendered geography of the English co-operative movement at the turn of the nineteenth century', *Women's History Review* 9:3 (2000), 559–83.

2834. Bowman, A. 'Company formation in the 19th century slate industry', *British Mining* 63 (1999), 48–55.

2835. Braine, P.M. 'Railways, coastal shipping and canals: the Bristol Channel coal trade in the nineteenth century', *Working Papers in Railway Studies* 7 (2000), 36–40.

2836. Braine, P.M. 'Sully's coal yard, Bridgwater', *Journal of the Railway and Canal Historical Society* 32 (1998), 524–44.

2837. Bunker, Stephen. 'Houses built of straw: the influence of the hat trade in the shaping of Luton', *Costume* 30 (1996), 106–11.

2838. Bunker, Stephen. *Strawopolis: Luton transformed, 1840–1876* (Publications of the Bedfordshire Historical Record Society, 78) ([Bedford]: Bedfordshire Historical Record Society, 1999), x, 290p.

2839. Burchardt, Jeremy F.S. 'Potato grounds and allotments in nineteenth-century southern England', *Agricultural History* 74:3 (2000), 667–84.

2840. Burt, Roger. 'British investment in the American mining frontier', *Business and Economic History* 26:2 (1997), 515–25.

2841. Cain, Peter J. 'The City of London, 1880–1914: tradition and innovation', A69, 189–204.

2842. Campbell, Alan. *The Scottish miners, 1874–1939* (London: Ashgate, 2000), 2 vols.

2843. Candee, R.M. 'British framework knitters in New England: technology transfer and machine knitting in America 1820–1900', *Textile History* 31:1 (2000), 27–53.

2844. Carnegie, G.D.; Parker, R.H. 'Accountants and empire: the case of co-membership of Australian and British accountancy bodies, 1885 to 1914', *Accountancy, Business and Financial History* 9 (1999), 77–133.

2845. Chase, Malcolm. *Early trade unionism: fraternity, skill and the politics of labour* (Aldershot: Ashgate, 2000), [viii], 286p.

2846. Church, Roy. 'Advertising consumer goods in nineteenth-century Britain: reinterpretations', *Economic History Review* 2nd ser. 53:4 (2000), 621–45.

2847. Church, Roy. 'Ossified or dynamic?: structure, markets and the competitive process in the British business system of the nineteenth century', *Business History* 42:1 (2000), 1–20.

2848. Clark, Anna. 'The new Poor Law and the breadwinner wage: contrasting assumptions', *Journal of Social History* 34:2 (2000), 261–82.

2849. Clendinning, Anne. '"Deft fingers" and "persuasive eloquence": the "lady demons" of the English gas industry, 1888–1918', *Women's History Review* 9:3 (2000), 501–37.

2850. Compton, Hugh. 'Staffing Oxford canal—around 1851', *Cake and Cockhorse* 14 (2000), 230–46.

2851. Cottrell, Philip Leonard. 'Cities of finance: Liverpool and the Atlantic economies', A65, 135–50.

2852. Coull, James R. 'Penetrating and monitoring the market: the development of the continental market for Scottish herring in the nineteenth and early twentieth centuries', *Scottish Economic & Social History* 19:2 (1999), 117–31.

2853. Crowhurst, Basil. *A history of the British ice cream industry* (Westerham: Food Trade, 2000), xiv, 194p.

2854. Daunton, Martin. 'Society and economic life', A145, 41–84.

2855. David, R.G. 'The ice trade and the northern economy, 1840–1914', *Northern History* 36 (2000), 113–27.

2856. Diamond, Bryan. 'Isaac Diamond and the Jews in the timber trade in the East End, 1880–1910', *Jewish Historical Studies* 35 (1998), 255–76.

2857. Eddershaw, David. *A country brewery: Hook Norton, 1849–1999: the story of a family brewing tradition, published to mark its 150th anniversary* (Banbury: Hook Norton Brewery Company, 1999), 124p.

2858. Fairbairn, R.A. 'Stotfield Burn and Brandon Walls mines, 1872–1882', *British Mining* 61 (1998), 101–9.

2859. Faudell, C.L. *Dairy goat husbandry literature, 1875 to 1988: a short history* (Tiverton: LR Enterprise, 1998), 20p. [Text privately circulated in 1988.]

2860. Fisher, John. 'Property rights in pheasants: landlords, farmers and the game laws, 1860–80', *Rural History* 11:2 (2000), 165–80.

2861. Fletcher, David. 'The archive of the invisible: the Ordnance Survey's Boundary Record Library', *Archives* 25:103 (2000), 98–116.

2862. Fletcher, Scott R.; Godley, Andrew. 'Foreign direct investment in British retailing, 1850–1962', *Business History* 42:2 (2000), 43–62.

2863. Forster, Margaret. *Rich desserts & captain's thin: a family and their times 1831–1931* [Carr's of Carlisle] (London: Chatto & Windus, 1997), xvii, 284p.

2864. French, Michael; Phillips, Jim. *Cheated not poisoned?: food regulation in the United Kingdom, 1875–1938* (Manchester: Manchester University Press, 2000), 213p.

2865. Galbraith, Spence. 'William Hardcastle (1794–1860) of Newcastle upon Tyne, and his pupil John Snow' [apothecaries], *Archaeologia Aeliana* 5th ser. 27 (1999), 155–70.

2866. Garside, W.R. 'Regional vs national perspectives on economic "decline" in late Victorian and Edwardian Britain', A69, 139–51.

2867. Gill, B.G. 'The venture of the Central Asian Trading Company in eastern Turkistan, 1874–5', *Asian Affairs* 31:2 (2000), 181–88.

2868. Gordon, Eleanor; Nair, Gwyneth. 'The economic role of middle-class women in Victorian Glasgow', *Women's History Review* 9:4 (2000), 791–814.

2869. Gough, John. 'Railways: documentation and observation', *Transactions of the Leicestershire Archaeological and Historical Society* 74 (2000), 99–111.

2870. Greasley, David; Oxley, Les. 'British industrialization, 1815–1860: a dis-aggregate time-series perspective', *Explorations in Economic History* 37 (2000), 98–119.

2871. Greasley, David; Oxley, Les. 'Competitiveness and growth: new perspectives on the late Victorian and Edwardian economy', A69, 65–84.

2872. Greenlees, Janet. 'Equal pay for equal work?: a new look at gender and wages in the Lancashire cotton industry, 1790–1855', A211, 167–90.

2873. Gwyn, David. 'The archive of the north Wales slate industry', *Archives* 24:101 (1999), 44–52.

2874. Hadfield, Alice Mary. *The Chartist Land Company*, revised edn. (Aylesbury: Square Edge, 2000), v, 11–248p. [1st published Newton Abbot: David and Charles, 1970.]

2875. Hair, Nick; Cotton, Julian. 'Excavations at Parton Colliery', *Transactions of the Cumberland & Westmorland Antiquarian & Archaeological Society* 100 (2000), 241–60.

2876. Harvey, Charles; Press, Jon. 'Management and the Taff Vale strike of 1900', *Business History* 42:2 (2000), 63–86.

2877. Herbert, Adrian. 'The life of J.C. Beadle', *Dartford Historical & Antiquarian Society Newsletter* 36 (1999), 27–32.

2878. Heywood, Colin. 'Age and gender at the workplace: the historical experiences of young people in western Europe and North America', A211, 48–65.

2879. Hill, Carol. 'Galloway shipping and regional development, 1750–1850', *Scottish Economic & Social History* 19:2 (1999), 95–116.

2880. Horrell, Sara; Oxley, Deborah. 'Work and prudence: household responses to income variation in nineteenth-century Britain', *European Review of Economic History* 4 (2000), 27–57.

2881.   Hosgood, C.P. 'Mrs Pooter's purchase: lower-middle-class consumerism and the sales, 1870–1914', A122, 146–63.
2882.   Howe, Anthony. 'Free trade and the international order: the Anglo-American tradition, 1846–1946', A135, 142–67.
2883.   Howlett, Peter. 'Evidence of the existence of an internal labour market in the Great Eastern Railway Company, 1875–1905', *Business History* 42:1 (2000), 21–40.
2884.   Hurren, Elizabeth T. 'Agricultural trade unionism and the crusade against outdoor relief: poor law politics in the Brixworth Union, Northamptonshire, 1870–75', *Agricultural History Review* 48:2 (2000), 200–22.
2885.   Hutchinson, P. 'The Violin Plant at the Steel Company of Wales', *Historical Methods* 33:1 (1999), 43–50.
2886.   Jacob, Margaret C. 'Commerce, industry, and the laws of Newtonian science: Weber revisited and revised', *Canadian Journal of History* 35:2 (2000), 275–92.
2887.   Jaffe, James A. 'Industrial arbitration, equity, and authority in England, 1800–1850', *Law and History Review* 18:3 (2000), 525–58.
2888.   Jaffe, James A. *Striking a bargain: work and industrial relations in England, 1815–1865* (Manchester: Manchester University Press, 2000), ix, 273p.
2889.   Jenkins, David. 'Shipbuilding and shipowning in Montgomeryshire: the Evans family of Morben Isaf, Derwenlas', *Montgomeryshire Collections* 88 (2000), 63–86.
2890.   Johnson, Paul. 'Civilizing Mammon: laws, morals, and the City in nineteenth-century England', A29, 301–19.
2891.   Jordan, Ellen. *The women's movement and women's employment in nineteenth century Britain* (London: Routledge, 1999), xv, 261p.
2892.   Killick, J. 'An early nineteenth-century shipping line: The Cope Line of Philadelphia and Liverpool packets, 1822–1872', *International Journal of Maritime History* 12:1 (2000), 61–88.
2893.   Kim, Dong-Woon. 'Board minute books as a source for the study of a multinational enterprise: the case study of J. & P. Coats before 1914', *Business Archives* 80 (2000), 1–14.
2894.   Kuntz, Tom. *The* Titanic *disaster hearings: the official transcripts of the 1912 Senate investigation* (New York: Pocket, 1998), xviii, 571p.
2895.   Ley, A.J. *A history of building control in England and Wales, 1840–1990* (Coventry: RICS Books, 2000), xvii, 222p.
2896.   Lloyd-Jones, Roger; Lewis, Mervyn J. *Raleigh and the British bicycle industry: an economic and business history, 1870–1960* (Modern Economic and Social History Series) (Aldershot: Ashgate, 2000), [xiii], 303p.
2897.   Loftus, Donna. 'The self-made man: businessmen and their autobiographies in nineteenth century Britain', *Business Archives* 80 (2000), 15–30.
2898.   Mackay, James Alexander. *Little boss: a life of Andrew Carnegie* (Edinburgh: Mainstream, 1997), 320p.
2899.   MacRaild, Donald M.; Martin, David E. *Labour in British society, 1830–1914* (Basingstoke: Macmillan, 2000), xi, 214p.
2900.   Maenpaa, S. 'Galley news: catering personnel on British passenger liners, 1860–1938', *International Journal of Maritime History* 12:1 (2000), 243–60.

2901.   Maltby, J. '"A sort of guide, philosopher and friend": the rise of the professional auditor in Britain', *Accountancy, Business and Financial History* 9 (1999), 29–50.

2902.   Martell, H.M. 'Researching mining history in the UK', *British Mining* 63 (1999), 147–55.

2903.   Matthews, Stephen. 'The administration of the livestock census of 1866', *Agricultural History Review* 48:2 (2000), 223–28.

2904.   McBain, C.S. 'A pioneer of the spirit: Charles Cree Doig' [distillery engineer], *Scottish Industrial History* 20 (2000), 47–51.

2905.   McCaughan, Michael. *The birth of the Titanic* (Belfast: Blackstaff, 1998), 184p.

2906.   Messenger, Thomas. *'Dear Daughter': the Messenger letters: voyages of a sailing ship captain, 1890–1898,* ed. & intro. by Graham Hindle (Blackburn: John Gray, 1998), 191p.

2907.   Millward, Robert. 'Industrial performance, the infrastructure and government policy', A69, 47–64.

2908.   Miskell, L.; Whatley, C.A. '"Juteopolis" in the making: linen and the industrial transformation of Dundee, c.1820–1850', *Textile History* 30:2 (1999), 176–98.

2909.   Mohun, Arwen. *Steam laundries: gender, technology, and work in the United States and Great Britain, 1880–1940* (Baltimore (MD) and London: Johns Hopkins University Press, 1999), x, 348p.

2910.   Moss, Michael S. *Standard Life 1825–2000: the building of Europe's largest mutual life company* (Edinburgh: Mainstream, 2000), 431p.

2911.   Munn, C.W. 'The emergence of Edinburgh as a financial centre', A65, 151–66.

2912.   Neaverson, Peter. 'Califat Colliery, Swannington Common: site history and excavation report', *Transactions of the Leicestershire Archaeological and Historical Society* 74 (2000), 79–98.

2913.   Nicholas, Tom. 'Businessmen and land ownership in the late nineteenth century revisited', *Economic History Review* 2nd ser. 53:4 (2000), 777–82. [Replies to no.2933.]

2914.   Nichols, M.J. 'Straw plaiting and the straw hat industry in Britain', *Costume* 30 (1996), 112–24.

2915.   Nutting, T. 'The British hosiery and knitwear machine building industry since 1850', *Textile History* 30:2 (1999), 207–33.

2916.   Ollerenshaw, Philip; Wardley, Peter. 'Economic growth and the business community in Bristol since 1840', A70, 124–55.

2917.   Osborne, Harvey. 'The seasonality of nineteenth-century poaching', *Agricultural History Review* 48:1 (2000), 27–41.

2918.   Osborne, Keith W. *The brewers of Cromwell's county: a directory of commercial breweries in Huntingdonshire* (Wellingborough: The author, 1999), 113p.

2919.   Palmer, Marilyn. 'Housing the Leicester framework knitters: history and archaeology', *Transactions of the Leicestershire Archaeological and Historical Society* 74 (2000), 59–78.

2920.   Parham, D. 'The Severn, a Welsh brig lost in the Baltic', *Maritime Wales* 20 (1999), 12–15.

2921. Pari Huws, G.D. 'Tramwyo Traeth Lafan' [Menai Straits crossings before the bridge], *Maritime Wales* 20 (1999), 56–61.

2922. Rappaport, Erika D. *Shopping for pleasure: women in the making of London's West End* (Princeton (NJ): Princeton University Press, 2000), xiii, 323p.

2923. Raveux, Olivier. 'Un technicien britannique en Europe meridionale: Philip Taylor (1786–1870)', *Histoire, économie et société* 19:2 (2000), 253–66.

2924. Roberts, O. 'Rescued near Ynys Enlli/Bardsey, 1866', *Maritime Wales* 20 (1999), 53–55.

2925. Roberts, O. 'The Cound of Frights of the Margerd Davies', *Maritime Wales* 20 (1999), 37–44.

2926. Roffey, Ron A. *The co-operative way: the origins and progress of the Royal Arsenal and South Surburban Co-operative Societies* ([London]: Co-operative Wholesale Society, South East Region, 1999), 218p.

2927. Ross, Duncan M. 'Penny banks in Glasgow, 1850–1914', *Scottish Industrial History* 21 (2000), 34–53.

2928. Sass, J.A. 'Moulton Mill', *Lincolnshire History and Archaeology* 34 (1999), 16–18.

2929. Schwartz, S. '"No place for a woman": gender at work in Cornwall's metalliferous mining industry', *Cornish Studies* 8 (2000), 69–96.

2930. Sharp, Robert. 'A sad anniversary: the death of Maudsley Sons & Field', *Mariner's Mirror* 86 (2000), 75–78.

2931. Shirlaw, Jean H. 'Brewing in the Nungate and Haddington during the 19th and 20th century', *Transactions of the East Lothian Antiquarian and Field Naturalists' Society* 23 (1996), 105–11.

2932. Smith, D. Ian. 'James and George Brooker: west Cumberland shipcarvers of the mid-19th century', *Transactions of the Cumberland & Westmorland Antiquarian & Archaeological Society* 100 (2000), 207–23.

2933. Smith, Julia A. 'Land ownership and social change in late nineteenth-century Britain', *Economic History Review* 2nd ser. 53:4 (2000), 767–76. [Reply: no.2913.]

2934. Solman, David. *Loddiges of Hackney: the largest hothouse in the world* (London: Hackney Society, 1995), 96p.

2935. Solomou, Solomos; Catao, Luis. 'Effective exchange rates 1879–1913', *European Review of Economic History* 4:3 (2000), 361–82.

2936. Squires, Stewart; Russell, Rex. 'Claxby ironstone mine, Lincolnshire' [1868–85], *Lincolnshire History and Archaeology* 34 (1999), 46–58.

2937. Stammers, Michael. 'Anthracite for Wells-next-the-Sea, a by-way of the Swansea coal trade', *Maritime Wales* 20 (1999), 77–79.

2938. Stammers, M.K. 'Coal for the Cape', *Maritime Wales* 21 (2000), 83–89.

2939. Stephens, W.B. '"An awful place for children?" Child labour in mid-nineteenth century Devon, Cornwall, Somerset and Dorset', *Devon Historian* 61 (2000), 3–9.

2940. not used

2941. Tissot, Laurent. 'Agences de voyages et conquetes touristiques, 1850–1914', *Relations internationales* 102 (2000), 185–99.

2942. Tran, Tri. 'Les pilotes du port de Londres au XIXe siècle', *Études Anglaises* 50:1 (1997), 62–70.

2943. Trebilcock, Clive. *Phoenix Assurance and the development of British insurance*, vol.2: *The era of the insurance giants, 1870–1984* (Cambridge: Cambridge University Press, 1998), 850p. [Vol. 1: *1782–1870* published 1985.]

2944. Turner, Michael. 'Corporate strategy or individual priority?: land management, income and tenure on Oxbridge agricultural land in the mid-nineteenth century', *Business History* 42:4 (2000), 1–26.

2945. Tusan, Michelle Elizabeth. '"Not the ordinary Victorian charity": The Society for Promoting the Employment of Women archive', *History Workshop Journal* 49 (2000), 220–30.

2946. Vourkatioti, Katerina. 'Anglo-Indian sea trade and Greek commercial enterprises in the second half of the nineteenth century', *International Journal of Maritime History* 11 (1999), 117–48.

2947. Wadsworth, Sarah. 'Charles Knight and Sir Frances Head: two early Victorian perspectives on printing and the allied trades', *Victorian Periodicals Review* 31 (1998), 369–86.

2948. Walker, F.M. 'The River Clyde: birthplace of an industry', A113, 31–45.

2949. Weir, R.B. 'Scotch on the records', *Scottish Industrial History* 20 (2000), 8–22.

2950. Wilkinson, A. 'The preternatural gardener: the life of James Shirley Hibberd (1825–90)', *Garden History* 26:2 (1998), 153–75.

2951. Williams, Chris. *Capitalism, community and conflict: the south Wales coalfield, 1898–1947* (Cardiff: University of Wales Press, 1998), x, 146p.

2952. Williams, John. 'The Fed: birth and first steps' [South Wales Miners' Federation, 1898], *Llafur* 7:3–4 (1999), 67–76.

2953. Wilson, R. Guerriero. *Disillusionment or new opportunities?: the changing nature of work in offices, Glasgow 1880–1914* (Aldershot: Ashgate, 1998), ix, 313p.

2954. Wingfield, T.C. '"You do not give answers that please me": British and American Boards of Inquiry into the Titanic sinking', *American Neptune* 59:4 (1999), 265–85.

2955. Winstanley, Michael. 'Temples of commerce: revolutions in shopping and banking', A210, 151–74.

2956. Wootton, C.W.; Wolk, C.M. 'The evolution and acceptance of the loose-leaf accounting system, 1885–1935', *Technology and Culture* 41:1 (2000), 80–98.

Eb. *Technology*

See also 423 (B); 2290 (G); 2748, 3560 (H)

2957. Cookson, Gillian. 'The transatlantic telegraph cable: eighth wonder of the world', *History Today* 50:3 (2000), 44–51.

2958. Foreman-Peck, James. 'The balance of technological transfers 1870–1914', A69, 114–38.

2959. Gwyn, David Rhys. 'From blacksmith to engineer: artisan technology in the Gwynedd slate industry', *Llafur* 7:3–4 (1999), 51–65.

2960. Hassam, Andrew. 'Portable iron structures and uncertain colonial spaces at the Sydenham Crystal Palace', A71, 174–93.

2961. Hewish, John. *Rooms near Chancery Lane: the Patent Office under the Commissioners, 1852–1883* (London: British Library, 2000), xii, 173p.

2962. Hodge, P.T. 'Power in Hebden Gill in the mid 19th century', *British Mining* 59 (1997), 148–55.

2963. Holden, Roger N. 'Stott and Sons: architects of the Lancashire cotton mill' [review], *Textile History* 30:1 (1999), 121.

2964. Lambert, A.D. 'Responding to the nineteenth century: the Royal Navy and the introduction of the screw propeller', *History of Technology* 21 (1999), 1–28.

2965. Luscombe, Edward W. 'Electricity in Plymouth: its origins and development', *Devonshire Association Report and Transactions* 131 (1999), 221–52.

2966. Mertens, J. 'From Tubal Cain to Faraday: William Whewell as a philosopher of technology', *History of Science* 38:3:121 (2000), 321–342.

2967. Noakes, R.J. 'Telegraphy is an occult art: Cromwell Fleetwood Varley and the diffusion of electricity to the other world', *British Journal for the History of Science* 32:4 (1999), 421–60.

2968. O'Neill, B.J. 'The development of the electrical supply industry in northwest Kent, 1882–1914', *The Local Historian* 30:1 (2000), 23–38.

2969. Probert, W.B.C. 'The evolution of rocket-based maritime rescue systems in the first half of the nineteenth century', *Mariner's Mirror* 83:2 (1997), 434–49.

2970. Russell, Iain. 'Technical transfer in the British optical instruments industry 1888–1914: the case of Barr & Stroud', *Scottish Industrial History* 21 (2000), 15–33.

2971. Scaife, W. Garrett. *From galaxies to turbines: science, technology and the Parsons family* (Bristol: Institute of Physics, 2000), xvi, 579p.

2972. Schwartzkopf, Jutta. 'Gender and technology: inverting established patterns. The Lancashire cotton weaving industry at the start of the twentieth century', A211, 151–66.

2973. Swade, Doron. *The cogwheel brain: Charles Babbage and the quest to build the first computer* (London: Little, Brown, 2000), x, 342p.

2974. Tortella, Teresa. 'Printing Spanish banknotes in England, 1850–1938', A104, 88–93.

2975. Widdowson, Brian. 'The Trent ketch', *Mariner's Mirror* 83:2 (1997), 450–9.

Fa. *Media and Communication*

See also 1548 (F); 2296, 2304–5, 2310 (G); 2765, 3065 (H); 3933, 4422 (I); 5608, 5769 (M)

2976. Anonymous. 'Luke Fildes and the launch of the Graphic', *Notes and Queries* 46:4 (1999), 482–84.

2977. Baird, C. 'Japan and Liverpool: James Lord Bowes and his legacy', *Journal of the History of Collections* 12:1 (2000), 127–38.

2978. Barnard, Robert (ed.) *The Meadley index to the Hull Times*, 7 vols.: I. *1857–1866*; III. *1877–1886*; IV. *1887–1896*; V. *1897–1906*; VI. *1907–1916*; VII. *1917–1927* (Hull: Hull College of Further Education Local History Unit and Kingston upon Hull City Council Local Studies Library, 1998).

2979. Briggs, Asa. 'Exhibiting the nation' [1851–2000], *History Today* 50:1 (2000), 16–25.

2980. Camlot, Jason Evan. 'Character of the periodical press: John Stuart Mill and Junius Redivivus in the 1830s', *Victorian Periodicals Review* 32 (1999), 166–76.

2981. Colby, Robert A. '"Into the blue water": the first year of *Cornhill Magazine* under Thackeray', *Victorian Periodicals Review* 32 (1999), 209–22.

2982. Curran, Eileen. 'Holding on by a pen: the story of a lady/reviewer: Mary Margaret Busk (1779–1863)', *Victorian Periodicals Review* 31 (1998), 9–30.

2983. Edwards, Peter David. *Dickens's 'young men': George Augustus Sala, Edmund Yates, and the world of Victorian journalism* (Aldershot: Ashgate, 1997), 229p.

2984. England, Steve. *Magnificent Mercury: history of a regional newspaper: the first 125 years of the* Leicester Mercury. (Leicester: Kairos, 1999), 140p.

2985. Fisher, Judith L. 'Thackeray as editor and author: *The adventures of Philip* and the inauguration of the *Cornhill Magazine*', *Victorian Periodicals Review* 33 (2000), 2–21.

2986. Frawley, Maria. 'The editor as advocate: Emily Faithful and *The Victoria Magazine*', *Victorian Periodicals Review* 31 (1998), 87–104.

2987. Garnett, Oliver. 'The letters and collection of William Graham: pre-Raphaelite patron and pre-Raphael collector', *Walpole Society* 62 (2000), 145–343.

2988. Heleniak, K.M. 'Victorian collections and British nationalism: Vernon, Sheepshanks and the National Gallery of British Art', *Journal of the History of Collections* 12:1 (2000), 91–107.

2989. Horn, Anne. 'Theater, journalism, and Thackeray's "man of the world magazine"' [*Cornhill Magazine*], *Victorian Periodicals Review* 32 (1999), 223–38.

2990. Howsam, L. 'An experiment with science for the nineteenth-century book trade: the International Scientific Series', *British Journal for the History of Science* 33:2:116 (2000), 187–207.

2991. Kaul, Chandrika. 'Popular press and empire: Northcliffe, India and the *Daily Mail*, 1896–1922', A38, 45–70.

2992. Linehan, Lawrence. '*The Bucks Herald*, its politics, supporters and finances, 1832–1867', *Records of Buckinghamshire* 40 (2000), 1–13.

2993. MacKenzie, John MacDonald. '"The second city of the empire": Glasgow—imperial municipality', A71, 215–37.

2994. Maunder, Andrew. '"Discourses of distinction": the reception of the *Cornhill Magazine*, 1859–60', *Victorian Periodicals Review* 32 (1999), 239–58.

2995. Morus, I.R. '"The nervous system of Britain": space, time and the electric telegraph in the Victorian age', *British Journal for the History of Science* 33:4:119 (2000), 455–76.

2996. Phegley, Jennifer. 'Clearing away "the briars and brambles": the education and professionalization of the *Cornhill Magazine*'s women readers, 1860–65', *Victorian Periodicals Review* 33 (2000), 22–43.

2997. Read, Donald. 'The relationship of Reuters and other news agencies with the British press, 1858–1984: service at cost or business for profit?', A38, 149–68.

2998. Reed, David. '"Rise and shine!": the birth of the glossy magazine', *British Library Journal* 24:2 (1998), 256–68.

2999. Ruth, Jennifer. '"Gross humbug" or "the language of truth": the case of the *Zoist*' [medical journal, 1840s], *Victorian Periodicals Review* 32 (1999), 299–323.

3000. Ryan, Deborah S. 'Staging the imperial city: the Pageant of London, 1911', A71, 117–35.

3001. Scholnick, Robert J. '"The fiery cross of knowledge": *Chambers's Edinburgh Journal*, 1832–58', *Victorian Periodicals Review* 32 (1999), 324–58.

3002. Sinnema, Peter W. 'Representing the railway: train accidents and trauma in the *Illustrated London News*', *Victorian Periodicals Review* 31 (1998), 142–68.

3003. Walkowitz, Judith R. 'The Indian woman, the flower girl, and the Jew: photojournalism in Edwardian London', *Victorian Studies* 42 (1998), 3–46.

Fb. *Science and Medicine*

See also 433 (B); 2316–18, 2322–3, 2326, 2329, 2338 (G); 2820, 3083, 3123, 3239 (H); 3873, 3952, 3955, 3961, 3967, 3972 (I)

3004. Aldridge, Don. *The rescue of Captain Scott* (East Linton: Tuckwell, 1999), 192p. [British Antarctic Expedition (1898–1900).]

3005. Anderson, K. 'The weather prophets: science and reputation in Victorian meteorology', *History of Science* 37 (1999), 179–216.

3006. Barr, W. 'Richard Cyriax's note concerning Thomas Simpson's claim of having discovered the Northwest Passage', *Polar Record* 197 (2000), 113–16.

3007. Baughman, T.H. *Before the heroes came: Antarctica in the 1890s* (Lincoln (NE) and London: University of Nebraska Press, 1994), xi, 160p.

3008. not used.

3009. Bliss, Michael. *William Osler: a life in medicine* (Oxford: Oxford University Press, 1999), xiv, 581p.

3010. Boylan, P.J. 'William Buckland (1784–1856) and the foundations of taphonomy and palaeoecology', *Archives of Natural History* 24:3 (1997), 361–72.

3011. Bristow, Ian. 'Colour theory in the mid-19th century', A3.

3012. Brody, Judit. 'A Victorian physician's struggle for the introduction of physiology, hygiene and Swedish gymnastics into the elementary schools', *History of Education Society Bulletin* 66 (2000), 80–88.

3013. Buchanan, Alexandrina. 'Science and sensibility: architectural antiquarianism in the early nineteenth century', A164, 169–80.

3014. Buchwald, Jed Z. (ed.) *Scientific credibility and technical standards in 19th- and 20th-century Germany and Britain* (Dordrecht and London: Kluwer Academic, 1996), ix, 182p.

3015. Bulmer, M. 'The development of Francis Galton's ideas on the mechanism of heredity', *Journal of the History of Biology* 32:2 (1999), 263–92.

3016. Burrow, John. 'Images of time: from Carlylean Vulcanism to sedimentary gradualism', A47, 198–223.

3017. Burton, Anthony. *Thomas Telford* (London: Aurum, 1999), viii, 232p.

3018. Bynum, William F.; Overy, Caroline (eds.) *The beast in the mosquito: the correspondence of Ronald Ross and Patrick Manson* (Clio Medica, 51) (Amsterdam: Rodopi, 1998), xxxv, 528p.

3019. Capelotti, P.J. 'Papers of Greely survivor Francis Joseph Long (1852–1916)', *Polar Record* 197 (2000), 157.

3020. Carpenter, P.K. 'The Bath Idiot and Imbecile Institution', *History of Psychiatry* 11:2 (2000), 163–88.

3021. Colp, R. 'More on Darwin's illness', *History of Science* 38:2:120 (2000), 219–36.

3022. Copp, C.J.T.; Taylor, M.A.; Thackray, J.C. 'Charles Moore (1814–1881), Somerset geologist', *Somerset Archaeology and Natural History* 140 (1997), 1–36.

3023. Crozier, Ivan D. 'Taking prisoners: Havelock Ellis, Sigmund Freud, and the construction of homosexuality, 1897–1951', *Social History of Medicine* 13:3 (2000), 447–66.

3024. Damkaer, D.M. 'Determination and enthusiasm: Richard Norris Wolfenden (1854–1926), his plankton studies and other things oceanographical', *Archives of Natural History* 27:2 (2000), 209–29.

3025. Dean, Dennis R. *Gideon Mantell and the discovery of dinosaurs* (Cambridge: Cambridge University Press, 1999), XIX, 290p.

3026. Desmond, Ray. *Sir Joseph Dalton Hooker: traveller & plant collector* (Woodbridge: Antique Collectors' Club and the Royal Botanic Gardens, Kew, 1999), 286p.

3027. Fa-ti, F. 'Hybrid discourse and textual practice: Sinology and natural history in the nineteenth century', *History of Science* 38:1:119 (2000), 25–56.

3028. Galbraith, Spence. 'Dr Joshua Parsons (1814–1891) of Beckington, Somerset general practitioner', *Somerset Archaeology and Natural History* 140 (1997), 105–19.

3029. Gaw, Jerry L. *"A time to heal": the diffusion of Listerism in Victorian Britain* (Transactions of the American Philosophical Society, 89:1) (Philadelphia (PA): American Philosophical Society, 1999), xii, 173p.

3030. Geary, L.M. 'Australian medical students in 19th century Scotland', *Proceedings of the Royal College of Physicians of Edinburgh* 26:3 (1996), 472–86.

3031. Gill, Geoff. 'Cholera and the fight for public health reform in mid-Victorian England', *The Historian* [London] 66 (2000), 10–16.

3032. Grierson, Janet. *Dr. Wilson and his Malvern Hydro: Park View in the water cure era* (Malvern: Cora Weaver, 1998), viii, 142p.

3033. Hagen, J.B. 'Naturalists, molecular biologists, and the challenges of molecular evolution', *Journal of the History of Biology* 32:2 (1999), 321–41.

3034. Harrison, Mark. 'Medicine and the management of modern warfare: an introduction', A52, 1–28.

3035. Haynes, Douglas M. 'Framing tropical disease in London: Patrick Manson, *Filaria perstans*, and the Uganda sleeping sickness epidemic, 1891–1902', *Social History of Medicine* 13:3 (2000), 467–93.

3036. Herrick, Claire. '"The conquest of the silent foe": British and American military medical reform rhetoric and the Russo-Japanese War', A52, 99–130.

3037. Hilton, Boyd. 'The politics of anatomy and an anatomy of politics *c*.1825–1850', A47, 179–97.

3038. Hirst, J. David. 'A medical "dead end" job?: the recruitment and career progression of the Edwardian school medical officer', *Medical History* 44:4 (2000), 443–60.

3039. Inkster, Ian. *Scientific culture and urbanisation in industrialising Britain* (Collected Studies, CS602) (Aldershot: Ashgate, 1997), xiii, 330p.

3040. Jackson, Mark. *The borderland of imbecility: medicine, society, and the fabrication of the feeble mind in late Victorian and Edwardian England* (Manchester: Manchester University Press, 2000), x, 273p.

3041. Jankovic, V. 'The place of nature and the nature of place: the chorographic challenge to the history of British provincial science', *History of Science* 38:1:119 (2000), 79–113.

3042. Jones, Claire. 'Grace Chisholm Young: gender and mathematics around 1900', *Women's History Review* 9:4 (2000), 675–92.

3043. Keynes, Richard Darwin (ed.) *Charles Darwin's zoology notes & specimen lists from H.M.S. Beagle* (Cambridge: Cambridge University Press, 2000), xxxiv, 428p.

3044. Knell, Simon J. *The culture of English geology, 1815–1851: a science revealed through its collecting* (Aldershot: Ashgate, 2000), xxi, 377p.

3045. Lee, Jeanette R. 'John Charles Bucknill: moral therapist, doctor, scientist, or Christian humanist?', *Devonshire Association Report and Transactions* 130 (1998), 81–94.

3046. Legg, A.W. 'The association between James Bolton of Halifax and Edward Robson of Darlington', *Archives of Natural History* 25:3 (1998), 355–60.

3047. Leone, M.; Robotti, N. 'Stellar, solar and laboratory spectra: the history of Lockyer's proto-elements', *Annals of Science* 57:3 (2000), 241–266.

3048. Livingstone, D.N. 'Science, region, and religion: the reception of Darwinism in Princeton, Belfast, and Edinburgh', A168, 7–38.

3049. MacGregor, A.; Headon, A. 'Re-inventing the Ashmolean: natural history and natural theology at Oxford in the 1820s to 1850's', *Archives of Natural History* 27:3 (2000), 369–406.

3050. MacLeod, Roy M. *The 'creed of science' in Victorian England* (Collected Studies series, CS598) (Aldershot: Variorum, 2000), 352p. [Reprints, not itemised.]

3051. Marsden, Barry M. *The early barrow-diggers* (Stroud: Tempus, 1999), 160p. [1st published Aylesbury: Shire Publications, 1974.]

3052. Mort, Frank. *Dangerous sexualities: medico-moral politics in England since 1830*, 2nd edn. (London: Routledge, 2000), xxviii, 250p.

3053. Oldroyd, David Roger. 'Adam Sedgwick and lakeland geology (1822–24)', A108, 197–204.

3054. Oldroyd, David Roger. 'Geikie and Judd, and controversies about the igneous rocks of the Scottish Hebrides: theory, practice, and power in the geological community', A156, 459–504.

3055. Preston, Rebecca. '"The scenery of the torrid zone": imagined travels and the culture of exotics in nineteenth-century British gardens', A71, 194–214.

3056. Roberts, M.B. 'I coloured a map: Darwin's attempts at geological mapping in 1831', *Archives of Natural History* 27:1 (2000), 69–80.

3057. Robertson, Edna. *Glasgow's doctor: James Burn Russell, MOH, 1837–1904* (East Linton: Tuckwell, 1998), xii, 248p.

3058. Ruse, Michael. *The Darwinian revolution: science red in tooth and claw*, 2nd edn. (Chicago (IL) and London: University of Chicago Press, 1999), xv, 346p. [1st published 1979.]

3059. Schwartz, J.S. 'Robert Chambers and Thomas Henry Huxley, science correspondents: the popularization and dissemination of nineteenth century natural science', *Journal of the History of Biology* 32:2 (1999), 343–83.

3060. Sibum, H. Otto. 'Les gestes de la mesure: Joule, les pratiques de la brasserie et la science', *Annales* 53 (1998), 745–74.

3061. Smyth, Albert Leslie. *John Dalton, 1766–1844: a bibliography of works by and about him with an annotated list of his surviving apparatus and personal effects* (Aldershot: Manchester Library and Philosophical Publications in association with Ashgate, 1998), xx, 167p.

3062. Stearn, William Thomas (ed.) *John Lindley, 1799–1865: gardener, botanist and pioneer orchidologist* (Woodbridge: Antique Collector's Club in association with the Royal Horticultural Society, 1998), 224p.

3063. Strange, Julie-Marie. 'Menstrual fictions: languages of medicine and menstruation, c.1850–1930', *Women's History Review* 9:3 (2000), 607–28.

3064. Swinney, G.N.; Wheeler, A. '"One of a bye-gone time": Richard Parnell (1810–82) and his fish collections', *Journal of the History of Collections* 12:2 (2000), 203–19.

3065. Topham, Jonathan R. 'Scientific publishing and the reading of science in nineteenth-century Britain: a historiographical survey and guide to sources', *Studies in History and Philosophy of Science Part A* 31:4 (2000), 559–612.

3066. Tully, I. 'A calendar of the letters of William Pamplin at the University of Wales, Bangor', *Archives of Natural History* 26:3 (1999), 299–348.

3067. Vass, Pamela. 'Rediscovering Thomas Fowler (1777–1843): mathematician and inventor', *Devonshire Association Report and Transactions* 131 (1999), 11–26.

3068.   Wilson, L.G. 'The critical role of Italian geology in the thought of Charles Lyell', A156, 653–74.
3069.   Winter, Alison. *Mesmerized: powers of mind in Victorian Britain* (Chicago (IL) and London: University of Chicago Press, 1998), xiv, 464p.
3070.   Woolley, Benjamin. *The bride of science: romance, reason and Byron's daughter* (London: Macmillan, 1999), viii, 416p.
3071.   Worboys, Michael. 'Almroth Wright at Netley: modern medicine and the military in Britain, 1892–1902', A52, 77–98.
3072.   Worboys, Michael. *Spreading germs: disease theories and medical practice in Britain, 1865–1900* (Cambridge: Cambridge University Press, 2000), xvi, 327p.

Fc. *Ideas and Learning*

See also 1631, 1658, 1663 (F); 2345, 2353, 2360, 2364, 2367, 2369, 2373, 2376, 2467 (G); 3271 (H); 4004, 4011, 4016, 4025, 4048, 4056, 4066, 4421 (I)

3073.   Albisetti, J.C. 'Un-learned lessons from the new world? English views of American coeducation and women's colleges, c.1865–1910', *History of Education* 29 (2000), 473–89.
3074.   Alter, Stephen G. *Darwinism and the linguistic image: language, race, and natural theology in the nineteenth century* (Baltimore (MD) and London: Johns Hopkins University Press, 1999), xiii, 193p.
3075.   not used.
3076.   Arnold, Matthew. *Culture and Anarchy and other writings*, ed. Stefan Collini. (Cambridge and New York: Cambridge University Press, 1993), xxxiv, 248p. [Contains *Democracy* (1861), *The Function of Criticism at the Present Time* (1864), 'Preface' to *Culture and Anarchy* (1864), *Culture and Anarchy* (1867–69) and *Equality* (1878).]
3077.   Austin, John. *The province of jurisprudence determined*, ed. Wilfrid E. Rumble. (Cambridge: Cambridge University Press, 1995), xxxix, 298p.
3078.   Bahners, P. '"A place among the English classics": Ranke's History of the Popes and its British readers', A201, 123–58.
3079.   Beard, Mary. *The invention of Jane Harrison* (Revealing Antiquity, 14) (Cambridge (MA) and London: Harvard University Press, 2000), xiii, 229p.
3080.   Briggs, C.S. 'Frenchmen student engineers in industrial Britain: a preliminary list of tours from the MS register of deposited journals at the Ecole des Mines, Paris', *British Mining* 61 (1998), 141–47.
3081.   Brock, Michael G.; Curthoys, Mark C. (eds.) *The history of the University of Oxford*, vol.7 part 2: *Nineteenth-century Oxford* (Oxford: Clarendon, 2000), 980p.
3082.   Brooks, Ron. 'Rochdale, Wrexham and the university tutorial class movement in north-west Wales, 1907–1914', *Welsh History Review* 20:1 (2000), 62–88.

3083. Bucchi, M. 'Images of science in the classroom: wallcharts and science education 1850–1920', *British Journal for the History of Science* 31:2 (1998), 161–84.

3084. Burrow, J. 'Historicism and social evolution', A201, 251–64.

3085. Bury, M.E.; Pickles, John Drayton (eds.) *Romilly's Cambridge diary 1848–1864: selected passages from the diary of the Rev. Joseph Romilly, Fellow of Trinity College and Registrary of the University of Cambridge* (Cambridgeshire Records Society, 14) (Cambridge: Cambridgeshire Records Society, 2000), xiii, 515p.

3086. Campbell, J. 'Stubbs, Maitland, and constitutional history', A201, 99–122.

3087. Chapman, Mark D. 'Concepts of the voluntary church in England and Germany, 1890–1920: a study of J.N. Figgis and Ernst Troeltsch', *Journal for the History of Modern Theology* 2:1 (1995), 37–59.

3088. Cox, Gordon. *A history of music education in England, 1872–1928* (Aldershot: Scolar, 1993), xi, 196p.

3089. Craik, A.D.D. 'James Ivory, F.R.S., mathematician: "the most unlucky person that ever existed"', *Notes & Records of the Royal Society* (of London) 54:2 (2000), 223–47.

3090. Daglish, Neil D. 'A "difficult and somewhat thankless task": politics, religion and the Education Bill of 1908', *Journal of Educational Administration and History* 31 (1999), 19–35.

3091. Draper, Jo. 'Bridport Literary and Scientific Institute', *Proceedings of the Dorset Natural History and Archaeological Society* 121 (1999), 136–8.

3092. Ebbatson, R. '"Trooped apparitions": Hardy and the Boer War', *Critical Survey* 11:3 (1999), 48–58.

3093. Entwistle, Dorothy. 'Counteracting the street culture: book prizes in English sunday schools at the turn of the century', *History of Education Society Bulletin* 55 (1995), 26–34.

3094. Evans, Margaret Kinnell. 'Lessons in image making: schooling through children's books', *History of Education Society Bulletin* 65 (2000), 26–34.

3095. Evans, W. Gareth. '"Organise the training of Welsh teachers and liberalise their education": Tom Ellis and the reform of teaching', *Welsh History Review* 19:4 (1999), 713–39.

3096. Fletcher, Allan. 'Caernarvonshire and the Education Act of 1870', *Caernarvonshire Historical Society Transactions* 61 (2000), 59–76.

3097. Fuchs, E. 'English positivism and German historicism: the reception of "scientific history" in Germany', A201, 229–50.

3098. Gardner, Philip; Cunningham, Peter. 'Teacher trainers and educational change in Britain, 1876–1996: "a flawed and deficient history"?', *Journal of Education for Teaching* 24:3 (1998), 231–55.

3099. Gay, H. 'Association and practice: the City and Guilds of London Institute for the Advancement of Technical Education', *Annals of Science* 57:4 (2000), 369–98.

3100. Goldman, L. 'Intellectuals and the English working class 1870–1945: the case of adult education', *History of Education* 29:4 (2000), 281–300.

3101. Hawthorne, E.J. 'Self-writing, literary traditions, and post-emancipation identity: the case of Mary Seacole', *Biography: an interdisciplinary quarterly* 23:2 (2000), 309–331.

3102. Heathorn, Stephen. 'An English paradise to regain?: Ebenezer Howard, the Town and Country Planning Association and English ruralism' [review article], *Rural History* 11 (2000), 113–28.

3103. Hickman, Mary J. 'Constructing the nation, segregating the Irish: the education of Irish Catholics in nineteenth-century Britain', *Aspects of Education* 54 (1997), 33–54.

3104. Ives, Eric William; Schwarz, Leonard D.; Drummond, Diane K. *The first civic university: Birmingham 1880–1980: an introductory history* (Birmingham: University of Birmingham Press, 2000), xviii, 462p.

3105. Jones, Diana K. 'Cotton, self-improvement and educational enterprise: a biographical study of the interests and initiatives of the Gregs of Styal in the promotion of useful knowledge (1780s-1870s)', *History of Education Society Bulletin* 66 (2000), 89–100.

3106. Jones, Peter Ellis. 'The established church and elementary education in Victorian Merioneth: a case-study of the Llansanffraid Glyndyfrdwg/ Carrog national school, part 1', *Journal of the Merioneth Historical and Record Society* 13 (2000), 274–85.

3107. Kennedy, Dane. '"Captain Burton's Oriental muck heap": *The Book of the Thousand Nights* and the uses of Orientalism', *Journal of British Studies* 39:3 (2000), 317–39.

3108. Lubenow, William C. 'University history and the history of universities in the nineteenth century' [review article], *Journal of British Studies* 39:2 (2000), 247–62.

3109. Marsden, William E. '"Poisoned history": a comparative study of nationalism, propaganda and the treatment of war and peace in the late nineteenth and early twentieth century school curriculum', *History of Education* 29:1 (2000), 29–48.

3110. Martin, Jane. 'Working for the people? Mrs Bridges Adams and the London School Board, 1897–1904', *History of Education* 29:1 (2000), 49–62.

3111. Matthews, E. Gwynn. *Yr Athro Alltud: Syr Henry Jones 1852–1922* (Dinbych: Gwasg Gee, 1998), ix, 161p.

3112. Miller, D.E. 'John Stuart Mill's civic liberalism', *History of Political Thought* 21 (2000), 88–113.

3113. Mitchell, G.A. 'Too little too late: the development of technical education and training in England and Wales prior to the twentieth century: II', *Welsh Journal of Education* 6:1 (1997), 93–105.

3114. Moore-Colyer, R.J. 'Feathered women and persecuted birds: the struggle against the plumage trade, c.1860–1922', *Rural History* 11 (2000), 57–73.

3115. Morris, William. *News from Nowhere, or an epoch of rest: being some chapters from a utopian romance*, ed. Krishnan Kumar. (Cambridge and New York: Cambridge University Press, 1995), xxxii, 229p.

3116. Morrish, Peter S. 'Dichotomy and status: Leeds University librarianship to 1934', *History of Universities* 15 (1999), 227–59.

3117. Muckle, James Y. '"Ladies' schools" in the London area in the 1870s: an archive at Bloomington, Indiana', *History of Education Society Bulletin* 66 (2000), 116–17.

3118.   Muckle, James Y. *Bold shall I stand: the education of young women in the Moravian settlement at Ockbrook since 1799* (Ockbrook: Ockbrook School, 2000), xii, 140p.

3119.   Muller, James W. '"Backward and precocious": Winston Churchill at school', *World and I* 12:12 (1997), 290–317.

3120.   Möller, Jes Fabricius. 'Teologiske reaktioner på darwinismen i Danmark 1860–1900' [Darwin and Danish theologians, 1860–1900], *Historisk Tidsskrift* [Copenhagen] 100 (2000), 69–92.

3121.   Oram, Alison. 'Women teachers and the suffrage campaign: arguments for professional equality', A178, 203–25.

3122.   Osterhammel, Jürgen. '"Peoples without history": in British and German historical thought', A201, 265–88.

3123.   Pennington, Carolyn. *The modernisation of medical teaching at Aberdeen in the nineteenth century* (Aberdeen: Aberdeen University Press, 1994), ix, 116p.

3124.   Radick, G. 'Morgan's canon, Garner's phonograph and the evolutionary original of language and reason', *British Journal for the History of Science* 33:1:116 (2000), 3–23.

3125.   Roberts, D. Hywel E. 'Sefydly Ysgol Ganolraddol yn Aberteifi, 1890–1898: "a denominational venture"?' [Intermediate school, Cardigan], *Ceredigion* 13:3 (1999), 47–63.

3126.   Roderick, Gordon W. 'A new college for South Wales—Cardiff versus Swansea: a battle of the sites, 1881–83', *Transactions of the Honourable Society of Cymmrodorion* ns 6 (1999), 90–103.

3127.   Roderick, Gordon W.; Allsobrook, David. 'Welsh society and university funding, 1860–1914', *Welsh History Review* 20:1 (2000), 34–61.

3128.   Rowold, K.J. '"The academic woman": minds, bodies and education in Britain and Germany c.1860–c.1914', *German History* 15:3 (1997), 392.

3129.   Sanderson, Michael. 'Education and economic decline 1870–1914: an innocent suspect?', A69, 155–74.

3130.   Sanderson, Michael. *Education and economic decline in Britain, 1870 to the 1990s* (Cambridge: Cambridge University Press, 1999), viii, 124p.

3131.   Schwarz, Bill. 'Philosophes of the conservative nation: Burke, Macaulay, Disraeli', *Journal of Historical Sociology* 12:3 (1999), 183–217.

3132.   Smith, John T. 'Brougham's expectations of the 1833 education grant', *Journal of Educational Administration and History* 31 (1999), 36–46.

3133.   Smith, John T. *Methodism and education, 1849–1902: J.H. Rigg, Romanism and Wesleyan schools* (Oxford: Clarendon, 1998), ix, 258p.

3134.   Spencer, Stephanie. 'Advice and ambition in a girls' public day school: the case of Sutton High School, 1884–1924', *Women's History Review* 9:1 (2000), 75–94.

3135.   Tribe, Keith. 'The Cambridge Economics Tripos 1903–55 and the training of economists', *Manchester School* 68:2 (2000), 222–48.

3136.   Tribe, Keith. 'The historicization of political economy?', A201, 211–28.

3137.   Tulloch, H. 'Lord Acton and German historiography', A201, 159–72.

3138.   Vance, N. 'Niebuhr in England: history, faith, and order', A201, 83–98.

3139.   Wende, Peter. 'Views and reviews: mutual perceptions of British and German historians in the late nineteenth century', A201, 173–89.

3140.   Williams, H.G. 'Nation-state versus national identity: state and inspec-
        torate in mid-Victorian Wales', *History of Education Quarterly* 40:2
        (2000), 145–68.

Fd. *Culture and the Arts*

See also 439, 445, 447, 456 (B); 816 (D); 1677, 1720, 1728 (F); 2369, 2380, 2397,
        2404, 2422, 2434, 2442, 2453, 2467, 2469, 2484–5, 2488, 2491 (G); 3437 (H);
        3873, 4085, 4087, 4113, 4120, 4124, 4158 (I); 5043, 5060 (J)

3141.   Airs, Malcolm. 'Introduction' [The Victorian great house], A3.
3142.   Allen, Kevin. *August Jaeger: portrait of Nimrod. A life in letters and other
        writings* (Aldershot: Ashgate, 2000), xvii, 318p.
3143.   Allien, Vivien (ed.) *Dear Mr Rosetti: the letters of Dante Gabriel Rosetti
        and Hall Caine 1878–1881* (Sheffield: Sheffield Academic Press, 2000), 336p.
3144.   Annand, Louise. 'Annie French', A30, 141–46.
3145.   Arthur, Liz. 'Ann Macbeth', A30, 153–58.
3146.   Arthur, Liz. 'Jessie Newbery', A30, 147–52.
3147.   Arthur, Liz. 'Kathleen Mann Crawford', A30, 183.
3148.   Barker, Juliet R.V. *Wordsworth: a life* (London: Viking, 2000), xvii, 971p.
3149.   Batchelor, John. *John Ruskin: no wealth but life* (London: Chatto &
        Windus, 2000), xiv, 369p. [Reprinted London: Pimlico, 2000.]
3150.   Bearman, C.J. 'Who were the folk?: the demography of Cecil Sharp's
        Somerset folk singers', *Historical Journal* 43:3 (2000), 751–76.
3151.   Black, Iain S. 'Spaces of capital: bank office building in the City of London,
        1830–1870', *Journal of Historical Geography* 26:3 (2000), 351–375.
3152.   Blissett, David. 'Veneerer-in-chief to the nobility: Sir Charles Barry's
        country houses', A3.
3153.   Bosbach, Franz; Büttner, Frank (eds.) *Künstlerische Beziehungen zwis-
        chen England und Deutschland in der viktorianische Epoche = Art in
        Britain and Germany in the age of Queen Victoria and Price Albert* (Prinz-
        Albert-Studien, 15) (München: K.G. Saur, 1998), 230p.
3154.   Boucher-Rivalain, O. 'Vision du passé dans les écrits architecturaux des
        années 1840 en France et en Angleterre' [Visions of the past in French and
        British architectural writings of the 1840s], *Cahiers victoriens et édouar-
        diens* 51 (2000).
3155.   Bowler, C.; Brimblecombe, P. 'Environmental pressures on building
        design and Manchester's John Rylands Library', *Journal of Design
        History* 13:3 (2000), 175–92.
3156.   Bradbury, Oliver. 'Paragon Buildings, Cheltenham', *The Georgian Group
        Journal* 10 (2000), 141–49.
3157.   Brooks, Ann; Haworth, Bryan. *Portico Library: a history* (Lancaster:
        Carnegie, 2000), vi, 151p.
3158.   Brown, R.A.; Hancock, E. 'The Crealocks: two soldier artists from the
        Crimea to the Zulu War', *Journal of the Society for Army Historical
        Research* 78:316 (2000), 243–51.
3159.   Burkhauser, Jude. 'Afterword: ghouls, gas pipes and guerilla girls—a wider
        legacy' [Glasgow girls: women in art and design, 1880–1920], A30, 240–45.

3160. Burkhauser, Jude. 'Blinkers on our imagination', A30, 214–19.

3161. Burkhauser, Jude. 'By women's hands: the metalworkers', A30, 178–82.

3162. Burkhauser, Jude; Taylor, Susan. 'De Courcy Lewthwaite Dewar', A30, 159–64.

3163. Burkhauser, Jude; Bird, Liz; Monie, Ian. 'Fra Newbery, Jessie Newbery & the Glasgow School of Art', A30, 63–80.

3164. Burkhauser, Jude; Helland, Janice. 'Frances Macdonald', A30, 123–32.

3165. Burkhauser, Jude. 'Introduction: "restored to a place of honour"' [Glasgow girls: women in art and design, 1880–1920], A30, 1–26.

3166. Burkhauser, Jude. 'Jessie M. King', A30, 133–40.

3167. Burkhauser, Jude. 'The "new woman" in the arts', A30, 45–54.

3168. Burkhauser, Jude. 'The Glasgow style', A30, 81–106.

3169. Burkhauser, Jude; Wickre, Bille. 'The Green Gate Close coterie', A30, 175–77.

3170. Burkhauser, Jude. 'The sister studios: their sole handwork. Margaret Gilmour, Mary Gilmour, the Begg sisters, the Walton sisters, Dorothy Carleton Smyth, Olive Carleton Smythe, Helen Paxton Brown', A30, 165–74.

3171. Burman, P. '"A stern thinker and most able constructor": Philip Webb, architect', *Architectural History* 42 (1999), 1–23.

3172. Cameron, Ewen A. 'The library of Charles Fraser Mackintosh, MP, 1828–1901', *Library History* 16 (2000), 133–42.

3173. Cameron, Neil. 'A Romantic folly to Romantic folly: the Glenfinnan Monument reassessed', *Proceedings of the Society of Antiquaries of Scotland* 129 (1999), 887–907.

3174. Ceadel, Martin. *Semi-detached idealists: the British peace movement and international relations, 1854–1945* (Oxford: Oxford University Press, 2000), 477p.

3175. Christiansen, Rupert. *The visitors: culture shock in nineteenth-century Britain* (London: Chatto & Windus, 2000), xi, 272p.

3176. Codell, J.F. 'Righting the Victorian artist: the Redgraves' *A Century of Painters of the English School* and the serialization of art history', *Oxford Art Journal* 23:2 (2000), 95–119.

3177. Docherty, L.J. 'Collecting as creation: Isabella Stewart Gardner's Fenway Court', A180, 217–22.

3178. Donald, Diana. 'Beastly sights: the treatment of animals and the image of London 1800–1840', A7, 48–78.

3179. Draper, Jo. 'Attempts at a Dorset County Museum in the 1820s', *Proceedings of the Dorset Natural History and Archaeological Society* 121 (1999), 138–40.

3180. Drury, John. 'Ruskin's way: *tout à fait comme un oiseau*', A47, 156–78.

3181. Ellis, Anne. 'Jane Younger', A30, 174–75.

3182. Epstein, James. '"America" in the Victorian cultural imagination', A135, 107–23.

3183. Fellows, Richard A. *Edwardian civic buildings and their details* (Oxford: Architectural Press, 1999), x, 129p.

3184. Fisher, Trevor. 'The mysteries of Oscar Wilde', *History Today* 50:12 (2000), 18–20.

3185. Flint, Kate. 'Literature, music, and the theatre', A145, 229–54.

3186.   Flint, Kate. *The Victorians and the visual imagination* (Cambridge: Cambridge University Press, 2000), xvi, 427p.

3187.   Francmanis, John. 'The "folk-song" competition: an aspect of the search for an English national music', *Rural History* 11:2 (2000), 181–206.

3188.   Franks, John. 'Jews in *Vanity Fair*', *Jewish Historical Studies* 35 (1998), 199–29.

3189.   Frazier, Adrian Woods. *George Moore, 1852–1933* (New Haven (CT) and London: Yale University Press, 2000), xix, 604p.

3190.   Gaimster, David. 'Sex and sensibility at the British Museum' [the 'secretum'], *History Today* 50:9 (2000), 10–15.

3191.   Gill, Michael H. 'Woodchester mansion: the French connection', A3.

3192.   Gilley, Sheridan. 'The legacy of William Hogarth, 1786–1866', *Recusant History* 25:2 (2000), 249–62.

3193.   Glasgow, Eric. 'Gladstone and public libraries', *Library History* 16 (2000), 57–63.

3194.   Gray, D.W.S. 'London and Paris illustrated in the first half of the nineteenth century', A20, 149–68.

3195.   not used.

3196.   Groves, D. '"Disgusted with all the cockneys": De Quincey, the London Magazine, and Blackwood's Magazine', *Notes and Queries* 47:3 (2000), 326–27.

3197.   Guy, J.M. '"Trafficking with merchants for his soul": Dante Gabriel Rossetti among the aesthetes', *Proceedings of the British Academy* 105 (2000), 171–86.

3198.   Gwyn, David. 'Vaunting and disrespectful notions: Charles Mercier's portrait of the Penrhyn Quarry Committee and Lord Penrhyn', *Caernarvonshire Historical Society Transactions* 61 (2000), 99–110.

3199.   Harvie, C. 'Enlightenment to renaissance: Scottish cultural life in the nineteenth century', A17, 214–43.

3200.   Heath, Desmond. *Roden Noel, 1834–1894: a wide angle: a background to Noel's life and work, featuring his poetry, his philosophy, correspondence with Tennyson, Browning, Hardy, and others, plus reminiscences of Noel's son, Conrad, the 'rebel priest' of Thaxted* (London: DB Books, 1998), xiv, 281p.

3201.   Hedley, Douglas. *Coleridge, philosophy and religion: aids to reflection and the mirror of the spirit* (Cambridge: Cambridge University Press, 2000), xiv, 330p.

3202.   Helland, Janice. *Professional women painters in nineteenth-century Scotland: commitment, friendship, pleasure* (Aldershot: Ashgate, 2000), xii, 212p.

3203.   Hewitt, Martin. 'Confronting the modern city: the Manchester Free Public Library, 1850–80', *Urban History* 27:1 (2000), 62–88.

3204.   Hill, K. '"Thoroughly imbued with the spirit of ancient Greece": symbolism and space in Victorian civic culture', A122, 99–111.

3205.   Hill, Roland. *Lord Acton* (New Haven (CT) and London: Yale University Press, 2000), xxiv, 548p.

3206.   Hilton, Timothy. *Ruskin: the later years* (New Haven (CT) and London: Yale University Press, 2000), xxiii, 656p. [Sequel to *The Early*

Years, 1819–1859 (New Haven (CT) and London: Yale University Press, 1985).]

3207. Howarth, Thomas. 'Some thoughts on Charles Rennie Mackintosh, "girls" and Glasgow', A30, 56–61.

3208. Howell, Peter. '"Masquerade" versus "straightforwardness": the country houses of Salvin and Scott', A3.

3209. Huggins, Mike J. 'Second-class citizens? English middle-class culture and sport, 1850–1910: a reconsideration', *International Journal of the History of Sport* 17:1 (2000), 1–35.

3210. Hughes, R. Elwyn. 'Arfonwyson: uchelgais a Siom' [John William Thomas], *National Library of Wales Journal* 31:2 (1999), 149–71.

3211. Hughes-Hallett, Penelope. *The immortal dinner: a famous evening of genius & laughter in literary London, 1817* (London: Viking, 2000), 352p.

3212. Hunt, Donald. *Elgar and the Three Choirs Festival* (Worcester: Osborne Heritage, 1999), 166p.

3213. Jansen, V. 'George Gilbert Scott and restoration at Chester Cathedral, 1819–1876', A204, 81–97.

3214. Jones, Martin. 'Edmund Scott and Brighton College chapel: a lost work rediscovered', *Sussex Archaeological Collections* 135 (1997), 309–11.

3215. Jones, Mervyn. *The amazing Victorian: a life of George Meredith* (London: Constable, 1999), 311p.

3216. Jones, Nigel H. *Rupert Brooke: life, death & myth* (London: R. Cohen, 1999), xvii, 462p.

3217. Kidd, Alan J.; Nicholls, D. 'Introduction: history, culture and the middle classes', A122, 1–11.

3218. Kidd, Sheila. 'The view from the inside' [review of books by Don E. Meeks on Gaelic poems & songs as historical sources], *Innes Review* 51:2 (2000), 188–93.

3219. King, Edmund M.B. 'The book cover designs of John Leighton, F.S.A', *British Library Journal* 24:2 (1998), 234–55.

3220. Kinna, Ruth. 'William Morris: art, work, and leisure', *Journal of the History of Ideas* 61:3 (2000), 493–512.

3221. Knight, William G. *A major London 'minor': the Surrey Theatre 1805–1865* (London: Society for Theatre Research, 1997), xii, 335p.

3222. Kurzer, F. 'A history of the Surrey Institution', *Annals of Science* 57:2 (2000), 109–41.

3223. Lambourne, Lionel. *Victorian painting* (London: Phaidon, 1999), 512p.

3224. Law, Graham. 'Before Tillotsons: novels in British provincial newspapers, 1855–1873', *Victorian Periodicals Review* 32 (1999), 43–79.

3225. Leoussi, Athena S. 'Pheidias and "l'esprit moderne": the study of human anatomy in nineteenth-century English and French art education', *European Review of History* 7:2 (2000), 167–88.

3226. Mace, Rodney. *British trade union posters: an illustrated history* (Stroud: Sutton, 1999), 184p.

3227. MacLennan, Heather. 'Antiquarianism, connoisseurship and the Northern Renaissance print: new collecting cultures in the early nineteenth century', A164, 149–62.

3228. Macleod, D.S. 'Homosexuality and middle-class in early Victorian patronage of the arts', A122, 65–80.

3229. Maguire, H. 'The Victorian theatre as a home from home', *Journal of Design History* 13:2 (2000), 107–21.

3230. Maitzen, Rohan Amanda. *Gender, genre, and Victorian historical writing* (New York: Garland, 1998), xvii, 229p.

3231. Marsh, Jan. *Dante Gabriel Rossetti: painter and poet* (London: Weidenfeld & Nicolson, 1999), xiii, 592p.

3232. Marshall, Philip. *Charles Marshall R.A. (1806–90): his origins, life and career as a panorama, diorama, landscape and scenic artist* (Truro: Aston, 2000), 80p.

3233. McKenzie, Ray. 'Introduction: the Glasgow boys', A30, 187–92.

3234. Mosselmans, B.; Mathijs, E. 'Jevons's music manuscript and the political economy of music', *History of Political Economy* 31 (suppl.) (2000), 121–156.

3235. Murray, Douglas K. *Bosie: a biography of Lord Alfred Douglas* (London: Hodder & Stoughton, 2000), x, 374p.

3236. Nenadic, Stana. 'English towns in the creative imagination', A210, 316–41.

3237. O'Donnell, Roderick. 'From "old English Catholic mansions" to castles in Connecticut": the country house practice of A.W. and E.W. Pugin, 1836–1875', A3.

3238. Onslow, Barbara. '"Humble comments for the ignorant": Margaret Oliphant's criticism of art and society', *Victorian Periodicals Review* 31 (1998), 55–74.

3239. Otis, Laura. *Membranes: metaphors of invasion in nineteenth-century literature, science, and politics* (Baltimore (MD) and London: Johns Hopkins University Press, 1999), x, 210p.

3240. Owen, A.E.B. 'Henry Bradshaw and his correspondents' [Librarian of Cambridge University], *Transactions of the Cambridge Bibliographical Society* 11:4 (1999), 480–96.

3241. Peach, Annette. 'Portraits of Byron', *Walpole Society* 62 (2000), 1–144.

3242. Poulson, C. 'Galahad and war memorial imagery of the nineteenth and early twentieth centuries', *Nineteenth Century Contexts* 21:4 (2000), 493–512.

3243. Pudney, Susan E. *The history of Bournemouth public libraries, 1893–1913* (Braintree: M.R. Stallion, 1999), 32p.

3244. Quigly, Isabel. *The Royal Society of Literature: a portrait* (Cambridge: Royal Society of Literature and the Cambridge University Library, 2000), 102p.

3245. Rees, H. 'Art exports and the construction of national heritage in late-Victorian and Edwardian Great Britain', *History of Political Economy* 31 (suppl.) (2000), 187–208.

3246. Reilly, Catherine W. *Mid-Victorian poetry, 1860–1879: an annotated bio-bibliography* (London: Mansell, 2000), xxi, 560p.

3247. Reynolds, Catriona; Burkhauser, Jude. 'Norah Neilson Gray', A30, 201–6.

3248. Reynolds, Siân. 'Running away to Paris: expatriate women artists of the 1900 generation, from Scotland and points south', *Women's History Review* 9:2 (2000), 327–44.

3249. Robertson, Pamela; Neat, Timothy. 'Margaret Macdonald', A30, 108–22.
3250. Robinson, Ainslie. 'Invoking the bard: the *Cornhill Magazine* and "revival" in the Victorian theatre, 1863', *Victorian Periodicals Review* 32 (1999), 259–68.
3251. Robinson, Hilary; Patrick, Adele. 'On visual iconography and the "Glasgow girls"', A30, 227–33.
3252. Rowan, Alistair. 'David Bryce and the Scottish baronial style', A3.
3253. Saint, Andrew. 'Cities, architecture, and art', A145, 255–92.
3254. Salmon, F. '"Storming the Campo Vaccino": British architects and the antique buildings of Rome after Waterloo', *Architectural History* 38 (1995), 146–75.
3255. Salmon, F. 'British architects, Italian fine arts academies and the foundation of the RIBA, 1816–43', *Architectural History* 39 (1996), 77–113.
3256. Sawyer, S. 'John Soane's symbolic Westminster: the apotheosis of George IV', *Architectural History* 39 (1996), 54–76.
3257. Schaffer, Talia. *The forgotten female aesthetes: literary culture in late-Victorian England* (Charlottesville (VA) and London: University Press of Virginia, 2000), x, 298p.
3258. Seymour, Miranda. *Mary Shelley* (London: John Murray, 2000), xvi, 655p.
3259. Sherlock, S.J. 'Nineteenth century workers' houses in Redcar, Cleveland', *Durham Archaeological Journal* 14:1 (1999), 177–86.
3260. Smith, Tori. '"A grand work of noble conception": the Victoria Memorial and imperial London', A71, 21–39.
3261. Smith, Tracy. 'Elusive sculptors: sources for identifying and accrediting architectural sculpture', *Scottish Archives* 5 (1999), 107–14.
3262. Spawn, Willman; Kinsella, Thomas E. *Ticketed bookbindings from nineteenth-century Britain* with an essay by Bernard C. Middleton (Bryn Mawr (PA): Bryn Mawr College Library and Oak Knoll Press, 1999), 206p.
3263. Stamp, Gavin. 'It looks like carelessness, or, in search of Alexander "Greek" Thomson', *Scottish Archives* 5 (1999), 12–28.
3264. Stashower, Daniel. *Teller of tales: the life of Arthur Conan Doyle* (London: Penguin, 2000), xv, 472p.
3265. Stevenson, Janet H. 'Alexander Nesbitt, a Sussex antiquary, and the Oldlands estate', *Sussex Archaeological Collections* 137 (1999), 161–73.
3266. Talbot, P.A. 'The Macclesfield Theatre Company and nineteenth century silk manufacturers', *Theatre Notebook* 54:1 (2000), 24–42.
3267. Tanner, Ailsa. 'Bessie Macnicol', A30, 193–200.
3268. Tanner, Ailsa. 'Eleanor Allen Moore', A30, 210–13.
3269. Tanner, Ailsa. 'Painters of flowers: Katharine Cameron, Maggie Hamilton, Lily Blatherwick, Constance Walton', A30, 220–26.
3270. Tanner, Ailsa; May, Jennifer. 'Stansmore Dean', A30, 207–9.
3271. Vickery, Margaret Birney. *Buildings for bluestockings: the architecture and social history of women's colleges in late Victorian England* (Newark (DE) and London: University of Delaware Press and Associated University Presses, 2000), xiii, 200p.
3272. Walker, David. 'William Burn', A3.

3273. Webster, C. 'The architectural profession in Leeds 1800–50: a case-study in provincial practice', *Architectural History* 38 (1995), 176–91.
3274. Weintraub, Stanley. *Shaw's people: Victoria to Churchill* (University Park (PA): Pennsylvania State University Press, 1996), 255p.
3275. White, M.V. 'Obscure objects of desire? Nineteenth-century British economists and the price(s) of "rare art"', *History of Political Economy* 31 (suppl.) (2000), 57–84.
3276. Wilson, A. '"The Florence of the north"? The civic culture of Liverpool in the early nineteenth century', A122, 34–46.
3277. Wilson, Richard. 'Building two Victorian country houses: Haveringland and Brodsworth', A3.
3278. Wimmer, C.A. 'Victoria, the empress gardener, or the Anglo-Prussian garden war 1858–88', *Garden History* 26:2 (1998), 192–207.
3279. Wood, Christopher. *Victorian painting* (London: Weidenfeld & Nicolson, 1999), 384p.
3280. Wood, J. 'Folklore studies at the Celtic dawn: the role of Alfred Nutt as publisher and scholar', *Folklore* 110 (1999), 3–12.
3281. Worsley, Giles. 'The mid-Victorian stable', A3.
3282. Yanni, Carla. 'On nature and nomenclature: William Whewell and the production of architectural knowledge in early Victorian Britain', *Architectural History* 40 (1997), 204–21.

G. *Religious Belief, Practice and Organisation*

See also 469, 492, 495 (B); 2497, 2499, 2509, 2511–13, 2518, 2522, 2524 (G); 2646, 2725, 2967, 3090, 3188, 3538, 3555 (H); 4155, 4158, 4182 (I); 6377, 6395 (P)

3283. Anonymous. 'Church charities in the diocese of Birmingham, 1800–1918', *Catholic Ancestor* 8:1 (2000), 28–36.
3284. Anonymous. 'Virginia Street Chapel, St George in the East, London: an introduction to the second baptismal register, 1832–1840', *Catholic Ancestor* 8:1 (2000), 24–28.
3285. Adshead, Samuel Adrian Miles. *The philosophy of religion in nineteenth-century England and beyond* (Basingstoke and New York: Macmillan and St Martin's Press, 2000), viii, 274p.
3286. Altholz, Josef L. 'Newman and the *Record*, 1828–1833', *Victorian Periodicals Review* 32 (1999), 160–5.
3287. Altholz, Josef L. 'Social Catholicism in England in the age of the devotional revolution', A27, 209–19.
3288. Ambler, R.W. '"This Romish business": ritual innovation and parish life in later nineteenth-century Lincolnshire', *Studies in Church History* 35 (1999), 384–95.
3289. Aspinwall, Bernard. 'Baptisms, marriages and Lithuanians; or, "Ghetto? What Ghetto?: some reflections on modern Catholic historical assumptions', *Innes Review* 51:1 (2000), 55–67.
3290. Aspinwall, Bernard. 'The ties that bind and loose: the Catholic community in Galloway, 1800–1998', *Records of the Scottish Church Historical Society* 29 (1999), 70–106.

3291. Aspinwall, Bernard. 'Towards an English Catholic social conscience, 1829–1920', *Recusant History* 25:1 (2000), 106–19.

3292. Barber, Lucille (ed.) *The diary: Christ Church, North Brixton, 1855–1995*, vol.2 ([London]: [Christ Church, North Brixton], 1998), viii, 241p.

3293. Bebbington, David William. *Holiness in nineteenth-century England* [The Didsbury Lectures 1998] (Carlisle: Paternoster, 2000), 97p.

3294. Bellenger, Aidan. '"The normal state of the Church": William Bernard Ullathorne, first Bishop of Birmingham', *Recusant History* 25:2 (2000), 325–34.

3295. Bellenger, Aidan. 'Cardinal Gasquet (1846–1929): an English Roman', *Recusant History* 24:4 (1999), 552–60.

3296. Bellenger, Aidan. 'England's Nazareth: the revival of the Roman Catholic shrine at Walsingham, 1897–1997', *Downside Review* 116 (1998), 271–78.

3297. Bradley, George. '*In vineam Domini*: Bishop Briggs and his visitations of the north', *Recusant History* 25:2 (2000), 174–91.

3298. Brown, Malcolm. 'The Jews of early St John's Wood', *Jewish Historical Studies* 35 (1998), 141–52.

3299. Brown, Malcolm. 'The Jews of Gravesend before 1915', *Jewish Historical Studies* 35 (1998), 119–40.

3300. Brown, Roger Lee. 'A reviving church?: the archdeaconry of Brecon in the year 1885', *Brycheiniog* 31 (1998–99), 109–32.

3301. Brown, Roger Lee. *David Howell: a pool of spirituality: a life of David Howell (Llawdden)* (Dinbych: Gwasg Gee, 1998), xiv, 318p.

3302. Cadle, Penelope J. 'A new broom in the Augean stable: Robert Gregory and liturgical changes at St Paul's Cathedral, London, 1868–1890', *Studies in Church History* 35 (1999), 361–73.

3303. Cesarani, David. 'British Jews', A136, 33–55.

3304. Champ, Judith F. 'Goths and Romans: Daniel Rock, Augustus Welby Pugin, and nineteenth-century English worship', *Studies in Church History* 35 (1999), 289–319.

3305. Clifton, Michael. 'Bishop Thomas Grant as a government negotiator', *Recusant History* 25:2 (2000), 304–11.

3306. Dackombe, Barry. 'A Quaker perspective on migration: Ampthill and Hitchin Preparative Meetings, 1811–1840', *Family & Community History* 3 (2000), 49–64.

3307. Dickson, Neil. '"Shut in with thee": the morning meeting among Scottish Open Brethren, 1840s–1960s', *Studies in Church History* 35 (1999), 275–88.

3308. Donis Ríos, Manuel Alberto. 'Sir Robert Ker Porter y los inicios del protestantismo en Venezuela' [Sir Robert Ker Porter and the beginnings of protestantism in Venezuela], *Boletin de la Academia Nacional de la Historia* [Venezuela] 82 (1999), 157–84.

3309. Doyle, Peter. '"A tangled skein of confusion": the administration of George Hilary Brown, Bishop of Liverpool 1850–1856', *Recusant History* 25:2 (2000), 294–303.

3310. Dudley, Martin. '"The Rector presents his compliments": worship, fabric, and furnishings of the Priory Church of St Bartholomew the Great, Smithfield, 1828–1938', *Studies in Church History* 35 (1999), 320–32.

3311. Finestein, Israel. 'Lucien Wolf (1857–1930): a study in ambivalence', *Jewish Historical Studies* 35 (1998), 239–54.

3312. Foley, Brian C. 'John Henry Newman and the Roman Oratory', *Recusant History* 25:1 (2000), 1–11.

3313. Foster, Stewart. '"In sad want of priests and money": Bishop Amherst at Northampton, 1858–1879', *Recusant History* 25:2 (2000), 281–93.

3314. Freeman, Peter. 'The Revd Richard Williams Morgan of Tregynon and his writings', *Montgomeryshire Collections* 88 (2000), 87–93.

3315. Garnett, Jane. 'Religious and intellectual life', A145, 195–228.

3316. Germain, Lucienne. *Réflexes identitaires et intégration: Les Juifs en Grande-Bretagne de 1830 à 1914* [The Jews in Great Britain, 1830–1914] (Paris: Honoré Champion, 2000), 248p.

3317. Gibbard, Noel. *Griffith John: apostle to central China* (Bridgend: Gwasg Bryntirion, 1998), 250p.

3318. Gilley, Sheridan. 'Roman Catholicism and the Irish in England', *Immigrants & Minorities* 18:2–3 (1999), 147–67.

3319. Hammond, Tony. 'F.H. Goldsmid and Archbishop Whately of Dublin: their significance in the emancipation debate', *Jewish Historical Studies* 35 (1998), 153–66.

3320. Hargreaves, John A. 'Methodism in Halifax: consolidation and decline, 1852–1914', *Transactions of the Halifax Antiquarian Society* ns 8 (2000), 133–49.

3321. Hilton, J. Anthony. 'Ruskin's influence on English Catholicism', *Recusant History* 25:1 (2000), 96–105.

3322. Holt, T.E. *Travelling folk: itinerant mission in the diocese of Salisbury, 1882, 1883*, ed. Rosemary Church (Devizes: Wiltshire Family History Society, 1999), 68p.

3323. Hood, Alban. '"Stirring up the pool": Bishop Thomas Joseph Brown O.S.B. (1798–1880) and the dispute between the hierarchy and the English Benedictines', *Recusant History* 25:2 (2000), 312–24.

3324. Horwood, Thomas. 'Public opinion and the 1908 Eucharistic Congress', *Recusant History* 25:1 (2000), 120–32.

3325. Hutton, Ronald. *The triumph of the moon: a history of modern pagan witchcraft* (Oxford: Oxford University Press, 1999), xv, 486p.

3326. Johnson, Dale A. 'Fissures in late-nineteenth-century English nonconformity: a case study in one congregation' [Halifax], *Church History* 66 (1997), 735–49.

3327. Jones, John Graham. 'Dean Charles Vaughan, A.J. Williams and the disestablishment debate of November 1885', *Journal of Welsh Religious History* 8 (2000), 43–61.

3328. Kessler, Edward. 'Claude Montefiore: defender of rabbinic Judaism', *Jewish Historical Studies* 35 (1998), 231–38.

3329. Knight, Frances. 'Anglican worship in late nineteenth-century Wales: a Montgomeryshire case study', *Studies in Church History* 35 (1999), 408–18.

3330. Kreller, Paul. 'The new rhetoric and the reception of Newman's *Apologia*', *Victorian Periodicals Review* 32 (1999), 80–100.

3331. Lannon, David. 'William Turner, first Bishop of Salford, pastor and educator', *Recusant History* 25:2 (2000), 192–217.

3332.   Larsen, Timothy. *Friends of religious equality: nonconformist politics in mid-Victorian England* (Woodbridge: Boydell, 1999), 300p.

3333.   Lazell, David. *Gypsy from the forest: a new biography of the international evangelist Gipsy Smith (1860–1947)* (Bridgend: Bryntirion, 1997), 256p.

3334.   Machin, Ian. 'British Catholics', A136, 11–32.

3335.   Mandle, W.F. 'Newman and his audiences: 1828–1845', *Journal of Religious History* 24:2 (2000), 143–58.

3336.   Marshall, George. 'Two autobiographical narratives of conversion: Robert Hugh Benson and Ronald Knox', *Recusant History* 24 (1998), 237–53.

3337.   Mason, Alistair. 'Milman's *History of the Jews*: a real place with real people', *Studies in Church History* 36 (2000), 319–28.

3338.   McClelland, V. '"Phylacteries of misery" or "mystic-eyed hierophants": some ecclesiastical and educational challenges in England of the Irish diaspora 1850–1902', *Aspects of Education* 54 (1997), 15–32.

3339.   McClelland, V. Alan. 'Changing concepts of the pastoral office: Wiseman, Manning and the Oblates of St. Charles', *Recusant History* 25:2 (2000), 218–36.

3340.   McClurken, K.M. 'For love of God and country: Bishop Charles McIlvaine's mission to England', *Anglican and Episcopal History* 69:3 (2000), 315–347.

3341.   McLennan, B. 'The response of the Dundee churches to the coming of state education', *Records of the Scottish Church Historical Society* 29 (1999), 39–69.

3342.   Moran, M.F. '"Light no Smithfield fires": some Victorian attitudes to witchcraft', *Journal of Popular Culture* 33:4 (2000), 123–52.

3343.   Morgan, Sue. 'Faith, sex and purity: the religio-feminist theory of Ellice Hopkins', *Women's History Review* 9:1 (2000), 13–34.

3344.   Morris, J.N. 'A "fluffy-minded Prayer Book fundamentalist"?: F.D. Maurice and the Anglican liturgy', *Studies in Church History* 35 (1999), 345–60.

3345.   Murray, Douglas M. 'Continuity and change in the liturgical revival in Scotland: John Macleod and the Duns case, 1875–6', *Studies in Church History* 35 (1999), 396–407.

3346.   Numbers, Ronald L. '"The most important Biblical discovery of our time": William Henry Green and the demise of Ussher's chronology', *Church History* 69:2 (2000), 257–76.

3347.   O'Donnell, Ellen. 'Clergy ministering to Lithuanian immigrants in Scotland, 1889–1989', *Innes Review* 51:2 (2000), 166–87.

3348.   Phillips, Peter. '"Or else we shall be bound hand and foot": Bishop James Brown and the oversight of seminaries', *Recusant History* 25:2 (2000), 237–48.

3349.   Plant, Helen. '"Ye are all one in Christ Jesus": aspects of Unitarianism and feminism in Birmingham, c.1869–90', *Women's History Review* 9:4 (2000), 721–42.

3350.   Railton, Nicholas M. *No North Sea: the Anglo-German evangelical network in the middle of the nineteenth century* (Leiden: Brill, 2000), xxii, 288p.

3351. Rimmington, Gerald T. 'Methodism and society in Leicester, 1881–1914', *The Local Historian* 30:2 (2000), 74–87.
3352. Rimmington, Gerald T. 'The Baptist churches and society in Leicester 1881–1914', *Baptist Quarterly* 38:7 (2000), 332–49.
3353. Roberts, Brynley F. 'Robert Jones, Rotherhithe' [vicar], *National Library of Wales Journal* 31:2 (1999), 135–48.
3354. Rowbotham, Judith. '"Soldiers of Christ"?: images of female missionaries in late nineteenth-century Britain: issues of heroism and martyrdom', *Gender & History* 12 (2000), 82–106.
3355. Rubinstein, Hilary L. 'A pioneering philosemite: Charlotte Elizabeth Tonna (1790–1846) and the Jews', *Jewish Historical Studies* 35 (1998), 103–18.
3356. Rubinstein, William D.; Rubinstein, Hilary L. *Philosemitism: admiration and support in the English-speaking world for Jews, 1840–1939* (Basingstoke and New York: Macmillan and St Martin's Press, 1999), xiii, 276p.
3357. Saer, D. Roy. 'A midnight *plygain* at Llanymawddwy church' [carol service], *Journal of the Merioneth Historical and Record Society* 13 (2000), 265–73.
3358. Skinner, S.A. 'Newman, the Tractarians and the *British Critic*', *Journal of Ecclesiastical History* 50:4 (1999), 716–59.
3359. Thomas, William. 'Religion and politics in the *Quarterly Review*, 1809–1853', A47, 136–55.
3360. Tracey, Gerard (ed.) *The letters and diaries of John Henry Newman*, vol. 8: *Tract 90 and the Jerusalem bishopric, January 1841 to April 1842* (Oxford: Clarendon, 1999).
3361. Turner, Garth. 'A Broad Churchman and the Prayer Book: the Reverend Charles Voysey', *Studies in Church History* 35 (1999), 374–83.
3362. Wasserstein, Bernard. 'Moses Samuel, Liverpool Hebraist', *Jewish Historical Studies* 35 (1998), 93–102.
3363. Whitehead, Maurice. 'Educational turmoil and ecclesiastical strife: the episcopal career of Joseph William Hendren, 1848–1853', *Recusant History* 25:2 (2000), 263–80.
3364. Williams, Michael E. 'Lisbon College: the penultimate chapter' [c.1900–15], *Recusant History* 25:1 (2000), 74–95.

Ha. *Law and Order*

See also 2191, 2629 (G); 2758 (H)

3365. Ainsley, Jill Newton. '"Some mysterious agency": women, violent crime, and the insanity acquittal in the Victorian courtroom', *Canadian Journal of History* 35:1 (2000), 37–55.
3366. Archer, John E. '"A reckless spirit of enterprise": game-preserving and poaching in nineteenth-century Lancashire', A111, 149–75.
3367. Arscott, C. 'Convict labour: masking and interchangeability in Victorian prison scenes', *Oxford Art Journal* 23:2 (2000), 120–42.
3368. Cairns, David J.A. *Advocacy and the making of the adversarial criminal trial, 1800–1865* (Oxford: Clarendon, 1998), xii, 215p.

3369. Dell, Simon. *Policing the peninsula (1850–2000): (a photographic celebration of Westcountry policing over the last 150 years)* (Newton Abbot: Forest Publishing in association with the Devon & Cornwall Constabulary, 2000), 144p.

3370. Emsley, Clive. 'The policeman as worker: a comparative survey, c.1800–1940', *International Review of Social History* 45:1 (2000), 89–110.

3371. Farmer, Lindsay. 'Reconstructing the English codification debate: the Criminal Law Commissioners, 1833–45', *Law and History Review* 18:2 (2000), 397–425.

3372. Fox, Warren. 'Murder in daily instalments: the newspapers and the case of Franz Müller (1864)', *Victorian Periodicals Review* 31 (1998), 271–98.

3373. Harris, Jonathan. 'Bernardino Rivadavia and Benthamite "discipleship"', *Latin American Research Review* 33:1 (1998), 129–49.

3374. Jones, Mark Ellis. '"Wales for the Welsh": the Welsh County Court judgeships, c.1868–1900', *Welsh History Review* 19:4 (1999), 643–78.

3375. Lawrence, Paul. '"Images of poverty and crime": police memoirs in England and France at the end of the nineteenth century', *Crime, Histoire et Sociétés* 4:1 (2000), 63–82.

3376. Lobban, Michael. 'Henry Brougham and law reform', *English Historical Review* 115 (2000), 1184–215.

3377. Mulhearn, R.M. 'Police and pilferers at the port of Liverpool, 1800–1850', *International Journal of Maritime History* 11:1 (1999), 149–62.

3378. Nellis, M.; Stephenson, D. 'The century of probation: continuity and change in the Probation Service in England and Wales 1877–1998', *Social Services Research* 3 (1998), 1–18.

3379. Noke, C. 'No value in par: a history of the no par value debate in the United Kingdom', *Accounting, Business & Financial History* 10:1 (2000), 13–36.

3380. Schramm, Jan-Melissa. *Testimony and advocacy in Victorian law, literature, and theology* (Cambridge: Cambridge University Press, 2000), xvi, 244p.

3381. Shore, Heather. 'Home, play and street life: causes of, and explanations for, juvenile crime in the early nineteenth century', A81, 96–114.

3382. Shore, Heather. 'The idea of juvenile crime', *History Today* 50:6 (2000), 21–29.

3383. Smith, Keith John Michael. *Lawyers, legislators and theorists: developments in English criminal jurisprudence 1800–1957* (Oxford: Clarendon, 1998), xxvi, 394p.

3384. Turrell, Rob. '"It's a mystery": the royal prerogative of mercy in England, Canada and South Africa', *Crime, Histoire et Sociétés* 4:1 (2000), 83–102.

3385. Upchurch, Charles. 'Forgetting the unthinkable: cross-dressers and British society in the case of the Queen vs. Boulton and others', *Gender & History* 12 (2000), 127–57.

3386. Waddams, S.M. 'English matrimonial law on the eve of reform (1828–57)', *Journal of Legal History* 21:2 (2000), 59–82.

3387. Weir, T. 'Roman and civil law and the development of Anglo-American jurisprudence in the nineteenth century', *Edinburgh Law Review* 3:3 (1999), 398–99.

3388.   Young, C. 'Middle-class "culture", law and gender identity: married women's property legislation in Scotland, c.1850–1920', A122, 133–45.

Hb. Public Administration

See also 2166, 2171, 2241, 2558 (G); 2907, 2951, 2961 (H); 4379 (I); 6340, 6457 (P)

3389.   Bowler, C.; Brimblecombe, P. 'Control of air pollution in Manchester prior to the Public Health Act, 1875', *Environment and History* 6:1 (2000), 71–98.

3390.   Colley, Robert. '"Destroy'd by time's devouring hand"?: mid-Victorian income tax records: a question of survival', *Archives* 25 (2000), 74–87.

3391.   Davies, Conway. 'Aspects of poor law provision in Carmarthenshire prior to 1834', A93, 105–30.

3392.   Englander, David. 'From the abyss: pauper petitions and correspondence in Victorian London', *London Journal* 25:1 (2000), 71–83.

3393.   Hamilton, C.I. 'John Wilson Croker: patronage and clientage at the Admiralty, 1809–1857', *Historical Journal* 43 (2000), 49–77.

3394.   Hankins, Fred. 'From parish pauper to union workhouse inmate, Pt. 2', *Brycheiniog* 31 (1998–99), 66–108.

3395.   Hore, Peter. 'Lord Melville, the Admiralty and the coming of steam navigation', *Mariner's Mirror* 86 (2000), 157–72.

3396.   Judd, Alan. *The quest for C: Sir Mansfield Cumming and the founding of the British secret service* (London: HarperCollins, 1999), 501p.

3397.   Killingback, Alan John. 'James Golsworthy and the Exeter city water supply during the 1832 cholera epidemic', *Devonshire Association Report and Transactions* 130 (1998), 95–109.

3398.   Lindsay, Jean. 'Poor relief in North Wales and East Lothian: a comparison of the East Lothian combination poorhouse and the Bangor and Beaumaris Union workhouse, 1865–1885', *Transactions of the East Lothian Antiquarian and Field Naturalists' Society* 24 (2000), 41–66.

3399.   Martin, Moira. 'Managing the poor: the administration of poor relief in Bristol in the nineteenth and twentieth centuries', A70, 156–83.

3400.   McParland, E. 'The office of the Surveyor General in Ireland in the eighteenth century', *Architectural History* 38 (1995), 91–101.

3401.   Pennant, E.H. Douglas. 'The second Lord Penrhyn and local government 1861–1902', *Caernarvonshire Historical Society Transactions* 61 (2000), 77–88.

3402.   Rubinstein, William D. 'The hunt for Jack the Ripper', *History Today* 50:5 (2000), 10–19.

3403.   Springhall, John. 'Wanted, the elusive Charlie Peace: a Sheffield killer of the 1870's as popular hero', *Historian* 65 (2000), 10–16.

3404.   Sunderland, David. '"A monument to defective administration"?: The London Commissions of Sewers in the early nineteenth century', *Urban History* 26 (1999), 349–72.

3405.   Webster, Eric. 'The Borough of Halifax, 1848–1900', *Transactions of the Halifax Antiquarian Society* ns 8 (2000), 105–24.

Hc. *Political and Constitutional*

See also 492, 513, 515 (B); 2006, 2063 (F); 2568, 2575, 2587, 2591, 2595, 2599–600, 2604 (G); 2719, 3037, 3239, 3332, 3359 (H); 3669, 3703, 4201, 4261, 4266, 4283, 4331, 4338, 4379, 4383, 4421–2 (I); 5608 (M)

3406. Adams, T. 'Labour vanguard, Tory bastion, or the triumph of New Liberalism? Manchester politics 1900 to 1914 in comparative perspective', *Manchester Region History Review* 14 (2000), 25–38.

3407. Ashton, Owen R. 'W.E. Adams, Chartist and republican in Victorian England', A111, 120–48.

3408. Barrow, Margaret. 'Teetotal feminists: temperance leadership and the campaign for women's suffrage', A76, 69–89.

3409. Beales, D. 'The idea of reform in British politics, 1829–1850', *Proceedings of the British Academy* 100 (1999), 159–74.

3410. Belchem, John. 'The little Manx nation: antiquarianism, ethnic identity, and Home Rule politics in the Isle of Man, 1880–1918', *Journal of British Studies* 39:2 (2000), 217–40.

3411. Betts, Robin. *Dr Macnamara, 1861–1931* (Liverpool: Liverpool University Press, 1999), vii, 414p.

3412. Bevir, Mark. 'Republicanism, socialism, and democracy in Britain: the origins of the Radical Left', *Journal of Social History* 34:2 (2000), 351–68.

3413. Bevir, Mark. 'Republicanism, Socialism, and democracy: the origins of the radical left', A165, 73–89.

3414. Biagini, Eugenio F. *Gladstone* (New York: St Martin's Press, 1999), ix, 138p. [Reprinted Basingstoke: Macmillan, 2000.]

3415. Blaszak, Barbara J. *The matriarchs of England's cooperative movement: a study in gender politics and female leadership, 1883–1921* (Contributions in Labor Studies, 56) (Westport (CT) and London: Greenwood, 2000), x, 209p.

3416. Blitz, D. 'Russell and the Boer War: from imperialist to anti-imperialist', *Russell: the Journal of the Bertrand Russell Archives* [Hamilton (Ont)] 19:2 (2000), 117–42.

3417. Bolt, Christine. 'The ideas of British suffragism', A178, 34–56.

3418. Bolt, Christine. 'Was there an Anglo-American feminist movement in the earlier twentieth century?', A135, 195–211.

3419. Bradley, J.M. 'Wearing the green: a history of nationalist demonstrations among the diaspora in Scotland', A83.

3420. Bradley, Katherine. '"If the vote is good for Jack, why not for Jill?": the women's suffrage movement in Cornwall 1870–1914', *Cornish Studies* 8 (2000), 127–46.

3421. Bradley, Katherine. *Friends and visitors: history of the women's suffrage movement in Cornwall, 1870–1914* (Penzance: Patten, 2000), 90p.

3422. Burns, Arthur. 'The costs and benefits of establishment: clergy-discipline legislation in Parliament, c.1830–c.1870', *Parliamentary History* 19 (2000), 81–95.

3423. Burton, Antoinette. 'Tongues untied: Lord Salisbury's "Black man" and the boundaries of imperial democracy', *Comparative Studies in Society and History* 42:3 (2000), 632–61.

3424. Catterall, Peter. 'The British electoral system, 1885–1970', *Historical Research* 73:181 (2000), 156–74.

3425. Catterall, Peter. 'The politics of electoral reform since 1885', A39, 129–57.

3426. Chadwick, Andrew. 'A "miracle of politics": the rise of Labour, 1900–1945', A24, 322–45.

3427. Chase, Malcolm. 'Republicanism: movement or moment?', A165, 35–50.

3428. Comninel, G.C. 'Marx's context', *History of Political Thought* 21:3 (2000), 467–84.

3429. Cowman, Krista. '"Crossing the great divide": inter-organizational suffrage relationships on Merseyside, 1895–1914', A76, 37–52.

3430. Cowman, Krista. '"Giving them something to do": how the early ILP appealed to women', A211, 119–34.

3431. Cowman, Krista. 'Women's suffrage campaigns in Britain' [review article], *Women's History Review* 9:4 (2000), 815–24.

3432. Cragoe, Matthew. 'George Osborne Morgan, Henry Richard, and the politics of religion in Wales, 1868–1874', *Parliamentary History* 19 (2000), 118–30.

3433. Davies, Keith. 'Rival prophets?: William Ferris Hay, Noah Ablett and the debate over working class political action in the South Wales Coalfield 1910–1914', *Llafur* 7:3–4 (1999), 89–100.

3434. Davis, Mary. *Sylvia Pankhurst: a life in radical politics* (London: Pluto, 1999), xv, 157p.

3435. Eustance, Claire; Ugolini, Laura; Ryan, Joan. 'Writing suffrage histories—the "British" experience', A76, 1–19.

3436. Faraut, Martine. 'Bringing the country to the city: Lord Brabazon's urban politics', A20, 181–95.

3437. Fisch, Audrey A. *American slaves in Victorian England: abolitionist politics in popular literature and culture* (Cambridge: Cambridge University Press, 2000), 139p.

3438. Fletcher, Ian Christopher. '"Some interesting survivals of a historic past?": republicanism, monarchism, and the militant Edwardian left', A165, 90–105.

3439. Frances, Hilary. '"Dare to be free!": The Women's Freedom League and its legacy', A178, 181–202.

3440. Fulmer, Constance M. 'Edith Simcox: feminist critic and reformer', *Victorian Periodicals Review* 31 (1998), 105–21.

3441. Gambles, Anna. *Protection and politics: conservative economic discourse, 1815–1852* (Royal Historical Society studies in history, ns) (Woodbridge: Royal Historical Society, 1999), xi, 291p.

3442. Goodchild, John. 'Scholar, squire and socialist: John Lister (1847–1933) of Shibden Hall', *Transactions of the Halifax Antiquarian Society* ns 8 (2000), 125–32.

3443. Goodway, David. 'A newly-discovered Chartist periodical' [*McDonall's Manchester Journal*, 1850], *Labour History Review* 64 (1999), 287–88.

3444. Hall, Lesley A. '"What a lot there is still to do": Stella Browne (1880–1955)—carrying the struggle ever onward', A76, 190–205.

3445. Hannam, June. '"An enlarged sphere of usefulness": the Bristol women's movement, c.1860–1914', A70, 184–209.

3446. Hannam, June. '"I had not been to London": women's suffrage—a view from the regions', A178, 226–45.

3447. Hannam, June. '"Suffragettes are splendid for any work": the Blathwayt diaries as a source for suffrage history', A76, 53–68.

3448. Hannam, June; Hunt, Karen. 'Gendering the stories of Socialism: an essay in historical criticism', A211, 102–18.

3449. Harrison, Royden. *The life and times of Sidney and Beatrice Webb: 1858–1905, the formative years* (Basingstoke: Macmillan, 2000), xii, 397p.

3450. Holton, Sandra Stanley. 'Reflecting on suffrage history', A76, 20–36.

3451. Holton, Sandra Stanley. 'The making of suffrage history', A178, 13–33.

3452. Howarth, Janet. 'Mrs Henry Fawcett (1847–1929): the widow as a problem in feminist biography', A178, 84–108.

3453. Hunt, Karen. 'Journeying through suffrage: the politics of Dora Montefiore', A76, 162–76.

3454. Hurren, Elizabeth T. 'Labourers are revolting: penalising the poor and a political reaction in the Brixworth union, Northamptonshire, 1875–1885', *Rural History* 11 (2000), 37–55.

3455. Jenkins, Terence Andrew. 'The whips in the early-Victorian House of Commons', *Parliamentary History* 19:2 (2000), 259–86.

3456. John, Angela V. 'Between the cause and the courts: the curious case of Cecil Chapman', A76, 145–61.

3457. Johnson, Graham. 'British social democracy and religion, 1881–1911', *Journal of Ecclesiastical History* 51:1 (2000), 94–115.

3458. Johnson, Graham. 'Social democracy and Labour politics in Britain, 1892–1911', *History* 85 (2000), 67–87.

3459. Jones, H. Stuart. *Victorian political thought* (Basingstoke: Macmillan, 2000), xv, 142p.

3460. Jones, John Graham. 'Entering the Cabinet: Lloyd George and the presidency of the Board of Trade', *Transactions of the Honourable Society of Cymmrodorion* ns 6 (1999), 104–18.

3461. Jones, Mark Ellis. 'Little Wales beyond Wales: the struggle of Selattyn, a Welsh parish in Shropshire', *National Library of Wales Journal* 31:2 (1999), 129–34.

3462. Kelly, Kieran; Richardson, Mike. 'The shaping of the Bristol labour movement, 1885–1985', A70, 210–36.

3463. Laybourn, Keith. 'Leaders of the Labour Party, 1900–22', A115, 1–18.

3464. Leighton, Denys P. 'Municipal progress, democracy, and radical identity in Birmingham, 1838–1886', *Midland History* 25 (2000), 115–42.

3465. Lopatin, Nancy P. 'Refining the limits of political reporting: the provincial press, and the Great Reform Act', *Victorian Periodicals Review* 31 (1998), 337–55.

3466. Macdonald, Catriona M.M. *The radical thread: political change in Scotland. Paisley politics, 1885–1924* (Scottish Historical Review monographs series, 7) (East Linton: Tuckwell, 2000), ix, 326p.

3467. MacRaild, Donald M. '"The bunkum of Ulsteria": the Orange marching tradition in late Victorian Cumbria', A83.

3468. Markham, Jan. 'James Clay, M.P. for Hull: a pioneering constituency member', *Northern History* 36 (2000), 147–57.

3469. Martin, Graham. 'The culture of the women's suffrage movement: the McKenzie letters', *Llafur* 7:3–4 (1999), 101–12.

3470. Martin, Ross Murdoch. *The Lancashire giant: David Shackleton, labour leader and civil servant* (Liverpool: Liverpool University Press, 2000), xv, 222p.

3471. Masson, Ursula. '"Political conditions in Wales are quite different . . .": party politics and votes for women in Wales, 1912–15', *Women's History Review* 9:2 (2000), 369–88.

3472. Masson, Ursula. 'Divided loyalties: women's suffrage and party politics in south Wales 1912–1915', *Llafur* 7:3–4 (1999), 113–26.

3473. Matthew, Colin. 'Public life and politics', A145, 85–134.

3474. Mayhall, Laura E. Nym. 'Defining militancy: radical protest, the constitutional idiom, and women's suffrage in Britain, 1908–1909', *Journal of British Studies* 39:3 (2000), 340–71.

3475. McCabe, M.A. 'A question of culture?: evangelicalism and the failure of socialist revivalism in Airdrie, c.1890–1914', *Records of the Scottish Church Historical Society* 29 (1999), 107–18.

3476. McFarland, Elaine W. 'Marching from the margins: twelfth July parades in Scotland, 1820–1914', A83.

3477. McHugh, D. 'The Labour Party in Manchester and Salford before the First World War: a case of unequal development', *Manchester Region History Review* 14 (2000), 13–24.

3478. Meisel, Joseph F. 'Words by the numbers: a quantitative analysis and comparison of the oratorical careers of William Ewart Gladstone and Winston Spencer Churchill', *Historical Research* 73:182 (2000), 262–95.

3479. Morrow, J. 'Community, class and Bosanquet's "New State"', *History of Political Thought* 21:3 (2000), 485–99.

3480. Mulvey-Roberts, Marie. 'Militancy, masochism or martyrdom? The public and private prisons of Constance Lytton', A178, 159–80.

3481. Nash, David S. 'Victorian republicanism: research avenues and sideways glances', A165, 12–24.

3482. Nym Mayhall, Laura E. 'The making of a suffragette: the uses of reading and the legacy of radicalism, 1890–1918', A13, 75–88.

3483. O'Day, A. 'Irish diaspora politics in perspective: the United Irish Leagues of Great Britain and America, 1900–14', *Immigrants & Minorities* 18:2–3 (1999), 214–39.

3484. Olechnowicz, Andrzej. 'Union first, politics after: Oldham cotton unions and the Labour Party before 1914', *Manchester Region History Review* 14 (2000), 3–12.

3485. Park, Sowon S. '"Doing justice to the real girl": the Women Writers' Suffrage League', A76, 90–104.

3486. Parry, J.P. 'Disraeli and England', *Historical Journal* 43:3 (2000), 699–728.

3487. Pearce, Edward. 'Eminent Edwardian editors' [A.G. Gardiner of the *Daily News* and J.L. Garvin of the *Observer*], *History Today* 50:4 (2000), 28–33.

3488. not used.

3489. Polkey, Pauline. 'Reading history through autobiography: politically active women of late nineteenth-cenury Britain and their personal narratives', *Women's History Review* 9:3 (2000), 483–500.

3490. Pollard, Sidney. *Labour history and the labour movement in Britain* (Variorum Collected Studies Series, CS 652) (Aldershot: Ashgate, 1999), xx, 313p.

3491. Pope, Robert. 'Facing the dawn: socialists, nonconformists and *Llais Llafur*, 1906–1914', *Llafur* 7:3–4 (1999), 77–88.

3492. Powell, Leogh Michael. 'Sir Michael Hicks Beach and Conservative politics 1880–1888', *Parliamentary History* 19:3 (2000), 377–404.

3493. Pugh, Martin. *The march of the women: a revisionist lanlysis of the campaign for women's suffrage, 1866–1914* (Oxford: Oxford University Press, 2000), 303p.

3494. Purbrick, L. 'The bourgeois body: civic portraiture, public men and the appearance of class power in Manchester, 1838–50', A122, 81–98.

3495. Purvis, June. '"Deeds, not words": daily life in the Women's Social and Political Union in Edwardian Britain', A178, 135–58.

3496. Purvis, June. 'Emmeline Pankhurst (1858–1928) and votes for women', A178, 109–34.

3497. Quinault, Roland. 'Anglo-American attitudes to democracy from Lincoln to Churchill', A135, 124–141.

3498. Rembold, Elfie. '"Home rule all round": experiments in regionalising Great Britain, 1886–1914', A39, 201–24.

3499. Rendall, Jane. 'Who was Lily Maxwell? Women's suffrage and Manchester politics, 1866–1867', A178, 57–83.

3500. Riedi, Eliza. 'Options for an imperialist woman: the case of Violet Markham, 1899–1914', *Albion* 32:1 (2000), 59–84.

3501. Roberts, Andrew. *Salisbury: Victorian titan* (London: Weidenfeld & Nicolson, 1999), xxi, 938p.

3502. Roberts, John Michael. 'The enigma of free speech: Speakers' Corner, the geography of governance and a crisis of rationality', *Social & Legal Studies* 9:2 (2000), 271–92.

3503. Rogers, Helen. *Women and the people: authority, authorship and the radical tradition in nineteenth-century England* (Aldershot: Ashgate, 2000), x, 342p.

3504. Salmon, Philip. 'Local politics and partisanship: the electoral impact of municipal reform, 1835', *Parliamentary History* 19:3 (2000), 357–76.

3505. Scherer, Paul. *Lord John Russell: a biography* (Selinsgrove (PA) and London: Susquehanna University Press and Associated University Presses, 1999), 427p.

3506. Self, Robert C. *The evolution of the British party system: class, ideology and electoral competition, 1885–1940* (Harlow: Longman, 2000), ix, 217p.

3507. Shannon, Richard. *Gladstone, vol.2: Heroic minister, 1865–1898* (London: Penguin, 1999), xvii, 702p.

3508. Smart, Judith. 'Jennie Baines: suffrage and an Australian connection', A178, 246–66.

3509. Smith, Harold L. *The British Women's Suffrage Campaign, 1866–1928* (London: Longman, 1998), 122p.

3510. Soffer, Reba N. 'The long nineteenth century of conservative thought', A13, 143–62.

3511. Stack, D.A. 'The first Darwinian Left: radical and socialist responses to Darwin, 1859–1914', *History of Political Thought* 21:4 (2000), 682–710.

3512. Stack, D.A. 'William Lovett and the National Association for the Political and Social Improvement of the People', *Historical Journal* 42:4 (1999), 1027–50.

3513. Stapleton, Julia. 'Political thought and national identity in Britain, 1850–1950', A47, 245–69.

3514. Steele, Edward David. *Lord Salisbury: a political biography* (London: UCL Press, 1999), xv, 455p.

3515. Steinberg, Marc W. 'The talk and back talk of collective action: a dialogic analysis of repertoires of discourse among nineteenth-century English cotton spinners', *American Journal of Sociology* 105 (1999), 736–80.

3516. Stokes, John (ed.) *Eleanor Marx (1855–1898): life, work, contacts* (Aldershot: Ashgate, 2000), xi, 196p.

3517. Symonds, Richard. *Inside the citadel: men and the emancipation of women, 1850–1920* (Basingstoke and New York: Macmillan and St Martin's Press, 1999), x, 208p.

3518. Taylor, Antony. '"The nauseating cult of the crown": republicanism, anti-monarchism and post-Chartist politics', A165, 51–72.

3519. Taylor, Antony. 'Medium and messages: republicanism's traditions and preoccupations', A165, 1–11.

3520. Taylor, B.W. 'Annabella, Lady Noel-Byron: a study of Lady Byron on education', *History of Education Quarterly* 38 (1998), 430–55.

3521. Taylor, Miles. 'Republics versus empires: Charles Dilke's republicanism', A165, 25–34.

3522. Taylor, Robert. 'Out of the bowels of the movement: the trade unions and the origins of the Labour Party 1900–1918', A24, 8–49.

3523. Thomas, William. *The quarrel of Macaulay and Croker: politics and history in the age of reform* (Oxford: Oxford University Press, 2000), vi, 339p.

3524. Trott, Michael. 'Political assassination in Lincoln?: the strange death of Coningsby Sibthorp' [1822], *Lincolnshire History and Archaeology* 34 (1999), 38–40.

3525. Ugolini, Laura. '"It is only justice to grant women's suffrage": Independent Labour Party men and women's suffrage, 1893–1905', A76, 126–44.

3526. Walton-Jordan, Ulrike; Schwarzkopf, Jutta. 'Transforming relations of gender: the feminist project of societal reform in turn-of-the-century Britain', A39, 158–78.

3527. Warren, Allen. 'Disraeli, the Conservatives and the national church, 1837–1881', *Parliamentary History* 19 (2000), 96–117.

3528. Weintraub, Stanley. *The importance of being Edward: king in waiting, 1841–1901* (London: John Murray, 2000), xv, 443p.

3529. Wende, Peter. '1848: reform or revolution in Germany and Great Britain', *Proceedings of the British Academy* 100 (1999), 145–58.

3530. Williams, J.Ll.W. 'W.J. Parry: quarryman's champion?', *Llafur* 8:1 (2000), 97–110.

3531. Worden, Blair. 'The Victorians and Oliver Cromwell', A47, 112–35.

3532.   Worden, Blair. 'Thomas Carlyle and Oliver Cromwell', *Proceedings of the British Academy* 105 (2000), 131–70.
3533.   Wrigley, Chris. 'William Morris, art and the rise of the British Labour movement', *The Historian* [London] 67 (2000), 4–10.
3534.   Ziegler, Paul R. 'The Palmerston papers in the Broadlands archives', *Archives* 25 (2000), 88–94.

J. Military

See also 2115, 2122 (F); 2615, 2621 (G); 2688, 2964, 3034, 3036, 3071, 3158, 3396, 3593 (H); 3955, 4555, 4562, 4798 (I); 5108 (J); 6581 (P)

3535.   Beckett, Ian F.W. 'Women and patronage in the late Victorian army', *History* 85:279 (2000), 463–80.
3536.   Edgerton, Robert B. *Death or glory: the legacy of the Crimean War* (Boulder (CO): Westview, 1999).
3537.   Evans, David. 'The Royal Navy and the developments of mobile logistics 1851–94', *Mariner's Mirror* 83:2 (1997), 318–27.
3538.   Gunten, André F. von. *La Validité des ordinations Anglicanes. Les documents de la Commission Préparatoire à la lettre 'Apostolicae Curae'*, vol.1: *Les Dossiers précédents* (Fontes Archivi Sancti Officii Romani, 1) (Florence: Olschki, 1997), xxv, 263p.
3539.   Hewitson, Thomas L. *A soldier's life: the story of Newcastle Barracks, established 1806* (Newcastle upon Tyne: Tyne Bridge, 1999), 96p.
3540.   Jenkins, David. 'Cardigan, Liverpool and Sydney: the career of Captain Lewis Davies 1833–1919', *Maritime Wales* 20 (1999), 16–36.
3541.   Kerbey, John. 'Useless toys: binoculars for the British army, 1856–1945', *Army Quarterly & Defence Journal* 129:1 (1999), 64–68.
3542.   Kochanski, Halik. *Sir Garnet Wolseley: Victorian hero* (London: Hambledon, 1999), xvii, 340p.
3543.   Lambert, A.D. 'The British naval strategic revolution, 1815–1854', A113, 145–61.
3544.   Leneman, Leah. *Elsie Inglis: founder of battlefield hospitals run entirely by women* (Edinburgh: National Museums of Scotland, 1998), 94p.
3545.   Lückhoff, Martin. *Anglikaner und Protestanten im Heligen Land. Das gemeinsame Bistum Jerusalem (1841–1886)* [Anglicans and Lutherans in the Holy Land: the combined bishopric of Jerusalem] (Wiesbaden: Harrassowitz, 1998), xiv, 357p.
3546.   McCaig, A.D. ' "The soul of artillery": Congreve's rockets and their effectiveness in warfare', *Journal of the Society for Army Historical Research* 78:316 (2000), 252–63.
3547.   Morris, A.J.A. (selected & ed.). *The letters of Lieutenant-Colonel Charles à Court Repington CMG military correspondent of* The Times *1903–1918* (Stroud: Sutton for the Army Records Society, 1999), xvi, 364p.
3548.   Mulholland, John; Jordan, Alan (eds.) *Victoria Cross bibliography* (London: Spink, 1999), xvii, 217p.
3549.   Oddy, Derek J. 'Gone for a soldier: the anatomy of the nineteenth-century army family', *Journal of Family History* 25 (2000), 39–62.

3550. Oldstone-Moore, Christopher. *Hugh Price Hughes: founder of a new Methodism, conscience of a new Nonconformity* (Cardiff: University of Wales Press, 1999), ix, 393p.

3551. Owen, Brian R. 'Shako of Colonel William Le Mesurier Tupper, 6th Scots Grenadiers, 1836', *Journal of the Society for Army Historical Research* 78:314 (2000), 77–80.

3552. Paris, Michael. *Warrior nation: images of war in British popular culture, 1850–2000* (London: Reaktion, 2000), 303p.

3553. Seligmann, Matthew S. 'A view from Berlin: Colonel Frederic Trench and the development of British perceptions of German aggressive intent, 1906–1910', *Journal of Strategic Studies* 23:2 (2000), 114–147.

3554. Sheffield, Gary D. (ed.) *Leadership and command: the Anglo-American military experience since 1861* (London: Brassey's, 1997), xiii, 242p.

3555. Sibery, Elizabeth. *The new crusaders: images of crusades in the 19th and early 20th centuries* (Aldershot: Ashgate, 2000), 252p.

3556. Stone, Ian R. ' "Our little uncommercial and unenterprising island": the Isle of Man history of Sir John Ross's *Victory*, 1826–7', *Mariner's Mirror* 86 (2000), 72–75.

3557. Strachan, Hew. 'Liberalism and conscription, 1789–1919', A200, 3–16.

3558. Talbot, Philip. 'Accounting for local management control in the late Victorian volunteer army', *Journal of the Society for Army Historical Research* 78:314 (2000), 115–23.

3559. Terrell, Christopher. 'Captain Bartholomew Sullivan and British hydrography in the Baltic war of 1854–56', *Journal of the International Map Collectors Society* 68:5 (1997), 7–15.

3560. Winton, Graham R. 'The British Army, mechanisation and a new transport system, 1900–14', *Journal of the Society for Army Historical Research* 78:315 (2000), 197–212.

3561. Yates, Nigel. *Anglican ritualism in Victorian Britain, 1830–1910* (Oxford: Clarendon, 1999), xiv, 455p.

K. *Foreign Affairs*

See also 2629 (G); 2747, 2840, 2946, 3153, 3248, 3254–5, 3308, 3488 (H); 4562, 4820, 4830, 4975 (I); 6687–8 (P)

3562. Arnstein, Walter L. 'Queen Victoria and the United States', A135, 91–106.

3563. Baumgart, Winfried. *The Crimean War, 1853–1856* (London: Arnold, 1999), xi, 244p.

3564. Bickers, Robert A. 'Chinese burns: the British in China 1842–1900', *History Today* 50:8 (2000), 10–17.

3565. Blinkhorn, Martin. 'Liability, responsibility and blame: British ransom victims in the Mediterranean periphery, 1860–81', *Australian Journal of Politics & History* 46:3 (2000), 336–56.

3566. Cobbing, Andrew John (trans. & adapted by) *The Japanese discovery of Victorian Britain: early travel encounters in the Far West* (Meiji Japan Series, 5) (Richmond (Sry): Japan Library, 1998), xiii, 257p.

3567.   Cobbing, Andrew John. *The Satsuma students in Britain: Japan's early search for the 'essence of the West'* (Meiji Japan Series, 9) (Richmond (Sry): Japan Library, 2000), xvi, 201p.

3568.   Forman, Ross G. 'When Britons brave Brazil: British imperialism and the adventure tale in Latin America, 1850–1918', *Victorian Studies* 42:3 (2000), 454–87.

3569.   Golicz, Roman. 'Napoleon III, Lord Palmerston and the Entente Cordiale', *History Today* 50:12 (2000), 10–17.

3570.   Goodlad, Graham David. *British foreign and imperial policy, 1865–1919* (London: Routledge, 2000), 118p.

3571.   Graham, L. 'Belittling Scotland: Scottish travellers in France in the nineteenth century', *Scottish Studies* (1994), 137–50.

3572.   Grailles, Bénédicte. 'Amis et ennemis avant 1914: l'exemple de la Russie, de l'Angleterre et de l'Allemagne', *Revue du Nord* 80 (1998), 255–83.

3573.   Grant, Alfred. *The American Civil War and the British press* (Jefferson (NC): McFarland, 2000), viii, 197p.

3574.   Hamilton, Keith. 'The poor relation: Spain in Anglo-French relations, 1898–1914', A191, 50–70.

3575.   Hawkins, Richard A. 'An English entrepreneur in the Hawaiian Islands: the life and times of John Kidwell, 1849–1922', *Hawaiian Journal of History* 31 (1997), 127–42.

3576.   Leventhal, Fred M.; Quinault, Roland. 'Introduction' [Anglo-American attitudes: from revolution to partnership], A135, 1–8.

3577.   Lynch, John. *Massacre in the Pampas, 1872: Britain and Argentina in the age of migration* (Norman (OK): University of Oklahoma Press, 1998), xiii, 237p.

3578.   Maisch, Christian J. 'The Falkland/Malvinas Islands clash of 1831–32: U.S. and British diplomacy in the South Atlantic', *Diplomatic History* 24 (2000), 185–209.

3579.   McDonough, Frank. 'The Conservative party and the Anglo-French entente, 1905–1914', A191, 36–49.

3580.   Meironke, Wolfgang. 'Lord Palmerston und die "Piratenflagge" Schwarz-Rot-Gold' [Palmerston and the [German republican] black, red and gold 'pirate flag'], *Schiff und Fahrt* 48 (1998), 1–8.

3581.   Melancon, Glenn T. 'Peaceful intentions: the first British trade commission in China, 1833–5', *Historical Research* 72 (2000), 34–47.

3582.   Morris, P. 'Some nineteenth century English views of French politics', *Collection École francaise de Rome* 240 (1997), 24–39.

3583.   Motono, Eiichi. *Conflict and cooperation in Sino-British business, 1860–1911: the impact of pro-British commercial network in Shanghai* (Basingstoke and New York: Macmillan and St Martin's Press in association with St Antony's College, Oxford, 2000), xiii, 229p.

3584.   Otte, T.G. 'A question of leadership: Lord Salisbury, the Unionist Cabinet and foreign policy making, 1895–1900', *Contemporary British History* 14:4 (2000), 1–26.

3585.   Otte, Thomas. 'The elusive balance: British foreign policy and the French entente before the First World War', A191, 11–35.

3586.   Pons, André. 'Bolívar y Blanco White', *Annuario de Estudios Americanos* 55:2 (1998).

3587. Preston, Diana. *Besieged in Peking: the story of the 1900 Boxer Rising* (London: Constable, 1999), xiv, 322p.

3588. Preston, Diana. 'The Boxer Rising', *Asian Affairs* 31:1 (2000), 26–36.

3589. Seldon, Anthony. *Foreign Office: the illustrated history* (London: HarperCollinsIllustrated, 2000), 240p.

3590. Urbach, Karina. *Bismarck's favourite Englishman: Lord Odo Russell's mission to Berlin* (London: I.B. Tauris, 1999), vii, 279p.

3591. Vale, Brian. *A war betwixt Englishmen: Brazil against Argentina on the River Plate 1825–1830* (2000).

3592. Vogt, Martin. 'Der Zollverein im Vormärz und England', *Mitteilungen des Bundesarchivs* (1998), 11–22.

3593. Wong, J.Y. 'The limits of naval power: British gunboat diplomacy in China from the *Nemesis* to the *Amethyst*, 1839–1949', *War & Society* 18:2 (2000), 93–120.

3594. Wrigley, Chris (ed. & intr.) *Struggles for supremacy: diplomatic essays by A.J.P. Taylor* (Aldershot: Ashgate, 2000), vii, 395p.

3595. Zachs, F. '"Novice" or "heaven-born" diplomat? Lord Dufferin and his plan for a "Province of Syria": Beirut, 1860–61', *Middle Eastern Studies* 36:3 (2000), 160–176.

I. BRITAIN SINCE 1914

A. *General*

See also 243 (B); 2633, 2636, 2639–40 (H)

3596. Annan, Noel. 'Our Age revisited', A138, 265–80.

3597. Black, Jeremy. *Modern British history since 1900* (Basingstoke: Palgrave, 2000), xx, 378p.

3598. Wynne Lewis, J. 'Dau Forwr Cymreig', *Maritime Wales* 20 (1999), 80–83.

B. *Historiography and Historical Methods*

See also 1338 (F); 2151, 2209 (G); 2641, 2645 (H); 3841, 3974, 4014, 4020, 4382, 4744 (I)

3599. Addison, Paul. 'British historians and the debate over the "postwar consensus"', A138, 255–64.

3600. Bagworth-Mann, Hazel. 'The Historical Manuscripts Commission', *History of Education Society Bulletin* 66 (2000), 110–13.

3601. Bell, Patricia L. 'Amy Joyce Godber (1906–1999)', *Journal of the Society of Archivists* 21:2 (2000), 221–5.

3602. Cantwell, John D. *The Public Record Office, 1959–1969* (Richmond: PRO, 2000), x, 172p. [Sequel to *The Public Record Office 1838–1958*, published London: HMSO, 1991.]

3603. Cohen, Ronald. *Bibliography of the works of Sir Winston Churchill* (London: Mansell, 2000)

3604. Green, David; Seddon, Peter (eds.) *History painting reassessed: the representation of history in contemporary art* (Manchester: Manchester University Press, 2000), 162p.

3605. Javurek, Teresa. 'A new Liberal descent: the "Labourer" trilogy by Lawrence and Barbara Hammond', *20th Century British History* 10:4 (1999), 375–403.

3606. Jones, Harriet. 'Free information', *History Today* 50:8 (2000), 18–19. [The Freedom of Information Act]

3607. Jordanova, Ludmilla. 'Public history', *History Today* 50:5 (2000), 20–21.

3608. Kaye, Harvey J. 'Fanning the spark of hope in the past: the British Marxist historians', *Rethinking History* 4:3 (2000), 281–94.

3609. Lebowitz, Arieh. 'Jews and the trade union movements in the UK and US: select bibliographical sources', A46, 158–77.

3610. Levitt, Ian. 'Scottish Air Services, 1933–75 and the Scottish New Towns, 1943–75: a guide to records at the National Archives of Scotland', *Scottish Archives* 5 (1999), 67–82.

3611. Lord, Evelyn. *Investigating the 20th century: sources for local historians* (Stroud: Tempus, 1999), 160p.

3612. Mathias, P. 'Sidney Pollard', *Journal of European Economic History* 28 (1999), 411–15.

3613. Navari, Cornelia. 'Arnold Toynbee (1889–1975): prophecy and civilization', *Review of International Studies* 26:2 (2000), 289–302.

3614. Obelkevich, Jim. 'New developments in history in the 1950s and 1960s', *Contemporary British History* 14:4 (2000), 125–42. [With witness seminar report, 143–67.]

3615. Pfaff, Richard W. 'The Lavington manual and its students', *Bodleian Library Record* 17:1 (2000), 10–23.

3616. Reid, Norman H. 'The photographic collections in St Andrews University Library', *Scottish Archives* 5 (1999), 83–90.

3617. Snowman, Daniel. 'John Keegan', *History Today* 50:5 (2000), 28–30.

3618. Soffer, Reba N. 'British Conservative historiography and the Second World War', A201, 373–99.

3619. Soffer, Reba N. 'Commitment and catastrophe: twentieth-century conservative historiography in Britain and America', A135, 227–42.

3620. Stuart, Flora Maxwell. 'Inside view', *Scottish Archives* 5 (1999), 7–11. [Archives (at Traquair) from the private owner's perspective.]

3621. Tate, T. 'Modernism, history, and the First World War', *Modernism/Modernity* 7:1 (2000), 174–75.

3622. Watters, Diane. 'Complexity and diversity: case studies in Scottish twentieth-century architectural archives', *Scottish Archives* 5 (1999), 91–99.

C. Population and Environment

See also 2649, 2651, 2657, 2661, 2665, 2668–71, 3209 (H); 4207, 4259, 4274 (I)

3623.   Brace, Catherine. 'A pleasure ground for the noisy herds?: incompatible encounters with the Cotswolds and England, 1900–1950', *Rural History* 11:1 (2000), 75–94.

3624.   Campbell, Sean. 'Beyond "Plastic Paddy": a re-examination of the second-generation Irish in England', *Immigrants & Minorities* 18:2–3 (1999), 266–88.

3625.   Chapman, David; et al. (eds.) *Region and renaissance: reflections on planning and development in the West Midlands, 1950–2000* (Studley: Brewin, 2000), 244p.

3626.   Connerly, C.E. '"One great city" or colonial economy? Explaining Birmingham's annexation struggles, 1945–1990', *Journal of Urban History* 26:1 (1999), 44–73.

3627.   Connolly, Tracey. 'Emigration from Ireland to Britain during the Second World War', A15, 51–64.

3628.   Delaney, Enda. '"Almost a class of helots in an alien land": the British state and Irish immigration, 1921–45', *Immigrants & Minorities* 18:2–3 (1999), 240–65.

3629.   Delaney, Enda. 'Placing postwar Irish migration to Britain in a comparative European perspective, 1945–1981', A15, 331–56.

3630.   Faulkner, Thomas. 'From Grainger to "Grainger Town": visions and visionaries of Newcastle upon Tyne', A20, 131–48.

3631.   Fry, D. 'Binley Woods: a Warwickshire example of inter-war "shack and track" development', *The Local Historian* 30:3 (2000), 139–149.

3632.   Gray, Breda. 'From "ethnicity" to "diaspora": 1980s emigration and "multicultural" London' [Irish migration], A15, 65–88.

3633.   Halpin, Brendan. 'Who are the Irish in Britain? Evidence from large-scale surveys', A15, 89–108.

3634.   Harris, Peter (ed.) *Post-war Bristol 1945–1965: twenty years that changed the city* (Local history pamphlets, 100) (Bristol: Bristol Branch of the Historical Association, 2000), 144p.

3635.   Hasegawa, Junichi. 'The reconstruction of Portsmouth in the 1940s', *Contemporary British History* 14:1 (1999), 45–62.

3636.   Hayes, Nick. 'Civic perceptions: housing and local decision-making in English cities in the 1920s', *Urban History* 27:2 (2000), 211–33.

3637.   Heathfield, John; Reboul, Percy. *Barnet: the twentieth century: including Finchley, Edgware and Hendon* (Stroud: Sutton, 1999), 128p.

3638.   Holbrook, A. *Tidal barrages in the Severn estuary: a bibliography 1904–1999* (Bath: University of Bath Press, 2000), i, 79p.

3639.   Homer, Andrew. 'Creating new communities: the role of the neighbourhood unit in post-war British planning', *Contemporary British History* 14:1 (1999), 63–80.

3640.   Johnes, Martin; McLean, Iain. 'Echoes of injustice' [aftermath of Aberfan disaster, 1966], *History Today* 50:12 (2000), 28–30.

3641. Jones, Harriet. "'This is magnificent!": 300,000 houses a year and the Tory revival after 1945', *Contemporary British History* 14:1 (1999), 99–121.

3642. Lambert, R.A. 'Conservation, recreation and tourism: Craigellachie National Nature Reserve, Aviemore, 1950–1980', *Northern Scotland* 20 (2000), 113–24.

3643. Lebas, Elizabeth. 'The making of a socialist arcadia: arboriculture and horticulture in the London borough of Bermondsey after the Great War', *Garden History* 27:2 (1999), 219–37.

3644. Mackey, Edward C.; Shewry, Michael C.; Tudor, Gavin J. *Land cover change: Scotland from the 1940s to the 1980s* (Natural Heritage of Scotland, 6) (Edinburgh: Stationery Office, 1998), xxvii, 263p.

3645. Maclean, Catherine. 'Getting out and getting on: Scottish Highland migration in the first half of the twentieth century', *Rural History* 11:2 (2000), 231–48.

3646. Martin, Geoffrey H. 'Destruction and reconstruction: debate and practice in Britain during and after World War II', A128, 409–22.

3647. Pooley, Colin G. 'From Londonderry to London: identity and sense of place for a Protestant Northern Irish woman in the 1930s', *Immigrants & Minorities* 18:2–3 (1999), 189–213.

3648. Rifkin, Adrian. 'Benjamin's Paris? Freud's Rome? Whose London? Imaging London after World War II', A7. [See also *Art History* 22:4 (1999), 619–32.]

3649. Tiratsoo, Nick. 'The reconstruction of blitzed British cities, 1945–55: myths and reality', *Contemporary British History* 14:1 (1999), 27–44.

3650. Tsubaki, Tatsuya. 'Planners and the public: British popular opinion on housing during the Second World War', *Contemporary British History* 14:1 (1999), 81–98.

Da. *Social Life and Conditions*

See also 2683, 2684, 2690–1, 2695–6, 2699, 2701, 2706, 2709, 2711, 2719–20, 2735–6, 2754, 2762, 2764 (H); 4147, 4279, 4425, 4544, 4621, 4653, 4706, 4724, 4733, 4769, 4790, 4801, 4806 (I)

3651. Atkins, Nicholas. 'L'accueil des réfugiés français en Grande-Bretagne' [The reception of French refugees in Britain in 1940], *Autrement Mémoires* 62 (2000), 113–25.

3652. Ayers, Pat. 'The making of men: masculinities in interwar Liverpool', A211, 66–83.

3653. Beaumont, Catriona. 'Citizens not feminists: the boundary negotiated between citizenship and feminism by mainstream women's organisations in England, 1928–39', *Women's History Review* 9:2 (2000), 411–29.

3654. Burman, Barbara. 'Racing bodies: dress and pioneer women aviators and racing drivers', *Women's History Review* 9:2 (2000), 299–326.

3655. Capet, Antoine. 'Logement et santé dans une ville sacrifiée: Jarrow dans les années 1930 vue par Ellen Wilkinson' [Housing and health in a 'murdered' town: 1930s Jarrow as seen by Ellen Wilkinson (from *The Town that was Murdered*, 1939)], A37, 175–89.

3656. Carré, Jacques. 'A.L. Bowley et A.R. Burnett-Hurst étudient les familles ouvrières à Reading en 1915' [A.L. Bowley and A.R. Burnett-Hurst's study of Reading working-class households in 1915 (from *Livelihood and Poverty: A Study in the Economic Conditions of Working-Class Households in Northampton, Warrington, Stanley and Reading*, 1915)], A37, 158–73.

3657. Charlot, Claire. 'La famille à l'épreuve de la libération des mœurs' [The family tested by the liberation of mores], A35, 53–68.

3658. Chassaigne, Philippe. *Pauvreté et inégalités en Grande-Bretagne de 1942 à 1990, 2 vols.: 1. Analyse et synthèse; 2. Textes et documents* [Poverty and inequality in Britain] (Paris: Messene, 2000).

3659. Clapson, Mark. 'The suburban aspiration in England since 1919', *Contemporary British History* 14:1 (1999), 151–74.

3660. Curcuru, Monique. 'Peter Willmott et Michael Young comparent anciennes et nouvelles banlieues ouvrières à Londres dans les années 1950' [Peter Willmott and Michael Young's comparison of old and new London suburbs in the 1950s (from *Family and Kinship in East London*, 1957)], A37, 191–200.

3661. Davies, Christie; Trivizas, Eugene; Wolfe, Roy. 'The failure of calendar reform (1922–1931): religious minorities, businessmen, scientists, and bureaucrats', *Journal of Historical Sociology* 12:3 (1999), 251–70.

3662. D'Cruze, Shani. 'Dainty little fairies: women, gender and the Savoy operas', *Women's History Review* 9:2 (2000), 345–68.

3663. Deakin, Nicholas (ed.) *Origins of the welfare state* (London: Routledge, 2000), 8 vols. [Reprints: 1. *The Next Five Years* (1935); 2. G.D.H. Cole, *Plan for Democratic Britain* (1939); E.F.M. Durbin, *What Have We to Defend?* (1942); 3. Margery Spring Rice, *Working Class Wives* (1939); 4. *Our Towns* (1942); *When We Build Again* (1942); 5. François Lafitte, *Britain's Way to Social Security*; William Beveridge, *Summary of Full Employment*; 6. Innes Pearce and Lucy Crocker, *The Peckham Experiment* (1943); 7. Ferdinand Zweig, *Life and Poverty* (1948); 8. George Watson, *The Unservile State* (1957).]

3664. Dean, Dennis. 'The race relations policy of the first Wilson Government', *20th Century British History* 11:3 (2000), 259–83.

3665. Evans, Ross. *Ross's story: 20th century farming in south west Scotland: an autobiography* (Dumfries: Dumfries and Galloway Libraries, Information and Archives, 1998), vii, 94p.

3666. Fink, Janet. 'Natural mothers, putative fathers, and innocent children: the definition and regulation of parental relationships outside marriage, in England, 1945–1959', *Journal of Family History* 25 (2000), 178–95.

3667. Finklestone, Joseph. *Ben Helfgott: from victim to champion* (London: Vallentine Mitchell, 2000).

3668. Fisher, Kate. '"She was quite satisfied with the arrangements I made": gender and birth control in Britain, 1920–1950', *Past & Present* 169 (2000), 161–93.

3669. Forbes, Grania. *My darling Buffy: the early life of the Queen Mother* (London: Richard Cohen, 1997), xvi, 206p.

3670. Francis, Martin. 'Labour and gender', A202, 191–220.

3671.   Goh, R.B. 'Peter O'Donnell, relations and national identity: the dynamics of representation in 1960s and 1970s Britain', *Journal of Popular Culture* 32:4 (1999), 29–44.

3672.   Gordon, Alan. 'Minimum wages, flexibility and social exclusion', A74, 145–61.

3673.   Green, Jeffrey. 'Before the *Windrush*' [the black presence in Britain prior to the arrival of the *Empire Windrush* from the West Indies in 1948], *History Today* 50:10 (2000), 29–35.

3674.   Greenfield, Jill; O'Connell, Sean; Reid, Chris. 'Gender, consumer culture and the middle-class male, 1918–39', A122, 183–97.

3675.   Grieves, K. 'Investigating local war memorial committees: demobilised soldiers, the bereaved and expressions of local pride in Sussex villages, 1918–1921', *The Local Historian* 30:1 (2000), 39–58.

3676.   Hansen, Randall A. *Citizenship and immigration in post-war Britain: the institutional origins of a multicultural nation* (Oxford: Oxford University Press, 2000), xiii, 301p.

3677.   Harrison, Brian. 'The public and private in modern Britain', A29, 337–58.

3678.   Horrell, Sara. 'Living standards in Britain 1900–2000: women's century?', *National Institute Economic Review* 172 (2000), 62–77.

3679.   Horwood, Catherine. '"Girls who arouse dangerous passions": women and bathing, 1900–39', *Women's History Review* 9:4 (2000), 653–74.

3680.   Houlbrook, Matt. 'The private world of public urinals: London 1918–1957', *London Journal* 25:1 (2000), 52–70.

3681.   Humphries, Steve; Hopwood, Beverley. *Green and pleasant land* (London: Channel 4 Books, 1999), 174p.

3682.   Hylton, Stuart. *Magical history tour: the 1960s revisited* (Stroud: Sutton, 2000), 182p.

3683.   Johnes, Martin. 'Eighty minute patriots? National identity and sport in modern Wales', *International Journal of the History of Sport* 17:4 (2000), 93–110.

3684.   Jones, Moya. 'The feminisation of poverty: increasing visibility', A84, 116–25.

3685.   Jones, William David; Williams, Chris. *B.L. Coombes* (Writers of Wales series (Cardiff: University of Wales Press, 1999), 128p. [Author of *These Poor Hands: The Autobiography of a Miner* (Left Book Club, Gollancz, 1939).]

3686.   Jones, William David. 'The B.L. Coombes archive', *Welsh Writing in English* 5 (1999), 150–57.

3687.   Kear, Adrian; Steinberg, Deborah Lynn (eds.) *Mourning Diana: nation, culture and the performance of grief* (London: Routledge, 1999), xi, 218p.

3688.   Kersaudy, François. 'Churchill et l'alcool: les coulisses de l'exploit' [Churchill and alcohol: finding an explanation for the exploit], *Historia* [Paris] 619 (1998), 76–81.

3689.   Leggett, Matthew. 'Immigration and race relations from World War II to 1990', A84, 79–90.

3690.   Lemosse, Michel. 'École et inégalités' [Schooling & inequality]', A42, 86–103.

3691. Lowerson, John. 'An outbreak of allodoxia? Operatic amateurs and middle-class musical taste between the wars', A122, 198–212.

3692. McKay, George. *Glastonbury: a very English fair* (London: Gollancz, 2000), 212p.

3693. Nicholson, Shirley. *An Edwardian bachelor: Roy Sambourne, 1878–1946* (London: Victorian Society, 1999), 120p.

3694. Nottage, Jane. *The Gleneagles Hotel: 75 years of Scottish excellence* (London: HarperCollins, 1999), 212p.

3695. Olechnowicz, Andrzej. 'Civic leadership and education for democracy: the Simons and the Wythenshawe Estate', *Contemporary British History* 14:1 (1999), 3–26.

3696. Palmer, Sarah. 'Women and the First World War', A218, 186–200.

3697. Pemberton, John; White, Jerry. 'The Boyd Orr survey of the nutrition of children in Britain, 1937–9, . . . with extracts from Gwen Pemberton's diaries', *History Workshop Journal* 50 (2000), 205–29.

3698. Physick, Ray; Holt, Richard. '"Big money": the tournament player and the PGA, 1945–75', *Contemporary British History* 14:2 (2000), 60–80.

3699. Plummer, Philip C. *A brief history of Courtenay Warner and Warner Estate: Walthamstow, Leyton, Woodford* (Walthamstow Historical Society monograph, ns, 31) (Walthamstow: Walthamstow Historical Society, 2000), 63p.

3700. Polley, Martin. '"The amateur rules": amateurism and professionalism in post-war British athletics', *Contemporary British History* 14:2 (2000), 81–114.

3701. Porter, Dilwyn. 'Amateur football in England, 1948–63: the Pegasus phenomenon', *Contemporary British History* 14:2 (2000), 1–30.

3702. Prum, Michel (ed.) *Exclure au nom de la race (États-Unis, Irlande, Grande-Bretagne)* [Exclusion on racial grounds (United States, Ireland, Britain)] (Paris: Syllepse, 2000), 159p.

3703. Rhodes, Rita M. *An arsenal for labour: the Royal Arsenal Co-operative Society and politics, 1896–1996* (Manchester: Holyoake Books, 1998), viii, 288p.

3704. Risoli, Mario. *When Pele broke our hearts: Wales and the 1958 World Cup* (Cardiff: Ashley Drake, 1998), vii, 161p.

3705. Roberts, O. 'The Royal Holyhead Yacht Club', *Maritime Wales* 21 (2000), 59–70.

3706. Rodger, Richard. 'Slums and suburbs: the persistence of residential apartheid', A210, 233–68.

3707. Sankey-Barker, Sarah. 'Life in Llangattock in the first half of the twentieth century', *Brycheiniog* 32 (2000), 112–52.

3708. Savage, Mike. 'Sociology, class and male manual work cultures', A32, 23–42.

3709. Scott, Peter. 'The state, internal migration, and the growth of new industrial communities in inter-war Britain', *English Historical Review* 115 (2000), 329–53.

3710. Seymour, Miranda. *Ottoline Morrell: life on the grand scale*, new edn. (London: Sceptre, 1998), 607p. [1st published by Hodder & Stoughton, 1992.]

3711. Smith, Adrian. 'Civil war in England: the clubs, the RFU and the impact of professionalism on Rugby Union, 1995–99', *Contemporary British History* 14:2 (2000), 146–88.

3712. Summerfield, Penny; Peniston-Bird, Corinna. 'Women in the firing line: the Home Guard and the defence of gender boundaries in Britain in the Second World War', *Women's History Review* 9:2 (2000), 231–55.

3713. Taylor, John A. *Diana, self-interest and British national identity* (Westport (CT): Praeger, 2000), x, 168p.

3714. Tizot, Jean-Yves. 'Le témoignage d'un médecin londonien, David Widgery, en 1991 sur les «moins favorisés»' [The 1991 testimony of a London physician, David Widgery, on the underprivileged (from *Some Lives! A GP's East End*, 1991)], A37, 217–31.

3715. Walton, John K. *The British seaside: holidays and resorts in the twentieth century* (Manchester: Manchester University Press, 2000), viii, 216p.

3716. Webster, Wendy. 'Defining boundaries: European volunteer worker women in Britain and narratives of community', *Women's History Review* 9:2 (2000), 257–76.

3717. White, Carol; Williams, Sian Rhiannon (eds.) *Struggle or starve: women's lives in the south Wales valleys between the two world wars* (Dinas Powys: Honno, 1998), 275p.

3718. Williams, Bill. *Sir Sidney Hamburger and Manchester Jewry: religion, city and community* (London: Vallentine Mitchell, 1999), xiii, 306p.

3719. Williamson, Margaret. '"Getting off at Loftus": sex and the working-class woman, 1920–1960', *Family & Community History* 3:1 (2000), 5–17.

3720. Wilson, Christopher. *Dancing with the devil: the Windsors and Jimmy Donahue* (London: HarperCollins, 2000), xv, 270p.

3721. Woodward, N. 'Why did south Wales miners have high mortality? evidence from the mid-twentieth century', *Welsh History Review* 20:1 (2000), 116–142.

3722. Yelling, Jim. 'The incidence of slum clearance in England and Wales, 1955–85', *Urban History* 27:2 (2000), 234–54.

3723. Zweiniger-Bargielowska, Ina. *Austerity in Britain: rationing, controls, and consumption, 1939–1955* (Oxford: Oxford University Press, 2000), xiii, 286p.

Db. *Social Structure*

See also 1438 (F); 2209 (G); 2768–9, 2773–5, 2784–5, 2787, 2789, 2795, 2797 (H); 3771, 3883, 4271, 4342, 4398 (I)

3724. Atkinson, A.B. 'Income inequality in the UK', A42, 76–85.

3725. Barret-Ducrocq, Françoise. 'Les femmes subissent-elles une inégalité spécifique?' [Do women suffer a specific inequality?], A42, 15–22.

3726. Bugler, Simon Peter. 'Relocation of immigrant and migrant labour and the social construction of ethnic identity: examples from British Africa and post-war Britain', *Cahiers du CICC* 12 (2000), 1–24.

3727. Capet, Antoine. 'Le débat sur les inégalités, 1942–1951' [The debate on inequality], *Revue française de civilisation britannique* 11–1 (2000), 19–40.

3728. Low, Eugenia. 'Class and the conceptualization of citizenship in twentieth-century Britain', *History of Political Thought* 21 (2000), 114–31.
3729. Mougel, François-Charles. 'Les indicateurs de la pauvreté, 1942–1990' [Indicators of poverty], A84, 67–77.
3730. Rubinstein, William D. 'Britain's elites in the interwar period, 1918–39', A123, 186–202.
3731. Spensky, Martine. 'Le genre de la pauvreté' [The gender of poverty], A197, 91–116.
3732. Trainor, Richard. 'Neither metropolitan nor provincial: the interwar middle class', A123, 203–13.
3733. Waters, Chris. 'Autobiography, nostalgia, and the changing practices of working-class selfhood', A13, 178–95.

Dc. *Social Policy and Welfare*

See also 2802, 2813, 2819, 2822 (H); 3697, 3783, 3949, 3965, 3973, 3976, 4192, 4268, 4273 (I)

3734. Abrams, Lynn. 'Lost childhoods: recovering children's experience of welfare in modern Scotland', A81, 152–72.
3735. Appleby, J. 'Government funding of the UK National Health Service: what does the historical record reveal?', *Journal of Health Services Research and Policy* 4:2 (1999), 79–89.
3736. Avril, Emmanuelle. 'L'attitude du Parti travailliste face à l'injustice sociale, 1942–1990' [Labour's position regarding social injustice], A84, 151–63.
3737. Avril, Emmanuelle. 'Le Parti travailliste et la pauvreté' [The Labour Party and poverty], A42, 51–75.
3738. Bridgen, Paul. 'The One Nation idea and state welfare: the Conservatives and pensions in the 1950s', *Contemporary British History* 14:3 (2000), 83–104.
3739. Busfield, Joan. *Health and health care in modern Britain* (Oxford: Oxford University Press, 2000), xiv, 199p.
3740. Capet, Antoine. '«Beveridge» et l'éradication de la pauvreté' ['Beveridge' and the elimination of poverty], A42, 23–50.
3741. Case, Philip. *A history of Dorking and district Age Concern: including Dorking Old Peoples Welfare Committee and Dorking and District Old People's Welfare Association, 1946 to 1996* (Dorking: Pre-School Supplies, 1999), 154p.
3742. Charlot, Claire. 'La pauvreté au Royaume-Uni: évolution d'un concept sociologique (1942–1990)' [Poverty in the United Kingdom: the evolution of a sociological concept], *Études anglaises* 53:4 (2000), 488–98.
3743. Charlot, Monica. 'Perceptions of Poverty', A42, 114–31.
3744. Crowley, Cornelius. 'La pauvreté dans une «ère d'abondance»: Science sociale et politiques publiques, 1942–1974' [Poverty in the 'affluent society': social science and public policies], A84, 36–50.
3745. Curcuru, Monique. 'Le logement social en Grande-Bretagne, 1945–1990' [Public housing in Britain], A84, 126–35.

3746. Cutler, Tony; James, Phillip; MacGregor, Susanne; Waine, Barbara. '«Modernisation» or insecurity: labour market deregulation and state retrenchment—the British case', A74, 75–93.

3747. Edwards, John. 'Conceptions of poverty, 1945–1990', Revue française de civilisation britannique 11:1 (2000), 7–18.

3748. Fraser, Derek. The welfare state (Stroud: Sutton, 2000), 128p.

3749. Freeman, Peggy. Good sense: the National Deafblind and Rubella Association, 1955–1995 (London: Sense, 1996), 200p.

3750. Frison, Danièle. 'Évolution du concept de pauvreté au XXe siècle' [The evolution of the concept of poverty in 20th-century Britain], A84, 9–21.

3751. Garside, Patricia L. 'The impact of philanthropy: housing provision and the Sutton Model Dwellings Trust, 1900–1939', Economic History Review 2nd ser. 53:4 (2000), 742–66.

3752. Ginn, Jay. 'Poverty and inequality among older people in post-war Britain: the gender dimension', Revue française de civilisation britannique 11:1 (2000), 101–14.

3753. Gladstone, David. 'Introduction: welfare before the welfare state', A90, 1–9.

3754. Gladstone, David. The twentieth-century welfare state (Basingstoke: Macmillan, 1999), ix, 176p.

3755. Green, David G. 'The friendly societies and Adam-Smith liberalism', A90, 18–25.

3756. Hall, Lesley A. (ed.) Marie Stopes: birth control and other writings (Bristol: Thoemmes Press, 2000), 5 vols.

3757. Hatton, Timothy J.; Bailey, Roy E. 'Seebohm Rowntree and the postwar poverty puzzle', Economic History Review 53:3 (2000), 517–43.

3758. Hutchings, Deborah. Monyhull, 1908–1998: a history of caring (Studley: Brewin, 1998), 167p.

3759. Jacobs, John. 'Beveridge slays the Giant Want—or does he?', A197, 63–90.

3760. King, Desmond S. In the name of liberalism: illiberal social policy in the USA and Britain (Oxford: Oxford University Press, 1999), xiii, 340p.

3761. Latham, Emma. 'The Liverpool Boys' Association and the Liverpool Union of Youth Clubs: youth organizations and gender, 1940–70', Journal of Contemporary History 35:3 (2000), 423–38.

3762. Leruez, Jacques. 'L'actualité de Beveridge: A propos de la réédition de la grande biographie de William Beveridge' [Beveridge's relevance today: on the new edition of Beveridge's great biography; review article], Vingtième Siècle 61 (1999), 135–39.

3763. Lewis, Jane. 'The voluntary sector in the mixed economy of welfare', A90, 10–17.

3764. Lister, Ruth. 'The politics of child poverty in Britain from 1965 to 1990', Revue française de civilisation britannique 11:1 (2000), 67–80.

3765. MacGregor, Susan. 'Shifting images of poverty and inequality in Britain 1942–1990: the political and institutional context', A197, 7–40.

3766. Macnicol, John. 'Reconstructing the «Underclass», 1942–90', A197, 117–38.

3767. Montgomery, George. Silent destiny: a brief history of Donaldson's College (Edinburgh: Scottish Workshop, 1997), 179p.

3768. Perry, Matt. *Bread and work: social policy and the experience of unemployment, 1918–39* (London: Pluto, 2000), xv, 244p.

3769. Powell, Martin. 'Wales and the National Health Service', *Llafur* 8:1 (2000), 33–44.

3770. Révauger, Jean-Paul. 'Interprétations culturelles de la pauvreté et stratégies politiques, 1970–1990' [Cultural interpretations of poverty and political strategies], A197, 139–59.

3771. Révauger, Jean-Paul. 'Pauvreté, égalité et universalisme de Beveridge à Wilson' [Poverty, equality and universalism from Beveridge to Wilson], *Revue française de civilisation britannique* 11:1 (2000), 115–27.

3772. Rodriguez, Jacques. 'Pauvreté et inégalité: Le rôle des sciences sociales dans les débats politiques britanniques, 1942–1990' [Poverty and inequality: the role of the social sciences in British political debates, 1942–90], A84, 221–31.

3773. Spicker, Paul. 'Poverty, inequality and the welfare state', A197, 41–62.

3774. Spicker, Paul. 'There and back again: the Welfare state, 1942–1990', *Revue française de civilisation britannique* 11:1 (2000), 41–56.

3775. Starkey, Pat. 'The feckless mother: women, poverty and social workers in wartime and post-war England', *Women's History Review* 9:3 (2000), 539–57.

3776. Stevens, R.A. 'Fifty years of the British National Health Service: mixed messages, diverse interpretations', *Bulletin of the History of Medicine* 74:4 (2000), 806–11.

3777. Thane, Pat. 'Labour and welfare', A202, 80–118.

3778. Tizot, Jean-Yves. 'De la question sociale à la question urbaine: Un regard sur l'émergence et l'évolution des «politiques sociales urbaines» dans la Grande-Bretagne d'après-guerre' [From the social question to the urban question: an examination of the emergence and evolution of 'urban social policies' in post-war Britain], A84, 192–206.

3779. Vincent, A.W. 'The poor law reports of 1909 and the social theory of the Charity Organisation Society', A90, 64–85. [1st published in *Victorian Studies* 27:3 (1984).]

3780. Whiteside, Noel. 'Private provision and public welfare: health insurance between the wars', A90, 26–42.

3781. Wilson, Peter. *Tale of two trusts: an account of the Frank Parkinson trusts* (Spennymoor: Memoir Club, 2000), xvi, 234p.

Ea. *Economic Activity and Organisation*

See also 378, 408, 418 (B); 2238, 2283 (G); 2683, 2823, 2828, 2832, 2842, 2853, 2857, 2859, 2862–4, 2873, 2878, 2882, 2895–6, 2900–1, 2907, 2910, 2915–16, 2918, 2922, 2929, 2943, 2948–9, 2951, 2955–6, 3388 (H); 3709, 3914–15, 3940, 4004, 4139, 4195, 4209, 4212, 4214, 4287, 4335, 4343, 4363, 4394, 4405, 4418, 4430, 4434, 4706, 4805, 4815, 4838, 4844, 4848, 4889, 4891, 4920, 4926, 4933, 4936, 4991 (I); 6252 (P)

3782. Anonymous. 'Index to the contents of Scottish Industrial History volumes 1–20 (1976–2000)', *Scottish Industrial History* 21 (2000), 54–78.

3783.   Alexander, Sally. 'Men's fears and women's work: responses to unemployment in London between the wars', *Gender & History* 12:2 (2000), 401–25.

3784.   Baines, Dudley; Johnson, Paul. 'Did they jump or were they pushed?: the exit of older men from the London labor market, 1919–1931', *Journal of Economic History* 59:4 (1999), 949–71.

3785.   Balisciano, M.L.; Medema, S.G. 'Positive science, normative man: Lionel Robbins and the political economy of art', *History of Political Economy* 31 (suppl.) (2000), 256–284.

3786.   Bamberg, James H. *British Petroleum and global oil, 1950–1975: the challenge of nationalism* (Cambridge: Cambridge University Press, 2000), xxviii, 637p. [3rd volume of *The History of the British Petroleum Company*. Vol.1: R.W. Ferrier, *The Developing Years 1902–1932* (Cambridge, 1982); vol.2: James H. Bamberg *The Anglo-Iranian Years, 1928–1954* (Cambridge, 1994).]

3787.   Beaudreau, B.C. 'Electric power, Keynes and the $4.86 pound: a reexamination of Britain's return to the Gold Standard', *Journal of European Economic History* 28 (1999), 383–408.

3788.   Beaven, Brad (ed.) 'Business records deposited in 1998', *Business Archives* 80 (2000), 64–80.

3789.   Beaven, Brad (ed.) 'Business records deposited in 1999', *Business Archives* 80 (2000), 81–98.

3790.   Bennett, John. 'Safety in numbers: educating safety representatives in the 1970s', *History of Education Society Bulletin* 66 (2000), 71–79.

3791.   Bennett, Robert. 'Gendering cultures in business and labour history: marriage bars in clerical employment', A211, 191–209.

3792.   Benson, J.; Alexander, A.; Shaw, G. 'Action and reaction: competition and the multiple retailer in 1920s Britain', *International Review of Retail Distribution and Consumer Research* 9:3 (1999), 245–59.

3793.   Black, Iain S. 'Imperial visions: rebuilding the Bank of England, 1919–39', A71, 96–116.

3794.   Black, Iain S. 'Rebuilding the heart of the empire: financial headquarters in the City of London 1919–1939', A7, 127–52. [See also *Art History* 22:4 (1999), 593–618.]

3795.   Bowden, S.; Turner, P. 'Real wage rigidities and the bargaining process: cotton spinning in the inter-war years', *Textile History* 31:1 (2000), 77–101.

3796.   Brassley, P. 'Output and technical change in twentieth-century British agriculture', *Agricultural History Review* 48:1 (2000), 60–84.

3797.   Brech, Edward F.L. 'Management history: an introduction', *Contemporary British History* 13:3 (1999), 1–9.

3798.   Brennan, Paul. 'Poverty and unemployment', A42, 104–13.

3799.   Bridel, P.; Presley, J. 'John Maynard Keynes and the French connection', *Manchester School of Economic and Social Studies* 65:4 (1997), 452–65.

3800.   Buck, Trevor; Tull, Malcolm. 'Anglo-American contributions to Japanese and German corporate governance after World War Two', *Business History* 42:2 (2000), 119–40.

3801.   Burge, Alun. 'A "subtle danger"?: the voluntary sector and coalfield society in south Wales, 1926–1939', *Llafur* 7:3–4 (1999), 127–42.

3802. Cairncross, A.K. 'A century of Scottish economics', *Scottish Journal of Political Economy* 45:3 (1998), 225–36.

3803. Callaghan, John. 'Rise and fall of the alternative economic strategy: from internationalisation of capital to "globalisation"', *Contemporary British History* 14:3 (2000), 105–30.

3804. Campbell, Alan; Fishman, Nina; McIlroy, John. 'The post-war compromise: mapping industrial politics, 1945–64', A31, 69–116.

3805. Capet, Antoine. 'The new employment flexibility: the perversion of an ideal?', A74, 51–61.

3806. Caruana, V.; Simmons, C. 'The promotion and development of Manchester Airport, 1929–1974: the local authority initiative', *The Local Historian* 30:3 (2000), 165–77.

3807. Chacksfield, J.E. *Sir Henry Fowler: a versatile life—the biography of Sir Henry Fowler* (Oakwood Library of Railway History, OL 110) (Usk: Oakwood, 2000), 168p.

3808. Chick, Martin. 'Reconstruction, modernisation et production dans une économie planifiée: le Royaume-Uni, 1945–1951' [Reconstruction, modernisation and production in a planned economy: the United Kingdom, 1945–1951], *Histoire, Économie et Société* 18:2 (1999), 303–24.

3809. Clark, Ernest. *Upgate and downgate: working the Chesterfield Canal in the 1930s* (Sheffield: Hallamshire, 2000), 191p.

3810. Collins, M. 'Bank of England autonomy: a retrospective', A107, 13–36.

3811. Coopey, Richard. 'Management and the introduction of computing in British industry, 1945–70', *Contemporary British History* 13:3 (1999), 59–71.

3812. Daniel, Sami; Arestis, Philip; Grahl, John (eds.) *The history and practice of economics: essays in honour of Bernard Corry and Maurice Peston*, vol.2 (Cheltenham: Edward Elgar, 1999), xxviii, 215p.

3813. Downs, Laura Lee. '«Boys will be men and girls will be boys»: Division sexuelle et travail dans la métallurgie (France et Angleterre, 1914–1939)' [Gender division and labour in engineering], *Annales* 54:3 (1999), 561–86.

3814. Dye, Jim (ed.) *150 years in struggle: the Liverpool labour movement, 1848–1998* (Liverpool: Liverpool Trades Union Council, 1998), 78p.

3815. Edwards, Roy. 'Conceptualising cost: the analysis of management information on Britain's railways, c.1935–56', *Contemporary British History* 13:3 (1999), 72–81.

3816. Eichengreen, Barry; Temin, Peter. 'The Gold Standard and the Great Depression', *Contemporary European History* 9:2 (2000), 183–207.

3817. Engert, Jeremy F.; Yalden, George A.; Long, Alan G. *Southern railway officials: a listing of Southern Railway officials with brief biographies* (Eastleigh: Railway Ancestors Family History Society, 1999), 56p.

3818. Fishman, Nina. '"Spearhead of the movement"?: The 1958 London busworkers' strike, the TUC and Frank Cousins', A31, 268–92.

3819. Fishman, Nina. '"The most serious crisis since 1926": the engineering and shipbuilding strikes of 1956', A31, 242–67.

3820. Fleischman, R.K.; Tyson, T.N. 'Parallels between US and UK cost accountancy in the World War I era', *Accounting, Business & Financial History* 10:2 (2000), 191–212.

3821. Fleming, A.I.M.; McKinstry, S.; Wallace, K. 'The decline and fall of the North British Locomotive Company, 1940–62: technological and financial mismanagement or institutional failure?', *Business History* 42:4 (2000), 67–90.

3822. Foster, John; Woolfson, Charles. 'How workers on the Clyde gained the capacity for class struggle: The Upper Clyde Shipbuilders' work-in, 1971–72', A32, 297–325.

3823. Fowler, Alan. 'Impact of the First World War on the Lancashire cotton industry and its workers', A218, 76–98.

3824. Gildart, Keith. 'Men of coal: miners' leaders in north-east Wales 1890–1961', *Llafur* 8:1 (2000), 111–30.

3825. Glover, Ian. 'British management and British history: assessing the responsibility of individuals for economic difficulties', *Contemporary British History* 13:3 (1999), 121–47.

3826. Greaves, J.I. '"Visible hands" and the rationalization of the British cotton industry 1925–1932', *Textile History* 31:1 (2000), 102–22.

3827. Harel, Joëlle. 'Le chômage en Grande-Bretagne de 1942 à 1990: L'action gouvernementale et la réalité économique' [Unemployment in Britain, 1942–90: government action and economic reality], A84, 91–101.

3828. Harris, R.I.D.; Andrew, B.P. 'Rates of return on plant and machinery in the regions of the UK, 1968–1991', *Scottish Journal of Political Economy* 47:3 (2000), 304–24.

3829. Higgins, David; Toms, Steven. 'Public subsidy and private divestment: the Lancashire cotton textile industry c.1950–c.1965', *Business History* 42:1 (2000), 59–84.

3830. Higgins, D.M. 'Competition, conflict and compromise: the Lancashire weaving industry during the inter-war years', *Textile History* 31:1 (2000), 54–76.

3831. Hyman, Richard. 'What went wrong', A32, 353–64.

3832. Jarvis, Anthea. 'British cotton couture: British fashion and the Cotton Board, 1941–1969', *Costume* 31 (1997), 92–99.

3833. Jenkins, David. *Shipowners of Cardiff: a class by themselves: a history of the Cardiff and Bristol Channel Incorporated Shipowners' Association* (Cardiff: University of Wales Press in association with the National Museums & Galleries of Wales, 1997), xii, 105p.

3834. Jones, Christine. 'Distilling the past', *Scottish Industrial History* 20 (2000), 23–36.

3835. Kelly, Scott. 'Ministers matter: Gaitskell and Butler at odds over convertibility, 1950–52', *Contemporary British History* 14:4 (2000), 27–53.

3836. Kennerley, Alston. 'Vocational further education and training for British Merchant Navy ratings: the National Sea Training Schools, 1942–1972', *History of Education* 29:4 (2000), 301–28.

3837. Kipping, Matthias. 'British economic declines: blame it on the consultants?', *Contemporary British History* 13:3 (1999), 23–38.

3838. Koerner, Steve. 'Business archives relating to the British motor cycle industry', *Business Archives* 80 (2000), 31–43.

3839. Kosky, Nathan. *Stansted Airport* (Stroud: Sutton, 2000), 160p.

3840. Lee, Martin. 'The ballasting of the twentieth-century deep water square rigger', *Mariner's Mirror* 86 (2000), 186–96.

3841. Light, Julie. 'Manufacturing the past—the representation of mining communities in history, literature and heritage: ". . . fantasies of a world that never was"?', *Llafur* 8:1 (2000), 19–32.

3842. Lunn, Ken. 'Complex encounters: trade unions, immigration and racism', A32, 70–92.

3843. Lyddon, Dave. '"Glorious summer", 1972: the high tide of rank-and-file militancy', A32, 326–52.

3844. Malchow, Howard L. 'Nostalgia, "heritage", and the London antiques trade: selling the past in Thatcher's Britain', A13, 196–216.

3845. Marrison, Andrew. 'Legacy—war, aftermath and the end of the nineteenth-century liberal trading order, 1914–32', A218, 119–64.

3846. Martin, John. 'British agricultural archives in the Second World War: lying fallow', *Archives* 25:103 (2000), 123–35.

3847. Martin, John. *The development of modern agriculture: British farming since 1931* (London: Macmillan, 1999), xvii, 236p.

3848. Matthews, Derek. 'Accountants v engineers: the professions in top management in Britain since the Second World War', *Contemporary British History* 13:3 (1999), 82–104.

3849. Mattioli, Marie-Annick. 'Le chômage féminin en Grande-Bretagne ou les raisons du taux de chômage inférieur à celui des hommes, 1942–1990' [Female unemployment in Britain: why it has been lower than male unemployment], A84, 102–15.

3850. McIlroy, John; Campbell, Alan; Fishman, Nina. 'Approaching post-war trade unionism', A32, 1–22.

3851. McIlroy, John. 'Making Trade Unionists: The politics of pedagogy, 1945–79', A31, 37–68.

3852. McIlroy, John; Campbell, Alan. 'The high tide of trade unionism: mapping industrial politics, 1964–79', A32, 93–132.

3853. McKinlay, Alan. 'Recasting the visible hand?: strategy, structure and process in UK manufacturing, c.1970–97', *Contemporary British History* 13 (1999), 148–63.

3854. McKinlay, Alan; Mercer, Helen; Rollings, Neil. 'Reluctant Europeans?: the Federation of British Industries and European integration, 1945–63', *Business History* 42:4 (2000), 91–116.

3855. McKinlay, Alan; Melling, Joseph. 'The shop floor politics of productivity: work, power and authority relations in British engineering, c.1945–57', A31, 222–41.

3856. Middleton, Roger. *The British economy since 1945: engaging with the debate* (Basingstoke: Macmillan, 2000), xix, 198p.

3857. Miller, David; Dinan, William. 'The rise of the PR industry in Britain, 1979–98', *European Journal of Communication* 15:1 (2000), 5–36.

3858. Mills, Terence C. 'Recent developments in modelling trends and cycles in economic time series and their relevance to quantitative economic history', A218, 34–51.

3859. Milward, A.S. 'Keynes, Keynesianism, and the international economy', *Proceedings of the British Academy* 105 (2000), 225–52.

3860. Mumby-Croft, R. 'The living conditions on board UK distant trawlers, 1945–1970', *Northern Mariner* 9 (1999), 25–34.

3861. Mumby-Croft, R. 'The working conditions on UK trawlers, 1950–1970', *International Journal of Maritime History* 11:1 (1999), 163–220.

3862. Nussbaumer, Marc. *Tensions et conflits autour des chemins de fer britanniques au XXe siècle* [Tensions and disputes in British railways in the 20th century] (Annales littéraires de l'Université de Franche-Comté, 691) (Besançon and Paris: Presses universitaires franc-comtoises diff. les Belles Lettres, 2000), 394p.

3863. O'Connell, Sean; Porter, Dilwyn. 'Cataloguing mail order's archives', *Business Archives* 80 (2000), 44–54.

3864. Payne, Peter L. 'The genesis and infancy of the Business Archives Council of Scotland', *Scottish Industrial History* 21 (2000), 10–14.

3865. Phillips, Jim. 'Democracy and trade unionism in the docks', A31, 293–310.

3866. Poirier, François. 'Les derniers seront-ils les premiers? Les syndicats britanniques face à l'inégalité des salaires' [Shall the last be the first?: British trade unions and wage inequality], A84, 232–46.

3867. Poirier, François. 'Syndicalisme et inégalités' [Trade unions and inequality], *Revue française de civilisation britannique* 11:1 (2000), 57–66.

3868. Pope, Rex. 'Unemployed women in inter-war Britain: the case of the Lancashire weaving district', *Women's History Review* 9:4 (2000), 743–60.

3869. Pratt, Derrick; Grant, Mike. *Wings across the Border: a history of aviation in north east Wales and the northern Marches*, vol.1 (Wrexham: Bridge Books, 1998), 97p.

3870. Pugh, Peter. *The magic of a name: the Rolls-Royce story, the first forty years* (Cambridge: Icon Books, 2000), xii, 340p.

3871. Reid, Alastair J. 'Labour and the trade unions', A202, 221–47.

3872. Révauger, Jean-Paul. 'Flexibility: in search of a new social settlement', A74, 15–32.

3873. Rhodes James, Robert. *Henry Wellcome* (London: Hodder and Stoughton, 1994), xix, 422p.

3874. Ritchie, Alex. 'Business history and the National Register of Archives', *Business Archives* 80 (2000), 55–56.

3875. Roberts, Brian. 'The "budgie train": women and wartime munitions work in a mining valley', *Llafur* 7:3–4 (1999), 143–52.

3876. Roper, Michael. 'Killing off the father: social science and the memory of Frederick Taylor in management studies, 1950–75', *Contemporary British History* 13:3 (1999), 39–58.

3877. Rudlin, Pernille. *The history of Mitsubishi Corporation in London: 1915 to present day* (Routledge Advances in Asia-Pacific Business, 10) (London: Routledge, 2000), x, 245p.

3878. Sampson, Karen (ed.) 'Select bibliography of new publications January—December 1999', *Business Archives* 79 (2000), 75–85.

3879. Scott, Peter; Reid, Chris. '"The white slavery of the motor world": opportunism in the interwar road haulage industry', *Social History* [London] 25:3 (2000), 300–15.

3880. Scott, Peter. 'The efficiency of Britain's "silly little bobtailed" coal wagons: a comment on Van Vleck', *Journal of Economic History* 59:4 (1999), 1072–80. [Responds to Va Nee L. Van Vleck, 'Delivering coal by road and rail in Britain: the efficiency of the "silly little bobtailed" coal wagons' *Journal of Economic History* 57 (1997), 139–60; with reply, no.3898.]

3881. Scott, Peter. 'Women, other "fresh" workers, and the new manufacturing workforce of interwar Britain', *International Review of Social History* 45:3 (2000), 449–74.

3882. Seargeant, Jacqui. 'Dewar's: the whisky of his forefathers', *Scottish Industrial History* 20 (2000), 37–46.

3883. Seddon, Jill. 'Mentioned, but denied significance: women designers and the "professionalisation" of design in Britain c. 1920–1951', *Gender & History* 12:2 (2000), 426–47.

3884. Supple, Barry. 'Moral choice and economic change: Britain in the twentieth century', *Historical Research* 73 (2000), 66–79.

3885. Taylor, Robert. '"What are we here for?": George Woodcock and trade union reform', A32, 187–215.

3886. Thompson, Paul. 'Snatching defeat from the jaws of victory: the last post of the old City financial elite, 1945–95', A123, 228–46.

3887. Thoms, David; Donnelly, Tom. *The Coventry motor industry* (Aldershot: Ashgate, 2000), 256p.

3888. Thomson, Peter. 'The changing face of a coastal port: Bridgwater shipping between the wars', *Mariner's Mirror* 86 (2000), 78–89.

3889. Thornett, Alan. *Inside Cowley—trade union struggle in the 1970s: who really opened the door to the Tory onslaught?* (London: Porcupine Press, 1998), xvi, 407p.

3890. Tipler, John. *Lotus racing cars: dominance and decline, 1968–2000* (Stroud: Sutton, 2000), 160p.

3891. Tiratsoo, Nick. '"Cinderellas at the ball": production managers in British manufacturing, 1945–80', *Contemporary British History* 13:3 (1999), 105–20.

3892. Tomlinson, Jim. 'Labour and the economy', A202, 46–79.

3893. Tomlinson, Jim. 'Marshall Aid and the "shortage economy" in Britain in the 1940s', *Contemporary European History* 9:1 (2000), 137–55.

3894. Turton, Alison. 'Connecting with schools: corporate archives as providers of educational resources', *Business Archives* 79 (2000), 1–21.

3895. Tweedale, Geoffrey. *Magic mineral to killer dust: Turner & Newall and the asbestos hazard* (Oxford: Oxford University Press, 2000), xx, 313p.

3896. Tweedale, Geoffrey. 'Sources in the history of occupational health: the Turner & Newall archive', *Social History of Medicine* 13:3 (2000), 515–534.

3897. Vamplew, Wray. 'Still crazy after all those years: continuity in a changing labour market for professional jockeys', *Contemporary British History* 14:2 (2000), 115–45.

3898. Van Vleck, Va Nee L. 'In defense (again) of "silly little bobtailed" coal wagons: reply to Peter Scott', *Journal of Economic History* 59:4 (1999), 1081–84. [Responds to no.3880.]

3899. Wapler, Claire. 'Montagu Norman, la Banque d'Angleterre et la question allemande de l'Armistice à l'occupation de la Ruhr (1919–1923)' [Montagu Norman, the Bank of England and the German question from the Armistice to the occupation of the Ruhr], *Histoire, Économie et Société* 18:4 (1999), 681–700.

3900.   Whiteside, Noel; Salais, Robert (eds.) *Governance, industry and labour markets in Britain and France: the modernising state in the mid-twentieth century* (London: Routledge, 1998), xi, 294p.

3901.   Whitton, Timothy. 'Les salaires de la pauvreté' [poverty wages], *Revue française de civilisation britannique* 11:1 (2000), 81–100.

3902.   Willis, Richard. 'Teachers rule OK' [teachers' professional organization], *History Today* 50:9 (2000), 26–27.

3903.   Wise, Ann. 'Dressmakers in Worthing, 1920–1950', *Costume* 32 (1998), 82–86.

3904.   Wood, Stewart. 'Why "indicative planning" failed: British industry and the formation of the National Economic Development Council (1960–64)', *20th Century British History* 11:4 (2000), 431–59.

3905.   Wright, Mike; Robbie, Ken; Chiplin, Brian; Albrighton, Mark. 'The development of an organisational innovation: management buy-outs in the UK, 1980–97', *Business History* 42:4 (2000), 137–84.

3906.   Wrigley, Chris. 'Organized labour and the international economy', A218, 201–16.

3907.   Wrigley, Chris. 'Women in the labour market and in the unions', A32, 43–69.

Eb. *Technology*

See also 423 (B); 2960, 2974 (H); 3838, 3869 (I)

3908.   Alexander, Robert Charles. *The inventor of stereo: the life and works of Alan Dower Blumlein* (Oxford: Focal, 1999), xxi, 421p.

3909.   Barnett, Correlli. 'The audit of the Great War on British technology', A69, 103–13.

3910.   Coates, Tim (ed.) *R101: the airship disaster—1930* (London: Stationery Office, 2000), 163p.

3911.   Divall, Colin; Donnelly, James F.; Johnston, Sean F. 'Professional identity and organisation in a technical occupation: the emergence of chemical engineering in Britain, ca.1915–30', *Contemporary British History* 13:4 (1999), 56–81.

3912.   Fern, Khinlyn. 'Lawrence of Arabia's fire tank / swimming pool at Clouds Hill, Dorset', *Proceedings of the Dorset Natural History and Archaeological Society* 121 (1999), 142–5.

3913.   Greenhalgh, Elizabeth. 'Technology development in coalition: the case of the First World War tank', *International History Review* 22:4 (2000), 806–36.

3914.   Horrocks, S.M. 'A promising pioneer profession? Women in industrial chemistry in inter-war Britain', *British Journal for the History of Science* 33:3:118 (2000), 351–67.

3915.   McKinstry, Sam. 'Engineering culture and accounting development at Albion Motors, 1900–c.1970', *Accounting, Business and Financial History* 9:2 (1999), 203–23.

3916.   Teichmann, Gabriela. *Britischer und deutscher Wohnungsbau in den Zwischenkriegsjahren: ein Vergleich* [British and German house building

between the wars: a comparison] (Europäische Hochschulschriften: Reihe 3, Geschichte und ihre Hilfswissenschaften, 740) (Frankfurt am Main: Peter Lang, 1997), 296p.
3917. Trubshaw, Brian. *Concorde: the inside story* (Stroud: Sutton, 2000), 187p.
3918. Walmsley, Nick. *R 101: a pictorial history* (Stroud: Sutton, 2000), 152p.

Fa. Media and Communication

See also 1548 (F); 2978–9, 2984, 2991, 2997 (H); 3857, 4133, 4258, 4369, 4422, 4772 (I); 5626 (M)

3919. Anderson, Peter J.; Weymouth, Tony. *Insulting the public? The British press and the European Union* (London: Longman, 1999), ix, 230p.
3920. Bryant, Mark (ed.) *Dictionary of twentieth century British cartoonists and caricaturists*, revised edn. (Aldershot: Ashgate, 2000), xvii, 254p. [1st published 1994, covering the period 1730–1980.]
3921. Burke, Michael; Haggith, Toby. 'Words divide, pictures unite: Otto Neurath and British propaganda films of the Second World War', *Imperial War Museum Review* 12 (1999), 59–71.
3922. Carpenter, Humphrey. *That was satire that was: Beyond the Fringe, the Establishment Club, Private Eye and That Was The Week That Was* (London: Gollancz, 2000), 378p.
3923. Caughie, John. *Television drama: realism, modernism, and British culture* (Oxford: Clarendon, 2000), ix, 257p.
3924. Chalaby, Jean. 'Northcliffe: proprietor as journalist', A38, 27–44.
3925. Emsley, Clive. 'PC Dixon and *Commissaire* Maigret: some myths and realities in the development of English and Continental police', A111, 97–119.
3926. Goodman, Geoffrey. 'The role of Industrial Correspondents', A31, 23–36.
3927. Grade, Michael. *It seemed like a good idea at the time* (London: Macmillan, 1999), xii, 432p.
3928. Greenfield, Jill; O'Connell, Sean; Reid, Chris. 'Fashioning masculinity: *Men Only*, consumption and the development of marketing in the 1930s', *20th Century British History* 10:4 (1999), 457–76.
3929. Harvey, A.D. 'Painted advertisements in Islington', *Transactions of the London and Middlesex Archaeological Society* 50 (1999), 153–61.
3930. L'Etang, J. 'State propaganda and bureaucratic intelligence: the creation of public relations in 20th century Britain', *Public Relations Review* 24:4 (1998), 413–42.
3931. Mackay, Robert. 'Leaving out the black notes: the BBC and "enemy music" in the Second World War', *Media History* 6:1 (2000), 75–80.
3932. Nicholas, Siân. 'All the news that's fit to broadcast: the popular press *versus* the BBC, 1922–45', A38, 121–48.
3933. Porter, Dilwyn. '"Where there's a tip there's a tap": the popular press and the investing public, 1900–60', A38, 71–96.
3934. Seymour-Ure, Colin. *Harlots revisited: media barons and the new politics* [1990–98] (Oxford: Green College, [1998]), 14p. [The Iain Walker Lecture 1998.]

3935. Seymour-Ure, Colin. 'Northcliffe's legacy', A38, 9–26.
3936. Smith, Adrian. 'The fall and fall of the third *Daily Herald* 1930–64', A38, 169–200.
3937. Smith, Robert. 'A mirror of Wales?: sound broadcasting by the BBC's Welsh Region 1937–1964', *Llafur* 8:1 (2000), 131–44.
3938. Thomas, James. 'The "Max factor"—a mirror image? Robert Maxwell and the *Daily Mirror* tradition', A38, 201–26.
3939. Twaites, Peter. 'Circles of confusion and sharp vision: British news photography, 1919–39', A38, 97–120.

Fb. *Science and Medicine*

See also 433 (B); 3009, 3014, 3023–4, 3034, 3036, 3052, 3063, 3083 (H); 3668, 3873, 3895–6, 4138, 4680, 4758 (I)

3940. Bloor, M. 'The South Wales Miners Federation, miners' lung and the instrumental use of expertise, 1900–50', *Social Studies of Science* 30:1 (2000), 125–40.
3941. Brain, W. Russell. 'Encounters with Winston Churchill', *Medical History* 44:1 (2000), 3–20. [Record of a consultant neurologist 1949–65.]
3942. Bryder, Linda. '"We shall not find salvation in inoculation": BCG vaccination in Scandinavia, Britain and the USA 1921–1960', *Social Science and Medicine* 49:9 (1999), 1157–68.
3943. Burcham, W.E. 'The Cavendish high-voltage laboratory, 1935–9', *Notes & Records of the Royal Society* (of London) 53:1 (1999), 121–34.
3944. Burnham, Dave. 'Cooling memories: why we still remember Scott and Shackleton', *Historian* 65 (2000), 17–22.
3945. Cain, J. 'For the "Promotion" and "Integration" of various fields: first years of Evolution, 1947–1949', *Archives of Natural History* 27:2 (2000), 231–60.
3946. Cain, J. 'Towards a "greater degree of integration": the Society for the Study of Speciation, 1939–41', *British Journal for the History of Science* 33:1:116 (2000), 85–108.
3947. Chamberlain, Geoffrey. *Victor Bonney: the gynaecological surgeon of the twentieth century* (Carnforth: Parthenon, 2000), x, 140p.
3948. Clark, D. 'Cradled to the grave? Terminal care in the United Kingdom, 1948–67', *Mortality* 4:3 (1999), 225–48.
3949. Crofts, Fay. *History of Hollymoor Hospital* (Studley: Brewin, 1998), 154p.
3950. Crozier, Ivan D. 'Havelock Ellis, Eonism and the patient's discourse; or writing a book about sex', *History of Psychiatry* 11:2 (2000), 125–54.
3951. Dixon, Shirley. 'The archive of the Queen's Nursing Institute in the Contemporary Medical Archives Centre', *Medical History* 44:2 (2000), 251–66.
3952. Dror, Othniel E. 'The affect of experiment: the turn to emotions in Anglo-American physiology, 1900–1940', *Isis* 90:2 (1999), 205–37.
3953. Edelson, Edward. *Francis Crick and James Watson and the building blocks of life* (Oxford: Oxford University Press, 2000), 112p. [Oxford Portraits in Science, intended for children.]

3954. Engineer, Amanda. 'Wellcome and "The Great Past"', *Medical History* 44:3 (2000), 389–404.

3955. Hall, Lesley A. '"War always brings it on": war, STDs, the military, and the civilian population in Britain, 1850–1950', A52, 205–24.

3956. Hammond, M. '"A soul stirring appeal to every Briton": the reception of The Birth of a Nation in Britain (1915–1916)', *Film History* 11:3 (1999), 353–70.

3957. Hardy, A. '"Straight back to barbarism": antityphoid inoculation and the Great War, 1914', *Bulletin of the History of Medicine* 74:2 (2000), 265–290.

3958. Harris, Tom (comp.) *A history of the West Somerset Medical Club, 1940–1997: compiled from the books of minutes of the meetings* ([Taunton]: [West Somerset Medical Club], [1999]), viii, 341p.

3959. Harrison, Mark. 'Disease, discipline and dissent: the Indian Army in France and England, 1914–1915', A52, 185–204.

3960. Harrison, Mark. 'Sex and the citizen soldier: health, morals and discipline in the British army during the Second World War', A52, 225–50.

3961. Higgs, Edward. 'Medical statistics, patronage and the State: the development of the MRC Statistical Unit, 1911–1948', *Medical History* 44:3 (2000), 323–40.

3962. Hopton, John. 'Prestwich Hospital in the twentieth century: a case study of slow and uneven progress in the development of psychiatric care', *History of Psychiatry* 10:3 (1999), 349–70.

3963. Hughes, Jonathan. 'The "matchbox on a muffin": the design of hospitals in the early NHS', *Medical History* 44:1 (2000), 21–56.

3964. Hull, A. 'War of words: the public science of the British scientific community and the origins of the Department of Scientific and Industrial Research, 1914–16', *British Journal for the History of Science* 32:4:115 (1999), 461–482.

3965. Jeffs, David (ed.) *One hundred years of health: the changing health of Guernsey 1899–1999* (Guernsey: Guernsey Board of Health, 1999), 202p.

3966. Leydier, Gilles. 'Isobel M.L. Robertson et l'accès aux services de santé à Glasgow durant l'ère Thatcher' [Isobel M.L. Robertson and access to health care in Glasgow during the Thatcher era (from *Regenerating the Inner City: Glasgow's Experience*, 1987)], A37, 201–16.

3967. Lorenzton, Maria. 'Nurse education at the London Homeopathic Hospital 1903–1947: preparation for professional specialists or marginalised Cinderellas?', *International History of Nursing Journal* 5:2 (2000), 20–27.

3968. Loughlin, Kelly. 'The history of health and medicine in contemporary Britain: reflections on the role of audio-visual sources', *Social History of Medicine* 13 (2000), 131–45.

3969. MacLeod, R. 'Sight and sound on the Western Front: surveyors, scientists and the "Battlefield Laboratory", 1915–1918', *War & Society* 18:1 (2000), 23–46.

3970. Mayer, Anna-K. 'Setting up a discipline: conflicting agendas of the Cambridge History of Science Committee, 1936–1950', *Studies in History and Philosophy of Science Part A* 31:4 (2000), 665–89.

3971.　McIntosh, Tania. '"An abortionist city": maternal mortality, abortion and birth control in Sheffield, 1920–1940', *Medical History* 44:1 (2000), 75–96.

3972.　Ogilvie, M.B. 'Annie Maunder (1868–1947) and British women astronomers at the dawn of professional astronomy', *British Journal for the History of Science* 33:1:116 (2000), 67–84.

3973.　Perry, Mark. 'Academic general practice in Manchester under the early National Health Service: a failed experiment in social medicine', *Social History of Medicine* 13:1 (2000), 111–29.

3974.　Porter, Roy. 'The Wellcome Trust Centre for the History of Medicine at UCL', *Medical History* 44:4 (2000), 441–42.

3975.　Prüll, Cay-Rüdiger. 'Pathology at war, 1914–1918: Germany and Britain in comparison', A52, 131–62.

3976.　Stanton, J. 'The cost of living: kidney dialysis, rationing and health economics in Britain, 1965–1996', *Social Science and Medicine* 49:9 (1999), 1169–82.

3977.　Stewart, John. '"Science fights death": David Stark Murray, science, and socialism in interwar Britain', *Annals of Science* 57:2 (2000), 143–62.

3978.　Varcoe, I. 'Practical proposals by scientists for reforming the machinery of scientific advice, 1914–17', *British Journal for the History of Science* 33:1:116 (2000), 109–14.

3979.　Washington, John Geoffrey. 'Northowram Hospital, 1934–2000', *Transactions of the Halifax Antiquarian Society* ns 8 (2000), 169–89.

3980.　Wheeler, Alwyne. 'The zoological collections of the British Museum (Natural History): evacuation of the collections during the war years 1939–1945', *Archives of Natural History* 27:1 (2000), 115–22.

3981.　White, Maurice W. *Years of caring: the Royal Orthopaedic Hospital* (Studley: Brewin, 1997), 282p.

3982.　Whitehead, Ian R. 'The British medical officer on the western front: the training of doctors for war', A52, 163–84.

3983.　Wilkinson, L. 'Burgeoning visions of global public health: the Rockefeller Foundation, the London School of Hygiene and Tropical Medicine, and the "hookworm connection"', *Studies in the History and Philosophy of Science part C: Biological and Biomedical Sciences* 31:3 (2000), 397–407.

3984.　Yates, David M. *Turing's legacy: a history of computing at the National Physical Laboratory 1945–1995* (London: Science Museum, 1997), 347p.

Fc. *Ideas and Learning*

See also 2360, 2367, 2376 (G); 3079, 3083, 3087–8, 3098–100, 3104, 3109, 3116, 3118, 3135 (H); 3600, 3615, 3767, 4130, 4262, 4373, 4421 (I)

3985.　Anonymous. 'Major accessions to repositories in 1998 relating to education', *History of Education Society Bulletin* 65 (2000), 44–54.

3986.　Armstrong, James. '"On account of literary indiscretions": Wyndham Lewis and the publication of Marjorie Firminger's Jam To-Day: A Novel (1930)', *The Library* 7th ser. 1:3 (2000), 308–21.

3987.　Besomi, Daniele (ed. & intr.) '"An Essay in Dynamic Theory": 1938 draft by Roy F. Harrod', *History of Political Economy* 28:2 (1996), 245–60.

3988. Besomi, Daniele. 'An additional note on the Harrod-Keynes correspondence', *History of Political Economy* 28:2 (1996), 281–94.
3989. Besomi, Daniele. 'From the trade cycle to the "Essay in Dynamic Theory": The Harrod-Keynes correspondence, 1937–1938', *History of Political Economy* 27:2 (1995), 309–43.
3990. Besomi, Daniele. 'Harrod on classification of technological progress: the origin of a wild-goose chase', *Banca Nazionale del Lavoro Quarterly Review* 208 (1999), 96–118.
3991. Besomi, Daniele. 'Inter-war trade cycle theories in a poem by James Meade', *European Journal of the History of Economic Thought* 6:2 (1999), 297–300.
3992. Besomi, Daniele. 'Keynes and Harrod on the classical theory of investment: more on the origin of the only diagram in the General Theory', *Journal of the History of Economic Thought* 22:3 (2000), 367–76.
3993. Besomi, Daniele. 'La teoria del ciclo e della crescita di Roy Harrod' [Roy Harrod's theory of the trade cycle and growth], A10.
3994. Besomi, Daniele. 'On the spread of an idea: the strange case of Mr. Harrod the multiplier', *History of Political Economy* 32:2 (2000), 347–79.
3995. Besomi, Daniele. 'Roy Harrod and the Oxford Economists' Research Group's inquiry on prices and interest, 1936–39', *Oxford Economic Papers* ns 50 (1998), 534–62.
3996. Besomi, Daniele. 'Roy Harrod and traditional theory', *European Journal of the History of Economic Thought* 4:1 (1997), 92–115.
3997. Besomi, Daniele. *The making of Harrod's dynamics* (Basingstoke: Macmillan, 1999).
3998. Boettke, Peter J.; et al. (eds.) *The legacy of Friedrich von Hayek*, 3 vols. [1: *Politics*; 2: *Philosophy*; 3. *Economics*.] (Intellectual Legacies in Modern Economics series, 6) (London: Edward Elgar, 2000).
3999. Bouckaert, Boudewijn; Godart-van der Kroon, Annette (eds.) *Hayek revisited* (The Locke Institute Series (London: Edward Elgar, 2000), xxi, 157p.
4000. Boussahba-Bravard, Myriam. 'L'Open University ou la grande «fierté» de Wilson' [The Open University, or Wilson's great 'pride'], A35, 209–26.
4001. Brock, Sebastian P. 'Hedley Frederick Davis Sparks, 1908–1996', *Proceedings of the British Academy* 101 (1999), 513–38.
4002. Buckingham, David; et al. *Children's television in Britain: history, discourse and policy* (London: British Film Institute, 1999), 200p.
4003. Bull, Christoph R. 'Swanscombe Library 1928–1998: the story of a public library pioneer', *Dartford Historical & Antiquarian Society Newsletter* 36 (1999), 4–15.
4004. Burge, Alun. 'Miners' learning in the South Wales Coalfield 1900–1947', *Llafur* 8:1 (2000), 69–96.
4005. Catterall, Peter. 'Management and engineering education in the 1950s and 1960s', *Contemporary British History* 13:3 (1999), 10–22.
4006. Coleman, J. 'The history of political thought in a modern university: the first Henry Tudor Memorial Lecture', *History of Political Thought* 21 (2000), 152–71.
4007. Cowdrey, Herbert Edward John. 'John Norman Davidson Kelly, 1909–1997', *Proceedings of the British Academy* 101 (1999), 419–40.

4008. Cretney, S.M. 'Lawrence Cecil Bartlett Gower, 1913–1997', *Proceedings of the British Academy* 101 (1999), 379–406.

4009. Cunningham, Peter. 'Making use of the past: memory, history and education', *History of Education Society Bulletin* 66 (2000), 68–70.

4010. Davies, Keith. '"An oasis of culture": the Aberdare valley educational settlement 1936–67', *Transactions of the Honourable Society of Cymmrodorion* ns 6 (1999), 135–48.

4011. Drower, Margaret S. *Flinders Petrie: a life in archaeology*, 2nd edn. (Madison (WI): Wisconsin University Press, 1995), xxiv, 500p. [1st published London: Gollancz, 1985.]

4012. Dyson, Brian. 'In the line of fire: the library of University College Hull during World War II', *Library History* 15:2 (1999), 113–23.

4013. Earlam, Patricia. *Ashford School, 1898–1998: a centenary history in words and pictures* (Ashford: Ashford School, 1998), 159p.

4014. Eastwood, David. 'History, politics and reputation: E.P. Thompson reconsidered', *History* 85:280 (2000), 634–54.

4015. Edwards, Brian. 'Names on the path to remembrance: the building of Marlborough College Memorial Hall' [First World War memorial], *Wiltshire Archaeological and Natural History Magazine* 93 (2000), 205–17.

4016. Edwards, Elizabeth. 'Women principals, 1900–1960: gender and power', *History of Education* 29:5 (2000), 405–14.

4017. Emmerick, Ronald Eric. 'Harold Walter Bailey, 1899–1996', *Proceedings of the British Academy* 101 (1999), 309–52.

4018. Felix, David. *Keynes: a critical Life* (Contributions in Economics and Economic History, 208) (London: Greenwood, 1999), xvii, 322p.

4019. Fletcher, Gordon. *Understanding Dennis Robertson: the man and his work* (London: Edward Elgar, 2000), 496p.

4020. Fourquet, François. 'Toynbee et la diversité des cultures' [Toynbee and cultural diversity], *Revue du MAUSS* 1 (1999), 323–32.

4021. Gerard, David. 'J.N.L. Myres (1902–1989)', *Library History* 15:2 (1999), 125–35.

4022. Green, S.J.D. 'The 1944 Education Act: a church-state perspective', *Parliamentary History* 19 (2000), 148–64.

4023. Greengrass, Mark. 'Kenneth Harold Dobson Haley, 1920–1997', *Proceedings of the British Academy* 101 (1999), 407–18.

4024. Gruffudd, Pyrs; Herbert, D.T.; Piccini, A. 'In search of Wales: travel writing and narratives of difference, 1918–50', *Journal of Historical Geography* 26:4 (2000), 589–604.

4025. Hair, Paul Edward Hedley (ed.) *Arts · Letters · Society: a miscellany commemorating the centenary of the Faculty of Arts at the University of Liverpool* (Liverpool Historical Studies, 15) (Liverpool: Liverpool University Press, 1996), 256p.

4026. Hardy, Richard; Gourvish, Terry. 'Michael R. Bonavia, 1909–99: an appreciation', *Journal of Transport History* 3rd ser. 21:1 (2000), 1–5.

4027. Haslam, Jonathan. *The vices of integrity: E.H. Carr, 1892–1982* (London: Verso, 1999), xiv, 306p.

4028. Holden, Hilda. 'Mr. Maltby at war', *Library History* 16:1 (2000), 65–69.

4029.   Holmes, Colin. 'Sidney Pollard 1925–1998', *History Workshop Journal* 49 (2000), 277–78.

4030.   Horn, Pamela. 'Training and status in domestic service: the role of the League of Skilled Housecraft, 1922–1942', *History of Education Society Bulletin* 65 (2000), 35–43.

4031.   Houlbrooke, Ralph. 'Lawrence Stone: historian of the family', *History of the Family* 5:2 (2000), 149–51.

4032.   Howkins, Alun. 'Stan Shipley 1930–1999', *History Workshop Journal* 49 (2000), 279–81.

4033.   Jackson, Robin; Woods, Sydney (eds.) *Images of Scotland* (Journal of Scottish Education Occasional Paper, 1) (Dundee: Northern College, 1997).

4034.   Jefcoate, Graham. 'Democracy at work: the Library Association's "centenary assessment" of 1950', *Library History* 15:2 (1999), 100–11.

4035.   Kaser, Michael. 'Peter John de la Fosse Wiles, 1919–1997', *Proceedings of the British Academy* 101 (1999), 539–56.

4036.   Kaye, Harvey J. *The British Marxist historians* (Basingstoke: Macmillan, 1995), xix, 316p. [1st published Cambridge: Polity, 1984; Reprinted with a new preface by the author and a foreword by Eric Hobsbawm.]

4037.   Knight, Ronald David. *T.E. Lawrence and the Max Gate circle*, 2nd edn. (Weymouth: The author, 1995), 213p. [1st published 1988.]

4038.   Lee, L.F. 'The Dalton Plan and the loyal, capable intelligent citizen', *History of Education* 29:2 (2000), 129–38.

4039.   Leeming, David. *Stephen Spender: a life in modernism* (London: Duckworth, 1999), xv, 288p.

4040.   Lees, Colin; Robertson, Alex. 'Manchester University and the city: aspects of policy-making in higher education, 1900–1930', *Bulletin of the John Rylands University Library of Manchester* 81:1 (1999), 85–112.

4041.   Lemosse, Michel. *Le système éducatif anglais depuis 1944* [The English educational system since 1944] (Paris: P.U.F., 2000), 247p.

4042.   Limond, David. '"It was the 'flappers' . . . who tilted the scales": gender and politics in the University of Glasgow Rectorial election of 1928', *History of Education Society Bulletin* 66 (2000), 101–9.

4043.   Limond, David. 'Only talk in the staffroom: "subversive" teaching in a Scottish school, 1939–40', *History of Education* 29:3 (2000), 239–52.

4044.   Loewe, Raphael. 'In memoriam Sir Isaiah Berlin, OM, CBE, MA, FBA', *Jewish Historical Studies* 35 (1998), xvi–xviii.

4045.   Margetson, John. *Gorty: Neville Gorton's years at Blundell's, 1934–1942* (Woodbridge: Letheringham, 1998), 131p.

4046.   Marlow, Lawrence; O'Day, Rosemary. 'David Englander 1949–1999', *History Workshop Journal* 49 (2000), 274–76.

4047.   Mayenburg, David von. *Schule, Berufsschule, Arbeitsmarkt: Die englische Debatte um die Elementarschulreform (1914–1939)* [Schools, vocational schools, labour market: the English debate on the reform of the elementary school] (Münchner Studien zur neueren und neuesten Geschichte, 16) (Frankfurt am Main and New York: Peter Lang, 1996), 307p.

4048.   Milligan, Susan. *Variety without disorder: St. Columba's School, Kilmacolm 1897–1997* (Kilmacolm: St. Columba's School, 1998), 272p.

4049. Monk, Ray. *Bertrand Russell*, vol.2: *The ghost of madness, 1921–1970* (London: Jonathan Cape, 2000), xiv, 574p. [Vol.1 *The Spirit of Solitude* published 1996.]

4050. Morrill, John S. 'John Philipps Kenyon, 1927–1996', *Proceedings of the British Academy* 101 (1999), 441–64.

4051. Moss, Annette E. (ed.) *A history of St John's RC Voluntary Aided Comprehensive School, Gravesend: its church, its land and its development* (Gravesend: St John's RC Comprehensive School, 1999), 100p.

4052. Newton, Jane. 'The Centre for the Study of Cartoons and Caricature, University of Kent at Canterbury' [archive report], *Contemporary British History* 13:4 (1999), 170–9.

4053. not used.

4054. Nicholls, Christine Stephanie. *The history of St Antony's College, Oxford, 1950–2000* (Basingstoke: Macmillan in association with St Antony's College, Oxford), xii, 316p.

4055. Nicholls, Mark. 'A reason for remembering: Francis Jenkinson and the War Reserve Collection', *Transactions of the Cambridge Bibliographical Society* 11:4 (1999), 497–515.

4056. Normandy Historians. *A century of Normandy in Surrey* (Normandy: Normandy Historians, 2000), 199p.

4057. O'Sullivan, L. 'Michael Oakeshott on European political history', *History of Political Thought* 21:1 (2000), 132–51.

4058. Payton, Philip. 'The ideology of language revival in modern Cornwall', A18, 395–424.

4059. Pearson, Paul M.; Sullivan, Danny; Thomson, Ian (eds.) *Thomas Merton, poet, monk, prophet* (Abergavenny: Three Peaks, 1998), 211p. [Papers presented at the Second General Conference of the Thomas Merton Society of Great Britain and Ireland at Oakham School, March 1998.]

4060. Perrin, Dennis. *A history of Acton Park Schools* (Wrexham: Acton Park Schools, 1998), 220p.

4061. Perry, C.R. 'In search of H.V. Morton: travel writing and cultural values in the first age of British democracy', *20th Century British History* 10:4 (1999), 431–56.

4062. Phillips, C.B. 'Thomas Stuart Willan, 1910–1994', *Proceedings of the British Academy* 101 (1999), 557–63.

4063. Powell, Anne (ed.) *Shadows of war: British women's poetry of the Second World War* (Stroud: Sutton, 1999), xxiii, 360p.

4064. Robertson, John. 'Colin Matthew, 1941–1999', *History Workshop Journal* 50 (2000), 307–11.

4065. Rose, Richard. 'William James Millar Mackenzie, 1909–1996', *Proceedings of the British Academy* 101 (1999), 465–88.

4066. Russell, Bertrand. *Autobiography* (London: Routledge, 1998), xv, 750p. [1st published in 3 vols. (1. 1872–1914; 2. 1914–1944; 3. 1944–1967) London: Allen & Unwin, 1967–69.]

4067. Ryder, B. 'The George Allen and Unwin collection: Reading University Library', *Publishing History* 47 (2000), 67–78.

4068. Samuel, Edgar. 'In memoriam Alfred Rubens, FRICS, FSA, FRHistS (1903–1998)', *Jewish Historical Studies* 35 (1998), xix–xxi.

4069.   Shepherd, Andrée. 'Les interprétations marxistes de la notion de pauvreté' [Marxist interpretations of the concept of poverty], A42, 5–14.
4070.   Shiel, J.B. 'The papers of T.W. Manson' [theologian], *Bulletin of the John Rylands University Library of Manchester* 81:2 (1999), 51–152.
4071.   Skrine, Peter. 'Leonard Wilson Forster, 1913–1997', *Proceedings of the British Academy* 101 (1999), 365–78.
4072.   Smith, P.J. 'Dorothy Garrod, first woman professor at Cambridge', *Antiquity* 74:283 (2000), 131–36.
4073.   Snowman, Daniel. 'Geoffrey Hosking talks to Daniel Snowman', *History Today* 50:7 (2000), 28–30.
4074.   Snowman, Daniel. 'Lady Antonia Fraser', *History Today* 50:10 (2000), 26–28.
4075.   Spencer, Stephanie. 'Women's dilemmas in postwar Britain: career stories for adolescent girls in the 1950s', *History of Education* 29:4 (2000), 329–42.
4076.   Steiner, Willi A. *The Institute of Advanced Legal Studies of the University of London, 1947–1976* (London: Institute of Advanced Legal Studies, 2000), 49p.
4077.   Stetz, M.D. 'Oscar Wilde at the movies: British sexual politics and The Green Carnation (1960)', *Biography: an interdisciplinary quarterly* 23:1 (2000), 90–107.
4078.   Stocks, J.C. 'Objective bees in psychological bonnets: intelligence testing and selection for secondary education in Scotland between the wars', *History of Education* 29:3 (2000), 225–38.
4079.   Theobald, Marjorie. 'Women, leadership and gender politics in the interwar years: the case of Julia Flynn', *History of Education* 29:1 (2000), 63–78.
4080.   Thomas, Colin. '"The end of history as we know it": Gwyn A. Williams as a television historian', *Llafur* 7:3–4 (1999), 5–19.
4081.   Trouvé, Susan. 'Education from Butler to Baker: Panacea, palliative, or privilege?', A84, 136–50.
4082.   Wilford, Hugh. '"Unwitting assets"?: British intellectuals and the Congress for Cultural Freedom', *20th Century British History* 11:1 (2000), 42–60.
4083.   Wilkes, J.J. 'Albert Lionel Frederick Rivet, 1915–1993', *Proceedings of the British Academy* 101 (1999), 489–512.
4084.   Woodland, Christine. 'The history of education: sources in the Modern Records Centre, University of Warwick', *History of Education Society Bulletin* 66 (2000), 114–15.

Fd. *Culture and the Arts*

See also 445, 447, 456 (B); 1125 (E); 1720 (F); 2442 (G); 3144–7, 3157, 3159–70, 3174, 3181, 3189, 3200, 3207, 3209, 3212, 3216–17, 3222, 3226, 3233, 3236, 3244, 3247, 3249, 3251, 3263, 3267–70, 3274 (H); 3604, 3873, 3986, 4158, 4218, 4288, 4662, 4684, 4919, 4944 (I)

4085.   Adamson, Keith I.P. *The Yorkshire Photographic Union: the first hundred years (1899–1999)* (Rotherham: Dearne Valley College, 1999), 237p.

4086.   Alexander, Jonathan J. 'Thomas Sherrer Ross Boase, 1898–1974', *Proceedings of the British Academy* 101 (1999), 353–64.
4087.   Baker, William; Womack, Kenneth (eds.) *Twentieth-century British book collectors and bibliographers* (Dictionary of Literary Biography, 201) (Detroit: Gale Research, 1999), xvii, 393p.
4088.   Bartram, Alan. *Making books: design in British publishing since 1945* (London: British Library, 1999), 160p.
4089.   Bell, Susan Groag. 'Vanessa's garden', A13, 103–22.
4090.   Benson, Timothy. 'Low and Churchill', *History Today* 50:2 (2000), 9–15.
4091.   Bergonzi, Bernard. *War poets and other subjects* (Aldershot: Ashgate, 1999), x, 211p.
4092.   Besomi, Daniele. 'Roy Harrod and the committee of enquiry into the Bodleian question 1930–31', *Bodleian Library Record* 17:1 (2000), 36–44.
4093.   Black, Alistair. *The public library in Britain, 1914–2000* (London: British Library, 2000), xii, 180p. [A sequel to his *A new history of the English public library: social and intellectual contexts, 1850–1914* (Leicester, 1996).]
4094.   Brandreth, Gyles. *John Gielgud: an actor's life* (Stroud: Sutton, 2000), 192p.
4095.   Broady, Maurice. 'Stained glass design in Wales', *Transactions of the Honourable Society of Cymmrodorion* ns 6 (1999), 149–66.
4096.   Brothers, Barbara; Gergits, Julia Marie (eds.) *British travel writers, 1940–1997* (Dictionary of Literary Biography, 204) (Detroit (MI): Gale, 1999), xxi, 398p.
4097.   Bryant, Christopher. *Glenda Jackson: the biography* (London: HarperCollins, 1999), xi, 292p.
4098.   Buckman, David. *Dictionary of artists in Britain since 1945* (Bristol: Art Dictionaries, 1998), 1344p.
4099.   Chibnall, Steve; Murphy, Robert (eds.) *British crime cinema* (London: Routledge, 1999), x, 251p.
4100.   Copp, Michael. 'No illusions: the war poetry of Edgell Rickword (1898–1982)', *Imperial War Museum Review* 12 (1999), 89–95.
4101.   Curtis, S. '"If it's not Scottish, it's crap!": Harry Lauder sings for Selig', *Film History* 11:4 (1999), 418–25.
4102.   Davies, Kevin. 'Twentieth century Danish furniture design and the English vernacular tradition', *Scandinavian Journal of Design History* 7 (1997), 41–57.
4103.   Dickason, Robert. 'New and Old Cinema', A35, 41–52.
4104.   Doctor, Jennifer R. *The BBC and ultra-modern music, 1922–1936: shaping a nation's tastes* (Cambridge: Cambridge University Press, 1999), xii, 508p.
4105.   Étienne, Anne. 'Les «Theatre Clubs» en Grande-Bretagne au XXe siècle', *Études anglaises* 53:3 (2000), 306–13.
4106.   Forster, Margaret. *Hidden lives: a family memoir* (London: Viking, 1995), 308p.
4107.   Frogley, Alain. '"Getting its history wrong": English nationalism and the reception of Ralph Vaughan Williams', A142, 145–62.
4108.   Garlake, Margaret. *New art, new world: British art in postwar society* (New Haven (CT): Yale University Press for the Paul Mellon Center for Studies in British Art, 1998), vii, 279p.

4109. Guilbert, Georges-Claude. 'Swinging London: rock, miniskirts, and gender-blurring for the People', A35, 7–16.

4110. Hansen, Peter H. 'Confetti of Empire: the conquest of Everest in Nepal, India, Britain, and New Zealand', *Comparative Studies in Society and History* 42:2 (2000), 307–32.

4111. Harrod, Tanya. *The crafts in Britain in the 20th century* (New Haven (CT) and London: Yale University Press for the Bard Graduate Center for Studies in the Decorative Arts, 1999), 496p.

4112. Hiscock, K. 'Modernity and "English" tradition: Betjeman at *The Architectural Review*', *Journal of Design History* 13:3 (2000), 193–212.

4113. Hobson, Patricia. *The first hundred years: a history of Sheffield Teachers' Operatic Society (affiliated to the National Operatic & Dramatic Association)* (Sheffield: Sheffield Teachers' Operatic Society, 2000), 196p.

4114. Jacques, Benoît. 'Poverty in British films, 1942–1955', A84, 261–70.

4115. Jenkins, Geraint H.; Williams, Mari A. (eds.) *"Let's do our best for the ancient tongue": the Welsh language in the twentieth century* (Cardiff: University of Wales Press, 2000), xiv, 700p.

4116. Kinghorn, Jonathan. 'The designers: into the 1930s', A30, 184–86.

4117. Lapp, A. 'Memories of a monument: the competition for a monument to the unknown political prisoner, London 1953—a discussion of the powers of sculpture . . .', A180, 1051–58.

4118. Leventhal, Fred M. 'British writers, American readers: women's voices in wartime', *Albion* 32:1 (2000), 1–18.

4119. MacDonald, Malcolm. 'Aspects of Scottish musical nationalism in the 20th century with special reference to the music of F.G. Scott, Ronald Center and Ronald Stevenson', A142, 111–32.

4120. Mackenney, Linda. *The activities of popular dramatists and drama groups in Scotland, 1900–1952* (Studies in the Theatre Arts, 9) (Lewiston (NY): Edwin Mellen, 2000), xv, 299p.

4121. McGregor, Robert Kuhn; Lewis, Ethan. *Conundrums for the long weekend: England, Dorothy L. Sayers and Lord Peter Wimsey* (Kent (OH): Kent State University Press, 2000), 248p.

4122. McKee, Vincent. *Gaelic nations: politics of the Gaelic language in Scotland and Northern Ireland in the 20th century* (London: Bluestock Press, 1997), ix, 127p.

4123. Moody, Michael. 'A dance of death: images of mortality in European graphics of the First World War', *Imperial War Museum Review* 12 (1999), 72–77.

4124. Moore, Jerrold Northrop. *F.L. Griggs, 1876–1938: the architecture of dreams* (Oxford: Clarendon, 1999), xii, 290p.

4125. Moriarty, C. 'A backroom service? the photographic library of the Council of Industrial Design, 1945–1965', *Journal of Design History* 13:1 (2000), 39–58.

4126. Nail, Sylvie. 'Le travail des apparences: L'esthétique des années soixante' [the insistence on appearance: aesthetics in the 1960s], A35, 17–39.

4127. Nicholson, Steve. *British theatre and the red peril: the portrayal of communism 1917–1945* (Exeter: University of Exeter Press, 1999), xx, 195p.

4128.   Normand, Tom. *The modern Scot: modernism and nationalism in Scottish art, 1928–1955* (Aldershot: Ashgate, 2000), xii, 195p.

4129.   O'Carroll, Susannah. 'Cathy Come Home de Ken Loach: Un déclencheur de la «redécouverte de la pauvreté» des années soixante?' [Ken Loach's *Cathy Come Home*: to what extent did it trigger the 'rediscovery of poverty' in the 1960s?], A84, 271–83.

4130.   Ouditt, Sharon. *Women writers of the First World War: an annotated bibliography* (London: Routledge, 2000), x, 230p.

4131.   Paris, Michael. 'Boys' books and the Great War', *History Today* 50:11 (2000), 44–49.

4132.   Porter, Vincent. 'The Robert Clark account: films released in Britain by Associated British Pictures, British Lion, MGM, and Warner Bros., 1946–1957', *Historical Journal of Film, Radio and Television* 20:4 (2000), 469–511.

4133.   Rothwell, Kenneth S. *A history of Shakespeare on screen: a century of film and television* (Cambridge: Cambridge University Press, 1999), xiv, 352p.

4134.   Saler, Michael. 'Whigs and surrealists: the "subtle links" of Humphrey Jennings's Pandaemonium', A13, 123–42.

4135.   Shellard, Dominic (ed.) *British theatre in the 1950s* (Sheffield: Sheffield Academic, 2000), 141p.

4136.   Smith, Barry (ed.) *Frederick Delius and Peter Warlock: a friendship revealed* [their correspondence, 1911–30] (Oxford: Clarendon, 2000), xxii, 542p.

4137.   Soden, Joanna; Keller, Victoria. *William Gillies* (Edinburgh: Canongate in collaboration with the Royal Scottish Academy, 1998), 160p.

4138.   Stirton, Charles. 'From ashes to icon', *Historian* 65 (2000), 4–9. [Middleton Hall's historic garden and the creation of the National Botanic Garden of Wales.]

4139.   Suga, Y. 'State patronage of design? the elitism/commercialism battle in the General Post Office's Graphic Production', *Journal of Design History* 13:1 (2000), 23–38.

4140.   Tanner, Ailsa; Burkhauser, Jude. 'The painters: between the wars. Agnes Miller Parker, Mary Viola Paterson, Josephine Haswell Miller, Jessie Alexandra Dick, Mary Armour', A30, 234–39.

4141.   Thomas, M. Wynn. 'Keeping the Rhondda for Wales: the case of J. Kitchener Davies', *Transactions of the Honourable Society of Cymmrodorion* ns 6 (1999), 119–34.

4142.   Tibbetts, John C. 'Kevin Brownlow's historical films: *It Happened Here* (1965) and *Winstanley* (1975)', *Historical Journal of Film Radio and Television* 20:2 (2000), 227–52.

4143.   Waddell, Heather. *The London art world, 1979–1999* (London: London Art and Artists Guide, 2000), 192p.

4144.   Wagg, Stephen. '"Time gentlemen please": the decline of amateur captaincy in English county cricket', *Contemporary British History* 14:2 (2000), 31–59.

4145.   Wykes, David. *Evelyn Waugh: a literary life* (Basingstoke and New York: Macmillan and St Martin's Press, 1999), xii, 224p.

G. Religious Belief, Practice and Organisation

See also 492, 495 (B); 3290, 3292, 3295–6, 3307, 3310–11, 3318, 3325, 3347, 3356
(H); 3718, 4001, 4007, 4059, 4070, 4344, 4693 (I)

4146. Bakewell, Kenneth Graham Bartlett. *St Hilda's Church, Hunts Cross, Liverpool, 1898–1998: a centenary publication* ([Liverpool?]: [The author?], [1999?]), 124p.

4147. Bethmont, Rémy. 'L'Église d'Angleterre face à la pauvreté et aux inégalités: Pensée et action, 1942–1990' [The Church of England's position regarding poverty and inequality: thought and action], A84, 247–59.

4148. Binfield, Clyde. 'Sir Makepeace Watermaster and the march of Christian people: an interaction of fiction, fact and politics', *Parliamentary History* 19 (2000), 165–84.

4149. Bruce, Alex. *The cathedral 'open and free': Dean Bennett of Chester* (Liverpool: Liverpool University Press, 2000), xiv, 286p.

4150. Chapman, Mark D. 'Anglo-German theological relations during the First World War', *Journal for the History of Modern Theology* 7:1 (2000), 109–26.

4151. Davies, John. 'Bishop Moriarty, Shrewsbury and World War Two', *Recusant History* 25:1 (2000), 133–58.

4152. Davies, John. 'Traditional religion, popular piety, or base superstition?: the cause for the beatification of Teresa Higginson', *Recusant History* 24:1 (1998), 123–44.

4153. Davies, Noel A. 'The search for Christian unity in Wales: the beginnings', *Journal of Welsh Religious History* 8 (2000), 63–76.

4154. Daykin, T.E. 'Reservation of the sacrament at Winchester Cathedral, 1931–1935', *Studies in Church History* 35 (1999), 464–77.

4155. Fagerberg, David W. *The size of Chesterton's Catholicism* (Notre Dame (IN): University of Notre Dame Press, 1998), vii, 214p.

4156. Finke, A.-K. 'Karl Barth and British theology', *Journal for the History of Modern Theology* 2:2 (1995), 193–224.

4157. Flinn, A. 'Irish Catholics in south east Lancashire: a conflict of loyalties?', *Manchester Region History Review* 14 (2000), 79–90.

4158. Freedman, Jonathan. *The temple of culture: assimilation and anti-semitism in literary Anglo-America* (New York: Oxford University Press, 2000), vi, 264p.

4159. Gaine, Simon G. *Obituary notices of the English Dominicans from 1952 to 1996* (Oxford: Blackfriars, 2000), 113p.

4160. Gray, Donald. *Ronald Jasper: his life, work and the ASB* [Alternative Service Book] (London: SPCK, 1997), x, 154p.

4161. Hayes, A.L. 'Tradition in the Anglican liturgical movement, 1945–1989', *Anglican and Episcopal History* 69:1 (2000), 22–43.

4162. Hazelgrove, Jennifer. 'Spiritualism after the Great War', *20th Century British History* 10:4 (1999), 404–30.

4163. Hazelgrove, Jennifer. *Spiritualism and British society between the wars* (Manchester: Manchester University Press, 2000), 294p.

4164.   Holmes, Heather. '"Unwearied investigations and interminable correspondence": the churches and clerical work in improving housing conditions for Irish migratory potato workers in Scotland', *Scottish Economic & Social History* 20:1 (2000), 31–57.

4165.   Hughes, Trystan Owain. '"No longer will we call ourselves Catholics in Wales but Welsh Catholics": Roman Catholicism, the Welsh language and Welsh national identity in the twentieth century', *Welsh History Review* 20:2 (2000), 336–65.

4166.   Hutchinson, Roger. *Aleister Crowley: the beast demystified* (Edinburgh: Mainstream, 1998), 216p.

4167.   Johnson, K.A. 'A question of authority: friction in the Catholic Family Life Movement, 1948–1962', *Catholic Historical Review* 86:2 (2000), 217–241.

4168.   Kaiser, Wolfram. 'Co-operation of European Catholic politicians in exile in Britain and the USA during the Second World War', *Journal of Contemporary History* 35:3 (2000), 439–66.

4169.   Kirby, Dianne. 'The Archbishop of York and Anglo-American relations during the Second World War and early Cold War, 1942–1955', *Journal of Religious History* 23:3 (1999), 327–345.

4170.   Lewis, Jane; Wallis, Patrick. 'Fault, breakdown, and the Church of England's involvement in the 1969 divorce reform', *20th Century British History* 11:3 (2000), 308–32.

4171.   Ling, Oi Ki. *The changing role of the British Protestant missionaries in China, 1945–1952* (Madison (NJ) and London: Farleigh Dickinson University Press and Associated University Presses, 1999), 303p.

4172.   Lyon, David H.S. *In pursuit of a vision: the story of the Church of Scotland's developing relationship with the churches emerging from the missionary movement in the twenty-five years from 1947 to 1972* (Edinburgh: Saint Andrew, 1998), 304p.

4173.   MacDonald, F. 'Scenes of ecclesiastical theatre in the Free Church of Scotland, 1981–2000', *Northern Scotland* 20 (2000), 125–148.

4174.   MacDonald, L.O. '"The most potent force of the future": the ministry and citizenship of Presbyterian women in the aftermath of the Great War', *Records of the Scottish Church Historical Society* 29 (1999), 119–38.

4175.   Machin, Ian. 'Reservation under pressure: ritual in the Prayer Book crisis, 1927–1928', *Studies in Church History* 35 (1999), 447–63.

4176.   McWhirr, Alan (ed.) *Century to millennium: St. James the Greater, Leicester 1899–1999* (Leicester: Parochial Church Council of St. James, 1999), vi, 234p.

4177.   Notare, Theresa. '"A revolution in Christian morals": resolution nr 15 of Lambeth 1930', *Revue d'Histoire Ecclésiastique* 94 (1999), 54–75, 471–501.

4178.   Parker, David. '"Stand therefore!" Bishop Michael Bolton Furse, the diocese of St Albans, and the church schools controversy, 1919–1939', *History of Education Quarterly* 39:2 (1999), 161–92.

4179.   Randall, Ian M. '"Austere ritual": the reformation of worship in inter-war English Congregationalism', *Studies in Church History* 35 (1999), 432–46.

4180.   Smith, Lyn. 'Quakers in uniform: the Friends Ambulance Unit', A25, 243–55.

4181.   Tessler, Gloria. *Amélie: the life of Lady Jakobovits* (London: Vallentine Mitchell, 1998), 352p.
4182.   Travell, John. *Doctor of souls: a biography of Dr Leslie Dixon Weatherhead* (Cambridge: Lutterworth, 1999), 327p.
4183.   Turner, Garth. 'Archbishop Lang's visit to the Holy Land in 1931', *Studies in Church History* 36 (2000), 343–57.
4184.   Williamson, Philip. 'Christian Conservatives and the totalitarian challenge, 1933–40', *English Historical Review* 115 (2000), 607–42.

Ha. *Law and Order*

See also 3369–70, 3378–9, 3383, 3388 (H); 3606, 3925, 4008, 4290 (I); 5774 (M)

4185.   Bailey, Victor. 'The shadow of the gallows: the death penalty and the British Labour Government, 1945–51', *Law and History Review* 18:2 (2000), 305–49.
4186.   Eddlestone, John J. *Blind justice: miscarriages of justice in 20th-century Britain* (Oxford: ABC-Clio, 2000), 445p.
4187.   Ewing, Keith D.; Gearty, Conor Anthony. *The struggle for civil liberties: political freedom and the rule of law in Britain, 1914–1945* (Oxford: Clarendon, 2000), xvii, 451p.
4188.   Jones, Dwyryd W. 'David Jones: a bibliography', A111, 238–40.
4189.   Stead, Peter. '"It's not all about nicking folks": dramatizing the police', A111, 207–37.
4190.   Thompson, Dorothy. 'David Jones: an appreciation', A111, 9–15.

Hb. *Public Administration*

See also 2907, 2951, 3399 (H); 4308, 4340, 4379, 4897 (I); 6442, 6457 (P)

4191.   Jones, Tim L. 'A comparative study of local authority preparations for nuclear war in north-eastern Wales, 1948–1968', *Welsh History Review* 20:1 (2000), 89–115.
4192.   Linehan, D. 'An archaeology of dereliction: poetics and policy in the governing of depressed industrial districts in interwar England and Wales', *Journal of Historical Geography* 26:1 (2000), 99–113.
4193.   Price, David. *Office of hope: a history of the public Employment Service in Great Britain* (PSI Research Report, 828) (London: Policy Studies Intitute, 2000), xviii, 370p.
4194.   Richards, David. *The civil service under the Conservatives, 1979–1997: Whitehall's political poodles?* (Brighton: Sussex Academic, 1997), xiii, 273p.
4195.   Short, Brian; Watkins, C.; Foot, W. *The National Farm Survey, 1941–1943: state surveillance and the countryside in England and Wales in the Second World War* (Wallingford: CABI, 2000), viii, 262p.

Hc. *Political and Constitutional*

See also 492, 513, 515 (B); 2575, 2591 (G); 2719, 3410–11, 3418, 3424–6, 3434, 3444,
3456, 3462–3, 3466, 3470–1, 3478–9, 3482, 3490, 3493, 3497, 3506, 3509,
3513, 3517, 3522, 3530 (H); 3603, 3669–70, 3687, 3703, 3777, 3835, 3871,
3892, 3900, 3904, 4097, 4127, 4184, 4187, 4194, 4646, 4705, 4807, 4819,
4857, 4884, 4953 (I); 5843, 5879 (M); 6471, 6492 (P)

4196. Alberti, Johanna. '"A symbol and a key": the suffrage movement in Britain, 1918–1928', A178, 267–90.

4197. Bale, Tim. 'Crimes and misdemeanours: managing dissent in the twentieth and twenty-first century Labour Party', A24, 268–91.

4198. Bale, Tim. 'Harold Wilson, 1963–76', A115, 116–32.

4199. Ball, Stuart (ed.) *Parliament and politics in the age of Churchill and Attlee: the Headlam diaries, 1935–1951* (Camden, 5th ser., 14) (Cambridge: Cambridge University Press for the Royal Historical Society, 1999), x, 665p.

4200. Barberis, Peter. 'The break-up of Britain: twentieth century perspectives', *Contemporary British History* 14:3 (2000), 1–9.

4201. Barrett, Buckley Barry. *Churchill: a concise bibliography* (Bibliographies and Indexes in World History, 50) (London: Greenwood, 2000), viii, 215p.

4202. Bashevkin, Sylvia. 'From tough times to better times: feminism, public policy, and New Labour politics in Britain', *International Political Science Review* 21:4 (2000), 407–24.

4203. Bashevkin, Sylvia. 'Tough times in review: the British women's movement during the Thatcher years', *Comparative Political Studies* 28:4 (1996), 525–52.

4204. Baston, Lewis. 'Labour local government 1900–1999', A24, 449–84.

4205. Baston, Lewis. 'The age of Wilson, 1955–1979', A24, 87–111.

4206. Beer, Samuel H. 'The rise and fall of party government in Britain and the United States, 1945–1996', A138, 281–302.

4207. Bell, Colin. *Scotland's century: an autobiography of the nation* (Glasgow: HarperCollins, 1999), 318p.

4208. Birke, Adolf M.; Brechtken, Magnus (eds.) *Kommunale Selbstverwaltung: Geschichte und Gegenwart im deutsch-britischen Vergleich = Local self-government* (Prinz-Albert-Studien, 13) (München: K.G. Saur, 1996), 164p.

4209. Blaazer, David. 'Guild socialists after guild socialism: the Workers' Control Group and the House of Industry League', *20th Century British History* 11:2 (2000), 135–55.

4210. Black, Lawrence. '"Still at the penny-farthing state in a jet-propelled era": branch life in 1950s socialism', *Labour History Review* 65:2 (2000), 202–26.

4211. Black, Lawrence. 'Social democracy as a way of life: fellowship and the Socialist Union, 1951–9', *20th Century British History* 10:4 (1999), 499–539.

4212. Booth, Alan. 'Inflation, expectations, and the political economy of Conservative Britain, 1951–1964', *Historical Journal* 43:3 (2000), 827–48.

4213. Brandreth, Gyles. *Breaking the code: Westminster Diaries, May 1990–May 1997* (London: Weidenfeld & Nicolson, 1999), xv, 527p.

4214. Bridgen, Paul. 'The State, redundancy pay, and economic policy-making in the early 1960s', *20th Century British History* 11:3 (2000), 233–58.

4215. Brivati, Brian. '"The future Labour offered": industrial modernization projects in the British Labour Party from Gaitskell to Blair', A24, 346–62.

4216. Brivati, Brian. 'Hugh Gaitskell, 1955–63', A115, 97–115.

4217. Brivati, Brian; Heffernan, Richard. 'Introduction' [the Labour Party], A24, 1–7.

4218. Brivati, Brian. 'Labour's literary dominance', A24, 485–502.

4219. Brivati, Brian. *Lord Goodman* (London: Richard Cohen, 1999), xvi, 320p.

4220. Budge, Ian. 'Party policy and ideology: reversing the 1950s?', in *Critical elections*, eds. Geoffrey Evans & Pippa Norris (London: Sage, 1999), 1–21.

4221. Burnham, Peter. 'Britain's external economic policy in the early 1950s: the historical significance of Operation Robot', *20th Century British History* 11:4 (2000), 379–408.

4222. Butler, David E.; Kitzinger, Uwe. *The 1975 referendum*, 2nd edn. (Basingstoke: Macmillan, 1996), xi, 315p. [1st edn. 1976.]

4223. Butler, David E. *The British general election of 1951* (The British General Elections, 1945–92) (Basingstoke: Macmillan, 1999), 289p. [1st published 1952.]

4224. Butler, David E. *The British general election of 1955* (The British General Elections, 1945–92) (Basingstoke: Macmillan, 1999), 236p. [1st published 1955.]

4225. Butler, David E.; Rose, Richard. *The British general election of 1959* (The British General Elections, 1945–92) (Basingstoke: Macmillan, 1999), viii, 293p. [1st published 1959.]

4226. Butler, David E.; King, Anthony. *The British general election of 1964* (The British General Elections, 1945–92) (Basingstoke: Macmillan, 1999), ix, 401p. [1st published 1964.]

4227. Butler, David E.; King, Anthony. *The British general election of 1966* (The British General Elections, 1945–92) (Basingstoke: Macmillan, 1999), xi, 338p.

4228. Butler, David E.; Pinto-Duschinsky, Michael. *The British general election of 1970* (The British General Elections, 1945–92) (Basingstoke: Macmillan, 1999), xvi, 493p. [1st published 1971.]

4229. Butler, David E.; Kavanagh, Dennis. *The British general election of 1979* (The British General Elections, 1945–92) (Basingstoke: Macmillan, 1999), ix, 443p. [1st published 1980.]

4230. Butler, David E.; Kavanagh, Dennis. *The British general election of 1983* (The British General Elections, 1945–92) (Basingstoke: Macmillan, 1999), xii, 388p. [1st published 1984.]

4231. Butler, David E.; Kavanagh, Dennis. *The British general election of 1987* (The British General Elections, 1945–92) (Basingstoke: Macmillan, 1999), xv, 379p. [1st published 1988.]

4232. Butler, David E.; Kavanagh, Dennis. *The British general election of 1992* (The British General Elections, 1945–92) (Basingstoke: Macmillan, 1999), xi, 380p. [1st published 1992.]

4233.   Butler, David E.; Kavanagh, Dennis. *The British general election of February 1974* (The British General Elections, 1945–92) (Basingstoke: Macmillan, 1999), ix, 354p. [1st published 1974.]

4234.   Butler, David E.; Kavanagh, Dennis. *The British general election of October 1974* (The British General Elections, 1945–92) (Basingstoke: Macmillan, 1999), 368p. [1st published 1975.]

4235.   Cabinet Office. *Cabinet papers: complete classes from the CAB & PREM series in the Public Record Office. Series 3. CAB 128 & CAB 129: Cabinet conclusions & Cabinet memoranda, 1945 and following* (Marlborough: Adam Matthew in association with the Public Record Office, 1997–98), 143p. [A listing and guide to the microfilm collection: Part 1. The Attlee government, August 1945–October 1951 (CAB 128/1–13 & CAB 129/1–20); Part 2. The Attlee government, August 1945–October 1951 (CAB 128/14–23 & CAB 129/21–47); Part 3. The Churchill and Eden governments, October 1951–January 1957 (CAB 128/23–30 & CAB 129/32–48); Part 4. The Macmillan and Douglas-Home governments, January 1957–October 1964 (CAB 128/31–38 & CAB 129/85–118; Part 5. The Harold Wilson government, October 1964–December 1968 (CAB 128/39–43, 46 & CAB 129/119–39); Part 6. The Harold Wilson government, January-May 1970, 2000 update for 1969 releases (CAB 128/44, 46 & CAB 129/140–46).]

4236.   Callaghan, John. 'The Left in Britain in the twentieth century' [conference report], *International Labor and Working-Class History* 57 (2000), 103–6.

4237.   Campbell, John. *Margaret Thatcher*, vol. 1: *The grocer's daughter* (London: Jonathan Cape, 2000), xv, 511p.

4238.   Campbell, John. *Nye Bevan* (London: Richard Cohen, 1997), xix, 409p. [1st published as *Nye Bevan and the mirage of British socialism* (London: Weidenfeld & Nicolson, 1987).]

4239.   Capet, Antoine. 'New Labour, National Labour et Middle Way: La voie mediane, 1931–1999: Voie vers le socialisme, vers le conservatisme ou vers le confusionnisme?' [The middle way: a way to socialism, conservatism or confusion], A212, 53–60.

4240.   Catsiapis, Hélène. *La Royauté anglaise au XXe siècle* [The English monarchy in the 20th century] (Paris: Ellipses, 2000), 160p.

4241.   Catterall, Peter. '"Efficiency with freedom"? Debates about the British constitution in the twentieth century', A39, 1–42.

4242.   Charlot, Monica. 'Let's Go With Labour', A35, 103–16.

4243.   Charmley, John. *Duff Cooper: the authorised biography* (London: Phoenix, 1997), xii, 265p. [1st published London: Weidenfeld & Nicolson, 1986.]

4244.   Churchill, Winston Spencer. *His father's son: the life of Randolph Churchill* (London: Weidenfeld & Nicolson, 1996), xii, 514p.

4245.   Collette, Christine. '"Le soleil du socialisme commence à se lever sur le monde": the utopian visions of Labour Zionism, British Labour and the Labour and Socialist International in the 1930s', A46, 71–92.

4246.   Collette, Christine. 'Questions of gender: Labour and women', A24, 402–21.

4247.   Collins, Tony. 'Return to manhood: the cult of masculinity and the British Union of Fascists', *International Journal of the History of Sport* 16:4

(2000), 145–62. [Special issue: 'Superhuman supreme: Fascist body as political icon—global fashion', also published as a book, ed. J.A. Mangan.]

4248.   Copsey, Nigel. *Anti-Fascism in Britain* (London: Macmillan, 1999), ix, 229p.

4249.   Coupland, Philip M. 'H.G. Wells' "Liberal Fascism"', *Journal of Contemporary History* 35:4 (2000), 541–58.

4250.   Coupland, Philip M. 'The Blackshirts in Northampton, 1933–1940', *Northamptonshire Past and Present* 53 (2000), 71–82.

4251.   Courtenay, Paul. 'The armorial bearings of Sir Winston Churchill: a ramble through heraldic byways', *Finest Hour: Journal of the Churchill Center and Societies* 102 (1999), 22–25.

4252.   Crago, T. '"Play the game as men play it": women in politics during the era of the "Cornish proto-alignment" 1918–1922', *Cornish Studies* 8 (2000), 147–60.

4253.   Creevy, Mathew. 'A critical review of the Wilson government's handling of the D-Notice affair of 1967' [research notes], *Intelligence and National Security* 14:3 (1999), 209–27.

4254.   Crew, Ivor; Thomson, Katarina. 'Party loyalties: dealignment or realignment?', in: *Critical elections*, eds. Geoffrey Evans & Pippa Norris (London: Sage, 1999), 64–86.

4255.   Crickhowell, Nicholas. *Westminster, Wales and water* (Cardiff: University of Wales Press, 1999), viii, 246p.

4256.   Croll, Andy. '"People's remembrancers" in a post-modern age: contemplating the non-crisis of Welsh labour history', *Llafur* 8:1 (2000), 5–17.

4257.   Cronin, J.E. 'Convergence by conviction: politics and economics in the emergence of the "Anglo-American model"', *Journal of Social History* 33:4 (2000), 781–804.

4258.   Crowson, Nicholas J. (ed.) *Fleet Street, press barons and politics: the journals of Collin Brooks, 1932–1940* (Camden Fifth Series, 11) (Cambridge: Cambridge University Press for the Royal Historical Society, 1998), ix, 311p.

4259.   Curtice, John; Park, Alison. 'Region: New Labour, new geography?', in: *Critical elections*, eds. Geoffrey Evans & Pippa Norris (London: Sage, 1999), 124–47.

4260.   Curtis, Sarah (ed.) *The journals of Woodrow Wyatt*, 3 vols.: 1. *1985–1988*; 2. *1989–1992*; 3. *1993–1997* (Basingstoke: Macmillan, 1998–2000).

4261.   Dale, Iain (ed.) *Conservative party general election manifestos, 1900–1997* (London: Routledge, 2000), vi, 479p.

4262.   Davies, John. 'John Davies and the Workers' Educational Association in south Wales', *Llafur* 8:1 (2000), 45–68.

4263.   Davies, S.; Morley, B. 'The politics of place: a comparative analysis of electoral politics in four Lancashire cotton textile towns, 1919–1939', *Manchester Region History Review* 14 (2000), 63–78.

4264.   Davis, Richard. 'The Conservative Party and social inequalities', A84, 164–78.

4265.   Deery, Philip. '"The secret battalion": communism in Britain during the Cold War', *Contemporary British History* 13:4 (1999), 1–28.

4266.   Dell, Edmund. *A strange eventful history: democratic socialism in Britain* (London: HarperCollins, 2000), 638p.

4267. Eccleshall, R. 'Party ideology and national decline', A75, 155–83.
4268. Ellison, Nick. 'Labour and welfare politics', A24, 422–48.
4269. English, Richard; Kenny, Michael. 'Conclusion: decline or declinism?', A75, 279–99.
4270. Espiet, Raphaële. 'Politique sociale des gouvernements Thatcher et incidences sur la pauvreté, 1979–1990' [The Thatcher Governments' social policy and its incidence on poverty], A84, 207–19.
4271. Evans, Geoffrey; Heath, Anthony; Payne, Clive. 'Class: Labour as a catch-all party?', in: *Critical elections*, eds. Geoffrey Evans & Pippa Norris (London: Sage, 1999), 87–101.
4272. Evans, Geoffrey; Norris, Pippa (eds.) *Critical elections: British parties and voters in long-term perspective* (London: Sage, 1999), 350p.
4273. Evans, Neil. '"South Wales has been roused as never before": marching against the means test, 1934–1936', A111, 176–206.
4274. Ewen, Shane. '"Mutual antagonism"?: an analysis of the relationship between Nottingham City and County during the interim development of Clifton housing estate, 1943 to 1951', *Midland History* 25 (2000), 162–79.
4275. Favretto, Ilaria. '"Wilsonism" reconsidered: Labour Party revisionism, 1952–64', *Contemporary British History* 14:4 (2000), 54–80.
4276. Fay, Marie-Therese; Meehan, Elizabeth. 'British decline and European integration', A75, 210–30.
4277. Fielding, Steven. 'New Labour and the past', A202, 367–92.
4278. Folly, Martin H. *Churchill, Whitehall and the Soviet Union, 1940–45* (Basingstoke: Macmillan, 2000), xi, 237p.
4279. Forbes, Grania. *Elizabeth the Queen Mother: a twentieth-century life* (London: Pavilion, 1999), 192p.
4280. Franklin, Mark; Hughes, Christina. 'Dynamic representation in Britain', in: *Critical elections*, eds. Geoffrey Evans & Pippa Norris (London: Sage, 1999), 240–58.
4281. Fraser, Derek. 'The Postwar consensus: a debate not long enough?', *Parliamentary Affairs* 53:2 (2000), 347–62.
4282. Gardiner, George. *A bastard's tale: the political memoirs of George Gardiner* (London: Aurum, 1999), 280p.
4283. Gilbert, Martin. *Churchill: a photographic portrait*, revised edn. (London: Pimlico, 1999), 364p. [1st published London: Heinemann, 1988.]
4284. Gottlieb, Julie V. *Feminine fascism: women in Britain's fascist movement, 1923–1945* (London: I.B. Tauris, 2000), x, 378p.
4285. Gottlieb, Julie V. 'Suffragette experience through the filter of fascism', A76, 105–25.
4286. Green, E.H.H. 'The Treasury resignations of 1958: a reconsideration', *20th Century British History* 11:4 (2000), 409–30.
4287. Griffiths, Clare. '"Red tape farm"? Visions of a socialist agriculture in 1920s and 1930s Britain', A217, 199–241.
4288. Hall, Douglas J. 'Bulldog Churchill: the evolution of a famous image', *Finest Hour: Journal of the Churchill Center and Societies* 106 (2000), 18–20.
4289. Harris, Jose. 'Labour's political and social thought', A202, 8–45.

4290.   Hart, Peter. '"Operations abroad": the IRA in Britain, 1919–23', *English Historical Review* 115 (2000), 71–102.

4291.   Heath, Anthony; Taylor, Bridget. 'New sources of abstention?', in: *Critical elections*, eds. Geoffrey Evans & Pippa Norris (London: Sage, 1999), 164–80.

4292.   Heath, Edward. *The course of my life: the autobiography of Edward Heath* (London: Hodder & Stoughton, 1998), xiii, 766p.

4293.   Heffernan, Richard. 'Beyond Euro-scepticism? Labour and the European Union since 1945', A24, 383–401.

4294.   Heffernan, Richard. 'Leaders and followers: the politics of the parliamentary Labour Party', A24, 246–67.

4295.   Hennessy, Peter. *Muddling through: power, politics and the quality of government in postwar Britain* (London: Gollancz, 1996), 317p.

4296.   Hennessy, Peter. *The Prime Minister: the office and its holders since 1945* (London: Allen Lane, 2000), xiv, 685p.

4297.   Henry, J. 'Salford Labour: a party in waiting 1919–1932', *Manchester Region History Review* 14 (2000), 47–62.

4298.   Heppell, Jason. 'A question of "Jewish politics"? The Jewish Section of the Communist Party of Great Britain, 1936–45', A46, 93–121.

4299.   Hilson, Mary; Melling, Joseph. 'Public gifts and political identities: Sir Richard Acland, Common Wealth, and the moral politics of land ownership in the 1940s', *20th Century British History* 11:2 (2000), 156–82.

4300.   Hope, John. 'Blackshirts, knuckle-dusters and lawyers: documentary essay on the Mosley versus Marchbanks papers', *Labour History Review* 65:1 (2000), 41–58, 19–36.

4301.   Hope, John. 'Cable Street, the BUF and the Italian subsidy', *Searchlight* 292 (1999), 20–21.

4302.   Howell, David. '"Shut your gob!": The Trade Unions and the Labour Party', A31, 117–44.

4303.   Hutchison, I.G.C. *Scottish politics in the twentieth century* (Basingstoke: Palgrave, 2000), 208p.

4304.   Jacob, Joe. 'Constitutional law reform: inside the motor', A39, 72–96.

4305.   Jefferys, Kevin. *Anthony Crosland: a new biography* (London: Richard Cohen, 1999), xvi, 270p.

4306.   Jefferys, Kevin. 'The Attlee years, 1935–1955', A24, 63–86.

4307.   Jefferys, Kevin. 'Winston Churchill and the war-time coalition', *History Review* 32 (1998), 44–49.

4308.   Johnes, Martin. 'Uneasy relationships: the Aberfan disaster 1966, Merthyr Tydfil Borough Council and local politics', *Welsh History Review* 20:1 (2000), 143–66.

4309.   Jones, John Graham. 'Clement Davies and Montgomeryshire politics, 1950–51', *Montgomeryshire Collections* 88 (2000), 95–116.

4310.   Jones, John Graham. 'Desmond Donnelly and the 1963 Labour Party leadership contest', *Llafur* 7:3–4 (1999), 153–9.

4311.   Jones, John Graham. 'Lloyd George, W. Llewelyn Williams M.P. and the 1916 Conscription Bill', *National Library of Wales Journal* 31:2 (1999), 173–88.

4312.   Jones, John Graham. 'The Earl Lloyd George of Dwyfor, A.J. Sylvester and the Caernarfon Boroughs vacancy of 1945', *Caernarvonshire Historical Society Transactions* 61 (2000), 111–33.

4313.   Jones, Tudor. 'Labour's constitution and public ownership: from "old" Clause Four to "new" Clause Four', A24, 292–321.

4314.   Kaiser, André. 'House of Lords and monarchy: British majoritarian democracy and the current reform debate about its pre-democratic institutions', A39, 97–128.

4315.   Kaiser, Wolfram. 'The decline and rise of radicalism: political parties and reform in the twentieth century', A39, 43–71.

4316.   Kampfner, John. *Robin Cook* (London: Gollancz, 1998), 256p.

4317.   Kean, Hilda. 'Suffrage autobiography: a study of Mary Richardson—suffragette, socialist and fascist', A76, 177–89.

4318.   Kelly, John. 'Social Democracy and anti-Communism: Allan Flanders and British industrial relations in the early post-war period', A31, 192–221.

4319.   Keohane, Dan. 'Labour's international policy: a story of conflict and contention', A24, 363–82.

4320.   Kersaudy, François. 'Un monument de contradictions, 2 parts: 1. Un monument de contradictions; 2. Le seigneur de la guerre' [Winston Churchill], *Historia* [Paris] 642 (2000), 54–59, 65–71.

4321.   Kersaudy, François. *Winston Churchill: Le pouvoir de l'imaginaire* [The power of imagination] (Paris: Tallandier, 2000), 602p.

4322.   Krockow, Christian *Graf* von. *Churchill: man of the century* (London: London House, 2000), 270p. [Translation of *Churchill: eine Biographie des 20. Jahrhunderts* (Hamburg: Hoffman & Campe, 1999).]

4323.   Kushner, Tony; Valman, Nadia. *Remembering Cable Street: Fascism and anti-Fascism in British society* (London: Vallentine Mitchell, 2000), 288p.

4324.   Lamont, Norman. *In office* (London: Little, Brown, 1999), viii, 597p.

4325.   Langworth, Richard M. 'Churchill and the art of the statesman-writer', *Finest Hour: Journal of the Churchill Center and Societies* 102 (1999), 14–21.

4326.   Langworth, Richard M. 'How Churchill saw others: Stanley Baldwin', *Finest Hour: Journal of the Churchill Center and Societies* 101 (1998–99), 29–31.

4327.   Laska, Vera. 'The private lives of Winston Churchill', *International Journal on World Peace* 12:4 (1995), 106–8.

4328.   Law, Cheryl. *Suffrage and power: the women's movement, 1918–1928* (London: I.B. Tauris, 1998), ix, 260p.

4329.   Lawrence, Jon. 'Labour—the myths it has lived by', A202, 341–66.

4330.   Lawrence, Jon. 'The politics of place and the politics of nation' [review article], *20th Century British History* 11:1 (2000), 83–94.

4331.   Laybourn, Keith. *A century of Labour: a history of the Labour Party, 1900–2000* (Stroud: Sutton, 2000), xv, 183p.

4332.   Laybourn, Keith. 'Labour in and out of government, 1923–1935', A24, 50–67.

4333.   Leruez, Jacques. 'French views on Thatcherism and Blairism', *Historical Research* 73:182 (2000), 296–311.

4334.   Levitt, I. 'H.G. Wells's "Liberal Fascism"', *Journal of Contemporary History* 35:4 (2000), 577–94.

4335.   Levitt, Ian. '"Taking a gamble": the Scottish Office, Whitehall and the Highlands and Islands Development Board, 1965–67', *Northern Scotland* 20 (2000), 87–112.

4336.   Levitt, Ian. 'Scottish papers submitted to the Cabinet, 1945–66: a guide to records held at the Public Record Office and National Archive of Scotland', *Scottish Economic & Social History* 20:1 (2000), 58–125.

4337.   Lineham, Thomas P. *British fascism, 1918–1939: parties, ideologies and culture* (Manchester: Manchester University Press, 2000), xiii, 306p.

4338.   List and Index Society. *Legislation index*, 2 vols.: 1. *1900–1913*; 2. *1914–1922* (List and Index Society, 277) (Kew: List and Index Society, 1999–2000).

4339.   Lomas, Janis. '"Delicate duties": issues of class and respectability in government policy towards the wives and widows of British soldiers in the era of the Great War', *Women's History Review* 9:1 (2000), 123–48.

4340.   London, Louise. *Whitehall and the Jews, 1933–1948: British immigration policy and the Holocaust* (Cambridge: Cambridge University Press, 2000), xiii, 313p.

4341.   Lovelock, Sir Douglas. *While I remember: Christmas Island, Customs & Excise and the Church Commissioners* (Edinburgh: Pentland, 1998), ix, 162p.

4342.   Low, Eugenia. 'The concept of citizenship in twentieth-century Britain: analysing contexts of development', A39, 179–200.

4343.   Ludlam, Steve. 'Norms and blocks: trade unions and the Labour Party since 1964', A24.

4344.   Machin, George Ian Thom. 'Parliament, the Church of England, and the Prayer Book Crisis, 1927–1928', *Parliamentary History* 19 (2000), 131–47.

4345.   Major, John Roy. *John Major: the autobiography* (London: HarperCollins, 1999), xxiii, 774p.

4346.   Mark, Graham. *British censorship of civil mails during World War I, 1914–1919* (Bristol: Stuart Rossiter Trust Fund, 2000), xxxv, 252p.

4347.   Marquand, David. *Ramsay MacDonald* (London: Richard Cohen, 1997), xx, 859p. [1st published London: Jonathan Cape, 1977.]

4348.   Mather, Janet. 'Labour and the English regions: centralised devolution?', *Contemporary British History* 14:3 (2000), 10–38.

4349.   Mawhinney, Brian. *In the firing line: politics, faith, power & forgiveness* (London: HarperCollins, 1999), xviii, 270p.

4350.   McCallum, Ronald B.; Readman, Alison. *The British general election of 1945* (The British General Elections, 1945–92) (Basingstoke: Macmillan, 1999), xv, 311p. [1st published by Oxford University Press, 1947.]

4351.   McHugh, J. 'The Stockport by-election of 1920: the Labour Party and the problem of Irish self-determination', *Manchester Region History Review* 14 (2000), 39–46.

4352.   McIlroy, John. '"Always outnumbered, always outgunned": The Trotskyists and the trade unions', A32, 259–298.

4353.   McIlroy, John. 'Notes on the Communist Party and industrial politics', A32, 216–58.

4354.   McIlroy, John. 'Reds at work: Communist factory organisation in the Cold War, 1947–56', *Labour History Review* 65:2 (2000), 181–201.

4355. McSmith, Andy. 'John Smith, 1992–94', A115, 193–207.
4356. Millman, Brock. 'The battle of Cory Hall, November 1916: patriots meet dissenters in wartime Cardiff', *Canadian Journal of History* 35:1 (2000), 57–83.
4357. Millon-Micalaudy, Isabelle. 'New Labour: New Lib-Labism? A nouveau travaillisme, nouveau pacte Lib-Lab?' [A new Lib-Lab pact for New Labour?], A212, 99–111.
4358. Mitchell, Austin. 'Reinterpreting Labour's history of failure', A24, 178–82.
4359. Mitchell, James. 'Devolution and the end of Britain?', *Contemporary British History* 14:3 (2000), 61–82.
4360. Mitchell, James. 'Territorial politics and change in Britain', A39, 225–54.
4361. Morgan, Kenneth O. 'James Callaghan, 1976–80', A115, 133–50.
4362. Motard, Anne-Marie. 'Les luttes internes au sein du Parti travailliste, 1964–1970' [in-fighting inside the Labour Party], A35, 117–34.
4363. Motard, Anne-Marie. 'Les syndicats: Les meilleurs ennemis du New Labour?' [the Trade Unions: New Labour's best enemies?], A212, 79–97.
4364. Mougel, François-Charles. 'Les enjeux de pouvoir' [power politics], A35, 77–102.
4365. Newman, Michael. *Harold Laski: a political biography* (Basingstoke: Macmillan, 1993), 456p.
4366. Nicholas, Herbert George. *The British general election of 1950* (Basingstoke: Macmillan, 1999), x, 353p. [1st published 1951.]
4367. Norris, Pippa. 'Gender: a gender-generation gap?', in: *Critical elections*, eds. Geoffrey Evans & Pippa Norris (London: Sage, 1999), 148–63.
4368. Norris, Pippa. 'New politicians? Changes in party competition at Westminster', in: *Critical elections*, eds. Geoffrey Evans & Pippa Norris (London: Sage, 1999), 22–43.
4369. Oborne, Peter. *Alastair Campbell: New Labour and the rise of the media class* (London: Aurum, 1999), ix, 230p.
4370. Osmond, Deborah. 'British Jewry and Labour politics, 1918–39', A46, 55–70.
4371. Overbeek, Henk. 'Globalization and Britain's decline', A75, 231–56.
4372. Owen, David. 'The legacy of the SDP', A24, 166–69.
4373. Owen, Ursula. 'An appreciation: Jill Craigie, 1914–99', *Women's History Review* 9:1 (2000), 9–12.
4374. Parker, Robert Alexander Clarke. 'Churchill and consensus', *Historical Journal* 39:2 (1996), 563–72.
4375. Parsons, Michael. 'Harold Wilson and the Labour Government: From enthusiasm to disillusion?', A35, 227–38.
4376. Pateman, M. 'Mancunians' perceptions of Labour in the Second World War', *Manchester Region History Review* 14 (2000), 91–102.
4377. Pateman, M. 'The Lancashire coalfield 1945–1972: NUM–Labour Party hegemony and industrial change', *Manchester Region History Review* 14 (2000), 103–16.
4378. Pearce, Robert. 'Clement Attlee, 1935–55', A115, 80–96.
4379. Peden, George Cameron. *The Treasury and British public policy, 1906–1959* (Oxford: Oxford University Press, 2000), xiv, 581p.

4380. Poirier, François. 'Retours sur *In Place of Strife*' [*In Place of Strife* revisited], A35, 135–52.
4381. Pottle, Mark Christopher (ed.) *Daring to hope: the diaries and letters of Violet Bonham Carter, 1946–1969* (London: Weidenfeld & Nicolson, 2000), xxxi, 431p. [Previous volumes: 1. *Lantern Slides* [1904–1914] (1996); 2. *Champion Redoubtable* [1914–1945] (1998).]
4382. Ramsden, John. '"That will depend on who writes the history": Winston Churchill as his own historian', A138, 241–54.
4383. Rasor, Eugene L. *Winston S. Churchill, 1874–1965: a comprehensive historiography and annotated bibliography* (Bibliographies of World Leaders, 6) (London: Greenwood, 2000), xxv, 704p.
4384. Renton, David. *Fascism, anti-fascism, and Britain in the 1940s* (Basingstoke: Macmillan, 2000), ix, 203p.
4385. Renton, David. *Fascism: theory and practice* [British Union of Fascists] (London: Pluto Press, 1999), vii, 150p.
4386. Renton, David. 'Necessary myth or collective truth?: Cable Street revisited', *Changing English* 5:2 (1998), 189–94.
4387. Renton, David. 'Not just economics but politics as well: trade unions, labour movement activists and anti-fascist protests, 1945–51', *Labour History Review* 65:2 (2000), 166–80.
4388. Renton, David. 'Was fascism an ideology?: British fascism reconsidered', *Race & Class* 41:3 (2000), 72–84.
4389. Rentoul, John. 'Tony Blair, 1994– ', A115, 208–28.
4390. Rhodes James, Robert (ed. & intr.) *Chips: the diary of Sir Henry Channon* (London: Phoenix, 1996), 495p. [1st published London: Weidenfeld & Nicolson, 1967.]
4391. Riddell, Neil. 'Arthur Henderson, 1931–32', A115, 41–60.
4392. Riddell, Neil. *Labour in Crisis: the second Labour Government, 1929–31* (Manchester: Manchester University Press, 1999), xi, 276p.
4393. Riddell, Neil. 'Walter Citrine and the British labour movement, 1925–1935', *History* 85 (2000), 285–306.
4394. Ringe, Astrid; Rollings, Neil. 'Responding to relative decline: the creation of the National Economic Development Council', *Economic History Review* 2nd ser. 53:2 (2000), 331–53.
4395. Rose, Norman. *The Cliveden set: portrait of an exclusive fraternity* (London: Cape, 2000), 277p.
4396. Rosen, Harold. 'A necessary myth: Cable Street revisited', *Changing English* 5:1 (1998), 27–34.
4397. Rubinstein, William D. 'The secret of Leopold Amery', *Historical Research* 73:181 (2000), 175–96.
4398. Saggar, Shamir; Heath, Anthony. 'Race: towards a multicultural electorate?', in: *Critical elections*, eds. Geoffrey Evans & Pippa Norris (London: Sage, 1999), 102–23.
4399. Sanders, David. 'The impact of Left-Right ideology', in: *Critical elections*, eds. Geoffrey Evans & Pippa Norris (London: Sage, 1999), 181–206.
4400. Seldon, Anthony; Collings, Daniel. *Britain under Thatcher* (London: Longman, 2000), xiv, 142p.

4401. Seldon, Anthony; Baston, Lewis. *Major: a political life* (London: Weidenfeld & Nicolson, 1997), xvii, 856p.

4402. Self, Robert C. (ed.) *The Neville Chamberlain diary letters*, 2 vols.: 1. *The making of a politician, 1915–20*; 2. *The reform years, 1921–27* (Aldershot: Ashgate, 2000).

4403. Shaw, Eric. 'Michael Foot, 1980–83', A115, 151–70.

4404. Shaw, Eric. 'The wilderness years, 1979–1994', A24, 112–42.

4405. Skidelsky, Robert. *John Maynard Keynes*, vol. 3: *Fighting for Britain 1937–1946* (Basingstoke: Macmillan, 2000), xxiii, 580p. [Volume 1: *Hopes Betrayed, 1883–1920* (1983 and 1992); Volume 2: *The Economist as Saviour, 1921–1937* (1992).]

4406. Smith, Martin J. 'From Old to New Labour, 1994–2000', A24, 143–62.

4407. Smith, Martin J. 'The impact of the state', A75, 184–209.

4408. Stewart, Graham. 'Churchill without the rhetoric' [review article], *Historical Journal* 43 (2000), 303–7.

4409. Storrs, Sir Ronald. *Middle East politics and diplomacy, 1904–1950: the papers of Sir Ronald Storrs (1881–1955) from Pembroke College, Cambridge* (Marlborough: Adam Matthew, 1999), 88p. [A listing and guide to the microfilm edition (26 reels).]

4410. Stuart, Mark. *Douglas Hurd: the public servant—an authorised biography* (Edinburgh: Mainstream, 1998), 472p.

4411. Surridge, Paula; Brown, Alice; McCrone, David; Paterson, Lindsay. 'Scotland: constitutional preferences and voting behaviour', in: *Critical elections*, eds. Geoffrey Evans & Pippa Norris (London: Sage, 1999), 223–39.

4412. Sutherland, Duncan. 'Peeresses, Parliament and prejudice: the admission of women to the House of Lords, 1918–1963', *Parliaments, Estates & Representation* 20 (2000), 215–32.

4413. Sykes, Patricia Lee. *Presidents and Prime Ministers: conviction politics in the Anglo-American tradition* (Lawrence (KS): University Press of Kansas, 2000), xiii, 399p.

4414. Tanner, Duncan; Thane, Pat; Tiratsoo, Nick. 'Introduction' [Labour's first century], A202, 1–7.

4415. Tanner, Duncan. 'Labour and its membership', A202, 248–80.

4416. Taylor, Andrew. 'The Conservative Party and the trade unions', A32, 151–86.

4417. Taylor, Miles. 'Labour and the constitution', A202, 151–90.

4418. Taylor, Robert. 'Trade union freedom and the Labour Party: Arthur Deakin, Frank Cousins and the Transport and General Workers' Union, 1945–1964', A24, 187–219.

4419. Thatcher, Carol. *Below the parapet: the biography of Denis Thatcher* (London: HarperCollins, 1996), x, 302p.

4420. Thibault, Charlotte. 'Churchill and Eisenhower at Gettysburg', *Finest Hour: Journal of the Churchill Center and Societies* 103 (1999), 24–27.

4421. Thomas, Mark; Lodge, Guy (eds.) *Radicals and reformers: a century of Fabian thought* (Fabian Special, 44) (London: Fabian Society, 2000), 58p. [Excerpts from pamphlets published between 1890 and 1999 by the Fabian Society, with new commentaries.]

4422. Thompson, J. Lee. *Northcliffe: press baron in politics, 1865–1922* (London: John Murray, 2000), xvi, 642p.

4423. Thompson, J. Lee. *Politicians, the press, and propaganda: Lord Northcliffe and the Great War, 1914–1919* (Kent (OH) and London: Kent State University Press, 1999), xii, 319p.

4424. Thompson, Willie. *The Communist movement since 1945* (Oxford: Blackwell, 1998), 262p.

4425. Thomson, Katharine. 'Racing to victory: Winston Churchill and the lure of the turf', *Finest Hour: Journal of the Churchill Center and Societies* 102 (1999), 26–30.

4426. Thorpe, Andrew. 'George Lansbury, 1932–35', A115, 61–79.

4427. Thorpe, Andrew. 'The Labour Party and the trade unions', A32, 133–50.

4428. Thorpe, Andrew. 'The membership of the Communist Party of Great Britain, 1920–1945', *Historical Journal* 43:3 (2000), 777–800.

4429. Thorpe, Jeremy. *In my own time: reminiscences of a Liberal leader* (London: Politico's, 1999), xx, 234p.

4430. Thorpe, Keir. '"Rendering the strike innocuous": the British government's response to industrial disputes in essential industries, 1953–55', *Journal of Contemporary History* 35:4 (2000), 577–600.

4431. Thurlow, Richard C. *Fascism in modern Britain* (Stroud: Sutton, 2000), 256p.

4432. Tiratsoo, Nick. 'Labour and the electorate', A202, 281–308.

4433. Tombs, Isabelle. 'Szmul Zygielbojm, the British Labour Party and the Holocaust', A46, 122–40.

4434. Toye, Richard. 'Gosplanners v. Thermostatters: Whitehall planning debates and their political consequences, 1945–49', *Contemporary British History* 14:4 (2000), 81–106.

4435. Toye, Richard. 'The Labour Party's external economic policy in the 1940s', *Historical Journal* 43:1 (2000), 189–215.

4436. Tregidga, G. '"Bodmin Man": Peter Bessell and Cornish politics in the 1950s and 1960s', *Cornish Studies* 8 (2000), 161–81.

4437. Trippier, David. *Lend me your ears* (Crook Town (Durham): Memoir Club, 1999), xii, 276p.

4438. Walden, George. *Lucky George: memoirs of an anti-politician* (London: Allen Lane, 1999), xiv, 401p.

4439. Walsha, Robert. 'The One Nation Group: a Tory approach to backbench politics and organization, 1950–1955', *20th Century British History* 11:2 (2000), 183–214.

4440. Ward-Smith, Gabriella. 'Essays on Stanley Baldwin: more than just a biography' [review article], *Contemporary British History* 14:2 (2000), 189–200.

4441. Webb, Martha Beatrice (ed.) *Pilgerfahrt nach Moskau: die Reise einer Fabierin in die Sowjetunion Stalins* [pilgrimage to Moscow: a Fabian's journey to Stalin's Soviet Union], ed. Ellen Beumelburg (KritBrit, 4) (Passau: Stutz, 1998), 173p. [Selection of texts translated into German.]

4442. Webb, Paul; Farrell, David M. 'Party members and ideological change', in: *Critical elections*, eds. Geoffrey Evans & Pippa Norris (London: Sage, 1999), 44–63.

4443. Weiler, Peter. 'The rise and fall of the Conservatives' "grand design for housing", 1951–64', *Contemporary British History* 14:1 (1999), 122–50.
4444. Weintraub, Stanley. 'Jesting and governing: Shaw and Churchill', *Costerus* 99 (1995), 15–32.
4445. Westlake, Martin. 'Neil Kinnock, 1983–92', A115, 171–92.
4446. Whiting, Richard C. *The Labour Party and taxation: party identity and political purpose in twentieth-century Britain* (Cambridge: Cambridge University Press, 2001), xii, 294p.
4447. Williams, A. Susan. *Ladies of influence: women of the elite in interwar Britain* (London: Allen Lane, 2000), xiv, 240p.
4448. Wood, Ian S. *Churchill* (Basingstoke: Palgrave, 2000), xii, 209p.
4449. Worley, Matthew. 'Left turn: a reassessment of the Communist Party of Great Britain in the third period, 1928–33', *20th Century British History* 11:4 (2000), 353–78.
4450. Wrench, David. '"Very peculiar circumstances": Walter Runciman and the National Government, 1931–3', *20th Century British History* 11:1 (2000), 61–82.
4451. Wrigley, Chris. 'James Ramsay MacDonald, 1922–31', A115, 19–40.
4452. Young, John. 'George Wigg, the Wilson government and the 1966 report into security in the diplomatic service and GCHQ' [research notes], *Intelligence and National Security* 14:3 (1999), 198–208.

J. *Military*

See also 517 (B); 3034, 3036, 3242, 3539–41, 3547–8, 3552, 3554, 3557, 3591 (H); 3667, 3712, 3723, 3875, 3913, 3931, 3955, 3957, 3959–60, 3969, 3975, 3980, 3982, 4012, 4055, 4091, 4100, 4123, 4150, 4180, 4253, 4290, 4320, 4339, 4397, 4452, 4809, 4811, 4825, 4831, 4834, 4838, 4843, 4851, 4853, 4863–6, 4868, 4877, 4882, 4890, 4896, 4898, 4905, 4922, 4929, 4932, 4938, 4943, 4947–8, 4950, 4952, 4958–60, 4966, 4968–9, 4974, 4977, 4984, 4987 (I); 5108 (J); 6610, 6654 (P)

4453. Anonymous. *Battlefront: Operation Market Garden: the bridges at Eindhoven, Nijmegen and Arnhem* (Kew: Public Record Office, 2000) [12 facsimiles of documents.]
4454. Anonymous. *Battlefront: the Battle of Britain* (London: Public Record Office, 2000) [12 facsimiles of documents.]
4455. Addison, Paul; Crang, Jeremy A. 'A battle of many nations' [Battle of Britain], A1, 243–266.
4456. Aldgate, Tony. 'The Battle of Britain on film', A1, 207–216.
4457. Aldrich, Richard J. *Intelligence and the war against Japan: Britain, America and the politics of secret service* (Cambridge: Cambridge University Press, 2000), xiv, 500p.
4458. Allen, Martin. *Hidden agenda: how the Duke of Windsor betrayed the allies* (Basingstoke: Macmillan, 2000), xxi, 343p.
4459. Amersfoort, Herman. 'Warfare in the Netherlands, Autumn 1944: old and new', A26, 153–74.

4460.   Andrew, Christopher; Aldrich, Richard J. (eds.) 'The intelligence services in the Second World War' [witness seminar], *Contemporary British History* 13:4 (1999), 130–69.

4461.   Ashby, John. *Seek glory, now keep glory: the story of the 1st Battalion Royal Warwickshire Regiment, 1914–1918* (Solihull: Helion, 2000), 256p.

4462.   Asher, Michael. *Lawrence: the uncrowned king of Arabia* (London: Viking, 1998), xix, 418p.

4463.   Ashplant, T.G.; Dawson, Graham; Roper, Michael (eds.) *The politics of war memory and commemoration* (Routledge Studies in Memory and Narrative, 7) (London: Routledge, 2000), xiv, 282p.

4464.   Ashton, J. Norman. *Only birds and fools: flight engineer, Avro Lancaster, World War II* (Shrewsbury: Airlife, 2000), 189p.

4465.   Badsey, Stephen (ed.) *The Hutchinson atlas of World War II battle plans: before and after* (London: Helicon, 2000), 284p.

4466.   Badsey, Stephen (ed.) *The media and international security* (London: Frank Cass, 2000), xxxii, 264p.

4467.   Bailey, Ian; et al. (comps.) *Never to return: a record of those commemorated on the war memorials of Audley, Talke, Scot Hay and Butt Lane* (Stoke-on-Trent: Audley & District Family History Society, 2000), 180p.

4468.   Bailey, Roderick. 'OSS-SOE relations, Albania 1943–44', *Intelligence and National Security* 15:2 (2000), 20–35.

4469.   Ball, Ernest Dieter. *Letters from a war child—Ernest Dieter Ball's correspondence, 1939–1941: a German Jewish refugee's account of growing up in wartime Horsham* (Horsham: Horsham Museum, 1999), 45p.

4470.   Ball, S.J. 'A rejected strategy: the army and National Service, 1946–1960', A200, 36–48.

4471.   Barnett, Correlli. 'Anglo-American strategy', A132, 174–89.

4472.   Battaglia, Mattea-Paola. 'Français, Italiens et Anglo-Américains en Méditerranée Occidentale (1940–1954)' [The French, Italians and Anglo-Americans in the Western Mediterranean], *Revue historique des armées* 215 (1999), 37–50.

4473.   Baxter, Colin F. (comp.) *Field Marshall Bernard Law Montgomery, 1887–1976: a selected bibliography* (Westport (CT): Greenwood, 2000), xii, 165p.

4474.   Baynes, John. 'Recruiting the professional army, 1960–1990', A200, 49–62.

4475.   Beach, Sir Hugh; Gurr, Nadine. *Flattering the passions: Or, the bomb and Britain's bid for a world role* (London: Tauris, 2000), 279p.

4476.   Bédoyère, Guy de la. *Battles over Britain: the archaelogy of the air war* (London: Tempus Publishing, 2000), 176p.

4477.   Beesly, Patrick. *Very special intelligence: the story of the Admiralty Operational Intelligence Centre, 1939–1945* (London: Greenhill, 2000), 296p. [1st published London: Hamish Hamilton, 1977.]

4478.   Bell, Christopher M. *The Royal Navy, strategy and seapower between the wars* (Basingstoke: Macmillan, 2000), xx, 232p.

4479.   Bell, Philip Michael Hett. 'Les Britanniques considéraient-ils la défaite de la France comme irrémédiable?' [Did the British consider the defeat of France as inevitable in 1940?], *Autrement Mémoires* 62 (Mars 2000), 126–44.

4480. Benton, Mary-Rose. *Family values: pillar to post evacuee—early stages for a touring actor* (Stourport-on-Severn: Thanet, 1998), 208p.

4481. Bickell, C. 'Operation "Fortitude South": an analysis of its influence upon German dispositions and conduct of operations in 1944', *War & Society* 18:1 (2000), 91–122.

4482. Biddle, Tami Davis. 'Allied air power: objectives and capabilities', A166, 35–51.

4483. Birke, Adolf M. 'British war-time planning and the "transfer of German populations"', A16, 157–80.

4484. Blacker, Sir Cecil. *Monkey business: the memoirs of General Sir Cecil Blacker* (London: Quiller, 1993), viii, 232p.

4485. Blandford, Edmund L. *SS intelligence: the Nazi spy organisation* (Shrewsbury: Airlife, 2000), 270p. [Includes British spy ring.]

4486. Blumenson, Martin. *The duel for France, 1944: the men and battles that changed the fate of Europe* (Cambridge (MA): Da Capo, 2000), 472p. [1st published as *The duel for France, 1944* (Boston (MA): Houghton Mifflin, 1963).]

4487. Bob, Hans-Ekkehard. 'Memories of a German veteran' [of the Battle of Britain], A1, 123–128.

4488. Bond, Brian. 'Comment on military operations to defeat Germany', A26, 141–52.

4489. Bond, Brian. 'Introduction' [The burning blue: a new history of the Battle of Britain], A1, 1–14.

4490. Boog, Horst. 'Invasion to surrender: the defense of Germany', A26, 115–40.

4491. Boog, Horst. 'The Luftwaffe's assault' [in the Battle of Britain], A1, 39–54.

4492. Boscowan, R. *Armoured guardsman* (London: Cooper, 2000), 224p.

4493. Bowyer, Chaz. *Albert Ball, VC* (Wrexham: Bridge Books, 1994), 197p. [1st published London: Kimber, 1977.]

4494. Bowyer, Chaz. *Coastal command at war* (Shepperton: Ian Allan, 2000), 160p.

4495. Bowyer, Michael. *Action stations revisited, 1: Eastern England* (Manchester: Crécy, 2000), 400p.

4496. Boyce, Rosalind. 'George Frederick Devaliant MC: the story of a soldier', *Lincolnshire History and Archaeology* 34 (1999), 19–23.

4497. Bradbeer, Grace. *The land changed its face: the evacuation of the South Hams 1943–44*, revised edn. (Dartmouth: Harbour, 1993), 144p. [1st published 1973.]

4498. Breitman, Richard. 'Auschwitz partially decoded', A166, 27–34.

4499. Brézet, François-Emmanuel. '21 juin 1919: le sabordage de Scapa Flow' [The scuttling at Scapa Flow, 21 June 1919], *Revue historique des armées* 216 (1999), 53–61.

4500. Brézet, François-Emmanuel. '3 septembre 1939: La Kriegsmarine entre dans la guerre' [3 September 1939: the Kriegsmarine enters the war], *Revue historique des armées* 217 (1999), 69–76.

4501. Brown, David (ed.) *Naval operations of the campaign in Norway: April-June 1940* (London: Cass, 2000), 188p. [Originally published 1951 as *Confidential Book No.3305* and deposited in the Public Record Office.]

4502. Brown, Louis. *A radar history of World War II: technical and military imperatives* (Bristol and Philadelphia (PA): Institute of Physics Publishing, 1999), xvi, 563p.

4503. Brown, Malcolm. *Spitfire summer: when Britain stood alone. Based on Imperial War Museum exhibition* (Birmingham: Carlton Books, 2000), 207p.

4504. Brown, Mike. *A child's war: Britain's children in the Second World War* (Stroud: Sutton, 2000), 128p.

4505. Brown, Mike. *Evacuees: evacuation in wartime Britain, 1939–1945* (Stroud: Sutton, 2000), 128p.

4506. Brown, Mike. *'Put that light out': Britain's Civil Defence services at war, 1939–1945* (Stroud: Sutton, 2000), 128p.

4507. Brugioni, Dino A. 'The aerial photos of the Auschwitz-Birkenau extermination complex', A166, 52–58.

4508. Budiansky, Stephen. *Battle of wits: the complete story of codebreaking in World War II* (London: Viking, 2000), 447p.

4509. Budiansky, Stephen. 'The difficult beginnings of US-British codebreaking co-operation', *Intelligence and National Security* 15:2 (2000), 49–73.

4510. Burridge, David. *20th century defences in Britain: Kent* (London: Brassey's, 1997), x, 85p.

4511. Caedel, Martin. 'A legitimate peace movement: the case of inter-war Britain, 1918–1945', A25, 134–48.

4512. Calder, Angus. 'The Battle of Britain and pilots' memoirs', A1, 191–206.

4513. Carroll, David. *The Home Guard* (Stroud: Sutton, 1999), 128p. [Pictorial album.]

4514. Carruthers, Bob; Trew, Simon. *The Normandy battles* (London: Cassell, 2000), 224p. [Pictorial album.]

4515. Carter, Ian. *Bomber Command, 1939–1945* (Shepperton: Ian Allan, 2000), 160p.

4516. Charles, Douglas. 'American, British and Canadian intelligence links: a critical annotated bibliography', *Intelligence and National Security* 15:2 (2000), 259–69.

4517. Chasseaud, Peter. *Artillery's astrologers: a history of British survey & mapping on the Western Front 1914–1918* (Lewes: Mapbooks, 1999), xviii, 558p.

4518. Chinnery, Philip. *March or die: the story of Wingate's Chindits* (Shrewsbury: Airlife, 1997), 256p.

4519. Clark, Freddie. *Agents by moonlight: the secret history of RAF Tempsford during World War II* (Stroud: Tempus Publishing, 1999), xxii, 336p.

4520. Clarke, Sir Rupert. *With Alex at war: from the Irrawaddy to the Po, 1941–1945* [Field Marshal Alexander] (London: Cooper, 2000), 224p.

4521. Clifford, J. Garry. 'Endings and beginnings', A169, 257–82.

4522. Cole, Benjamin. 'British technical intelligence and the Soviet intermediate range ballistic missile threat, 1952–1960', *Intelligence and National Security* 14:2 (1999), 70–93.

4523. Collingwood, Donald J. *The Captain class frigates in the Second World War: an operational history of the American built destroyer escorts serving under the White Ensign from 1943–1946* (London: Leo Cooper, 1998), xvi, 208p.

4524. Commeau, Jean-Marie. *L'aéronautique navale française au Royaume-Uni, 1940–1946* [The French Fleet Air Arm in the United Kingdom] (Paris: ARDHAN, 2000), 230p.

4525. Cook, T. '"Against God-inspired conscience": the perception of gas warfare as a weapon of mass destruction, 1915–1939', *War & Society* 18:1 (2000), 47–70.

4526. Cook, Theodore F. 'The Japanese perspective' [on the Battle of Britain], A1, 108–122.

4527. Corrigan, Gordon. *Sepoys in the trenches: the Indian Corps on the Western Front, 1914–1915* (Staplehurst: Spellmount, 1999), xiv, 328p.

4528. Cox, Sebastian. 'The RAF's response' [in the Battle of Britain], A1, 55–70.

4529. Craig, Phil; Clayton, Tim. *Finest Hour* [Battle of Britain] (London: Hodder & Stoughton, 1999), x, 418p.

4530. Crang, Jeremy A. *The British army and the people's war, 1939–1945* (Manchester: Manchester University Press, 2000), 161p.

4531. Crang, Jeremy A. 'The British army as a social institution, 1939–1945', A200, 16–35.

4532. Cull, Brian; Malizia, Nicola; Galea, Frederick. *Spitfires over Sicily: the crucial role of the Malta Spitfires in the Battle of Sicily, January-August 1943* (London: Grub Street, 2000), 240p.

4533. Cunningham, Wallace. 'Memories of a British veteran' [of the Battle of Britain], A1, 129–137.

4534. Danchev, Alex. 'Liddell Hart's big idea', *Review of International Studies* 25:1 (1999), 29–48.

4535. Dandeker, Christopher. 'On "the need to be different": recent trends in military culture', A200, 16–35.

4536. Davis, Richard G. 'The bombing of Auschwitz: comments on a historical speculation', A166, 214–26.

4537. de Lee, N. 'Command in central Norway, 1940: a cautionary tale', *Strategic and Combat Studies Institute Occasional Paper* 38 (1999), 52–59.

4538. Delaforce, Patrick. *Churchill's secret weapons: the story of Hobart's Funnies* (London: Hale, 2000), 256p.

4539. Deseyne, Alex. 'Britse tanks tijdens de slag van Passendale: succes of mislukking?' [British tanks during the Battle of Passchendaele: success or failure?], *Het Zonneheem* 26:3 (1997), 1–12.

4540. Devereux, Joseph; Sacker, Graham. *Roll of honour land forces World War 2*, 3 vols.: 1. *Cavalry, Yeomanry, Royal Armoured Corps, Reconnaissance Corps, Royal Tank Regiment, Brigade of Guards*; 2. *Cambridgeshire Regiment, Devonshire Regiment, King's Own Royal Regiment (Lancaster), King's Regiment (Liverpool), Lincolnshire Regiment, Queen's Royal Regiment, Queen's Royal Regiment (West Surrey), Royal East Kent Regiment (The Buffs), Royal Fusileers (City of London Regiment), Royal Norfolk Regiment, Royal Northumberland Fusiliers, Royal Scots (The Royal Regiment), Royal Warwickshire Regiment, Somerset Light Infantry (Prince Albert's), Suffolk Regiment*; 3. *West Yorkshire Regiment, East Yorkshire Regiment, Bedfordshire and Hertfordshire Regiment, Hertfordshire Regiment, Leicestershire Regiment, Green Howards, Lancashire Fusiliers, Royal Scots Fusiliers, Cheshire Regiment, Royal*

Welch Fusiliers, South Lancashire Regiment, South Wales Borderers, Monmouthshire Regiment, Brecknockshire Battalion, King's Own Scottish Borderers, Cameronians (Scottish Rifles), Royal Inniskilling Fusiliers, Gloucestershire Regiment, Worcestershire Regiment, East Lancashire Regiment (Cheltenham: Promenade, 1999–2000).

4541. Dibbs, John M.; Holmes, Tony. *Spitfire: flying legend 60th anniversary 1936–96* (London: Osprey Aerospace, 1996), 192p. [Pictorial album]

4542. Doherty, Richard. *A noble crusade: the history of Eighth Army, 1941 to 1945* (Staplehurst: Spellmount, 1999), xv, 368p.

4543. Downing, Taylor; Johnston, Andrew. 'The Spitfire legend', *History Today* 50:9 (2000), 19–25.

4544. Duchen, Claire; Bandhauer-Schöffmann, Irene (eds.) *When the war was over: women, war, and peace in Europe, 1940–1956* (London: Leicester University Press, 2000), x, 260p.

4545. Dudgeon, A.G. (Air Vice-Marshal). *Hidden victory: the Battle of Habbaniya, May 1941* (London: Tempus Press, 2000), 146p.

4546. Dudley Edwards, Owen. 'The Battle of Britain and children's literature', A1, 163–190.

4547. Dunning, James. *'It had to be tough': the fascinating story of the origins of the Commandos and their special training in World War II* (Edinburgh: Pentland, 2000), xii, 212p.

4548. Eglin, Josephine. 'Women pacifists in inter-war Britain', A25, 149–68.

4549. Eisenhower, David. 'The broad-front controversy revisited', A26, 69–94.

4550. Eisenhower, John S.D. *Allies: Pearl Harbor to D-Day* (Cambridge (MA): Da Capo, 2000), 528p. [1st published New York: Doubleday, 1982.]

4551. English, John A. 'Cinderella campaign: the genesis and conduct of First Canadian Army operations leading to the opening of the Scheldt estuary, 1944', A26, 175–208.

4552. Erdheim, Stuart G. 'Could the allies have bombed Auschwitz-Birkenau?', A166, 127–56.

4553. Erwood, Peter. *A fury of guns: the war diary of the 75th (Cinque Ports) Heavy Anti-Aircraft Regiment, Royal Artillery, (Territorial Army), Dover, 1939–40* [including the Battle of Britain] (Fleet Hargate: Arcturus, 1999), iv, 128p.

4554. Etschmann, Wolfgang. '«Spitfires over Austria»: Die Royal Air Force in Österreich 1945–1947' [The Royal Air Force in Austria], *Österreichische Militärische Zeitschrift* 37 (1999), 183–90.

4555. Evans, B. 'Captain Richard Owen Jones, 1861–1943', *Maritime Wales* 20 (1999), 45–52.

4556. Evans, Nicholas. 'The deaths of qualified staff officers 1914–18', *Journal of the Society for Army Historical Research* 78 (2000), 29–37.

4557. Farndale, Sir Martin. *A history of the Royal Regiment of Artillery: Far East theatre, 1941–1946* (London: Brassey's, 2000). [Vol. 6 of *History of the Royal Regiment of Artillery* (1986–96).]

4558. Fedorowich, Kent. 'Axis prisoners of war as sources for British military intelligence, 1939–42', *Intelligence and National Security* 14:2 (1999), 156–78.

4559. Feingold, Henry L. 'Bombing Auschwitz and the politics of the Jewish question during World War II', A166, 193–203.

4560. Ferguson, Niall. *The pity of war* [First World War] (London: Allen Lane, 1998), xlv, 623p.

4561. Fish, Jane. '"It looked more natural": Miss Rosie Newman's colour film of the Second World War', *Imperial War Museum Review* 11 (1999), 27–39.

4562. Fisher, John. 'On the Baghdad road: on the trail of W.J. Childs. A study in British Near Eastern intelligence and historical analysis, c.1900–1930', *Archives* 24:101 (1999), 53–70.

4563. Foot, Michael Richard Daniel. *SOE: an outline history of the Special Operations Executive 1940–46* (London: Pimlico, 1999), xxii, 401p. [1st published London: BBC Books, 1984.]

4564. Ford, Ken. *Battle-Axe division: from Africa to Italy with the 78th Division, 1942–1945* (Stroud: Sutton, 1999), vi, 218p.

4565. Fowler, Simon. 'New MI5 Records at the Public Record Office' [Second World War records], *Labour History Review* 63 (1999), 288–96.

4566. Franks, Norman Leslie Robert. *Royal Air Force Fighter Command losses of the Second World War*, vol.2: *Operational losses: aircraft and crews, 1942–43* (Leicester: Midland, 1998), 155p.

4567. Franks, Norman Leslie Robert. *Royal Air Force Fighter Command losses of the Second World War*, vol.3: *Operational losses: aircraft and crews (incorporating ADGB and 2nd TAF) 1944–1945* (Hinckley: Midland Counties Publications, 1999), 192p.

4568. Freedman, Lawrence; Gearson, John. 'Interdependence and independence: Nassau and the British nuclear deterrent', A28, 179–206.

4569. French, David. '"You cannot hate the bastard who is trying to kill you. . ." Combat and ideology in the British army in the war against Germany, 1939–45', *20th Century British History* 11:1 (2000), 1–22.

4570. French, David. *Raising Churchill's army: the British army and the war against Germany, 1939–1945* (Oxford: Oxford University Press, 2000), xii, 319p.

4571. Furse, Anthony. *Wilfrid Freeman: the genius behind Allied air supremacy, 1939–1945* (Staplehurst: Spellmount, 2000), 384p.

4572. Gallagher, Donat. 'Sir Robert Laycock and the evacuation of Crete from Sphakia', *Journal of the Society for Army Historical Research* 78 (2000), 38–55.

4573. Gander, Terry. *Allied infantry weapons of World War II* (Marlborough: Crowood, 2000), 192p.

4574. Garbett, Mike; Goulding, Brian. *Lincoln at war, 1944–1966* (Shepperton: Ian Allan, 2000), 176p. [Reissue of 1979 edn.]

4575. Garden, Timothy. 'Last post for the chiefs' [the chiefs of staff system in the 20th century], *Journal of the Royal United Services Institute for Defence Studies* 144:1 (1999), 47–51.

4576. Gardner, W.J.R. *Decoding history: the Battle of the Atlantic and Ultra* (Basingstoke and Annapolis (MD): Macmillan and Naval Institute Press, 1999), xvii, 263p.

4577. Gardner, W.J.R. (ed.) *The evacuation from Dunkirk: 'Operation*

Dynamo', 26 May–4 June 1940 (London: Cass, 2000), xiv, 210p. [From official account of 1949.]

4578.   Gat, Azar. *British armour theory and the rise of the Panzer arm: revising the revisionists* (Basingstoke: Macmillan, 1999), xii, 125p.

4579.   Geddes, James D. *Colours of British regiments*, vol.2: *Units raised during World War I* (Easingwold: The author, 2000), xiv, 208p.

4580.   Gilbert, Martin. 'The contemporary case for the feasibility of bombing Auschwitz', A166, 65–75.

4581.   Gliddon, Gerald. *Arras & Messines, 1917* (VCs of the First World War series) (Stroud: Sutton, 1998), x, 222p.

4582.   Gliddon, Gerald. *The road to victory, 1918* [8 August to 26 September] (VCs of the First World War series) (Stroud: Sutton, 2000), 224p.

4583.   Gliddon, Gerald. *The final days, 1918* [27 September to 11 November] (VCs of the First World War series) (Stroud: Sutton, 2000), 224p.

4584.   Gliddon, Gerald. *VCs of the First World War: 1914* (VCs of the First World War series) (Stroud: Sutton, 1994), xiii, 230p.

4585.   Gliddon, Gerald. *VCs of the First World War: the Somme* (VCs of the First World War series) (Stroud: Sutton, 1994), viii, 212p. [1st published Norwich: Gliddon Books, 1991.]

4586.   Golda, E. Michael. 'The Dardanelles campaign: a historical analogy for littoral mine warfare', *Naval War College Review* 51:3 (1998), 82–96.

4587.   Gordon, A. 'Ratcatchers and regulators at the Battle of Jutland', *Strategic and Combat Studies Institute Occasional Paper* 38 (1999), 44–51.

4588.   Goss, Chris (ed.) *The bombers' battle: personal accounts of the Battle of Britain by Luftwaffe bomber crews, July-October 1940* (Manchester: Crécy, 2000), 208p.

4589.   Goss, Chris (ed.) *The fighters' battle: personal accounts of the Battle of Britain by Luftwaffe fighter crews, July-October 1940* (Manchester: Crécy, 2000), 208p.

4590.   Goulter, C. 'Sir Arthur Harris: different perspectives', *Strategic and Combat Studies Institute Occasional Paper* 38 (1999), 75–85.

4591.   Green, Christopher. 'Scheme of complement for "Captain" class frigates', *Mariner's Mirror* 86 (2000), 85–87.

4592.   Greenfield, George. *Chasing the beast: one man's war* (London: Richard Cohen, 1998), 212p.

4593.   Gregory, Adrian. 'The commemoration of the Battle of Britain', A1, 217–228.

4594.   Gregory, R.G. *Evacuee: a wartime's evacuation from Southampton to Bournemouth*, 2 vols. [1. *1939–42*; 2. *1942–45*] (RGG Chapbooks, 9–10) (Wimborne: Wanda, 1998).

4595.   Gretzyngier, Robert. *Poles in defence of Britain: a day-by-day chronology of Polish day and night fighter pilot Operations, July 1940–June 1941* (London: Grub Street, 2000), 288p.

4596.   Griehl, Manfred. *German bombers over England, 1940–1944* (London: Greenhill, 1999), 72p.

4597.   Guelton, Frédéric. 'Psychologische Kriegführung und Suezkrise. Das 5. Bureau der Force A bei der französisch-britischen Intervention in Ägypten'

[Psychological warfare and the Suez Crisis: the 5th Bureau of Force A during the Anglo-French intervention in Egypt], A101, 235–56.

4598. Haase, Norbert. '"Freiheit hinter Stacheldraht": Widerstand und Selbstbehauptung von deutschen Gegnern des NS-Regimes in westalliierten Kriegsgefangenenlagern' ['Freedom behind barbed wire': resistance and self-assertiveness of German opponents of the Nazi regime in the prisoner of war camps of the Western Allies], A173, 413–40.

4599. Hack, Karl. '"Iron claws on Malaya": the historiography of the Malayan Emergency', *Journal of Southeast Asian Studies* 30:1 (1999), 99–146.

4600. Hague, Arnold. *The Allied convoy system: its organization, defence, and operation* (London: Chatham, 2000), 208p.

4601. Haig, Dawyck (Earl Haig). *My father's son: the memoir of Dawyck Haig* [Field Marshal Haig's only son] (London: Cooper, 2000), 256p.

4602. Hallion, Richard P. 'The American perspective' [on the Battle of Britain], A1, 82–107.

4603. Hamilton, C.I. 'The character and organization of the Admiralty Operational Intelligence Centre during the Second World War', *War in History* 7:3 (2000), 295–324.

4604. Harbord, Frank. *Familiar voices* (Knebworth (Herts): Able Publishing, 1998), 283p.

4605. Harding, Richard. 'Learning from the war: the development of British amphibious capability, 1919–29', *Mariner's Mirror* 86 (2000), 173–85.

4606. Harper, Stephen. *Capturing Enigma: how HMS Petard seized the German naval codes* (Stroud: Sutton, 1999), xii, 180p.

4607. Harris, J.P. 'Das britische Expeditionsheer in der Hundert-Tage-Schlacht vom 8. August 1918 bis 11. November 1918' [The British Expeditionary Force in the hundred-days' battle from 8 August to 11 November 1918], A73, 115–34.

4608. Hart, Dennis A. *Clash of arms: how the Allies won in Normandy* (The Art of War Series (New York: Lynne Rienner, 2000), 460p.

4609. Hart, Peter. *The heat of battle: the 16th Battalion Durham Light Infantry: the Italian campaign, 1943–1945* (Barnsley: Leo Cooper, 1999), 224p.

4610. Hart, Stephen Ashley. *Montgomery and 'Colossal Cracks': The 21st Army Group in north-west Europe, 1944–1945* (Praeger Studies in War Series) (Westport (CT): Praeger, 2000), 244p.

4611. Hatch, David A. 'Enigma and Purple: how the allies broke German and Japanese codes during the war', A117, 53–61.

4612. Hatcher, Patrick Lloyd. *North Atlantic civilization at war: the World War II battles of sky, sand, snow, sea, and shore as experienced by a soldier, a ship and some spirits through the Battle of Britain, El Alamein, Stalingrad, the Atlantic and Normandy* (Armonk (NY): M.E. Sharpe, 1998), xvi, 171p.

4613. Havers, R.P.W. 'Allied prisoners of war attitudes to the fall of Singapore and the "Selerang Barrack Square Incident"', *Imperial War Museum Review* 11 (1999), 59–78.

4614. Hay, John. *On Big Flowery Hill: a soldier's journal of a secret mission into occupied China, 1942* (Reading: Two Rivers, 2000), 90p.

4615. Hershberg, James G. 'Their men in Havana: Anglo-American intelligence exchanges and the Cuban crises, 1961–62', *Intelligence and National Security* 15:2 (2000), 121–76.

4616. Heuser, Beatrice. 'John Bull und Marianne: Das Auseinanderleben zweier alter Verbündeter' [The estrangement of two old allies], A101, 553–71.

4617. Heywood, Samantha. 'Forts or follies? Government citadels in the Second World War', *Imperial War Museum Review* 12 (1999), 18–28.

4618. Hiley, Nicholas. ' "Kitchener Wants You" and "Daddy, what did YOU do in the Great War?": the myth of British recruiting posters', *Imperial War Museum Review* 11 (1999), 40–58.

4619. Hilton, Peter. 'Reminiscences and reflections of a codebreaker', A117, 1–8.

4620. Hoare, Oliver (ed.) *Camp O20: MI5 and the Nazi spies: the official history of MI5's wartime interrogation centre* (Richmond: Public Record Office, 2000), vii, 376p.

4621. Hodson-Pressinger, S. 'War & peace memorials: Captain Adrian Jones, 1845–1938', *Army Quarterly & Defence Journal* 129:3 (1999), 327–30.

4622. Hogan, David. 'Berlin revisited—and revisited: Eisenhower's decision to halt at the Elbe', A169, 77–102.

4623. Holloway, David. 'The atomic bomb and the end of the wartime alliance', A132, 207–25.

4624. Hopkins, Michael F. 'Britain and the Korean War after 50 years: the slow emergence of an intelligence dimension' [review article], *Intelligence and National Security* 15:1 (2000), 177–82.

4625. Horn, M. 'The concept of total war: national effort and taxation in Britain and France during the First World War', *War & Society* 18:1 (2000), 1–22.

4626. Houghton, Michael A. 'HMS *Vanguard*', *Warship International* 35 (1998), 225–47.

4627. Hughes, David; Broshot, James; Philson, Alan. *The British armies in World War Two: an organisational history*, vol.1: *British armoured and cavalry divisions* (West Chester (OH): Nafziger, 1999), 100p.

4628. Hughes, Matthew. 'Lloyd George, the generals and the Palestine campaign, 1917–1918', *Imperial War Museum Review* 11 (1999), 4–17.

4629. Hughes, Matthew; Seligmann, Matthew. 'The battle for the Dodecanese, 1943: a reassessment', *Imperial War Museum Review* 12 (1999), 109–13.

4630. Hughes Wilson, John. 'Intelligence blunders: from Stalin to the Falklands War', *Journal of the Royal United Services Institute for Defence Studies* 144:5 (1999), 61–64.

4631. Hunter, David J. *Queen's Own Highlanders* (Famous Regiments on Cigarette & Trade Cards Series) (Nottingham: Privately published, 2000), 56p.

4632. Hunter, David J. *The Royal Regiment of Fusiliers*, 2 vols. (Famous Regiments on Cigarette & Trade Cards Series) (Nottingham: Privately published, 1999).

4633. Hunter, Robin. *True Stories of the Commandos* (London: Virgin, 2000).

4634. *Irish Guards: their first hundred years 1900–2000* (Staplehurst: Spellmount, 2000), 223p.

4635. Jahr, Christoph. 'Bei einer geschlagenen Armee ist der Klügste, wer zuerst davonläuft: Das Problem der Desertion im deutschen und britischen Heer

1918' [In a defeated army the cleverest are those who run away first: the problem of desertion in the German and British land forces in 1918], A73, 241–71.

4636.   Jahr, Christoph. 'Zivilisten als Kriegsgefangene: Die Internierung von "Feindstaaten-Ausländern" in Deutschland während des Ersten Weltkrieges am Beispiel des "Engländerlagers" in Ruhleben' [Civilians as prisoners of war: The internment of 'enemy aliens' in Germany during the First World War as exemplified by the 'Englishmen's camp' at Ruhleben], A173, 297–321.

4637.   James, T.C.G. *Air defence of Britain*, vol.2: *The Battle of Britain* (Royal Air Force Official Histories) (London: Cass, 2000), 350p.

4638.   Jeffreys, Alan. '"The Jungle Book": jungle training in South East Asia, 1941–1943', *Imperial War Museum Review* 12 (1999), 48–58.

4639.   Jeffreys-Jones, Rhodri. 'The role of British intelligence in the mythologies underpinning the OSS and early CIA', *Intelligence and National Security* 15:2 (2000), 5–19.

4640.   Johnson, Gaynor. '"Das Kind" revisited: Lord D'Abernon and German security policy, 1922–1925', *Contemporary European History* 9:2 (2000), 209–24.

4641.   Johnstone-Bryden, Richard. *Britain's greatest warship: HMS Ark Royal IV*, foreword by Admiral of the Fleet Sir Michael Pollock (Stroud: Sutton, 1999), ix, 262p.

4642.   Jones, Kevin. 'From the horse's mouth: Luftwaffe prisoners of war as sources for Air Ministry intelligence during the Battle of Britain', *Intelligence & National Security* 15:1 (2000), 60–80.

4643.   Jones, Simon. '"The right medicine for the Bolshevist": British air-dropped chemical weapons in north Russia, 1919', *Imperial War Museum Review* 12 (1999), 78–88.

4644.   Kaplan, Philip. *Bombers: the air crew experience* (London: Aurum, 2000), 240p.

4645.   Kennedy, Ludovic. *Pursuit: the chase and sinking of the Bismarck* (Annapolis (MD): Naval Institute Press, 2000), 252p. [1st published London: Collins, 1974.]

4646.   Keohane, Dan. *Security in British politics, 1945–99* (Basingstoke: Macmillan, 2000), ix, 240p.

4647.   Kerbey, John. '1918—year of victory', *Army Quarterly & Defence Journal* 129:3 (1999), 290–95.

4648.   Kerbey, John. 'Dunkirk: look back', *Army Quarterly & Defence Journal* 129:3 (1999), 307–309.

4649.   Kersaudy, François. 'En 1943, Tito réussit à mystifier Churchill' [How Tito hoodwinked Churchill in 1943], *Historia* [Paris] 603 (1997), 28–35.

4650.   Kersaudy, François. 'La Norvège, obsession de Churchill et d'Hitler, 2 parts' [Norway: Churchill's and Hitler's obsession], *Historia* [Paris] 614–15 (1998), 18–23, 18–23.

4651.   Kimball, Warren F. 'Anglo-American war aims, 1941–43, "the first review": Eden's mission to Washington', A132, 1–21.

4652.   Kitchens, James H. (III). 'The bombing of Auschwitz re-examined', A166, 80–100.

4653. Knight, Ronald D. *The home front: life in Dorset, 1939–1944: an evacuee's experience—with additional biographical details* (Weymouth: The author, 1999), 60p.

4654. Kop, H.J.E. van der. 'Operatie Cerberus/Filler: een Duits succes, een Britse afgang' [Operation Cerberus/Filler: a German success, a British disaster], *Mars et Historia* 33:3 (1999), 29–35.

4655. Krasker, Sarah. 'How Britain and the US attacked Moscow via Albania', *Army Quarterly & Defence Journal* 129:1 (1999), 50–54. [Part 1 in volume 128:4 (1998), 441–44.]

4656. Krumeich, Gerd. '«Die Stunde der Abrechnung ist da»: Die Friedensverhandlungen in Versailles 1919 und die Fortführung des Krieges in den Köpfen' ['The hour of reckoning has come': the peace negotiations at Versailles in 1919 and the continuation of the war in the mind], *Militärgeschichte* 9 (1999), 48–55.

4657. Kudryashov, Sergei. 'The Soviet perspective' [on the Battle of Britain], A1, 71–80.

4658. Lacquer, Walter. 'Auschwitz', A166, 186–92.

4659. Lake, Alan. *Flying units of the RAF: the ancestry, formation and disbandment of all flying units from 1912* (Shrewsbury: Airlife, 1999), 316p.

4660. Lake, Jeremy; Schofield, John. 'Conservation and the Battle of Britain', A1, 229–242.

4661. Lake, Jon. *Sunderland squadrons of World War II* (Combat Aircraft Series, 19) (Reading: Osprey, 2000), 112p. [Pictorial album.]

4662. Lambourne, Nicola. 'First World War propaganda and the use and abuse of historic monuments on the Western Front', *Imperial War Museum Review* 12 (1999), 96–108.

4663. Largent, Jesse Willard (ed.) *RAF wings over Florida: memories of World War II British air cadets* (West Lafayette (IN): Purdue University Press, 2000), 256p.

4664. Lee, Eric C.B. (ed.) *The Cruiser experience: life aboard Royal Navy cruisers during World War Two* (Fleet Hargate, Spalding (Lincs): Arcturus Press, 2000), 214p.

4665. Lee, John. *A soldier's life: General Sir Ian Hamilton, 1853–1947* (Basingstoke: Macmillan, 2000), xxviii, 292p.

4666. Lehmkuhl, Ursula. '«Vom Umgang mit dem Niedergang»: Strategien der Sicherung britischer Machtpositionen in der internationalen Politik vor und nach Suez' [Facing decline: the strategy of assuring British power positions in international politics before and after Suez], A101, 589–613.

4667. Levine, Alan J. *From the Normandy beaches to the Baltic Sea: the North-West Europe campaign, 1944–1945* (Westport (CT) and London: Praeger, 2000), xi, 223p.

4668. Levy, James. 'Ready or not? The Home Fleet at the outset of World War II', *Naval War College Review* 52:4 (1999), 90–108.

4669. Levy, Richard H. 'The bombing of Auschwitz revisited: a critical analysis', A166, 101–26.

4670. Lihou, Maurice. *It's dicey flying Wimpys (in Italian skies): operations of No. 205 Group RAF, 1944–45* (Edinburgh: Pentland, 2000), 258p. [1st published Walton on Thames: Air Research, 1993.]

4671.   Lindsay, Sir Martin. *So few got through: the personal diary of Lt.-Col. Martin Lindsay, DSO, MP who served with the Gordon Highlanders in the 51st Highland Division from July, 1944, to May, 1945* (London: Cooper, 2000), 224p. [1st published London: Collins, 1946.]

4672.   Lloyd Owen, David. *The Long Range Desert Group, 1940–1945: Providence their Guide*, revised edn. (London: Harrap, 2000), 256p. [1st published London: Harrap, 1980.]

4673.   Loridan, Dominique. 'Octobre 1914–avril 1915: la quatrième division britannique à Ploegsteert' [October 1914–April 1915: the British 4th Division at Ploegsteert], *Mémoires de la Société d'Histoire de Comines-Warneton et de la Région* 27 (1997), 275–312.

4674.   Lowe, Peter C. 'The war against Japan and allied relations', A132, 190–206.

4675.   Lowry, Bullit. *Armistice 1918* (Kent (OH): Kent State University Press, 1996), xv, 245p.

4676.   Lowry, Thomas; Wellham, John W.G. *The attack on Taranto: blueprint for Pearl Harbor* (Mechanicsburg (PA): Stackpole, 1995), 143p.

4677.   Lucas, W. Scott; Morey, A. 'The hidden "alliance": the CIA and MI6 before and after Suez', *Intelligence and National Security* 15:2 (2000), 95–120.

4678.   Macdonald, William James. *The true 'Intrepid': Sir William Stephenson and the unknown agents* (Surrey (British Columbia): Timberholme Books, 1998), 432p.

4679.   Mackay, Ron. *Ridgewell's Flying Fortresses: The 381st Bombardment Group (H) in World War II* [June 1943–May 1945] (Atglen (Pennsylvania): Schiffer, 2000), 256p.

4680.   Maddrell, Paul. 'British-American scientific collaboration during the occupation of Germany', *Intelligence and National Security* 15:2 (2000), 74–94.

4681.   Maier, Klaus A. 'The Luftwaffe' [in the Battle of Britain], A1, 15–21.

4682.   Maiolo, Joseph A. 'Deception and intelligence failure: Anglo-German preparation for U-boat warfare in the 1930s', *Journal of Strategic Studies* 22:4 (1999), 55–76.

4683.   Malvern, Sue. 'Memorizing the Great War: Stanley Spencer at Burghclere', *Art History* 23:2 (2000), 182–204.

4684.   Malvern, Sue. 'War, memory and museums: art and artefact in the Imperial War Museum', *History Workshop Journal* 49 (2000), 177–203.

4685.   Marchant, David John. *Rise from the east: the story of No.247 (China-British) Squadron, Royal Air Force* (Tunbridge Wells: Air-Britain, 1996), 176p.

4686.   Marx, Roland. 'La nouvelle politique de défense, 1967–1970: Forces et positions à l'Est de Suez' [The new defence policy: forces and positions East of Suez], A35, 181–92.

4687.   McCart, Neil. *Three 'Ark Royals', 1938–1999* (Cheltenham: Fan Publications, 1999), 208p.

4688.   McCart, Neil. Tiger, Lion *and* Blake, *1942–1986: the Royal Navy's last cruisers* (Cheltenham: Fan Publications, 1999), 144p.

4689.   McCrery, Nigel. *All the king's men: one of the greatest mysteries of the First World War finally solved* [1/5th Battalion, Norfolk Regiment at Gallipoli] (London: Pocket Books, 1999), xiii, 140p. [1st published as *The Vanished Battalion* (London: Simon & Schuster, 1992).]

4690.   McKale, Donald M. *War by revolution: Germany and Great Britain in the Middle East in the era of World War I* (Kent (OH) and London: Kent State University Press, 1998), xxii, 332p.

4691.   McManus, B. 'The loss of the Cadet School Training Ship HMS Conway', *Maritime Wales* 20 (1999), 84–95.

4692.   McNair, Ronald. *1944: La poursuite alliée—La Libération de la Seine à la Meuse* [The Allied chase: the liberation campaign from the Seine to the Meuse] (Bayeux: Heimdal, 2000), 168p. [Pictorial Album; Sequel to: Ronald McNair [pseudonym] *Le repli sur la Seine* [the German retreat on the Seine, summer 1944] (Bayeux: Heimdal, 1990).]

4693.   McNaught, Kenneth. 'J.S. Woodsworth and war' [Methodist pacifist], A25, 186–98.

4694.   Meilinger, Phillip S. 'Between the Devil and the deep blue sea: the Fleet Air Arm before the Second World War', *Journal of the Royal United Services Institute for Defence Studies* 144:5 (1999), 73–78.

4695.   Middeke, Michael. 'Anglo-American nuclear weapons cooperation after the Nassau Conference: the British policy of interdependence', *Journal of Cold War Studies* 2:2 (2000), 69–96.

4696.   Middlebrook, Martin. *Your country needs you: from 6 to 65 divisions* (Barnsley: Cooper, 2000), 174p.

4697.   Miller, Russell. *Nothing less than victory: the oral history of D-Day* (London: Pimlico, 2000), 496p. [1st published London: Michael Joseph and New York: Morrow, 1993.]

4698.   Millgate, Helen D. (ed.) *Mr Brown's war: a diary of the Second World War* (Stroud: Sutton, 1998), x, 277p.

4699.   Mitcham, Samuel W. *Retreat to the Reich: the German defeat in France, 1944* (New York: Praeger, 2000), viii, 277p.

4700.   Mole, W.G. 'Singapore to Southampton via Tokyo: A POW's odyssey', *Army Quarterly & Defence Journal* 129:1 (1999), 58–63.

4701.   Moore, B. 'Unruly allies: British problems with the French treatment of Axis prisoners of war, 1943–1945', *War in History* 7:2 (2000), 180–98.

4702.   Morgan, Mike. *Daggers drawn: Second World War heroes of the SAS and SBS;* foreword by Major Roy Farran (Stroud: Sutton, 2000), 247p.

4703.   Morgan, Mike. *Sting of the scorpion: the inside story of the Long Range Desert Group;* foreword by Major General David Lloyd Owen (Stroud: Sutton, 2000), 213p.

4704.   Morris, Richard. *Cheshire: the biography of Leonard Cheshire, VC, OM* (London: Viking, 2000), xxv, 530p.

4705.   Müller, Klaus-Jürgen. 'Militär und Politik im deutsch-britischen Vergleich' [Military and political affairs in Britain and Germany: a comparison], A185, 189–202.

4706.   Murphy, Hugh. '"From the crinoline to the boilersuit": women workers in British shipbuilding during the Second World War', *Contemporary British History* 13:4 (1999), 82–104.

4707.   Murray, Williamson. 'Monday-morning quarterbacking and the bombing of Auschwitz', A166, 204–13.

4708.   Nagl, John A. 'Learning to eat soup with a knife: British and American army counterinsurgency during the Malayan Emergency and the Vietnam War', *World Affairs* 161:4 (1999), 193–99.

4709.   Neillands, Robin. *The Great War generals on the Western Front 1914–18* (London: Robinson, 1999), ix, 549p.

4710.   Nesbit, Roy Conyers. *RAF in Action, 1939–1945: images from air cameras and war artists* (London: Public Record Office, 2000), 256p.

4711.   Nesbit, Roy Conyers. *The Battle of Britain* (Stroud: Sutton, 2000), 265p. [Pictorial album.]

4712.   Oram, Gerard. *Worthless men: race, eugenics and the death penalty in the British Army during the First World War* (London: Francis Boutle, 1998), 142p.

4713.   Osborne, John Morton. 'Continuity in British sport: The experience of the first World War', A13, 89–102.

4714.   Osborne, Mike. *20th century defences in Britain: Lincolnshire* (London: Brassey's, 1997), xi, 84p.

4715.   O'Shea, Stephen. *Back to the front: an accidental historian walks the trenches of World War I* (London: Robson, 1997), 205p.

4716.   O'Sullivan, Patrick. *'Lusitania': unravelling the mysteries* (Cork: Collins, 1998), 140p.

4717.   Overy, Richard James. 'How significant was the battle?' [Battle of Britain], A1, 267–280.

4718.   Overy, Richard James. *The battle: Summer 1940* (London: Penguin, 2000), xiv, 177p.

4719.   Page, Christopher. *Command in the Royal Naval Division: a military biography of Brigadier General A.M. Asquith DSO* (Staplehurst: Spellmount, 1999), xiv, 194p.

4720.   Parsons, Michael. *The Falklands War* (Sutton Pocket Histories) (Stroud: Sutton, 2000), 118p.

4721.   Parsons, Reg. *Z for Zebra* (London: Minerva Press, 1999), 190p.

4722.   Paul, Septimus H. *Nuclear rivals: Anglo-American atomic relations, 1941–1952* (Columbus (OH): Ohio State University Press, 2000), 272p.

4723.   Pawley, Margaret. *In obedience to instructions: F.A.N.Y. with the S.O.E. in the Mediterranean* [First Aid Nursing Yeomanry; Special Operations Executive] (London: Leo Cooper, 1999), xiii, 178p.

4724.   Perry, Colin. *Boy in the Blitz: the 1940 diary of Colin Perry* (Stroud: Sutton, 2000), 224p. [1st published London: Cooper, 1972.]

4725.   Perry, Nicholas. 'General Nugent and the Ulster Division in the March 1918 retreat', *Imperial War Museum Review* 12 (1999), 4–17.

4726.   Pogge von Strandmann, Hartmut. 'The role of British and German historians in mobilizing public opinion in 1914', A201, 335–72.

4727.   Pommerin, Reiner. 'Zur Einsicht bomben?: Die Zerstörung Dresdens in der Luftkriegsstrategie des Zweiten Weltkriegs' [Bombing to bring people to their senses? The destruction of Dresden in the air war strategy of the Second World War], A185, 227–47.

4728. Price, Alfred. *Battle of Britain Day, 15 September 1940* (London: Greenhill, 2000), 192p. [1st published 1990.]

4729. Price, Alfred. *Blitz on Britain: 1939–1945* (Stroud: Sutton, 2000), 221p. [Revised edn. of *Blitz on Britain: the bomber attacks on the United Kingdom, 1939–1945* (Shepperton: Ian Allan, 1977).]

4730. Radice, Peter. 'The Radice papers' [German occupation], *Alderney Society Bulletin* 32 (1997), 52–59.

4731. Ratcliff, R.A. 'Searching for security: the German investigation into Enigma's security', *Intelligence & National Security* 14:1 (1999), 146–67.

4732. Rčĕsevskij, O.A. 'Sekretnye voennye plany U. Čerčillja protiv SSSR v mae 1945 g.' [Churchill's secret war plans against the USSR in May 1945], *Novaja i novejšaja storia* 3 (1999), 98–123.

4733. Regelous, Ken. *To the long pond: the adventures of an evacuee* (Dereham: Larks Press, 1999), 165p.

4734. Reid, Brian Holden. *Studies in British military thought: debates with Fuller and Liddell Hart* (Lincoln (NE): University of Nebraska Press, 1998), xviii, 287p.

4735. Reid, Stuart. '"I shall never forget this place": the diary of Private Jack Milton, 2nd Battalion Highland Light Infantry, 1914–1915', *Journal of the Society for Army Historical Research* 78:314 (2000), 124–35.

4736. Reynolds, David. 'Churchill and allied grand strategy in Europe, 1944–1945: the erosion of British influence', A26, 39–54.

4737. Reynolds, Leonard C. 'Breakout from encirclement: The 2nd Motor Torpedo Boat Flotilla in the Far East, 1939–1942', *Imperial War Museum Review* 11 (1999), 99–108.

4738. Reynolds, Leonard C. *Home waters MTBs & MGBs at war, 1939–1945* (Stroud: Sutton, 2000), 224p.

4739. Riegner, Gerhart M. 'The allies and Auschwitz: a participant's view', A166, 76–79.

4740. Rigby, Andrew. 'The Peace Pledge Union: from peace to war, 1936–1945', A25, 169–85.

4741. Robertson, K.G. (ed.) *War, resistance and intelligence: collected essays in honour of M.R.D. Foot* (Barnsley: Cooper, 1999), xxv, 262p.

4742. Robinson, Anthony. *RAF fighter squadrons in the Battle of Britain*, 2nd edn. (London: Brockhampton Press, 1999), 287p. [1st published London: Arms & Armour, 1987.]

4743. Rogers, Anthony. *Battle over Malta: aircraft losses and crash sites, 1940–1942* (Stroud: Sutton, 2000), 256p.

4744. Roper, Michael. 'Re-remembering the soldier hero: the psychic and social construction of memory in personal narratives of the Great War', *History Workshop Journal* 50 (2000), 181–204.

4745. Rose, Nigel. 'Dear Mum and Dad: an RAF pilot's letters to his parents, June-December 1940', A1, 138–162.

4746. Ross, David. *Richard Hillary: the authorised biography of a Second World War fighter pilot and author of* The Last Enemy (London: Grub Street, 2000), 414p.

4747. Rudhall, Robert J. *Battle of Britain: the movie* (Worcester: Ramrod Publications, 2000), 192p.

4748.   Saxon, Timothy D. 'Anglo-Japanese naval co-operation, 1914–1918', *Naval War College Review* 53:1 (2000), 62–92.

4749.   Schellenberg, Walter. *Invasion 1940: the Nazi invasion plan for Britain*, introduction by John Erickson (London: St Ermin's, 2000), xxxv, 272p. [Translation of and commentary on 1940 Gestapo handbook for German occupation forces in Great Britain.]

4750.   Schulten, C.M. 'Commentary on the liberation of the Netherlands', A26, 209–20.

4751.   Scott, Stuart R. *Mosquito Thunder: No.105 Squadron RAF at war, 1942–45* (Stroud: Sutton, 1999), xii, 212p. [Sequel to: Scott, Stuart R. *Battle-Axe Blenheims: No.105 Squadron RAF at War, 1940–41* (Stroud: Sutton, 1996).]

4752.   Seaman, Mark. *Bravest of the brave: the true story of Wing Commander Tommy Yeo-Thomas, SOE secret agent, codename 'the White Rabbit'* (London: Michael O'Mara, 1997), 256p.

4753.   Sebag-Montefiore, Hugh. *Enigma: the battle for the code* (London: Weidenfeld & Nicolson, 2000), xii, 403p.

4754.   Sheffield, Gary D. 'British high command in the First World War: an overview', *Strategic and Combat Studies Institute Occasional Paper* 38 (1999), 15–25.

4755.   Sheffield, Gary D. *Leadership in the trenches: officer-man relations, morale and discipline in the British army in the era of the First World War* (Basingstoke: Palgrave in association with King's College London, 2000), xxiv, 270p.

4756.   Sheffy, Yigal. 'The spy who never was: an intelligence myth in Palestine, 1914–18', *Intelligence and National Security* 14:3 (1999), 123–42.

4757.   Shephard, Ben. '"Pitiless psychology": the role of prevention in British military psychiatry in the Second World War', *History of Psychiatry* 10:4 (1999), 491–524.

4758.   Shephard, Ben. *A war of nerves: soldiers and psychiatry, 1914–1994* (London: Jonathan Cape, 2000), 480p.

4759.   Shipster, John Neville. *Mist over the rice fields: a soldier's story of the Burma campaign, 1943–1945 & Korean War, 1950–1951* (London: Cooper, 2000), 224p.

4760.   Slessor, Tim. 'The Tragedy of HMS Glorious' [sunk 8 June 1940], *Journal of the Royal United Services Institute for Defence Studies* 144:1 (1999), 68–74.

4761.   Slocombe, I. 'Recruitment into the armed forces during the First World War: the work of the military tribunals in Wiltshire, 1915–1918', *The Local Historian* 30:2 (2000), 105–23.

4762.   Smith, Angela K. 'Women and World War I: new perspectives' [review article], *European English Messenger* 9:2 (2000), 35–40.

4763.   Smith, Arthur Lee. 'Angloamerikanische Umerziehungsprogramme für deutsche Kriegsgefangene: Ein Vergleich' [Anglo-American re-education programmes for German prisoners of war: a comparison], A161, 974–89.

4764.   Smith, Eric. *First things first: the story of RAF Hornchurch and RFC Suttons Farm, 1915–1962* (Romford: Ian Henry, 2000), 185p. [1st edn. 1992.]

4765. Smith, Malcolm. 'The RAF' [in the Battle of Britain], A1, 22–38.

4766. Smith, Michael. *The emperor's codes: Bletchley Park and the breaking of Japan's secret ciphers* (London: Bantam, 2000), 322p.

4767. Spence, Richard B. 'Secret agent 666: Aleister Crowley and British intelligence in America, 1914–18', *International Journal of Intelligence and Counterintelligence* 13:3 (2000), 359–71.

4768. Spencer, William. *Air force records for family historians* (Public Record Office Reader's Guide, 21) (Kew: PRO, 2000), xiv, 114p.

4769. Sponza, Lucio. *Divided loyalties: Italians in Britain during the Second World War* (Frankfurt am Main: Peter Lang, 2000), 358p.

4770. Starns, Penny. *Nurses at war: women on the frontline, 1939–1945* (Stroud: Sutton, 2000), 224p.

4771. Steinbach, Peter. '"Die Brücke ist geschlagen": Die Konfrontation deutscher Kriegsgefangener mit der Demokratie in amerikanischer und britischer Kriegsgefangenschaft' ['The bridge is built': the confrontation of German prisoners of war with democracy in American and British captivity], *Historical Social Research* 22:3–4 (1997), 275–99. Reprinted in Müller, Rolf-Dieter; Volkmann, Hans-Erich (eds.) [*Die Wehrmacht: Mythos und Realität. Im Auftrag des Militärgeschichtlichen Forschungsamtes* (München: Oldenbourg, 1999), 990–1011.]

4772. Stenton, Michael. *Radio London and resistance in occupied Europe: British political warfare, 1939–1943* (Oxford: Oxford University Press, 2000), 423p.

4773. Stone, David. *Cold War warriors: the story of the Duke of Edinburgh's Royal Regiment (Berkshire and Wiltshire) 9th June 1959–27th April 1994* (London: Leo Cooper, 1998), 434p.

4774. Strachan, Hew. 'Die Vorstellungen der Anglo-Amerikaner von der Wehrmacht' [How the British and Americans saw the Wehrmacht], A161, 92–104.

4775. Strachan, Hew. 'The First World War', *Historical Journal* 43:3 (2000), 889–904.

4776. Sugarman, Martin. 'The SIG: behind the lines with Jewish commandos', *Jewish Historical Studies* 35 (1998), 287–307.

4777. Sugarman, Martin. 'Two Jewish heroines of the SOE', *Jewish Historical Studies* 35 (1998), 309–28.

4778. Sutherland, John; Simons, Roy W. '40 years of Marconi radar: 1946–86— part 1', *Army Quarterly & Defence Journal* 129:3 (1999), 310–14.

4779. Tavender, Ian. *Distinguished Flying Medal: register for the Second World War*, 2 vols. 1: *A-J*; 2: *K-Z* (London: Savannah Publications, 2000).

4780. Termote, Tomas. *Duinkerken en Dynamo: De evacuatie aan de hand van scheepswrakken voor de Belgische kust* [Dunkirk and Dynamo: The evacuation in the light of the shipwrecks off the Belgian coast] (België in oorlog, 16) (Erpe-Mere: De Krijger, 2000), 96p. [Pictorial album.]

4781. Thomas, Martin. 'France in British signals intelligence, 1939–1945', *French History* 14:1 (2000), 41–66.

4782. Thurlow, Richard C. 'The evolution of the mythical British Fifth Column 1939–46', *20th Century British History* 10:4 (1999), 477–98.

4783. Till, G. 'The Gallipoli campaign: command performances', *Strategic and Combat Studies Institute Occasional Paper* 38 (1999), 26–43.

4784. Timpson, Alastair. *In Rommel's backyard: behind the lines with the Long Range Desert Group* [September 1941–December 1942] (London: Cooper, 2000), 193p.

4785. Tout, Ken. *The bloody Battle for Tilly: Normandy 1944* (Stroud: Sutton, 2000), 256p.

4786. Troy, Thomas F. 'Churchill and Britain's secret agents', *International Journal of Intelligence and Counterintelligence* 11:4 (1999), 495–97.

4787. Tsouras, Peter. *Disaster at D-Day: the Germans defeat the Allies, June 1944* (London: Greenhill, 2000), 236p. [Counterfactual history, 1st published 1994.]

4788. Van der Vat, Dan. *Standard of power: the Royal Navy in the twentieth century* (London: Hutchinson, 2000), xx, 460p.

4789. Walker, D.B. 'The riddle of Amy Johnson's last day', *Army Quarterly & Defence Journal* 129:3 (1999), 268–71.

4790. Wallace, Lorne A. (ed.) *Here come the Glasgow Keelies* (Dunning (Perthshire): Dunning Parish Historical Society, 1999), xvi, 163p.

4791. Waller, John H. 'Britain's World War II intelligence network', *International Journal of Intelligence and Counterintelligence* 12:1 (1999), 113–19.

4792. Weight, Angela. 'Anthony Gross, RA, CBE: A war artist's diary, Europe 1944–1945', *Imperial War Museum Review* 11 (1999), 18–26.

4793. Weinberg, Gerhard L. 'The allies and the Holocaust', A166, 15–26.

4794. Wert, Hal E. 'Military expediency, the "Hunger Winter", and Holland's belated liberation', A169, 117–44.

4795. Wilkinson, Bill. 'Exeter's Baedeker raid', *Army Quarterly & Defence Journal* 129:2 (1999), 201–5.

4796. Wilkinson, Richard. 'The downfall of Hore-Belisha', *Journal of the Royal United Services Institute for Defence Studies* 144:1 (1999), 63–67.

4797. Williams, George Kent. *Biplanes and bombsights: British bombing in World War I* (Maxell Air Force Base (Alabama): Air University Press, 1999), xiv, 312p.

4798. Wilson, J. 'A soldier-historian's view of the British army since 1900', *Army Quarterly & Defence Journal* 129:3 (1999), 318–20.

4799. Wilson, Patrick. *Dunkirk: from disaster to deliverance* (London: Cooper, 1999), 192p.

4800. Wilson, Theodore A. 'Endgames: V-E Day and war termination', A169, 11–46.

4801. Winfield, Pamela. *Melancholy baby: the unplanned consequences of the G.I.'s arrival in Europe for World War II* (Westport (CT): Bergin & Garvey, 2000), xv, 158p.

4802. Winter, Jay. 'Shell-shock and the cultural history of the Great War', *Journal of Contemporary History* 35:1 (2000), 7–12.

4803. Woodman, Richard. *Malta convoys, 1940–1943* (London: John Murray, 2000), xx, 532p.

4804. Wragg, David. *Snatching defeat from the jaws of victory: 20th century military blunders* (Stroud: Sutton, 2000), 288p.

4805. Wrigley, Chris. 'The war and the international economy' [First World War], A218, 1–33.
4806. Young, Neil. '"A splendid response"? County cricket and the First World War', *Imperial War Museum Review* 12 (1999), 36–47.
4807. Ziegler, Philip. 'Mountbatten revisited', A138, 185–202.
4808. Zugbach de Sugg, Reggie von; Ishaq, Mohammed. 'Officer recruitment: the decline in social eliteness in the senior ranks of the British army', A200, 75–86.

K. Foreign Affairs

See also 3553, 3576, 3594 (H); 3627, 3629, 3632–3, 3786, 3854, 4096, 4150, 4169, 4183, 4184, 4221, 4245, 4265, 4276, 4278, 4293, 4319, 4333, 4371, 4433, 4471, 4475, 4483, 4509, 4516, 4521–2, 4549–50, 4554, 4562, 4568, 4599, 4615–16, 4623, 4639–40, 4643, 4649, 4651, 4655–6, 4662, 4666, 4674, 4677, 4680, 4690, 4695, 4722, 4736, 4763, 4771, 4781 (I); 5885 (M); 6471, 6492, 6654, 6687, 6694 (P)

4809. Andrew, Christopher. 'Anglo-American-Soviet intelligence relations', A132, 108–35.
4810. Arcidiacono, Bruno. 'La Grande-Bretagne, les Balkans et le partage de l'Europe: à propos d'un paradigme et de quelques volte-face', *Storia delle Relazioni Internazionali* 11–12:1 (1997), 37–74.
4811. Arnn, Larry P. 'True politics and strategy', A163, 129–38.
4812. Ashton, Nigel J.; Hellema, Duco. 'Hanging the Kaiser: Anglo-Dutch relations and the fate of Wilhelm II, 1918–20', *Diplomacy & Statecraft* 11:2 (2000), 53–78.
4813. Avery, Donald H. 'The Quebec conferences and the Anglo-Canadian Montreal laboratory, 1942–46', A216, 119–41.
4814. Bange, Oliver. *The EEC crisis of 1963: Kennedy, Macmillan, de Gaulle and Adenauer in conflict* (Basingstoke: Macmillan, 2000), xv, 291p.
4815. Barton, J.R. 'Struggling against decline: British business in Chile, 1919–33', *Journal of Latin American Studies* 32:1 (2000), 235–64.
4816. Beck, Peter J. 'Going to war, peaceful co-existence or virtual membership? British football and FIFA, 1928–46', *International Journal of the History of Sport* 17:1 (2000), 113–34.
4817. Bell, Peter. *Chamberlain, Germany and Japan, 1933–4* (Basingstoke: Macmillan in association with King's College, London, 1996), xii, 240p.
4818. Bell, Philip Michael Hett. 'Entente broken and renewed: Britain and France, 1940–1945', A191, 223–43.
4819. Berger, Stefan. 'Labour in comparative perspective', A202, 309–40.
4820. Bickers, Robert A. *Britain in China: community, culture and colonialism 1900–1949* (Manchester and New York: Manchester University Press, 1999), xii, 276p.
4821. Birke, Adolf M. 'Britain and German unity', A16, 279–92.
4822. Birke, Adolf M. 'Britain's influence on the West German constitution', A16, 222–65.

4823. Birke, Adolf M. 'Der Beitrag der Alliierten zur Neuordnung der Kommunal- und Länderverfassungen in Deutschland' [The Allied contribution to the reorganisation of municipal and 'Land' institutions in Germany], A16, 206–21.

4824. Birke, Adolf M. 'Der britische Weg in den kalten Krieg' [the British road to the Cold War], A16, 181–93.

4825. Birke, Adolf M. 'Die britische Demokratisierungspolitik in Westdeutschland bis 1949' [The British policy of democratisation in West Germany until 1949], A16, 194–205. [1st published in Oberreuter, Heinrich; Weber, Jürgen (eds.) *Freundliche Feinde?: Die Alliierten und die Demokratiegründung in Deutschland* (Landsberg am Lech: Olzog, 1996), 217–31.]

4826. Birke, Adolf M. 'Geschichtsauffassung und Deutschlandbild im Foreign Office Research Department' [Interpretation of history and perception of Germany in the Foreign Office Research Department], A16, 140–56. [1st published in *Historisches Jahrbuch* 104 (1984): 372–91.]

4827. Birke, Adolf M. 'Sir Frank Roberts: diplomat and architect of British policy towards Germany', A16, 266–78.

4828. Birke, Adolf M. 'Warum Deutschlands Demokratie versagte: Geschichtsanalyse im britischen Außenministerium, 1943–1945' [Why Germany's democracy failed: historical analysis in the British Foreign Office], A16, 127–139. Originally published in *Historisches Jahrbuch* 103 (1983), 395–410.]

4829. Bitar, Mona. 'Bombs, plots and Allies: Cambodia and the western powers, 1958–59', *Intelligence and National Security* 14:4 (1999), 149–80.

4830. Boutin, Christophe. 'L'extrême-droite sous la IIIe République face à l'Angleterre: entre rejet et fascination' [The French extreme Right of the Third Republic and England: between rejection and fascination], *Revue française d'histoire des idées politiques* 12 (2000), 327–46.

4831. Breitman, Richard. *Official secrets: what the Nazis planned, what the British and Americans knew* (London: Allen Lane, 1999), viii, 325p. [1st published New York: Hill and Wang, 1998.]

4832. Brind, Harry. *Lying abroad: diplomatic memoirs* (London: Radcliffe, 1999), xi, 260p.

4833. Bromund, Ted R. '"This somewhat embarrassing ship": the British Foreign Office and the *Mayflower II*, 1954–1957', *New England Quarterly* 82 (1999), 42–60.

4834. Bünger, Siegfried. 'Großbritannien und die "Garantie" für die Tschechoslowakei im Jahre 1938' [Great Britain and the 'guarantee' to Czechoslovakia in 1938], *Bulletin für Faschismus- und Weltkriegsforschung* 11 (1998), 36–49.

4835. Bullard, Julian Leonard; Bullard, Margaret (eds.) *Inside Stalin's Russia: the diaries of Reader Bullard, 1930–1934* (Charlbury: Day, 2000), x, 310p.

4836. Buller, Jim. *National statecraft and European integration: the Conservative government and the European Union, 1979–97* (London: Pinter, 2000), viii, 190p.

4837. Burk, Kathleen. 'American foreign economic policy and lend/lease', A132, 43–68.

4838. Burk, Kathleen. 'War and Anglo-American financial relations in the twentieth century', A135, 243–60.

4839. Carew, Anthony. 'The Trades Union Congress in the international labour movement', A31, 145–167.

4840. Carlton, David. *Churchill and the Soviet Union* (Manchester: Manchester University Press, 2000), 234p.

4841. Carty, Anthony; Smith, Richard A. *Sir Gerald Fitzmaurice and the world crisis: a legal advisor in the Foreign Office, 1932–1945* (The Hague: Kluwer, 2000), xi, 689p.

4842. Charmley, John. 'Churchill's Roosevelt', A132, 90–107.

4843. Churchill, Winston Spencer. 'The sinews of peace' [The text of his 1946 Fulton 'Iron Curtain' speech], A163, 1–14.

4844. Citino, Nathan J. 'Defending the "postwar petroleum order": the US, Britain and the 1954 Saudi-Onassis tanker deal', *Diplomacy & Statecraft* 11:2 (2000), 137–160.

4845. Conradi, Peter J.; Martin, Stoddard (eds.) *Cold war, common pursuit: British Council lecturers in Poland, 1938–1998* (London: Starhaven, 1999), 164p.

4846. Corbett, Anne; Johnson, Douglas (eds.) *A Day in June: Britain and de Gaulle* [18 June 1940] (London: Franco-British Council, 2000), 64p.

4847. Danchev, Alex. 'Special pleading', A28, 271–88.

4848. David, Thomas; Etemad, Bouda. 'Les relations commerciales de la Suisse avec les Grandes puissances durant l'entre-deux-guerres. Un survol chiffré', A95, 31–58.

4849. De Vries, David. 'White-collar and Labour: clerks and the Histadrut in British-ruled Palestine', A46, 21–54.

4850. Denniston, R. 'Diplomatic intercepts in peace and war: Chanak 1922', *Diplomacy & Statecraft* 11:1 (2000), 241–56.

4851. Dixon, P. 'Britain's Vietnam syndrome? Public opinion and British military intervention—from Palestine to the former Yugoslavia', *Review of International Studies* 26:1 (1999), 99–122.

4852. Dockrill, Michael. 'France's economic and financial crisis: the view from the Foreign Office, the Treasury and the Bank of England, 1936–1939', A191, 205–22.

4853. Dockrill, Saki. 'Britain's power and influence: dealing with three roles and the Wilson government's defence debate at Chequers in November 1964', *Diplomacy & Statecraft* 11:1 (2000), 211–240.

4854. Dunthorn, David J. 'The Prieto-Gil-Robles meeting of October 1947: Britain and the failure of the Spanish Anti-Franco Coalition, 1945–50', *European History Quarterly* 30:1 (2000), 49–75.

4855. Dutton, David. 'Britain and France at war, 1914–1918', A191, 71–88.

4856. Eayrs, James. 'The Atlantic Conference and its charter: a Canadian's reflections', A22, 151–172.

4857. Edmunds, June. 'The evolution of British Labour Party policy on Israel from 1967 to the Intifada', *20th Century British History* 11:1 (2000), 23–41.

4858. Ellison, James. *Threatening Europe: Britain and the creation of the European Community, 1955–58* (London: Macmillan, 2000), 272p.

4859. English, John. 'Atlanticism at high tide: the Quebec conference, 1944', A216, 105–18.

4860. Eskander, Saad. 'Britain's policy in southern Kurdistan: the formation and the termination of the first Kurdish government, 1918–1919', *British Journal of Middle Eastern Studies* 27:2 (2000), 139–63.

4861. Fielding, Jeremy. 'Coping with decline: US policy towards the British defence reviews of 1966', *Diplomatic History* 22:4 (1999), 633–56.

4862. Fielding, Jeremy. 'The primacy of national security? American responses to the British financial crisis of 1949', *Diplomacy & Statecraft* 11:1 (2000), 163–88.

4863. Folly, Martin H. 'The Red Air Force in Italy, 1944: a case study in the formation of British policy to the Soviet Union in World War II', *Diplomacy & Statecraft* 11:2 (2000), 105–136.

4864. French, David. '"Had we known how bad things were in Germany, we might have got stiffer terms": Great Britain and the German Armistice', A19, 69–86.

4865. Fry, Michael Graham. 'British revisionism', A19, 565–601.

4866. Gardner, Lloyd C. 'The Atlantic Charter: idea and reality, 1942–1945', A22, 45–82.

4867. Ginanneschi, Marco. 'La politica estera della Banca d'Inghilterra tra le due guerre' [The external policy of the Bank of England between the wars], *Storia delle Relazioni Internazionali* 11–12:1 (1997), 209–46.

4868. Goldstein, Erik. 'Great Britain: the home front', A19, 147–66.

4869. Gowland, David A.; Turner, Arthur S. (eds.) *Britain and European integration, 1945–1998: a documentary history* (London: Routledge, 2000), xvi, 252p.

4870. Gowland, David A.; Turner, Arthur S. *Reluctant Europeans: Britain and European integration, 1945–1998* (Harlow: Longman, 2000), x, 393p.

4871. Graebner, N.A. 'Yalta, Potsdam and beyond: the British and American perspectives', A132, 226–54.

4872. Greenwood, Sean. *Britain and the Cold War, 1945–91* (Basingstoke: Macmillan, 2000), ix, 227p.

4873. Greenwood, Sean. 'The most important of the western nations: France's place in Britain's post-war foreign policy, 1945–1949', A191, 244–63.

4874. Hahn, Peter L. 'Discord or accomodation? Britain and the United States in world affairs, 1945–92', A135, 276–94.

4875. Halkin, Ariela. *The enemy reviewed: German popular literature through British eyes between the two world wars* (Westport (CT) and London: Praeger, 1995), 211p.

4876. Hannay, Sir David (ed.) *Britain's entry into the European Community: report by Sir Con O'Neill on the negotiations of 1970–1972* (London: Frank Cass, 2000), xxxi, 464p.

4877. Harris, John; Trow, M.J. *Hess: the British conspiracy* (London: André Deutsch, 1999), 287p.

4878. Harrison, Mark. 'The Soviet economy and relations with the United States and Britain 1941–45', A132, 69–89.

4879. Henig, Ruth. 'Britain, France and the League of Nations in the 1920s', A191, 139–57.

4880. Heuser, Beatrice. 'Britain, France and the bomb: the parting of the ways between Suez and Nassau', *Storia delle Relazioni Internazionali* 11–12:1 (1997), 75–93.

4881. Heuser, Beatrice. 'What price solidarity? European-American nuclear interdependence in NATO', A28, 153–79.

4882. Hills, Alice. *Britain and the occupation of Austria, 1943–45* (Basingstoke: Macmillan in association with King's College London, 2000), xi, 222p.

4883. Hopkins, Michael F. '"Worlds apart": the British Embassy in Moscow and the search for east-west understanding', *Contemporary British History* 14:3 (2000), 131–48.

4884. Howe, Stephen. 'Labour and international affairs', A202, 119–50.

4885. Hughes, Michael. 'The virtues of specialization: British and American diplomatic reporting on Russia, 1921–39', *Diplomacy & Statecraft* 11:2 (2000), 79–104.

4886. Hughes, Phillip. 'Division and discord: British policy, Indochina, and the origins of the Vietnam War, 1954–56', *Journal of Imperial and Commonwealth History* 28:3 (2000), 94–112.

4887. Hurwitz, D.L. 'Churchill and Palestine', *Judaism* 44:1 (1995), 3–35.

4888. James, Alan. 'Britain, the Cold War, and the Congo crisis, 1960–63', *Journal of Imperial and Commonwealth History* 28:3 (2000), 152–68.

4889. Jayne, Catherine E. *Oil, war, and Anglo-American relations: American and British reactions to Mexico's expropriation of foreign oil properties, 1937–1941* (Contributions to Latin American Studies, 19) (London: Greenwood, 2000), 264p.

4890. Jespersen, Knud J.V. *Med hjælp fra England: SOE og den danske mod-standskamp 1940–1945, vol.2: Den væbnede kamp, 1943–1945* [With help from England: SOE and the Danish resistance, 2: Fighting Denmark] (Odense: Odense University Press, 2000), 493p.

4891. Jones, Geoffrey. 'Multinational cross-investment between Switzerland and Britain 1914–1945', A95, 427–60.

4892. Kaiser, Wolfram; Staerck, Gillian (eds.) *British foreign policy, 1955–64: contracting options* (Basingstoke: Macmillan in association with the Institute of Contemporary British History, 2000), xix, 296p.

4893. Kaufman, Victor S. '"Chirep": the Anglo-American dispute over Chinese representation in the United Nations, 1950–71', *English Historical Review* 115 (2000), 354–77.

4894. Kelly, Saul. 'Britain, the United States, and the end of the Italian empire in Africa, 1940–52', *Journal of Imperial and Commonwealth History* 28:3 (2000), 51–70.

4895. Kelly, Saul. *Cold War in the desert: Britain, the United States, and the Italian colonies, 1945–52* (Basingstoke: Macmillan, 2000), ix, 207p.

4896. Kelly, Saul. 'No ordinary Foreign Office official: Sir Roger Makins and Anglo-American atomic relations 1945–55', *Contemporary British History* 14:4 (2000), 107–24.

4897. Kelly, Saul; Gorst, Antony (eds.) *Whitehall and the Suez Crisis* (London: Frank Cass, 1999), 279p. [Special issue of *Contemporary British History* 13:2 (1999).]

4898. Kimball, Warren F. 'Churchill, the Americans, and self-determination', A169, 213–32.

4899. Kimball, Warren F. 'The two-sided octagon: Roosevelt and Churchill at Quebec, September 1944', A216, 3–16.

4900. Kirby, Dianne. 'Divinely sanctioned: the Anglo-American Cold War alliance and the defence of western civilization and Christianity, 1945–48', *Journal of Contemporary History* 35:3 (2000), 385–412.

4901. Kirk-Greene, Anthony Hamilton Millard. 'Accredited to Africa: British diplomatic representation and African experience, c.1960–95', *Diplomacy & Statecraft* 11:1 (2000), 79–128.

4902. Kitching, Carolyn. 'The search for disarmament: Anglo-French relations, 1929–1934', A191, 158–79.

4903. Krauss, H. Alexander. *Whitehall zwischen 'Commonwealth' und 'Common Market': die Commonwealth- und Westeuropapolitik der Regierung Macmillan und die britische Regierungsbürokratie 1957–1963* [Whitehall between 'Commonwealth' and 'Common Market': the Commonwealth and western European policies of the Macmillan government and the bureaucracy] (Europäische Hochschulschriften: Reihe 3, Geschichte und ihre Hilfswissenschaften, 846) (Frankfurt am Main: Peter Lang, 1999), xi, 332p.

4904. Lamont-Brown, Raymond. *Tutor to the Dragon Emperor: the life of Sir Reginald Fleming Johnston at the court of the last emperor of China* (Stroud: Sutton, 1999), xiii, 176p.

4905. Langley, H.D. 'Roosevelt and Churchill and the fight for victory and stability', A143, 131–46.

4906. Le Mahieu, D.L. 'America and the representation of British history in film and television', A135, 261–75.

4907. Lehmkuhl, Ursula. *Pax Anglo-Americana: Machtstrukturelle Grundlagen anglo-amerikanischer Asien- und Fernostpolitik in den 1950er Jahren* [Power foundations of Anglo-American policy in Asia and the Far East in the 1950s] (Studien zur internationalen Geschichte, 7) (Munich: Oldenbourg, 1999), 304p.

4908. Lentin, Anthony. 'Lloyd George, Clemenceau and the elusive Anglo-French guarantee treaty, 1919: "a disastrous episode"?', A191, 104–19.

4909. Leruez, Jacques. 'Franco-Scottish relations in the late twentieth century and in the twenty-first century', A130, 143–53.

4910. Leventhal, Fred M. 'Essential democracy: the 1939 royal visit to the United States', A13, 163–77.

4911. Leventhal, Fred M. 'Public face and public space: the projection of Britain in America before the Second World War', A135, 212–26.

4912. Louis, Wm. Roger. 'Harold Macmillan and the Middle East crisis of 1958', *Proceedings of the British Academy* 94 (1997), 207–28.

4913. Ludlow, N. Piers. '"Ne pleurez pas, Milord": Macmillan and France from Algiers to Rambouillet', A5, 95–112.

4914. Ludlow, N. Piers. 'A mismanaged application: Britain and EEC membership (1961–3)', A152, 271–85.

4915. Ludlow, N. Piers. 'A slow reassessment: British views of Italy's European policy 1950–1963', *Storia delle Relazioni Internazionali* 13:2–14:1 (1998–99), 383–406.

4916. Ludlow, N. Piers. 'British policy and the first application to the EEC (1961–63)', A63, 107–26.

4917. Ludlow, N. Piers. 'Cena późnego akcesu: Wielka Brytania a Wspólnoty Europejskie 1950–1973' [Paying the cost of late arrival: Britain and the European Community, 1950–1973], A129.

4918. Ludlow, N. Piers. 'Le Paradoxe Anglais: Great Britain and political union', *Revue de Allemagne* 29:2 (1997), 259–72.

4919. MacKay, Robert. 'Being beastly to the Germans: music, censorship and the BBC in World War II', *Historical Journal of Film, Radio and Television* 20:4 (2000), 513–25.

4920. MacKenzie, Hector. 'Sinews of war and peace: the politics of Canadian economic aid to Britain, 1939–1945', *International Journal* 54:4 (1998–99), 648–70.

4921. Magee, Frank. 'Conducting Locarno diplomacy: Britain and the Austro-German customs union crisis, 1931', *20th Century British History* 11:2 (2000), 105–34.

4922. Mahoney, Daniel J. 'Moral principle and realistic judgment', A163, 69–92.

4923. Mallett, Robert. 'Fascist foreign policy and official Italian views of Anthony Eden in the 1930s', *Historical Journal* 43:1 (2000), 157–87.

4924. Malmgreen, Gail. 'Comrades and kinsmen: the Jewish Labour Committee and anti-Nazi activity, 1934–1941', A46, 4–20.

4925. Mariager, Rasmus. 'Danmark som besættelsesmagt?: dansk-britiske forhandlinger om Dansk deltagelse i besættelsen af Tyskland' [Anglo-Danish relations, 1946–49], *Historisk Tidsskrift* [Copenhagen] 98 (1998), 78–98.

4926. Mazbouri, Malik. 'Place financière suisse et crédits aux belligérants durant la Première Guerre mondiale', A95, 59–90.

4927. McNamara, Robert. 'Britain, Nasser and the outbreak of the Six Day War', *Journal of Contemporary History* 35:4 (2000), 619–39.

4928. Medawar, Jean; Pyke, David. *Hitler's gift* [refugee Jewish scientists] (London: Richard Cohen in association with the European Jewish Publication Society, 2000), 288p.

4929. Melissen, Jan. 'The politics of US missile deployment in Britain, 1955–59', *Storia delle Relazioni Internazionali* 13:1 (1998), 151–85.

4930. Menon, Anand. 'Triomphant malgré lui? Le Royaume-Uni et l'émergence d'une Europe anglo-saxonne' [Triumphant in spite of itself? The United Kingdom and the emergence of an Anglo-Saxon Europe], *Pouvoirs* [Paris] 93 (2000), 177–193.

4931. Minion, Mark. 'The Fabian Society and Europe during the 1940s: the search for a "Socialist foreign policy"', *European History Quarterly* 30:2 (2000), 237–70.

4932. Moscrop, John James. *Measuring Jerusalem: the Palestine Exploration Fund and British interests in the Holy Land* (Leicester: Leicester University Press, 1999), 256p.

4933. Natmeßnig, Charlotte. *Britische Finanzinteressen in Österreich: die Anglo-Österreichische Bank* [British financial interests in Austria: the Anglo-Austrian Bank] (Studien zur Wirtschaftsgeschichte und zur Wirtschaftspolitik, 5) (Vienna: Böhlau, 1998), 302p.

4934. Neville, Peter. *Appeasing Hitler: the diplomacy of Sir Nevile Henderson, 1937–39* (Basingstoke: Macmillan, 2000), xv, 237p.

4935. Neville, Peter Patrick. 'Nevile Henderson in Constantinople, Cairo and Belgrade: the prototype appeaser?', *Byzantine and Modern Greek Studies* 24 (2000), 194–210.

4936. Newton, Scott. 'A "visionary hope" frustrated: J.M. Keynes and the origins of the postwar international monetary order', *Diplomacy & Statecraft* 11:1 (2000), 189–210.

4937. Nouailhat, Yves-Henri. 'Les «relations spéciales» entre la Grande-Bretagne et les États-Unis pendant les années Wilson' [The Anglo-American 'special relationship' during the Wilson years], A35, 167–80.

4938. Offner, Arnold A. 'From Reims to Potsdam: Victory, atomic diplomacy, and the origins of the Cold War', A169, 233–56.

4939. Ortuño Anaya, Pilar. 'The Labour Party, the TUC and Spain, 1959–1977', *Labour History Review* 64:3 (1999), 269–86.

4940. Osborn, Patrick A. *Operation Pike: Britain versus the Soviet Union, 1939–1941* (Contributions in Military History, 190) (London: Greenwood, 2000), xxxvi, 274p.

4941. Pagedas, Constantine A. *Anglo-American strategic relations and the French problem, 1960–1963: a troubled partnership* (London: Cass, 2000), xvii, 308p.

4942. Parker, Robert Alexander Clarke. *Churchill and Appeasement* (Basingstoke: Macmillan, 2000), xi, 290p.

4943. Parrish, Thomas. *Berlin in the balance, 1945–1949: the blockade, the airlift, the first major battle of the Cold War* (Reading (MA): Perseus Books, 1998), 394p.

4944. Peck, Robert E. 'The banning of *Titanic*: a study of British postwar film censorship in Germany', *Historical Journal of Film Radio and Television* 20:3 (2000), 427–44.

4945. Petersen, Tore Tingvold. 'Crossing the Rubicon?: Britain's withdrawal from the Middle East, 1964–1968: a bibliographical review', *International History Review* 22:2 (2000), 318–40.

4946. Petersen, Tore Tingvold. *The Middle East between the great powers: Anglo-American conflict and cooperation, 1952–7* (Basingstoke and New York: Macmillan and St Martin's Press, 2000), xiii, 170p.

4947. Powers, Patrick J.C. 'Rhetorical statesmanship', A163, 139–50.

4948. Rahe, Paul A. 'The beginning of the Cold War', A163, 49–68.

4949. Ramsden, John. 'Mr Churchill goes to Fulton' [Missouri, 1946], A163, 15–48.

4950. Reynolds, David. 'The Atlantic "flop": British Foreign Policy and the Churchill-Roosevelt meeting of August 1941', A22, 129–150.

4951. Roberts, John Charles Quentin. *Speak clearly into the chandelier: cultural politics between Britain and Russia 1973–2000* (Richmond: Curzon, 2000), xiii, 272p.

4952. Robinson, David. 'The Atlantic Charter meeting: an eyewitness account', A22.

4953. Rouvillois, Frédéric. 'Se choisir un modèle: Michel Debré et le parlementarisme anglais en 1958' [Choosing a model: Debré and British parliamentarianism in 1958], *Revue française d'histoire des idées politiques* 12 (2000), 347–66.

4954. Ruane, Kevin. 'Anthony Eden, the Foreign Office and Anglo-French relations, 1951–1954', A191, 280–300.

4955. Rychlík, Jan; Marzik, Thomas D.; Bielik, Miroslav (eds.) *R.W. Seton-Watson and his relations with the Czechs and Slovaks*, 2 vols.: 1. *Documents 1906–1918*; 2. *Documents 1906–1951* (Prague: T.G. Masaryka, 1995) [Text in Czech and English; documents in English, French, German, Czech and Slovak.]

4956. Sarkisyanz, Manuel. *Adolf Hitlers englische Vorbilder: vom britischen zum ostmärkisch-bajuwarischen Herrenmenschentum. Vorlesungen gehalten an der Heidelberger Universität* [Adolf Hitler's English models: from a British to a Bavarian-Eastern Marches race of supermen] (Ketsch am Rhein: The author, 1997), iii, 350p.

4957. Schnapper, Pauline. *La Grande-Bretagne et l'Europe: Le grand malentendu* [Britain and Europe: the great misunderstanding] (Paris: Presses de la Fondation nationale des sciences politiques, 2000), 218p.

4958. Schrafstetter, Susanna. *Die dritte Atommacht: britische Nichtverbreitungspolitik im Dienst von Statussicherung und Deutschlandpolitik 1952–1968* [The third atomic power: British non-proliferation policy as a means of securing status and policy towards Germany] (Schriftenreihe der Vierteljahrshefte für Zeitgeschichte, 79) (Munich: Oldenbourg, 1999), 254p.

4959. Schrafstetter, Susanna; Twigge, Stephen. 'Trick or truth? The British ANF proposal, West Germany and US nonproliferation policy, 1964–68' [Atlantic Nuclear Force], *Diplomacy & Statecraft* 11:2 (2000), 161–184.

4960. Schweitzer, Carl-Christoph. 'Britische Deutschlandbilder im Zweiten Weltkrieg' [British images of Germany in the Second World War], A185, 203–25.

4961. Sharp, Alan. 'Anglo-French relations from Versailles to Locarno, 1919–1925: the quest for security', A191, 120–38.

4962. Sharp, Alan; Stone, Glyn. 'Introduction' [Anglo-French relations in the twentieth century], A191, 1–10.

4963. Shogan, Robert. *Hard bargain: how FDR twisted Churchill's arm, evaded the law, and changed the role of the American presidency* (Boulder (CO): Westview, 1999), 320p. [1st published New York: Simon & Schuster, 1994.]

4964. Sikorsky, Jonathan. 'From British Cassandra to American hero: the Churchill legend in the World War II American media', *Finest Hour: Journal of the Churchill Center and Societies* 108 (2000), 30–35.

4965. Staerck, Gillian (ed.) 'The role of HM Embassy in Moscow', *Contemporary British History* 14:3 (2000), 149–61.

4966. Stafford, David. 'Roosevelt, Churchill and Anglo-American intelligence: the strange case of Juan March', *Intelligence and National Security* 15:2 (2000), 36–48.

4967. Stevens, Richard. 'Cold War politics: Communism and anti-Communism in the trade unions', A31, 168–91.

4968.   Stoler, Mark A. *Allies and adversaries: the Joint Chiefs of Staff, the grand alliance, and U.S. strategy in World War II* (Chapel Hill (NC) and London: University of North Carolina Press, 2000), xxii, 380p.
4969.   Stoler, Mark A. 'Allies or adversaries? The Joint Chiefs of Staff and Soviet-American relations, Spring 1945', A169, 145–66.
4970.   Stone, Glyn. 'Britain and Portuguese Africa, 1961–65', *Journal of Imperial and Commonwealth History* 28:3 (2000), 169–92.
4971.   Stone, Glyn. 'From entente to alliance: Anglo-French relations, 1935–1939', A191, 180–204.
4972.   Strobl, Gerwin. *The Germanic isle: Nazi perceptions of Britain* (Cambridge: Cambridge University Press, 2000), 284p.
4973.   Subritzky, John. *Confronting Sukarno: British, American, Australian and New Zealand diplomacy in the Malaysian-Indonesian confrontation, 1961–5* (Basingstoke: Macmillan, 2000), xix, 246p.
4974.   Swain, Geoffrey. '"An interesting and plausible proposal": Bruce Lockhart, Sidney Reilly and the Latvian riflemen, Russia 1918', *Intelligence and National Security* 14:3 (1999), 81–102.
4975.   Taylor, Alan John Percivale. *Struggles for supremacy: diplomatic essays*, ed. Chris Wrigley. (Aldershot: Ashgate, 2000), vii, 395p.
4976.   Taylor, Eva Haraszti (comp.) *Britain and Hungary in the post-war years, 1945–51: a parallel history in narrative and documents*, 2 vols.: 1. *The narrative*; 2. *The documents* (Nottingham: Astra, 2000).
4977.   Thatcher, Margaret Hilda (1st baroness Thatcher of Kesteven). 'New threats for old', A163, 151–68.
4978.   Thomas, Martin. 'Divisive decolonization: the Anglo-French withdrawal from Syria and Lebanon, 1944–46', *Journal of Imperial and Commonwealth History* 28:3 (2000), 71–93.
4979.   Tilea, Viorel Virgil. *Envoy extraordinary: memoirs of a Romanian diplomat* [The Romanian minister in Britain, 1939–1940], ed. Ileana Tilea (London: Haggerston, 1998), xiii, 315p.
4980.   Tomaru, Junko. *The postwar rapproachment of Malaya and Japan, 1945–61: the roles of Britain and Japan in south-east Asia* (Basingstoke: Macmillan in association with St Antony's College, Oxford, 2000), xiv, 317p.
4981.   Tombs, Isabelle. '"Morituri vos salutant": Szmul Zygielbojm's suicide in May 1943 and the international socialist community in London', *Holocaust and Genocide Studies* 14:2 (2000), 242–65.
4982.   Vanthoor, Willem F.V. *A chronological history of the European Union, 1946–1998* (Cheltenham: Edward Elgar, 1999), xxi, 244p.
4983.   Warner, Isabel; Bevins, Richard. 'Das Foreign Office und der ungarische Volksaufstand von 1956' [The Foreign Office and the Hungarian popular rising of 1956], A101, 375–94.
4984.   Warren, Spencer. 'A philosophy of international politics', A163, 93–128.
4985.   Wasserstein, Bernard. *Britain and the Jews of Europe, 1939–1945*, 2nd edn. (London: Leicester University Press, 1999), [xv], 352p. [1st published Oxford University Press, 1979.]
4986.   Watson, David. 'Britain, France and the Russian Civil War, 1918–1920', A191, 89–103.

4987.   Whitaker, Reg. 'Cold War alchemy: how America, Britain and Canada transformed espionage into subversion', *Intelligence and National Security* 15:2 (2000), 177–210.

4988.   Woolner, David B. 'Coming to grips with the "German problem": Roosevelt, Churchill, and the Morgenthau Plan at the second Quebec conference', A216, 65–104.

4989.   Worley, Matthew. 'The Communist International, the Communist Party of Great Britain, and the "Third Period", 1928–1932', *European History Quarterly* 30:2 (2000), 185–208.

4990.   Wright, Joanne. 'The Cold War, European Community and Anglo-French relations, 1958–1998', A191, 324–44.

4991.   Wylie, Neville. 'The Swiss Franc and British policy towards Switzerland 1939–1945', A95, 461–80.

4992.   Young, John. 'The failure of the new entente cordiale, 1947–1950', A191, 264–79.

4993.   Young, John W. *Britain and European unity, 1945–1999*, 2nd edn. (Basingstoke: Palgrave, 2000), xii, 237p. [1st published 1993.]

4994.   Zimmermann, Hubert. 'The sour fruits of victory: sterling and security in Anglo-German relations during the 1950s and 1960s', *Contemporary European History* 9:2 (2000), 225–44.

J. MEDIEVAL WALES

A. *General*

See also 5290 (L)

4995.   Arnold, Christopher J.; Davies, Jeffrey L. *Roman and early medieval Wales* (Stroud: Sutton, 2000), viii, 216p.

4996.   Davies, R. Rees. 'Owain Glyn Dŵr a'i apêl' [Owain Glyn Dwr and his appeal], *Y Traethodydd* 155 (2000), 198–209.

4997.   Davies, R. Rees. 'Shakespeare's Glendower and Owain Glyn Dŵr', *The Historian* [London] 66 (2000), 22–25.

4998.   Jones, John Gwynfor. 'Owain Glyndŵr a gwrthryfel y Cymry 1400–1415' [Owain Glyndwr and the revolt of the Welsh 1400–1415], *Taliesin* 110 (2000), 24–40.

4999.   White, Richard. 'Caernarfon and the origins of the kingdoms of Gwynedd', *Caernarvonshire Historical Society Transactions* 61 (2000), 23–39.

5000.   Wyatt, David. 'Gruffudd ap Cynan and the Hiberno-Norse world', *Welsh History Review* 19:4 (1999), 595–617.

B. Historiography and Historical Methods

See also 274, 304 (B)

5001. Griffiths, Ralph Alan. 'The authors of urban records in medieval Wales', A177, 157–76.
5002. Holder, Nick; Wardle, Peter. 'A disputed early-medieval inscribed stone from Barry, Vale of Glamorgan', *Medieval Archaeology* 43 (1999), 216–22.

C. Population and Environment

See also 954 (E)

5003. Andrews, Phil. 'Excavations at Cosmeston medieval village, near Penarth, South Glamorgan, 1993', *Archaeology in Wales* 36 (1996), 11–35.
5004. Coe, Jon. 'River and valley terms in the Book of Llandaf', *Nomina* 23 (2000), 5–21.
5005. Griffiths, Ralph Alan. 'Wales and the marches', A174, 681–714.
5006. Hamilton, Mike; Howell, Ray. 'Trelech: the geophysical survey of a possible medieval hospice site', *Medieval Archaeology* 44 (2000), 229–33.
5007. Johnstone, Neil. 'Cae Llys, Rhosyr: a court of the princes of Gwynedd', *Studia Celtica* 33 (1999), 251–95.
5008. Jones, Sue; Thompson, David. 'The archaeology of deserted rural settlement in north-west Wales', A8, 50–57.
5009. Lilley, Keith D. '"Non urbe, non vico, non castris": territorial control and the colonization and urbanization of Wales and Ireland under Anglo-Norman lordship', *Journal of Historical Geography* 26:4 (2000), 517–31.
5010. Ludlow, Neil. 'Excavations within medieval Talgarth, Powys 1997–98', *Brycheiniog* 32 (2000), 11–48.
5011. Murphy, Kenneth. 'The rise and fall of the medieval town in Wales', A194, 193–213.
5012. Pierce, Gwynedd O. 'The Welsh *mystwyr*', *Nomina* 23 (2000), 121–39.
5013. Redknap, Mark. 'Further work at Glyn, Llanbedrgoch, Anglesey', *Archaeology in Wales* 39 (1999), 56–61.
5014. Sambrook, Paul. 'Medieval or later deserted rural settlement in west Wales', A8, 90–95.
5015. Silvester, R.J. 'Deserted rural settlements of medieval or later date in north-eastern and central Wales', A8, 100–108.
5016. Wilson, Julia C. 'Trelech: a new location for the old town', *Archaeology in Wales* 38 (1998), 67–70.

Da. Social Life and Conditions

See also 1376, 1420 (F)

5017. de Lewandowicz, Martin. 'A survey of Castell Prysor, Meirionnydd', *Archaeology in Wales* 38 (1998), 36–42.

5018. Jenkins, Dafydd. 'Hawk and hound: hunting in the laws of court', A41, 255–80.
5019. Kissock, Jonathan; Johnston, R.A.S. 'Excavation of a house platform on Cefn Drum, Pontardulais', *Archaeology in Wales* 38 (1998), 71–3.
5020. Kissock, Jonathan. 'Farmsteads of a presumed medieval date on Cefn Drum, Gower: an interim review', *Studia Celtica* 34 (2000), 223–248.
5021. Longley, D.M.T. 'Rescue excavations at 29 High Street, Caernarfon, Gwynedd', *Caernarvonshire Historical Society Transactions* 61 (2000), 41–57.
5022. Smith, Llinos Beverley. 'Towards a history of women in late medieval Wales', A186, 14–49.

Db. *Social Structure*

5023. Hines, John. 'Welsh and English: mutual origins in post-Roman Britain?', *Studia Celtica* 34 (2000), 81–104.
5024. Hughes, R. Elfyn. 'Self-created changes in the structure of cognate tenurial land holding systems in fifteenth-century Merioneth', *Journal of the Merioneth Historical and Record Society* 13:3 (2000), 207–26.
5025. Redknap, Mark. *Vikings in Wales: an archaeological quest* (Cardiff: National Museums and Galleries of Wales, 2000), 116p.

Ea. *Economic Activity and Organisation*

See also 1029 (E)

5026. Charles-Edwards, T.M. 'Food, drink and clothing in the laws of court', A41, 319–37.
5027. Howell, Raymond. 'Development by design: an investigation of thirteenth-century industrialization and urban growth at Trelech, Gwent', *Studia Celtica* 34 (2000), 211–22.

Eb. *Technology*

5028. Breeze, Andrew. 'Cefnllys and the Hereford map', *Radnorshire Society Transactions* 69 (1999), 173–75.
5029. O'Loughlin, Thomas. 'An early thirteenth-century map in Dublin: a window into the world of Giraldus Cambrensis', *Imago Mundi* 51 (1999), 24–39.

Fa. *Media and Communication*

See also 5002, 5049, 5081 (J)

5030. Huws, Daniel. 'Descriptions of the Welsh manuscripts', A41, 415–24.
5031. Huws, Daniel. *Medieval Welsh manuscripts* (Cardiff: University of Wales Press, 2000), xvi, 352p.
5032. McKee, Helen. 'Scribes and glosses from Dark Age Wales: the Cambridge Juvencus manuscript', *Cambrian Medieval Celtic Studies* 39 (2000), 1–22.

Fb. *Science and Medicine*

5033. Carr, A.D. 'The Black Death in Caernarfonsire', *Caernarvonshire Historical Society Transactions* 61 (2000), 7–22.
5034. Owen, Morfydd E. 'Medics and medicine', A41, 116–41.

Fc. *Ideas and Learning*

5035. Howlett, David. 'A Brittonic curriculum: a British child's ABC 123', *Cambrian Medieval Celtic Studies* 40 (2000), 21–26.

Fd. *Culture and the Arts*

See also 5035, 5110 (J); 5379, 5385 (L)

5036. Booth, P.H.W. 'The corporation of Holt, the manor of Farndon, and the bridge over the Dee, Denbighshire', *Archaeologia Cambrensis* 146 (2000 for 1997), 109–16.
5037. Breeze, Andrew. 'The battle of Brunanburh and Welsh tradition', *Neophilologus* 83 (1999), 479–82.
5038. Breeze, Andrew. 'The Lady Beryke and Sir Meneduke in *the Awntrys off Arthur*', *Transactions of the Cumberland & Westmorland Antiquarian & Archaeological Society* 100 (2000), 281–5.
5039. Breeze, Andrew. 'Two English carols in a Radnorshire deed of 1471 at Bridgwater, Somerset', *National Library of Wales Journal* 31:2 (1999), 117–19.
5040. Bryant-Quinn, Paul. '"Y mab o Emlyn": golwg ar waith Syr Phylib, bardd-offeiriad' ['The son from Emlyn: a look at the work of Syr Phylib, poet-priest], *Ceredigion* 13:3 (1999), 18–42.
5041. Bryant-Quinn, Paul (ed.) *Gwaith Ieuan Brydydd Hir* [The works of Ieuan Brydydd Hir] (Aberystwyth: Canolfan Uwchefrydiau Cymreig a Cheltaidd, 2000), xx, 213p.
5042. Davies, Morgan Thomas. 'Plowmen, patrons, and poets: Iolo Goch's *Cywydd y Llafurwr* and some matters of Wales in the fourteenth century', *Medievalia et Humanistica, ns* 24 (1997), 51–74.
5043. Edwards, Huw M. 'Dwyn marwnadau adref' [Bringing elegies home], *Llên Cymru* 23 (2000), 21–38.
5044. Evans, Dylan Foster. 'Ail-lunio'r Cymry—y beirdd ar ôl methiant Glyndŵr' [Reconstructing the Welsh—the poets after the failure of Glyndwr], *Taliesin* 110 (2000), 43–57.
5045. Evans, Dylan Foster. 'Rhoi eich troed ynddi: camau cyntaf ar drywydd ffasiwn yng Nghymru'r oesoedd canol' [Putting your foot in it: first steps in search of fashion in medieval Wales], *Tu Chwith* 14 (2000), 21–34.
5046. Hallam, Tudur. 'Ysgrifen(nu) Lewys Glyn Cothi' [The writing of Lewys Glyn Cothi], *Llên Cymru* 23 (2000), 74–94.
5047. Ifans, Rhiannon (ed.) *Gwaith Gruffudd Llwyd a'r Llygliwiaid eraill* [The works of Gruffudd Llwyd and the other Llygliwiaid] (Aberystwyth: Canolfan Uwchefrydiau Cymreig a Cheltaidd, 2000), xxii, 359p.

5048.   Jenkins, Dafydd. '*Bardd teulu* and *pencerdd*', A41, 142–66.
5049.   Johnston, Dafydd. '"Ceidwaid yr hen iaith"? Beirdd yr uchelwyr a'r iaith Saesneg' ['Guardians of the old language'? The poets of the uchelwyr and the English language], Y *Traethodydd* 155 (2000), 16–24.
5050.   Lloyd, Lowri W. 'Beth yw perthyn? Pedwar term teuluol ym marddoniaeth yr oesoedd canol' [What is belonging? Four family terms in medieval poetry], *Dwned* 6 (2000), 25–53.
5051.   Lynch, Peredur I. 'Court poetry, power and politics', A41, 167–90.
5052.   Nagy, Joseph Falaky. 'Esyllt observed', A18, 222–32.
5053.   Olding, Frank. 'Penrhos castle', *Gwent Local History* 88 (2000), 3–16.
5054.   Phillips, Manon. '*Defod a moes y llys*', A41, 347–61.
5055.   Phillips, Neil. 'Abergavenny castle 1087–1537', *Gwent Local History* 88 (2000), 17–31.
5056.   Roberts, Brynley F. 'Writing in Wales', A209, 182–207.
5057.   Russell, Paul. '*Canu i Swyddogion Llys y Brenin*', A41, 552–60.
5058.   Spurgeon, C.J.; Roberts, D.J.; Thomas, H.J. 'Supposed castles in Glamorgan: a review', *Archaeology in Wales* 39 (1999), 27–40.
5059.   Stacey, Robin Chapman. 'Clothes talk from medieval Wales', A41, 338–46.
5060.   Thomas, Howard J. 'The manor and castle of Fonmon, near Barry', *Morgannwg* 43 (1999), 63–82.
5061.   Thomas, Owen. 'Dafydd Epynt: bardd llythrennog o Frycheiniog' [Dafydd Epynt: a literate poet from Brycheiniog], *Dwned* 6 (2000), 77–94.
5062.   Turner, Rick. 'St Davids bishop palace, Pembrokeshire', *Antiquaries Journal* 80 (2000), 87–194.
5063.   Williams, Gruffydd Aled. 'Adolygu'r canon: cywydd arall gan Iolo Goch i Owain Glyndŵr' [Revising the canon: another cywydd by Iolo Goch to Owain Glyndwr], *Llên Cymru* 23 (2000), 39–73.
5064.   Williams, P. Lynne. '"Ar ganghennau'r gynghanedd": agweddau ar y goedwig yn llenyddiaeth yr oesoedd canol' ['On the branches of the cynghanedd': aspects of the wood in medieval literature], *Dwned* 6 (2000), 55–76.

G. Religious Belief, Practice and Organisation

See also 1167, 1177 (E); 5039 (J)

5065.   Goering, Joseph; Pryce, Huw. 'The *De modo confitendi* of Cadwgan, bishop of Bangor', *Mediaeval Studies* 62 (2000), 1–27.
5066.   Insley, Charles. 'Fact and fiction in thirteenth-century Gwynedd: the Aberconwy charters', *Studia Celtica* 33 (1999), 235–50.
5067.   Kay, Richard. 'Gerald of Wales and the fourth Lateran council', *Viator* 29 (1998), 79–93.
5068.   O'Loughlin, Thomas. 'Giraldus Cambrensis and the sexual agenda of the twelfth century reformers', *Journal of Welsh Religious History* 8 (2000), 1–15.
5069.   O'Loughlin, Thomas. 'Rhygyfarch's *Vita Dauidis*: an *apparatus biblicus*', *Studia Celtica* 32 (1998), 179–88.

5070. Pearson, Matthew J. 'The creation and development of the St Asaph cathedral chapter, 1141–1293', *Cambrian Medieval Celtic Studies* 40 (2000), 35–56.

5071. Pearson, Matthew J. 'The creation of the Bangor cathedral chapter', *Welsh History Review* 20:1 (2000), 167–81.

5072. Pryce, Huw. 'The household priest (*offeiriad teulu*)', A41, 82–93.

5073. Rees, Elizabeth. *Celtic saints: passionate wanderers* (London: Thames & Hudson, 2000), 208p.

5074. Richter, Michael. 'William ap Rhys, William de Braose and the lordship of Gower, 1289 and 1307', *Studia Celtica* 32 (1998), 189–209.

5075. Roberts, Dylan; Suggett, Richard. 'A late-medieval monastic hall house rediscovered: the King's Court, Talyllychau', *The Carmarthenshire Antiquary* 35 (1999), 5–11.

5076. Wedell, Nina. 'St Ailworth: a Celtic saint in the Black Mountains?', *Archaeologia Cambrensis* 146 (2000 for 1997), 79–100.

5077. Winward, Fiona. 'The lives of St. Wenefred (*BHL* 8847–8851)', *Analecta Bollandiana* 117 (1999), 89–132.

Ha. *Law and Order*

5078. Jenkins, Dafydd. 'Excursus: the lawbooks and their relation', A41, 10–14.

5079. Jenkins, Dafydd. 'Prolegomena to the laws of court', A41, 15–28.

5080. Owen, Morfydd E. 'The laws of court from Cyfnerth', A41, 425–77.

5081. Pryce, Huw. 'Lawbooks and literacy in medieval Wales', *Speculum* 75 (2000), 29–67.

5082. Pryce, Huw. 'The context and purpose of the earliest Welsh lawbooks', *Cambrian Medieval Celtic Studies* 39 (2000), 39–63.

5083. Russell, Paul. 'The laws of court from Latin B', A41, 478–526.

5084. Smith, J.B. '*Ynad Llys, Brawdwr Llys, Iudex Curie*', A41, 94–115.

Hb. *Public Administration*

5085. Insley, Charles. 'From *Rex Wallie* to *Princeps Wallie*: charters and state formation in thirteenth-century Wales', A141, 179–96.

5086. Johnstone, Neil. '*Llys* and *maerdref*: the royal courts of the princes of Gwynedd', *Studia Celtica* 34 (2000), 167–210.

5087. Jones, Glanville R.J. '*Llys* and *maerdref*', A41, 296–318.

5088. Jones, Rhys. 'Changing ideologies of medieval state formation: the growing exploitation of land in Gwynedd c.1100–c.1400', *Journal of Historical Geography* 26:4 (2000), 505–16.

5089. Jones, Rhys. 'The formation of the cantref and the commote in medieval Gwynedd', *Studia Celtica* 32 (1998), 169–77.

Hc. *Political and Constitutional*

5090. Charles-Edwards, T.M.; Owen, Morfydd E.; Russell Paul. 'Introduction' [The Welsh king and his court], A41, 1–9.

5091. Charles-Edwards, T.M.; Jones, Nerys Ann. '*Breintiau Gwŷr Powys*: the liberties of the men of Powys', A41, 191–223.

5092. Crump, J.J. 'Repercussions of the execution of William de Braose: a letter from Llywelyn ab Iorwerth to Stephen de Segrave' [c.1230–1], *Historical Research* 73 (2000), 197–212.

5093. Davies, R. Rees. 'Brecon, Owain Glyn Dŵr, and Dafydd Gam', *Brycheiniog* 32 (2000), 51–60.

5094. Edwards, Anthony. *Letters of a peacemaker: the intervention of Archbishop John Peckham in the Welsh war of 1282* (Tregarth: Anthony Edwards, 1998), 50p.

5095. Hill, David. 'Offa's dyke: pattern and purpose', *Antiquaries Journal* 80 (2000), 195–206.

5096. Holden, Brock W. 'The making of the middle march of Wales, 1066–1250', *Welsh History Review* 20:2 (2000), 207–26.

5097. Maund, Kari. *The Welsh kings* (Stroud: Tempus, 2000), 160p.

5098. Maund, K.L. 'Dynastic segmentation and Gwynedd c.950–c.1000', *Studia Celtica* 32 (1998), 155–167.

5099. Owen, Morfydd E. 'Royal propaganda: stories from the law-texts', A41, 224–54.

5100. Rowlands, I.W. 'The 1201 peace between King John and Llywelyn ap Iorwerth', *Studia Celtica* 34 (2000), 149–66.

5101. Russell, Paul. '*Swydd, swyddog, swyddwr*: office, officer and official', A41, 281–95.

5102. Stacey, Robin Chapman. 'King, queen and *edling* in the laws of court', A41, 29–62.

5103. Stephenson, David. 'The laws of court: past reality or present ideal?', A41, 400–14.

5104. Thornton, David E. 'Who was Rhain the Irishman?', *Studia Celtica* 34 (2000), 131–48.

5105. Walters, D.B. 'Comparative aspects of the tractates on the laws of court', A41, 382–99.

J. *Military*

5106. Carr, A.D. '*Teulu* and *Penteulu*', A41, 63–81.

5107. Mathieu, James R. 'New methods on old castles: generating new ways of seeing', *Medieval Archaeology* 43 (1999), 115–42.

5108. Miles, Trevor J. 'Flint: excavations at the castle and on the town defences 1971–1974', *Archaeologia Cambrensis* 145 (1998 for 1996), 67–151.

5109. Stephenson, David. 'The Walwayns of Hay and the Chronicle of Walter of Guisborough: a note', *Brycheiniog* 32 (2000), 49–50.

5110. Walker, R.F. 'Bwlchyddinas Castle, Breconshire, and the survey of 1337', *Brycheiniog* 31 (1998–99), 19–30.

K. SCOTLAND BEFORE THE UNION

A. *General*

See also 1332–4, 1336 (F); 5290 (L)

5111. Ballantyne, John H.; Smith, Brian (eds.) *Shetland documents 1195–1579* (Lerwick: Shetland Islands Council & the Shetland Times, 1999), xxii, 359p.
5112. Cowan, Edward J.; McDonald, Russell Andrew (eds.) *Alba: Celtic Scotland in the middle ages* (East Linton: Tuckwell, 2000), xiv, 282p.
5113. Cummins, Walter Arthur. *The Picts and their symbols* (Stroud: Sutton, 1999), 218p.
5114. Emery, N. 'The impact of the outside world on St Kilda: the artefact evidence', A8, 161–66.
5115. Macdougall, Norman. 'L'Ecosse à la fin du XIIIe siècle: un royaume menacé', A130, 9–22.
5116. Sharpe, R. 'The thriving of Dalriada', A203, 47–61.
5117. Smout, T. Christopher. *A history of the Scottish people, 1560–1830* (London: Fontana, 1998), 540p. [1st published London: Collins, 1969.]
5118. Taylor, Simon; Henderson, J.M. 'The medieval marches of Wester Kinnear, Kilmany parish, Fife', *Tayside Fife Archaeological Journal* 4 (1998), 232–47.

B. *Historiography and Historical Methods*

See also 304 (B)

5119. Boardman, Steve; Lynch, Michael. 'The state of late medieval and early modern Scottish history', A66, 44–59.
5120. Crone, Anne. 'Native tree-ring chronologies from some Scottish medieval burghs', *Medieval Archaeology* 44 (2000), 201–16.
5121. Dumville, D.N. 'The Chronicle of the Kings of Alba', A203, 73–86.
5122. Duncan, A.A.M. 'Sources and uses of the Chronicle of Melrose, 1165–1297', A203, 146–85.
5123. Forsyth, K.; Koch, J.T. 'Evidence of a lost Pictish source in the Historia Regum Anglorum of Symeon of Durham', A203, 19–34.
5124. Grant, Alexander. 'Acts of lordship: the records of Archibald, fourth earl of Douglas', A66, 235–74.
5125. Gray, Iain. 'Dean of Guild Court records: a unique source for Scottish urban history', *Scottish Archives* 5 (1999), 41–48.
5126. Koch, John T. 'The place of "Y Gododdin" in the history of Scotland', A18, 199–210.
5127. Lowrey, John. 'Archives and archaeology: the prehistory of Queensberry House, Edinburgh', *Scottish Archives* 5 (1999), 29–40.
5128. Macfarlane, Leslie. 'The Vatican Archives as a source for Scottish medieval historians: an update', A66, 183–89.

5129.   McAndrew, Bruce A. 'The sigillography of the Ragman Roll', *Proceedings of the Society of Antiquaries of Scotland* 129 (1999), 663–752.
5130.   Oram, Richard D. 'Gold into lead? The state of early medieval Scottish history', A66, 32–43.
5131.   Symonds, J. 'The dark island revisited: an approach to the historical archaeology of Milton, South Uist', A8, 197–210.
5132.   Watt, Donald Elmslie Robertson (ed.) *A history book for Scots: selections from Scottichronicon* (Edinburgh: Mercat, 1998), xiii, 306p.

C. Population and Environment

See also 707, 726 (D); 1346, 1347, 1354, 1359–62, 1367 (F)

5133.   Atkinson, John Andrew. 'Rural settlement in north Lochtayside: understanding the landscapes of change', A8, 150–60.
5134.   Bangor-Jones, M. 'Settlement history of Assynt, Sutherland', A8, 211–26.
5135.   Breeze, Andrew. 'Four Brittonic place-names from south-west Scotland', *Transactions of the Dumfriesshire and Galloway Natural History and Antiquarian Society* 74 (2000), 55–60.
5136.   Breeze, Andrew. 'Some Celtic place-names of Scotland, including *Dalriada, Kincarden, Abercorn, Coldingham* and *Girvan*', *Scottish Language* 18 (1999), 34–51.
5137.   Caldwell, D.H. 'Post-medieval settlement in Islay—some recent research', A8, 58–68.
5138.   Carter, Stephen P. 'The burgh of Inverurie, Aberdeenshire: archaeological evidence from a medieval lordship', *Proceedings of the Society of Antiquaries of Scotland* 129 (1999), 649–61.
5139.   Dennison, E. Patricia. 'Recreating the urban past', A66, 275–84.
5140.   Dennison, E. Patricia; Simpson, Grant G. 'Scotland', A174, 715–40.
5141.   Devine, Thomas Martin. 'Scotland', A43, 151–66.
5142.   Ditchburn, David. 'Scotland 1300–1540', A174, 495–504.
5143.   Durkan, John. 'What's in a name?: Thaney or Enoch' [Scottish saints], *Innes Review* 51:1 (2000), 80–83.
5144.   Hingley, R. 'Medieval or later rural settlement in Scotland: the value of the resource', A8, 11–19.
5145.   Lelong, O. 'A township through time: excavation and survey at the deserted settlement of Easter Raitts, Badenoch, 1995–99', A8, 40–49.
5146.   Perry, David. 'Dunfermline: from "Saracen" castle to "populous manufacturing royal burrow"', *Proceedings of the Society of Antiquaries of Scotland* 129 (1999), 779–815.
5147.   Sandnes, B. 'Place-names in Orkney as evidence for language contact', *Northern Studies* 34 (1999), 23–34.
5148.   Scott, Margaret. '"Bullion" in Scottish place-names', *Nomina* 23 (2000), 37–48.
5149.   Sharples, N.; Parker Pearson, M. 'Norse settlement in the Outer Hebrides', *Norweigan Archaeological Review* 32:1 (1999), 41–62.
5150.   Waugh, D.J. 'Settlement names in the south-west: Dumfries and Galloway', *Scottish Language* 17 (1998), 40–54.

5151.   Whyte, Ian D. 'Historical geographical dimensions of medieval or later rural settlement in lowland Scotland', A8, 145–49.

Da. Social Life and Conditions

5152.   Bunyan, Stephen. 'The Fletchers of Saltoun', *Transactions of the East Lothian Antiquarian and Field Naturalists' Society* 24 (2000), 67–76.

5153.   Coutts, W. 'Wife and widow: the evidence of testaments and marriage contracts c.1600', A77, 176–86.

5154.   DesBrisay, G. 'Wet nurses and unwed mothers in seventeenth-century Aberdeen', A77, 210–20.

5155.   Desbrisay, Gordon. 'City limits: female philanthropists and wet nurses in seventeenth-century Scottish towns', *Journal of the Canadian Historical Association* ns 8 (1997), 39–60.

5156.   Dorward, D. 'Scottish surnames in the context of Scottish culture, historical and contemporary', *Onoma* 34 (1998–99), 77–90.

5157.   Ewan, Elizabeth. 'Mons Meg and merchant Meg: women in later medieval Edinburgh', A66, 131–42.

5158.   Hughson, Irene I. 'Pictish horses and Pictish society', A18, 211–21.

5159.   Leneman, Leah. *Sin in the city: sexuality and social control in urban Scotland 1660–1780* (Edinburgh: Scottish Cultural Press, 1998), vii, 163p.

5160.   Mitchison, Rosalind; Leneman, Leah. *Girls in trouble: sexuality and social control in rural Scotland 1660–1780* (Edinburgh: Scottish Cultural Press, 1998), viii, 133p.

5161.   Reddington-Wilde, Roxanne L. 'A woman's place: birth order, gender and social status in Highland houses', A77, 201–9.

5162.   Roberts, Alasdair. 'The Knights of the Mortar: an alternative suggestion', *Scottish Historical Review* 79:1 (2000), 82–86.

5163.   Stiubhart, D.U. 'Women and gender in the early modern western Gaidhealtachd', A77, 233–50.

5164.   Todd, Margo. 'Profane pastimes and the reformed community: the persistence of popular festivities in early modern Scotland', *Journal of British Studies* 39:2 (2000), 123–56.

Db. Social Structure

See also 1361 (F)

5165.   Barrett, J.H.; Beukens, R.P. 'Radiocarbon dating and marine reservoir correction of Viking age Christian burials from Orkney', *Antiquity* 74:285 (2000), 537–543.

5166.   James, Heather F. 'Excavations of a medieval cemetery at Skaill House, and a cist in the Bay of Skaill, Sandwick, Orkney', *Proceedings of the Society of Antiquaries of Scotland* 129 (1999), 753–77.

5167.   MacGregor, Martin. 'Genealogies of the clans: contributions to the study of MS 1467', *Innes Review* 51:2 (2000), 131–46.

5168.   Ó Muraíle, Nollaig. 'Irish genealogical connections: the Scottish dimension', A18, 251–64.

Ea. *Economic Activity and Organisation*

See also 1476, 1490, 1507 (F); 5188, 5245 (K)

5169.   Adamson, Duncan. 'Some early teind lists: NAS Vol. CS 7 335', *Transactions of the Dumfriesshire and Galloway Natural History and Antiquarian Society* 74 (2000), 95–103.

5170.   Cheape, Hugh. 'Logboats in history: West Highland evidence', *Proceedings of the Society of Antiquaries of Scotland* 129 (1999), 851–60.

5171.   Cormack, W.F. 'Drengs and drings' [forms of landholding], *Transactions of the Dumfriesshire and Galloway Natural History and Antiquarian Society* 74 (2000), 61–67.

5172.   Dingwall, H. 'The power behind the merchant? Women and the economy in late seventeenth-century Edinburgh', A77, 152–64.

5173.   Dodgshon, R.A. 'Traditional highland field systems: their constraints and thresholds', A8, 109–16.

5174.   Ewan, E. '"For whatever ales ye": women as consumers and producers in late medieval Scottish towns', A77, 125–36.

5175.   Hall, D.W. 'Scottish medieval pottery industries', A8, 173–77.

5176.   Harris, Bob. 'Scotland's herring fisheries and the prosperity of the nation, c.1660–1760', *Scottish Historical Review* 79:1 (2000), 39–60.

5177.   Harvey, W.S. 'Lead mining in mediaeval Scotland', *British Mining* 59 (1997), 123–27.

5178.   Holmes, Nicholas. *Scottish coins: a history of small change in Scotland* (Edinburgh: NMS [National Museums of Scotland], 1998), 112p.

5179.   Holmes, N.M.McQ. 'Scottish coin hoards, 1996–97', *British Numismatic Journal* 68 (1998), 77–94.

5180.   Laing, William; Urquhart, Robert H.J. 'A seventeeth-century description of herring fishing off the west coast of Scotland', *Scottish Archives* 5 (1999), 100–6.

5181.   Lane, A. 'Trade, gifts, and cultural exchange in dark-age western Scotland', A56, 103–13.

5182.   Mann, A.J. 'Embroidery to enterprise: the role of women in the book trade of early modern Scotland', A77, 137–51.

5183.   Meikle, M.M. '"Holde her at the Oeconomicke rule of the House": Anna of Denmark and Scottish court finances, 1589–1603', A77, 105–11.

5184.   Shirlaw, Jean H. 'The glassworks at Morrison's Haven', *Transactions of the East Lothian Antiquarian and Field Naturalists' Society* 24 (2000), 39–40.

5185.   Thomas, Jane. 'The craftsmen of Elgin, 1540–1660', A66, 143–54.

5186.   Whittington, G.; McManus, J. 'Dark Age agricultural practices and environmental change: evidence from Tentsmuir, Fife, eastern Scotland', A150, 111–20.

Fa. *Media and Communication*

See 1561 (F)

Fb. *Science and Medicine*

5187.   Harrison, G. 'Public hygiene and drainage in Stirling and other early modern Scottish towns', *Review of Scottish Culture* 11 (1998–99), 67–77.
5188.   Whitfield, Niamh. 'Design and units of measure on the Hunterston Brooch', A100, 296–314.

Fc. *Ideas and Learning*

See also 1650 (F)

5189.   Allan, David. '"In the bosome of a shaddowie grove": Sir George Mackenzie and the consolations of retirement', *History of European Ideas* 25:5 (1999), 251–73.
5190.   McLaren, Colin. 'Visiting the charter chest: the early records of the University and King's College, Aberdeen', A66, 190–202.
5191.   Morét, Ulrike. 'Historians and languages: medieval and humanist views of Celtic Britain', A66, 60–74.
5192.   Vance, S.M. 'Godly citizens and civic unrest: tensions in schooling in Aberdeen in the era of the Reformation', *European Review of History* 7:1 (2000), 123–37.

Fd. *Culture and the Arts*

See also 821 (D); 1141 (E); 1694 (F); 5225 (K)

5193.   Ager, Barry. 'Pierowell, Orkney: the re-discovered provenance of a "pair" of ninth-century Viking oval brooches in the Department of Medieval and Later Antiquities of the British Museum', *Archaeological Journal* 156 (1999), 359–62.
5194.   Allan, David. 'A commendation of the private country life: philosophy and the garden in seventeenth-century Scotland', *Garden History* 25:1 (1997), 59–80.
5195.   Atkins, S.N. 'A fragment of medieval church music in Stranraer Museum', *Transactions of the Dumfriesshire and Galloway Natural History and Antiquarian Society* 74 (2000), 69–75.
5196.   Banderier, Gilles. 'Du Bartas et la littérature écossaise: une hypothèse', *Bibliotheque d'Humanisme et Renaissance* 62 (2000), 89–92.
5197.   Barbour, John. *The Bruce*, ed. & transl. Archibald Alexander McBeth Duncan (Canongate Classics, 78) (Edinburgh: Canongate, 1997), viii, 792p.
5198.   Brown, Michael. '"Vile times": Walter Bower's last book and the minority of James II', *Scottish Historical Review* 79:2 (2000), 165–88.
5199.   Clancy, T.O. 'Scotland, the "Nennian" recension of the Historia Brittonum, and the Lebor Bretnach', A203, 87–107.
5200.   Cox, Richard A.V. *The language of the ogam inscriptions of Scotland: contributions to the study of ogam, runic and Roman alphabet inscrip-*

tions in Scotland (Aberdeen: Department of Celtic, University of Aberdeen, 1999), xvi, 187p.

5201. Donaldson, William. 'Manuscript material in the University of Aberdeen for the study of piping', *Northern Scotland* 20 (2000), 167–178.

5202. Frater, A.C. 'Women of the Gaidhealtachd and their songs to 1750', A77, 67–82.

5203. Gammeltoft, Peder. 'Why the difference?: an attempt to account for the variations in the phonetic development of place-names in Old Norse böl-staddr in the Hebrides', *Nomina* 23 (2000), 107–19.

5204. Goldstein, James. 'Writing in Scotland, 1058–1560', A209, 229–54.

5205. Henderson, Isabel. 'The insular and continental context of the St Andrews sarcophagus', A56, 71–102.

5206. Henderson, Isabel; Scott, I.G. 'Towards defining the function of sculpture in Alba: the evidence of St Andrews, Brechin and Rosemarkie', A203, 35–46.

5207. Howlett, David. 'The structure of *De Situ Albanie*', A203, 124–45.

5208. Laing, Lloyd. 'The chronology and context of Pictish relief sculpture', *Medieval Archaeology* 44 (2000), 81–114.

5209. McKean, C. 'Sir James Hamilton of Finnart: a renaissance courtier-architect', *Architectural History* 42 (1999), 141–72.

5210. Newlyn, E.S. 'Images of women in sixteenth-century Scottish literary manuscripts', A77, 56–66.

5211. Reddington-Wilde, Roxanne L. 'Violent death and damning words: women's lament in Scottish Gaelic poetry', A18, 265–86.

5212. Scott, Cooper. 'Ornamental structure in the medieval gardens of Scotland', *Proceedings of the Society of Antiquaries of Scotland* 129 (1999), 817–39.

5213. Thomson, D.S. 'Scottish Gaelic traditional songs from the 16th to the 18th century', *Proceedings of the British Academy* 105 (2000), 93–114.

5214. Trench-Jellicoe, Ross. 'A missing figure on slab fragment no 2 from Monifieth, Angus, the a'Chill Cross, Canna, and some implications of the development of a variant form of the Virgin's hairstyle and dress in early medieval Scotland', *Proceedings of the Society of Antiquaries of Scotland* 129 (1999), 597–647.

5215. van Buuren, Catherine (ed.) *The Buke of the Chess: edited from the Asloan Manuscript (NLS MS 16500)* (Scottish Text Society, 4th ser., 27) (Edinburgh: Scottish Text Society, 1997), clv, 234p.

5216. von den Steinen, K. 'In search of the antecedents of women's political activism in early eighteenth-century Scotland: the daughters of Anne, Duchess of Hamilton', A77, 112–24.

G. *Religious Belief, Practice and Organisation*

See also 821 (D); 1874 (F); 2511 (G); 5073 (J); 5169, 5214, 5279 (K)

5217. Anonymous. 'Catholic converts in Islay, Colonsay and Jura', *Catholic Ancestor* 8:1 (2000), 8–11.

5218. Bertie, David M. 'A previously undescribed Scottish communion token from Keithhall, Aberdeenshire', *Proceedings of the Society of Antiquaries of Scotland* 129 (1999), 847–9.

5219. Bourke, Cormac. 'Fergna Epscop', *Innes Review* 51:1 (2000), 68–71. [Suggests that the 4th abbot of Iona was a bishop.]

5220. Broun, D. 'The church of St Andrews and its foundation legend in the early twelfth century: recovering the full text of Version A of the foundation legend', A203, 108–14.

5221. Dilworth, Mark. 'Fearn Abbey as a monastic institution', *Innes Review* 51:1 (2000), 40–54. [List of abbots.]

5222. Fitch, A.-B. 'Power through purity: the virgin martyrs and women's salvation in pre-Reformation Scotland', A77, 16–28.

5223. Graham, M.F. 'Women and the church courts in Reformation-era Scotland', A77, 187–200.

5224. Harrison, Stuart A. 'The early Gothic church at Dundrenan Abbey', *Journal of the British Archaeological Association* 151 (1998), 137–48.

5225. Henderson, Isabel. 'Monasteries and sculpture in the insular pre-Viking age: the Pictish evidence', A205, 75–96.

5226. Macquarrie, Alan. 'The Offices for St Columba (9 June) and St Adomnan (23 September) in the Aberdeen Breviary', *Innes Review* 51:1 (2000), 1–39.

5227. Mason, Roger A. (ed.) *John Knox and the British reformations* (Aldershot: Ashgate, 1998), xvi, 297p.

5228. McDonald, R.A. 'The foundation and patronage of nunneries by native elites in twelfth- and early thirteenth-century Scotland', A77, 3–15.

5229. Mullan, David George. *Scottish Puritanism, 1590–1638* (Oxford: Oxford University Press, 2000), xiii, 371p.

5230. Mullan, David George. 'Women in Scottish divinity, c.1590–c.1640', A77, 29–44.

5231. Normand, Lawrence; Roberts, Gareth (eds.) *Witchcraft in early modern Scotland: James VI's demonology and the North Berwick witches* (Exeter: Exeter University Press, 2000), xiii, 454p.

5232. Taylor, Simon. 'Columba east of Drumalban: some aspects of the cult of Columba in eastern Scotland', *Innes Review* 51:2 (2000), 109–30.

5233. Taylor, Simon. 'The coming of the Augustinians to St Andrews and version B of the St Andrews foundation legend', A203, 115–23.

5234. Veitch, K. 'The conversion of native religious communities to the Augustinian rule in twelfth- and thirteenth-century Alba', *Records of the Scottish Church Historical Society* 29 (1999), 1–22.

5235. Weatherhead, Rennie. 'Baldred: the recorded facts and his "miracles" told in Alciun's York poem', *Transactions of the East Lothian Antiquarian and Field Naturalists' Society* 24 (2000), 27–28.

5236. Weatherhead, Rennie. 'St. Bey and her well at Dunbar', *Transactions of the East Lothian Antiquarian and Field Naturalists' Society* 24 (2000), 23–26.

5237. Whyte, Ian D.; Whyte, K.A. 'Wed to the manse: the wives of Scottish ministers, c.1560–c.1800', A77, 221–32.

5238. Wormald, Jenny. 'The witches, the Devil and the king', A66, 165–82.

Ha. *Law and Order*

See also 1325 (E); 5223 (K)

5239.   Feenstra, R. 'Teaching the civil law at Louvain as reported by Scottish students in the 1430s', *Tijdschrift voor Rechtsgeschiedenis* 65 (1997), 245–80.
5240.   Finlay, J. 'Women and legal representation in early sixteenth-century Scotland', A77, 165–75.
5241.   Finlay, John. 'James Henryson and the origins of the office of King's Advocate', *Scottish Historical Review* 79:1 (2000), 17–38.

Hb. *Public Administration*

5242.   McHarg, James F. *In search of Dr John MakLuire: pioneer Edinburgh physician, forgotten for over 300 years* (Wellcome Unit for the History of Medicine, University of Glasgow publication, 9) (Glasgow: Wellcome Unit for the History of Medicine, University of Glasgow, 1997), xxxiv, 239p.
5243.   Murray, Athol L. 'The Town Clerk of Perth's *Liber omne gaderum* 1425', *Scottish Archives* 5 (1999), 63–66.
5244.   Truckell, A.E. 'Dumfries Burgh Court Books in the 16th century. Part II', *Transactions of the Dumfriesshire and Galloway Natural History and Antiquarian Society* 74 (2000), 77–93.
5245.   Wilson, J.B. 'Lochmaben Town Council minutes 1612–1721: the economy of Lochmaben', *Transactions of the Dumfriesshire and Galloway Natural History and Antiquarian Society* 74 (2000), 114–9.

Hc. *Political and Constitutional*

See also 1985, 1991–2, 2018, 2038, 2040, 2044, 2053, 2072, 2081, 2104 (F); 5276 (K)

5246.   Aitchison, Nicholas B. *Macbeth: man and myth* (Stroud: Sutton, 1999), viii, 216p.
5247.   Brotherstone, Terry; Ditchburn, David. '1320 and a' that: the Declaration of Arbroath and the remaking of Scottish history', A66, 10–31.
5248.   Brotherstone, Terry; Ditchburn, David. 'The steam behind the spectacles: Grant G. Simpson, freedom and authority', A66, 3–9.
5249.   Broun, D. 'The origin of Scottish identity in its European context', A56, 21–32.
5250.   Glozier, Matthew. 'The Earl of Melfort, the Court Catholic party and the foundation of the Order of the Thistle, 1687', *Scottish Historical Review* 79:2 (2000), 233–38.
5251.   Grant, Alexander. 'The construction of the early Scottish state', A141, 47–71.
5252.   Grant, R. 'Politicking Jacobean women: Lady Ferniehirst, the Countess of Arran and the Countess of Huntly, c.1580–1603', A77, 95–104.
5253.   Herbert, M. 'Ri Eirenn, Ri Alban: kingship and identity in the ninth and tenth centuries', A203, 62–72.

5254. Imsen, Steinar. 'Earldom and kingdom: Orkney in the realm of Norway 1195–1379', *Historisk tidsskrift* [Norway] 79 (2000), 163–80.
5255. MacDougall, Norman. *James IV* (East Linton: Tuckwell, 1997), xi, 339p. [1st published Edinburgh: John Donald, 1989.]
5256. Macinnes, Allan I. 'Covenanting ideology in seventeenth-century Scotland', A170, 191–220.
5257. Macpherson, Robin. 'Francis Stewart, fifth earl Bothwell, and James VI: perception politics', A66, 155–64.
5258. Neville, Cynthia J. 'A Celtic enclave in Norman Scotland: Earl Gilbert and the Earldom of Strathearn, 1171–1223', A66, 75–92.
5259. Ouston, Hugh. '"From Thames to Tweed departed": the court of James, Duke of York in Scotland, 1679–82', A58, 266–79.
5260. Owen, Douglas David Roy. *William the Lion, 1143–1214: kingship and culture* (East Linton: Tuckwell, 1997), xii, 218p.
5261. Pittock, Murray G.H. 'From Edinburgh to London: Scottish court writing and 1603', A58, 13–28.
5262. Stringer, Keith J. 'Acts of lordship: the records of the lords of Galloway to 1234', A66, 203–34.
5263. Tanner, Roland. 'The Lords of the Articles before 1540: a reassessment', *Scottish Historical Review* 79:2 (2000), 189–212.
5264. Thomas, A. '"Dragonis baith and dowis ay in double forme": women at the court of James V, 1513–1542', A77, 83–94.
5265. Wedgwood, Cicely Veronica. *Montrose*, new edn. (Stroud: Alan Sutton, 1995), xii, 172p. [Illustrated edition.]
5266. Woolf, Alex. 'The "Moray question" and the kingship of Alba in the tenth and eleventh centuries', *Scottish Historical Review* 79:2 (2000), 145–64.

J. *Military*

See also 1325 (E); 2109, 2113–15 (F); 2617 (G)

5267. Brockington, William S. (ed.) *Monro: his expedition with the worthy Scots regiment called Mac-Keys* (New York: Praeger, 1999), xlix, 429p.
5268. Chevalier, Bernard. 'Les Alliés écossais au service du roi de France au XV siècle', A130, 47–58.
5269. Driscoll, Stephen T.; Yeoman, Peter A. *Excavations within Edinburgh Castle in 1988–91* (Monograph Series, 12) (Edinburgh: Society of Antiquaries of Scotland, 1997), xv, 251p.
5270. Macdonald, Alastair J. 'Profit, politics and personality: war and the later medieval Scottish nobility', A66, 118–30.
5271. MacIvor, Iain; Gallagher, Dennis. 'Excavations at Caerlaverock Castle, 1955–66', *Archaeological Journal* 156 (1999), 143–245.
5272. Pringle, Denys. 'Rothesay Castle and the Stewarts', *Journal of the British Archaeological Association* 151 (1998), 149–69.
5273. Ross, A. 'Men for all seasons? The Strathbogie Earls of Atholl and the Wars of Independence, c.1290–c.1335', *Northern Scotland* 20 (2000), 1–30.
5274. Traquair, Peter. *Freedom's sword: Scotland's wars of independence* (London: HarperCollins, 1998), 352p.

K. *Foreign Affairs*

See also 5239, 5254, 5267–8 (K); 5471 (L)

5275.   Autrand, Françoise. 'Aux origines de l'Europe moderne: l'alliance France-Ecosse au XIVe siècle', A130, 33–46.
5276.   Bawcutt, P.; Henisch, B. 'Scots abroad in the fifteenth century: the Princesses Margaret, Isabella and Eleanor', A77, 45–55.
5277.   Cameron, Sonja. 'Sir James Douglas, Spain, and the Holy Land', A66, 108–17.
5278.   Contamine, Philippe. 'Entre France et Ecosse: Bérault Stuart, siegneur d'Aubigny (vers 1452–1508), chef de guerre, diplomate, écrivain militaire', A130, 59–76.
5279.   Dilworth, Mark. 'Walter Malin, diplomatic agent and monastic reformer', *Innes Review* 51:2 (2000), 147–65.
5280.   Duchein, Michel. 'Le Traité franco-écossais de 1295 dans son contexte international', A130, 23–32.
5281.   MacDonald, A.J. 'The apogee of the "Auld Alliance" and the limits of policy, 1369–1402', *Northern Scotland* 20 (2000), 31–46.
5282.   Macdougall, Simone; Macdougall, Norman. 'Les liaisons dangereuses: Jacques IV d'Ecosse, Louis XII de France, et l'Angleterre—1498–1513', A130, 77–88.
5283.   Stevenson, Alexander. 'Medieval Scottish associations with Bruges', A66, 93–107.

L. IRELAND TO *c*.1640

A. *General*

See also 1334, 1336 (F); 5000 (J); 5476, 5480, 5495 (M)

5284.   Altholz, Josef L. (ed.) *Selected documents in Irish history* (London: M.E. Sharpe, 2000), viii, 152p.
5285.   *Archaeological inventory of County Cork,* volume 4 (Dublin: Stationery Office, 2000).
5286.   Duffy, Seán; et al. *Atlas of Irish history* (Dublin: Gill & Macmillan, 1997), 144p.
5287.   Ivic, Christopher. 'Incorporating Ireland: cultural conflict in Holinshed's Irish *Chronicles*', *Journal of Medieval and Early Modern Studies* 29:3 (1999), 473–98.
5288.   Lydon, James. 'Historical revisit: Edmund Curtis, A history of medieval Ireland (1923, 1938)', *Irish Historical Studies* 31 (1999), 535–48.
5289.   Mac Annaidh, Séamus. *Irish history* (Bath: Parrogon, 2000), 320p.
5290.   Maier, Bernhard. *Die Kelten: ihre Geschichte von den Anfängen bis zur Gegenwart* [The Celts: their history from the beginning to the present] (München: C.H. Beck, 2000), 320p.

5291. Ó Dálaigh, Brian (ed.) *The strangers gaze: travels in County Clare 1534–1950* (Ennis: Clasp, 1998), vii, 370p.
5292. O'Keeffe, Tadhg. *Medieval Ireland: an archaeology* (Stroud: Tempus, 2000), 192p.

B. *Historiography and Historical Methods*

5293. Herity, Michael. 'The return of the Cathach to Ireland: conflicting accounts of the repatration of the Cathach from the Continent', A196, 454–64.
5294. Kelly, James. 'Introduction: the historiography of the diocese of Dublin', A121, 1–18.
5295. McLeod, Wilson. 'The rhetorical geography of the late medieval Irish chronicles', *Cambrian Medieval Celtic Studies* 40 (2000), 57–68.
5296. Morgan, Hiram. 'Beyond Spenser? A historiographical introduction to the study of political ideas in early modern Ireland', A157, 9–21.
5297. Morgan, Hiram. 'Giraldus Cambrensis and the Tudor conquest of Ireland', A157, 22–44.
5298. Ó Concheanainn, Tomás. 'A medieval Irish historiographer: Giolla Íosa Mac Fhir Bhisigh', A196, 387–95.
5299. Ó Riain, Pádraig. 'The *Catalogus praecipuorum sanctorum Hiberniae*, sixty years on', A196, 396–430.
5300. O'Sullivan, William. 'The manuscript catalogue of Dubhaltach Mac Fhirbhisigh', A196, 439–47.
5301. Simpson, Linzi. 'Forty years a-digging: a preliminary synthesis of archaeological investigations in medieval Dublin', A72, 11–68.

C. *Population and Environment*

See also 996 (E); 1367 (F); 5009 (J)

5302. Aalen, F.H.A.; Whelan, Kevin; Stout, Matthew (eds.) *Atlas of the Irish rural landscape* (Cork: Cork University Press, 1997), 352p.
5303. Barry, T. 'Excavations at Piperstown Deserted Medieval Village, Co. Ltd 1987', *Proceedings of the Royal Irish Academy, section C* 100:3 (2000) [entire issue]
5304. Caball, Marc. 'Innovation and tradition: Irish Gaelic responses to early modern conquest and colonization', A157, 62–82.
5305. Clarke, Howard B. 'Decolonisation and the dynamics of urban decline in Ireland, 1300–1550', A194, 157–92.
5306. Clinton, Mark. 'Settlement patterns in the early historic kingdom of Leinster (seventh-mid twelfth centuries)', A196, 275–98.
5307. Geraghty, Siobhán. *Viking Dublin: botanical evidence from Fishamble Street* (Medieval Dublin Excavations, 1962–81, Series C, 2) (Dublin: Royal Irish Academy, 1996), viii, 115p.
5308. Holm, Poul. 'Viking Dublin and the city-state concept: parameters and significance of the Hiberno-Norse settlement', A98, 251–62.
5309. McKay, Patrick. *A dictionary of Ulster place-names* (Belfast: Institute of Irish Studies, Queen's University of Belfast, 1999), xiv, 159p.

5310. McKay, Patrick. 'Some Belfast place-names', *Nomina* 23 (2000), 49–54.
5311. Mitchell, Fraser. 'An introduction to human and climate impacts in the Irish quaternary', A154, 10.05–10.25.
5312. Monk, M. 'Some aspects of the interaction between early medieval Irish society and the environment', A154, 15.05–15.30.
5313. Ó Mórdha, Eoghan. 'The placenames in the Book of Cuanu', A196, 189–91.
5314. Ó Muraíle, Nollaig. 'Some early Connacht population-groups', A196, 161–77.
5315. O'Sullivan, A. 'Prehistoric and medieval coastal settlement and wetland exploitation in the Shannon estuary, Ireland', *Warp Occasional Paper* 12 (1999), 177–84.
5316. O'Sullivan, A. 'The exploitation and evolution of coastal landscapes on the Shannon estuary 5000BC-1500AD', A154, 14.15–14.40.
5317. Ryan, Michael. 'Furrows and browse: some archaeological thoughts on agriculture and population in early medieval Ireland', A196, 30–36.
5318. Stalmans, Nathalie. 'La description de la région de Slieve Bloom (Irlande) dans l'hagiographie de quelques fondateurs: une clef de datation des sources?', *Revue Belge de Philologie et d'Histoire* 76 (1998), 895–906.

Da. *Social Life and Conditions*

See also 5543 (M)

5319. Bradley, John. *The topography and layout of medieval Drogheda* ([Drogheda]: Old Drogheda Society, 1997), 38p.
5320. Carey, Vincent. '"Neither good English nor good Irish": bi-lingualism and identity formation in sixteenth-century Ireland', A157, 45–61.
5321. Coughlan, Tim. 'The Anglo-Norman houses of Dublin: evidence from Back Lane', A72, 203–33.
5322. Doyle, I. 'The early medieval activity at Dalkey Island, Co. Dublin: a re-assessment', *Journal of Irish Archaeology* 9 (1998), 89–104.
5323. Eogan, George. 'Life and living at Lagore', A196, 64–82.
5324. Hayden, Alan. 'West Side story: archaeological excavations at Cornmarket and Bridge Street Upper, Dublin—a summary account', A72, 84–116.
5325. Herity, Michael; Kelly, Dorothy; Mattenberger, Ursula. 'List of early Christian cross slabs in seven north-western counties', *Journal of the Royal Society of Antiquaries of Ireland* 127 (1997), 80–124.
5326. King, Heather A. (ed.) *Clonmacnoise studies*, vol.1: *Seminar papers 1994* (Dublin: Dúchas, the Heritage Service, 1998), ix, 148p.
5327. Mac Cuarta, Brian. 'A planter's funeral, legacies, and inventory: Sir Matthew De Renzy (1577–1634)', *Journal of the Royal Society of Antiquaries of Ireland* 127 (1997), 18–34.
5328. Ó Floinn, Raghnall. 'Freestone Hill, C. Kilkenny: a reassessment', A196, 12–29.
5329. Sweetman, P. David. 'The fortified house in Ireland', A196, 448–53.
5330. Wallace, Patrick F. '*Garrda* and *airbeada*: the plot thickens in Viking Dublin', A196, 261–74.

Db. *Social Structure*

See also 996 (E); 1456 (F); 5025 (J); 5168 (K); 5543, 5566, 5753 (M)

5331. Charles-Edwards, T.M. 'Britons in Ireland, c.550–800', A36, 15–26.
5332. Fenlon, Jane. 'Episodes of magnificence: the material worlds of the dukes of Ormonde', A12, 137–59.
5333. Landwehr, Achim. '"Becoming a liege and true Englishman": Englische Assimilationspolitik in Irland 1534–1547' [English assimilation policy in Ireland], *Historische Mitteilungen der Ranke-Gesellschaft* 12 (1999), 1–34.
5334. Mac Cuarta, Brian. 'A settler's land disputes in a Gaelic lordship: Matthew De Renzy in Delvin Mac Coghlan, 1613–18', *Studia Hibernica* 30 (1998–99), 63–88.
5335. Ó Canann, Tomás G. 'Ua Canannáin genealogies in the Irish manuscript tradition', *Studia Hibernica* 30 (1998–99), 167–229.

Ea. *Economic Activity and Organisation*

See also 1020 (E)

5336. Ferguson, Lydia. '*Custodes librorum*: service, staff and salaries, 1601–1855' [Trinity College Dublin library], A125, 25–38.
5337. Gillespie, Raymond. 'Urban destruction by war in early modern Ireland', A128, 275–88.
5338. Hall, V.; Pilcher, J. 'Tephra dated vegetational changes associated with medieval agriculture in Ireland', A154, 15.60–16.15.
5339. Lyons, Mary Ann. 'Franco-Irish relations in the sixteenth century', *Irish Economic and Social History* 25 (1998), 284.
5340. Lyons, Mary Ann. 'Maritime relations between Ireland and France, c.1480–c.1630', *Irish Economic and Social History* 27 (2000), 1–24.
5341. McCutcheon, Clare. 'Medieval pottery in Dublin: new names and some dates', A72, 117–25.
5342. O'Brien, B. 'Early metal mining and its impact on the Irish landscape', A154, 11.55–12.20.
5343. Ohlmeyer, Jane H. 'Calculating debt: the Irish statute Staple records', *Irish Economic and Social History* 27 (2000), 63–65.
5344. Swan, D.L. 'Archaeological excavations at Usher's Quay, 1991' [Dublin], A72, 126–58.
5345. Valante, Mary. 'Dublin's economic relations with hinterland and periphery in the later Viking age', A72, 69–83.

Eb. *Technology*

See also 5029 (J)

5346. Fry, Malcolm. *Coití: logboats from northern Ireland*, ed. Brian Scott (N.I. Archaeological Monographs, 4) (Antrim: Greystone, 2000), xi, 152p.

5347.   Rynne, Colin. 'Horizontal mills in medieval Ireland', *Transactions of the Newcomen Society* 70:2 (1999), 251–56.

Fa. *Media and Communication*

See also 5032 (J); 5769 (M)

5348.   Boran, Elizabethanne. 'The function of the library in the early seventeenth century' [Trinity College Dublin library], A125, 39–52.
5349.   Cains, Anthony. 'The Long Room survey of sixteenth- and seventeenth-century books of the first collections' [Trinity College Dublin library], A125, 53–71.
5350.   Crowley, Tony. *The politics of language in Ireland 1366–1922: a sourcebook* (London: Routledge, 2000), xvi, 236p.
5351.   Drennan, A.S. 'Bibliographical note. On the identification of the first Belfast printed book', *The Library* 7th ser. 1:2 (2000), 193–96.
5352.   Fox, Peter. 'The librarians of Trinity College', A125, 11–24.
5353.   Grimes, Brendan. 'The library buildings up to 1970' [Trinity College Dublin library], A125, 72–90.
5354.   Harpur, Isolde. 'A select chronology' [Trinity College Dublin library], A125, 177–84.
5355.   Maxwell, Jane. 'A guide to the manuscript sources in TCD for the history of the library', A125, 91–103.
5356.   Meehan, Bernard. 'Lost and found: a stray of the thirteenth century from Trinity College Library', A125, 116–19.

Fb. *Science and Medicine*

5357.   Isler, H.; Hasenfratz, H.; O'Neil, T. 'A sixth-century Irish headache cure and its use in a south German monastery', *Cephalalgia* 16:8 (1996), 536–40.

Fc. *Ideas and Learning*

See also 5646, 5663–4 (M)

5358.   Carey, Vincent. 'The Irish face of Machiavelli: Richard Beacon's *Solon his follie* and republican ideology in the conquest of Ireland', A157, 83–109.
5359.   Clarke, Aidan. 'Patrick Darcy and the constitutional relationship between Ireland and Britain', A170, 35–55.
5360.   Daintree, David. 'Virgil and Virgil scholia in early medieval Ireland', *Romanobarbarica* 16 (1999), 347–61.
5361.   Edwards, David. 'Ideology and experience: Spenser's *View* and martial law in Ireland', A157, 127–57.
5362.   McKenna, Catherine. 'Learning lordship: the education of Manawydan', A36, 101–20.

Fd. *Culture and the Arts*

See also 1141 (E); 1705 (F); 5332, 5401, 5419, 5459 (L)

5363. Bhreathnach, Edel. 'Kings, the kingship of Leinster and the regnal poems of *laídshenchas Laigen*: a reflection of dynastic politics in Leinster, 650–1150', A196, 299–312.

5364. Brannon, P.V. 'Medieval Ireland: music in cathedral, church and cloister', *Early Music* 28:2 (2000), 193–204.

5365. Buckley, A. 'Music and musicians in medieval Irish society', *Early Music* 28:2 (2000), 165–92.

5366. Canny, Nicholas P. 'Poetry as politics: a view of the present state of *The Faerie Queene*', A157, 110–26.

5367. Carey, John. 'The finding of Arthur's grave: a story from Clonmacnoise?', A36, 1–14.

5368. Cosart, J.; Mariani, A.; Smith, C.; Stattelman, D. 'Reconstructing the music of medieval Ireland: Altramar's crossroads of the Celts', *Early Music* 28:2 (2000), 270–82.

5369. Crilly, Oliver. 'The Christ of Maghera: a preliminary study of the lintel of the old church of St Lurach at Maghera, County Derry', A114, 73–84.

5370. Deevy, Mary B.; Baker, Christine. 'Ring brooches and finger rings from medieval Dublin', A72, 159–84.

5371. Dolan, Terence. 'Writing in Ireland', A209, 208–28.

5372. Eoin, G.M. 'Poet and prince in medieval Ireland', A162, 3–16.

5373. Evans, D. Ellis. '*Onomaris*: name of story and history?', A36, 27–37.

5374. Fletcher, Alan J. *Drama, performance, and polity in pre-Cromwellian Ireland* (Cork and Toronto (Ont): Cork University Press and University of Toronto Press, 2000), xv, 520p.

5375. Hourihane, Colum. *The mason and his mark: masons' marks in the medieval Irish archbishoprics of Cashel and Dublin* (British Archaeological Reports, British Series, 294) (Oxford: Archaeopress, 2000), viii, 83p.

5376. *The Hunt Museum Limerick—North Thomond church silver 1425–1820, September-November 2000* (Limerick: The Hunt Museum, 2000).

5377. Kelly, Dorothy. 'The crosses of Tory Island', A196, 53–63.

5378. Ní Dhonnchadha, Máirín. 'On Gormfhlaith daughter of Flann Sinna and the lure of the sovereignty goddess', A196, 225–37.

5379. Ní Mhaonaigh, Máire. '*Nósa Ua Maine*: fact or fiction?', A41, 362–81.

5380. Ó Catháin, Séamas. 'Searmanas Cois Teallaigh Choigilt na Tine', A36, 157–67.

5381. O'Keeffe, Tadhg. 'Diarmait Mac Murchada and Romanesque Leinster: four twelfth-century churches in context', *Journal of the Royal Society of Antiquaries of Ireland* 127 (1997), 52–79.

5382. Ó Muraíle, Nollaig. 'Court poets and historians in late medieval Connacht', A162, 17–26.

5383. Ó Riain, Pádraig. 'Finnio and Winniau: a return to the subject', A36, 187–202.

5384. O'Sullivan, William. 'John Madden's manuscripts', A125, 104–15.

5385. Russell, Paul. '*Nósa Ua Maine*: "the customs of the Uí Mhaine"', A41, 527–51.
5386. Simms, Katharine. 'The dating of two poems on Ulster chieftains', A196, 381–86.
5387. Stalley, Roger. 'The 1562 collapse of the nave and its aftermath' [Christ Church Cathedral, Dublin], A151, 218–36.
5388. Stalley, Roger. 'The architecture of the cathedral and priory buildings, 1250–1530' [Christ Church Cathedral, Dublin], A151, 95–129.
5389. Stalley, Roger. 'The construction of the medieval cathedral, c.1030–1250', A151, 52–74.
5390. Toner, Gregory. 'The Ulster cycle: historiography or fiction?', *Cambrian Medieval Celtic Studies* 40 (2000), 1–20.
5391. Tristram, Hildegard L.C. 'Mimesis and diegesis in the *Cattle Raid of Cuailnge*', A36, 263–76.
5392. Williams, Gruffydd Aled. 'The feasting aspects of *Hirlais Owein*', A36, 289–302.

G. Religious Belief, Practice and Organisation

See also 867 (D); 1177 (E); 5073 (J); 5543, 5663, 5753, 5755 (M)

5393. Bottigheimer, Karl. 'Revisionism and the Irish Reformation', *Journal of Ecclesiastical History* 51:3 (2000), 581–86.
5394. Bourke, Cormac. 'The bells of Saints Caillín and Cuana: two twelfth-century cups', A196, 331–40.
5395. Boydell, Barra. 'Music in the medieval cathedral priory', A151, 142–50.
5396. Boydell, Barra. 'The establishment of the choral tradition, 1480–1647' [Christ Church Cathedral, Dublin], A151, 237–54.
5397. Bradshaw, Brendan. 'Revisionism and the Irish Reformation: a rejoinder', *Journal of Ecclesiastical History* 51:3 (2000), 587–91.
5398. Bray, Dorothy Ann. 'The manly spirit of St Monenna', A18, 171–81.
5399. Breatnach, Pádraig A. 'An inventory of Latin lives of Irish saints from St Anthony's College, Louvain, c.1643', A196, 431–38.
5400. Clarke, Howard B. 'Conversion, church and cathedral: the diocese of Dublin to 1152', A121, 19–50.
5401. Czernin, M. 'Fragments of liturgical chant from medieval Irish monasteries in continental Europe', *Early Music* 28:2 (2000), 217–25.
5402. De Paor, Máire (ed.) *Patrick the pilgrim Apostle of Ireland: St Patrick's Confessio and* Epistola. (Dublin: Veritas, 1998), 313p.
5403. Devlin, Ciarán. 'Some episcopal lives' [bishops of Derry], A114, 114–39.
5404. Devlin, Ciarán. 'The formation of the diocese' [of Derry], A114, 85–113.
5405. Diamond, Ciaran. 'The Reformation charter of Christ Church Cathedral, Dublin, 1541' [with text and translation], *Archivium Hibernicum* 53 (1999), 20–35.
5406. Doherty, Charles. 'Cluain Dolcáin: a brief note', A196, 182–88.
5407. Edwards, David. 'The poisoned chalice: the Ormond inheritance, sectarian division and the emergence of James Butler, 1614–1642', A12, 55–82.

5408. Etchingham, Colmán. *Church organisation in Ireland, A.D. 650 to 1000* ([Maynooth]: Laigin Publications, 1999), viii, 538p.
5409. FitzPatrick, Elizabeth; O'Brien, Caimin. *The medieval churches of County Offaly* (Dublin: Government of Ireland, 1998), xiv, 186p.
5410. Fletcher, Alan J. 'Liturgy in the late medieval cathedral priory', A151, 129–41.
5411. Ford, Alan. 'Dependent or independent? The Church of Ireland and its colonial context, 1536–1649', *Seventeenth Century* 10:2 (1995), 163–87.
5412. Gillespie, Raymond. 'The coming of reform, 1500–58' [Christ Church Cathedral, Dublin], A151, 151–73.
5413. Gillespie, Raymond. 'The crisis of reform, 1625–60' [Christ Church Cathedral, Dublin], A151, 195–217.
5414. Gillespie, Raymond. 'The religion of the first duke of Ormond', A12, 101–13.
5415. Gillespie, Raymond. 'The shaping of reform, 1558–1625' [Christ Church Cathedral, Dublin], A151, 174–94.
5416. Hall, Dianne. 'Towards a prosopography of nuns in medieval Ireland', *Archivium Hibernicum* 53 (1999), 3–15.
5417. Herbert, Máire. 'Literary sea-voyages and early Munster hagiography', A18, 182–89.
5418. Hickey, Elizabeth. *Clonard: the story of an early Irish monastery, 520–1202* (Leixlip (Co. Kildare): The author, 1998), 69p.
5419. Hourihane, C. '"Holye crossys": a catalogue of processional, altar, pendant and crucifix figures for late medieval Ireland', *Proceedings of the Royal Irish Academy, section C* 100:1 (2000) [entire issue].
5420. Jefferies, Henry A.; Johnston, Ethna. 'Early churches in the Faughan River valley, County Derry', A114, 49–72.
5421. Jefferies, Henry A. 'Erenaghs in pre-plantation Ulster: an early seventeenth-century account', *Archivium Hibernicum* 53 (1999), 16–19.
5422. Jefferies, Henry A. 'George Montgomery, first Protestant bishop of Derry, Raphoe and Clogher (1605–10)', A114, 140–66.
5423. Johnson, Ruth. 'On the dating of some early-medieval Irish crosiers', *Medieval Archaeology* 44 (2000), 115–58.
5424. Kinsella, Stuart. 'From Hiberno-Norse to Anglo-Norman, c.1030–1300' [Christ Church Cathedral, Dublin], A151, 25–52.
5425. Lacey, Brian. 'Colum Cille and the diocese of Derry', A114, 17–29.
5426. Lennon, Colm. 'Mass in the manor house: the Counter-Reformation in Dublin, 1560–1630', A121, 112–26.
5427. Lennon, Colm. 'Political thought of Irish counter-reformation churchmen: the testimony of the "Analecta" of Bishop David Rothe', A157, 181–202.
5428. Lydon, James. 'Christ Church in the later medieval Irish world, 1300–1500', A151, 75–94.
5429. Lyons, Mary Ann. *Church and society in County Kildare, c.1480–1547* (Dublin: Four Courts, 2000), 208p.
5430. Mac Shamhráin, Ailbhe. 'The emergence of the metropolitan see: Dublin, 1111–1216', A121, 51–71.
5431. Manning, Conleth. 'References to church buildings in the Annals', A196, 37–52.

5432. Massey, Eithne. *Prior Roger Outlaw of Kilmainham, 1314–1341* (Maynooth Studies in Irish Local History, 30) (Dublin: Irish Academic Press, 2000), 64p.

5433. Masterson, Rory. 'The alien priory of Fore, Co. Westmeath, in the middle ages', *Archivium Hibernicum* 53 (1999), 73–79.

5434. Meckler, Michael. 'Carnal love and priestly ordination on sixth-century Tiree', *Innes Review* 51:2 (2000), 95–108.

5435. Murphy, Margaret. 'Archbishops and Anglicanisation: Dublin, 1181–1271', A121, 72–91.

5436. Murray, James. 'The diocese of Dublin in the sixteenth century: clerical opposition and the failure of the Reformation', A121, 92–111.

5437. O'Carroll, Michael. 'Our Lady in early medieval Ireland', A196, 178–81.

5438. O'Keeffe, Tadhg. 'Romanesque as metaphor: architecture and reform in early twelfth-century Ireland', A196, 313–22.

5439. O'Loughlin, Thomas. 'The plan of the New Jerusalem in the Book of Armagh', *Cambrian Medieval Celtic Studies* 39 (2000), 23–38.

5440. Ó Néill, Pádraig. 'The Old Irish tract on the mass in the Stowe Missal: some observations on its origins and textual history', A196, 199–204.

5441. Ó Riain-Raedel, Dagmar. 'German influence on Munster church and kings in the twelfth century', A196, 323–30.

5442. Picard, Jean-Michel. '*Princeps* and *principatus* in the early Irish church: a reassessment', A196, 146–60.

5443. Refaussé, Raymond. 'Introduction' [history of Christ Church Cathedral, Dublin], A151, 1–24.

5444. Richter, Michael. 'Gilbert of Limerick revisited', A196, 341–47.

5445. Swift, Catherine. 'Forest and fields: a study of "monastic towns" in seventh and eighth century Ireland', *Journal of Irish Archaeology* 9 (1998), 105–26.

5446. Walsh, Claire. 'Archaeological excavations at the abbey of St Thomas the Martyr, Dublin', A72, 185–202.

5447. Walsh, John R. 'The early church' [in the diocese of Derry], A114, 30–48.

5448. Wilson, Henry Albert (ed.) *The calendar of St Willibrord from MS. Paris Lat. 10837: facsimile with transcription, introduction and notes* (Woodbridge: Boydell for the Henry Bradshaw Society, 1998), 96p. [1st published 1918.]

Ha. *Law and Order*

See also 5766, 5774 (M)

5449. Mac Cana, Proinsias. 'The motif of trivial causes', A196, 205–11.

5450. Murray, Kevin. 'A Middle Irish tract on *cró* and *díbad*', A196, 251–60.

Hb. *Public Administration*

See also 5407 (L)

5451. Aylmer, Gerald E. 'The first duke of Ormond as patron and administrator', A12, 115–35.

5452. Flanagan, Marie Therese. 'Household favourites: Angevin royal agents in Ireland under Henry II and John', A196, 357–80.
5453. McCavitt, John. *Sir Arthur Chichester: Lord Deputy of Ireland, 1605–1616* (Belfast: Institute of Irish Studies, The Queens University of Belfast, 1998), viii, 282p.
5454. Nagy, Joseph Falaky. 'The Irish herald', A36, 121–30.
5455. O'Sullivan, Harold. *A history of local government in County Louth: from earliest times to the present time* (Dublin: IPA, 2000), 377p.

Hc. *Political and Constitutional*

See also 936 (D); 2008, 2038, 2058 (F); 5090, 5104 (J); 5284 (L); 5646 (M)

5456. Barnard, Toby C. 'Introduction: the dukes of Ormonde', A12, 1–53.
5457. Byrne, Paul. 'Ciannachta Breg before Síl náeda Sláine', A196, 121–26.
5458. Byrnes, Michael. 'The árd Ciannachta in Adomnán's *Vita Columbae*: a reflection of Iona's attitude to the Síl náeda Sláine in the late seventh century', A196, 127–36.
5459. Carroll, Clare. 'Irish and Spanish cultural and political relations in the work of O'Sullivan Beare', A157, 229–53.
5460. Connon, Anne. 'The *Banshenshas* and the Uí Néill queens of Tara', A196, 98–108.
5461. Flanagan, Eugene. 'The anatomy of Jacobean Ireland: Captain Barnaby Rich, Sir John Davies and the failure of reform, 1609–22', A157, 158–80.
5462. Ford, Alan. 'James Ussher and the Godly prince in early seventeenth-century Ireland', A157, 203–28.
5463. Jaski, B. 'Kings over overkings: propaganda for pre-eminence in early medieval Ireland', *Mediaevalia Groningana* 23 (1997), 163–76.
5464. Lennon, Colm. *An Irish prisoner of conscience of the Tudor era: Archbishop Richard Creagh of Armagh, 1523–1586* (Dublin: Four Courts, 2000), 166p.
5465. Mac Shamhráin, Ailbhe. '*Nebulae discutiuntur*? The emergence of Clann Cholmáin, sixth-eighth centuries', A196, 83–97.
5466. Ó Corráin, Donnchadh. 'Muirchertach Mac Lochlainn and the *Circuit of Ireland*', A196, 238–50.
5467. Ó Cróinín, Dáibhí. 'Three weddings and a funeral: rewriting Irish political history in the tenth century', A196, 212–24.
5468. Ó hAodha, Donncha. 'Rechtgal ú Síadail, a famous poet of the Old Irish period', A196, 192–98.
5469. Orr, D. Alan. 'England, Ireland, Magna Carta, and the common law: the case of Connor, Lord Maguire, second Baron of Enniskillen', *Journal of British Studies* 39:4 (2000), 389–421.
5470. Swift, Catherine. '*Óenach Tailten*, the Blackwater Valley and the Uí Néill king of Tara', A196, 109–20.

J. *Military*

See 2127 (F)

K. *Foreign Affairs*

See also 936 (D)

5471. Duffy, Seán. 'Ireland and Scotland, 1014–1169: contacts and caveats', A196, 348–56.
5472. Marongiu, Paula. 'Relationes inter Italiam et Hiberniam: de Donato Scoto Faesularum episcopo', *Romanobarbarica* 15 (1998), 105–15.
5473. Picard, Jean-Michel. 'L'Irlande et la Normandie avant les normands (VIIe–IXe siecles)', *Annales de Normandie* 47 (1997), 3–24.

M. IRELAND SINCE c.1640

A. *General*

See also 1333 (F); 5284–6, 5288–9 (L); 6040, 6050, 6052, 6059–60 (P)

5474. Anonymous. 'Major accessions to repositories relating to Irish history, 1997 and 1998', *Irish Historical Studies* 31 (1999), 558–61.
5475. Anonymous. 'Public Record Office of Northern Ireland: recent accessions of interest to the social and economic historian', *Irish Economic and Social History* 27 (2000), 75–76.
5476. Brennan, Michael. *Dearc Fhearna its history and environs: Dunmore caves an epitome of local history* (Ballyfoyle: The author, 2000), 64p.
5477. Browne, Bernard. *Living by the pen: a biographical dictionary of County Wexford authors* (Old Ross: The author, 1997), iv, 168p.
5478. Canavan, Tony. 'The profession of history: the public and the past', A188, 226–41.
5479. Coogan, Tim Pat. *Wherever green is worn: the story of the Irish diaspora* (London: Hutchinson, 2000).
5480. Cunningham, Bernadette; Gillespie, Raymond. 'Select bibliography of writings on Irish economic and social history published in 1999', *Irish Economic and Social History* 27 (2000), 90–121.
5481. Day, Angélique; McWilliams, Patrick (eds.) *Ordnance Survey memoirs of Ireland*, vol.30: *Parishes of County Londonderry* (Belfast: Institute of Irish Studies, Queen's University of Belfast, in association with the Royal Irish Academy, 1995), xv, 132p.
5482. Day, Angélique; McWilliams, Patrick (eds.) *Ordnance Survey Memoirs of Ireland*, vol.31: *Parishes of County Londonderry, XI: 1821, 1833, 1836–7: South Londonderry* (Belfast: Institute of Irish Studies in association with the Royal Irish Academy, 1995), xiv, 144p.

5483.   Day, Angélique; McWilliams, Patrick; English, Lisa (eds.) *Ordnance Survey Memoirs of Ireland*, vol.33: *Parishes of County Londonderry, XII 1829–30, 1832, 1834–36: Coleraine and Mouth of the Bann* (Belfast: Institute of Irish Studies in association with the Royal Irish Academy, 1995), xiv, 173p.

5484.   Day, Angélique (ed.) *Ordnance Survey Memoirs of Ireland*, vol.34: *Parishes of County Londonderry, XIII 1831–8: Clondermot and the Waterside* (Belfast: Institute of Irish Studies in association with the Royal Irish Academy, 1996), xiii, 133p.

5485.   Day, Angélique; McWilliams, Patrick (eds.) *Ordnance Survey memoirs of Ireland*, vol.37: *Parishes of County Antrim, XIV: 1832, 1839–40: Carrickfergus* (Belfast: Institute of Irish Studies, Queen's University of Belfast, in association with the Royal Irish Academy, 1996), xii, 194p.

5486.   Day, Angélique; McWilliams, Patrick (eds.) *Ordnance Survey Memoirs of Ireland*, vol.38: *Parishes of County Donegal, I: 1833–5: North-east Donegal* (Belfast: Institute of Irish Studies in association with the Royal Irish Academy, 1997), xiv, 153p.

5487.   Day, Angélique; McWilliams, Patrick. *Ordnance Survey Memoirs of Ireland*, vol.39: *Parishes of County Donegal, II: 1835–6: Mid, west and south Donegal* (Belfast: Institute of Irish Studies in association with the Royal Irish Academy, 1997), xiii, 200p.

5488.   Dickson, D. *New foundations: Ireland 1660–1800*, 2nd revised & enlarged edn. (Dublin: Irish Academic Press, 2000), xvi, 248p.

5489.   Donnelly, Brian; Ó hOgartaigh, Margaret. 'Medical archives for the socio-economic historian', *Irish Economic and Social History* 27 (2000), 66–72.

5490.   Donnelly, Brian. 'National Archives: survey of business records', *Irish Economic and Social History* 27 (2000), 73–74.

5491.   Durell, Penelope; Kelly, Cornelius. *The grand tour of Beara* (Cork: Cailleach Books, 2000), x, 214p.

5492.   Herity, Michael (ed.) *Ordnance Survey letters of Donegal: letters containing information relative to the antiquities of the County of Donegal collected during the progress of the Ordnance Survey of 1835* (Dublin: Four Masters, 2000), xxiv, 148p.

5493.   Kennealy, Thomas. *The great shame: a story of the Irish in the old world and the new* (London: Chatto & Windus, 1998), xii, 732p.

5494.   King, Carla. 'Introduction: famine, land and culture in Ireland', A126, 1–5.

5495.   Luddy, Maria. 'The Women's History Project: an update', *Irish Archives* 6:2 (1999), 34–37.

5496.   Mac Éinrí. 'Introduction' [The Irish diaspora], A15, 1–16.

5497.   Nevin, Monica. 'Joseph Cooper Walker, 1761–1810. Part II', *Journal of the Royal Society of Antiquaries of Ireland* 127 (1997), 34–51.

5498.   Ó Néill, Pádraig. *Knockbridge miscellany* (Knockbridge, Co. Louth: Pádraig ó Néill, 1998), ix, 312p.

5499.   O'Sullivan, Harold. *John Bellew, a seventeenth century man of many parts, 1605–1679* (Dublin: Irish Academic, 2000), xiii, 229p.

5500.   Power, Patrick C. *A history of Dungarvan, town and district* (Dungarvan: De Paor, 2000), vi, 330p.

5501. Reid, Gerard (ed.) *Great Irish voices: over 400 years of Irish oratory* (Dublin: Irish Academic, 1999), xi, 402p.
5502. Stanley, Derek. *South Dublin from the Liffey to Greystones* (Dublin: Gill & Macmillan, 2000), 128p.

B. *Historiography and Historical Methods*

See also 286, 287, 304 (B); 1338 (F); 5293, 5300 (L); 5567, 5797, 5808 (M); 6080 (P)

5503. Anonymous. 'Ninth biennial report (sixtieth and sixty-first years) of the Irish Committee of Historical Sciences, May 1997–May 1999', *Irish Historical Studies* 32 (2000), 141–42.
5504. Anonymous. 'Theses on Irish history completed in Irish universities, 1997 and 1998', *Irish Historical Studies* 31 (1999), 562–4.
5505. Bardon, Jonathan. *A guide to local history sources in the Public Record Office of Northern Ireland* (Belfast: Blackstaff, 2000), 119p.
5506. Heuston, John. 'Oral history: a new focus for the archivist?', *Irish Archives* 6:2 (1999), 30–33.
5507. Howe, Stephen. 'Viewpoint: the politics of historical "revisionism": comparing Ireland and Israel/Palestine', *Past & Present* 168 (2000), 227–53.
5508. Peatling, G.K. 'New Liberalism, J.L. Hammond and the Irish problem, 1897–1949', *Historical Research* 73 (2000), 48–65.
5509. Quaggin, Helen. 'The Françoise Henry Collection: a database cataloguing and digitisation project by the Archaeology Department, University College Dublin', *Irish Archives* 6:2 (1999), 3–8. [Documenting early Irish Christian art.]
5510. Quinn, James. 'Theobald Wolfe Tone and the historians' [review article], *Irish Historical Studies* 32:125 (2000), 113–28.

C. *Population and Environment*

See also 1367 (F); 2652, 2670 (H); 3624, 3627–9, 3632–3, 3647 (I); 5302, 5309–10 (L); 5545, 5563, 5565, 5579 (M); 5907, 5915 (N); 6110–11 (P)

5511. Akenson, Donald Harman. 'Irish migration to North America, 1800–1920', A15, 111–38.
5512. Bell, Jonathan. 'The spread of cultivation into the marginal land in Ireland during the 18th and early 19th centuries', A150, 39–44.
5513. Bradley, John. *Kilkenny*, eds. J.H. Andrews; Anngret Simms; H.B. Clarke; Raymond Gillespie; Sarah Gearty (Irish Historic Towns Atlas, 10) (Dublin: Royal Irish Academy, 2000), 28p.
5514. Casteleyn, Mary. 'The parish register and family history collections of the late Michael Leader', *Irish Genealogist* 10 (1999), 173–201.
5515. Cawley, Mary; Ní Scannláin, Eibhlín. 'North-west Connemara: processes and patterns of landscape change in the nineteenth century', A48, 98–112.
5516. Courtney, Damien. 'A quantification of Irish migration with particular emphasis on the 1980s and 1990s', A15, 287–316.

5517.   Delaney, Enda. *Demography, state and society: Irish migration to Britain, 1921–1971* (Liverpool: Liverpool University Press, 2000), xiv, 345p.

5518.   Delaney, Tom. *Castlecomer, Co. Kilkenny, 1901 census* (Irish Genealogical Sources, 19) (Dun Laoghaire: Dun Laoghaire Genealogical Society, 2000), 286p.

5519.   Garry, James. *The streets and lanes of Drogheda*, 2nd edn. (Drogheda: Old Drogheda Society, 2000), 120p.

5520.   Gray, Breda. 'Gendering the Irish diaspora: questions of enrichment, hybridization and return', *Women's Studies International Forum* 23:2 (2000), 167–85.

5521.   Kennedy, Líam. 'Bastardy and the Great Famine: Ireland 1845–50', A126, 6–28.

5522.   Keogh, Marie. *Crosserlough, Co. Cavan, 1821 census* (Irish Genealogical Sources, 17) (Dun Laoghaire: Dun Laoghaire Genealogical Society, 2000), 296p.

5523.   Mac Laughlin, Jim. 'Changing attitudes to "new wave" emigration? Structuralism versus voluntarism in the study of Irish emigration', A15, 317–30.

5524.   McDonald, Frank. *The construction of Dublin* (Dublin: Gandon Editions, 2000), 384p.

5525.   McKenna, Patrick. 'Irish emigration to Argentina: a different model', A15, 195–212.

5526.   Ó Gráda, Cormac. 'Fertility control early in marriage in Ireland a century ago', *Journal of Population Economics* 8:4 (1995), 423.

5527.   O'Neill, Tim P. 'Famine evictions', A126, 29–70.

5528.   Rees, Jim. *Surplus people: the Fitzwilliam clearances 1847–1856* (Cork: Collins, 2000), iv, 156p.

5529.   Reid, R. '"That famine is pressing each day more heavily upon them": the emigration of Irish convict families to New South Wales, 1848–1852', *Visible Immigrants* 2 (1991), 69–96.

5530.   Thomas, C. 'Family formation in a colonial city: Londonderry 1650–1750', *Proceedings of the Royal Irish Academy, section C* 100:2 (2000) [whole issue].

5531.   Walsh, Brendan M. 'Urbanization and the regional distribution of population in post-Famine Ireland', *Journal of European Economic History* 29 (2000), 109–27.

5532.   Whelan, Kevin. 'Settlement patterns in the west of Ireland in the pre-Famine period', A48, 60–78.

Da. *Social Life and Conditions*

See also 381 (B); 2193 (G); 2686, 2723, 2736 (H); 5515, 5582, 5642 (M); 5923 (N); 6159, 6171 (P)

5533.   Barnard, Toby C. 'Aristocratic values in the careers of the dukes of Ormonde', A12, 161–75.

5534.   Bishop, Erin I. (ed.) *'My darling Danny': letters from Mary O'Connell to her son Daniel, 1830–1832* (Cork: Cork University Press, 1998), vi, 108p.

5535. Clear, Caitríona. *Women of the house: women's household work in Ireland 1922–1961* (Dublin and Portland (OR): Irish Academic Press, 2000), x, 278p.

5536. Clear, Caitríona. 'Women, work and memory in rural Ireland, 1921–61', A126, 180–93.

5537. Coldrey, B. ' "A strange mixture of caring and corruption": residential care in Christian Brothers orphanages and industrial schools during their last phase, 1940s to 1960s', *History of Education* 29:4 (2000), 343–56.

5538. Connolly, S.J. 'A woman's life in mid-eighteenth-century Ireland: the case of Letitia Bushe', *Historical Journal* 43:2 (2000), 433–51.

5539. Cronin, Michael; O'Connor, Barbara. 'From Gombeen to Gubeen: tourism, identity and class in Ireland, 1949–99', A188, 165–84.

5540. Cronin, Mike. *Sport and nationalism in Ireland: Gaelic games, soccer and Irish identity since 1884* (Dublin: Four Courts, 1999), 214p.

5541. Davis, Richard; Davis, Marianne. *The rebel in his family: selected papers of William Smith O'Brien* (Cork: Cork University Press, 1998), vi, 94p.

5542. Dudley, Rowena. 'The Dublin parishes and the poor, 1660–1740', *Archivium Hibernicum* 53 (1999), 80–94.

5543. Elliott, Marianne. *The Catholics of Ulster: a history* (London: Allen Lane, 2000), xliii, 641p.

5544. FitzGerald, Elizabeth. *Lord Kildare's grand tour: the letters of William Fitzgerald, 1766–1769* (Cork: Collins, 2000), 155p.

5545. Garrett, Paul Michael. 'The abnormal flight: the migration and repatriation of Irish unmarried mothers', *Social History* [London] 25:3 (2000), 330–43.

5546. Helle, Andreas. *Ulster, die blockierte Nation: Nordirlands Protestanten zwischen britischer Identität und irischem Regionalismus (1868–1922)* [Northern Irish Protestants between British identity and Irish regionalism] (Frankfurt am Main: Campus, 1999), 430p.

5547. Kinealy, Christine; Gerard, MacAtasney. *The hidden famine: poverty, hunger, and sectarianism in Belfast, 1840–50* (London: Pluto, 2000), xi, 242p.

5548. Lawlor, Chris. *Canon Frederick Donovan's Dunlavin, 1884–1896: a west Wicklow village in the late nineteenth century* (Maynooth Studies in Irish Local History, 29) (Dublin: Irish Academic Press, 2000), 64p.

5549. Magennis, Eoin. 'In search of the "moral economy": food scarcity in 1756–57 and the crowd', A118, 189–211.

5550. Mokyr, Joel; Ó Gráda, Cormac. *Famine disease and famine mortality: lessons from the Irish experience, 1845–1850* (Centre for Economic Research Working Paper Series, WP99/12) (Dublin: Department of Economics, University College Dublin, 1999), 40p.

5551. Mulvey, Con (ed.) *The memorial inscriptions and related history of Kiltullagh, Killimordaly and Esker graveyards* (Kiltullagh, Co. Galway: Kiltullagh Community Council, 1998), ix, 146p.

5552. Ó Cathaoir, Brendán. *Famine diary* (Dublin and Portland (OR): Irish Academic, 1999), xix, 201p. [An unabridged collection of the 120 diary entries which appeared in the *Irish Times*.]

5553. Somerville-Large, Peter. *Irish voices: fifty years of Irish life 1916–1966* (London: Chatto & Windus, 1999), xii, 289p.

5554. Throop, Elizabeth A. *Net curtains and closed doors: intimacy, family, and public life in Dublin* (Westport (CT) and London: Bergin & Garvey, 1999), xvii, 168p.

5555. Tyers, Padraig. *Blasket memories: the life of an Irish island community* (Cork: Mercier, 2000), 190p.

Db. *Social Structure*

See also 1637 (F); 2773, 2785, 2788–9 (H); 5332 (L); 5532, 5540, 5543, 5551, 5563, 5587–9, 5597, 5649, 5670, 5753, 5773, 5784 (M); 6183 (P)

5556. Anonymous. *Memorial inscriptions of Deansgrange Cemetery, Blackrock, Co. Dublin, Ireland*, vol.4, *South section* (Dun Laoghaire: Dun Laoghaire Genealogical Society, 2000), 195p.

5557. Anonymous. *Memorial inscriptions of Dun Laoghaire-Rathdown, Co. Dublin*, vol.1 (Dun Laoghaire: Genealogical Society of Ireland, 2000), 112p.

5558. Busteed, Mervyn A. 'Identity and economy on an Anglo-Irish estate: Castle Caldwell, Co. Fermanagh, c.1750–1793', *Journal of Historical Geography* 26:2 (2000), 174–202.

5559. Clark, Mary. 'Foreigners and freedom: the Huguenot refuge in Dublin city, 1660–1700', *Proceedings of the Huguenot Society of Great Britain & Ireland* 27:3 (2000), 382–91.

5560. Fannin, Samuel. 'The Ryan and Terry families in Spain', *Irish Genealogist* 10 (1999), 245–9.

5561. Glazier, Michael (ed.) *The encyclopedia of the Irish in America* (Notre Dame (IN): University of Notre Dame Press, 1999), xxi, 988p.

5562. Goodall, David. 'An Irishman in India: Abraham Goodall, F.R.C.S. 1801–1892', *Irish Genealogist* 10 (1999), 133–43.

5563. Gurrin, Brian. *A century of struggle in Delgany and Kilcoole: an exploration of the social implications of population change in north-east Wicklow 1666–1779* (Maynooth Studies in Irish Local History, 34) (Dublin: Irish Academic Press, 2000), 80p.

5564. Hall, Brendan; O'Reilly, G.H. (comps.) *Dublin's riviera in the mid 19th century* (Irish Genealogical Sources, 18) (Dun Laoghaire: Dun Laoghaire Genealogical Society, 2000), 152p.

5565. Kenny, Kevin. *The American Irish: a history* (Harlow: Longman, 2000), xix, 328p.

5566. Knight, Ronald David. *T.E. Lawrence's Irish ancestry and relationship to Sir Walter Raleigh* (Weymouth: The author, 2000), iv, 153p.

5567. Ludington, Charles C. 'Between myth and margin: the Huguenots in Irish history', *Historical Research* 73 (2000), 1–19.

5568. Mac Laughlin, Jim. 'Social and ideological constructs of "slum-dwellers" in nineteenth-century Ireland', *Journal of Historical Geography* 26:4 (2000), 631–36.

5569. Malcolmson, A.P.W. 'The Irish peerage and the Act of Union, 1800–1971', *Transactions of the Royal Historical Society* 6th ser. 10 (2000), 289–327.

5570. Mark, Gordon St. George. 'The Joyces of Merview. Part IV', *Irish Genealogist* 10 (1999), 202–14.

5571. McCan, Anthony. 'Scully tombstones on the Rock of Cashel', *Irish Genealogist* 10 (1999), 240–4.

5572. Morris, H.F. 'Faulkner's Dublin Journal 1762' [births, marriages and deaths], *Irish Genealogist* 10 (1999), 144–72.

5573. Moulinas, René. 'James Butler, second duke of Ormonde in Avignon', A12, 255–62.

5574. Proudfoot, Lindsay. 'Hybrid space? Self and other in narratives of landownership in nineteenth-century Ireland', *Journal of Historical Geography* 26:2 (2000), 203–21.

5575. Ryder, Seán. 'The politics of landscape and region in nineteenth-century poetry', A137, 169–84.

5576. Whelan, Ruth. 'The current state of research on the Huguenots and Ireland: the Round Table at Maynooth, 17 May 1999', *Proceedings of the Huguenot Society of Great Britain & Ireland* 27:3 (2000), 418–33.

Dc. *Social Policy and Welfare*

See also 5537, 5542, 5750 (M)

5577. Hatton, Helen E. *The largest amount of good: Quaker relief in Ireland, 1654–1921* (Kingston (Ont) and London: McGill-Queen's University Press, 1993), xii, 367p.

5578. Kelly, Adrian. 'Catholic action and the development of the Irish welfare state in the 1930s and 1940s', *Archivium Hibernicum* 53 (1999), 107–17.

5579. O'Connell, Anne. 'Charlotte Grace O'Brien', A59, 231–62.

5580. O'Connor, Anne V. 'Anne Jellicoe', A59, 125–59.

5581. O'Driscoll, Finín. 'Social Catholicism and the social question in independent Ireland: the challenge to the fiscal system', A57, 121–43.

5582. O'Rourke, Kevin Hjortshøj. *Culture, politics and innovation: creamery diffusion in late 19th century Denmark and Ireland* (Centre for Economic Research Working Paper Series, WP99/23) (Dublin: Department of Economics, University College Dublin, 1999), [77]p.

Ea. *Economic Activity and Organisation*

See also 381 (B); 2905 (H); 5336–7, 5343 (L); 5490, 5512, 5515, 5528, 5558, 5582, 5588, 5597, 5620, 5654, 5848 (M); 5915 (N)

5583. Bielenberg, Andy. 'Entrepreneurship, power and public opinion in Ireland: the career of William Martin Murphy', *Irish Economic and Social History* 27 (2000), 25–43.

5584. Crean, Tom. 'Crowds and the labour movement in the southwest, 1914–23', A118, 249–68.

5585. Cronin, Mike. 'Golden dreams, harsh realities: economics and informal empire in the Irish Free State', A57, 144–63.

5586. Cullen, L.M. *The Irish brandy houses of eighteenth-century France* (Dublin: Lilliput, 2000), xi, 244p.

5587. Dooley, Terence A.M. 'Landlords and the land question, 1879–1909', A126, 116–39.

5588. Dooley, Terence A.M. *Sources for the history of landed estates in Ireland,* ed. Mary Ann Lyons (Maynooth Research Guides for Irish Local History, 2) (Dublin: Irish Academic Press, 2000).

5589. Friel, Patricia. *Frederick Trench (1746–1836) and Heywood, Queen's County: the creation of a romantic demesne* (Maynooth Studies in Irish Local History, 32) (Dublin: Irish Academic Press, 2000), 72p.

5590. Hasson, Gerald. *Thunder & clatter: the history of shipbuilding in Derry* (Londonderry: Guildhall, 1997), 52p.

5591. Holmes, Heather. 'Organising the Irish migratory potato workers: the efforts in the early twentieth century', *Rural History* 11:2 (2000), 207–29.

5592. Hood, Susan. 'Ringing in the new millennium at the RCB Library: the Dukes Bell Archive' [Church of Ireland, Representative Church Body Library], *Irish Archives* 6:2 (1999), 9–17.

5593. Hunt, Tom. *Portlaw, County Waterford, 1825–1876: portrait of an industrial village and its cotton industry* (Maynooth Studies in Irish Local History, 33) (Dublin: Irish Academic Press, 2000)

5594. King, Carla. 'The Recess Committee, 1895–6', *Studia Hibernica* 30 (1998–99), 21–46.

5595. Lane, Pádraig G. 'Agricultural labourers and the land question', A126, 101–15.

5596. Martin, Sheila. *Directory of merchants and traders of Dublin in 1798, from the Gentleman's and Citizen's Almanack compiled by John Watson Stewart for the year of our Lord 1798* (Irish Genealogical Sources, 20) (Dun Laoghaire: Dun Laoghaire Genealogical Society, 2000), 232p.

5597. McCartney, Donal. 'Parnell, Davitt and the land question', A126, 71–82.

5598. Murphy, Gary. *Towards a corporate state? Seán Lemass and the realignment of interest groups in the policy process, 1948–1964* (Research Papers (Dublin City University Business School), 23) (Dublin: Dublin City University Business School, [1997]), 14p.

5599. O'Connell, Maurice. 'Irish banking and monetary union', A50, 56–64.

5600. Ó Gráda, Cormac. 'From "frugal comfort" to ten thousand a year: trade and growth in the Irish economy', A188, 263–82.

5601. Ó Gráda, Cormac. *From 'frugal comfort' to ten thousand a year: trade and growth in the Irish economy* (Centre for Economic Research Working Paper Series, WP98/16) (Dublin: Department of Economics, University College Dublin, 1998), 33p.

5602. Ó Gráda, Cormac. *Immigrants, savers, and runners: the Emigrant Industrial Savings Bank in the 1850's* (Centre for Economic Research Working Paper Series, WP98/2) (Dublin: Department of Economics, University College Dublin, 1998), 27p.

5603. Ollerenshaw, Philip. 'Businessmen and the development of Ulster Unionism, 1886–1921', *Journal of Imperial and Commonwealth History* 28 (2000), 35–64.

5604.   Quinn, John; Reilly, Alan; Cattley, Tim. *Wings over the Foyle: a history of Limavady Airfield* (Belfast: World War II Irish Wreckology Group, 1995), 149p.
5605.   Whelan, Bernadette. *Ireland and the Marshall Plan, 1947–1957* (Dublin: Four Courts, 2000), [iii], 426p.

Eb. *Technology*

See 2971 (H); 5635 (M)

Fa. *Media and Communication*

See also 5349–50, 5352–5 (L); 5572–3, 5655–6, 5686, 5769 (M)

5606.   Barton, Ruth. 'The Ballykissangelization of Ireland', *Historical Journal of Film Radio and Television* 20:3 (2000), 413–26.
5607.   Cole, Robert. '1922 and all that: the inner war in feature films of independence' [review essay], *Historical Journal of Film Radio and Television* 20:3 (2000), 445–51.
5608.   Cormack, M. 'Minority languages, nationalism and broadcasting: the British and Irish examples', *Nations and Nationalism* 6:3 (2000), 383–98.
5609.   Donnelly, K.J. 'The policing of cinema: troubled film exhibition in Northern Ireland', *Historical Journal of Film Radio and Television* 20:3 (2000), 385–96.
5610.   Drennan, A.S. 'On the identification of the first Belfast printed book', *The Library* 7th ser. 1:2 (2000), 193–96.
5611.   Fennessy, Ignatius. 'More printed items from the Wadding Papers (FLK MSS D 1–2, and others)' [in the Franciscan Library, Killiney], *Collectanea Hibernica* 41 (1999), 36–57.
5612.   Fennessy, Ignatius. 'News from Rome, 1691: books and friars', *Collectanea Hibernica* 41 (1999), 58–64.
5613.   Fenning, Hugh. 'Dublin imprints of Catholic interest: 1740–59', *Collectanea Hibernica* 41 (1999), 65–116.
5614.   Finlayson, Alan; Hughes, Eamonn. 'Advertising for peace: the state and political advertising in Northern Ireland, 1988–1998', *Historical Journal of Film Radio and Television* 20:3 (2000), 397–412.
5615.   Harris, Ruth-Ann M. 'Searching for missing friends in the Boston *Pilot* newspaper, 1831–1863', A15, 158–75.
5616.   Herr, Cheryl Temple. 'Addressing the eye in Ireland: Thaddeus O'Sullivan's *On a paving stone mounted* (1978)', *Historical Journal of Film Radio and Television* 20:3 (2000), 367–74.
5617.   Hill, John. '"Purely Sinn Fein propaganda": the banning of *Ourselves Alone* (1936)', *Historical Journal of Film Radio and Television* 20:3 (2000), 317–33.
5618.   Horgan, John. 'The media and the state: television and the press 1949–99', A188, 242–59.
5619.   Hyland, A. 'European influences on Irish education in the nineteenth and twentieth centuries', *Aspects of Education* 47 (1992), 50–66.

5620. Litvack, Leon. 'Exhibiting Ireland, 1851–3: colonial mimicry in London, Cork and Dublin', A137, 15–57.

5621. Maillot, Agnès. 'Punk on celluloid: John Davis' *Shell Shock Rock* (1979)', *Historical Journal of Film Radio and Television* 20:3 (2000), 375–84.

5622. McLoone, Martin. 'Music hall dope and British propaganda?: Cultural identity and early broadcasting in Ireland', *Historical Journal of Film Radio and Television* 20:3 (2000), 301–16.

5623. O'Brien, Harvey. 'Projecting the past: historical documentary in Ireland', *Historical Journal of Film Radio and Television* 20:3 (2000), 335–50.

5624. Ó hAodha, Mícheál. 'Irish rural libraries: glimpses of the past', *Library History* 16 (2000), 49–56.

5625. Patterson, Henry. 'Party versus order: Ulster Unionism and the Flags and Emblems Act' [1954], *Contemporary British History* 13:4 (1999), 105–29.

5626. Pettitt, Lance. 'Philip Donnellan, Ireland and dissident documentary', *Historical Journal of Film Radio and Television* 20:3 (2000), 351–66.

5627. Rockett, Kevin. 'Protecting the family and the nation: the official censorship of American cinema in Ireland, 1923–1954', *Historical Journal of Film Radio and Television* 20:3 (2000), 283–300.

5628. Saris, A. Jamie. 'Imagining Ireland in the Great Exhibition of 1853', A137, 66–86.

5629. Schulz, Thilo. *Das Deutschlandbild der* Irish Times *1933–1945* [The image of Germany in the *Irish Times*] (Frankfurt am Main: Peter Lang, 1999), x, 382p.

5630. Steele, Karen. 'Constance Markievicz's allegorical garden: femininity, militancy, and the press, 1909–1915', *Women's Studies* 29:4 (2000), 423–47.

5631. Tilley, Elizabeth. 'Charting culture in the *Dublin University Magazine*', A137, 58–65.

Fb. *Science and Medicine*

See also 3048 (H); 5489, 5550, 5807 (M)

5632. Bowler, Peter J. 'Biology in an age of revolution', A219, 1–6.

5633. Burns, D. Thorburn. 'John Patten Emmet (1796–1842): foundation Professor of Chemistry in the University of Virginia', A219, 25–33.

5634. Crean, Edward J. *Breaking the silence: the education of the deaf in Ireland 1816–1996* (Dublin: Irish Deaf Society, 1997), xx, 235p.

5635. Dooge, James C.I. 'Science, engineering and the military in Ireland: 1760–1800', A219, 51–77.

5636. Fenning, Hugh. 'Typhus epidemic in Ireland, 1817–19: priests, ministers and doctors', *Collectanea Hibernica* 41 (1999), 117–52.

5637. Flannery, Sarah; Flannery, David. *In code: a mathematical journey* (London: Profile, 2000), xi, 271p.

5638. Houston, Ken (ed.) *Creators of mathematics: the Irish connection* (Dublin: University College Dublin Press, 2000), 150p.

5639. Nelson, E.C. 'A caricature of an Irish naturalist: Revd Dr William Richardson (1740–1820)', *Archives of Natural History* 27:1 (2000), 149–51.

5640.   Nelson, S. 'Pastoral care and moral government: early nineteenth century nursing and solutions to the Irish question', *Journal of Advanced Nursing* 26:1 (1997), 6–14.

5641.   Riordan, Susannah. '"A political blackthorn": Seán MacEntee, the Dignan plan and the principle of ministerial responsibility', *Irish Economic and Social History* 27 (2000), 44–62.

5642.   Saris, A. Jamie. 'Culture and history in the halfway house: ethnography, tradition and the rural middle class in the west of Ireland', *Journal of Historical Sociology* 13:1 (2000), 10–36.

5643.   Whyte, Nicholas. '"Lords of ether and of light": the Irish astronomical tradition of the nineteenth century', *Irish Review* 17–18 (1995), 127–41.

5644.   Wyse Jackson, Patrick N. 'Tumultuous times: geology in Ireland and the debate on the nature of basalt and other rocks of north-east Ireland between 1740 and 1816', A219, 35–50.

Fc. *Ideas and Learning*

See also 1607, 1637, 1652 (F); 3103 (H); 5497, 5611–13, 5619, 5634, 5682, 5689, 5698, 5710, 5725, 5727, 5749, 5795–6 (M)

5645.   Beale, George; Phoenix, Eamon. *Stran: Stranmillis College 1922–1998: an illustrated history* (Belfast: Stranmillis, 1998), xi,130p.

5646.   Casway, Jerrold. 'Gaelic Maccabeanism: the politics of reconciliation', A170, 176–88.

5647.   Cohen, Marilyn. '"Drifting with denominationalism": a situated examination of Irish National Schools in nineteenth-century Tullylish, County Down', *History of Education Quarterly* 40:1 (2000), 49–70.

5648.   Coleman, Marie. *IFUT: a history* [Irish Federation of University Teachers] (Dublin: IFUT, 2000), 110p.

5649.   Coughlan, Patricia. 'Counter-currents in colonial discourse: the political thought of Vincent and Daniel Gookin', A170, 56–82.

5650.   Cunningham, Bernadette. 'Representations of king, parliament and the Irish people in Geoffrey Keating's *Foras Feasa ar Éirinn* and John Lynch's *Cambrensis Eversus* (1662)', A170, 131–54.

5651.   Dempsey, Pauric. 'Trinity College Dublin and the new political order', A57, 217–31.

5652.   Eagleton, Terry. *Scholars and rebels in nineteenth-century Ireland* (Oxford: Blackwell, 1999), vi, 177p.

5653.   English, Richard. 'Socialist republicanism in independent Ireland, 1922–49', A57, 84–97.

5654.   Forest, Mary; Ingram, Valerie. 'Education for lady gardeners in Ireland', *Garden History* 27:2 (1999), 206–18.

5655.   Gillespie, Raymond. 'Political ideas and their social contexts in seventeenth-century Ireland', A170, 107–27.

5656.   Hislop, Harold. 'Kildare Place Society chapbooks: curriculum and Irish identity 1811–1831', *Aspects of Education* 54 (1997), 98–117.

5657.   Kelly, Patrick. 'Recasting a tradition: William Molyneux and the sources of *The Case of Ireland . . . Stated* (1698)', A170, 83–106.

5658.   Kennedy, Máire. 'Charles Praval: an eighteenth-century French teacher in Dublin', *Dublin Historical Record* 52 (1999), 126–37.

5659.   Koeper-Saul, Veronika. 'The study of German in TCD and the acquisition of German language works by the library in the nineteenth century', A125, 151–66.

5660.   O'Connor, T. 'The role of Irish clerics in Paris University politics 1730–40', *History of Universities* 15 (1999), 193–226.

5661.   O'Donoghue, T.A. 'Catholic influence and the secondary school curriculum in Ireland, 1922–1962', *History of Education Review* 28:2 (1999), 16–29.

5662.   O'Donoghue, Thomas A. *The Catholic Church and the secondary school curriculum in Ireland, 1922–1962* (Irish Studies, 5) (New York: Peter Lang, 1999), 183p.

5663.   Ó hAnnracháin, Tadhg. '"Though hereticks and politicians should misinterpret their good zeale": political ideology and Catholicism in early modern Ireland', A170, 155–75.

5664.   Ohlmeyer, Jane H. 'Introduction' [Political thought in seventeenth-century Ireland], A170, 1–34.

5665.   Pašeta, Senia. 'The Catholic hierarchy and the Irish university question, 1880–1908', *History* 85 (2000), 268–84.

5666.   Pašeta, Senia. 'Trinity College, Dublin, and the education of Irish Catholics, 1873–1908', *Studia Hibernica* 30 (1998–99), 7–20.

5667.   Pocock, J.G.A. 'The third kingdom in its history: an afterword', A170, 271–80.

5668.   Raftery, Deirdre. 'Home education in nineteenth century Ireland: the role and status of the governess', *Irish Educational Studies* 19 (2000), 308–17.

Fd. *Culture and the Arts*

See also 1730 (F); 2458 (G); 3189 (H); 4122 (I); 5332, 5371, 5376, 5387 (L); 5558, 5575, 5621, 5631, 5642, 5652, 5756–7, 5827 (M)

5669.   Allison, Jonathan. 'Acts of memory: poetry and the republic of Ireland since 1949', A188, 44–63.

5670.   Backus, Margot Gayle. *The gothic family romance: heterosexuality, child sacrifice, and the Anglo-Irish colonial order* (Durham (NC): Duke University Press, 1999), xi, 291p.

5671.   Belanger, Jacqueline. 'The desire of the west: the Aran Islands and Irish identity in *Grania*', A137, 95–107.

5672.   Beranger, Gabriel. *Drawings of the principal antique buildings of Ireland: National Library of Ireland MS 1958 TX*, ed. Peter Harbison (Dublin: Four Courts, 1998), 228p.

5673.   Botkin, Frances. 'Edgeworth and Wordsworth: plain unvarnished tales', A137, 140–55.

5674.   Boydell, Barra. 'Music in the nineteenth-century cathedral, 1800–70' [Christ Church Cathedral, Dublin], A151, 339–52.

5675.   Boydell, Barra. 'Optimism and decline: music, 1870–c.1970' [Christ Church Cathedral, Dublin], A151, 374–85.

5676.	Boydell, Barra. 'The flourishing of music, 1660–1800' [Christ Church Cathedral, Dublin], A151, 298–314.

5677.	Campbell, M. 'Thomas Moore's wild song: the 1821 *Irish Melodies*', *Bullán: an Irish Studies Review* 4:2 (2000), 83–104.

5678.	Caraher, Brian. 'Edgeworth, Wilde and Joyce: reading Irish regionalism through "the cracked lookingglass" of a servant's art', A137, 123–35.

5679.	Clutterbuck, Catriona. 'Irish women's poetry and the republic of Ireland: formalism as form', A188, 17–43.

5680.	Corbett, Mary Jean. *Allegories of Union in Irish and English writing, 1790–1870: politics, history, and the family from Edgeworth to Arnold* (Cambridge: Cambridge University Press, 2000), x, 228p.

5681.	Cullen, Fintan (ed.) *Sources in Irish art: a reader* (Cork: Cork University Press, 2000).

5682.	Cunningham, Bernadette. *The world of Geoffrey Keating: history, myth and religion in seventeenth-century Ireland* (Dublin: Four Courts, 2000), xv, 263p.

5683.	Dibble, J. 'Musical nationalism in Ireland in the twentieth century: complexities and contradictions', A142, 133–44.

5684.	Fleischmann, Ruth. *Aloys Fleischmann (1910–92): a life for music in Ireland remembered by contemporaries* (Dublin: Mercier, 2000), 430p.

5685.	Harbison, Peter. *Cooper's Ireland: drawings and notes from an eighteenth-century gentleman* [National Library of Ireland Mss. 2122TX (1) and (2)] (Dublin: The O'Brien Press in association with the National Library of Ireland, 2000).

5686.	Haslam, Richard. 'Irish film: screening the republic', A188, 130–46.

5687.	Heyck, Thomas William. 'The genealogy of Irish modernism: the case of W.B. Yeats', A27, 220–51.

5688.	Kennedy, S.B. 'An Irish school of art? Depictions of the landscape in a critical period, 1880–1930', A126, 153–68.

5689.	Kinane, Vincent. 'Legal deposit, 1801–1922' [of books in Trinity College Dublin Library], A125, 120–37.

5690.	Kirkland, R. '"The shanachie of Belfast and its red-brick Gaeltacht": Cathal O'Byrne', *Bullán: an Irish Studies Review* 4:2 (2000), 67–82.

5691.	Klein, A. 'An "old eminence among musical nations": nationalism and the case for a musical history in Ireland', A142, 233–36.

5692.	Maume, Patrick. 'The papish minister: Shan Bullock, John Haughton Steele, and the literary portrayal of the nineteenth-century clergyman', A137, 108–22.

5693.	McAteer, Michael. '"Ireland and the hour": paternalism and nationality in Standish James O'Grady's *Toryism and the Tory Democracy*', A137, 199–214.

5694.	McBride, Lawrence W. 'Imagining the nation in Irish historical fiction, c.1870–c.1925', A27, 81–107.

5695.	McCarthy, Conor. *Modernisation, crisis and culture in Ireland, 1969–1992* (Dublin: Four Courts, 2000), 240p.

5696.	McCormack, W.J. *Fool of the family: a life of J.M. Synge* (London: Weidenfeld & Nicolson, 2000), xii, 500p.

5697.	Morash, Chris. '"Something's missing": theatre and the Republic of Ireland Act', A188, 64–81.

5698. Nicholson, Ciaran; O'Brien, Ann. 'A select bibliography of the library' [Trinity College Dublin Library], A125, 167–76.

5699. Nicholson, Ciaran. 'A selection of published illustrations relating to the library: buildings, people, and some artifacts' [Trinity College Dublin], A125, 177–85.

5700. Norman, Paralee. *Marmion Wilme Savage, 1804–1872: Dublin's Victorian satirist* (Lewiston (NY): Edwin Mellen, 2000), xii, 133p.

5701. Ó Catháin, Diarmaid. 'General Baron Edmund Harold (1737–1808): a "Celtic" writer in Germany', *Studia Hibernica* 30 (1998–99), 119–53.

5702. Ó Giolláin, Diarmuid. *Locating Irish folklore, tradition, modernity, identity* (Cork: Cork University Press, 2000), 228p.

5703. O'Neill, Marie. *Grace Gifford Plunkett and Irish freedom* (Dublin and Portland (OR): Irish Academic Press, 2000), 117p.

5704. Pappas, George S. *Berkeley's thought* (Ithaca (NY): Cornell University Press, 2000), xi, 261p.

5705. Ryan, Ray. 'Introduction: state and nation: the republic and Ireland, 1949–99', A188, 1–13.

5706. Ryan, Ray. 'The republic and Ireland: pluralism, politics, and narrative form', A188, 82–100.

5707. Sagarra, Eda. 'Modern languages in Ireland: yesterday, today, tomorrow', A50, 30–43.

5708. Sheehy, David C. 'The "brick palace" at Drumcondra: Archbishop Walsh and the building of archbishop's house', A121, 313–30.

5709. Taaffe, Seamus. 'Commemorating the fallen: public memorials to the Irish dead of the Great War', *Archaeology Ireland* 13:3 (1999), 18–22.

5710. Walsh, Anne. 'The library as revealed in the Parliamentary Commission report of 1853' [Trinity College Dublin Library], A125, 138–50.

5711. Whelan, Kevin. 'Writing Ireland: reading England', A137, 185–98.

G. *Religious Belief, Practice and Organisation*

See also 485 (B); 3318, 3338 (H); 4157, 4164 (I); 5403, 5413–14, 5443 (L); 5543, 5548, 5577, 5611–13, 5636, 5640, 5663, 5682, 5692, 5708, 5727, 5734, 5749, 5756–7, 5794, 5825, 5831, 5835, 5862, 5865, 5887 (M)

5712. Biletz, Frank A. 'The *Irish Peasant* and the conflict between Irish-Ireland and the Catholic bishops', A27, 108–29.

5713. Bolster, Angela. 'The story of Mercy in Derry', A114, 187–207.

5714. Brown, Stewart J. 'The New Reformation Movement in the Church of Ireland, 1801–29', A27, 180–208.

5715. Costello, Con. *Faith or fatherhood? Bishop Dunboyne's dilemma: the story of John Butler, Catholic bishop of Cork 1763–1787* (Dublin: Woodfield, 2000), xxi, 105p. [Revised edition of *In Quest of an Heir: The Life and Times of John Butler, Catholic Bishop of Cork, Protestant Bishop of Dunboyne* (Cork: Tower Books, 1978).]

5716. Donnelly, James S. (Jr.) 'The peak of Marianism in Ireland, 1930–60', A27, 252–83.

5717. Dooley, Terence A.M. *The plight of Monaghan protestants, 1912–1926* (Maynooth Studies in Irish Local History, 31) (Dublin: Irish Academic Press, 2000), 64p.

5718. Enright, Séamus. 'Women and Catholic life in Dublin, 1766–1852', A121, 268–93.

5719. Fennessy, Ignatius. 'Receptions and professions at the Ennis Novitiate of the Friars Minor, 1877–85 (FLK, MS C 622, int.3)', *Collectanea Hibernica* 41 (1999), 225–30.

5720. Fenning, Hugh. 'The archbishops of Dublin, 1693–1786', A121, 175–214.

5721. Firtéar, Pádraig (ed.) *Na Bráithre Críostaí i gCorca Dhuibhne: a scéal* (An Daingean: An Sagart, 2000)

5722. Geary, Trevor R. *Armaghbreague Presbyterian Church: 150 years of Christian witness, 1847–1997* (Armagh: Armaghbreague Presbyterian Church 150th Committee, 1997), vi, 318p.

5723. Gillespie, Raymond. 'Catholic religious cultures in the diocese of Dublin, 1614–97', A121, 127–43.

5724. Greaves, Richard L. 'The "Great Persecution" reconsidered: the Irish Quakers and the Ethic of suffering', A147, 211–33.

5725. Griffin, Patrick. 'Defining the limits of Britishness: the "new" British history and the meaning of the Revolution Settlement in Ireland for Ulster's Presbyterians', *Journal of British Studies* 39:3 (2000), 263–87.

5726. Hartigan, Maurice. 'The religious life of the Catholic laity of Dublin, 1920–40', A121, 331–48.

5727. Kelly, James. 'Conservative Protestant political thought in late eighteenth-century Ireland', A51, 185–220.

5728. Kelly, James. 'The impact of the penal laws' [in the diocese of Dublin], A121, 144–74.

5729. Keogh, Dáire. '"The pattern of the flock": John Thomas Troy, 1786–1823', A121, 215–36.

5730. Kerr, Donal. 'Dublin's forgotten archbishop: Daniel Murray, 1768–1852', A121, 247–67.

5731. Laheen, Kevin A. 'Jesuit parish mission memoirs 1863–76, part II', *Collectanea Hibernica* 41 (1999), 153–24.

5732. Ledwidge, John. 'The Christian Brothers and the diocese of Derry', A114, 208–23.

5733. Madden, Finbar J.; Bradley, Thomas. 'The diocese of Derry in the twentieth century', A114, 240–58.

5734. McCarthy, Michael. 'Dublin's Greek pro-cathedral', A121, 237–46.

5735. McCormack, Bridget. *Perceptions of St Patrick in eighteenth-century Ireland* (Dublin: Four Courts, 2000), 119p.

5736. McLaughlin, Stephen. 'The development of the Catholic church in Derry under the leadership of Bishop Francis Kelly (1849–88)', A114, 224–39.

5737. McMahon, Deirdre. 'John Charles McQuaid: archbishop of Dublin, 1940–72', A121, 349–80.

5738. Miller, David W. 'Mass attendance in Ireland in 1834', A27, 158–79.

5739. Millett, Benignus. 'Calendar of volume 16 of the *Fondo di Vienna* in Propaganda Archives: Part 3, ff 217–80', *Collectanea Hibernica* 41 (1999), 10–35.

5740. Millett, Benignus. 'Lease of the Friary of Crevalea (Dromahaire) in County Leitrim to Owen Wynne, 1 April 1658', *Collectanea Hibernica* 41 (1999), 7–9.

5741. Milne, Kenneth. 'Restoration and reorganisation, 1660–1830' [Christ Church Cathedral, Dublin], A151, 255–97.

5742. Milne, Kenneth. 'The stripping of the assets, 1830–1960' [Christ Church Cathedral, Dublin], A151, 315–38.

5743. Mirala, Petri. '"A large mob, calling themselves freemasons": masonic parades in Ulster', A118, 117–38.

5744. Moloney, R. 'Charles Stokes (1852–1895): an Irishman in 19th century Africa', *Studies* [Dublin] 87:346 (1998), 128–34.

5745. Morrissey, Thomas J. *William J. Walsh, Archbishop of Dublin, 1841–1921, no uncertain voice* (Dublin: Four Courts, 2000).

5746. O'Carroll, Ciaran. 'The pastoral politics of Paul Cullen', A121, 294–312.

5747. Ó Doibhlin, Diarmaid. 'Penal days' [in the diocese of Derry], A114, 167–86.

5748. O'Glaisne, Risteard. *De Bhunadh Protastúnach nó rian Chonradh na Gaeilge* (Carbad, n.d.)

5749. Pocock, J.G.A. 'Protestant Ireland: the view from a distance', A51, 221–30.

5750. Prunty, Jacinta. 'Margaret Louisa Aylward', A59, 55–88.

5751. Purcell, Mary. 'Dublin Diocesan Archives: Hamilton papers (10)', *Archivium Hibernicum* 53 (1999), 36–72. Extracts 1843 and 1844 from calendar of the papers of Dr John Hamilton (1800–62).]

5752. Rafferty, Oliver P. 'Carleton's ecclesiastical context: the Ulster Catholic experience', *Bullán: an Irish Studies Review* 4:2 (2000), 105–124.

5753. Rafferty, Oliver P. *Catholicism in Ulster, 1603–1983: an interpretative history* (Dublin: Gill & Macmillan, 1994), xiv, 306p.

5754. Refaussé, Raymond. *Church of Ireland records* (Maynooth Research Guides for Irish Local History, 1) (Dublin: Irish Academic Press, 2000).

5755. Ryan, Christopher. *The Parish of St. John the Evangelist, Ballinteer: Silver Jubilee of the Parish (1973–1998)* (Ballinteer, Dublin: Ballinteer Family History Society, 1998), 124p.

5756. Stalley, Roger (ed.) *George Edmund Street and the restoration of Christ Church Cathedral, Dublin* (Dublin: Four Courts, 2000).

5757. Stalley, Roger. 'George Edmund Street and the restoration of the cathedral, 1868–78' [Christ Church Cathedral, Dublin], A151, 353–73.

5758. Watters, Enda (ed.) *Go teach all nations: a history of the Irish Province of the Congregation of the Holy Spirit* (Dublin: Paraclete, 2000), xi, 464p.

5759. Whelan, Ruth. 'L'Irlande religieuse à l'époque de Édit de Nantes, ou le refus ambigu de la diversité', A64, 108–26.

Ha. *Law and Order*

See also 4290 (I); 5609 (M); 6531 (P)

5760. Allen, Gregory. *The Gárda Síochána: policing independent Ireland, 1922–82* (Dublin: Gill & Macmillan, 1999), xii, 306p.

5761. Brewer, J.D.; Lockhart, Bill; Rodgers, Paula. 'Crime in Ireland 1945–95', *Proceedings of the British Academy* 98 (1999), 161–86.
5762. Carroll-Burke, Patrick. *Colonial discipline: the making of the Irish convict system* (Maynooth Historical Studies (Dublin: Four Courts, 2000), 256p.
5763. Devereaux, Simon. 'Irish convict transportation and the reach of the state in late Hanoverian Britain', *Journal of the Canadian Historical Association* ns 8 (1997), 61–85.
5764. Dowling, J.A. 'The Irish Court of Appeal in Chancery 1857–77', *Journal of Legal History* 21:2 (2000), 83–118.
5765. Hanafin, Patrick. 'Legal texts as cultural documents: interpreting the Irish constitution', A188, 147–64.
5766. Hart, A.R. *A history of the king's sergeants at law in Dublin: honour rather than advantage* (Dublin: Four Courts, 2000), xvi, 213p.
5767. Herlihy, Jim. *The Royal Irish Constabulary: a complete alphabetical list of officers and men, 1816–1922* (Dublin: Four Courts, 1999), xxxi, 488p.
5768. Hogan, Gerard. 'The Supreme Court and the reference of the Offences against the State Bill, 1940', *Irish Jurist* 35 (2000), 238–79.
5769. Ibbetson, David. 'Legal printing and legal doctrine', *Irish Jurist* 35 (2000), 345–54.
5770. Jackson, John; Quinn, Katie; O'Malley, Tom. 'The jury system in contemporary Ireland: in the shadows of a troubled past', *Law and Contemporary Problems* 62:2 (1999), 203–32.
5771. Jeffery, Keith. 'Parades, police and government in Northern Ireland, 1922–1969', A83, 78–94.
5772. Malcolm, Elizabeth. '"The reign of terror in Carlow": the politics of policing Ireland in the late 1830s', *Irish Historical Studies* 32 (2000), 59–74.
5773. McMahon, Richard. 'The regional administration of a central legal policy', A137, 158–68.
5774. Osborough, W.N. 'Law and the spread of literacy: millennial reflections on Boddington's plight', *Irish Jurist* 35 (2000), 36–61.
5775. Osborough, W.N. *Studies in Irish legal history* (Dublin: Four Courts, 1999), xi, 340p.
5776. Osborough, W.N. 'The history of Irish legal publishing: a challenge unmet', *Irish Jurist* 35 (2000), 355–74.
5777. Ryder, Chris. *The RUC 1922–2000: a force under fire*, revised (4th) edn. (London: Arrow, 2000), xviii, 536p.
5778. Scanlon, Mary. *The Dublin Metropolitan Police* (London: Minerva, 1998), 75p.

Hb. *Public Administration*

See also 5451, 5455 (L)

5779. Barnard, Toby C. 'The viceregal court in later seventeenth-century Ireland', A58, 256–65.
5780. Costello, Peter. *Dublin Castle in the life of the Irish nation* (Dublin: Wolfhound, 2000), 160p.

5781.   Cronin, Mike; Regan, John M. 'Introduction' [Ireland: the politics of independence, 1922–49: new perspectives and re-considerations], A57, 1–12.
5782.   McCavery, Trevor. 'Politics, public finance and the British-Irish Act of Union of 1801', *Transactions of the Royal Historical Society* 6th ser. 10 (2000), 353–75.
5783.   O'Callaghan, Antóin. *The lord mayors of Cork, 1900–2000* (Cork: Inversnaid Publications, 2000), 180p.

Hc. *Political and Constitutional*

See also 1991, 2008, 2014, 2024, 2038, 2040, 2044, 2050 (F); 2568, 2570, 2583, 2590 (G); 3483 (H); 4200, 4290, 4351 (I); 5284, 5456, 5469 (L); 5508, 5569, 5591, 5597, 5603, 5608, 5622, 5625, 5629, 5646, 5653, 5680, 5700, 5703, 5743, 5749, 5781, 5795–6, 5877 (M); 6531 (P)

5784.   Adolph, Anthony R.J.S. 'The Earl of St. Alban's, the Marquess of Antrim and the Irish Acts of Settlement and Explanation, 1660–1684', *Irish Genealogist* 10 (1999), 234–39.
5785.   Ball, Stephen. 'Crowd activity during the Irish Land War, 1879–90', A118, 212–48.
5786.   Barnard, Toby C. *Cromwellian Ireland: English government and reform in Ireland, 1649–1660* (Oxford: Clarendon, 2000), xxxii, 349p.
5787.   Bernstein, George L. 'British Liberal politics and Irish Liberalism after O'Connell', A27, 43–64.
5788.   Blackstock, Allan. '"The invincible mass": loyal crowds in mid-Ulster, 1795–1796', A118, 83–114.
5789.   Blackstock, Allan. 'The Union and the military, 1801–c.1830', *Transactions of the Royal Historical Society* 6th ser. 10 (2000), 329–51.
5790.   Bryan, Dominic. 'Drumcree and the "right to march": Orangeism, ritual and politics in Northern Ireland', A83, 191–207.
5791.   Campbell, Fergus. 'The hidden history of the Irish land war: a guide to local sources', A126, 140–52.
5792.   Campbell, Malcolm. 'Emigrant responses to war and revolution, 1914–21: Irish opinion in the United States and Australia', *Irish Historical Studies* 32:125 (2000), 75–92.
5793.   Chambers, Ian. 'Winston Churchill and Irish Home Rule, 1899–1914', *Parliamentary History* 19:3 (2000), 405–21.
5794.   Conlon, Larry. 'Dissension, radicalism, and republicanism in Monaghan and the role of freemasonry up to and during the 1798 rebellion', *Clogher Record* 16:3 (1999), 86–111.
5795.   Connolly, S.J. 'Introduction: varieties of Irish political thought', A51, 11–26.
5796.   Connolly, S.J. 'Precedent and principle: the patriots and their critics', A51, 130–58.
5797.   Connolly, S.J. 'Reconsidering the Irish Act of Union', *Transactions of the Royal Historical Society* 6th ser. 10 (2000), 399–408.
5798.   Connolly, S.J. 'The Glorious Revolution in Irish Protestant political thinking', A51, 27–63.

5799. Costello, Peter. 'Land and Liam O'Flaherty', A126, 169–79.
5800. Côté, Jane; Hearne, Dana. 'Anna Parnell', A59, 263–93.
5801. Coulter, Colin. '"A miserable failure of a state": unionist intellectuals and the Irish republic', A188, 204–25.
5802. Cox, Adrian; Guelke, Fiona. *A farewell to arms? From 'long war' to long peace in Northern Ireland* (Manchester and New York: Manchester University Press and St Martin's Press, 2000), 360p.
5803. Cronin, Maura. '"Of one mind?": O'Connellite crowds in the 1830s and 1840s', A118, 139–72.
5804. Cullen, L.M. 'Alliances and misalliances in the politics of the Union', *Transactions of the Royal Historical Society* 6th ser. 10 (2000), 221–41.
5805. Cullen, Mary. 'Anna Maria Haslam', A59, 161–96.
5806. Daly, Edward. 'The "troubles"', A114, 259–96.
5807. Davis, William J. 'William James MacNeven: chemist and United Irishman', A219, 7–24.
5808. Devine, Francis. 'An index to the sources for labour historians in *Saothar*: a working journal' [Journal of the Irish Labour History Society], *Irish Archives* 6:2 (1999), 18–29.
5809. Dooley, Dolores. 'Anna Doyle Wheeler', A59, 19–53.
5810. Doyle, John. *"Ulster like Israel can only lose once": Ulster unionism, security and citizenship, 1972–97* (Research Papers, 31) (Dublin: Dublin City University Business School, 1997), 29p.
5811. Doyle, William. 'The Union in a European context', *Transactions of the Royal Historical Society* 6th ser. 10 (2000), 167–80.
5812. Dunn, Seamus. 'Bloody Sunday and its commemoration parades', A83, 129–41.
5813. Dunphy, Richard. 'The enigma of Fianna Fail: party strategy, social classes and the politics of hegemony', A57, 67–83.
5814. Farry, Michael. *The aftermath of revolution: Sligo 1921–23* (Dublin: University College Dublin Press, 2000), 270p.
5815. Flynn, M.K. *Ideology, mobilization and the nation: the rise of Irish, Basque and Carlist nationalist movements in the nineteenth and early twentieth centuries* (Basingstoke: Macmillan, 2000), xiii, 238p.
5816. Foy, Michael; Barton, Brian. *The Easter Rising* (Stroud: Sutton, 1999), 274p.
5817. Fraser, Grace; Morgan, Valerie. '"Miracle on the Shankill": the Peace March and Rally of 28 August 1976', A83, 142–57.
5818. Fraser, T.G. 'The apprentice boys and the relief of Derry parades', A83, 173–90.
5819. Garvin, Tom. 'A quiet revolution: the remaking of Irish political culture', A188, 187–203.
5820. Geoghegan, Patrick. 'The Catholics and the Union', *Transactions of the Royal Historical Society* 6th ser. 10 (2000), 243–58.
5821. Girvin, Brian. 'The British state and Northern Ireland: can the national question be reformed?', A39, 255–94.
5822. Hayes, William Joseph. *Tipperary in the year of rebellion 1798* (Roscrea (Co. Tipperary): Lisheen, 1998), 110p.
5823. Hill, Jacqueline. 'Corporatist ideology and practice in Ireland, 1660–1800', A51, 64–82.

5824. Hooper, Glenn. 'The pursuit of signs: searching for Ireland after the Union', A137, 215–32.

5825. Hoppen, K. Theodore. 'Riding a tiger: Daniel O'Connell, reform, and popular politics in Ireland, 1800–1847', *Proceedings of the British Academy* 100 (1999), 121–43.

5826. Inoue, Keiko. 'Sinn Féin propaganda and the "Partition Election", 1921', *Studia Hibernica* 30 (1998–99), 47–61.

5827. Jarman, Neil. 'For God and Ulster: blood and thunder bands and loyalist political culture', A83, 158–72.

5828. Jarman, Neil; Bryan, Dominic. 'Green parades in an Orange state: nationalist and republican commemorations and demonstrations from Partition to the Troubles, 1920–1970', A83, 95–110.

5829. Jeffery, Keith. *Ireland and the Great War* (Cambridge: Cambridge University Press, 2000), xiv, 208p.

5830. Jupp, Peter; Magennis, Eoin. 'Introduction: crowds in Ireland c.1730–1920', A118, 1–42.

5831. Kearney, Hugh F. '1875: faith or fatherland? The contested symbolism of Irish nationalism', A27, 65–80.

5832. Kelly, James. 'Introduction: the emergence of political parading, 1660–1800', A83, 9–26.

5833. Kelly, James. 'Popular politics in Ireland and the Act of Union', *Transactions of the Royal Historical Society* 6th ser. 10 (2000), 259–88.

5834. Kelly, Patrick. 'The politics of political economy in mid-eighteenth-century Ireland', A51, 105–29.

5835. Kerr, Donal A. 'Priests, pikes and patriots: the Irish Catholic church and political violence from the Whiteboys to the Fenians', A27, 16–42.

5836. Kinsella, Anna. *Women of Wexford 1798–1998* (Courtown: Courtown Publications, 1998), xv, 126p.

5837. Lee, J.J. 'On the birth of the modern Irish state: the Larkin thesis', A27, 130–57.

5838. Legg, Marie-Louise (ed.) *Alfred Webb: the autobiography of a Quaker nationalist* (Cork: Cork University Press, 2000), 100p.

5839. Little, Patrick. 'The first unionists? Irish Protestant attitudes to union with England, 1653–9', *Irish Historical Studies* 32 (2000), 44–58.

5840. Little, Patrick. 'The Marquess of Ormond and the English parliament, 1645–1647', A12, 83–99.

5841. Loughlin, James. 'Parades and politics: Liberal governments and the Orange Order, 1880–1886', A83, 27–43.

5842. Luddy, Maria. 'Isabella M.S. Tod', A59, 197–230.

5843. MacCormick, D. Neil. 'Stands Scotland still where she did? New unions for old in the islands', *Irish Jurist* 35 (2000), 1–16.

5844. Magennis, Eoin. *The Irish political system, 1740–1765: the golden age of the undertakers* (Dublin: Four Courts, 2000), 231p.

5845. Mahony, Robert. 'Protestant dependence and consumption in Swift's Irish writings', A51, 83–104.

5846. Matthew, Colin. 'Gladstone, O'Connell and Home Rule', A50, 11–29.

5847. Maume, Patrick. *Rebel on the run: T.J. Quinn and the IRB/Land League diaspora in America* (Working Papers in Irish Studies, 1) (Fort Lauderdale (FL): Nova Southeastern University, 2000), 12p.

5848. McGrath, Charles Ivar. *The making of the eighteenth-century Irish constitution: government, parliament and the revenue, 1692–1714* (Dublin: Four Courts, 2000), 314p.

5849. McBride, Ian. 'The harp without the crown: nationalism and republicanism in the 1790s', A51, 159–84.

5850. McDonald, Henry. *Trimble* (London: Bloomsbury, 2000), [vii], 342p.

5851. McDonnell, A.D. *The life of Sir Denis Henry: Catholic Unionist* (Belfast: Ulster Historical Foundation, 2000), [iv], 156p.

5852. McIntosh, Gillian. 'Symbolic mirrors: commemorations of Edward Carson in the 1930s', *Irish Historical Studies* 32 (2000), 93–112.

5853. Michelucci, Riccardo. 'Una repubblica nel Commonwealth: le relazioni diplomatiche tra la Gran Bretagna e lo Stato Libero d'Irlanda dal 1932 al 1938' [The diplomatic relations between Great Britain and the Irish Free State, 1932–1938], *Storia delle Relazioni Internazionali* 11–12:2 (1997), 39–84.

5854. Mulholland, Marc. 'Assimilation versus segregation: Unionist strategy in the 1960s', *20th Century British History* 11:3 (2000), 284–307.

5855. Murphy, Clare. 'Varieties of crowd activity from Fenianism to the Land War, 1867–79', A118, 173–86.

5856. O'Callaghan, M. 'Old parchment and water: the Boundary Commission of 1925 and the copperfastening of the Irish border', *Bullán: an Irish Studies Review* 4:2 (2000), 27–55.

5857. Ó Ciardha, Éamonn. '"The Unkinde Deserter" and "The Bright Duke": contrasting views of the dukes of Ormonde in the Irish royalist tradition', A12, 177–93.

5858. O'Donnell, Ruán. *Aftermath: post-rebellion insurgency in Wicklow, 1799–1803* (Dublin and Portland (OR): Irish Academic, 2000), xiv, 272p.

5859. O'Neill, Bairbre. 'The referendum process in Ireland', *Irish Jurist* 35 (2000), 305–44.

5860. O'Shea, James. *Prince of swindlers: John Sadleir MP 1813–1856* (Templeogue (Dub): Geography Publications, 2000), x, 509p.

5861. Pašeta, Senia. 'Ireland's last Home Rule generation: the decline of constitutional nationalism in Ireland, 1916–30', A57, 13–31.

5862. Rafferty, Oliver P. *The church, the state and the Fenian threat, 1861–75* (Basingstoke: Macmillan, 1999), xviii, 229p.

5863. Raftery, Deirdre. 'Frances Power Cobbe', A59, 89–123.

5864. Regan, John M. 'The politics of utopia: party politics, executive autonomy and the new administration', A57, 32–66.

5865. Riordan, Susannah. 'The unpopular front: Catholic revival and Irish cultural identity, 1932–48', A57, 98–120.

5866. Rose, Peter. *How the troubles came to Northern Ireland* (Basingstoke: Macmillan, 2000), xviii, 216p.

5867. Saison, Ghislaine. 'La ville de New York vue par les nationalistes irlandais dans la seconde moitié du XIXe siècle' [the city of New York as seen by Irish Nationalists in the second half of the 19th century], A34, 85–97.

5868.   Sloan, Robert. *William Smith O'Brien and the Young Ireland rebellion of 1848* (Dublin: Four Courts, 2000), 320p.
5869.   Stöter, Eva Maria. 'Region vs. nation: nineteenth-century "Germany" as a mirror for Irish regional/national politics', A137, 87–94.
5870.   Tonge, Jonathan. 'From Sunningdale to the Good Friday agreement: creating devolved government in Northern Ireland', *Contemporary British History* 14:3 (2000), 39–60.
5871.   Travers, Pauric. 'Davitt after the Land League', A126, 83–100.

J. Military

See also 2109, 2113 (F); 4290 (I); 5635, 5780, 5789 (M); 6609 (P)

5872.   Bell, J. Bowyer. *The IRA, 1968–2000: analysis of a secret army* (Ilford: Frank Cass, 2000), xx, 351p.
5873.   Canny, Liam. 'Pariah dogs: deserters from the Irish Defence Forces who joined the British Armed Forces during "The Emergency"', *Studia Hibernica* 30 (1998/99), 231–49.
5874.   Clifton, R. '"An indiscriminate blackness"? Massacre, counter-massacre, and ethnic cleansing in Ireland, 1640–1660', *War and Genocide* 1 (1999), 107–26.
5875.   Doherty, Richard. *Irish men and women in the Second World War* (Dublin: Four Courts, 1999), 319p.
5876.   Hall, Brendan (comp.) *The Louth Rifles, 1877–1908* (Irish Genealogical Sources, 21) (Dun Laoghaire: Dun Laoghaire Genealogical Society, 2000), 160p.
5877.   Mac Suibhne, Breandán. 'Whiskey, potatoes and true-born patriot paddies: volunteering and the construction of the Irish nation in northwest Ulster, 1770–1789', A118, 45–82.
5878.   Wheeler, James Scott. *Cromwell in Ireland* (Dublin: Gill & Macmillan, 1999), ix, 305p.

K. Foreign Affairs

See also 3627, 3629, 3632–3 (I); 5525, 5573, 5599, 5605, 5701, 5811 (M)

5879.   Doerries, Reinhard R. *Prelude to the Easter Rising: Sir Roger Casement in imperial Germany* (London: Cass, 2000), xiv, 233p.
5880.   Fanning, Ronan. 'Dublin: the view from a neutral capital', A169, 103–16.
5881.   Kennedy, Michael. *Division and consensus: the politics of cross border relations in Ireland, 1925–1969* (Dublin: Institute of Public Administration, 2000), 422p.
5882.   Lowry, Donal. 'New Ireland, old empire and the outside world, 1922–49: the strange evolution of a "dictionary republic"', A57, 164–216.
5883.   Miller, Kerby A. '"Scotch-Irish", "black Irish" and "real Irish": emigrants and identities in the old South', A15, 139–57.
5884.   O'Brien, Miriam Hederman. 'Ireland's contribution to the evolution of Europe', A50, 44–55.

5885. O'Duffy, Brendan. 'British and Irish conflict regulation from Sunningdale to Belfast, part II: Playing for a draw, 1985–1999', *Nations and Nationalism* 6:3 (2000), 399–435.

5886. Rouffiac, Nathalie Genet. 'The Irish Jacobite exile in France, 1692–1715', A12, 195–209.

5887. Wiel, Jerome de. 'Monsignor O'Riordan, Bishop O'Dwyer and the shaping of new relations between nationalist Ireland and the Vatican during World War I', *Archivium Hibernicum* 53 (1999), 95–106.

N. EMPIRE TO 1783

A. *General*

See also 1336 (F); 2150 (G); 5897 (N); 6045 (P)

5888. Appiah, Kwame Anthony; Gates, Henry Louis (Jr.) (eds.) *Africana: the encyclopedia of the African and African American experience* (New York: Basic Civitas Books, 1999), xxxvii, 2095p.

5889. Armitage, David. 'The British conception of Empire in the eighteenth century', A6, 91–107.

5890. Bailyn, Bernard. 'The first British empire: from Cambridge to Oxford. An essay-review of The Oxford History of the British Empire, volume I: The Origins of Empire: British Overseas Enterprise to the Close of the Seventeenth Century, and volume II: The Eighteenth Century', *William and Mary Quarterly* 57:3 (2000), 647–59.

5891. Bowen, H.V. '400 years of the East India Company', *History Today* 50:7 (2000), 47–53.

5892. Jaffee, David. *People of the Wachusett: greater New England in history and memory, 1630–1860* (Ithaca (NY): Cornell University Press, 1999), xiii, 306p.

5893. Macintyre, Stuart. *A concise history of Australia* (Cambridge: Cambridge University Press, 1999), xiii, 320p.

5894. Marshall, Peter James. 'Britain and the world in the eighteenth century: III. Britain and India', *Transactions of the Royal Historical Society* 6th ser. 10 (2000), 1–16.

5895. Mays, Terry M. *Historical dictionary of the American Revolution* (Lanham (MD) and London: Scarecrow Press, 1998), xxxvi, 555p.

B. *Historiography and Historical Methods*

5896. Ben-Atar, Doron. 'The American Revolution' [Historiography], A214, 94–113.

5897. Canny, Nicholas P. 'Writing Atlantic history; or, reconfiguring the history of colonial British America', *Journal of American History* 86 (1999), 1093–114.

5898. Drayton, Richard. 'Science, medicine, and the British empire' [Historiography], A214, 264–76.
5899. Foster, Stephen. 'British North America in the seventeenth and eighteenth centuries' [Historiography], A214, 73–93.
5900. Frykenberg, Robert Eric. 'India to 1858' [Historiography], A214, 194–213.
5901. Higman, Barry W. 'The British West Indies' [Historiography], A214, 134–45.
5902. Marshall, Peter James. 'The first British empire' [Historiography], A214, 43–53.

C. Population and Environment

See also 2159 (G); 5565 (M); 5888, 5956, 6009 (N); 6229 (P)

5903. Abrams, Ann Uhry. *The pilgrims and Pocahontas: rival myths of American origin* (Boulder (CO): Westview, 1999), xxii, 378p.
5904. Archer, Christon A. 'Whose scourge? Smallpox epidemics on the northwest coast', A85, 165–91.
5905. Baseler, Marilyn C. *'Asylum for mankind': America, 1607–1800* (Ithaca (NY): Cornell University Press, 1998), xi, 353p.
5906. Beiler, Rosalind J. 'Distributing aid to believers in need: the religious foundations of transatlantic migration', A33, 73–87.
5907. Bielenberg, Andy. 'Irish emigration to the British empire, 1700–1914', A15, 215–34.
5908. Canny, Nicholas P. 'Fashioning "British" worlds in the seventeenth century', A33, 26–45.
5909. Davies, Wayne K.D. 'Capt. William Owen and the settlement of Campobello: Montgomeryshire's connection with New Brunswick, Canada. Part I' [1760s], *National Library of Wales Journal* 31:2 (1999), 189–211.
5910. Games, Alison. *Migration and the origins of the English Atlantic world* (Cambridge (MA) and London: Harvard University Press, 1999), xiii, 322p.
5911. Games, Alison. 'The English Atlantic world: a view from London', A33, 46–72.
5912. Gragg, Larry. 'The Port Royal earthquake of 1692', *History Today* 50:9 (2000), 28–34.
5913. Haynes, D.E. 'Conceiving mobility: weavers' migrations in pre-colonial and colonial India', *Indian Economic and Social History Review* 36:1 (1999), 35–68.
5914. Kupperman, Karen Ordahl. 'Needs and opportunities: British expansion', *Itinerario* 18 (1994), 130–36.
5915. Mannion, John. 'Victualling a fishery: Newfoundland diet and the origins of the Irish provisions trade, 1675–1700', *International Journal of Maritime History* 12:1 (2000), 1–60.
5916. Marshall, Peter James. 'The white town of Calcutta under the rule of the East India Company', *Modern Asian Studies* 34:2 (2000), 307–32.
5917. Merrell, James Hart. *Into the American woods: negotiators on the Pennsylvania frontier* (New York and London: Norton, 1999), 463p.

5918.   Raková, Svatava. *Anglické Kolonie v Severní Americe v 17. století: modely politické kultury* (Práce Historického ústavu CAV, Rada A, Monographia, 14) (Praha: Historicky ústav AV CR, 1997), 398p. [With English summary.]

Da. Social Life and Conditions

See also 1375, 1407 (F)

5919.   Crane, Elaine Forman. *Ebb tide in New England: women, seaports, and social change, 1630–1800* (Boston (MA): Northeastern University Press, 1998), x, 333p.
5920.   Dening, Greg. 'The hegemony of laughter: Purea's theatre', A85, 127–46.
5921.   Foster, Thomas A. 'Deficient husbands: manhood, sexual incapacity, and male sexuality in seventeenth-century New England', *William and Mary Quarterly* 56:4 (1999), 723–44.
5922.   Hodges, Graham Russell. *Root & branch: African Americans in New York and east Jersey, 1613–1863* (Chapel Hill (NC): University of North Carolina Press, 1999), xii, 413p.
5923.   Hoffman, Ronald; Mason, Sally D. *Princes of Ireland, planters of Maryland: a Carroll saga, 1500–1782* (Chapel Hill (NC) and London: University of North Carolina Press for the Omohundro Institute of Early American History and Culture, Williamsburg, Virginia, 2000), xxvi, 429p.
5924.   Illick, Joseph E. 'Childhood in the three cultures in early America', A33, 308–23.
5925.   Imbarrato, Susan Clair. *Declarations of independency in eighteenth-century American autobiography* (Knoxville (TN): University of Tennessee Press, 1998), xix, 171p.
5926.   Langford, Paul. 'Manners and character in Anglo-American perceptions, 1750–1850', A135, 76–90.
5927.   Levy, Barry. 'Girls and boys: poor children and the labor market in colonial Massachusetts', A33, 287–307.
5928.   Little, Ann M. 'Men on top? The farmer, the minister, and marriage in early New England', A33, 123–50.
5929.   Nolte, Paul. 'Soziale und kulturelle Identität in der atlantischen Kolonialgesellschaft: das Werk von Jack P. Greene' [Social and cultural identity in Atlantic colonial society: the work of Jack P. Greene], *Zeitschrift für Historische Forschung* 26 (1999), 99–108.
5930.   Northrup, D. 'Igbo and myth Igbo: culture and ethnicity in the Atlantic world, 1600–1850', *Slavery & Abolition* 21:3 (2000), 1–20.
5931.   Oberg, Michael Leroy. *Dominion and civility: English imperialism and native America, 1585–1685* (Ithaca (NY): Cornell University Press, 1999), x, 239p.
5932.   Picart, Lennox O'Riley. 'The Trelawny Maroons and Sir John Wentworth: the struggle to maintain their culture, 1796–1800', *Collections of the Royal Nova Scotia Historical Society* 44 (1995), 165–87.
5933.   Smith, Mark M. 'Culture, commerce, and calendar reform in colonial America', *William and Mary Quarterly* 55 (1998), 557–84.

5934.   Thompson, Peter. *Rum punch & revolution: taverngoing & public life in eighteenth-century Philadelphia* (Philadelphia (PA): University of Pennsylvania Press, 1998), ix, 265p.

5935.   Ward, Harry M. *The War for Independence and the transformation of American society* (London: UCL Press, 1999), x, 310p.

5936.   Wilheit, Mary Catherine. 'Obedience Robins of Long Buckby: a seventeenth-century Virginian', *Northamptonshire Past and Present* 53 (2000), 7–18.

5937.   Zuckerman, M.; et al. 'Deference or defiance in eighteenth-century America? A round table', *Journal of American History* 85 (1998), 13–97.

Db. *Social Structure*

See also 1456 (F); 2550 (G); 5561, 5565 (M); 5888, 5908, 5928, 5937, 5946, 5963, 5981, 6002 (N)

5938.   Beach, A.R. 'A profound pessimism about the empire: the Isle of Pines, English degeneracy and Dutch supremacy', *The Eighteenth Century* 41:1 (2000), 21–36.

5939.   Bracken, Christopher. *The Potlatch papers: a colonial case history* (Chicago (IL): University of Chicago Press, 1997), 276p.

5940.   Cogliano, Francis D. '"We all hoisted the American flag": national identity among American prisoners in Britain during the American Revolution', *Journal of American Studies* 32:1 (1998), 19–37.

5941.   Gould, Eliga H. 'The American revolution in Britain's imperial identity', A135, 23–37.

5942.   Greene, Jack Phillip. 'Liberty, slavery and the transformation of British identity in the eighteenth-century West Indies', *Slavery & Abolition* 21:1 (2000), 1–31.

5943.   Rajan, Balachandra; Sauer, Elizabeth (eds.) *Milton and the imperial vision* (Pittsburgh (PA): Duquesne University Press, 1999), vi, 376p.

Ea. *Economic Activity and Organisation*

See also 1488 (F); 2159, 2239, 2245, 2262, 2272, 2277, 2285 (G); 5888, 5913, 5915–16, 5942, 6003 (N); 6223, 6229 (P)

5944.   Baladouni, Vahé; Makepeace, Margaret (eds.) *Armenian merchants of the seventeenth and early eighteenth centuries: English East India Company sources* (Transactions of the American Philosophical Society, 88:5) (Philadelphia (PA): American Philosophical Society, 1998), xxxvii, 294p.

5945.   Bazis-Selfa, John. 'Slavery and the disciplining of free labor in the colonial mid-Atlantic iron industry', A33, 270–86.

5946.   Bush, Barbara. '"Sable Venus", "she devil" or "drudge"?: British slavery and the "fabulous Fiction" of black women's identities, c.1650–1838', *Women's History Review* 9:4 (2000), 761–90.

5947. Cant, Jeff (ed.) *His Majesty's grant of the Island of St. Helena to the East India Company, 16th December, 1673* (London: The Wanderer, 1999), 141p. [A limited edition of 100 copies.]

5948. Dunn, E.E. '"Grasping at the shadow": the Massachusetts currency debate, 1690–1751', *New England Quarterly* 71 (1998), 54–76.

5949. Egnal, Marc. *New world economies: the growth of the thirteen colonies and early Canada* (New York: Oxford University Press, 1998), xix, 236p.

5950. Eltis, David; Engerman, Stanley L. 'The importance of slavery and the slave trade to industrialising Britain', *Journal of Economic History* 60:1 (2000), 123–44.

5951. Eltis, David. *The rise of African slavery in the Americas* (Cambridge: Cambridge University Press, 2000), 353p.

5952. Faber, Eli. *Jews, slaves, and the slave trade: setting the record straight* (New York: New York University Press, 1998), xvii, 266p.

5953. Finkelman, Paul; Miller, Joseph Calder (eds.) *Macmillan encyclopedia of world slavery* (New York and London: Macmillan Reference USA, Simon & Schuster Macmillan, & Prentice Hall International, 1998), 2 vols.

5954. Fiske, Jo-Anne; Sleeper-Smith, Susan; Wicken, William (eds.) *New faces of the fur trade: selected papers of the Seventh North American Fur Trade Conference, Halifax, Nova Scotia, 1995* (East Lansing (MI): Michigan State University Press, 1998), ix, 358p.

5955. Galvin, Peter R. *Patterns of pillage: a geography of Caribbean-based piracy in Spanish America, 1536–1718* (New York: Peter Lang, 1999), xiv, 271p.

5956. Govier, M. 'The Royal Society, slavery, and the island of Jamaica 1660–1700', *Notes & Records of the Royal Society* (of London) 53:2 (1999), 203–17.

5957. Grant, Hugh. 'Bookkeeping in the eighteenth century: the grand journal and grand ledger of the Hudson's Bay Company', *Archivaria* 43 (1997), 143–57.

5958. Hancock, David. '"A world of business to do": William Freeman and the foundations of England's commercial empire, 1645–1707', *William and Mary Quarterly* 3rd ser. 57:1 (2000), 3–34.

5959. Hancock, David. 'Transatlantic trade in the era of the American revolution', A135, 38–75.

5960. Higman, Barry W. *Montpelier, Jamaica: a plantation community in slavery and freedom, 1739–1912* (Mona, Jamaica: University Press of the West Indies, 1998), xv, 384p.

5961. Karras, Alan L. 'Caribbean contraband, slavery property, and the state, 1767–1792', A33, 250–69.

5962. Linebaugh, Peter; Rediker, Marcus. *The many-headed hydra: the hidden history of the revolutionary Atlantic* (London: Verso, 2000), 433p.

5963. Markovits, Claude. *The global world of Indian merchants, 1750–1947: traders of Sind from Bukhara to Panama* (Cambridge: Cambridge University Press, 2000), xv, 327p.

5964. Ryden, D.B. '"One of the fertiliest, pleasentest Spotts": an analysis of the slave economy in Jamaica's St Andrew Parish, 1753', *Slavery & Abolition* 21:1 (2000), 32–55.

5965. Sutton, Jean. *Lords of the east: the East India Company and its ships 1600–1874* (London: Conway Maritime, 2000), i, 160p. [Revised and enlarged version of a book first published in 1981.]

5966. Van Dyke, P.A. 'Pigs, chickens, and lemonade: the provisions trade in Canton, 1700–1840', *International Journal of Maritime History* 12:1 (2000), 111–144.

5967. Walvin, James. *Making the black Atlantic: Britain and the African diaspora* (London: Cassell, 2000), xi, 180p.

5968. Williams, Oscar R. *African Americans and colonial legislation in the middle colonies* (New York: Garland, 1998), x, 120p.

Eb. *Technology*

See 5976 (N)

Fb. *Science and Medicine*

See also 5898, 5993 (N)

5969. David, Andrew. 'James Cook's 1762 survey of St. John's harbour and adjacent parts of Newfoundland', *Terrae Incognitae* 30 (1998), 63–71.

5970. Fisher, Robin. 'Vancouver's vision of native peoples: the northwest coast and Hawai'i', A85, 147–63.

5971. Jobson, Richard *The discovery of River Gambra (1623)*, edited, with additional material, by David P. Gamble & Paul Edward Hedley Hair. (Works issued by the Hakluyt Society, 3rd ser., 2) (London: Hakluyt Society, 1999), xvi, 341p.

5972. Kriz, Kay Dian. 'Curiosities, commodities, and transplanted bodies in Hans Sloane's *Natural history of Jamaica*', *William and Mary Quarterly* 3rd ser. 57 (2000), 35–78.

5973. Mackay, David. 'Exploring the Pacific, exploring James Cook', A85, 251–69.

5974. Milton, Giles. *Nathaniel's nutmeg: how one man's courage changed the course of history* (London: Hodder & Stoughton, 1999), xi, 388p.

5975. Neill, A. 'Buccaneer ethnography: nature, culture, and nation in the journals of William Dampier', *Eighteenth Century Studies* 33:2 (2000), 165–80.

5976. Rahman, A. (ed.) *History of Indian science, technology and culture, A.D. 1000–1800* (History of Science, Philosophy and Culture in Indian Civilization, III: 1) (New Delhi: Oxford University Press, 1999), xx, 445p.

5977. Savours, Ann. *The search for the North West Passage* (London: Chatham, 1999), ix, 342p.

5978. Williams, Glyndwr. '"To make discoveries of countries hitherto unknown": The Admiralty and Pacific exploration in the eighteenth century', A85, 13–31.

5979. Williams, Glyndwr (ed.) *Captain Cook's voyages, 1768–1779* (London: Folio Society, 1997), xxxiv, 552p.

5980. Williams, Glyndwr. *The prize of all the oceans: the triumph and tragedy of Anson's voyage round the world* (London: HarperCollins, 1999), xxi, 264p.

Fc. *Ideas and Learning*

See also 5890, 5948 (N); 6437 (P)

5981.   Armitage, David. *The ideological origins of the British empire* (Cambridge: Cambridge University Press, 2000), 257p.
5982.   Drayton, Richard. *Nature's government: science, British imperialism and the 'improvement' of the world* (New Haven (CT) and London: Yale University Press, 2000), xxi, 346p.
5983.   Ferguson, Robert A. 'The commonalities of *Common Sense*' [the influence of Thomas Paine], *William and Mary Quarterly* 3rd ser. 57:3 (2000), 465–504.
5984.   Landsman, Ned C. *From colonials to provincials: American thought and culture 1680–1760* (New York: Twayne, 1997), 223p.

Fd. *Culture and the Arts*

See also 1719, 1762 (F); 2463 (G); 5903, 5934 (N)

5985.   Marshall, Peter James. 'The great map of mankind: the British encounter with India', A85, 237–50.
5986.   Morris, Elaine L.; et al. '". . . the old stone fortt at Newcastle . . .": The Redoubt, Nevis, eastern Caribbean', *Post-Medieval Archaeology* 33 (1999), 194–221.
5987.   Rohatgi, Pauline; Godrej, Pheroza (eds.) *Under the Indian sun: British landscape artists and India* (Bombay: Marg, 1995), viii, 168p.
5988.   Sarudy, Barbara Wells. *Gardens and gardening in the Chesapeake, 1700–1805* (Baltimore (MD): Johns Hopkins University Press, 1998), xiv, 206p.

G. *Religious Belief, Practice and Organisation*

See also 1407 (F); 2512 (G); 5906, 5925 (N)

5989.   Banerjee, Pompa. 'Hard to swallow: women, poison, and Hindu widow-burning, 1500–1700', *Continuity and Change* 15:2 (2000), 187–208.
5990.   Brekus, Catherine A. *Strangers and pilgrims: female preaching in America, 1740–1845* (Chapel Hill (NC): University of North Carolina Press, 1998), x, 466p.
5991.   Dreisbach, D.L. 'George Mason's pursuit of religious liberty in revolutionary Virginia', *Virginia Magazine of History and Biography* 108:1 (2000), 5–44.
5992.   Evans, E.D. 'A providential rescue?: Griffith Jones and the Malabar Mission', *Journal of Welsh Religious History* 8 (2000), 35–42.
5993.   Gevitz, N. '"The Devil hath laughed at the physicians": witchcraft and medical practice in seventeenth-century New England', *Journal of the History of Medicine and Allied Sciences* 55:1 (2000), 5–36.

5994.   Hambye, Edward René. *History of Christianity in India*, vol.3: *The eighteenth century* (Bangalore: Church History Association of India, 1997), xxiii, 562p.

5995.   Hanson, Charles P. *Necessary virtue: the pragmatic origins of religious liberty in New England* (Charlottesville (VA): University Press of Virginia, 1998), x, 277p.

5996.   James, Sydney V. *John Clarke and his legacies: religion and law in colonial Rhode Island, 1638–1750*, ed. Theodore Dwight Bozeman (University Park (PA): Pennsylvania State University Press, 1999), xiv, 202p.

5997.   Landsman, Ned C. 'Presbyterians, Evangelicals, and the educational culture of the middle colonies', A33, 168–82.

5998.   O'Connor, Daniel; et al. *Three centuries of mission: the United Society for the Propagation of the Gospel 1701–2000* (London: Continuum, 2000), xvi, 448p.

5999.   Smaby, Beverly Prior. 'Female piety among eighteenth-century Moravians', A33, 151–67.

6000.   Westerkamp, Marilyn J. 'Engendering Puritan religious culture in Old and New England', A33, 105–22.

6001.   Westerkamp, Marilyn J. *Women and religion in early America, 1600–1850: the Puritan and evangelical traditions* (London: Routledge, 1999), ix, 219p.

Ha. *Law and Order*

See also 2539, 2550 (G); 5968, 5975, 5996 (N)

6002.   Colley, Linda. 'Going native, telling tales: captivity, collaborations and empire', *Past & Present* 168 (2000), 170–93.

6003.   Kuiters, W.G.J. 'Law and empire: The Armenians contra Verelst, 1769–77', *Journal of Imperial and Commonwealth History* 28:2 (2000), 1–22.

6004.   Maxwell, C.V.H. '"The horrid villainy": Sarah Bassett and the poisoning conspiracies in Bermuda, 1727–30', *Slavery & Abolition* 21:3 (2000), 48–74.

Hb. *Public Administration*

See also 6019 (N); 6223, 6229 (P)

6005.   Hermes, Katherine A. 'Jurisdiction in the colonial northeast: Algonquian, English and French governance', *American Journal of Legal History* 43 (1999), 52–73.

6006.   Nelson, Larry Lee. *A man of distinction among them: Alexander McKee and British-Indian affairs along the Ohio country frontier, 1754–1799* (Kent (OH) and London: Kent State University Press, 1999), xv, 262p.

Hc. *Political and Constitutional*

See also 2004, 2050 (F); 2568–9 (G); 5940–1, 5962, 5967 (N)

6007. Barnes, Ian. *The historical atlas of the American Revolution* (New York: Routledge, 2000), 223p.

6008. Bourke, Richard. 'Liberty, authority, and trust in Burke's idea of empire', *Journal of the History of Ideas* 61:3 (2000), 453–71.

6009. Burdiel, Isabel; Church, Roy A. (ed.) *Viejos y nuevos imperios: Espana y Gran Bretana (Siglo XVII–XX)* (Valencia: Ediciones Episteme, 1998), 229p.

6010. Butler, Jon. *Becoming America: the revolution before 1776* (Cambridge (MA): Harvard University Press, 2000), x, 324p.

6011. Cornog, Evan. *The birth of empire: DeWitt Clinton and the American experience, 1769–1828* (New York: Oxford University Press, 1998), x, 224p.

6012. Gordon, Stewart. *Marathas, marauders, and state formation in eighteenth-century India* (Delhi: Oxford University Press, 1994), xi, 223p.

6013. Grasso, Christopher. *A speaking aristocracy: transforming public discourse in eighteenth-century Connecticut* (Chapel Hill (NC): University of North Carolina Press for the Omohundro Institute of Early American History and Culture, 1999), viii, 511p.

6014. Greene, Jack Phillip. '"A plain and natural right to life and liberty": an early natural rights attack on the excesses of the slave system in colonial British America', *William and Mary Quarterly* 3rd ser. 57:4 (2000), 793–98.

6015. Greene, Jack Phillip; Pole, Jack Richon (eds.) *Companion to the American Revolution* (Malden (MA) and Oxford: Blackwell, 2000), xvi, 778p.

6016. Holton, Woody. *Forced founders: Indians, debtors, slaves, and the making of the American revolution in Virginia* (Chapel Hill (NC): University of North Carolina Press for the Omohundro Institute of Early American History and Culture, Williamsburg, Virginia, 1999), xxi, 231p.

6017. Kamensky, Jane. *Governing the tongue: the politics of speech in early New England* (New York: Oxford University Press, 1997), 291p.

6018. Marshall, Peter James. 'Eighteenth-century Britain and its empire', *The Historian* [London] 68 (2000), 12–17.

6019. Morgan, Edmund Sears; Morgan, Helen. *The Stamp Act crisis: prologue to revolution*, 3rd edn. (Chapel Hill (NC): University of North Carolina Press, 1995), xiv, 327p. [1st published 1953.]

6020. O'Shaughnessy, Andrew Jackson. *An empire divided: the American revolution and the British Caribbean* (Philadelphia (PA): University of Pennsylvania Press, 2000), xvi, 357p.

6021. Phillips, Kevin P. *The cousins' wars: religion, politics, and the triumph of Anglo-America* (New York: Basic Books, 1999), xxviii, 707p.

6022. Quinn, David Beers. 'Thomas Harriot and the problem of America', A82, 9–27.

6023. Schulze, David. 'L'application de la Proclamation royale de 1763 dans les frontières originales de la province de Québec: la décision du Conseil privé dans l'affaire Allsopp' [The application of the royal proclamation of 1763 on the original frontiers of the province of Quebec: the decision of the Privy Council in the Allsopp affair], *Revue Juridique Thémis* 31 (1997), 511–74.

6024. Starr, Rebecca. *A school for politics: commercial lobbying and political culture in early South Carolina* (Baltimore (MD): Johns Hopkins University Press, 1998), x, 218p. [Mainly considers the post-Revolution period.]

6025. Tully, Alan. *Forming American politics: ideas, interests, and institutions in colonial New York and Pennsylvania* (Baltimore (MD): Johns Hopkins University Press, 1994), xiii, 566p.

6026. Young, Alfred Fabian. *The shoemaker and the tea party: memory and the American revolution* (Boston (MA): Beacon Press, 1999), xvii, 262p.

J. *Military*

See also 5940 (N)

6027. Anderson, Fred. *Crucible of war: the Seven Years' War and the fate of empire in British North America, 1754–1766* (New York: Alfred A. Knopf, 2000), xxv, 862p.

6028. Babits, Lawrence Edward. *A devil of a whipping: the Battle of Cowpens* (Chapel Hill (NC): University of North Carolina Press, 1998), xxi, 231p.

6029. Buckley, Roger Norman. *The British army in the West Indies: society and the military in the revolutionary age* (Gainesville (FL): University Press of Florida, 1998).

6030. Conrad, Dennis M.; Parks, Roger N.; King, Martha J. (eds.) *The papers of General Nathanael Greene*, vol. 9, *11 July 1781–2 December 1781*; vol.10, *3 December 1781–6 April 1782* (Chapel Hill (NC) and London: University of North Carolina Press).

6031. Karr, Ronald Dale. '"Why should you be so furious?" The violence of the Pequot War', *Journal of American History* 85 (1998), 876–909.

6032. Lewis, James Allen. *Neptune's militia: the frigate South Carolina during the American revolution* (Kent (OH) and London: Kent State University Press, 1999), x, 235p.

6033. Nester, William R. *The first global war: Britain, France and the fate of North America, 1756–1775* (Westport (CT): Praeger, 2000), ix, 308p.

6034. Nester, William R. *The great frontier war: Britain, France and the imperial struggle for North America, 1607–1755* (Westport (CT): Praeger, 2000), xiii, 326p.

6035. Syrett, David. 'The raising of American troops for service in the West Indies during the War of Austrian Succession, 1740–1', *Historical Research* 72 (2000), 20–32.

6036. Way, Peter. 'Rebellion of the regulars: working soldiers and the mutiny of 1763–1764', *William and Mary Quarterly* 3rd ser. 57:4 (2000), 761–92.

K. *Foreign Affairs*

6037. Frost, Alan. 'The Spanish yoke: British schemes to revolutionise Spanish America, 1739–1807', A85, 33–52.

P. EMPIRE AND COMMONWEALTH POST 1783

A. *General*

See also 5479, 5493 (M); 5888–9, 5893–4 (N)

6038. Ambler, Charles H. 'East Africa: metropolitan Action and local initiative' [Historiography], A214, 500–12.

6039. Austen, Ralph A.; Derrick, Jonathan. *Middlemen of the Cameroons rivers: the Duala and their hinterland, c.1600–c.1900* (African Studies Series, 96) (Cambridge: Cambridge University Press, 1999), xii, 252p.

6040. Bayly, Christopher Alan. 'Ireland, India and the Empire, 1780–1914', *Transactions of the Royal Historical Society* 6th ser. 10 (2000), 377–98.

6041. Bridges, Roy C. (ed.) *Imperialism, decolonization and Africa: studies presented to John Hargreaves: with an academic memoir and bibliography* (Basingstoke and New York: Macmillan and St Martin's Press, 2000), xv, 213p.

6042. Chakravarti, Uma. *Rewriting history: the life and times of Pandita Ramabai* (New Delhi: Kali for Women in association with the Book Review Literary Trust, 1998), xiii, 370p.

6043. Connah, Graham; Burke, Christine. *Kibiro: the salt of Bunyoro, past and present* (British Institute in Eastern Africa, memoir, 13) (London: British Institute in Eastern Africa, 1996), xv, 224p.

6044. Daly, M.W. (ed.) *Modern Egypt, from 1517 to the end of the twentieth century* (The Cambridge History of Egypt, II) (Cambridge: Cambridge University Press, 1998).

6045. Denoon, Donald; Mein Smith, Philippa; Wyndham, Marivic. *A history of Australia, New Zealand and the Pacific* (Oxford and Malden (MA): Blackwell, 2000), xiv, 523p.

6046. Douglas, Bronwen. 'Imperial flotsam? The British in the Pacific islands' [Historiography], A214, 366–78.

6047. El-Sohl, Raghid (ed.) *The Sultanate of Oman, 1939–1945* (Reading: Ithaca Press, 2000), 376p.

6048. Guha, Ranajit (ed.) *A subaltern studies reader, 1986–1995* (Minneapolis (MN) and London: University of Minnesota Press, 1997), xxii, 303p.

6049. Hayes, Patricia; et al. (eds.) *Namibia under South African rule: mobility & containment, 1915–46* (Oxford and Athens (OH): James Currey and Ohio University Press, 1998), xx, 330p. [The 'Trees Never Meet' project.]

6050. Holmes, Michael. 'The Irish and India: imperialism, nationalism and internationalism', A15, 235–50.

6051. Hopkins, Antony Gerald. 'From Africa to empire', A138.

6052. Howe, Stephen. *Ireland and empire: colonial legacies in Irish history and culture* (Oxford: Oxford University Press, 2000), 333p.

6053. Hughes, J. 'Ten myths about the preservation of historic sites in Antarctica and some implications for Mawson's huts at Cape Denison', *Polar Record* 197 (2000), 117–30.

6054. King, Robert J. 'Francisco Muñoz y San Clemente and his "Reflections on the English settlements of New Holland"', *British Library Journal* 25:1 (1999), 55–76.

6055. Klein, I. 'Materialism. Mutiny and modernization in British India', *Modern Asian Studies* 34:3 (2000), 545–580.

6056. Macintyre, Stuart. 'Australia in the Empire' [Historiography], A214, 163–81.

6057. Mackenzie, John MacDonald. 'India's Role in the Victorian Concept of Empire', A6, 119–132.

6058. Mann, Michael. *British rule on Indian soil: north India in the first half of the nineteenth century* (New Delhi: Manohar, 1999), 244p. [1st published as *Britische Herrschaft auf indischem Boden.*]

6059. McCarthy, Angela. '"The desired haven"? Impressions of New Zealand in letters to and from Ireland, 1840–1925', A15, 272–84.

6060. McCracken, Donal P. 'Odd man out: the South African experience' [Irish migration], A15, 251–71.

6061. Nowell, Sybil Hall. *An inquisitive eye: travels of an American lady in the British Empire of the 1930s*, ed. Robert N. White (London: Radcliffe, 1999), 151p.

6062. Owram, Douglas. 'Canada and the Empire' [Historiography], A214, 146–62.

6063. Parsons, Timothy. *The British imperial century, 1815–1914: a world history perspective* (Lanham (MD) and Oxford: Rowman & Littlefield, 1999), xi, 153p.

6064. Pons, Xavier. *L'Australie: Entre Occident et Orient* (Paris: La Documentation française, 2000), 133p.

6065. Porter, Andrew Neil. 'Birmingham, Westminster and the City of London: visions of empire compared', *Journal of Historical Geography* 21:1 (1995), 83–87.

6066. Porter, Andrew Neil. 'From Empire to the Commonwealth of Nations', A6, 167–178.

6067. Porter, Andrew Neil. 'The empire and the world', A145, 135–62.

6068. Ramdin, Ron. *Arising from bondage: a history of the Indo-Caribbean people* (London: I.B. Tauris, 2000), x, 387p.

6069. Saunders, Christopher. 'African attitudes to Britain and the empire before and after the South African War', A139, 140–49.

6070. Shennan, Margaret. *Out in the midday sun: the British in Malaya, 1880–1960* (London: John Murray, 2000), 426p.

6071. Sluglett, Peter. 'Formal and informal empire in the Middle East' [Historiography], A214, 416–36.

6072. Tolron, Francine. *La Nouvelle-Zélande: Du duel au duo? Essai d'histoire culturelle* [New Zealand from duel to duo: an essay in cultural history] (Toulouse: Presses universitaires du Mirail, 2000), 338p.

6073.   Worden, Nigel; Van Heyningen, Elizabeth; Bickford-Smith, Vivian. *Cape Town: the making of a city: an illustrated social history* (Claremont and Hilversum: David Philip and Verloren, 1998), 283p.

B. *Historiography and Historical Methods*

See also 5898, 5900–1 (N); 6310, 6488 (P)

6074.   Bayly, Christopher Alan. 'The second British empire' [Historiography], A214, 54–72.
6075.   Belich, James. 'Colonization and history in New Zealand' [Historiography], A214, 182–93.
6076.   Bell-Gam, Ruby A.; Iyam, David Uru. *Nigeria* (World Bibliographical Series, 100) (Oxford and Santa Barbara (CA): Clio, 1999), xxvii, 342p. [1st published 1985, compiled by Robert A. Myers.]
6077.   De Silva, Kingsley M. 'Ceylon (Sri Lanka)' [Historiography], A214, 243–52.
6078.   Falola, Toyin. 'West Africa' [Historiography], A214, 486–99.
6079.   Grotpeter, John J.; Siegel, Brian V.; Pletcher, James R. *Historical dictionary of Zambia*, 2nd edn. (African Historical Dictionaries, 19) (Lanham (MD) and London: Scarecrow, 1998), xxxv, 571p. [1st published 1979.]
6080.   Harkness, David. 'Ireland' [Historiography], A214, 114–33.
6081.   Helyer, Patrick J.; Swales, Michael K. *A bibliography of Tristan da Cunha* (Oswestry: Anthony Nelson, 1998), 175p.
6082.   Higman, Barry W. *Writing West Indian histories* (London: Macmillan Education, 1999), xiv, 289p.
6083.   Hudson, William James; Bolton, Geoffrey Curgenven (eds.) *Creating Australia: changing Australian history* (St Leonards (NSW): Allen & Unwin, 1997), xiii, 187p.
6084.   Joyce, Peter. *A concise dictionary of South African biography* (Cape Town: Francolin, 2000).
6085.   Louis, William Roger. 'Introduction' [historiography of the British Empire], A214, 1–42.
6086.   McIntyre, William David. 'The Commonwealth' [Historiography], A214, 558–70.
6087.   Middleton, John (ed.) *Encyclopedia of Africa south of the Sahara* (New York: Charles Scribner's Sons, 1997), 4 vols.
6088.   Moore, Robin James. 'India in the 1940s' [Historiography], A214, 231–42.
6089.   Raychaudhuri, Tapan. 'India, 1858 to the 1930s' [Historiography], A214, 214–30.
6090.   Roberts, Andrew Dunlop. 'The British empire in tropical Africa: a review of the literature to the 1960s' [Historiography], A214, 462–85.
6091.   Talbot, Ian Arthur. 'Pakistan's Emergence' [Historiography], A214, 253–63.
6092.   Tarling, Peter Nicholas. 'The British empire in south-east Asia' [Historiography], A214, 403–15.
6093.   Thornton, Archibald Paton. 'The shaping of imperial history' [Historiography], A214, 612–34.

6094.   Turnbull, Constance Mary. 'Formal and informal empire in East Asia' [Historiography], A214, 379–402.
6095.   Uche, Chibuike Ugochukwu. 'A threat to historical research' [private versus official accounts of events], *Archives* 25:103 (2000), 136–41.
6096.   Washbrook, David Anthony. 'Orients and occidents: colonial discourse theory and the historiography of the British empire' [Historiography], A214, 596–611.
6097.   Winks, Robin William. 'The future of imperial history' [Historiography], A214, 653–68.
6098.   Worger, William H. 'Southern and Central Africa' [Historiography], A214, 513–40.

C. Population and Environment

See also 2663 (H); 5511, 5529 (M); 5888, 5907, 5913, 5916, 6009 (N); 6165, 6229, 6244, 6246, 6271, 6396 (P)

6099.   Barton, G.A. 'Empire forestry and American environmentalism', *Environment and History* 6:2 (2000), 187–204.
6100.   Bennett, Jason Patrick. 'Apple of the empire: landscape and imperial identity in turn-of-the-century British Columbia', *Journal of the Canadian Historical Association* ns 9 (1998), 63–92.
6101.   Bennett, Judith A. *Pacific forest: a history of resource control and contest in the Solomon Islands, c.1800–1997* (Knapwell: White Horse, 2000), 512p.
6102.   Biswas, S. 'Environment & imperialism—the complexity exposed: a critique of Jim Corbett's "My India"', *Proceedings of the Indian History Congress* 56 (1995), 636–42.
6103.   Carter, Sarah. *Aboriginal people and colonizers of western Canada to 1900* (Toronto (Ont) and London: University of Toronto Press, 1999), 195p.
6104.   Clayton, D. 'The creation of imperial space in the Pacific Northwest', *Journal of Historical Geography* 26:3 (2000), 327–50.
6105.   Davies, Wayne K.D. 'Falling on deaf ears?: Canadian promotion and Welsh emigration to the prairies', *Welsh History Review* 19:4 (1999), 679–712.
6106.   Dunlap, Thomas R. *Nature and the English diaspora: environment and history in the United States, Canada, Australia, and New Zealand* (Cambridge: Cambridge University Press, 1999), xv, 350p.
6107.   Elliot, Bruce S. 'English immigration to Prince Edward Island. Pt 1', *Island Magazine* 40 (1996), 3–11.
6108.   Elliot, Bruce S. 'English immigration to Prince Edward Island. Pt 2', *Island Magazine* 41 (1997), 3–9.
6109.   Endersby, J. 'A garden enclosed: botanical barter in Sydney, 1818–39', *British Journal for the History of Science* 33:3:118 (2000), 313–34.
6110.   Fraser, Lyndon. *A distant shore: Irish migration & New Zealand settlement* (Dunedin (NZ): University of Otago Press, 2000), 196p.
6111.   Fraser, Lyndon. 'Irish migration to the west coast, 1864–1900', *New Zealand Journal of History* 34:2 (2000), 197–225.

6112. Indra, Doreen Marie (ed.) *Engendering forced migration: theory and practice* (New York and Oxford: Berghahn, 1999), xx, 390p.

6113. Jacobs, N. 'Grasslands and thickets: bush encroachment and herding in the Kalahari Thornveld', *Environment and History* 6:3 (2000), 289–316.

6114. Kisling, V.N. 'Colonial menageries and the exchange of exotic faunas', *Archives of Natural History* 25:3 (1998), 303–20.

6115. Little, J.I. 'From the Isle of Arran to Inverness Township: a case study of Highland emigration and North American settlement, 1829–34', *Scottish Economic & Social History* 20:1 (2000), 3–30.

6116. Mackenzie, A. Fiona D. *Land, ecology and resistance in Kenya, 1880–1952* (Edinburgh: Edinburgh University Press for the International African Institute, 1998), xiii, 286p.

6117. Majumdar, E. 'In search of a new resort: emergence of Kalimpong as a hill station (1865–1920)', *Proceedings of the Indian History Congress* 54 (1994), 574–81.

6118. Margalit, H. 'Planning, anxiety and imperial identity in early twentieth century Sydney', *Architectural Theory Review* 4:1 (1999), 51–60.

6119. McCann, James. *Green land, brown land, black land: an environmental history of Africa, 1800–1900* (Portsmouth (NH) and Oxford: Heinemann and James Currey, 1999), xv, 201p.

6120. McCracken, Donal P. *Gardens of empire: botanical institutions of the Victorian British empire* (London: Leicester University Press, 1997), x, 242p.

6121. McLean, Gavin. *Wellington: the first years of European settlement, 1840–1850* (Auckland (NZ): Penguin, 2000), 96p.

6122. Neumann, Roderick P. *Imposing wilderness: struggles over livelihood and nature preservation in Africa* (Berkeley (CA) and London: University of California Press, 1998), xii, 256p.

6123. Pigott, L.J. 'John White's Journal of a Voyage to New South Wales (1790): comments on the natural history and the artistic origins of the plates', *Archives of Natural History* 27:2 (2000), 157–74.

6124. Roberts, J. 'English gardens in India', *Garden History* 26:2 (1998), 115–35.

6125. Robertshaw, Peter; Taylor, David. 'Climate change and the rise of political complexity in western Uganda', *Journal of African History* 41:1 (2000), 1–28.

6126. Sangwan, S. 'Making of a popular debate: the Indian forester and the emerging agenda of state forestry in India, 1875–1904', *Indian Economic and Social History Review* 36:2 (1999), 187–238.

6127. Schug, D.M. 'The bureaucratisation of forest management in India', *Environment and History* 6:2 (2000), 229–42.

6128. Singh, M. 'Basutoland: a historical journey into the environment', *Environment and History* 6:1 (2000), 31–70.

6129. Subash Chandran, M.D.; Hughes, J.D. 'Sacred groves and conservation: the comparative history of traditional reserves in the Mediterranean area and in south India', *Environment and History* 6:2 (2000), 169–86.

6130. Watts, Sheldon J. *Epidemics and history: disease, power, and imperialism* (New Haven (CT) and London: Yale University Press, 1997), xvi, 400p.

6131.   Widdis, Randy William. *With scarcely a ripple: Anglo-Canadian migra-tion into the United States and western Canada, 1880–1920* (Montreal (Ont) and London: McGill-Queen's University Press, 1998), xxii, 418p.
6132.   Wylie, Diana. 'Disease, diet, and gender: late twentieth-century perspec-tives on empire' [Historiography], A214, 277–89.

Da. *Social Life and Conditions*

See also 3673 (I); 5930 (N); 6285, 6529, 6544, 6617, 6645, 6647 (P)

6133.   Banerjee, Pompa. 'Burning questions: widows, witches, and early modern European travel narratives of India', *Journal of Medieval and Early Modern Studies* 29:3 (1999), 529–62.
6134.   Barnes, Teresa A. *'We women worked so hard': gender, urbanization, and social reproduction in colonial Harare, Zimbabwe, 1930–1956* (Ports-mouth (NH) and Oxford: Heinemann and James Currey, 1999), xlv, 204p.
6135.   Baskerville, Peter A.; Sager, Eric W. *Unwilling idlers: the urban unem-ployed and their families in late Victorian Canada* (Toronto (Ont) and London: University of Toronto Press, 1998), xiv, 294p.
6136.   Binney, Judith. *Redemption songs: a life of Te Kooti Arikirangi Te Turuki* (Auckland (NZ): Auckland University Press, 1995), 666p.
6137.   Black, David R.; Nauright, John (eds.) *Rugby and the South African nation: sport, cultures, politics, and power in the old and new South Africas* (Manchester: Manchester University Press, 1998), xii, 163p.
6138.   Blunt, A. 'Embodying war: British women and domestic defilement in the Indian "Mutiny", 1857–8', *Journal of Historical Geography* 26:3 (2000), 403–28.
6139.   Blunt, A. 'Imperial geographies of home: British domesticity in India, 1886–1925', *Transactions of the Institute of British Geographers* 24:4 (1999), 421–40.
6140.   Buettner, Elizabeth. 'Parent-child separations and colonial careers: the Talbot family correspondence in the 1880s and 1890s', A81, 115–32.
6141.   Bush, Julia. *Edwardian ladies and imperial power* (London: Leicester University Press, 2000), xi, 242p.
6142.   Campbell, Christopher. *The maharajah's box: an imperial story of conspir-acy, love and a guru's prophecy* (London: HarperCollins, 2000), xvii, 474p.
6143.   Casella, E.C. '"Doing trade": a sexual economy of nineteenth-century Australian female convict prisons', *World Archaeology* 32:2 (2000), 209–21.
6144.   Dagut, S. 'Gender, colonial "women's history" and the construction of social distance: middle-class British women in later nineteenth-century South Africa', *Journal of Southern African Studies* 26:3 (2000), 555–72.
6145.   Damousi, Joy. *The labour of loss: mourning, memory and wartime bereavement in Australia* (Cambridge: Cambridge University Press, 1999), x, 212p.
6146.   Daniels, Kay. *Convict women* (St Leonards (NSW): Allen & Unwin, 1998), xi, 276p.
6147.   Delius, Peter. *A lion amongst the cattle: reconstruction and resistance in*

the northern Transvaal (Portsmouth (NH) and London: Heinemann and James Currey, 1996), xvi, 268p.

6148. Denwood, P. 'William Moorcroft—an assessment', A172, 39–54.

6149. Diamond, Marion. *Emigration and empire: the life of Maria S. Rye* (New York and London: Garland, 1999), xix, 304p.

6150. Downes, A.D. '"Flannelled fools"? Cricket and the political economy of the British West Indies c.1895–1906', *International Journal of the History of Sport* 17:4 (2000), 59–80.

6151. Fisher, M.H. 'Representing "his" women: Mirza Abu Talib Khan's 1801 "Vindication of the Liberties of Asiatic Women"', *Indian Economic and Social History Review* 37:2 (2000), 215–238.

6152. Fleischmann, E.L. 'The emergence of the Palestinian women's movement, 1929–39', *Journal of Palestine Studies* 29:3:115 (2000), 16–32.

6153. Frost, Diane. *Work and community among West African migrant workers since the nineteenth century* (Liverpool: Liverpool University Press, 1998), 278p.

6154. Furedi, Frank. 'The demobilized African soldier and the blow to white prestige', A124, 179–97.

6155. Getz, T.R. 'The case for Africans: the role of slaves and masters in emancipation on the Gold Coast, 1874–1900', *Slavery & Abolition* 21:1 (2000), 128–45.

6156. Ghosh, A. 'Valorising the "vulgar": nationalist appropriations of colloquial Bengali traditions, c.1870–1905', *Indian Economic and Social History Review* 37:2 (2000), 151–184.

6157. Gupta, C. 'Hindu women, Muslim men: cleavages in shared spaces of everyday life, United Provinces, c.1890–1930', *Indian Economic and Social History Review* 37:2 (2000), 121–150.

6158. Hendrickson, Hildi (ed.) *Clothing and difference: embodied identities in colonial and post-colonial Africa* (Durham (NC) and London: Duke University Press, 1996), viii, 268p.

6159. Horton, P.A. 'The "green" and the "gold": the Irish-Australians and their role in the emergence of the Australian sports culture', *International Journal of the History of Sport* 17:2–3 (2000), 65–92.

6160. Hunt, Nancy Rose; Liu, Tessie P.; Quataert, Jean Helen (eds.) *Gendered colonialisms in African history* (Oxford and Malden (MA): Blackwell, 1997), x, 138p.

6161. Jeater, D. 'No place for a woman: Gwelo Town, Southern Rhodesia, 1894–1920', *Journal of Southern African Studies* 26:1 (2000), 29–42.

6162. Jobling, I. 'In pursuit of status, respectability and idealism: pioneers of the Olympic movement in Australasia', *International Journal of the History of Sport* 17:2–3 (2000), 142–166.

6163. Jones, B. 'Welsh identities in Ballarat, Australia, during the late nineteenth century', *Welsh History Review* 20:2 (2000), 283–307.

6164. Kimmerling, B. 'The formation of Palestinian collective identities: the Ottoman and Mandatory periods', *Middle Eastern Studies* 36:2 (2000), 48–81.

6165. Kranidis, Rita S. *The Victorian spinster and colonial emigration: contested subjects* (Basingstoke and New York: Macmillan and St Martin's Press, 1999), x, 228p.

6166. Krikler, Jeremy. 'The inner mechanic of a South African racial massacre (1922)', *Historical Journal* 42:4 (1999), 1051–75.

6167. Langdon, R. '"Dusky damsels": Pitcairn Island's neglected matriarchs of the Bounty saga', *Journal of Pacific History* 35:1 (2000), 29–48.

6168. Lenta, Margaret; Le Cordeur, Basil (eds.) *The Cape diaries of Lady Anne Barnard 1799–1800*, 2 vols. (Van Riebeeck Society, 2nd ser., 29–30) (Cape Town, 1999).

6169. Mangan, J.A.; Hickey, C. 'A pioneer of the proletariat: Herbert Milnes and the games cult in New Zealand', *International Journal of the History of Sport* 17:2–3 (2000), 31–48.

6170. Maxwell, David James. *Christians and chiefs in Zimbabwe: a social history of the Hwesa people c.1870s-1990s* (Edinburgh: Edinburgh University Press, 1999), x, 291p.

6171. McClaughlin, Trevor (ed.) *Irish women in colonial Australia* (St Leonards (NSW): Allen & Unwin, 1998), xvii, 229p.

6172. Midgley, Clare. 'Female emancipation in an imperial frame: English women and the campaign against sati (widow-burning) in India, 1813–30', *Women's History Review* 9:1 (2000), 95–122.

6173. Ndee, H.S. 'Sport in Africa: western influences, British middle-class educationalists and the diffusion of adapted athleticism in Tanzania', *International Journal of the History of Sport* 17:1 (2000), 69–93.

6174. Newton, M. '"New ideas of correctness": gender, amelioration and emancipation in Barbados, 1810s-50s', *Slavery & Abolition* 21:3 (2000), 94–124.

6175. Pitot, Geneviève. *The Mauritian shekel: the story of the Jewish detainees in Mauritius, 1940–1945*, transl. Donna Edouard, ed. Helen Topor (Port Louis (Mauritius): Vizavi, 1998), 259p.

6176. Raychaudhuri, T. 'Love in a colonial climate: marriage, sex and romance in nineteenth-century Bengal', *Modern Asian Studies* 34:2 (2000), 349–78.

6177. Robinson, Jane (ed.) *Parrot pie for breakfast: an anthology of women pioneers* (Oxford: Oxford University Press, 1999), xiv, 177p.

6178. Saiyid, Dushka Hyder. *Muslim women of the British Punjab: from seclusion to politics* (Basingstoke: Macmillan, 1998), 192p.

6179. Van Kirk, Sylvia. 'Colonised lives: the native wives and daughters of five founding families of Victoria' [Canada], A85, 215–33.

Db. *Social Structure*

See also 2550 (G); 2787 (H); 5888, 5946, 5963, 6002 (N); 6230, 6366, 6576, 6594, 6616, 6629 (P)

6180. Badru, Pade. *Imperialism and ethnic politics in Nigeria, 1960–96* (Trenton (NJ): Africa World Press, 1998), xiv, 174p.

6181. Bravman, Bill. *Making ethnic ways: communities and their transformations in Taita, Kenya, 1800–1950* (Portsmouth (NH) and Oxford: Heinemann and James Currey, 1998), xiv, 283p.

6182. Buettner, Elizabeth. 'Problematic spaces, problematic races: defining "Europeans" in late colonial India', *Women's History Review* 9:2 (2000), 277–98.

6183. Campbell, Malcolm. 'Immigrants on the land: a comparative study of Irish rural settlement in nineteenth-century Minnesota and New South Wales', A15, 176–94.

6184. Darwin, John Gareth. 'Civility and empire', A29, 321–36.

6185. du Toit, Brian M. *The Boers in east Africa: ethnicity and identity* (Westport (CT) and London: Bergin & Garvey, 1998), viii, 209p.

6186. Fomin, E.D.S.; Ngoh, Victor Julius. *Slave settlements in the Banyang country, 1800–1950* (Limbe: University of Buea Publications, 1998).

6187. Forward, Alan. *'You have been allocated Uganda': letters from a district officer* (Poyntington (Dor): Poyntington Publishing, 1999), vi, 176p.

6188. Füredi, Frank. *The silent war: imperialism and the changing perception of race* (London: Pluto, 1998), 282p.

6189. Gorlizki, Y. 'Class and nation in the Jewish settlement of Palestine: the case of Merhavia, 1910–30', *Journal of Historical Geography* 26:4 (2000), 572–88.

6190. Jeffery, Roger (ed.) *The social construction of Indian forests* (Edinburgh and New Delhi: Centre for South Asian Studies and Manohar, 1998), 187p.

6191. Lentz, Carola. *Die Konstruktion von Ethnizität: eine politische Geschichte Nord-West Ghanas, 1870–1990* [The construction of ethnicity: a political history of north-west Ghana] (Köln: R. Köppe, 1998), 690p.

6192. Mindenhall, D. 'Choosing the group: nineteenth-century non-mining Cornish in British Columbia', *Cornish Studies* 8 (2000), 40–53.

6193. Pridmore, J. '"The military wanted to see a Zulu dance": white history and black anthropology in the Natal narrative, c.1890–1905', *South African Historical Journal* 41 (1999), 72–82.

6194. Stiansen, Endre; Kevane, Michael (eds.) *Kordofan invaded: peripheral incorporation and social transformation in Islamic Africa* (Leiden: Brill, 1998), x, 303p.

Dc. Social Policy and Welfare

See also 6335, 6417 (P)

6195. Howell, P. 'Prostitution and racialised sexuality: the regulation of prostitution in Britain and the British empire before the Contagious Diseases Acts', *Environment and Planning D: Society and Space* 18:3 (2000), 321–40.

6196. Lewis, Joanna E. '"Tropical East Ends" and the Second World War: some contradictions in Colonial Office welfare initiatives', A195, 61–91.

6197. Lewis, Joanna E. '"Tropical East Ends" and the Second World War: some contradictions in Colonial Office welfare initiatives', *Journal of Imperial and Commonwealth History* 28:2 (2000), 42–66. [A revised version of no.6196.]

6198. Mills, J.H. 'Re-forming the Indian: treatment regimes in the lunatic asylums of British India, 1857–1880', *Indian Economic and Social History Review* 36:4 (1999), 407–30.

6199. Nag, S. 'Bamboo, rats and famines: famine relief and perceptions of British paternalism in the Mizo Hills (India)', *Environment and History* 5:2 (1999), 245–52.

6200. Watts, Sheldon J. 'British development policies and malaria in India 1897–c.1929', *Past & Present* 165 (1999), 141–81.

Ea. *Economic Activity and Organisation*

See also 2239, 2285 (G); 2844, 2851, 2908, 2938, 2946 (H); 4815, 4920 (I); 5585, 5620, 5628 (M); 5888, 5913, 5916, 5946, 5953, 5955, 5960–1, 5963, 5965–7 (N); 6065, 6126–7, 6289, 6427–8, 6506, 6522, 6544, 6605, 6692, 6698 (P)

6201. Amit, I. 'Economic and Zionist ideological perceptions: private initiative in Palestine in the 1920s and 1930s', *Middle Eastern Studies* 36:2 (2000), 82–102.
6202. Bashir Hasan, S. 'The Muzaffaris in Malwa and the shift to imperial currency', *Proceedings of the Indian History Congress* 56 (1995), 338–52.
6203. Benjamin, N. 'Trading activities of Indians in east Africa (with special reference to slavery) in the nineteenth century', *Indian Economic and Social History Review* 35:4 (1998), 405–20.
6204. Bennett, J.A. ' "The grievous mistakes of the Vanikoro concession": the Vanikoro Kauri Timber Company, Solomon Islands, 1926–1964', *Environment and History* 6:3 (2000), 317–348.
6205. Bennett, J.A. 'Across the Bougainville Strait: commercial interests and colonial rivalry, c.1880–1930', *Journal of Pacific History* 35:1 (2000), 67–82.
6206. Blake, Robert. *Jardine Matheson: traders of the Far East* (London: Weidenfeld & Nicolson, 2000), xii, 280p.
6207. Boot, H.M. 'Government and the colonial economies: a reply to Frost' [no.6217], *Australian Economic History Review* 40:1 (2000), 86–92.
6208. Bulley, Anne. *The Bombay country ships: 1790–1833* (Richmond: Curzon, 2000), xvi, 288p.
6209. Butler, L.J. 'Reconstruction, development and entrepreneurial state: the British colonial model, 1939–51', *Contemporary British History* 13:4 (1999), 29–55.
6210. Capling, A. 'The "enfant terrible": Australia and the reconstruction of the multilateral trade system, 1946–8', *Australian Economic History Review* 40:1 (2000), 1–21.
6211. den Otter, Andy Albert von. *The philosophy of railways: the transcontinental railway idea in British North America* (Toronto and London: University of Toronto Press, 1997), xi, 292p.
6212. Dickinson, A.B.; Sanger, C.W. 'Newfoundland and Labrador shore-station whaling: the third major phase, 1937–1951', *International Journal of Maritime History* 11:1 (1999), 101–16.
6213. Drabble, John H. *An economic history of Malaysia, c.1800–1990: the transition to modern economic growth* (Basingstoke and New York: Macmillan and St Martin's Press in association with the Australian National University, 2000), xxiii, 320p.
6214. Drescher, Seymour. *From slavery to freedom: comparative studies in the rise and the fall of Atlantic slavery* (Basingstoke: Macmillan, 1999), xxv, 454p.

6215.   Engdahl, Torbjörn. *The exchange of cotton: Uganda peasants, colonial market regulations and the organisation of the international cotton trade, 1904–1918* (Acta Universitatis Upsaliensis, Uppsala Studies in Economic History, 48) (Uppsala: Acta Universitatis Upsaliensis, 1999), 246p.

6216.   Fieldhouse, David Kenneth. *The west and the third world: trade, colonialism, dependence and development* (Oxford: Blackwell, 1999), xii, 378p.

6217.   Frost, L. 'Government and the colonial economies: an alternative view', *Australian Economic History Review* 40:1 (2000), 71–85p. [With reply, no.6207; a response to H.M. Boot, 'Government and the colonial economies' *Australian Economic History Review* 38:1 (1998), 74–101.]

6218.   Gélinas, Claude. 'L'aventure de la North West Company en Mauricie, 1799–1814', *Revue d'Histoire de l'Amérique Française* 53 (1999), 401–19.

6219.   Goodall, Heather. *Invasion to embassy: land in aboriginal politics in New South Wales, 1770–1972* (St Leonards (NSW): Allen & Unwin in association with Black Books, 1996), xxiv, 421p.

6220.   Gray, A.C. '"Light airs from the south": whalers' logs in Pacific history', *Journal of Pacific History* 35:1 (2000), 109–114.

6221.   Green, Edwin; Kinsey, Sara. *The paradise bank: the Mercantile Bank of India, 1893–1984* (Studies in Banking History) (London: Ashgate, 1999), 272p.

6222.   Griggs, Peter. 'Sugar plantations in Queensland, 1864–1912: origins, characteristics, distribution, and decline', *Agricultural History* 74:3 (2000), 609–47.

6223.   Guha, S. 'Weak states and strong markets in south Asian development, c.1700–1970', *Indian Economic and Social History Review* 36:3 (1999), 335–54.

6224.   Hall-Matthews, D. 'Colonial ideologies of the market and famine policy in Ahmednagar district, Bombay Presidency, c.1870–1884', *Indian Economic and Social History Review* 36:3 (1999), 303–34.

6225.   Haynes, D.E. 'Market formation in Khandesh, c.1820–1930', *Indian Economic and Social History Review* 36:3 (1999), 275–302.

6226.   Heap, Simon. 'Transport and liquor in colonial Nigeria', *Journal of Transport History* 3rd ser. 21:1 (2000), 28–53.

6227.   Heuman, Gad J. 'Slavery, the slave trade, and abolition' [Historiography], A214, 315–26.

6228.   Higman, Barry W. 'The sugar revolution' [West Indies], *Economic History Review* 2nd ser. 53:2 (2000), 213–36.

6229.   Hill, Christopher V. *River of sorrow: environment and social control in riparian north India, 1770–1994* (Ann Arbor (MI): Association for Asian Studies, 1997), xii, 200p.

6230.   Hodgson, Dorothy L. 'Taking stock: state control, ethnic identity and pastoralist development in Tanganyika, 1948–1958', *Journal of African History* 41:1 (2000), 55–78.

6231.   Hoefte, Rosemarijn. *In place of slavery: a social history of British Indian and Javanese laborers in Suriname* (Gainesville (FL): University Press of Florida, 1998), xii, 275p.

6232.   Hopkins, Antony Gerald. 'Development and the utopian ideal, 1960–1999' [Historiography], A214, 635–51.

6233. Houtkamp, John A. *Tropical Africa's emergence as a banana supplier in the inter-war period* (Aldershot: Avebury, 1996), xi, 164p.

6234. Husain Jafri, S.Z. 'The British intervention and agrarian instability in the kingdom of Awadh (1801–56)', *Proceedings of the Indian History Conference* 54 (1994), 545–52.

6235. Ineson, John. *Paper currency of the Anglo-Boer War, 1899–1902* (London: Spink, 1999), ix, 102p.

6236. Jaekel, Francis. *The history of the Nigerian railway* (Ibadan: Spectrum Books, 1997), 3 vols.

6237. Jayashree, C.H. 'Colonial perspectives on slavery in Malabar in the 19th century', *Proceedings of the Indian History Congress* 54 (1994), 516–25.

6238. John, N. 'The campaign against British bank involvement in apartheid South Africa', *African Affairs* 396 (2000), 415–434.

6239. Kale, Madhavi. *Fragments of empire: capital, slavery and Indian indentured labor in the British Caribbean* (Phildelphia (PA): University of Pennsylvania Press, 1998).

6240. Karlinsky, N. 'California dreaming: adapting the "California model" to the Jewish citrus industry in Palestine, 1917–1939', *Israel Studies* 5:1 (2000), 24–40.

6241. Klippel, Walter E.; Schroedl, Gerald F. 'African slave craftsmen and single-hole bone discs from Brimstone Hill, St Kitts, West Indies', *Post-Medieval Archaeology* 33 (1999), 222–32.

6242. Kranton, R.E. 'The hazards of piecemeal reform: British civil courts and the credit market in colonial India', *Journal of Development Economics* 58:1 (1999), 1–24.

6243. Kurup, K.K.N. 'The beginnings of the colonial agrarian system in south India', *Proceedings of the Indian Historical Congress* 54 (1994), 387–97.

6244. Lanz, T.J. 'The origins, development and legacy of scientific forestry in Cameroon', *Environment and History* 6:1 (2000), 99–120.

6245. Lera, N. 'The Baluchistan "white elephant": the Chappar Rift and other strategic railways on the border of British India', *Asian Affairs* 31:2 (2000), 170–80.

6246. Manchuelle, Edouard François. *Willing migrants: Soninke labor diasporas, 1848–1960* (Athens (OH) and London: Ohio University Press and James Currey, 1997), xvii, 371p.

6247. Misra, A.M. ' "Business culture" and entrepreneurialism in British India, 1860–1950', *Modern Asian Studies* 34:2 (2000), 333–48.

6248. Mitra, I. 'Peoples war (1941 to 1945) and the Indian trade union movement in Bengal: a case study', *Proceedings of the Indian History Congress* 56 (1995), 657–64.

6249. Monteith, Kathleen E.A. 'Competition between Barclays Bank (DCO) and the Canadian banks in the West Indies, 1926–45', *Financial History Review* 7:1 (2000), 67–88.

6250. Monteith, Kathleen E.A. 'Emancipation and labour on Jamaican coffee plantations, 1838–48', *Slavery & Abolition* 21:3 (2000), 125–135.

6251. Moore-Colyer, R.J. 'Aspects of the trade in British pedigree draught horses with the United States and Canada, c.1850–1920', *Agricultural History Review* 48:1 (2000), 42–59.

6252. Muirhead, Bruce. 'From dreams to reality: the evolution of Anglo-Canadian trade during the Diefenbaker era', *Journal of the Canadian Historical Association* ns 9 (1998), 243–66.

6253. Nakazato, Nariaki. *Agrarian system in eastern Bengal c.1870–1910* (Calcutta: K.P. Bagchi, 1994), xix, 337p.

6254. Ojo, Oladeji O. (ed.) *Africa and Europe: the changing economic relationship* (London: Zed Books in association with the African Development Bank, 1996), xii, 180p.

6255. Orvis, Stephen Walter. *The agrarian question in Kenya* (Gainesville (FL): University Press of Florida, 1997), xiv, 209p.

6256. Panda, Chitta. *The decline of the Bengal zamindars: Midnapore 1870–1920* (Delhi and Oxford: Oxford University Press, 1996), xix, 231p.

6257. Phimister, Ian. 'Corners and company-mongering: Nigerian tin and the City of London, 1909–12', *Journal of Imperial and Commonwealth History* 28:2 (2000), 23–41.

6258. Pomfret, R. 'Trade policy in Canada and Australia in the twentieth century', *Australian Economic History Review* 40:2 (2000), 114–26.

6259. Porter, Andrew Neil. 'London and the British empire: c.1815–1914', A65, 53–68.

6260. Reeves, P.; Pokrant, B.; McGuire, J. 'The auction lease system in Lower Burma's fisheries, 1870–1904: implications for artisanal fishers and lessees', *Journal of Southeast Asian Studies* 30:2 (1999), 249–62.

6261. Robb, P. 'Credit, work and race in 1790s Calcutta: early colonialism through a contemporary European view', *Indian Economic and Social History Review* 37:1 (2000), 1–26.

6262. Robb, Peter G. *Ancient rights and future comfort: Bihar, the Bengal Tenancy Act of 1885, and British rule in India* (Richmond (Surrey): Curzon, 1997), xxvii, 378p.

6263. Rockel, S.J. '"A nation of porters": the Nyamwezi and the labour market in nineteenth-century Tanzania', *Journal of African History* 41:2 (2000), 173–196.

6264. Rooth, T. 'Australia, Canada, and the international economy in the era of postwar reconstruction, 1945–50', *Australian Economic History Review* 40:2 (2000), 127–52.

6265. Salmon, M.S. '"This unsatisfactory condition:" the formation and financing of Canada Steamship Lines, 1910–1915', *International Journal of Maritime History* 12:1 (2000), 145–76.

6266. Samson, Jane. 'Too zealous guardians? The Royal Navy and the South Pacific labour trade', A124, 70–90.

6267. Sarkar, S. 'Land revenue and land prices in Bengal in the era of the Permanent Settlement', *Proceedings of the Indian History Congress* 54 (1994), 510–15.

6268. Schenk, C.R. 'Another Asian financial crisis: monetary links between Hong Kong and China 1945–50', *Modern Asian Studies* 34:3 (2000), 739–764.

6269. Sen, Samita. *Women and labour in late colonial India: the Bengal jute industry* (Cambridge: Cambridge University Press, 1999), xviii, 265p.

6270.   Simelane, Hamilton Sipho. 'Landlords, the state, and child labor in colonial Swaziland, 1914–1947', *International Journal of African Historical Studies* 31:3 (1998), 571–94.

6271.   Soluri, J. 'People, plants, and pathogens: The eco-social dynamics of export banana production in Honduras, 1875–1950', *Hispanic American Historical Review* 80:3 (2000), 463–502.

6272.   Swallow, Deborah. 'The India Museum and the British-Indian textile trade in the late nineteenth century', *Textile History* 30:1 (1999), 29–45.

6273.   Tripp, Aili Mari. *Changing the rules: the politics of liberalization and the urban informal economy in Tanzania* (Berkeley (CA) and London: University of California Press, 1997), xxii, 260p.

6274.   Troy, Patrick Nicol (ed.) *A history of European housing in Australia* (Cambridge: Cambridge University Press, 2000), 325p.

6275.   Tull, Malcolm. *A community enterprise: the history of the port of Fremantle, 1897 to 1997* (St John's (Newfoundland): International Maritime Economic History Association, 1997), x, 334p.

6276.   Turnell, S. 'F.L. McDougall: eminence grise of Australian economic diplomacy', *Australian Economic History Review* 40:1 (2000), 51–70.

6277.   Vahed, G. 'Control and repression: the plight of Indian hawkers and flower sellers in Durban, 1910–1948', *International Journal of African Historical Studies* 32:1 (1999), 19–48.

6278.   Werner, Wolfgang. *No one will become rich: economy and society in the Herero reserves in Namibia, 1915–1946* (Basel Namibia Studies series, 2) (Basel: P. Schlettwein, 1998), 254p.

6279.   Wharton, A. 'Economy, architecture, and politics: colonialist and Cold War hotels', *History of Political Economy* 31 (suppl.) (2000), 285–302.

6280.   White, Michael. 'Agricultural societies in colonial Western Australia 1831–70', *History of Education* 29:1 (2000), 3–28.

6281.   White, Nicholas J. 'The business and the politics of decolonization: the British experience in the twentieth century', *Economic History Review* 53:3 (2000), 544–64.

6282.   Wilkinson, Glenn R. '"To the front": British newspaper advertising and the Boer War', A91, 203–12.

6283.   Yaxley, John. 'Finance and empire in the Far East: some aspects of financial and development issues in the western Pacific and Hong Kong 1960–1990', A195, 323–30.

6284.   Yazbak, M. 'From poverty to revolt: economic factors in the outbreak of the 1936 rebellion in Palestine', *Middle Eastern Studies* 36:3 (2000), 93–113.

Eb. *Technology*

See 5976 (N)

Fa. *Media and Communication*

See also 2991 (H)

6285. Andrewes, F. ' "They play in your home": cricket, media and modernity in pre-war Australia', *International Journal of the History of Sport* 17:2–3 (2000), 93–110.

6286. Badsey, Stephen. 'War correspondents in the Boer War', A91, 187–202.

6287. Beaumont, Jacqueline. 'The British Press and Censorship during the South African War 1899–1902', *South African Historical Journal* 41 (1999), 267–89.

6288. Beaumont, Jacqueline. '*The Times* at war, 1899–1902', A139, 67–83.

6289. Boyce, Robert W.D. 'Imperial dreams and national realities: Britain, Canada and the struggle for the Pacific Telegraph Cable, 1879–1902', *English Historical Review* 115 (2000), 39–70.

6290. Dugmore, Charles. 'From pro-Boer to jingo: an analysis of small town English-language newspapers on the Rand before the outbreak of war in 1899', *South African Historical Journal* 41 (1999), 246–66.

6291. Harrington, Peter. 'Pictorial journalism and the Boer War: the London illustrated weeklies', A91, 224–44.

6292. Helly, Dorothy O.; Callaway, Helen. 'Journalism as active politics: Flora Shaw, *The Times* and South Africa', A139, 50–66.

6293. not used.

6294. Sargent, Paul. '*Indian News Parade*: the first Indian newsreel', *Imperial War Museum Review* 12 (1999), 29–35.

6295. Sutcliffe, Derek; Jarvis, Steve (eds.) *Encyclopaedia of Jamaican philately: including postal history & postcards*, vol.1: *Postage stamps to 1935* (St Neots: British West Indies Study Circle, 1997)

6296. Switzer, Les (ed.) *South Africa's alternative press: voices of protest and resistance, 1880s–1960s* (Cambridge: Cambridge University Press, 1996), xv, 400p.

6297. Williams, John Frank. *The ANZACs, the media and the Great War* (Kensington (NSW): University of New South Wales Press, 1999), x, 302p.

6298. Wong, W.S. 'Establishing modern advertising languages: patent medicine newspaper advertisements in Hong Kong, 1945–1969', *Journal of Design History* 13:3 (2000), 213–26.

Fb. *Science and Medicine*

See also 3030, 3035, 3071 (H); 3959 (I); 5898, 5976, 5977 (N); 6120 (P)

6299. Arnold, David. *Science, technology, and medicine in colonial India* (The new Cambridge history of India, III, 5) (Cambridge: Cambridge University Press, 2000), xii, 234p.

6300. Barr, William. 'A warrant officer in the Arctic: the journal of George Ford, 1850–1854', A85, 101–23.

6301. Bashford, A. ' "Is white Australia possible?" race, colonialism and tropical medicine', *Ethnic and Racial Studies* 23:2 (2000), 248–71.

6302. Chakraborty, P. 'Science, nationalism, and colonial contestations: P.C. Ray and his Hindu chemistry', *Indian Economic and Social History Review* 37:2 (2000), 185–214.

6303. Cohen, A. 'Mary Elizabeth Barber: South Africa's first lady natural historian', *Archives of Natural History* 27:2 (2000), 187–208.

6304. Cook, Andrew. 'Alexander Dalrymple and the Hydrographic Office', A85, 53–68.

6305. Cookman, Scott. *Ice blink: the tragic fate of Sir John Franklin's lost polar expedition* (New York: John Wiley & Sons, 2000), xii, 244p.

6306. D'Arcy, Patrick Francis. *Laboratory on the Nile: a history of the Wellcome Tropical Research Laboratories* (New York and London: Pharmaceutical Products Press, 1999), xv, 281p.

6307. Driver, Felix. *Geography militant: cultures of exploration and empire* (Oxford and Malden (MA): Blackwell, 2001), viii, 258p. [Published in 2000.]

6308. Jones, Margaret. 'The Ceylon malaria epidemic of 1934–35: a case study in colonial medicine', *Social History of Medicine* 13:1 (2000), 87–110.

6309. Keay, John. *The great arc: the dramatic tale of how India was mapped and Everest was named* (London: HarperCollins, 2000), 208p.

6310. Keenleyside, Anne; Fricke, Henry C. 'The final days of the Franklin expedition: new skeletal evidence', *Arctic* 50 (1997), 36–46.

6311. Kirchberger, Ulrike. 'Deutsche Naturwissenschaftler im britischen Empire: die Erforschung der aussereuropäischen Welt im Spannungsfeld zwischen deutschem und britischem Imperialismus' [German naturalists in the British empire], *Historische Zeitschrift* 271:3 (2000), 621–60.

6312. Knight, R.J.B. 'John Lort Stokes and the New Zealand Survey, 1848–1851', A85, 87–99.

6313. Kochhar, R.K. 'Science in British India', *Indian Journal of History of Science* 34:4 (1999), 317–46.

6314. Korsmo, F.L.; Sfraga, M.P. 'Churchill Peaks and the politics of naming', *Polar Record* 197 (2000), 131–38.

6315. McEwan, Cheryl. *Gender, geography and empire: Victorian women travellers in West Africa* (Aldershot: Ashgate, 2000), 256p.

6316. Murray, Colin; Sanders, Peter. 'Medicine murder in Basutoland: colonial rule and moral crisis', *Africa* 70:1 (2000), 49–78.

6317. Royle, S.A. 'Health and health care in Pitcairn Island in 1841: the report of Surgeon William Gunn of HMS Curacoa', *Journal of Pacific History* 35:2 (2000), 213–18.

6318. Samson, Jane. 'An empire of science: the voyage of HMS *Herald*, 1845–1851', A85, 69–85.

6319. Sheel, A. 'Bubonic plague in south Bihar: Gaya and Shahabad districts, 1900–1924', *Indian Economic and Social History Review* 35:4 (1998), 421–42.

6320. Smith, James Raymond. *Everest: the man and the mountain* (Latheronwheel: Whittles, 1999), xiv, 306p.

6321. Stafford, Robert A. 'Exploration and empire' [Historiography], A214, 290–302.

6322. Stone, Ian R.; Tammiksaar, E. 'Correspondence concerning the publication of Wrangell's narrative of an expedition to the polar sea in the years 1820, 1821, 1822 & 1823', *Polar Record* 197 (2000), 155–56.

6323. Tennent, W.J. 'Charles Morris Woodford C.M.G. (1852–1927): Pacific adventurer and forgotten Solomon Islands naturalist', *Archives of Natural History* 26:3 (1999), 419–32.

6324. Wheeler, B.; Young, L. 'Antarctica in museums: the Mawson collections in Australia', *Polar Record* 198 (2000), 193–202.

Fc. *Ideas and Learning*

See also 634 (C); 3092, 3107 (H); 5982 (N); 6646 (P)

6325. Ambirajan, S. 'Mill and India', A155, 221–64.

6326. Campbell, Carl C. *The young colonials: a social history of education in Trinidad and Tobago, 1834–1939* (Barbados: The Press, University of the West Indies, 1996), 387p.

6327. Carson, P. 'Golden casket or pebbles and trash? J.S. Mill and the Anglicist/Orientalist controversy', A155, 149–72.

6328. Chakrabarti, D.K. 'Colonial Indology and identity', *Antiquity* 74:285 (2000), 667–670.

6329. Charton, Hélène. *Le désir d'école: les initiatives africaines dans l'éducation au Kenya* (Paris: Publications de l'Université Paris-7-Denis Diderot, 1997), 134p.

6330. Doniger, W. '"I have Scinde": flogging a dead (white male Orientalist) horse', *Journal of Asian Studies* 58:4 (1999), 940–60.

6331. Durrill, Wayne K. 'Shaping a settler elite: students, competition and leadership at South African College, 1829–95', *Journal of African History* 41:2 (2000), 221–239.

6332. Elboim-Dror, R. 'British educational policies in Palestine', *Middle Eastern Studies* 36:2 (2000), 28–47.

6333. Hitchen, P. 'State and church in British Honduran education, 1931–39: a British colonial perspective', *History of Education* 29:3 (2000), 195–212.

6334. Joy, R.J. Hepzi. *History and development of education of women in Kerala (1819–1947)* (Thiruvananthapuram: Seminary Publications, 1995), 275p.

6335. Kosambi, Meera. 'A window in the prison-house: women's education and the politics of social reform in nineteenth-century western India', *History of Education* 29 (2000), 429–42.

6336. Majeed, J. 'James Mill's The History of British India: a reevaluation', A155, 53–71.

6337. Marker, M. 'Ethnohistory and indigenous education: a moment of uncertainty', *History of Education* 29:1 (2000), 79–86.

6338. McLean, David. *Education and empire: naval tradition and England's elite society* (London: British Academic Press, 1999), viii, 184p.

6339. Mirza, Q. 'Colonial fantasies: towards a feminist reading of Orientalism', *Women's Studies International Forum* 23:2 (2000), 259–60.

6340. Munro, D. 'J.W. Davidson and Western Samoa: university politics and the travails of a constitutional adviser', *Journal of Pacific History* 35:2 (2000), 195–212.

6341. Raj, K. 'L'orientalisme en Inde au tournant du XIXe siecle: la reponse du mondialisme britannique a l'universalisme de la Revolution francaise', *Annales historiques de la Révolution française* 320 (2000), 89–100.

6342. Rimmer, Douglas; Kirk-Greene, Anthony Hamilton Millard (eds.) *The British intellectual engagement with Africa in the twentieth century* (Basingstoke: Macmillan in association with the Royal African Society, 2000), [xiv], 267p.

6343. Zastoupil, Lynn; Moir, Martin (eds.) *The great Indian education debate: documents relating to the Orientalist-Anglicist controversy, 1781–1843* (Richmond: Curzon, 1999), xvi, 357p.

Fd. *Culture and the Arts*

See also 3158 (H); 4110 (I); 5987 (N); 6123, 6279, 6419 (P)

6344. Auerbach, Jeffrey. 'Art and Empire' [Historiography], A214, 571–83.

6345. Burns, J. 'Biopics and politics: the making and unmaking of the Rhodes movies', *Biography: an interdisciplinary quarterly* 23:1 (2000), 108–126.

6346. Burns, James. 'Watching Africans watch films: theories of spectatorship in British colonial Africa', *Historical Journal of Film Radio and Television* 20:2 (2000), 197–212.

6347. Butchart, Alexander. *The anatomy of power: European constructions of the African body* (London: Zed Books, 1998), xiv, 220p.

6348. Chowdhry, Prem. *Colonial India and the making of empire cinema: image, ideology and identity* (Manchester: Manchester University Press, 2000), viii, 294p.

6349. Ganachari, A. 'British official view of Bhagwat Gita as "text-book for the mental training of revolutionary recruits"', *Proceedings of the Indian History Congress* 56 (1995), 601–10.

6350. Hedges, P.M. 'Architecture, inculturation and Christian mission: the buildings of the Cambridge Mission to Delhi, and their meaning for the church today', *International Review of Mission* 90:353 (2000), 180–89.

6351. Inglis, Kenneth Stanley. *Sacred places: war memorials in the Australian landscape* (Carlton (Vic): Miegunyah Press at Melbourne University Press, 1998), xvi, 522p.

6352. Kallman, D. 'Projected moralities, engaged anxieties: Northern Rhodesia's reading publics, 1953–1964', *International Journal of African Historical Studies* 32:1 (1999), 71–118.

6353. Kirk-Greene, Anthony Hamilton Millard. 'The colonial service in the novel', A195, 19–48.

6354. Metcalf, Thomas R. 'Architecture in the British Empire' [Historiography], A214, 584–95.

6355. Pfisterer, Susan; Mahony, Edel (eds.) *A fringe of papers: offshore perspectives on Australian history & literature* (London: Sir Robert Menzies Centre for Australian Studies and the British Australian Studies Association, 1999), iv, 106p.

6356. Ramakrishna, V. 'Construction of colonial culture and ideology', *Proceedings of the Indian History Congress* 56 (1996), 487–526.

6357. Rosen, F. 'Eric Stokes, British utilitarianism, and India', A155, 18–33.
6358. Stearn, Roger T. 'Boer War Image-maker: Richard Caton Woodville', A91, 213–23.
6359. Subramanian, L. 'The reinvention of a tradition: nationalism, Carnatic music and the Madras Music Academy, 1900–1947', *Indian Economic and Social History Review* 36:2 (1999), 131–64.
6360. Van Wyk Smith, Malvern. 'Telling the Boer War: narrative indeterminacy in Kipling's stories of the South African War', *South African Historical Journal* 41 (1999), 349–69.
6361. Welter, V.M. 'Arcades for Lucknow: Patrick Geddes, Charles Rennie Mackintosh and the reconstruction of the city', *Architectural History* 42 (1999), 316–32.
6362. Wood, Marcus. *Blind memory: visual representations of slavery in England and America, 1780–1865* (Manchester: Manchester University Press, 2000), 341p.
6363. Zastoupil, Lynn. 'India, J.S. Mill, and "western" culture', A155, 111–48.

G. *Religious Belief, Practice and Organisation*

See also 3354 (H); 4171 (I); 5744 (M); 5994, 5998 (N); 6170, 6350, 6422, 6479, 6483, 6504, 6518, 6523, 6526 (P)

6364. Adderley, Rosanne Marion. 'Orisha worship and "Jesus time": remaking African religious conversion in the nineteenth-century Caribbean', A33, 183–206.
6365. Brock, Peter. 'Mission encounters in the colonial world: British Columbia and south-west Australia', *Journal of Religious History* 24:2 (2000), 159–79.
6366. Bugge, Henriette. *Mission and Tamil society: social and religious change in south India (1840–1900)* (Richmond: Curzon, 1994), 223p.
6367. Comaroff, John L.; Comaroff, Jean. 'Cultivation, Christianity and colonialism: towards a new African genesis', A62, 55–81.
6368. Cox, James Leland (ed.) *Rites of passage in contemporary Africa: interaction between Christian and African traditional religions* (Cardiff: Cardiff Academic Press, 1998) A168, xx, 259p.
6369. Cuthbertson, Greg. 'Pricking the "nonconformist conscience": religion against the South African War', A139, 169–87.
6370. de Gruchy, John W. 'Remembering a legacy' [The London Missionary Society in Southern Africa], A62, 1–6.
6371. Douglas, S.; LeMarquand, G. 'A bibliography of Anglicanism outside continental North America and the British Isles', *Anglican and Episcopal History* 68:4 (1999), 517–43.
6372. Elbourne, Elizabeth. 'Whose gospel? Conflict in the LMS in the early 1840s', A62, 132–55.
6373. Erlank, Natasha. 'Jane and John Philip: partnership, usefulness & sexuality in the service of God', A62, 82–98.
6374. Etherington, Norman A. 'The standard of living question in nineteenth-century missions in KwaZulu-Natal', A62, 156–65.

6375. Etherington, Norman A. 'Missions and empire' [Historiography], A214, 303–14.

6376. Falola, Toyin. *Violence in Nigeria: the crisis of religious politics and secular ideologies* (Rochester (NY): University of Rochester Press, 1998), xxi, 386p.

6377. Francis-Dehqani, Gulnar Eleanor. *Religious feminism in an age of empire: CMS women missionaries in Iran, 1869–1934* (Bristol: Centre for Comparative Studies in Religion and Gender, 2000), 251p.

6378. Hiney, Tom. *On the missionary trail: the classic Georgian adventure of two Englishmen, sent on a journey around the world, 1821–29* (London: Chatto & Windus, 2000), xiv, 367p.

6379. Lange, R. 'Indigenous agents of religious change in New Zealand, 1830–1860', *Journal of Religious History* 24:3 (2000), 279–95.

6380. Ludlow, Helen. '"Working at the heart": the London Missionary Society in Cape Town, 1842–3', A62, 99–119.

6381. Lutz, J.G. 'The legacy of Karl Friedrich August Gutzlaff', *International Bulletin of Missionary Research* 24:3 (2000), 123–127.

6382. Malik, Jamal. *Colonialization of Islam: dissolution of traditional institutions in Pakistan* (New Delhi: Manohar, 1998), xiv, 359p.

6383. Porter, Andrew Neil. 'The career of William Ellis: British missions, the Pacific, and the American connection', A85, 193–214.

6384. Ride, Lindsay; Ride, May. 'An East India Company cemetery: Protestant burials in Macao', *Nineteenth Century Contexts* 21:4 (2000), 617–19.

6385. Roe, Jeremy (comp. & ed.) *Daniel Allen: pastor and pioneer* (Australia's Particular Baptist Heritage, 4) (Ryde (NSW): CBO Publications, 1998), 86p.

6386. Ross, Andrew. 'David Livingstone: the man behind the mask', A62, 37–54.

6387. Ross, Robert. 'Congregations, missionaries and the Grahamstown schism of 1842–3', A62, 120–31.

6388. Rountree, K. 'Re-making the Maori female body: Marianne William's mission in the Bay of Islands', *Journal of Pacific History* 35:1 (2000), 49–66.

6389. Saunders, Christopher. 'Looking back: 170 years of historical writing on the LMS in South Africa', A62, 7–16.

6390. Schoffeleers, Matthew. *In search of truth and justice: confrontations between church and state in Malawi 1960–1994* (Kachere Books, 8) ([Blantyre (Malawi)]: Christian Literature Association in Malawi, 1999), 383p.

6391. Southerwood, William Terrance. *Catholics in British colonies: planting a faith where no sun sets—islands and dependencies of Britain till 1900* (London: Minerva, 1998), xii, 385p.

6392. Spear, Thomas T.; Kimambo, Isaria N. (eds.) *East African expressions of Christianity* (Oxford and Athens (OH): James Currey and Ohio University Press, 1999), xi, 340p.

6393. Switzer, Les. 'American missionaries and the making of an African church in colonial Natal', A62, 166–88.

6394. Ward, Kevin; Stanley, Brian (eds.) *The Church Mission Society and world Christianity, 1799–1999* (Grand Rapids (MI) and Richmond (Sry): W.B. Eerdmans and Curzon Press, 2000), xviii, 382p.

6395. Young, Brian William. '"The lust of empire and religious hate": Christianity, history, and India, 1790–1820', A47, 91–111.
6396. Zaman, Muhammad Qasim. 'Religious education and the rhetoric of reform: the Madrasa in British India and Pakistan', *Comparative Studies in Society and History* 41:2 (1999), 294–323.

Ha. *Law and Order*

See also 2550 (G); 3384 (H); 5763 (M); 6002 (N); 6242, 6277, 6531 (P)

6397. *The Amritsar massacre, 1919: General Dyer in the Punjab*, abridged edn. (London: The Stationery Office, 2000), 167p. [1st published 1920.]
6398. Anderson, Clare. *Convicts in the Indian Ocean: transportation from south Asia to Mauritius, 1815–53* (Basingstoke and New York: Macmillan and St Martin's Press, 2000), xii, 192p.
6399. Bailey, Mark W. 'John Reeves, Esq., Newfoundland's first chief justice: English law and politics in the eighteenth century', *Newfoundland Studies* 14:1 (1998), 28–49.
6400. Chatterjee, Indrani. *Gender, slavery and law in colonial India* (New Delhi and Oxford: Oxford University Press, 1999), xii, 286p.
6401. De, B. '"Maintenance of order" in early wartime Bengal, 1939–1942', *Proceedings of the Indian History Congress* 56 (1995), 646–56.
6402. Kituai, August Ibrum K. *My gun, my brother: the world of the Papua New Guinea colonial police, 1920–1960* (Pacific Islands Monograph series, 15) (Honolulu (HI): University of Hawai'i Press, 1998), xx, 414p.
6403. Kostal, R.W. 'A jurisprudence of power: martial law and the Ceylon controversy of 1848–51', *Journal of Imperial and Commonwealth History* 28 (2000), 1–34.
6404. Macoun, Michael J. *Wrong place, right time: policing the end of empire* (London: Radcliffe, 1996), xxiii, 184p.
6405. Miller, P. 'Inventing mastery: patriarchal precedents and the legal status of indigenous people in Australia', *Journal of Historical Sociology* 13:3 (2000), 264–288.
6406. Mitchell, Robin. 'The Nigerian police: profile of a police detachment', A195, 213–27.
6407. Munn, Christopher. 'The transportation of Chinese convicts from Hong Kong, 1844–1858', *Journal of the Canadian Historical Association* ns 8 (1997), 113–45.
6408. Olukoju, Ayodeji. 'Self-help criminality as resistance?: Currency counterfeiting in colonial Nigeria', *International Review of Social History* 45:3 (2000), 385–408.
6409. Picker, Gregory. 'A state of infancy: the anti-transportation movement in New Zealand, 1848–1852', *New Zealand Journal of History* 34:2 (2000), 226–40.
6410. Ramakrishna, Kumar. 'Content, credibility and context: propaganda, government surrender policy and the Malayan Communist terrorist mass surrenders of 1958', *Intelligence and National Security* 14:4 (1999), 242–66.

6411.   Reece, Bob. '"Such a banditti": Irish convicts in Newfoundland, 1789. Pt. 1', *Newfoundland Studies* 13:1 (1997), 1–29.
6412.   Reece, Bob. '"Such a banditti": Irish convicts in Newfoundland, 1789. Pt. 2', *Newfoundland Studies* 13:2 (1997), 127–41.
6413.   Richardson, Sam. 'Indirect rule and law reform in northern Nigeria', A195, 209–12.
6414.   Shadle, B.L. '"Changing traditions to meet current altering conditions": customary law, African courts and the rejection of codification in Kenya, 1930–60', *Journal of African History* 40:3 (1999), 411–32.
6415.   Shamir, Ronen. *The colonies of law: colonialism, Zionism, and law in early mandate Palestine* (Cambridge: Cambridge University Press, 2000), xiii, 216p.
6416.   Skuy, D. 'Macaulay and the Indian penal code of 1862: the myth of the inherent superiority and modernity of the English legal system compared to India's legal system in the nineteenth century', *Modern Asian Studies* 32:3 (1998), 513–58.
6417.   Strange, Carolyn; Loo, Tina Merrill. *Making good: law and moral regulation in Canada, 1867–1939* (Toronto (Ont) and London: University of Toronto Press, 1997), x, 170p.
6418.   Tollefson, Harold. *Policing Islam: the British occupation of Egypt and the Anglo-Egyptian struggle over control of the police, 1882–1914* (Contributions in Comparative Colonial Studies (Westport (CT) and London: Greenwood, 1999), xiv, 200p.
6419.   Walsh, M. 'The empire of the censors: film censorship in the Dominions', *Journal of Popular British Cinema* 3 (2000), 45–58.
6420.   Ward, Iain. *Mariners: the Hong Kong Marine Police, 1948–1997* (Wivenhoe: IEW, 1999), ix, 271p.

Hb. *Public Administration*

See also 6223, 6229, 6262, 6567 (P)

6421.   Auchterlonie, P. 'A turk of the west: Sir Edgar Vincent's career in Egypt and the Ottoman empire', *British Journal of Middle Eastern Studies* 27:1 (2000), 49–68.
6422.   Cassels, N.G. 'John Stuart Mill, religion, and law in the Examiner's Office', A155, 173–97.
6423.   Clark, Trevor. 'Chalk and cheese? The colonial and diplomatic services', A195, 49–59.
6424.   Davey, Kenneth. 'Colonial development and good government [in Uganda]: a personal perspective', A195, 119–27.
6425.   Davies, Philip H.J. 'The SIS Singapore station and the SIS Far Eastern controller', *Intelligence and National Security* 14:4 (1999), 105–29.
6426.   Fedorowich, Kent. 'Decolonization deferred?: the re-establishment of colonial rule in Hong Kong, 1942–45', *Journal of Imperial and Commonwealth History* 28:3 (2000), 25–50.
6427.   Gullick, John. 'Colonial administrators and businessmen in postwar Malaya', A195, 287–93.

6428. Hannam, K. 'Utilitarianism and the identity of the Indian Forest Service', *Environment and History* 6:2 (2000), 205–28.

6429. Johnson, John. 'The Mau Mau emergency and the administration', A195, 103–8.

6430. Judd, Denis (ed.) *A British tale of Indian and foreign service: the memoirs of Sir Ian Scott* (London: Radcliffe, 1999), xiii, 287p.

6431. Khan, M.M. 'Civil service reforms in British India and united Pakistan', *International Journal of Public Administration* 22:6 (1999), 947–54.

6432. Kirk-Greene, Anthony Hamilton Millard. *Britain's imperial administrators, 1858–1966* (Basingstoke: Macmillan in association with St Antony's College, Oxford, 2000), xv, 347p.

6433. Kruijer-Poesiat, Lies. 'An inauguration in Suriname, 1804', *Studia Rosenthaliana* 34 (2000), 194–7.

6434. Lonsdale, John. 'British colonial officials and the Kikuyu people', A195, 95–102.

6435. Lynn, Martin R.S. 'Nigerian complications: the Colonial Office, the colonial service and the 1953 crisis in Nigeria', A195, 181–208.

6436. Marshall, Peter James. 'The British experience of imperial rule', A195, 1–18.

6437. Marshall, Peter James. 'The case for coercing America before the revolution', A135, 9–22.

6438. Miller, Rory. 'Sir Ronald Storrs and Zion: the dream that turned into a nightmare', *Middle Eastern Studies* 36:3 (2000), 114–144.

6439. Milne, Malcolm. *No telephone to heaven: from apex to nadir—colonial service in Nigeria, Aden, the Cameroons and the Gold Coast, 1938–61* (Stockbridge: Meon Hill, 1999), 464p.

6440. Moir, Martin. 'John Stuart Mill's draft despatches to India and the problem of bureaucratic authorship', A155, 72–86.

6441. Moore, R. 'The debris of empire: the 1981 Nationality Act and the Oceanic Dependent Territories', *Immigrants & Minorities* 19:1 (2000), 1–24.

6442. Murphy, Philip. *Alan Lennox-Boyd: a biography* (London: I.B. Tauris, 1999), xi, 276p.

6443. Newman, Joanna. 'The Colonial Office and British refugee policy in the 1930s', A195, 259–67.

6444. Nsibambi, Apolo (ed.) *Decentralisation and civil society in Uganda: the quest for good governance* (Kampala: Fountain, 1998), vi, 154p.

6445. O'Brien, P.K. 'Balance sheets for the acquisition, retention and loss of european empires overseas', *Itinerario* 23:3–4 (1999), 25–52.

6446. Pachauri, S.K. 'British relations with princely states in the 19th century: case study of relation of trust and fealty with the rule of Patiala', *Proceedings of the Indian History Congress* 56 (1995), 532–44.

6447. Rathbone, Richard. 'The colonial service and the transfer of power in Ghana', A195, 149–66.

6448. Rathbone, Richard. 'The transfer of power and colonial civil servants in Ghana', *Journal of Imperial and Commonwealth History* 28:2 (2000), 67–84.

6449. Read, James. 'Indirect rule and the search for justice in east Africa', A195, 109–18.

6450. Stuart, Andrew. 'French & English: a colonial game or a colonial war?', A195, 295–303.

6451. Taylor, David. 'Governing Montserrat: a case study', A195, 249–57.

6452. Taylor, D.G.P. 'British colonial policy in the Caribbean: the insoluble dilemma—the case of Montserrat', *Round Table* 355 (2000), 337–344.

6453. Taylor, John. 'Ottawa: Canada's evolving capital', *The Historian* [London] 66 (2000), 17–21.

6454. Thomas, Graham F. (ed.) *The Sudan journal of Ismay Thomas* (Lewes: Book Guild, 2000), 177p.

6455. Thompson, Gardner. 'Governing Uganda: the Second World War and its aftermath', A195, 129–46.

6456. Turnbull, Mary. 'The Malayan civil service and the transition to independence', A195, 271–86.

6457. Waley, Daniel Philip. *A Liberal Life: Sydney, Earl Buxton, 1853–1934: statesman, Governor-General of South Africa* (Hassocks: Newtimber, 1999), 376p.

6458. Waters, Michael. 'Hong Kong: administrative preparations for 1997', A195, 331–40.

6459. Worby, Eric. '"Discipline without oppression": sequence, timing and marginality in Southern Rhodesia's post-war development regime', *Journal of African History* 41:1 (2000), 101–25.

6460. Wrangham, Elizabeth. 'The colonial service and the First World War: "carrying on": the service under strain', A195, 167–80.

Hc. *Political and Constitutional*

See also 2568 (G); 3416, 3423, 3508 (H); 4341, 4370, 4447, 4807 (I); 5792 (M); 5967, 6009, 6018 (N); 6065, 6116, 6168, 6178, 6281, 6284, 6296, 6314, 6345, 6376, 6390, 6637, 6640 (P)

6461. Ahmad, A. 'The non-cooperation, Gandhi and Aligarh (1920)', *Proceedings of the Indian History Congress* 54 (1994), 428–32.

6462. Ali, S. 'The Ottoman caliphate and British imperialism in India', *Proceedings of the Indian History Congress* 54 (1994), 739–47.

6463. Antlöv, Hans; Tonnesson, Stein (eds.) *Imperial policy and Southeast Asian nationalism 1930–1957* (Studies on Asian Topics, 19) (London: Curzon, 1995), xiii, 322p.

6464. Ashton, Stephen. 'If the price is right: the West Indies Federation and decolonisation in the British Caribbean', A195, 231–47.

6465. Bandyopadhyay, S. 'Transfer of power and the crisis of Dalit politics in India, 1945–47', *Modern Asian Studies* 34:4 (2000), 893–942.

6466. Beckles, H. 'Just cricket: black struggles for racial justice and equality', *African Studies* 58:2 (1999), 171–90.

6467. Benyon, John. '"Intermediate" imperialism and the test of empire: Milner's "excentric" High Commission in South Africa', A139, 84–103.

6468. Bhattacharya, S. '"A great destiny": the British colonial state and the advertisement of post-war reconstruction in India, 1942–45', *South Asia Research* 19:1 (1999), 71–100.

6469. Blyth, Robert J. 'Redrawing the boundary between India and Britain: the succession crisis at Zanzibar, 1870–1873', *International History Review* 22:4 (2000), 785–805.

6470. Buckner, Philip. 'The Royal Tour of 1901 and the construction of an imperial identity in South Africa', *South African Historical Journal* 41 (1999), 324–48.

6471. Butler, L.J. 'Britain, the United States, and the demise of the Central African Federation, 1959–63', *Journal of Imperial and Commonwealth History* 28:3 (2000), 131–51.

6472. Callahan, Michael Dennis. *Mandates and empire: the League of Nations and Africa, 1914–1931* (Brighton: Sussex Academic Press, 1999), ix, 297p.

6473. Campbell, I.C. 'The ASOPA controversy: a pivot of Australian policy for Papua and New Guinea, 1945–49', *Journal of Pacific History* 35:1 (2000), 83–100.

6474. Chamberlain, Muriel Evelyn. *Decolonisation: the fall of the European empires*, 2nd edn. (Malden (MA): Blackwell, 1999), xvi, 140p. [1st published 1985.]

6475. Chester, Lucy. 'Parting of the ways' [drawing the Indo-Pakistan border, 1947], *History Today* 50:3 (2000), 36–7.

6476. Dappa-Biriye, Harold J.R. *Minority politics in pre- and post-independence Nigeria* (Port Harcourt: University of Port Harcourt Press, 1995), ix, 67p.

6477. Darwin, John Gareth. 'Decolonization and the end of empire' [Historiography], A214, 541–57.

6478. Darwin, John Gareth. 'What was the late colonial state?', *Itinerario* 23:3–4 (1999), 73–82.

6479. de Gruchy, Steve. 'The alleged political conservatism of Robert Moffat', A62, 17–36.

6480. Dobell, Lauren. *SWAPO's struggle for Namibia, 1960–1991: war by other means* (Basel Namibia Studies series, 3) (Basel: P. Schlettwein, 1998), 175p.

6481. Ducharme, Michel. 'L'État selon Lord Durham: liberté et nationalité dans l'empire britannique', *Cahiers d'Histoire* [Montreal] 18:2 (1998), 39–64.

6482. Dyson, Sally (comp. & ed.) *Nigeria: the birth of Africa's greatest country: from the pages of Drum magazine* (Ibadan and Oxford: Spectrum Books, 1998), 2 vols.

6483. Elbourne, Elizabeth. '"Race", warfare, and religion in mid-nineteenth-century Southern Africa: the Khoikhoi rebellion against the Cape Colony', *Journal of African Cultural Studies* 13:1 (2000), 17–42.

6484. Fraser, Cary. 'The "new frontier" of Empire in the Caribbean: the transfer of power in British Guiana, 1961–1964', *International History Review* 22:3 (2000), 583–610.

6485. Gocking, Roger. 'A chieftaincy dispute and ritual murder in Elmina, Ghana, 1945–6', *Journal of African History* 41:2 (2000), 197–219.

6486. Grigg, John. 'Myths about the approach to Indian independence', A138.

6487. Gurney, C. '"A great cause": the origins of the Anti-Apartheid Movement, June 1959–March 1960', *Journal of Southern African Studies* 26:1 (2000), 123–44.

6488. Hamilton, Carolyn. *Terrific majesty: the powers of Shaka Zulu and the limits of historical invention* (Cape Town and Johannesburg; Cambridge (MA): David Philip and Harvard University Press, 1998), xii, 278p.

6489. Hazareesingh, S. 'The quest for urban citizenship: civic rights, public opinion and colonial resistance in early twentieth-century Bombay', *Modern Asian Studies* 34:4 (2000), 797–830.

6490. Hiller, James K.; Harrington, Michael F. (eds.) *The Newfoundland National Convention, 1946–1948: debates, papers and reports* (Montréal: McGill-Queen's University Press on behalf of Memorial University of Newfoundland, 1994), 2 vols.

6491. Holland, Robert F. 'The decolonizing metropole: British experience from India to Hong Kong, 1947–1997', *European Review* [Chichester] 8:1 (2000), 65–76.

6492. Jackson, Michael. *A Scottish life: Sir John Martin, Churchill and empire*, ed. Janet Jackson (London: Radcliffe, 1999), xiv, 279p.

6493. Jones, Matthew. 'Creating Malaysia: Singapore security, the Borneo Territories, and the contours of British policy, 1961–63', *Journal of Imperial and Commonwealth History* 28:2 (2000), 85–109.

6494. Kelemen, Paul. 'Looking the other way: the British Labour Party, Zionism and the Palestinians', A46, 141–57.

6495. Kotzin, D.P. 'An attempt to Americanize the Yishuv: Judah L. Magnes in mandatory Palestine', *Israel Studies* 5:1 (2000), 1–23.

6496. Kozhuvanal, Antony. 'Gandhi's Satyagraha and its roots in India's past', A25, 440–54.

6497. Loewenstein, A.B. ' "The veiled protectorate of Kowait": liberalized imperialism and British efforts to influence Kuwaiti domestic policy during the reign of Sheikh Ahmad al-Jaber, 1938–50', *Middle Eastern Studies* 36:2 (2000), 103–23.

6498. Low, Donald Anthony; Brasted, Howard (eds.) *Freedom, trauma, continuities: northern India and independence* (New Delhi and London: Sage, 1998) [ix], 237p.

6499. Lowry, Donal. ' "These colonies are practically democratic republics" (James Bryce): republicanism in the British colonies of settlement in the long nineteenth century', A165, 125–39.

6500. Madden, A. Frederick (ed.) *The end of empire: dependencies since 1948, part 1: the West Indies, British Honduras, Hong Kong, Fiji, Cyprus, Gibraltar, and the Falklands* (Select Documents on the Constitutional History of the British Empire and Commonwealth, 8) (Westport (CT) and London: Greenwood, 2000), xxxv, 555p.

6501. Marshall, Peter James. *The writings and speeches of Edmund Burke*, vol.7: *India: the Hastings trial, 1789–1794* (Oxford: Clarendon, 2000), xiv, 728p.

6502. Martel, Gordon. 'Decolonisation after Suez: retreat or rationalisation?', *Australian Journal of Politics & History* 46:3 (2000), 403–17.

6503. Martin, Allan William. *Robert Menzies: a life*, vol.2: *1944–1978* (Carlton (Vic): Melbourne University Press, 2000). [Volume 1 published 1993.]

6504. Maxwell, David James. ' "Catch the cockerel before dawn": pentecostalism and politics in post-colonial Zimbabwe', *Africa* [London] 70:2 (2000), 249–277.

6505. McIntyre, W. David. 'Britain and the creation of the Commonwealth Secretariat', *Journal of Imperial and Commonwealth History* 28 (2000), 135–58.

6506. McKnight, Glenn H. 'Land, politics, and Buganda's "indigenous" colonial state', *Journal of Imperial and Commonwealth History* 28 (2000), 65–89.

6507. McMinn, Winston Gregory. *Nationalism and federalism in Australia* (Melbourne (Vic) and Oxford: Oxford University Press, 1994), vi, 317p.

6508. Mehta, Uday Singh. *Liberalism and empire: a study in nineteenth-century British liberal thought* (Chicago (IL) and London: University of Chicago Press, 1999), xii, 237p. [Also published with subtitle *India in British liberal thought* (New Delhi: Oxford University Press, 1999).]

6509. Merle, Isabelle. 'Le Mabo case: l'australie face à son passé colonial', *Annales* 53 (1998), 209–29.

6510. Moore, Brian L. *Cultural power, resistance and pluralism: colonial Guyana, 1838–1900* (Kingston (Jamaica): The Press, University of the West Indies, 1995), xiii, 376p.

6511. Moore, Erin. *Gender, law, and resistance in India* (Tucson (AZ): University of Arizona Press, 1998), x, 205p.

6512. Moore, R. 'John Stuart Mill and royal India', A155, 87–110.

6513. Morris, Benny. *Righteous victims: a history of the Zionist-Arab conflict, 1881–1999* (London: John Murray, 1999), xiv, 751p.

6514. Mungazi, Dickson A. *The last British liberals in Africa: Michael Blundell and Garfield Todd* (Westport (CT) and London: Praeger, 1999), xvi, 285p.

6515. Nafi, Basheer M. *Arabism, Islamism and the Palestine question, 1908–1941: a political history* (Reading: Ithaca Press, 1998), vii, 459p.

6516. Nash, David S. 'Charles Bradlaugh, India and the many chameleon destinations of republicanism', A165, 106–24.

6517. Nitzan-Shiftan, A. 'Contested Zionism—alternative modernism: Erich Mendelsohn and the Tel Aviv Chug in mandate Palestine', *Architectural History* 39 (1996), 147–80.

6518. Oddie, Geoffrey A. *Missionaries, rebellion and proto-nationalism: James Long of Bengal 1814–87* (Richmond: Curzon, 1999), xiv, 261p.

6519. Otieno, Wambui Waiyaki. *Mau Mau's daughter: a life history*, ed. Cora Ann Presley. (Boulder (CO) and London: Lynne Reinner Publications, 1998), xiii, 255p.

6520. Pandey, S.N. 'Tribal uprising in north-east India during the British rule: Kuki and Naga revolts in Manipur', *Proceedings of the Indian History Congress* 56 (1995), 545–50.

6521. Peers, Douglas M. 'Imperial epitaph: John Stuart Mill's defence of the East India Company', A155, 198–220.

6522. Phimister, Ian; Raftopoulos, B. '"Kana sora ratswa ngaritswe": African nationalists and black workers—the 1948 general strike in colonial Zimbabwe', *Journal of Historical Sociology* 13:3 (2000), 289–324.

6523. Rafferty, Oliver P. 'Fenianism in North America in the 1860s: problems for church and state', *History* 84 (1999), 257–77.

6524. Ram Singh, S. 'Gandhi, the colonial middle class and the Indian people', *Proceedings of the Indian History Congress* 54 (1994), 1–33.

6525. Rama Rathan, G.G. 'Mysore state and Indian National Congress before Gandhi's advent', *Proceedings of the Indian History Congress 56* (1995), 551–56.

6526. Saillant, John. 'Antiguan Methodism and antislavery activity: Anne and Elizabeth Hart in the eighteenth-century black Atlantic', *Church History* 69:1 (2000), 86–115.

6527. Samaddara, Ranabira. *Memory, identity, power: politics in the jungle Mahals (West Bengal), 1890–1950* (London: Sangam, 1998), viii, 295p.

6528. Schneer, Jonathan. 'Anti-imperial London: the Pan-African Conference of 1900', A71, 254–67.

6529. Segev, Tom. *One Palestine, complete: Jews and Arabs under the British mandate* (New York and London: Little, Brown, 2000), viii, 612p. [1st published in Hebrew: *Yamei Kalaniot* (Jerusalem: Keter, 1999).]

6530. Sharma, K.K. 'Legislative politics & agrarian agitation in Bihar, 1917–1931', *Proceedings of the Indian History Congress 56* (1995), 773–76.

6531. Silvestri, Michael. '"The Sinn Féin of India": Irish nationalism and the policing of revolutionary terrorism in Bengal', *Journal of British Studies* 39:4 (2000), 454–86.

6532. Simoni, M. 'At the roots of division: a new perspective on Arabs and Jews, 1930–39', *Middle Eastern Studies* 36:3 (2000), 52–92.

6533. Singh, S.B. 'Clash between Indian judiciary and executive during Second World War', *Proceedings of the Indian History Conference 54* (1994), 451–57.

6534. Sinha, Mrinalini. 'Suffragism and internationalism: the enfranchisement of British and Indian women under an imperial state', *Indian Economic and Social History Review* 36:4 (1999), 461–84.

6535. Smith, John. 'Preparation for independence: West African experience applied to the Pacific', A195, 305–22.

6536. Smith, Simon C. 'Revolution and reaction: South Arabia in the aftermath of the Yemeni revolution', *Journal of Imperial and Commonwealth History* 28:3 (2000), 193–208.

6537. Stromberg, J.R. 'Maatskappy, state, and empire: a Pro-Boer revision', *Journal of Libertarian Studies* 14:1 (1999), 1–26.

6538. Subritzky, John. 'Britain, *Konfrontasi*, and the end of empire in southeast Asia, 1961–65', *Journal of Imperial and Commonwealth History* 28:3 (2000), 209–27.

6539. Talbot, Ian Arthur; Singh, Gurharpal (eds.) *Region and partition: Bengal, Punjab and the partition of the subcontinent* (Oxford: Oxford University Press, 1999), viii, 407p.

6540. Tamarkin, Mordechai. 'The Cape Afrikaners and the British empire from the Jameson raid to the South African War', A139, 121–39.

6541. Tarling, Nicholas. *Nations and states in Southeast Asia* (Cambridge: Cambridge University Press, 1998), x, 136p.

6542. Taylor, Miles. 'The 1848 revolutions and the British empire', *Past & Present* 166 (2000), 146–80.

6543. Thompson, Andrew Stuart. *Imperial Britain: the empire in British politics, c.1880–1932* (Harlow: Longman, 2000), xvii, 219p.

6544. Tollenaere, Herman Ary Oscar de. *The politics of divine wisdom: theosophy and labour, national, and women's movements in Indonesia and South Asia, 1875–1947* (Nijmegen: Uitgeverij Katholieke Universiteit, 1996), xxiii, 459p.

6545. Watson, Ruth. 'Murder and the political body in early colonial Ibadan', *Africa* 70:1 (2000), 25–48.

6546. Watts, R. 'Breaking the boundaries of Victorian imperialism or extending a reformed "paternalism"? Mary Carpenter and India', *History of Education* 29 (2000), 443–56.

6547. Weaver, Stewart. 'The pro-Boers: war, empire, and the uses of nostalgia in turn-of-the-century England', A13, 43–57.

6548. Weiss, Ruth (with Parpart, Jane L.). *Sir Garfield Todd and the making of Zimbabwe* (London: British Academic, 1999), xx, 234p.

6549. Wolton, Suke. *Lord Hailey, the Colonial Office and the politics of race and empire in the Second World War: the loss of white prestige* (Basingstoke: Macmillan in association with St Antony's College, Oxford, 2000), xii, 221p.

6550. Wood-Ellem, Elizabeth. *Queen Salote of Tonga: the story of an era, 1900–1965* (Auckland (NZ): Auckland University Press, 1999), xix, 376p.

6551. Worden, Nigel. *The making of modern South Africa: conquest, segregation, and apartheid*, 3rd edn. (Oxford: Blackwell, 2000), xiv, 194p. [2nd edn. 1995.]

J. Military

See also 517 (B); 3071, 3158, 3548, 3593 (H); 3959, 4518, 4527, 4551, 4562, 4599, 4610, 4685, 4692, 4756, 4785, 4807, 4851, 4856 (I); 6154, 6235, 6266, 6282, 6286–8, 6291, 6297, 6351, 6358, 6360, 6369, 6403, 6426, 6460, 6480, 6493, 6547, 6683, 6691, 6693 (P)

6552. Anonymous. *The Boer War: Ladysmith & Mafeking 1900* (London: Stationery Office, 1999), 212p.

6553. Anonymous. *The British invasion of Tibet: Colonel Younghusband, 1904*, abridged edn. (London: Stationery Office, 1999), 249p. [1st published 1904 as Cd.1920.]

6554. Aldrich, Richard J. *Legacies of secret service: renegade SOE and the Karen struggle in Burma, 1948–50 Intelligence and National Security* 14:4 (1999), 130–48p.

6555. Allen, Charles. *Soldier sahibs: the men who made the North-West Frontier* (London: John Murrary, 2000), xii, 368p.

6556. Anderson, D. 'The very model of a modern manoeuvrist general: William Slim and the exercise of high command in Burma', *Strategic and Combat Studies Institute Occasional Paper* 38 (1999), 60–74.

6557. Antal, Sandy. *A wampum denied: Procter's War of 1812* (Ottawa (Ont) and East Lansing (MI): Carleton University Press and Michigan State University Press, 1997), xv, 450p.

6558. Beckett, Ian F.W. 'Buller and the politics of command', A91, 41–55.

6559. Benn, Carl. *The Iroquois in the War of 1812* (Toronto (Ont), London and Buffalo (NY): University of Toronto Press, 1998), xi, 272p.

6560. Bennett, William. *Absent minded beggars: volunteers in the Boer War* ([South Yorkshire]: Leo Cooper, 1999), 260p.

6561. Benyon, John. 'The "walkover" that wasn't: "miscalculation" and the "unneccessary" South African War', *South African Historical Journal* 41 (1999), 106–29.

6562. Bhattacharya, S. 'British military information management techniques and the south Asian soldier: eastern India during the Second World War', *Modern Asian Studies* 34:2 (2000), 483–510.

6563. Bhebe, Ngwabi; Ranger, Terence Osborn (eds.) *Society in Zimbabwe's liberation war* (Oxford: Currey, 1996), vi, 250p.

6564. Bierman, John; Smith, Colin. *Fire in the night: Wingate of Burma, Ethiopia, and Zion* (New York: Random House, 1999), 434p.

6565. Blackburn, George G. *The guns of war* (London: Constable, 2000), 1056p. [Originally published in two volumes: *The guns of Normandy* (Toronto: McClelland & Stewart, 1995), 511p.; *The guns of Victory* (1996), 506p.]

6566. Bose, B. 'Royal Indian uprising in 1946: last blow to British raj', *Proceedings of the Indian History Congress* 56 (1995), 766–68.

6567. Boyce, D.G. 'From Assaye to the Assaye: reflections on British government, force, and moral authority in India', *Journal of Military History* 63:3 (1999), 643–68.

6568. Bridge, T. 'Kitchener: the road to Omdurman', *Army Quarterly & Defence Journal* 129:3 (1999), 340–42.

6569. Brock, Peter; Saunders, Malcolm. 'Pacifists as conscientious objectors in Australia', A25, 272–91.

6570. Bryant, Geoffrey J. 'Indigenous mercenaries in the service of European imperialists: the case of the Sepoys in the early British Indian Army, 1750–1800', *War in History* 7 (2000), 2–28.

6571. Bussemaker, H.T. 'Paradise in peril: the Netherlands, Great Britain and the defence of the Netherlands East Indies, 1940–41', *Journal of Southeast Asian Studies* 31:1 (2000), 115–36.

6572. Carruthers, Jane. 'A kaleidoscopic commentary: the South African War journals of James Stevenson-Hamilton', *South African Historical Journal* 41 (1999), 196–221.

6573. Carter, David J. *POW: behind Canadian barbed wire: alien, refugee and prisoner of war camps in Canada, 1914–1946* (Elkwater (Alta.): Eagle Butte Press, 1998), ii, 253p.

6574. Carver, Michael. *The National Army Museum book of the Boer War* (London: Sidgwick & Jackson in association with the National Army Museum, 1999), 301p.

6575. Chandramohan, Balasubramanyam. '"Hamlet with the Prince of Denmark left out"?: The South African War, empire and India', A139, 150–68.

6576. Chene, M.D. 'Military ethnology in British India', *South Asia Research* 19:2 (1999), 121–36.

6577. Cookson, J.E. 'Pacifism and conscientious objection in New Zealand', A25, 272–91.

6578. Crawford, John (ed.). *Kia Kaha: New Zealand in the Second World War* (Auckland (NZ): Oxford University Press, 2000), xiv, 330p.
6579. Cuthbertson, Greg; Jeeves, Alan. 'The many-sided struggle for Southern Africa, 1899–1902', *South African Historical Journal* 41 (1999), 2–21.
6580. Dedering, Tilman. 'The Ferreira raid of 1906: Boers, Britons and Germans in southern Africa in the aftermath of the South African War', *Journal of Southern African Studies* 26:1 (2000), 43–60.
6581. Downham, John. *Red roses on the Veldt: Lancashire regiments in the Boer War, 1899–1902* (Lancaster: Carnegie, 2000), xiv, 338p.
6582. Drysdall, Alan R. *Rhodesia's role in the Second Anglo-Boer War* (Anglo-Boer War Philatelic Society publications, 9) (Chester: Anglo-Boer War Philatelic Society, 2000), 103p.
6583. Dyde, Brian. *The empty sleeve: the story of the West India regiments of the British army* (St John's (Antigua) and London: Hansib and Readers Book Club, 1997).
6584. Easter, David. 'British and Malaysian covert support for rebel movements in Indonesia during the "Confrontation", 1963–66', *Intelligence and National Security* 14:4 (1999), 195–210.
6585. Farndale, Sir Martin. *The Far East theatre, 1941–1946* (History of the Royal Regiment of Artillery, ns, 6) (London: Brassey's, 2000), xix, 464p.
6586. Fisher, John. 'Major Norman Bray and eastern unrest in the aftermath of World War I', *Asian Affairs* 31:2 (2000), 189–97.
6587. Flower-Smith, Malcolm; Yorke, Edmund. *Mafeking!: the story of a siege* (Weltevredenpark: Covos-Day, 2000), 174p.
6588. Gooch, John. 'Introduction' [The Anglo-Boer War], A91, xi–xxi.
6589. Gough, Barry M. *HMCS Haida: battle ensign flying* (St. Catharines (Ont): Vanwell, 2000).
6590. Gough, Barry M. 'The Royal Navy and the British empire' [Historiography], A214, 327–41.
6591. Gould, Tony. *Imperial warriors: Britain and the Gurkhas* (London: Granta, 1999), 480p.
6592. Grey, Jeffrey. *A military history of Australia*, revised edn. (Cambridge: Cambridge University Press, 1999), xi, 300p.
6593. Griffiths, R.J. 'The white man's burden—the story of the capture of German Cameroun, 1914', *Army Quarterly & Defence Journal* 129:3 (1999), 343–46.
6594. Grundlingh, Albert. 'The king's Afrikaners? Enlistment and ethnic identity in the Union of South Africa's defence force during the Second World War, 1939–45', *Journal of African History* 40:3 (1999), 351–66.
6595. Hack, Karl. 'British intelligence and counter-insurgency in the era of decolonisation: the example of Malaya', *Intelligence and National Security* 14:2 (1999).
6596. Hack, Karl. 'Corpses, prisoners of war and captured documents: British and Communist narratives of the Malayan Emergency, and the dynamics of intelligence transformation', *Intelligence and National Security* 14:4 (1999), 211–41.
6597. Harfield, Alan. 'Raffles and the Java Light Cavalry', *Journal of the Society for Army Historical Research* 78:315 (2000), 173–96.

6598. Harris, John. 'The Nile Expedition of 1898 and Omdurman: the diary of Sergeant S.W. Harris', *Journal of the Society for Army Historical Research* 78 (2000), 11–28.

6599. Heal, S.C. *A great fleet of ships: the Canadian Forts and Parks* [merchant vessels built from 1941 to 1945] (Annapolis (MD): Naval Institute Press, 2000), 312p.

6600. Healy, M.S. 'Colour, climate, and combat: the Caribbean Regiment in the Second World War', *International History Review* 22:1 (2000), 65–85.

6601. Hopkins, Pat; Dugmore, Heather. *The boy: Baden-Powell and the siege of Mafeking* (Rivonia: Zebra, 1999), xviii, 222p.

6602. Horner, David Murray. *Blamey: the Commander-in-Chief* (St Leonards (NSW): Allen & Unwin, 1998), xviii, 686p.

6603. Howard, N. 'Military aspects of the Dogra conquest of Ladakh 1834–1839', A172, 349–62.

6604. Hughes, Matthew. *Allenby and British strategy in the Middle East, 1917–1919* (London: Frank Cass, 1999), xii, 224p.

6605. Hull, Richard W. 'American Enterprise and the South African War 1895–1902', *South African Historical Journal* 41 (1999), 130–48.

6606. Iacovetta, Franca; Perin, Roberto; Principe, Angelo (eds.) *Enemies within: Italian and other internees in Canada and abroad* (Toronto (Ont) and Buffalo (NY): University of Toronto Press, 2000), viii, 429p.

6607. Jablonsky, D. 'Churchill's initial experience with the British conduct of small wars: India and the Sudan, 1897–1898', *Small Wars and Insurgencies* 11:1 (2000), 1–25.

6608. Jeffery, Keith. 'Kruger's farmers, Strathcona's Horse, Sir George Clarke's camels and the Kaiser's battleships: the impact of the South African war in imperial defence', A139, 188–202.

6609. Jeffery, Keith. 'The Irish soldier in the Boer War', A91, 141–51.

6610. Jeffreys, Alan. '"*The Jungle Book*": jungle training in south east Asia, 1941–1943', *Imperial War Museum Review* 12 (1999), 48–58.

6611. Johnson Barker, Brian. *A concise dictionary of the Boer War* (Cape Town: Francolin, 1999), 143p.

6612. Johnston, Mark. *Fighting the enemy: Australian soldiers and their adversaries in World War II* (Cambridge: Cambridge University Press, 2000), 232p.

6613. Jones, Randolph. 'The Bourbon Regiment and the Barbados Slave Revolt of 1816', *Journal of the Society for Army Historical Research* 78 (2000), 3–10.

6614. Jordan, D. '"A particularly exacting operation": British forces and the Battle of Surabaya, November 1945', *Small Wars and Insurgencies* 11:3 (2000), 89–114.

6615. Kamtekar, I. 'Military ingredient of communal violence in Punjab, 1947', *Proceedings of the Indian History Congress* 56 (1995), 568–72.

6616. Kelly, Wayne Edward. 'Race and segregation in the Upper Canada militia', *Journal of the Society for Army Historical Research* 78:316 (2000), 264–77.

6617. Killingray, David. 'Gender issues and African colonial armies', A124, 221–48.

6618. Killingray, David. 'Guardians of empire', A124, 1–24.

6619. Killingray, David. 'Imperial defence' [Historiography], A214, 342–53.

6620. Kirby, June (comp. & ed.) *A special job: the Wheatstone girls, 1943–1945* [Australian army] (Henley Beach (South Australia): Seaview Press, 1999), xii, 122p.

6621. Kochanski, Halik. 'Wolseley and the South African War', A91, 56–69.

6622. Kundu, Apurba. *Militarism in India: the army and civil society in consensus* (London: Tauris Academic, 1998), viii, 230p.

6623. Laband, John. 'Zulus and the War' [South African War, 1899–1902], A91, 107–25.

6624. Lord, Cliff; Birtles, David. *The armed forces of Aden, 1839–1967* (Solihull: Helion, 2000), 112p.

6625. Lowry, Donal. '"The Boers were the beginning of the end"?: the wider impact of the South African War', A139, 203–46.

6626. Lowry, Donal. '"The play of forces world-wide in their scope and revolutionary in their operation [J.A. Hobson]": the South African War as an international event', *South African Historical Journal* 41 (1999), 82–105.

6627. Lowry, Donal. 'Introduction: not just a "teatime war"' [the South African War], A139, 1–22.

6628. Malcomson, Robert. *Lords of the lake: the naval war on Lake Ontario, 1812–1814* (London: Chatham, 1999), xx, 411p.

6629. Manson, A.H. 'The South African War and the re-shaping of Hurutshe society, 1899–1907', *South African Historical Journal* 41 (1999), 56–71.

6630. Maphalala, Jabulani. 'Zulus and the Boer War', *History Today* 50:1 (2000), 46–51.

6631. Mark, Chi-Kwan. 'A reward for good behaviour in the Cold War: bargaining over the defence of Hong Kong, 1949–1957', *International History Review* 22:4 (2000), 837–61.

6632. Marshall, P. 'The British Commonwealth Air Training Plan', *Round Table* 354 (2000), 267–78.

6633. Martyn, Errol W. *For your tomorrow: a record of New Zealanders who have died while serving with the RNZAF & allied air services since 1915*, 2 vols. 1: *Fates 1915–1942*; 2: *Fates 1943–1998* (Wellington (NZ): Volplane Press, 1998–99).

6634. Mileham, Patrick J.R. (ed.) *'Clearly my duty': the letters of Sir John Gilmour from the Boer War 1900–1901* (East Linton: Tuckwell, 1996), xx, 200p.

6635. Miller, Carman. 'Loyalty, Patriotism and Resistance: Canada's Response to the Anglo-Boer War, 1899–1902', *South African Historical Journal* 41 (1999), 312–23.

6636. Milner, Marc. *Canada's navy: the first century* (Toronto (Ont) and London: University of Toronto Press, 1999), xiii, 356p.

6637. Mohamed, Jama. 'The 1944 Somaliland Camel Corps mutiny and popular politics', *History Workshop Journal* 50 (2000), 93–113.

6638. Moreman, Tim. '"Watch and ward": the army in India and the North-West Frontier, 1920–1939', A124, 137–56.

6639. Moreman, T.R. *The army in India and the development of frontier warfare, 1849–1947* (Basingstoke: Macmillan in association with Kings College London, 1998), xxiii, 258p.

6640. Morgan, Kenneth O. 'Lloyd George, Keir Hardy and the importance of the "Pro-Boers"', *South African Historical Journal* 41 (1999), 290–311.

6641. Nasson, William. 'Africans at War' [South African War (1899–1902)], A91, 126–40.

6642. Omissi, David Enrico (ed.) *Indian voices of the Great War: soldiers' letters, 1914–18* (Basingstoke and New York: Macmillan and St Martin's Press, 1999), xxvii, 382p.

6643. Ovendale, Ritchie. 'The Empire-Commonwealth and the two world wars' [Historiography], A214, 354–65.

6644. Parsons, Neil. 'Not quite all quiet on the North West Frontier: Khama's Bangwato and the Waterberg Commando', *South African Historical Journal* 41 (1999), 44–55.

6645. Parsons, Timothy. 'All *askaris* are family men: sex, domesticity and discipline in the King's African Rifles, 1902–1964', A124, 157–78.

6646. Parsons, Timothy. 'Dangerous education?: The army as school in colonial East Africa', *Journal of Imperial and Commonwealth History* 28 (2000), 112–34.

6647. Peers, Douglas M. 'Imperial vice: sex, drink and the health of British troops in north Indian cantonments, 1800–1858', A124, 25–52.

6648. Pinfold, John. 'Archives in Oxford Relating to the South African War', *South African Historical Journal* 41 (1999), 422–42.

6649. Powell, Geoffrey. *Buller: a scapegoat? A life of General Sir Redvers Buller 1839–1908* (London: Leo Cooper, 1994), 245p.

6650. Pressinger, Selwyn Philip Hodson. *Major W.S.R. Hodson, 1821–1858: in memoriam* (London: Sandilands, 2000), 98p.

6651. Pretorius, Fransjohan. 'Boer attitudes to Africans in wartime', A139, 104–20.

6652. Pretorius, Fransjohan. 'The experience of the bitter-ender Boer in the guerilla phase of the South African War', A91, 166–83.

6653. Robins, Colin. 'Overland to India—by donkey: a journey by Lance Sergeant Samuel Robert Taylor, 46th (South Devon) Regiment', *Journal of the Society for Army Historical Research* 78:314 (2000), 102–14.

6654. Sarty, Roger. 'The ghosts of Fisher and Jellicoe: the Royal Canadian Navy and the Quebec conferences', A216, 143–70.

6655. Saxena, K.M.L. *The military system of India, 1900–1939* (New Delhi: Reliance, 1999), xix, 539p. [Sequel to *The military system of India, 1850–1900.*]

6656. Schurman, Donald M. *Imperial defence, 1868–1887*, ed. John Beeler (London: Cass, 2000), xx, 192p.

6657. Smith, Iain R. 'A century of controversy over origins' [of the South African War], A139, 23–49.

6658. Smith, Iain R. 'Jan Smuts and the South African War', *South African Historical Journal* 41 (1999), 172–95.

6659. Spiers, Edward M. 'The Scottish Soldier in the Boer War', A91, 152–65.

6660. Steele, David. 'Salisbury and the Soldiers', A91, 3–20.

6661. Stewart, Brian. 'Winning in Malaya: an intelligence success story', *Intelligence and National Security* 14:4 (1999), 267–83.

6662.   Stuchtey, Benedikt. 'The International of Critics: German and British Scholars during the South African War (1899–1902)', *South African Historical Journal* 41 (1999), 149–71.

6663.   Surridge, Keith Terrance. 'Lansdowne at the War Office', A91, 21–40.

6664.   Taaffe, S.R. *Macarthur's jungle war: the 1944 New Guinea campaign* (Lawrence (KS): University Press of Kansas, 1998), xiii, 312p.

6665.   Tai-Yong, T. 'An imperial home-front: Punjab and the First World War', *Journal of Military History* 64:2 (2000), 371–410.

6666.   Tennyson, Brian Douglas; Sarty, Roger Flynn. *Guardian of the gulf: Sydney, Cape Breton, and the Atlantic wars* (Toronto (Ont) and London: University of Toronto Press, 2000), x, 495p.

6667.   Teulié, Gilles. *Les Afrikaners et la guerre anglo-boer (1899–1902): étude des cultures populaires et des mentalités en présence* [The Afrikaners and the Anglo-Boer War: a study of popular cultures and mentalities] (Montpellier: Presses de l'université Paul Valéry, 2000), 496p.

6668.   Trew, Peter. *The Boer War generals* (Stroud: Sutton, 1999), 288p.

6669.   van Heyningen, Elizabeth. 'The voices of women in the South African War', *South African Historical Journal* 41 (1999), 22–43.

6670.   Vietzen, Sylvia. 'The letters speak: Mary Moore, war and the Battle of Colenso, December 1899', *South African Historical Journal* 41 (1999), 222–45.

6671.   Warren, Alan. 'Archives and the Indian army in Waziristan', *Archives* 22:96 (1997), 45–50.

6672.   Webb, Denver A. *Fortifications in the Province of Queen Adelaide and British Kaffraria, 1835–1866* ([Cape Town]: Castle Military Museum, 1998), 104p.

6673.   Wessels, André. 'Afrikaners at War' [South African War, 1899–1902], A91, 73–106.

K. Foreign Affairs

See also 2628 (G); 2946, 3568, 3570, 3577–8, 3588, 3593 (H); 4562, 4599, 4813, 4815, 4820, 4851, 4859–60, 4886–7, 4894–5, 4920, 4945, 4970, 4973, 4978 (I); 5882 (M); 6037 (N); 6210, 6218, 6238, 6276, 6446, 6471–3, 6487, 6492, 6497, 6505, 6542, 6571, 6605, 6654, 6662 (P)

6674.   Banton, Mandy. *Imperial and Commonwealth conferences* (List & Index Society, 280) (Kew: List and Index Society, 2000), 198p.

6675.   Blyth, Robert J. 'Britain versus India in the Persian Gulf: the struggle for political control, c.1928–48', *Journal of Imperial and Commonwealth History* 28 (2000), 90–111.

6676.   Buzpinar, S.T. 'The repercussions of the British occupation of Egypt on Syria, 1882–83', *Middle Eastern Studies* 36:1 (2000), 82–91.

6677.   Chakrabarti, S. 'From Robert Shaw to George Nathaniel Curzon: British penetration to eastern Turkestan in the late 19th century', *Proceedings of the Indian History Congress* 56 (1995), 813–24.

6678.   Darwin, John Gareth. 'Diplomacy and decolonization', *Journal of Imperial and Commonwealth History* 28:3 (2000), 5–24.

6679. Davie, Michael. *Anglo-Australian attitudes* (London: Secker & Warburg, 2000), 250p.

6680. Flint, John Edgar. 'Britain and the Scramble for Africa' [Historiography], A214, 450–62.

6681. Gil-Har, Y. 'Boundaries delimitation: Palestine and Trans-Jordan', *Middle Eastern Studies* 36:1 (2000), 68–81.

6682. Granatstein, J.L. 'Happily on the margins: Mackenzie King and Canada at the Quebec conferences', A216, 49–64.

6683. Granatstein, J.L. 'The man who wasn't there: Mackenzie King, Canada, and the Atlantic Charter', A22, 115–28.

6684. Hiller, James K. *The historical background to the Canada-France maritime boundary decision* (Canada House lecture series, 56) ([London]: [Canadian High Commission], [1994]), 18p.

6685. Hopkins, Antony Gerald. 'Quasi-states, weak states and the partition of Africa', *Review of International Studies* 26:2 (2000), 311–20.

6686. Johnson, Edward. 'Britain and the Cyprus problem at the United Nations, 1954–58', *Journal of Imperial and Commonwealth History* 28:3 (2000), 113–30.

6687. Karsh, Efraim; Karsh, Inari. *Empires of the sand: the struggle for mastery in the Middle East, 1789–1923* (Cambridge (MA) and London: Harvard University Press, 1999), 409p.

6688. Kuleshov, N.S. 'The Tibet policies of Britain and Russia, 1900–14', *Asian Affairs* 31:1 (2000), 41–48.

6689. Lloyd, Lorna. '"What's in a name?": the curious tale of the office of High Commissioner', *Diplomacy & Statecraft* 11:1 (2000), 47–78.

6690. Lombardo, Johannes R. 'A mission of espionage, intelligence and psychological operations: the American consulate in Hong Kong, 1949–64', *Intelligence and National Security* 14:4 (1999), 64–81.

6691. Marquis, Greg. *In Armageddon's shadow: the civil war and Canada's maritime provinces* (Halifax (NS) and London: Gorsebrook Research Institute for Atlantic Canada Studies, Saint Mary's University and McGill-Queen's University Press, 1998), xx, 389p.

6692. Miller, Rory. 'Informal empire in Latin America' [Historiography], A214, 437–49.

6693. Perras, Galen Roger. *Franklin Roosevelt and the origins of the Canadian-American security alliance, 1933–1945: necessary, but not necessary enough* (Westport (CT): Praeger, 1998), viii, 156p.

6694. Robertson, P.; Singleton, J. 'The Old Commonwealth and Britain's first application to join the EEC, 1961–3', *Australian Economic History Review* 40:2 (2000), 153–77.

6695. Rogan, Eugene L. *Frontiers of the state in the late Ottoman Empire: Transjordan, 1850–1921* (Cambridge: Cambridge University Press, 1999), xiv, 274p.

6696. Seligmann, Matthew S. *Rivalry in Southern Africa, 1893–99: the transformation of German colonial policy* (Basingstoke and New York: Macmillan and St Martin's Press, 1998), vii, 200p.

6697. Shamir Hasan, S. 'Britain and the Iraq–Kuwait dispute', *Proceedings of the Indian History Congress* 56 (1995), 881–88.

6698. Sinha, A. 'Anglo-French collaboration in Europe and the floating of the Nouvelle Compagnie des Indes in 1785', *Proceedings of the Indian History Congress* 54 (1994), 714–21.

6699. Tarling, Nicholas. '"Cold storage": British policy and the beginnings of the Irian Barat/West New Guinea dispute', *Australian Journal of Politics & History* 46:2 (2000), 175–93.

6700. Thomas, Martin. 'From Dien Bien Phu to Evian: Anglo-French imperial relations, 1954–1962', A191, 301–23.

6701. Yi-Hua, F.K. 'The position of Hong Kong in Britain's policy towards two rival Chinese regimes during the early years of the Cold War', *Civil Wars* 2:4 (1999), 106–37.

JOURNALS CONSULTED

Africa
African Affairs
African Studies
Agricultural History
Agricultural History Review
Albion
American Historical Review
The Americas
Analecta Bollandiana
Analecta Cartusiana
Analecta Hibernica
Anglican and Episcopal History
Anglo-Norman Studies
Anglo-Saxon England
Annales
Annales de Démographie Historique
Annales Historiques de la Révolution
  Française
Annals of Science
Annuarium Historiae Conciliorum
Anselm Studies
Anthologia Annua
Antiquaries Journal
Antiquity
Archaeologia
Archaeologia Aeliana
Archaeologia Cambrensis
Archaeologia Cantiana
Archaeological Journal
Archiv für Diplomatik
Archiv für Reformationsgeschichte
Archives
Archives of Natural History
Archivium Hibernicum
Armed Forces and Society
Army Quarterly & Defence Journal
Art History
Asian Affairs
Australian Economic History Review
Australian Historical Studies
Australian Journal of Politics & History
Ayrshire Archaeological & Natural

History Collections

Baptist Quarterly
Bath History
Bengal Past and Present
Biblion: the Bulletin of the New York
  Public Library
Bibliotheque de l'Ecole des Chartes
Bibliotheque d'Humanisme et Renaissance
Biography: an interdisciplinary quarterly
Birmingham and Warwickshire
  Archaeological Society Transactions
Bodleian Library Record
Book History
Book of the Old Edinburgh Club
Breifne: Journal of Cumann Seanchais
  Bhréifne
Britannia
British Historical Society of Portugal
  Annual Report
British Journal for Eighteenth-Century
  Studies
British Journal for the History of Science
British Journal of Criminology
British Journal of Educational Studies
Brritish Journal of Political Science
British Library Journal
British Numismatic Journal
Brycheiniog
Bullán: an Irish Studies Review
Bulletin of the Board of Celtic Studies
Bulletin of the History of Medicine
Bulletin of the John Rylands University
  Library of Manchester
Bulletin of the S.O.A.S.
Business Archives
Business History
Business History Review

Caernarvonshire Historical Society
  Transactions
Cahiers d'Études africaines

Journals consulted

Cahiers de Civilisation Medievale
Cahiers Élisabéthains
Cake and Cockhorse
The Carmarthenshire Antiquary
Cambrian Medieval Celtic Studies
Cambridge Antiquarian Society
   Proceedings
Cambridge Archaeological Journal
Canadian Historical Review
Canadian Journal of History
Cantium
Cathair na Mart: Journal of the Westport
   Historical Society
Catholic Ancestor
Catholic Archives
Catholic Historical Review
Ceredigion
Church History
Church Monuments
Clio [Napoli]
Clogher Record: Journal of the Clogher
   Historical Society
Collectanea Hibernica
Comparative Studies in Society & History
Construction History
Contemporary British History
Contemporary European History
Continuity and Change
Crime, Histoire et Sociétés
Criminal Justice History

Decies: Journal of the Waterford
   Archaeological and Historical Society
Derbyshire Archaeological Journal
Devon Historian
Diplomacy & Statecraft
Diplomatic History
Dorset Natural History and Archaeological
   Society Proceedings
Dumfriesshire & Galloway Natural
   History & Antiquarian Society
   Transactions

Early Medieval Europe
East Midland Historian
Economic History Review
The Eighteenth Century
Eighteenth Century Life
Eighteenth Century Studies
Éire-Ireland
English Historical Review
English Place-Name Society Journal
Enlightenment and Dissent

Environment and History
Environment and Planning C: Government
   and Policy
Environment and Planning D: Society and
   Space
Essex Archaeology and History
European History Quarterly
European Journal of the History of
   Economic Thought
European Journal of Women's Studies
The European Legacy
European Review of Economic History
European Review of History
European Romantic Review
European Sports History Review
Explorations in Economic History

Family & Community History
Financial History Review
Finest Hour: Journal of the Churchill
   Center and Societies
Francia
French Historical Studies
French History

Gaelic Society of Inverness Transactions
Garden History
Gender & History
Genealogists' Magazine
The Georgian Group Journal
German History
Glasgow Archaeological Journal
Guerres Mondiales et Conflits
   Contemporains

Hampshire Studies
Hansische Geschichtsblätter
Haskins Society Journal
Hawick Archaeological Society
   Transactions
Hertfordshire Archaeology
Hispania: Revista Española de Historia
Hispanic American Historical Review
Histoire, Economie et Société
Histoire Sociale / Social History
Historia [Pretoria]
Historia Contemporánea
Historian
The Historian [East Lansing (MI)]
Historical Journal
Historical Journal of Film, Radio &
   Television
Historical Methods

Journals consulted

Historical Research
Historical Social Research
Historical Studies in Industrial Relations
Historisches Jahrbuch
Historisches Zeitschrift
Historisk Tidskrift [Sweden]
Historisk Tidsskrift [Copenhagen]
History
History & Anthropology
History and Computing
History & Memory
History and Technology
History and Theory
History Ireland
History of Economic Ideas
History of Education
History of Education Quarterly
History of Education Society Bulletin
History of Political Thought
History of Political Economy
History of Psychiatry
History of Science
The History Teacher [Long Beach, CA]
History of Technology
History of the Family
History of Universities
History Today
History Workshop Journal
Holocaust and Genocide Studies
Huguenot Society Proceedings
Huntington Library Quarterly

IEEE Annals of the History of Computing
Immigrants & Minorities
Innes Review
Intelligence and National Security
International Bulletin of Missionary
    Research
International History Review
International Journal of African Historical
    Studies
International Journal of the History of
    Sport
International Journal of Maritime History
    [St. John's, Newfoundland]
International Labor and Working Class
    History
International Review of Mission
International Review of Social History
Irish Archives
Irish Economic and Social History
Irish Genealogist
Irish Historical Studies

Irish Studies Review
Irish Sword
Isis
Israel Studies
Itinerario

Jamaican Historical Review
Jewish Historical Studies
Jewish History
Journal de la Société des Océanistes
Journal of African History
Journal of American History
Journal of American Studies
Journal of Asian Studies
Journal of Australian Studies
Journal of British Studies
Journal of Caribbean Studies
Journal of Commonwealth and
    Comparative Politics
Journal of Conflict Resolution
Journal of Contemporary History
Journal of Design History
Journal of Early Modern History
Journal of Ecclesiastical History
Journal of Economic History
Journal of European Economic History
Journal of Family History
Journal of Garden History
Journal of Historical Geography
Journal of Historical Sociology
Journal of Holocaust Education
Journal of Imperial and Commonwealth
    History
Journal of Interdisciplinary History
Journal of Israeli History
Journal of Latin American Studies
Journal of Legal History
Journal of Medieval History
Journal of Medieval and Early Modern
    Studies
Journal of Military History
Journal of Modern African Studies
Journal of Modern History
Journal of Pacific History
Journal of Palestine Studies
Journal of Peasant Studies
Journal of Popular Culture
Journal of Religion in Africa
Journal of Religious History
Journal of Social History
Journal of Southeast Asian Studies
Journal of Southern African Studies
Journal of Sport History

Journals consulted

Journal of Strategic Studies
Journal of the British Archaeological
  Association
Journal of the Canadian Historical
  Association
Journal of the Cork Historical and
  Archaeological Society
Journal of the County Louth
  Archaeological and Historical Society
Journal of the Friends' Historical Society
Journal of the Galway Archaeological and
  Historical Society
Journal of the History of Biology
Journal of the History of Collections
Journal of the History of Ideas
Journal of the History of Medicine and
  Allied Sciences
Journal of the History of Sexuality
Journal of the Hong Kong Branch of the
  Royal Asiatic Society
Journal of the Malaysian Branch of the
  Royal Asiatic Society
Journal of the Merioneth Historical and
  Record Society
Journal of the Pakistan Historical Society
Journal of the Polynesian Society
Journal of the Royal Society of Antiquaries
  of Ireland
Journal of the Royal Asiatic Society
Journal of the Royal Australian Historical
  Society
Journal of the Society for Army Historical
  Research
Journal of the Society of Archivists
Journal of the Warburg and Courtauld
  Institutes
Journal of Transport History
Journal of Urban History
Journal of Victorian Culture
Journal of Welsh Religious History
Journal of Women's History
Journal of World History

Labour History Review
Landscape History
Law and History Review
Leicestershire Archaeological & Historical
  Society Transactions
The Library
Library History
Lincolnshire History and Archaeology
Lincolnshire Past & Present
Llafur

The Local Historian
Local Population Studies
London and Middlesex Archaeological
  Society Transactions
London Journal
London Topographical Record

Mariner's Mirror
Maritime Wales
Media History
Mediaeval Studies
Medical History
Medieval Archaeology
Medieval Prosopography
Medieval Settlement Research Group
  Annual Report
Medievalia et Humanistica
Mediterranean Historical Review
Medium Aevum
Melin: Journal of the Welsh Mills Society
Melita Historica
Merioneth Historical and Record Society
  Journal
Merseyside Archaeological Society Journal
Methodist History
Middle Eastern Studies
Midland History
Minerva
Modern Asian Studies
Modern History Review
Monastic Research Bulletin
The Monmouthshire Antiquary
Montgomeryshire Collections
Moyen Age
The Muslim World

National Library of Wales Journal
Nations and Nationalism
Nederlands Archief voor Kerkgeschiedenis
New York History
New Zealand Journal of History
New York History
Nieuwe West-Indische Gids / New West
  Indian Guide
Nomina
Norfolk Archaeology
Northamptonshire Past and Present
Northern History
Northern Mariner
Northern Scotland
Northern Studies
Notes and Queries

Journals consulted

Old Kilkenny Review: Journal of the Kilkenny Archaeological Society
Oral History
Oxford Art Journal
Oxford Journal of Archaeology
Oxoniensia

Pacific Historical Review
Parergon
Parliamentary History
Parliaments, Estates & Representation
Past & Present
Pennsylvania Magazine of History and Biography
Peritia
Post-Medieval Archaeology
Proceedings of the British Academy
Proceedings of the Cambridge Antiquarian Society
Proceedings of the Consortium on Revolutionary Europe 1750–1850
Proceedings of the Devon Archaeological Society
Proceedings of the Dorset Natural History & Archaeological Society
Proceedings of the Huguenot Society of Great Britain and Ireland
Proceedings of the Royal Irish Academy, section C
Proceedings of the Society of Antiquaries of Scotland
Prometheus
Prophile
Prose Studies
Publishing History

Quarterly Bulletin of the South African Library
Quarendo
QWERTY [Pau]

Race and Class
Radical History Review
Records of Buckinghamshire
Records of the Scottish Church Historical Society
Research in Economic History
Recusant History
Renaissance and Reformation
Renaissance Quarterly
Renaissance Studies
Rethinking History
Review of European Economic History

Review of International Studies
Revolutionary History
Revolutionary Russia
Revue Benedictine
Revue d'histoire ecclesiastique
Revue française de civilisation britannique
Revue française d'histoire d'outre-mer
Revue Historique
Ríocht na Midhe [Journal of the County Meath Historical Society]
Rivista Storica Italiana
Round Table
Royal Society of Antiquaries of Ireland Journal
Rural History

Saothar: Journal of the Irish Labour History Society
Scandia
Scandinavian Economic History Review
Scandinavian Journal of History
Science & Society
Scotlands
Scottish Economic and Social History
Scottish Geographical Magazine
Scottish Historical Review
Scottish Industrial History
Scottish Journal of Political Economy
Scriptorium
Seanchas Ardmhacha: Journal of the Armagh Diocesan Historical Society
Shropshire History and Archaeology
Sixteenth Century Journal
Slavery and Abolition
Small Wars and Insurgencies
Social History
Social History of Medicine
Social & Legal Studies
Social Studies of Science
Socialist History
Société Guernesiaise Report and Transactions
Society of Antiquaries of Scotland Proceedings
Somerset Archaeology and Natural History
Southern History
Speculum
Staffordshire Studies
Studia Celtica
Studia Hibernica
Studies in Anglo-Saxon History
Studies in Church History

Journals consulted

Studies in History and Philosophy of
    Science
Surrey Archaeological Collections
Sussex Archaeological Collections

Technology and Culture
Textile History
Tijdschrift voor Geschiedenis
Tijdschrift voor Rechtsgeschiedenis
Tijdschrift voor Zeegeschiedenis
Tipperary Historical Journal
Town Planning Review
Traditio
Transactions of the Bristol and
    Gloucestershire Archaeological Society
Transactions of the Cambridge
    Bibliographical Society
Transactions of the Caernarvonshire
    Historical Society
Transactions of the Cambridge
    Bibliographical Society
Transactions of the Cumberland &
    Westmorland Antiquarian and
    Archaeological Society
Transactions of the East Lothian
    Antiquarian Society
Transactions of the English Ceramic Circle
Transactions of the Halifax Antiquarian
    Society
Transactions of the Honourable Society of
    Cymmrodorion
Transactions of the Institute of British
    Geographers
Transactions of the Leicestershire
    Archaeological and Historical Society
Transactions of the London and Middlesex
    Archaeological Society

Transactions of the Royal Historical
    Society
Transactions of the Thoroton Society of
    Nottingham
Transactions of the Worcestershire
    Archaeological Society
20th Century British History

Urban History

Vernacular Architecture
Vesalius
Viator
Victorian Periodicals Review
Victorian Studies
Vierteljahrschrift für Zeitgeschichte
Vingtième Siècle
Virginia Magazine of History and
    Biography

Walpole Society
War & Society
War in History
Welsh History Review
William & Mary Quarterly
Wiltshire Archaeological & Natural
    History Magazine
Women's History Review
Women's Studies International Forum
World Archaeology

York Historian
Yorkshire Archaeological Journal
Yorkshire Numismatist

Zeitschrift für Geschichtswissenschaft

INDEX OF AUTHORS

Index of Authors

Andrew, B.P. 3828 (I)
Andrew, Christopher 4460, 4809 (I)
Andrewes, F. 6285 (P)
Andrewes, Jane 1474 (F)
Andrews, D.D. 224, 467 (B)
Andrews, Frank W.G. 2825 (H)
Andrews, J.H. 5513 (M)
Andrews, Ken 2826 (H)
Andrews, Phil 696 (D), 1013 (E), 5003 (J)
Annan, Noel 3596 (I)
Annand, Louise 3144 (H)
Ansprenger, Franz 6 (A)
Antal, Sandy 6557 (P)
Antlöv, Hans 6463 (P)
Appelbaum, Robert 1606 (F)
Appiah, Kwame Anthony 5888 (N)
Appleby, J. 3735 (I)
Archer, Christon A. 5904 (N)
Archer, Ian 2649 (H)
Archer, Ian W. 1437, 1475, 1985–6 (F)
Archer, John E. 3366 (H)
Arcidiacono, Bruno 4810 (I)
Arel, Maria Salomon 1476 (F)
Arestis, Philip 3812 (I)
Armitage, David 1607 (F), 5889, 5981 (N)
Armstrong, James 3986 (I)
Armstrong, John 2827–8 (H)
Arnn, Larry P. 4811 (I)
Arnold, A.J. 2829 (H)
Arnold, Christopher J. 4995 (J)
Arnold, Dana 7 (A), 2156 (G)
Arnold, David 6299 (P)
Arnold, Hilary 1014 (E)
Arnold, Janet 1672 (F)
Arnold, Matthew 3076 (H)
Arnstein, Walter L. 3562 (H)
Arscott, C. 3367 (H)
Arthur, Liz 3145–7 (H)
Ash, Eric H. 1477 (F)
Ashbee, Andrew 439 (B), 1098 (E)
Ashby, John 4461 (I)
Ashdown, Dulcie M. 1987 (F)
Ashelford, Jane 333 (B)
Asher, Michael 4462 (I)
Ashley, Maurice 2106 (F)
Ashplant, T.G. 4463 (I)
Ashton, J. Norman 4464 (I)
Ashton, Nigel J. 4812 (I)
Ashton, Owen R. 3407 (H)
Ashton, Stephen 6464 (P)
Ashworth, William J. 2290 (G)
Asleson, Robyn 2380 (G)
Aspin, Richard 1563 (F)

Aspinwall, Bernard 3289–91 (H)
Astell, Ann W. 1270 (E)
Astill, Grenville 697 (D)
Aston, Mick 305 (B)
Atkins, Nicholas 3651 (I)
Atkins, S.N. 5195 (K)
Atkinson, A.B. 3724 (I)
Atkinson, Colin B. 1773 (F)
Atkinson, Jo B. 1773 (F)
Atkinson, John Andrew 8 (A), 5133 (K)
Attard, Bernard 365 (B)
Auchterlonie, P. 6421 (P)
Auerbach, Jeffrey 6344 (P)
Aughton, Peter 225 (B)
Auksi, Peter 1774–5 (F)
Aurell, Martin 9 (A), 1271 (E)
Austen, Ralph A. 6039 (P)
Austern, Linda Phyllis 1673 (F)
Austin, John 3077 (H)
Autrand, Françoise 5275 (K)
Avery, Donald H. 4813 (I)
Avril, Emmanuelle 3736–7 (I)
Ayers, Pat 3652 (I)
Aylmer, Gerald E. 468 (B), 1988 (F), 5451 (L)

Babits, Lawrence Edward 6028 (N)
Backouche, Isabelle 299 (B)
Backus, Margot Gayle 5670 (M)
Bacon, Francis 1564 (F)
Bacot, Guillaume 2623 (G)
Badham, Sally 1099 (E)
Badru, Pade 6180 (P)
Badsey, Stephen 4465–6 (I), 6286 (P)
Bagenal, T.B. 2766, 2830 (H)
Bagworth-Mann, Hazel 3600 (I)
Bahners, P. 3078 (H)
Bailey, Ian 4467 (I)
Bailey, K.A. 698, 778 (D)
Bailey, Mark W. 6399 (P)
Bailey, Roderick 4468 (I)
Bailey, Roy E. 3757 (I)
Bailey, Victor 4185 (I)
Baillie, James 2341 (G)
Bailyn, Bernard 5890 (N)
Bain, P. 1368 (F)
Baines, Dudley 3784 (I)
Baird, C. 2977 (H)
Baker, Christine 5370 (L)
Baker, John Hamilton 1957 (F)
Baker, M. 2381 (G)
Baker, William 4087 (I)
Baker-Jones, Leslie 334 (B)

Index of Authors

Index of Authors

Index of Authors

Index of Authors

Index of Authors

Dibble, J. 5683 (M)
Dibbs, John M. 4541 (I)
Dick, John A.R. 1815 (F)
Dickason, Robert 4103 (I)
Dickens, Alison 1171 (E)
Dickinson, A.B. 6212 (P)
Dickinson, Brenda 656 (C)
Dickinson, Patric L. 1442 (F)
Dickson, D. 5488 (M)
Dickson, Neil 3307 (H)
Diederiks, Herman A. 65 (A)
Dietz, K. 715 (D)
Dilley, Robert S. 2237 (G)
Dillon, Janette 1388 (F)
Dils, Joan A. 1575 (F)
Dilworth, Mark 5221, 5279 (K)
Dinan, William 3857 (I)
Dingwall, H. 5172 (K)
Dingwall, Helen M. 2300 (G)
Dintenfass, Michael 69 (A), 2642,
    2775–6 (H)
Ditchburn, David 66 (A), 5142, 5247–8 (K)
Ditchfield, G.M. 2496, 2573 (G)
Divall, Colin 3911 (I)
Dixon, P. 4851 (I)
Dixon, Shirley 3951 (I)
Doane, A.N. 809 (D)
Dobell, Lauren 6480 (P)
Dobney, Keith 552 (C), 690 (D)
Dobranski, Stephen B. 67 (A), 1816–17 (F)
Dobson, Barrie 1024, 1167 (E)
Docherty, L.J. 3177 (H)
Dockrill, Michael 4852 (I)
Dockrill, Saki 4853 (I)
Doctor, Jennifer R. 4104 (I)
Dodgshon, R.A. 5173 (K)
Dodsworth, Martin 1570–1 (F)
Dodwell, Charles Reginald 810 (D)
Doe, Norman 476 (B)
Doerries, Reinhard R. 5879 (M)
Doherty, Charles 5406 (L)
Doherty, Richard 4542 (I), 5875 (M)
Dolan, Brian 2322 (G)
Dolan, Frances E. 1389, 1818 (F)
Dolan, Terence 5371 (L)
Domville, Edward Alan 339 (B)
Donagan, Barbara 2017 (F)
Donald, Diana 3178 (H)
Donaldson, William 447 (B), 5201 (K)
Doniger, W. 6330 (P)
Donis Ríos, Manuel Alberto 3308 (H)
Donnelly, Brian 5489–90 (M)
Donnelly, James F. 3911 (I)

Donnelly, James S. (Jr.) 5716 (M)
Donnelly, K.J. 5609 (M)
Donnelly, Tom 3887 (I)
Doody, G.A. 2806 (H)
Doody, Margaret Anne 2407 (G)
Dooge, James C.I. 5635 (M)
Dooley, Dolores 5809 (M)
Dooley, Terence A.M. 5587–8, 5717 (M)
Dor, Juliette 68 (A)
Doran, Susan 2018, 2137 (F)
Dore, J.N. 674 (C)
Dormois, Jean-Pierre 69 (A)
Dorward, D. 5156 (K)
Douglas, Alistair 2238 (G)
Douglas, Bronwen 6046 (P)
Douglas, Hugh 2144, 2557 (G)
Douglas, Roy 378 (B)
Douglas, S. 6371 (P)
Dowling, J.A. 5764 (M)
Dowling, Maria 1168 (E)
Downes, A.D. 6150 (P)
Downes, Kerry 1685 (F)
Downham, John 6581 (P)
Downing, Mark 1113 (E)
Downing, Taylor 4543 (I)
Downs, Laura Lee 3813 (I)
Doyle, A.I. 1303 (E)
Doyle, Barry 311 (B)
Doyle, I. 5322 (L)
Doyle, John 5810 (M)
Doyle, Peter 3309 (H)
Doyle, William 5811 (M)
Drabble, John H. 6213 (P)
Drage, Christopher 651 (C)
Draper, Jo 3091, 3179 (H)
Drayton, Richard 5898, 5982 (N)
Dreisbach, D.L. 5991 (N)
Drennan, A.S. 5351 (L), 5610 (M)
Drescher, Seymour 6214 (P)
Dresser, Madge 70 (A), 2239, 2497 (G)
Driscoll, Stephen T. 5269 (K)
Driver, Felix 71 (A), 2654 (H), 6307 (P)
Driver, J.T. 1284 (E)
Driver, T.G. 616 (C)
Dror, Othniel E. 3952 (I)
Drower, Margaret S. 4011 (I)
Drummond, Diane K. 3104 (H)
Drury, John 3180 (H)
Drysdall, Alan R. 6582 (P)
du Toit, Brian M. 6185 (P)
Dubois, Pierre 2408 (G)
Ducharme, Michel 6481 (P)
Duchein, Michel 5280 (K)

Index of Authors

Hassan, John 2657 (H)
Hasson, Gerald 5590 (M)
Hatch, David A. 4611 (I)
Hatcher, Patrick Lloyd 4612 (I)
Hatton, Helen E. 5577 (M)
Hatton, Timothy J. 3757 (I)
Havers, R.P.W. 4613 (I)
Hawkes, Emma 985 (E)
Hawkes, Jane 100 (A), 820 (D)
Hawkings, David T. 2249 (G)
Hawkins, Richard A. 3575 (H)
Hawkins, Richard 381 (B)
Haworth, Bryan 3157 (H)
Hawthorne, E.J. 3101 (H)
Hay, D. 2544 (G)
Hay, John 4614 (I)
Haycock, D. 2337 (G)
Haycock, David 2355, 2437 (G)
Hayden, Alan 5324 (L)
Hayden, J.M. 1183 (E)
Haydon, Colin 2506, 2582 (G)
Haydon, E. 1322 (E)
Hayes, A.L. 4161 (I)
Hayes, Graham 267 (B)
Hayes, Nick 3636 (I)
Hayes, Patricia 6049 (P)
Hayes, William Joseph 5822 (M)
Hayman, Richard 2160, 2250 (G)
Haynes, D.E. 5913 (N), 6225 (P)
Haynes, Douglas M. 3035 (H)
Hayton, D.W. 2583 (G)
Hayward, Maria 1695, 2133 (F)
Haywood, John 915 (D)
Hazareesingh, S. 6489 (P)
Hazelgrove, Jennifer 4162–3 (I)
Headon, A. 3049 (H)
Heal, Felicity 1396 (F)
Heal, S.C. 6599 (P)
Healy, M.S. 6600 (P)
Healy, Simon 1910 (F)
Heap, Simon 6226 (P)
Heard, Kieron 538 (C)
Hearn, Karen 1696 (F)
Hearne, Dana 5800 (M)
Heath, Anthony 4271, 4291, 4398 (I)
Heath, Desmond 3200 (H)
Heath, Edward 4292 (I)
Heathcote, Thomas Anthony 518 (B)
Heathfield, John 3637 (I)
Heathorn, Stephen 3102 (H)
Hedges, P.M. 6350 (P)
Hedley, Douglas 3201 (H)
Heffernan, Brian 24 (A)

Heffernan, Richard 4217, 4293–4 (I)
Heffernan, T. 2356 (G)
Heighway, Carolyn 1118 (E)
Heinemann, Winfried 101 (A)
Heiser, Richard R. 1261 (E)
Heleniak, K.M. 2988 (H)
Helland, Janice 3164, 3202 (H)
Helle, Andreas 5546 (M)
Hellema, Duco 4812 (I)
Hellinga, Lotte 453 (B)
Hellmuth, Eckhart 2584 (G)
Helly, Dorothy O. 6292 (P)
Hellyer, Roger 428 (B)
Helyer, Patrick J. 6081 (P)
Hen, Y. 102 (A)
Henderson, D.M. 2330 (G)
Henderson, Isabel 821 (D), 5205–6, 5225 (K)
Henderson, J.M. 5118 (K)
Henderson, Paula 1697 (F)
Hendrickson, Hildi 6158 (P)
Henig, Martin 539, 638, 643–7 (C)
Henig, Ruth 4879 (I)
Henisch, B. 5276 (K)
Hennessy, Peter 4295–6 (I)
Hennock, E. Peter 2658 (H)
Henriet, Patrick 103 (A)
Henry, J. 4297 (I)
Heppell, Jason 4298 (I)
Hepple, Leslie W. 1629 (F)
Herbert, Adrian 2877 (H)
Herbert, D.T. 4024 (I)
Herbert, M. 5253 (K)
Herbert, Máire 5417 (L)
Herbert, Nicholas 2251 (G)
Herity, Michael 5293, 5325 (L), 5492 (M)
Herlihy, Jim 5767 (M)
Herman, Peter C. 2033 (F)
Hermes, Katherine A. 6005 (N)
Herr, Cheryl Temple 5616 (M)
Herrick, Claire 3036 (H)
Herrmann, Frank 454 (B)
Hershberg, James G. 4615 (I)
Heslop, David 986 (E)
Hesse, Mary 383 (B)
Heuman, Gad J. 6227 (P)
Heuser, Beatrice 4616, 4880–1 (I)
Heuston, John 5506 (M)
Hewish, John 2961 (H)
Hewitson, Thomas L. 3539 (H)
Hewitt, Martin 3203 (H)
Hewitt, Virginia 104 (A)
Hewlings, Richard 2252 (G)
Heyck, Thomas William 5687 (M)

388

Index of Authors

Index of Authors

James, Tom Beaumont 1043 (E)
Janacek, Bruce 1584 (F)
Jankovic, V. 3041 (H)
Jansen, A.M. 869 (D)
Jansen, V. 3213 (H)
Janssen, Frans A. 1545 (F)
Jarman, Neil 5827–8 (M)
Jarvie, G. 2719 (H)
Jarvis, Anthea 3832 (I)
Jarvis, Steve 6295 (P)
Jaski, B. 5463 (L)
Javurek, Teresa 3605 (I)
Jayashree, C.H. 6237 (P)
Jayne, Catherine E. 4889 (I)
Jeater, D. 6161 (P)
Jeeves, Alan 6579 (P)
Jefcoate, Graham 4034 (I)
Jefferies, Henry A. 114 (A), 5420–2 (L)
Jeffery, Keith 5771, 5829 (M), 6608–9 (P)
Jeffery, Roger 6190 (P)
Jefferys, Kevin 115 (A), 4305–7 (I)
Jeffreys, Alan 4638 (I), 6610 (P)
Jeffreys-Jones, Rhodri 4639 (I)
Jeffs, David 3965 (I)
Jenkins, Dafydd 5018, 5048, 5078–9 (J)
Jenkins, David 2889, 3540 (H), 3833 (I)
Jenkins, Geraint H. 4115 (I)
Jenkins, John 2438 (G)
Jenkins, Philip 1357 (F)
Jenkins, Terence Andrew 3455 (H)
Jenks, S. 1264 (E)
Jenks, Timothy 2588 (G)
Jenks, W.E. 630 (C)
Jenner, Mark S.R. 94 (A), 1358, 1406, 1632 (F)
Jennings, Paul 2786 (H)
Jervis, Simon 440 (B)
Jespersen, Knud J.V. 4890 (I)
Jobling, I. 6162 (P)
Jobson, Richard 5971 (N)
John, Angela V. 3456 (H)
John, N. 6238 (P)
Johnes, Martin 2720 (H), 3640, 3683, 4308 (I)
Johns, Adrian 1546 (F)
Johns, Catherine 560 (C)
Johnson Barker, Brian 6611 (P)
Johnson, Dale A. 3326 (H)
Johnson, David 2510 (G)
Johnson, Douglas 4846 (I)
Johnson, Edward 6686 (P)
Johnson, Gaynor 4640 (I)
Johnson, Graham 3457–8 (H)

Johnson, John 6429 (P)
Johnson, K.A. 4167 (I)
Johnson, Lesley 68 (A), 1122 (E)
Johnson, Paul 2890 (H), 3784 (I)
Johnson, Ruth 5423 (L)
Johnson, V.S. 1547 (F)
Johnston, Andrew 4543 (I)
Johnston, Dafydd 5049 (J)
Johnston, Ethna 5420 (L)
Johnston, Mark 6612 (P)
Johnston, R.A.S. 5019 (J)
Johnston, Sean F. 3911 (I)
Johnstone, E.C. 2806 (H)
Johnstone, Neil 5007, 5086 (J)
Johnstone-Bryden, Richard 4641 (I)
Jones, Ann Rosalind 1705 (F)
Jones, B. 6163 (P)
Jones, Christine 3834 (I)
Jones, Christopher A. 871 (D)
Jones, Christopher 870 (D), 1324 (E)
Jones, Claire 3042 (H)
Jones, Clyve 2589 (G)
Jones, Diana K. 3105 (H)
Jones, Dot 2721 (H)
Jones, Dwyryd W. 4188 (I)
Jones, E.D. 1000 (E)
Jones, Evan T. 964, 1044 (E)
Jones, Geoffrey 4891 (I)
Jones, Glanville R.J. 5087 (J)
Jones, Graham 1186 (E)
Jones, H. Stuart 3459 (H)
Jones, Harriet 3606, 3641 (I)
Jones, Helen 285 (B)
Jones, John Graham 3327, 3460 (H), 4309–12 (I)
Jones, John Gwynfor 4998 (J)
Jones, Judith 1454 (F)
Jones, Kathleen 484 (B)
Jones, Kevin 4642 (I)
Jones, Malcolm 1045 (E)
Jones, Margaret 6308 (P)
Jones, Mark Ellis 3374, 3461 (H)
Jones, Martin 3214 (H)
Jones, Matthew 6493 (P)
Jones, Mervyn 3215 (H)
Jones, Michael A. 2043 (F)
Jones, Michael J. 561, 583 (C)
Jones, Moya 3684 (I)
Jones, Nerys Ann 5091 (J)
Jones, Nigel H. 3216 (H)
Jones, P. 2511 (G)
Jones, Peris 2223 (G)
Jones, Peter Ellis 3106 (H)

Index of Authors

Index of Authors

Keohane, Dan 4319, 4646 (I)
Keppie, Lawrence 682 (C)
Kerbey, John 3541, 4647–8 (I)
Kerby-Fulton, Kathryn 1296 (E)
Kerhervé, Alain 2358 (G)
Kermode, Jennifer 734, 965 (E)
Kerr, Donal A. 5730, 5835 (M)
Kerrigan, William 1847 (F)
Kerry, David A. 485 (B)
Kersaudy, François 3688, 4320–1, 4649–50 (I)
Kershaw, Roger 501 (B)
Kesselring, Krista 1970 (F)
Kessler, Edward 3328 (H)
Kevane, Michael 6194 (P)
Key, Newton E. 2045 (F)
Keynes, Richard Darwin 3043 (H)
Keynes, Simon 456 (B)
Khan, M.M. 6431 (P)
Kibata, Yoichi 526 (B)
Kidd, Alan J. 122–3 (A), 2209 (G), 2643, 3217 (H)
Kidd, Sheila 3218 (H)
Kiessling, Nicolas K. 1548 (F)
Killick, J. 2892 (H)
Killingback, Alan John 3397 (H)
Killingray, David 124 (A), 6617–19 (P)
Kim, Dong-Woon 2893 (H)
Kimambo, Isaria N. 6392 (P)
Kimball, Warren F. 4651, 4898–9 (I)
Kimmerling, B. 6164 (P)
Kinane, Vincent 125 (A), 5689 (M)
Kinchin, Juliet 2661 (H)
Kinealy, Christine 5547 (M)
King, Anthony 4226–7 (I)
King, Carla 126 (A), 5494, 5594 (M)
King, Desmond S. 3760 (I)
King, Edmund 1123, 1297 (E)
King, Edmund M.B. 3219 (H)
King, Heather A. 5326 (L)
King, John N. 1848 (F)
King, M. 606 (C)
King, Martha J. 6030 (N)
King, P.W. 1531 (F)
King, Robert J. 6054 (P)
King, Steve 1355 (F)
King, Steven 2331 (G)
Kinghorn, Jonathan 4116 (I)
Kingsley, Margery 1849 (F)
Kinna, Ruth 3220 (H)
Kinney, Arthur F. 1709, 1850 (F)
Kinsella, Anna 5836 (M)
Kinsella, Stuart 5424 (L)

Kinsella, Thomas E. 3262 (H)
Kinsey, Sara 6221 (P)
Kipping, Matthias 3837 (I)
Kirby, Dianne 4169, 4900 (I)
Kirby, June 6620 (P)
Kirchberger, Ulrike 6311 (P)
Kirk, James 486 (B)
Kirk, Tim 40 (A)
Kirk-Greene, Anthony Hamilton Millard 4901, 6342, 6353, 6432 (P)
Kirkland, R. 5690 (M)
Kirkus, M. Gregory 1851, 2513 (G)
Kisby, Fiona 1710–11 (F)
Kisling, V.N. 6114 (P)
Kissock, Jonathan 5019–20 (J)
Kitchens, James H. (III) 4652 (I)
Kitching, Carolyn 4902 (I)
Kitching, Christopher 288 (B)
Kitsikopoulos, Harry 989 (E)
Kituai, August Ibrum K. 6402 (P)
Kitzinger, Uwe 4222 (I)
Klein, A. 5691 (M)
Klein, I. 6055 (P)
Klein, Peter 1124, 1712 (F)
Klippel, Walter E. 6241 (P)
Knapp, Alexander 487 (B)
Knell, Simon J. 3044 (H)
Knight, Caroline 1634 (F)
Knight, Frances 3329 (H)
Knight, Gershom A. 1265 (E)
Knight, Jeremy K. 649 (C)
Knight, R.J.B. 6312 (P)
Knight, Ronald D. 2181, 4653 (I)
Knight, Ronald David 4037, 5566 (M)
Knight, Stephen Thomas 1125, 1713 (F)
Knight, William G. 3221 (H)
Knighton, C.S. 127 (A), 1852, 2119–20 (F)
Knoppers, Laura Lunger 2046 (F)
Knowles, James 2047 (F)
Knowles, Nigel 1853 (F)
Knox, William W. 2636 (H)
Koch, John T. 36 (A), 5123, 5126 (K)
Kochanski, Halik 3542, 6621 (P)
Kochhar, R.K. 6313 (P)
Koehler, M. 2440 (G)
Koeper-Saul, Veronika 5659 (M)
Koerner, Steve 3838 (I)
Kop, H.J.E. van der 4654 (I)
Körner, Martin 128 (A)
Korshin, Paul 2441 (G)
Korsmo, F.L. 6314 (P)
Korte, Barbara 437 (B)
Kosambi, Meera 6335 (P)

Index of Authors

Index of Authors

Index of Authors

Ling, Oi Ki 4171 (I)
Linney-Drouet, C.A. 2616 (G)
Linstrum, Derek 1720 (F)
Lipkes, Jeff 2730 (H)
Lippincott, Kristen 424 (B)
Lister, Ruth 3764 (I)
Little, Ann M. 5928 (N)
Little, J.I. 2256, 6115 (P)
Little, Katherine C. 1195 (E)
Little, Patrick 5839–40 (M)
Litton, Pauline 2515 (G)
Litvack, Leon 137 (A), 5620 (M)
Litzenberger, Caroline 1860 (F)
Liu, Tai 1861 (F)
Liu, Tessie P. 6160 (P)
Livingstone, D.N. 3048 (H)
Llewellyn, Charles 393 (B)
Llewellyn, Sacha 2444 (G)
Lloyd Owen, David 4672 (I)
Lloyd, Campbell F. 2558 (G)
Lloyd, Howell A. 1587 (F)
Lloyd, Lorna 6689 (P)
Lloyd, Lowri W. 5050 (J)
Lloyd, Richard 1862 (F)
Lloyd, T.H. 1498 (F)
Lloyd-Jones, Roger 2896 (H)
Llwyd, Rheinallt 1550 (F)
Loades, David Michael 127 (A), 2052, 2121 (F)
Lobban, Michael 3376 (H)
Lockhart, Bill 5761 (M)
Lodge, Guy 4421 (I)
Loewe, Raphael 4044 (I)
Loewen, Brad 1067 (E)
Loewenstein, A.B. 6497 (P)
Loewenstein, David 1863 (F)
Loftus, Donna 2897 (H)
Logan, Deborah 2731–2 (H)
Logan, George M. 1645 (F)
Lomas, Janis 4339 (I)
Lomas, Richard 1052 (E)
Lombardo, Johannes R. 6690 (P)
London, Louise 4340 (I)
Long, Alan G. 3817 (I)
Long, R. James 1196 (E)
Longhorn, Victor 1864 (F)
Longley, D.M.T. 5021 (J)
Lonsdale, John 6434 (P)
Loo, Tina Merrill 6417 (P)
Lopatin, Nancy P. 3465 (H)
Lord, Cliff 6624 (P)
Lord, Evelyn 3611 (I)
Lorenzton, Maria 3967 (I)

Loridan, Dominique 4673 (I)
Lorrey, Haidee 1197 (E)
Lösch, Doris 1636 (F)
Loughlin, James 5841 (M)
Loughlin, Kelly 3968 (I)
Louis, Wm. Roger 138 (A), 4912 (I), 6085 (P)
Loussouarn, Sophie 2362 (G)
Lovegrove, Deryck 2516–17 (G)
Lovelock, Sir Douglas 4341 (I)
Low, Donald Anthony 6498 (P)
Low, Eugenia 3728 (I), 4342 (I)
Lowe, C.E. 683 (C)
Lowe, M.C. 394 (B)
Lowe, Peter C. 4674 (I)
Lowe, Raymond 237 (B)
Lowerson, John 3691 (I)
Lowrey, John 5127 (K)
Lowry, Bullit 4675 (I)
Lowry, Donal 139 (A), 5882 (M), 6499, 6625–7 (P)
Lowry, Thomas 4676 (I)
Loyn, Henry Royston 877 (D)
Lualdi, Katharine Jackson 140 (A)
Lubenow, William C. 3108 (H)
Luborsky, Ruth Samson 1551 (F)
Lucas, Peter J. 1552 (F)
Lucas, W. Scott 4677 (I)
Luckett, Larry 652 (C)
Lückhoff, Martin 3545 (H)
Lucy, Samantha J. 770–3 (D)
Luddy, Maria 59 (A), 5495, 5842 (M)
Ludington, Charles C. 1637 (F), 5567 (M)
Ludlam, Steve 4343 (I)
Ludlow, Helen 6380 (P)
Ludlow, N. Piers 4913–18 (I)
Ludlow, Neil 5010 (J)
Luffingham, John 238 (B)
Lund, Eric 61 (A), 1865 (F)
Lundgren, Karen 1198 (E)
Lunn, Ken 3842 (I)
Luscombe, Edward W. 2965 (H)
Lutterkort, Karl 878 (D)
Luttmer, Frank 1866 (F)
Lutz, J.G. 6381 (P)
Lyddon, Dave 3843 (I)
Lydon, James 5288, 5428 (L)
Lynch, Beth 1553 (F)
Lynch, Jack 1721 (F)
Lynch, John 3577 (H)
Lynch, Michael 1507, 5119 (K)
Lynch, Peredur I. 5051 (J)

Index of Authors

Index of Authors

Index of Authors

Index of Authors

Miller, Naomi J. 149 (A)
Miller, P. 6405 (P)
Miller, Rory 6438, 6692 (P)
Miller, Russell 4697 (I)
Miller, S. 292 (B)
Millett, Benignus 5739–40 (M)
Millett, Martin 563 (C)
Millgate, Helen D. 4698 (I)
Milligan, Susan 4048 (I)
Millman, Brock 4356 (I)
Millon-Micalaudy, Isabelle 4357 (I)
Mills, Coralie M. 150 (A)
Mills, J.H. 6198 (P)
Mills, Susan 100 (A), 793 (D)
Mills, Terence C. 3858 (I)
Millward, Robert 2907 (H)
Milne, Kenneth 151 (A), 5741–2 (M)
Milne, Malcolm 6439 (P)
Milner, Marc 6636 (P)
Milton, Anthony 1886 (F)
Milton, Giles 5974 (N)
Milton, Philip 2062 (F)
Milward, A. 152 (A)
Milward, A.S. 3859 (I)
Mindenhall, D. 6192 (P)
Minion, Mark 4931 (I)
Minnis, Alastair J. 153 (A)
Mirala, Petri 5743 (M)
Mirza, Q. 6339 (P)
Miskell, L. 2908 (H)
Misra, A.M. 6247 (P)
Mitcham, Samuel W. 4699 (I)
Mitchell, Austin 4358 (I)
Mitchell, Fraser 154 (A), 5311 (L)
Mitchell, G.A. 3113 (H)
Mitchell, James 4359–60 (I)
Mitchell, L.G. 2595 (G)
Mitchell, Robin 6406 (P)
Mitchell, Rosemary 2644 (H)
Mitchison, Rosalind 2257 (G), 5160 (K)
Mitra, I. 6248 (P)
Moesgaard, Jens-Christian 1054 (E)
Moffatt, Douglas 1071 (E)
Mohamed, Jama 6637 (P)
Mohun, Arwen 2909 (H)
Moir, Martin 155 (A), 6343, 6440 (P)
Mokyr, Joel 5550 (M)
Mole, W.G. 4700 (I)
Møbarller, Jes Fabricius 3120 (H)
Moloney, R. 683 (C), 5744 (M)
Money, John 2185, 2291 (G)
Monie, Ian 3163 (H)
Monk, M. 5312 (L)

Monk, Ray 4049 (I)
Monteith, Kathleen E.A. 6249–50 (P)
Montgomery, George 3767 (I)
Moody, Michael 4123 (I)
Moore, B. 4701 (I)
Moore, Brian L. 6510 (P)
Moore, D. 2455 (G)
Moore, Donald 2456 (G)
Moore, Erin 6511 (P)
Moore, J. 2292 (G)
Moore, Jerrold Northrop 4124 (I)
Moore, Lucy 2186 (G)
Moore, Peter 241 (B), 2122 (F)
Moore, R. 6441, 6512 (P)
Moore, Robin James 6088 (P)
Moore-Colyer, R.J. 3114 (H), 6251 (P)
Moran, M.F. 3342 (H)
Moran, Madge 242 (B)
Morash, Chris 5697 (M)
More, Sir Thomas 1645 (F)
Morello, Nicoletta 156 (A)
Moreman, T.R. 6639 (P)
Moreman, Tim 6638 (P)
Morét, Ulrike 5191 (K)
Morey, A. 4677 (I)
Morgan, D. Densil 1887 (F)
Morgan, Edmund Sears 6019 (N)
Morgan, Gerald 1458 (F)
Morgan, Helen 6019 (N)
Morgan, Hiram 157 (A), 5296–7 (L)
Morgan, Kenneth 2258 (G)
Morgan, Kenneth O. 111 (A), 513 (B),
    4361 (I), 6640 (P)
Morgan, Mike 4702–3 (I)
Morgan, N. 1202 (E)
Morgan, Prys 2063 (F)
Morgan, Sue 3343 (H)
Morgan, Valerie 5817 (M)
Moriarty, C. 4125 (I)
Moriceau, Jean-Marc 401 (B)
Morley, B. 4263 (I)
Morley, Beric M. 943 (E)
Morrill, John Stephen 1888 (F), 4050 (I)
Morris, A.J.A. 3547 (H)
Morris, Benny 6513 (P)
Morris, Carole A. 794 (D)
Morris, Christopher D. 739 (D)
Morris, Christopher W. 158 (A)
Morris, Elaine L. 5986 (N)
Morris, H.F. 5572 (M)
Morris, J.N. 3344 (H)
Morris, M. 2123 (F)
Morris, P. 3582 (H)

Index of Authors

Index of Authors

405

Index of Authors

Overbeek, Henk 4371 (I)
Overell, M.A. 1896 (F)
Overhoff, Jürgen 1897 (F)
Overmans, Rüdiger 173 (A)
Overy, Caroline 3018 (H)
Overy, Richard James 4717–18 (I)
Owen, A.E.B. 3240 (H)
Owen, Brian R. 3551 (H)
Owen, David 4372 (I)
Owen, David Lloyd 4703 (I)
Owen, Douglas David Roy 5260 (K)
Owen, Morfydd E. 41 (A), 5034, 5080, 5090, 5099 (J)
Owen, Ursula 4373 (I)
Owens, Alastair 199 (A)
Owram, Douglas 6062 (P)
Oxley, Deborah 2880 (H)
Oxley, G.W. 2263 (G)
Oxley, Les 2870–1 (H)
Oz-Salzburger, Fania 2368 (G)

Pachauri, S.K. 6446 (P)
Padel, O.J. 1031 (E)
Page, Christopher 4719 (I)
Page, Mark 1304 (E)
Pagedas, Constantine A. 4941 (I)
Painter, Kenneth 666 (C)
Palliser, David M. 141, 174 (A), 589 (C), 741, 795–6 (D), 1058 (E)
Palmer, Frances 1676 (F)
Palmer, Marilyn 2919 (H)
Palmer, Martin 491 (B)
Palmer, Nicholas 1324 (E)
Palmer, Nigel 491 (B)
Palmer, Sarah 3696 (I)
Palmer, Stuart 1324 (E)
Palmer, Stuart C. 246 (B)
Palmer, Susann 247 (B)
Palmer, William 1971 (F)
Panayotova, Stella 1132 (E)
Panda, Chitta 6256 (P)
Pandey, S.N. 6520 (P)
Panton, F.H. 2559 (G)
Pappas, George S. 5704 (M)
Parham, D. 2920 (H)
Pari Huws, G.D. 2921 (H)
Paris, Michael 3552 (H), 4131 (I)
Parish, Helen L. 1898–9 (F)
Park, Alison 4259 (I)
Park, D. 1159 (E)
Park, Sowon S. 3485 (H)
Parker Pearson, M. 5149 (K)
Parker, Christopher 2645 (H)

Parker, David 4178 (I)
Parker, Derek 2066 (F)
Parker, Douglas Harold 1900, 1918 (F)
Parker, Kenneth L. 1901 (F)
Parker, R.H. 2844 (H)
Parker, Robert Alexander Clarke 4374, 4942 (I)
Parkinson-Bailey, John J. 457 (B)
Parks, Roger N. 6030 (N)
Parpart, Jane L. 6548 (P)
Parratt, C.M. 2737 (H)
Parrish, Thomas 4943 (I)
Parrott, Vivienne 2778 (H)
Parry, Charles 609 (C)
Parry, J.P. 492 (B), 3486 (H)
Parsloe, John 2303 (G)
Parsons, David 890–1 (D)
Parsons, David N. 320–1 (B)
Parsons, Michael 4375, 4720 (I)
Parsons, Neil 6644 (P)
Parsons, Reg 4721 (I)
Parsons, Timothy 6063, 6645–6 (P)
Partridge, Michael 381 (B)
Paseta, Senia 5665–6, 5861 (M)
Pasquarello, Michael 1902 (F)
Passmore, Susan C. 2188 (G)
Paster, Gail Kern 1591 (F)
Patchett, John H. 248 (B)
Pateman, M. 4376–7 (I)
Paterson, Lindsay 4411 (I)
Patrick, Adele 3251 (H)
Pattacini, L. 1732 (F)
Patterson, Annabel 1733 (F)
Patterson, Catherine F. 1981, 2069 (F)
Patterson, Henry 5625 (M)
Patterson, W.B. 1903 (F)
Paul, Septimus H. 4722 (I)
Paulson, Ronald 2465 (G)
Paviot, Jacques 175 (A)
Pawley, Margaret 4723 (I)
Payne, Ann 2126 (F)
Payne, Clive 4271 (I)
Payne, Peter L. 3864 (I)
Payton, Philip 4058 (I)
Peacey, Jason T. 1648, 2070–2 (F)
Peach, Annette 3241 (H)
Pearce, Edward 3487 (H)
Pearce, Jacqueline 1501 (F), 2264 (G)
Pearce, Robert 4378 (I)
Pearsall, Mark 501 (B)
Pearson, Lynn F. 458 (B)
Pearson, Matthew J. 5070–1 (J)
Pearson, Paul M. 4059 (I)

Index of Authors

Index of Authors

Raftis, J. Ambrose 950 (E)
Raftopoulos, B. 6522 (P)
Rahe, Paul A. 4948 (I)
Rahman, A. 5976 (N)
Rahtz, Philip 610 (C), 744 (D)
Railton, Nicholas M. 3350 (H)
Raj, K. 6341 (P)
Rajan, Balachandra 5943 (N)
Rak, J. 2147 (G)
Raková, Svatava 5918 (N)
Ram Singh, S. 6524 (P)
Rama Rathan, G.G. 6525 (P)
Ramakrishna, Kumar 6410 (P)
Ramakrishna, V. 6356 (P)
Ramdin, Ron 6068 (P)
Ramsay, N. 1059 (E)
Ramsden, John 4382, 4949 (I)
Ramsey, Keith 2649 (H)
Randall, Adrian 179 (A), 2550 (G)
Randall, Ian M. 4179 (I)
Randolph, Gregory 1769 (F)
Ranfurley, Hermione, countess of 2744 (H)
Ranger, Terence Osborn 6563 (P)
Ransom, Bill 406 (B)
Rappaport, Erika D. 2922 (H)
Rasche, Ulrich 1210 (E)
Rasor, Eugene L. 4383 (I)
Ratcliff, R.A 4731 (I)
Rathbone, Richard 6447–8 (P)
Raven, James 2469 (G)
Ravenhill, Mary R. 426 (B)
Ravenhill, William L.D. 285 (B)
Raveux, Olivier 2923 (H)
Ravilious, C.P. 2745 (H)
Raw, Barbara C. 893 (D)
Rawcliffe, Carole 1078 (E)
Rawlings, Mick 249 (B)
Raychaudhuri, Tapan 6089, 6176 (P)
Razovsky, Helaine 1913 (F)
Razzell, Peter 355 (B)
Rčeševskij, O.A. 4732 (I)
Read, Donald 2997 (H)
Read, James 6449 (P)
Readman, Alison 4350 (I)
Reboul, Percy 3637 (I)
Reddington-Wilde, Roxanne L. 5161, 5211 (K)
Redford, Bruce 2470 (G)
Rediker, Marcus 5962 (N)
Redknap, Mark 5013, 5025 (J)
Redwood, Pamela 1503 (F)
Reece, Bob 6411–12 (P)
Reece, Richard 564 (C)

Reed, David 2998 (H)
Reed, Michael 1360 (F), 2162 (G)
Reeder, David 65 (A)
Rees, Elizabeth 5073 (J)
Rees, Graham 1564 (F)
Rees, H. 3245 (H) .
Rees, Jim 5528 (M)
Reeves, Eileen 1654 (F)
Reeves, P. 6260 (P)
Refaussé, Raymond 5443 (L), 5754 (M)
Regan, John M. 57 (A), 5781, 5864 (M)
Regelous, Ken 4733 (I)
Reid, A. 2667 (H)
Reid, Alastair J. 3871 (I)
Reid, Brian Holden 4734 (I)
Reid, Chris 3674, 3879, 3928 (I)
Reid, Gerard 5501 (M)
Reid, Norman H. 3616 (I)
Reid, R. 5529 (M)
Reid, Stuart 4735 (I)
Reilly, Alan 5604 (M)
Reilly, Catherine W. 3246 (H)
Reinink, Adriaan Wessel 180 (A)
Reiter, J. 129 (A)
Rembold, Elfie 3498 (H)
Renaud, Emma 1335 (F)
Rendall, Jane 3499 (H)
Rendel, Margherita 2746 (H)
Renevey, D. 1133 (E)
Renshaw, Alison 1211 (E)
Renton, David 4384–8 (I)
Rentoul, John 4389 (I)
Renwick, John 2423 (G)
Révauger, Cécile 2471 (G)
Révauger, Jean-Paul 74, 181 (A), 3770–1, 3872 (I)
Revell, Louise 80 (A)
Rey, Michel 1373 (F)
Reynolds, Andrew 745 (D)
Reynolds, Catriona 3247 (H)
Reynolds, David 4736, 4950 (I)
Reynolds, Julie 655 (C)
Reynolds, Leonard C. 4737–8 (I)
Reynolds, Siân 3248 (H)
Rhodes James, Robert 3873, 4390 (I)
Rhodes, Rita M. 3703 (I)
Rice Young, Charles 1260 (E)
Rice, A.L. 432 (B)
Richards, David 4194 (I)
Richards, Julian D. 746–9 (D)
Richardson, J. 2472 (G)
Richardson, Joan 344, 296 (B)
Richardson, Malcolm 1266 (E)

Index of Authors

Index of Authors

Index of Authors

Index of Authors

INDEX OF PERSONAL NAMES

Index of Personal Names

Beranger, Gabriel (fl. 1730–1817) 5672 (M)
Bere, Thomas (fl. 1799–1802) 2530 (G)
Berengaria of Navarre (queen) (d. 1230) 1280 (E)
Beresford, William Carr, viscount 2626 (G)
Berkeley, George (bishop) (d. 1753) 5704 (M)
Berkeley, Sir Richard (d. 1604) 1643 (F)
Berlin, Sir Isaiah (d. 1997) 4044 (I)
Besse, Antonin 4054 (I)
Bessell, Peter Joseph (d. 1985) 4436 (I)
Betjeman, Sir John (d. 1984) 4112 (I)
Beuno (saint) 5073 (J)
Bevan, Aneurin (d. 1960) 4238 (I)
Bevan, Charles (d. 1711) 2607 (G)
Beveridge, William Henry, 1st baron (d. 1963) 3740, 3759, 3762 (I)
Bevin, Ernest (d. 1951) 4900 (I)
Bey (saint) 5236 (K)
Bicknell, Alexander (d. 1796) 2220 (G)
Bigger, Francis Joseph 5748 (M)
Biggs family 2698 (H)
Birchenshawe, John (Abbot of St Werburgh's, Chester) (fl. 1493) 2095 (F)
Bismarck, Otto, Fürst von (d. 1898) 3590 (H)
Blacker, Sir Cecil (b. 1916) 4484 (I)
Blackwood, Frederick Temple Hamilton-Temple, 1st marquess of Dufferin and Ava (d. 1902) 3595 (H)
Blair, Anthony Charles Lynton (b. 1953) 212 (A), 4202, 4296, 4333, 4389, 4993 (I)
Blake, William (d. 1827) 2596 (G)
Blamey, Sir Thomas (d. 1951) 6602 (P)
Blatherwick, Lily (d. 1934) 3269 (H)
Bleddyn ap Cynfyn (king) (d. 1075) 5097 (J)
Blind, Mathilde 3516 (H)
Bloch, Denise 4777 (I)
Bloch, Marc (d. 1944) 950 (E)
Blow, James (d. 1759) 5610 (M)
Blumlein, Alan Dower (d. 1942) 3908 (I)
Blundell, Sir Michael (d. 1993) 6514 (P)
Blundell, William (d. 1638) 1923 (F)
Boase, Thomas Sherrer Ross (d. 1974) 4086 (I)
Boddington, M.R. 5774 (M)
Bodin, Jean 1627 (F)
Bolivar, Simon 3586 (H)
Bolton, James (fl. 1775–95) 3046 (H)
Bonaparte, Napoleon (d. 1821) 2627 (G)
Bonavia, Michael R. (d. 1999) 4026 (I)
Bone, Henry (d. 1834) 2488 (G)
Bonham Carter, Violet (d. 1969) 4381 (I)
Bonney, Victor (d. 1953) 3947 (I)
Bonsanquet, Bernard (d. 1923) 3479 (H)

Boole, George (d. 1864) 5638 (M)
Booth, Charles (d. 1916) 2743 (H)
Boswell, James (d. 1795) 2170, 2470 (G)
Bothwell, James Stewart Hepburn, 5th earl of (d. 1624) 5257 (K)
Bottome, Phyllis (d. 1963) 4118 (I)
Boudicca (queen of the Iceni) (d. 62) 1457 (F)
Boulton, Ernest (fl. 1870–71) 3385 (H)
Boumphrey, Joe 251 (B)
Bower, Walter (abbot of Inchcolm) (d. 1449) 5132, 5198 (K)
Bowes, John (d. 1899) 2977 (H)
Bowler, Jonathan B. (d. 1911) 2826 (H)
Boyd Orr, John, 1st baron (d. 1971) 3697 (I)
Boyle, Richard, 3rd earl of Burlington and 4th earl of Cork (d. 1753) 1728 (F)
Boyle, Robert (d. 1691) 1566, 1572, 1577, 1583, 1585 (F)
Brabazon, Reginald, 12th earl of Meath (d. 1929) 3436 (H)
Brackley, Elizabeth (d. 1663) 1688 (F)
Bradlaugh, Charles (d. 1891) 6516 (P)
Bradshaw, Henry (d. 1886) 3240 (H)
Bradshaw, Henry (monk of Chester) (fl. 1509–13) 2095 (F)
Brand, Robert Henry, 1st baron (d. 1963) 4395 (I)
Brandreth, Gyles Daubeney (b. 1948) 4213 (I)
Braose (Briouze) family 1204 (E)
Bray, Norman Napier Evelyn (b. 1885) 6586 (P)
Brevint, Daniel (d. 1695) 1830 (F)
Bridges-Adams, Mary (d. 1939) 3110 (H)
Bridgman, Charles (d. 1738) 1728 (F)
Briggs, John (bishop) (d. 1861) 3297 (H)
Brind, Arthur Henry (b. 1927) 4832 (I)
Brittain, Vera (d. 1970) 4118 (I)
Bromwich, Andrew (d. 1702) 1917 (F)
Brontë, Charlotte (d. 1855) 2398 (G)
Brook, Rupert Chawner (d. 1915) 3216 (H)
Brooke, Fulke Greville, 1st baron (d. 1628) 1642 (F)
Brooke, Ralph (d. 1624) 1655 (F)
Brooke, William, 10th lord Cobham (d. 1597) 1704 (F)
Brooker, George (d. 1912) 2932 (H)
Brooker, James (d. 1860) 2932 (H)
Brooks, Collin (b. 1893) 4258 (I)
Brougham, Henry Peter, baron Brougham & Vaux (d. 1868) 3132, 3376 (H)
Brown, George Alfred George-, baron George-Brown (d. 1985) 4362 (I)

Index of Personal Names

Fanshawe, Sir Richard (d. 1666) 2141 (F)
Fawcett, Millicent, dame (d. 1929) 3452 (H)
Fawkener, Sir Everard (d. 1758) 2146 (G)
Febvre, Lucien (d. 1955) 950 (E)
Fell, Margaret (d. 1702) 1844 (F)
Ferguson, Adam (d. 1816) 2368 (G)
Ferguson, Samuel (d. 1886) 5575 (M)
Ferniehirst, lady 5252 (K)
Ferrers family (of Tutbury and Groby)
   1003 (E)
Féthgna (bishop of Armagh) (d. 874) 5032 (J)
Fielding, Henry (d. 1754) 2361, 2465 (G)
Figgis, John Neville (d. 1919) 3087 (H)
Fildes, Luke (d. 1927) 2976 (H)
Firminger, Marjorie (d. 1976) 3986 (I)
Fishacre, Richard (d. 1248) 1196 (E)
Fisher, John (cardinal & saint) (d. 1535)
   1168 (E), 1871 (F)
Fitter, Daniel (d. 1700) 1917 (F)
Fitter, Francis (d. 1711) 1917 (F)
Fitzalan, Henry, 12th earl of Arundel
   (d. 1580) 1928 (F)
Fitzgerald, James (d. 1835) 5766 (M)
Fitzgerald, William Robert, marquis of
   Kildare (d. 1804) 5544 (M)
Fitzmaurice, Sir Gerald Gray (d. 1982)
   4841 (I)
Fitzsimon, Henry (SJ) (d. 1643) 5299 (L)
Flanders, Allan David (d. 1973) 4318 (I)
Fleischmann, Aloys (d. 1992) 5684 (M)
Fletcher, John (d. 1848?) 2522 (G)
Flynn, Julia 4079 (I)
Folkes, Martin (d. 1754) 2437 (G)
Foot, Michael (b. 1913) 4403–4 (I)
Foot, Michael Richard Daniell (b. 1919)
   4741 (I)
Forbes, Sir Charles Morton (d. 1960) 4668 (I)
Ford, George (b. 1821) 6300 (P)
Forster, Georg (d. 1794) 2319 (G)
Forster, Johann Reinhold (d. 1798) 2319 (G)
Forster, Leonard Wilson (d. 1997) 4071 (I)
Fortescue family (of Devon) 341 (B)
Fortescue, M.A. (d. 1849) 5498 (M)
Forward, Alan 6187 (P)
Fouke Fitz Waryn 1250 (E)
Foulkes, Robert (fl. 1676–79) 1433 (F)
Fowler, Sir Henry (d. 1938) 3807 (I)
Fowler, Thomas (d. 1843) 3067 (H)
Foxe, John (d. 1587) 1627, 1827, 1905 (F)
Frank, Fritz (d. 1968) 4756 (I)
Franklin, Benjamin (d. 1790) 2150 (G)
Franklin, Sir John (d. 1847) 6300, 6305,
   6310 (P)

Fraser, Antonia, lady (b. 1932) 4074 (I)
Frederick Louis (Prince of Wales) (d. 1751)
   2400 (G)
Frederick, Sir Charles (d. 1785) 2309 (G)
Freeman, Sir Wilfrid Rhodes (d. 1953)
   4571 (I)
Freeman, William (d. 1707) 5958 (N)
French, Annie (d. 1965) 3144 (H)
French, John Denton Pinkstone, 1st earl of
   Ypres (d. 1925) 4709 (I)
Freud, Sigmund (d. 1939) 3023 (H)
Frith, Francis 2640 (H)
Frith, John (d. 1533) 1813 (F)
Fry, Charles Burgess (d. 1956) 2764 (H)
Fuller, Isaac (d. 1672) 1748 (F)
Fuller, John Frederick Charles (d. 1966)
   4734 (I)
Furse, Michael Bolton (bishop) (d. 1955)
   4178 (I)

Gaitskell, Hugh Todd Naylor (d. 1963)
   3835, 4216 (I)
Galahad (Arthurian knight) 3242 (H)
Gale, George Alexander (d. 1896) 417 (B)
Galileo 1559 (F)
Galton, Sir Francis (d. 1911) 3015 (H)
Galwey family 5586 (M)
Gamelyn 1250 (E)
Gandhi, Mohandas Karamchand (d. 1948)
   6461, 6524 (P)
Garbett, Cyril Forster (archbishop) (d.
   1955) 4169 (I)
Gardiner, Alfred G. (d. 1946) 3487 (H)
Gardiner, Sir George Arthur (b. 1935)
   4282 (I)
Gardner, Isabella Stewart (d. 1924) 3177 (H)
Gardner, Richard Lynch (d. 1920) 3124 (H)
Garrod, Dorothy Annie Elizabeth (d. 1968)
   4072 (I)
Garvin, James Louis (d. 1947) 3487 (H)
Gasquet, Francis Aidan (cardinal) (d. 1929)
   3295 (H)
Gay, John (d. 1732) 2472 (G)
Geddes, Sir Patrick (d. 1932) 6361 (P)
Geikie, Sir Archibald (d. 1924) 3054 (H)
Geoffrey Gaimar (fl. c.1140) 1105 (E)
Geoffrey of Monmouth (bishop) (d. 1156)
   1239 (E)
Geoffrey, duke of Brittany (son of Henry
   III) (d. 1186) 1286, 1315 (E)
George (saint) (d. c.303) 1212 (E)
George III (king) (d. 1820) 2536 (G)
George V (king) (d. 1936) 6470 (P)

COUNTY ABBREVIATIONS

Abd	Aberdeenshire	Fer	Fermanagh
Agy	Anglesey	Fif	Fifeshire
Ans	Angus	Fln	Flint
Ant	Antrim	Gal	Galway
Arl	Argyllshire	Gla	Glamorgan
Arm	Armagh	Gls	Gloucestershire
Ayr	Ayrshire	Ham	Hampshire
Ban	Banffshire	Hef	Herefordshire
Bdf	Bedfordshire	Hrt	Hertfordshire
Bew	Berwickshire	Hun	Huntingdonshire
Bkm	Buckinghamshire	Inv	Inverness-shire
Bre	Brecknockshire	IoM	Isle of Man
Brk	Berkshire	IoS	Isles of Scilly
But	Buteshire	IoW	Isle of Wight
Cae	Caernarfonshire	Kcd	Kincardineshire
Cai	Caithness	Ken	Kent
Cam	Cambridgeshire	Ker	Kerry
Car	Carlow	Kid	Kildare
Cav	Cavan	Kik	Kilkenny
Cgn	Cardiganshire	Kkd	Kirkcudbrightshire
Che	Cheshire	Krs	Kinross-shire
CI	Channel Islands	Lan	Lancashire
Cla	Clare	Las	Laois
Clk	Clackmannanshire	Lec	Leicestershire
Cmn	Carmarthenshire	Let	Leitrim
Con	Cornwall	Lim	Limerick
Cor	Cork	Lin	Lincolnshire
Cul	Cumberland	Lks	Lanarkshire
Dby	Derbyshire	Log	Longford
Den	Denbigh	Lou	Louth
Dev	Devon	May	Mayo
Dfs	Dumfries-shire	Mdx	Middlesex
Dmb	Dumbartonshire	Mea	Meath
Don	Donegal	Mer	Merioneth
Dor	Dorset	Mgy	Montgomeryshire
Dow	Down	Mln	Midlothian
Dry	Derry	Mog	Monaghan
Dub	Dublin	Mon	Monmouth
Dmb	Dunbartonshire	Mor	Morayshire
Dur	Durham	Nai	Nairnshire
Eln	East Lothian	Nbl	Northumberland
Ess	Essex	Nfk	Norfolk

County Abbreviations

Nth	Northamptonshire	Ssx	Sussex
Ntt	Nottinghamshire	Sti	Stirlingshire
Off	Offaly	Sts	Staffordshire
Ork	Orkney	Sut	Sutherland
Oxf	Oxfordshire	Tip	Tipperary
Pee	Peebles-shire	Tyr	Tyrone
Pem	Pembrokeshire	War	Warwickshire
Per	Perthshire	Wat	Waterford
Rad	Radnorshire	Wem	Westmeath
Rfw	Renfrewshire	Wes	Westmorland
Roc	Ross & Cromarty	Wex	Wexford
Ros	Roscommon	Wic	Wicklow
Rox	Roxburghshire	Wig	Wigtownshire
Rut	Rutland	Wil	Wiltshire
Sel	Selkirkshire	Wis	Hebrides
Sfk	Suffolk	Wln	West Lothian
Shr	Shropshire	Wor	Worcestershire
Sli	Sligo	Yks	Yorkshire
Som	Somerset	Zet	Shetland
Sry	Surrey		

INDEX OF PLACES

Index of Places

INDEX OF SUBJECTS

Index of Subjects

Index of Subjects

Pacifism 2377 (G), 4180, 4511, 4548, 4665, 4693, 4740 (I), 6569, 6577 (P)

Paganism 481 (B), 663, 667 (C), 849 (D)

Pageants 1314 (E); civic 2096 (F)

Painting 1747–8 (F), 2480 (G), 2710, 3159–60, 3163, 3165, 3167–8, 3170, 3207, 3223, 3233, 3249, 3251, 3253, 3267–70, 3279, 3308 (H), 4683 (I), 6358 (P); genre 2422 (G); *see also* Art

Painters 2417 (G), 3202, 3231 (H), 4140 (I)

Palaces 1756 (F); royal 1674 (F)

Palaeography 689, 693–4, 809, 811, 816, 818, 833, 904 (D), 3615 (I)

Palaeontology 3025 (H)

Palatinates 1249 (E)

Palatines 5906 (N)

Palestine Exploration Fund 4932 (I)

Palestine Liberation Organisation 4857 (I)

Pamphlets 1412, 1553, 1650, 1936 (F)

Pan-African Conference (1900) 6528 (P)

Pan-Arabism 6515 (P)

Panzers 4578 (I)

Papacy 888 (D), 3538 (H), 5067 (J); Papal elections 1878–9 (F)

Papal provisions 1182 (E)

Parachute troops 4453 (I)

Parades 5771, 5790, 5812, 5817–18, 5827–8, 5832, 5841 (M)

Parasitology 3018 (H)

Parenthood 1371, 1382 (F), 3666 (I), 5545 (M)

Parishes 493 (B), 1736 (F); monastic 1155 (E); Parish registers 483 (B), 1339 (F), 2204 (G)

Parks 328 (B), 3253 (H); public 2378 (G); national 3642 (I)

Parliament 492, 506 (B), 1512, 1781–2, 1786, 1920, 1929, 1972, 2044, 2049, 2051, 2059, 2061, 2070–1, 2077, 2081–2, 2138 (F), 2586 (G), 2812 (H), 4412 (I), 5848 (M), 6501 (P); House of Commons 4368 (I), 6501 (P); House of Lords 4314, 4412 (I); Irish parliament 5844 (M); *History of Parliament* 506 (B)

Members of Parliament 506 (B), 2592 (G), 4199 (I); biography 5860 (M); Conservative 4213, 4390, 4437, 4438 (I)

Parliamentary: records 6501 (P); reform 2595, 2599 (G); seats 4312 (I)

Parliamentarianism 1554, 1777, 1782, 1894, 1989, 1999, 2010, 2016, 2022, 2034–5, 2037, 2044, 2051, 2072–3, 2078, 2082, 2092 (F)

Partition: Africa 6680, 6685 (P); India 6091, 6475, 6486, 6539, 6615 (P); Ireland 5826 (M)

Past & Present (journal) 3614 (I)

Pastimes 5215 (K)

Pastoralism 1065 (E)

Patent Office 2961 (H)

Patriotism: *see* Nationalism

Patriots, Irish 5796 (M)

Patristic literature 4007 (I)

Patron saints 925 (D), 1212 (E)

Patronage 926 (D), 1943, 1981, 1988, 2015, 2061 (F); aristocratic 1754 (F); artistic 645 (C), 842 (D), 5332, 5372, 5375, 5382, 5451 (L); ecclesiastical 1204, 1210 (E); of nunneries 5228 (K); literary 811 (D), 1105, 1136 (E); political 909 (D), 1659, 2021 (F); royal 997, 1317 (E)

Peace 5614 (M)

Peace: ballot 4184 (I); movements 3174 (H); process 5802, 5850, 5870 (M)

Peace Pledge Union 4740 (I)

Peasantry 401 (B), 979, 989, 1000, 1008, 1440–1, 1455, 1459, 1462, 1466 (F)

Peasants' Revolt 1096 (E)

Pedlars 2231 (G); textile 2231 (G)

Peeresses 4412 (I)

Penal laws 5728, 5747 (M)

Penal policy and reform 2224, 2553 (G); Penal code 6416 (P)

Penance 1285 (E)

Penitentials 1211 (E)

Pensions 3738 (I)

Pentecostalism 6504 (P)

Performers 450 (B)

Periodicals 1532–3, 1536, 1542, 1544, 1546, 1624, 2031 (F), 2305–6, 2441 (G), 2731–2, 2980–2, 2985–6, 2989, 2994, 2996, 2999, 3001–2, 3250, 3286 (H), 5572, 5631 (M); illustrated 6291 (P)

Permanent Settlement (Bengal) 6267 (P)

Petitioning 2100 (F)

Petroleum 4889 (I); industry 3786 (I); supplies 4844 (I)

Pew rights 472 (B)

Philanthropy 2220 (G), 2751 (H), 3751 (I), 6149 (P); Philanthropists 2898 (H), 5155 (K)

Philately 6295 (P)

Philhellenism 1746 (F)

Philology, classical 3079 (H)

Index of Subjects

Regional history 3366 (H), 3623, 3645, 3717, 3721, 3828, 3868, 3888, 3937, 4058, 4330, 4360 (I); *see also* Local history
Regional: development 3806 (I); policy 4348 (I)
Regionalisation 3498 (H)
Regionalism 5678 (M)
Registration, vital 355 (B); registration documents 483 (B), 1339 (F), 4540 (I), 5514 (M)
Relations, central-local 919, 921 (D), 1353, 1490, 1506, 1686, 1971, 1981–2, 1985, 1996, 2020–2, 2037, 2041, 2043, 2057, 2061, 2069, 2073, 2078, 2081, 2092, 2094, 2101, 2118 (F); church-state 1803 (F), 2504 (G), 4022, 4344 (I); civil-military 2020, 2051, 2091, 2111, 2134 (F), 2609 (G)
Relics 872 (D), 1224 (E)
Religion 546 (C), 658 (C), 888 (D), 1332–4, 1382, 2006, 2036, 2088 (F), 2534 (G), 3201, 3285, 3325, 3359 (H), 5984, 5996 (N), 6422 (P); pagan 668 (C); traditional African 6368 (P)
Religion: and politics 4148, 4344 (I); and society 1072 (E)
Religious: art 803, 810, 813, 828, 831, 833, 884, 886, 889 (D), 1206 (E), 1682, 1726 (F); change 6366 (P); communities 5234 (K); conversion 849, 861, 880, 883, 891, 900, 908, 913, 916, 932 (D), 1197 (E), 1840, 1874, 1909, 1927, 1945 (F), 2507 (G), 5217 (K), 5402 (L), 6364, 6379 (P); cults 869, 881, 897, 899, 925 (D), 2095 (F), 5073, 5076–7 (J); festivals 1403 (F); history 2154 (G), 4001 (I); houses 494 (B), 699, 737, 754, 847, 854, 856–8, 866, 872, 916 (D), 1500, 1677, 1790, 1799, 1807, 1809, 1873, 1943, 2095 (F), 5066, 5075 (J), 5221, 5225, 5279 (K), 5357, 5398, 5412, 5418, 5433, 5445–6 (L), 5537, 5611–12, 5719, 5721, 5740 (M); female religious houses 859 (D), 1851 (F), 5228 (K); images, pagan 643–4, 655 (C); liberty 5995 (N); life 4059 (I); literature 826, 840–1, 847, 850–1, 860, 867–8, 876, 879, 907 (D), 1407, 1478, 1718, 1773, 1780, 1788, 1820, 1830, 1850, 1902, 1913, 1923, 1931, 1946 (F); music 439 (B), 1676, 1706, 1781, 1862, 1928, 1952 (F), 5039 (J), 5364, 5395–6, 5401, 5410 (L), 5675–6 (M); persecution 1791, 1797, 1821, 1831, 1837, 1840, 1846, 1855, 1881, 1884–6, 1907, 1911, 1923, 1942, 1945, 1954, 1956

(F), 5724, 5753 (M); polemics 1663, 1789–90, 1796, 1802–3, 1815, 1818, 1831–2, 1849, 1871–2, 1886, 1891, 1896, 1898–9, 1902, 1909, 1927, 1944–5, 2087 (F); practice and piety 664 (C), 666 (C), 883 (D), 1193, 1228, 1233 (E), 1377, 1389, 1400, 1588, 1619, 1684, 1694, 1772, 1774, 1779, 1790, 1794, 1801, 1804–5, 1807, 1810, 1813, 1826, 1833, 1838–9, 1854, 1857–8, 1860, 1866, 1869, 1873, 1880, 1882, 1890, 1901, 1913, 1917–18, 1921, 1925, 1935, 1944, 1946, 1955–6, 1985, 2087, 2093 (F), 3315 (H), 5414 (L), 5716, 5718, 5726, 5731, 5738 (M), 5906, 5997, 5999, 6000 (N); piety, elite 1912 (F); piety, female 1771, 1773, 1798, 1818, 1872, 1912, 1931, 1943, 1950 (F), 2512 (G), 6001 (N); popular 1462, 1783, 1834, 1912, 1916, 1938, 1986 (F); devotion 1194, 1206, 1209 (E); protest 1142 (E); reform 898 (D), 1929 (F); refugees 1804, 1823 (F); studies 485 (B); thought 847–8, 898 (D), 1569, 1581, 1600, 1616, 1621, 1639, 1653, 1667, 1746, 1777, 1782, 1792, 1795, 1798–1800, 1802, 1816, 1819, 1820, 1827, 1830, 1834, 1842–5, 1849, 1865, 1866, 1874, 1889, 1893, 1894, 1897, 1904, 1905, 1915, 1919, 1921, 1940, 1946 (F), 2178, 2495, 2510, 2512, 2514, 2523, 2525–6 (G), 3120 (H); toleration 1791, 1876, 1882 (F)
Religious orders 2520 (G), 4159 (I), 5732, 5758 (M); female 5416 (L); mendicant 1217 (E); Augustinians 5233 (K); Carmelite 1121 (E); Cistercians 1046, 1157 (E); Dominicans 4159 (I); Franciscans 1799 (F); Gregorian 2500 (G); Hospitallers 5432 (L); Jesuits 2502–3 (G); Carmelites 1162 (E); Hospitallers 1204 (E); Institute of the Blessed Virgin Mary 2513 (G); Trinitarian friars 1183 (E)
Republicanism 510, 515 (B), 1989, 2031, 2040, 2046, 2082 (F), 3407, 3413, 3427, 3438, 3481, 3518–19, 3521 (H), 5653, 5849 (M), 6052, 6499, 6516 (P)
Research, historical 6095 (P); scientific 3943, 3952–3, 3977 (I)
Resistance: *see* Rebellion
Resistance movements, Continental 4741 (I)
Resource control 6101 (P)
Restoration, architectural 5757 (M)
Retailing 1038 (E), 1494, 1503, 1555, 1611 (F), 2233, 2251, 2273, 2304 (G), 2862,